The Silent Peacemaker: Intellectual Property Rights and the Interwar International Legal Order, 1919–1939

Legal History Library

VOLUME 72

Studies in the History of International Law

VOLUME 26

The titles published in this series are listed at *brill.com/shil*

The Silent Peacemaker: Intellectual Property Rights and the Interwar International Legal Order, 1919–1939

Edited by

P. Sean Morris

BRILL | NIJHOFF

LEIDEN | BOSTON

Cover illustration: Ferdinand von Wright, Stonecrop, 1840–1849. Available via the Finnish National Gallery.

Library of Congress Cataloging-in-Publication Data

Names: Morris, P. Sean, editor.
Title: The silent peacemaker : intellectual property rights and the interwar international legal order, 1919-1939 / P. Sean Morris.
Description: Leiden ; Boston : Brill/Nijhoff, 2025. | Series: Studies in the history of international law ; volume 26 | Includes index.
Identifiers: LCCN 2024039195 (print) | LCCN 2024039196 (ebook) | ISBN 9789004714656 (hardback) | ISBN 9789004714663 (ebook)
Subjects: LCSH: Intellectual property (International law)–History. | Intellectual property–Japan–History. | International law–Japan–History. | International law–History.
Classification: LCC K1401 .S523 2025 (print) | LCC K1401 (ebook) | DDC 346.04/809042–dc23/eng/20240826
LC record available at https://lccn.loc.gov/2024039195
LC ebook record available at https://lccn.loc.gov/2024039196

Typeface for the Latin, Greek, and Cyrillic scripts: "Brill". See and download: brill.com/brill-typeface.

ISSN 1874-1793
ISBN 978-90-04-71465-6 (hardback)
ISBN 978-90-04-71466-3 (e-book)
DOI 10.1163/9789004714663

Contents

Acknowledgements

This book would not have been possible without the contributors and external reviewers. The contributors waited patiently for the external reports and diligently carried out the suggestions made. At the same time, the contributors also formed the "internal review board", where, in lieu of a workshop, each contributor was assigned to a colleague's paper to read, comment and make further suggestions to improve the final version. While it was impossible to please all the reviewers, external and internal, or that some chapters touched upon delicate matters, the process itself was fair and gave everyone a voice. In addition, contributors from all regions of the world engages with some of the developments on intellectual property during period. Not all issues could be covered, but we managed to get something that is noteworthy for the intellectual property curious minds or perhaps those interested in aspects of international IP legal relations which are often not the subject matter of most books. The editor is truly grateful to the contributors, the external and internal reviewers, and the team at Brill for their work on this volume.

The contributors would like to thank their colleagues, friends and families for various support and especially colleagues who read or shared their thoughts on different versions of their chapters.

The editor would like to acknowledge sponsorship from the Faculty of Law, University of Helsinki for language revision carried out on chapters six, seven and eleven. In this regard, the services of the University's Language Revision Centre are acknowledged.

The chapter by Veronique Pouillard received funding from the research project ERC CoG Creative IPR, The History of Intellectual Property in the Creative Industries (2018–2025). Thus, the chapter "Intellectual Property Rights in Belgium and in the Congo: Between Internationalism and Colonialism" is provided in open access.

Figures and Tables

Figures

Tables

Notes on Contributors

Michael Blakeney
is Winthrop Professor of Law at the Faculty of Law, UWA. He has held academic positions at a number of Universities in Australia and the UK and formerly worked in the Asia Pacific Bureau of the World Intellectual Property Organization. He is an arbitrator with the International Court of Arbitration.

Enrico Bonadio
is Reader in Law at City, University of London. He teaches, researches, and advises in the field of intellectual property (IP) law. His research agenda is wide-ranging, having recently focused on the intersection between IP and technology and IP protection of non-conventional forms of creativity, amongst other areas. Enrico has been delivering classes and talks in more than 130 universities and research institutions in six continents.

Patricia Covarrubia
is a Reader in Law at The University of Buckingham and an IP consultant at the Latin America IPR SME Helpdesk, co-funded by the EU Commission. She holds an LLM in European Law and PhD in Intellectual Property. Previously, she worked at the University of Brunel teaching IP Law and European Law. She has worked at BPP, School of Law, London where she was EU leader tutor for the Graduate Diploma in Law (GDL). She taught in Bucks New University and in Holborn College, North Greenwich where she ran Liverpool John Moores, Wales University and London University programmes.

Christine Haight Farley
is a Professor of Law at American University Washington College of Law where she serves as Co-Faculty Director of the Program on Information Justice and Intellectual Property and teaches Intellectual Property, Trademark Law, Contracts, Art Law, and Advertising law. Her scholarship has focused on the international aspects of intellectual property law, conflicts between intellectual property rights and freedom of expression, intellectual property law's treatment of art, and the expansion of intellectual property rights. She has been a visiting professor at Boston University, the University of Paris West, the University of Puerto Rico, the University of Havana, Monash University, and the National Law University in Lucknow, India, and serves on the Board of Directors for the Center for Inter-American Legal Education.

Laura Ford
is a Scholar at C-IP2 and an Associate Professor of Law at Faulkner University's Thomas Goode Jones School of Law. With a background in both law and sociology, Laura's research and teaching interests include: law & religion; economic sociology; social theory; the history and development of intellectual property; and historical sociology.

Giacomo Gabbuti
is a Assistant Professor at the Institute of Economics, Scuola Superiore Sant'Anna, Pisa. He was awarded a DPhil in Economic and Social History at the University of Oxford His research focus on economic inequality, social mobility and wellbeing in Modern Italian history, with a focus on the Fascist period.

Johanna Gibson
is Herchel Smith Professor of Intellectual Property Law, Academic Director of the Intellectual Property Law LLM and the Deputy Director of the Queen Mary Intellectual Property Research Institute at the Centre for Commercial Law Studies (CCLS). She is also Editor-In-Chief of the Queen Mary Journal of Intellectual Property (QMJIP). She has consulted widely to industry, government, NGOs and practitioners, and has been a visiting professor to institutions around the world, including the Queensland University of Technology (Australia), Monash University (Australia), the University of Toronto (Canada) and the Institute of Musical Research (School of Advanced Studies, UK). Johanna's research interests are in intellectual property and the creative industries, particularly fashion and film, and animal welfare law and companion animal behaviour and science.

Phillip Johnson
is a Professor of Commercial Law at Cardiff University. He has written extensively on intellectual properrty history, including *Privatised Law Reform: A History of Patent Law through Private Legislation* (Routledge 2017), *Parliament, Inventions and Patents: A Research Guide and Bibliography* (Routledge 2018) and *Booksellers' Bill 1774 Legislating in the 18th Century: A view from Sir Henry Cavendish's Parliamentary Diary* (Wiley 2022).

Ekaterina Kirsanova
is an Associate Professor in the Faculty of Law/ School of Digital Law and Bio-Law, Higher School of Economics Moscow. She completed her doctoral studies at the Moscow State University including a residential programme in

Intellectual Property at the University of Oxford. She has published widely in Russian on intellectual property and teaches on the International Intellectual Property Law module at the Higher School of Economics in Moscow.

Anat Lior

is an AI Schmidt Visiting Scholar and Lecturer in Global Affairs with the Jackson School at Yale, and a Yale Affiliated fellow at the Yale Information Society Project. Her research interests include AI governance and liability, the intersection of insurance and emerging technologies and intellectual property law.

P. Sean Morris

is a Research Scholar in the Faculty of Law, University of Helsinki and an Affiliated Fellow at the Erik Castren Institute of International Law and Human Rights, University of Helsinki. Sean is a generalist international lawyer and works in international intellectual property, legal history and contemporary practices of international law.

Alessandro Nuvolari

is Professor of Economic History and Director of the Institute of Economics at Scuola Superiore Sant'Anna. He was educated at Bocconi University, Milan, Italy and at Eindhoven University of Technology, the Netherlands, where he received a PhD in Economics.

Emmanuel Kolawole Oke

is a Senior Lecturer in International Intellectual Property Law at Edinburgh Law School. His research interests include international and comparative aspects of intellectual property law. Specifically, his research explores the interface between intellectual property and other branches of international law such as international trade law, international investment law, and international human rights law.

Véronique Pouillard

is Professor of Modern International History at the Institute for Archaeology, Conservation, and History, University of Oslo. She research and has published books and articles in business and economic history, with focus on topics including the media, fashion, and the history of intellectual property rights. She is the author of *Paris to New York: The Transatlantic Fashion Industry in the Twentieth Century*, Harvard University Press, 2021. She is also the co-editor of the *Oxford Handbook of Luxury Business*, Oxford University Press, 2021.

Akshita Rohatgi
is a Student of Law at Guru Gobind Singh Indraprastha University, Delhi, India. She has a background of internships in different facets of commercial law at practice area-specific and full-service law firms. She has also worked on multiple research projects and authored publications dealing with emerging legal issues in the fields of Arbitration, Intellectual Property Rights and Technology law.

Anele Simon
is a legal researcher who earned her LL.B degree from the University of Pretoria and an LLM in International Trade and Investment Law from the Catholic University of Lyon, France. Her research focuses on international Intellectual Property (IP) law and international trade law. She currently serves as the Secretary General of the Independent Continental Youth Advisory Council on the AfCFTA (ICOYACA).

Caterina Sganga
is Professor of Comparative Private Law at Scuola Superiore Sant'Anna since August 2024. She joined Sant'Anna as an Associate Professor in October 2018. Prior to her appointment at Sant' Anna, she was Assistant and later Associate Professor of Law at the Department of Legal Studies and Department of Economics and Business of Central European University (CEU, 2012–2018). She holds a Ph.D. in Comparative Private Law from Sant'Anna, an LL.M. from Yale Law School, and an LL.B. and J.D. from University of Pisa.

Noppanun Supasiripongchai
is an Associate Professor of Business Law, School of Law, University of Phayao, Thailand. He holds a Ph.D. in Law from University of Edinburgh, an LL.M. in Intellectual Property Law from Australian National University, an LL.M. in Commercial Law from Monash University and an LL.B. from Bangkok University.

Masabumi Suzuki
is a Professor, Faculty of Law, Waseda University, Tokyo Japan. He is a leading expert on Japanese and international intellectual property law, and published a number of works in both English and Japanese. He was for several years an official at the Japanese Ministry of Economy, Trade and Industry.

Lior Zemer
is the Dean and Professor of Law at the Harry Radzyner School of Law, Reichman University (IDC), Herzliya, Israel. Prof. Zemer is the Founder and Director of the MA Program in Law, Technology and Business Innovation, an innovative and multidisciplinary program bridging between law, science, technology and business innovation for both law and non-law graduates.

The Interwar Peacemaking Epoch of International Intellectual Property (1919–1939): Ambiguities and Markets

P. Sean Morris

History has always been at the very centre of the existence of intellectual property law and its evolution. This is even more so when scholars in the twenty first-century looked back on how the science and law of intellectual property evolved in the past half a milieu.[1] From the origins of the first Venetian patent,[2] the making of the Statute of Anne for Copyrights,[3] the role of the Statute of Monopolies,[4] the rise of international intellectual property treaties and polices,[5] trademarks ambitions,[6] to the making of the intellectual property provisions in contemporary trade treaties;[7] the role and history in intellectual

1 E.g., May, Christopher and Sell, Susan. *Intellectual Property Rights: A Critical History* (Boulder: Lynne Rienner, 2005).

2 See Mandich, Giulio, 'Venetian Patents (1440–1550)'. *Journal of the Patent Office Society* 30(3) (1948) 166–224; Mossoff, Adam, 'Rethinking the Development of Patents: An Intellectual History, 1550–1800'. *Hastings Law Journal* 52(6) (2001) 1255–1322; Johnson, Phillip. *Privatised Law Reform: A History of Patent Law Through Private Legislation, 1620–1907* (Abingdon: Routledge, 2019).

3 See also, Joyce, Craig, 'The Statute of Anne: Yesterday and Today'. *Houston Law Review* 47(4) (2010) 779–792; Seville, Catherine. *The Internationalisation of Copyright Law: Books, Buccaneers and the Black Flag in the Nineteenth Century* (Cambridge: Cambridge University Press, 2006).

4 Kyle, Chris, 'But a New Button to an Old Coat: The Enactment of the Statute of Monopolies, 21 James I cap.3'. *Journal of Legal History* 19(3) (1988) 203–223; Fisher, Matthew, 'The Statute of Monopolies and Modern Patent Law: Foundation or Elaborate Folly?' *Intellectual Property Quarterly* (2022), Issue 4, 176–207.

5 Duncan, Louise. *The Role of Theoretical Debate in the Evolution of National and International Patent Protection: From the French Revolution to the Paris Convention of 1883* (Leiden: Brill 2021); Morris, P. Sean (ed)., *Intellectual Property and the Law of Nations, 1860–1920* (Leiden: Brill 2022).

6 Bently, Lionel. 'The Making of Modern Trade Mark Law: The Construction of the Legal Concept of Trade Mark 1860–80'. In *Trade Marks and Brands: An Interdisciplinary Critique*, Bently, Lionel, Davis, Jennifer, and Ginsburg, Jane eds. (Cambridge: Cambridge University Press, 2007) 3; see also, Schechter, Franck. *The Historical Foundations of the Law Relating to Trademarks* (Columbia University Press 1925).

7 Hicks, Laurinda and Holbein, James, 'Convergence of National Intellectual Property Norms in International Trading Agreements'. *American University Journal of International Law and Policy* 12(5) (1997) 769–814; Heath, Christopher, Sanders, Anselm, eds. *Intellectual Property and Free Trade Agreements* (Oxford: Hart Publishing, 2007).

 | DOI:10.1163/9789004714663_002

property sits at the very progress and function of markets and industrialisation in society.

At the same, peacemaking, as such, has also been at the centre of international intellectual property treaties – at least in the form declarations or tacit support for peace and access to markets. In the Berne Convention for example,[8] when the negotiations were concluded in the 1880s, some states declared that copyright creates the possibilities for 'the cause of peace'.[9] Given the significance of international intellectual property treaties in international law the treatment of intellectual property peacemaking efforts would seem rather straightforward. Yet, it is not as simple as first appeared, as there are ambiguities, legal norms, markets, and expansion that raises more questions than answers are readily available.

In recent times the role and function of intellectual property law has gained the attention of scholars who are now presenting a new historical approach from the perspective of international law.[10] At least, it is somewhat a nascent approach, but sits broadly within emerging trends that have been looking at the history of international law. Scholars in international law have been looking at the past using historical methods, or at least, the international lawyer's version of historical method, and in the process, have opened up new debates and methods on the use of history in international law.[11] Although international historians as such might sometimes be baffled by international lawyers methodological approaches, or (American) international lawyers may intellectually disagree with what they see as "non-legal" by some European international lawyers approaches to the history of international law,[12] the fact remains, attempts are being made to carve out a history of international law in methodological approaches.

8 Berne Convention for the Protection of Literary and Artistic Works, 9 September 1886, 828 UNTS 221 (hereinafter "Berne Convention").

9 The declaration of states reads, inter alia, '… that international respect for the law of copyright opens paths across frontiers for works of the mind, thus contributing to a better international understanding and to the cause of peace', as quoted in, Ricketson, Samuel, *The Berne Convention for the Protection of Literary and Artistic Works: 1886–1986* (Centre for Commercial Law Studies, Queen Mary College/Kluwer, 1987) 891.

10 See (n 5).

11 But see, Orford, Anne. *International Law and the Politics of History* (Cambridge: Cambridge University Press, 2021) 18–69.

12 See e.g., Dunoff, Jeffrey, 'From Interdisciplinarity to Counterdisciplinarty: Is there Madness in Martti's Method?' *Temple Journal of International and Comparative Law Journal* 27(2) (2013) 309–338, 316 (noting the non-legal use of methods Martti often employ in his supposedly "legal" works of international law).

Taking cue from the rise of historical approaches to international law, the history of international intellectual property law is making some inroads by using historical approaches. The limited output so far on this history of international intellectual property law takes into account examination of archival data to tell how the international treaty on industrial policy – the Paris Convention was formed.[13] Other outputs examined some of the different elements that makes up international intellectual property especially in the latter part of the nineteenth century.[14] For other outputs, the history of international intellectual property law definitely have some connections with 'world peace'[15] (more on this anon). Thus, the emerging scholarship on the historical approaches to international intellectual property reveals a number of opportunities for various aspects of the field of international intellectual property law to develop in parallel with the history of international law.

One of the common features that international intellectual property law has with international law as a field is that both fields are relatively broad. First, it should be understood that international intellectual property law is a field of international law. The latter encompasses all forms of state relations in both public and private law spheres or what nineteenth century scholars of international law such as Thomas Holland describes as the law of nations as essentially private law.[16]

This traditional meaning of international law has not changed, and international law is still, in contemporary times, about contracts, international conventions or customs, as pointedly said by the World Court in the late 1920s in *Various Serbian Loans*.[17] Moreover, international

---

13 Duncan (n 5); Ricketson, Samuel. *The Paris Convention on the Protection of Industrial Property – A Commentary* (Oxford: Oxford University Press, 2015); Ladas, Stephen, *The Protection of Industrial Property* (Harvard University Press, 1930).

14 Morris (n 5).

15 Ricketson, Sam, and Ginsburg, Jane. 'The Berne Convention: Historical and Institutional Aspects'. In *International Intellectual Property*, Gervais, Daniel, ed. (Cheltenham: Edward Elgar 2015) 20.

16 Holland, Thomas. *Studies in International Law* (Oxford: Clarendon Press, 1898) 152: 'The Law of Nations is but private law "writ large." It is an application to political communities of those legal ideas which were originally applied to the relations of individuals. Its leading distinctions are therefore naturally those with which Private law has long ago rendered us familiar'. See also Holland, Thomas. *The Elements of Jurisprudence, 12th edn* (Oxford: Oxford University Press, 1958) 390: 'Although, as being concerned with the relations of States, "International" is in a sense a department of "public" law, its analogies are rather to the private than to the public brand of law municipal'.

17 PCIJ, *Payment of Various Serbian Loans Issued in France* (*France v Yugoslavia*), Judgment, 1929 P.C.I.J. (ser. A) No. 20 (12 July 1929) para. 86.

law,[18] is further made up of a network of treaties, which among other things, imposes obligations on states. In this context, the legality of international law cannot be mistaken. And, it is also in this process, where a network of treaties exists for international law as a field, that the field of international intellectual property law emerged in the late nineteenth century with the Paris and Berne Conventions.[19]

If there was ever a moment to definitely point to as the exact rise of international law based on multilateral treaties, then the processes of the 1880s on the negotiations of multilateral treaties for intellectual property and the subsequent Paris and Berne Conventions was that moment. But in this regard, the field of international intellectual property law is also very broad in that along with the three major areas of patents, copyrights and trademarks, there are also a number of sub-fields and processes that requires legislative activities and treaties that further adds to the layers of international intellectual property law. Most contemporary writers on the field of intellectual property often do so through the prism of the national law – where domestic legislative activities emerged and sometimes transplanted or internationalised.[20] But such prism is only part of the narratives that contributes to the historical approaches, and there is further need on how the international legislative activities are seen.

The growth of the international intellectual property regimes through treaties from the latter part of the nineteenth century through to the early 1910s has been largely due to events in Paris and Berne.[21] At the same time bilateral and trans-regional efforts such as those in Europe and Latin America also signalled that the pre-World War One regime of international intellectual property was in expansive mode.[22] For instance, the South American Patent

18 For the purposes of the discussions here, I am not taking into account 'customs', but for general views on international law and intellectual property see e.g., Morris, P. Sean, 'Private Intellectual Property Regulation in Public International Law'. *UC Davis Journal of International Law and Policy* 26(1) (2020) 147–190; Grosse Ruse-Khan, Henning. 'The Role of Customary International Law for Intellectual Property Protection Beyond Borders'. In *Intellectual Property Beyond Borders*, Grosse Ruse-Khan, Henning, and Metzger, Axel, eds. (Cambridge: Cambridge University Press, 2022).

19 Berne Convention (n 8); Paris Convention for the Protection of Industrial Property, adopted 20 March 1883, 828 UNTS 305.

20 E.g., Seville (n 3).

21 See Morris (n 5); Ricketson, Sam. 'The Trademark Provisions in the Paris Convention for the Protection of Industrial Property'. In *The Cambridge Handbook of International and Comparative Trademark Law,* Caliboli, Irene, and Ginsburg, Jane, eds. (Cambridge: Cambridge University Press, 2020) 5–6.

22 E.g., Treaty of Commerce and Navigation between Her Majesty and the King of Italy, 15 June 1883, Article 17.

Convention lead to "Paris norms";[23] and the Paris Convention revisions of 1897 and 1900 resulted in the legalist form of the Paris Convention more appealing.[24] Another pre-war revision of the Paris Convention in 1911 made intellectual property more international as in previous years and thus, among other things, showed that intellectual property joined international law in its quest to organizes a world order around economic internationalism. However, with the start of hostilities in 1914 the world order changed and, in some ways, the international legal regime for intellectual property emerged unscathed.[25]

To settle major conflicts states are often drawn to a negotiating process where treaties are drawn-up and during that process the treaties that were in force prior to an armed conflict are often taken into account. This may be the case for example, requiring a losing party to accede to an international convention for protecting intellectual property rights.[26] But the general point is that peace treaties as such tend to make provisions for property related questions including those of intellectual property rights.[27] The Versailles system[28] – that

---

23 Treaty on Patents of Invention (Signed at Montevideo, 16 January 1889); for further discussions see, Morris, P. Sean. 'Innovation Diplomacy: International Exhibitions and the Rise of Innovation in the Law of Nations'. In *Intellectual Property and the Law of Nations, 1860–1920*, Morris, P. Sean, ed. (Leiden: Brill 2022) 99, 131–133. See also, Ladas, Stephen, 'Pan American Conventions on Industrial Property'. *American Journal of International Law* 22(4) (1928) 803–821 (1928).

24 The revision conferences of the Paris Convention took place in Brussels, also discussed in, Ricketson (n 21) 6.

25 See also, Simonson, *Paul. Private Property and Rights in Enemy Countries under the Peace Treaties with Germany, Austria, Hungary, Bulgaria, and Turkey* (London: Sweet and Maxwell, 1921) Chapter 4 (discussing industrial, literary and artistic property); McNair, Arnold, 'The Effects of Peace Treaties upon Private Rights'. *Cambridge Law Journal* 7(3) (1941) 379–398.

26 See, The Treaty of Peace between the Allied and Associated Powers and Austria, Signed at Saint-Germain-en-Laye, 10 September 1919 (hereinafter "The Treaty of Saint-Germain"), Article 239.

27 Ibid.

28 I am referring to the five treaties signed during the Paris Peace Conference and shortly thereafter, with the main one being, The Treaty of Versailles 28 June 2019; and then, The Treaty of Peace between the Allied and Associated Powers and Austria, Signed at Saint-Germain-en-Laye, 10 September 1919 (hereinafter "The Treaty of Saint-Germain"); Treaty of Peace Between the Allied and Associated Powers and Bulgaria, and Protocol and Declaration, Signed at Neuilly-Sur-Seine, 27 November 1919 (hereinafter "Treaty of Neuilly"); Treaty of Peace Between The Allied and Associated Powers and Hungary and Protocol and Declaration, Signed at Trianon 4 June 1920, (hereinafter "Treaty of Trianon"); The Peace Treaty of Sèvres, 10 August 1920, and Treaty of Peace with Turkey, Signed at Lausanne 24 July 1923. For some general readings see e.g., Kleinlein, Thomas, 'The Versailles Peace Treaty before the Permanent Court of International Justice: Tracing the Legalism of the Paris Settlement'. *German Yearbook of International Law* 62(1) (2019) 129–162; Almond, Nina,

is the five main treaties to conclude the First World War contained provisions for property including those of an intellectual property nature.[29]

The general parameters of this book are on the role of intellectual property as silent peacemaker in the aftermath of the first world war. In other words, we are looking at the role and function of intellectual property in this period, and broadly classifying such functions performed by intellectual property protection and enforcement as peacemaking. This does not mean that all chapters will go about setting out discussions on peace or armed conflict. We are interested in the development, problems, functions and other identifiable evolutionary norms and rules on intellectual property in the period.

The term "silent peacemaker" may appear to be in conflict (or full of ambiguities) with what some of what we uncovered in the volume, such as Nazi confiscated art works, but when other developments are examined, then, peacemaking for the purposes of this volume is both a term of art and also a reference to widening participation of the world community in international intellectual property protection and enforcement. Moreover, peacemaking also captures the turn to markets for goods and the required international cooperation and treaties necessary to protect them.

Peacemaking is a process of intervention to diffuse a conflict or prevent the expansion of conflicts. Moreover, peacemaking requires cooperation by states, private parties or other subjects that are necessary to ensure that good relations exist in society.[30] This broad outline of peacemaking is to demonstrate

---

and Haswell Lutz, Ralph. *The Treaty of St. Germain: A Documentary History of its Territorial and Political Clauses* (Stanford University Press, 1935); Swanson, John. *The Remnants of the Habsburg Monarchy: The Shaping of Modern Austria, 1918–1922* (New York: Columbia University Press, 2001); Sturchier, Nikolas, 'Neuilly Peace Treaty (1919)'. *Max Planck Encyclopaedia of Public International Law* (2008); Montgomery, EA, 'The Making of the Treaty of Sevres of 10 August 1920'. *The Historical Journal* 15(4) (1972) 775–787; Wu, Albert, and Sawyer, Stephen. *The Making of a World Order: Global Historical Perspectives on the Paris Peace Conference and the Treaty of Versailles* (Abingdon: Routledge 2024).

29 E.g., The Treaty of Peace between the Allied and Associated Powers and Austria, Signed at Saint-Germain-en-Laye, 10 September 1919, Article 239.

30 The processes and or definitions of peace-making may vary and fit only certain situation, but for general arguments see e.g., Mayer, Arno. *The Politics and Diplomacy of Peacemaking: Containment and Counterrevolution at Versailles, 1918–1919* (New York: Alfred Knopf 1967); Thomson, David, Meyer, Ernest, and Briggs, Asa. *Patterns of Peacemaking* (London: Kegan Paul, 1945); Randle, Robert. *The Origins of Peace: A Study of Peacemaking and the Structure of Peace Settlements* (New York: The Free Press, 1973); Mosely, Philip, 'Peacemaking 1946'. *International Organization* 1(1) (1947) 22–32 (discussing peace-making between the two world wars). Contemporary writers often view peace-making as a political process where 'power and persuasion' are often tools used in the process, see Reisman, Michael, 'Peacemaking'. *Yale Journal of International Law* 18(1) (1993) 415–424, 420.

that the same argument can apply to intellectual property activities during the interwar. Peacemaking in international intellectual property should be seen as a form of cooperation for the protection and enforcement of intellectual property and how states engage in the adoption of international treaties. Moreover, peacemaking in international intellectual property necessary entails when the owners of intellectual property rights are taken into account, the access they have to markets and intellectual property leads to further international obligations.

Thus, peacemaking in international intellectual property can also be viewed as legal cooperation among states for economic opportunities in order to prevent conflict and engages in the formal application of international legal rules during the process of cooperation and economic activities. There is no right conception of peacemaking for international intellectual property, since a definition of "peace" or "peacemaking" may vary and how the process can be borne out in situations where there are genuine intellectual property conflicts or ambiguities. By pointing out one or more forms and processes of how international intellectual property are elements of peacemaking then it should be easier to move the conversation further or unearth some of the more difficult situations in intellectual property protection, enforcement, and as activities of international legalism that arose during the interwar period.

Furthermore, when the context of the Berne Convention declarations are taken into account and the references to understanding 'peace' there are good reasons to think that previous conflicts were in the minds of negotiators. First, the late 1870s and early 1880s were periods in which two major conflicts were settled by peace treaties. These include the Franco-Prussian War[31] or the Russo-Turkish War of 1877[32] and they would have been still fresh in the minds of the intellectual property negotiators in the early 1880s. Secondly, international (legal thought) was partly shaped by these two conflicts and their historical developments underscore the importance of peace treaties to other treaties in the international legal order – then and now, but as was seen in the Versailles Treaty.

Peace treaties tends to create dynamics in international legal relations where private property on the one hand is part of the larger settlement, and, on the other, peace treaties set conditions for accession to international treaties, such as that of the Berne Convention after World War One.[33] In both type

31 Treaty of Frankfurt (1871).

32 Treaty of Berlin (1878).

33 E.g., Treaty on Trianon, Article 17; see also, Drost, Pieter, *Contracts and Peace Treaties: The General Clause on Contracts in the Peace Treaties of Paris 1947 and in the Peace Treaty of*

of situations, the presence of intellectual property is paramount, yet forms part of international law peacemaking efforts.

In this regard, the private actors, for example that would have been more dominant in international intellectual property treaties would now see their role and interactions with the state actors of international law on generally the same level. Thus, interactions and markets-based connections between peace treaties and international intellectual property law forms a process of norm-relations while pointing to the virtues of peacemaking. This process in turn generates additional questions on the extent additional factors in international law such as the extent states can participate in intellectual property treaty revisions or how the moral inventions of patents are subjected to negotiation under international law.

But the most important is whether these types of developments will breach the peace, as it were. In other words, would efforts for additional intellectual property rules and regulations be subject to a lack of consensus in an international negotiating process? If so, then, how much or to what extent would a breach of the peace occur? These are all important questions, yet we cannot provide correct answers to them let alone cover them in sufficient detail. Instead, we are left to focus on developments that touches the surface of many questions relating to the peacemaking activities of international intellectual property in the period chosen. Naturally, there are also controversial aspects of intellectual property enforcement or protection that may not seem as peacemaking given that they take into account the role of The Third Reich or Italian Fascism. These discussions are fully taken up in chapters seven and eight.

When the guns were silenced in 1918 the victorious powers went about setting out the terms for peace and a new world order in the aftermath of the conflict. The resulting Treaty of Versailles comprised of over four-hundred articles and among those articles were terms on intellectual property rights. Among the economic matters in Part X of Treaty of Versailles, the role of industrial property in the peace process was set out Articles 306–311, and intellectual property rights would maintain the same international character as set out in the international treaties on intellectual property.

The tone for the peacemaking functions of intellectual property rights were already established in Article 286 of the Treaty of Versailles which recognised

Versailles 1919. A Comparison in Outline with Some Suggestions for the Future of Peace Treaties (The Hague: Martinus Nijhoff, 1948); Lesaffer, Randall, ed. *Peace Treaties and International Law in European History: From the Late Middle Ages to World War One* (Cambridge: Cambridge University Press, 2004).

the existing international treaties on intellectual property rights.[34] It was important that international treaties that were either suspended by the belligerent states or treaties that went into a form of hibernation regained their legal status if the post-war economic situation would have some semblance of peace and recovery.

The protection of intellectual property rights had been a bedrock of the pre-war international legal system and the Versailles drafters were keen that the international treaties on intellectual property rights would regain their status by coming 'into effect' without conditions immediately. Thus, as the drafters of the Treaty of Versailles set about the scope of industrial property, it was noted in the first paragraph of Article 306 that intellectual property rights 'shall be re-established or restored'.[35] The restoration or reestablishment of intellectual property rights in the Treaty of Versailles along with the other provisions on private property would signal a new epoch of economic peace in a general context while enforcement measures were being implemented in later years.

The "war" over confiscation and general property rights as such still surfaced due to how provisions of the Treaty of Versailles were applied as per Articles 297 and 298.[36] The peacemaking functions of intellectual property on the other hand as set out in Articles 306–311 of the Treaty of Versailles did not have the same fanfare as those on private property in Articles 297–298 for instance. Although, there were property claims disputes in the Mixed Arbitral Tribunals and the Permanent Court of International Justice (PCIJ), the issue of intellectual property claims under the PCIJ is still debated.[37] However it is the

34 Treaty of Versailles, Article 286, stating: 'The International Convention of Paris March 20, 1883, for the protection of industrial property, revised at Washington on June 2, 1911; and the International Convention of Berne of September 9, 1886, for the protection of literary and artistic works, revised at Berlin on November 13, 1908, completed by the additional Protocol signed at Berne on March 20, 1914, will again come into effect as from the coming into force of the present Treaty, in so far as they are not affected or modified by the exceptions and restrictions resulting therefrom'.

35 Treaty of Versailles, Article 306: 'Subject to the stipulations of the present Treaty, rights of industrial, literary and artistic property, as such property is defined by the International Conventions of Paris and Berne, mentioned in Article 286, shall be re-established or restored, as from the coming into force of the Present Treaty, in the territories of the High Contracting Parties, in favour of the persons entitled to the benefit of them at the moment when the state of war commenced or their legal representatives. '…".

36 See, Mulder, Nicholas, "A Retrograde Tendency': The Expropriation of German Property in the Versailles Treaty'. *Journal of the History of International Law* 22(4) (2019) 507–535.

37 For discussions on mixed tribunals see, Ruiz Fabri, Helene, and Erpelding, Michel, eds. *The Mixed Arbitral Tribunals, 1919–1939* (Baden and Baden: Nomos 2023); and on intellectual property, see Morris, P. Sean, 'Chorzow Factory – Intellectual Property and the

broader development of intellectual property rights and the effects of the provisions under the Treaty of Versailles that needs to be assessed along the lines of the progressive development of international rules on intellectual property during the interwar period.

When such accounts are considered, then, there is reason to believe that intellectual property played the role of a silent peacemaker as rules of intellectual property expanded and integrated the interwar world. Moreover, it was also an opportunity for economic treaties to resurrect themselves and help to shape the opportunities for reconstruction and greater commercial relations with states near and far while at the same time enforcing the common rules of intellectual property protection which survived the Great War.

For the purposes of the arguments here, what is important is that after the war and per the Versailles Treaty, the rules of international intellectual property law emerged unscathed and were restored. Moreover, as part of the peace settlement, The Versailles Treaty required states to accede to the international intellectual property conventions. This, in my view, was a part of the pacifist form of interwar internationalism based on economic activities and market access.

The interwar period was complex and there are divergent views on how it shaped international society. Notably works such as that or Carr, Wright and Bull have shown that the period was one of failures, crises, economic depression, and all those factors also contributed to the causes for the second world war.[38] These views have also been further supported by how the quintessential

Continuity of International Law in Investor-State Dispute Settlement'. *Queen Mary Journal of Intellectual Property* 11(2) (2020) 179–199; and Ferguson, Alexander, 'A Reply to: Chorzow Factory – Intellectual Property and the Continuity of International Law in Investor-State Dispute Settlement'. *Queen Mary Journal of Intellectual Property* 11(4) (2021) 505–508.

38 Carr, Edward. *The Twenty Years' Crisis, 1919–1939* (London: MacMillan, 1946); Wright, Quincy, *The Study of International Relations* (New York: Appleton-Century-Crofts, 1955); Bull, Headley. 'The Theory of International Politics, 1919–1969'. In *The Aberystwyth Papers: International Politics 1919–1969*, Porter, Brian, ed. (London: Oxford University Press, 1972); Adamthwaite, Anthony. *The Making of the Second World War* (London: Unwin Hyman, 1977); Steiner, Zara. *The Lights that Failed: European International History 1919–1933* (Oxford: Oxford University Press, 2005). The origins of the second world war are attributed to various factors including the "weaknesses" of the League of Nations and different interwar developments, however, those arguments are not relevant here, but for some legal discussions, see e.g., Stone, Julius. *Legal Controls of International Conflict: A Treatise on the Dynamics of Disputes and War Law* (London: Stevens and Sons, 1954); Korovin, Eugene, 'The Second World War and International Law'. *American Journal of International Law* 40(4) (1946) 742–755; Friedmann, Wolfgang, 'International Law and

international organization of the period, the League of Nations was unable to fully disarm states and war was only inevitable.[39] The pessimistic assessment of the interwar period increased in the literature and the general consensus remained virtually the same and that the period contributed to the collapse of international society and paused the rise of globalization in the twentieth century.[40] These narratives are however only part of the story and many successful developments in the mid and latter part of the twentieth century can trace their origins to the progressive liberal and legal developments of the interwar period. These include, environmental,[41] minorities,[42] human rights,[43] food security, among many others.

Some of the reflections on the success of the interwar period have only taken up in recent times by scholars, whilst liberating the intellectual flux that troubled the interwar period for nearly a century. But there were other major developments that limited the intellectual investigations on the interwar due to the Cold War and the subsequent dissolution of the Soviet Union. The fast-moving pace of international law then became one of human rights, security, terrorism, dispute settlement in world trade, and perhaps a bit of irony, "transnational European law". For international legal scholars, they were hardly looking back at the internationalism that emerged in the 1920s. But in any case, as the 2020s began to roar the academic community were all looking for great ways to reflect on the events that took place nearly a century earlier.[44]

---

the Present War'. *Modern Law Review* 3(3) (1940) 177–194, especially, 182–183, discussing the role of 'property'.

39 But see, Shotwell, James, and Salvin, Marina. *Lessons on Security and Disarmament from the History of the League of Nations* (New York: Carnegie Endowment for International Peace, 1949); Sare, Sami. *The League of Nations and the Debate on Disarmament (1918–1919)* (Roma: Ezizioni Nuova Cultura, 2013).

40 On globalization in the league era see e.g., d'Alessandro, Michele. 'Global Economic Governance and the Private Sector: The League of Nations' Experiment in the 1920s'. In *The Foundations of Worldwide Economic Integration: Power, Institutions, and Global Markets, 1850–1930*, Dejung, Christof, and Petersson, Niels, eds. (Cambridge: Cambridge University Press, 2013) 249–270; Gorman, Daniel. *The Emergence of International Society in the 1920s* (Cambridge: Cambridge University Press, 2012).

41 See Aloni, Omer. *The League of Nations and the Protection of the Environment* (Cambridge: Cambridge University Press, 2021).

42 Rosting, Helmer, 'Protection of Minorities by the League of Nations'. *American Journal of International Law* 17(4) (1923) 641–660.

43 Mazower, Mark, 'The Strange Triumph of Human Rights, 1933–1950'. *The Historical Journal* 47(2) (2004) 79–398.

44 E.g., Morris, P. Sean, ed. *The League of Nations and the Development of International Law: A New Intellectual History of the Advisory Committee of Jurists* (Abingdon: Routledge, 2022).

The start of hostilities in 2022 with the Russia-Ukraine conflict then hasten to dampen the post-mortem analysis of the interwar period and echoing the issues around Ukrainian statehood that surfaced in the 1920s, global economic sanctions,[45] armed-conflict, and food security: in 2022 it appeared as if it was déjà vu.

Regardless, of the problems and conflicts in world society, intellectual property rights have a reputation of endurance and rigidity, and part of it comes from the fact that as private rights, states and individuals have an obligation to ensure that the legal rules providing for their protection are enforced. In other words, the protection of intellectual property rights had become a default rule of law force on their own, whether in war or in peace, the protection and enforcement of private (intellectual) property rights remains remarkably resilient.

The 1920s was relatively free of major (world-war type) conflicts and most societies having just experienced the horrors of the Great War shared a desire for peace, even if such peace, relates to the restoration of industrial property as in Articles 306–311 of Treaty of Versailles. Given that industrial property is linked with economic progress then pacifism was part of the liberal project to seize the moment of a new international society.

In one of the first major works to document the economic relationship between war and peace after the great conflict, Keynes wrote that private property as such that the Treaty of Versailles contained was unprecedented and 'artificial'[46] but conceded that in general represented 'the logical completion of Germany's outlawry'.[47] So, even where the general economic articles on private property in the Treaty of Versailles were much detested in the academic works including that of Keynes, the same cannot be said of the industrial property provisions since they represents what the Paris Convention refers to as 'Union for the protection of industrial property'.[48] Hence, it is only natural to also identify this union as part of the healing and integration of world society in the developments of the 1920s and 1930s where the liberalism of international law was taking shape.

Beyond the Treaty of Versailles, some of the other notable developments on the expansion of international intellectual property law during the

45 Mulder, Nicholas. *The Economic Weapon: The Rise of Sanctions as a Tool of Modern War* (Yale University Press, 2022).

46 Keynes, John. *The Economic Consequences of the Peace* (Cambridge: Cambridge University Press, 2013) 44.

47 Ibid, 51.

48 Paris Convention, Article 1(1).

interwar period including those discussed in the volume are the Pan American Conventions,[49] the issue of broadcasting and performers rights,[50] and the London Conference on the Paris Convention.[51] These developments were part of the move toward the internationalisation of intellectual property rules at a time when the liberal expansion of the international legal order was taking shape.[52] At the same time questions on Italian Fascism or how the Third Reich confiscated art works can hardly be seen as peacemaking efforts in international intellectual property but they form part of the narrative on the developments during the interwar.

In light of these developments, the history of international intellectual property presents an opportunity to cast light on foundational elements that shaped treaties on intellectual property from their origins in the 1880s and how those foundations were restored after the Great War to signal continuity. Hence, important examples such as geographical indications (GI) and their legal status was not a matter of few countries, rather, the new world also embarked on forging a new international relation on these new types of intellectual property rights.[53] These developments not only contributed to how the narratives on the history of international intellectual property rights are framed within the international legal order. They also inform us on how states formed new modes of international relations based on legal principles and the common desire to concentrate on legal norms and rules that are based on treaties or just to protect commodities within the liberal international legal order.

One of the factors that connected how the liberal international legal order was truly "international" in the sense of the interwar period was the speed and progress in which non-European nations such as Japan, Nigeria, Thailand and even Colonial Congo became part of the advancement of international intellectual property rules through their interactions with the more powerful nations of Britain, the US and Europe during the interwar years.[54] This form of internationalization helps to frame a liberal picture of the world order in the 1920s and 1930s where progress and economic developments could be attained

49 See Covarrubia, Chapter 6 in this volume.

50 See Gibson, Chapter 14 in this volume.

51 See Johnson, Chapter 3 in this volume.

52 But see, Sylvest, Casper. *British Liberal Internationalism, 1880–1930: Making Progress?* (Manchester: Manchester University Press, 2009).

53 See, Farley, Chapter 5 in this volume.

54 But see, Donze, Pierre-Yves. 'The International Patent System and the Global Flow of Technologies: The Case of Japan, 1880–1930'. In *The Foundations of Worldwide Economic Integration: Power, Institutions, and Global Markets, 1850–1930,* Christof Dejung and Niels Petersson, eds. (Cambridge: Cambridge University Press, 2013) 179–203.

through how much protections exists for intellectual property rights such as those in the Berne and Paris Conventions. Thus, these historical interactions and outward look to the wider world by non-European nations became part of how the international legal order was more tolerant to nations that share a vision of the progress of the science and rules of the international legal system necessary to maintain world peace.

As a work in the history of international legal discourse the volume entertains the expansion and history of international intellectual property law during the interwar period and attempts to carve out some of the unknown or largely forgotten developments in the field. The accounts are not purely about the developments that took place in Europe or largely in conjunction with North America. Rather, as in the previous volume,[55] there are accounts on colonial and imperial narratives in the areas of trademarks and copyrights, Soviet conceptions of intellectual property as "public", and intellectual property as war policy. Difficult questions are also raised concerning how the Nazis plundered artworks and the curious behaviour of intellectual property rights in Fascist Italy, and the gradual liberal international expansion of intellectual property rights through treaties such as the Pan-American Conventions in the 1920s and on inventor's moral rights in the 1934 London Conference on the Paris Convention. Part of what emerged from some the discussions are ambiguities, markets and internationalisation in the interwar epoch.

All these accounts in the volume are designed to show the relationship between intellectual property rights at the national level and their expansion at the international level through treaty accession, obligations and specifically the role of intellectual property in the international legal order as a form of international cooperation through which peacemaking and market access promotes liberal legal internationalism. There are off course ambiguities in some of the developments especially those on the early Soviet period (and even after); Nazim and Fascism. Yet, in all these ambiguities – intellectual property norms and rules of enforcement remains resilient.

To this end, the chapters are arranged under specific sections where thematic narratives show how historical and international cooperation emerged from the interwar period in international intellectual property. These thematic engagements with intellectual property rights and the interwar international legal order are only part of the broader developments during the era. Not all of it can be captured in the volume, however, it is hoped that there is room for

55 Morris (n 5).

the additional stories to be explored by enterprising scholars on the history of intellectual property and international law.

Bibliography

Adamthwaite, Anthony. *The Making of the Second World War* (London: Unwin Hyman, 1977).

Almond, Nina, and Haswell Lutz, Ralph. *The Treaty of St. Germain: A Documentary History of its Territorial and Political Clauses* (Stanford University Press, 1935).

Aloni, Omer. *The League of Nations and the Protection of the Environment* (Cambridge: Cambridge University Press, 2021).

Bently, Lionel. 'The Making of Modern Trade Mark Law: The Construction of the Legal Concept of Trade Mark 1860–80'. In *Trade Marks and Brands: An Interdisciplinary Critique,* Bently, Lionel, Davis, Jennifer, and Ginsburg, Jane eds. (Cambridge: Cambridge University Press, 2007).

Bull, Headley, 'The Theory of International Politics, 1919–1969'. In *The Aberystwyth Papers: International Politics 1919–1969*, Porter, Brian, ed. (London: Oxford University Press, 1972).

Carr, Edward. *The Twenty Years' Crisis, 1919–1939* (London: MacMillan, 1946).

d'Alessandro, Michele. 'Global Economic Governance and the Private Sector: The League of Nations' Experiment in the 1920s'. In *The Foundations of Worldwide Economic Integration: Power, Institutions, and Global Markets, 1850–1930*, Dejung, Christof, and Petersson, Niels, eds. (Cambridge: Cambridge University Press, 2013).

Drost, Pieter. *Contracts and Peace Treaties: The General Clause on Contracts in the Peace Treaties of Paris 1947 and in the Peace Treaty of Versailles 1919. A Comparison in Outline with Some Suggestions for the Future of Peace Treaties* (The Hague: Martinus Nijhoff, 1948).

Duncan, Louise. *The Role of Theoretical Debate in the Evolution of National and International Patent Protection: From the French Revolution to the Paris Convention of 1883* (Leiden: Brill 2021).

Dunoff, Jeffrey, 'From Interdisciplinarity to Counterdisciplinarty: Is there Madness in Martti's Method?' *Temple Journal of International and Comparative Law Journal* 27(2) (2013) 309–338.

Ferguson, Alexander, 'A Reply to: Chorzow Factory – Intellectual Property and the Continuity of International Law in Investor-State Dispute Settlement'. *Queen Mary Journal of Intellectual Property* 11(4) (2021) 505–508.

Fisher, Matthew, 'The Statute of Monopolies and Modern Patent Law: Foundation or Elaborate Folly?' *Intellectual Property Quarterly* (4) (2022) 176–207.

Friedmann, Wolfgang, 'International Law and the Present War'. *Modern Law Review* 3(3) (1940) 177–194.

Gorman, Daniel. *The Emergence of International Society in the 1920s* (Cambridge: Cambridge University Press, 2012).

Grosse Ruse-Khan, Henning. 'The Role of Customary International Law for Intellectual Property Protection Beyond Borders'. In *Intellectual Property Beyond Borders*, Grosse Ruse-Khan, Henning, and Metzger, Axel, eds. (Cambridge: Cambridge University Press, 2022).

Johnson, Phillip. *Privatised Law Reform: A History of Patent Law Through Private Legislation, 1620–1907* (Abingdon: Routledge, 2019).

Joyce, Craig, 'The Statute of Anne: Yesterday and Today'. *Houston Law Review* 47(4) (2010) 779–792.

Korovin, Eugene, 'The Second World War and International Law'. *American Journal of International Law* 40(4) (1946) 742–755.

Kyle, Chris, 'But a New Button to an Old Coat: The Enactment of the Statute of Monopolies, 21 James I cap.3'. *Journal of Legal History* 19(3) (1988) 203–223.

Heath, Christopher, and Sanders, Anselm, (Eds.). *Intellectual Property and Free Trade Agreements* (Oxford: Hart Publishing, 2007).

Hicks, Laurinda, and Holbein, James, 'Convergence of National Intellectual Property Norms in International Trading Agreements'. *American University Journal of International Law and Policy* 12(5) (1997) 769–814.

Holland, Thomas. *Studies in International Law* (Oxford: Clarendon Press, 1898).

Holland, Thomas. *The Elements of Jurisprudence, 12th edn* (Oxford: Oxford University Press, 1958).

Keynes, John. *The Economic Consequences of the Peace* (Cambridge: Cambridge University Press, 2013).

Kleinlein, Thomas, 'The Versailles Peace Treaty before the Permanent Court of International Justice: Tracing the Legalism of the Paris Settlement'. *German Yearbook of International Law* 62(1) (2019) 129–162.

Ladas, Stephen, 'Pan American Conventions on Industrial Property'. *American Journal of International Law* 22(4) (1928) 803–821.

Ladas, Stephen. *The Protection of Industrial Property* (Harvard University Press, 1930).

Lesaffer, Randall, (Ed.). *Peace Treaties and International Law in European History: From the Late Middle Ages to World War One* (Cambridge: Cambridge University Press, 2004).

Mandich, Giulio, 'Venetian Patents (1440–1550)'. *Journal of the Patent Office Society* 30(3) (1948) 166–224.

May, Christopher, and Sell, Susan. *Intellectual Property Rights: A Critical History* (Boulder: Lynne Rienner, 2005).

Mayer, Arno. *The Politics and Diplomacy of Peacemaking: Containment and Counterrevolution at Versailles, 1918–1919* (New York: Alfred Knopf, 1967).

Mazower, Mark, 'The Strange Triumph of Human Rights, 1933–1950'. *The Historical Journal* 47(2) (2004) 379–398.

McNair, Arnold, 'The Effects of Peace Treaties upon Private Rights'. *Cambridge Law Journal* 7(3) (1941) 379–398.

Montgomery, E.A., 'The Making of the Treaty of Sevres of 10 August 1920'. *The Historical Journal* 15(4) (1972) 775–787.

Morris, P. Sean, 'Chorzow Factory – Intellectual Property and the Continuity of International Law in Investor-State Dispute Settlement'. *Queen Mary Journal of Intellectual Property* 11(2) (2020) 179–199.

Morris, P. Sean, 'Private Intellectual Property Regulation in Public International Law'. *UC Davis Journal of International Law and Policy* 26(1) (2020) 147–190.

Morris, P. Sean. 'Innovation Diplomacy: International Exhibitions and the Rise of Innovation in the Law of Nations'. In *Intellectual Property and the Law of Nations, 1860–1920,* Morris, P. Sean, ed. (Leiden: Brill, 2022).

Morris, P. Sean. (Ed.). *The League of Nations and the Development of International Law: A New Intellectual History of the Advisory Committee of Jurists* (Abingdon: Routledge, 2022).

Mosely, Philip, 'Peacemaking 1946'. *International Organization* 1(1) (1947) 22–32.

Mossoff, Adam, 'Rethinking the Development of Patents: An Intellectual History, 1550–1800'. *Hastings Law Journal* 52(6) (2001) 1255–1322.

Mulder, Nicholas, "A Retrograde Tendency': The Expropriation of German Property in the Versailles Treaty'. *Journal of the History of International Law* 22(4) (2019) 507–535.

Mulder, Nicholas. *The Economic Weapon: The Rise of Sanctions as a Tool of Modern War* (Yale University Press, 2022).

Potter, Pitman. *The League of Nations and Other International Organizations* (Geneva: Geneva Research Center, 1934).

Randle, Robert. *The Origins of Peace: A Study of Peacemaking and the Structure of Peace Settlements* (New York: The Free Press 1973).

Reisman, Michael, 'Peacemaking'. *Yale Journal of International Law* 18(1) (1993) 415–424.

Ricketson, Sam. 'The Trademark Provisions in the Paris Convention for the Protection of Industrial Property'. In *The Cambridge Handbook of International and Comparative Trademark Law,* Caliboli, Irene, and Ginsburg, Jane, eds. (Cambridge: Cambridge University Press, 2020).

Ricketson, Sam, and Ginsburg, Jane. 'The Berne Convention: Historical and Institutional Aspects'. In *International Intellectual Property*, Gervais, Daniel, ed. (Cheltenham: Edward Elgar 2015) 20.

Ricketson, Samuel. *The Berne Convention for the Protection of Literary and Artistic Works: 1886–1986* (Centre for Commercial Law Studies, Queen Mary College/ Kluwer, 1987).

Ricketson, Samuel. *The Paris Convention on the Protection of Industrial Property – A Commentary* (Oxford: Oxford University Press, 2015).

Rosting, Helmer, 'Protection of Minorities by the League of Nations'. *American Journal of International Law* 17(4) (1923) 641–660.

Ruiz Fabri, Helene, and Erpelding, Michel. (Eds.). *The Mixed Arbitral Tribunals, 1919–1939* (Baden and Baden: Nomos 2023).

Sare, Sami. *The League of Nations and the Debate on Disarmament* (*1918–1919*) (Roma: Ezizioni Nuova Cultura, 2013).

Schechter, Franck. *The Historical Foundations of the Law Relating to Trademarks* (Columbia University Press, 1925).

Seville, Catherine. *The Internationalisation of Copyright Law: Books, Buccaneers and the Black Flag in the Nineteenth Century* (Cambridge: Cambridge University Press, 2006).

Simonson, Paul. *Private Property and Rights in Enemy Countries under the Peace Treaties with Germany, Austria, Hungary, Bulgaria, and Turkey* (London: Sweet and Maxwell, 1921).

Shotwell, James, and Salvin, Marina. *Lessons on Security and Disarmament from the History of the League of Nations* (Carnegie Endowment for International Peace, 1949).

Steiner, Zara. *The Lights that Failed: European International History 1919–1933* (Oxford: Oxford University Press, 2005).

Stone, Julius. *Legal Controls of International Conflict: A Treatise on the Dynamics of Disputes and War Law* (London: Stevens and Sons, 1954).

Sturchier, Nikolas, 'Neuilly Peace Treaty (1919)'. *Max Planck Encyclopaedia of Public International Law* (2008).

Swanson, John. *The Remnants of the Habsburg Monarchy: The Shaping of Modern Austria, 1918–1922* (New York: Columbia University Press 2001).

Sylvest, Casper. *British Liberal Internationalism, 1880–1930: Making Progress?* (Manchester: Manchester University Press, 2009).

Thompson, James. *Great Britain and the World Disarmament Conference, 1932–1934* (University of North Carolina, 1961).

Thomson, David, Meyer, Ernest, and Briggs, Asa. *Patterns of Peacemaking* (London: Kegan Paul, 1945).

Wright, Quincy. *The Study of International Relations* (New York: Appleton-Century-Crofts, 1955).

Wu, Albert, and Sawyer, Stephen. *The Making of a World Order: Global Historical Perspectives on the Paris Peace Conference and the Treaty of Versailles* (Abingdon: Routledge 2024).

Treaties, Legislations and Cases

Berne Convention for the Protection of Literary and Artistic Works, 9 September 1886, 828 UNTS 221 (Berne Convention).

Paris Convention for the Protection of Industrial Property, adopted 20 March 1883, 828 UNTS 305.

Treaty of Frankfurt (1871).

Treaty of Berlin (1878).

The Treaty of Peace between the Allied and Associated Powers and Austria, Signed at Saint-Germain-en-Laye, 10 September 1919, Article 239.

The Treaty of Versailles 28 June 2019.

The Treaty of Peace between the Allied and Associated Powers and Austria, Signed at Saint-Germain-en-Laye, 10 September 1919.

Treaty of Peace Between the Allied and Associated Powers and Bulgaria, and Protocol and Declaration, Signed at Neuilly-Sur-Seine, 27 November 1919.

Treaty of Peace Between The Allied and Associated Powers and Hungary and Protocol and Declaration, Signed at Trianon 4 June 1920.

The Peace Treaty of Sèvres, 10 August 1920, and Treaty of Peace with Turkey, Signed at Lausanne 24 July 1923.

The Treaty of Peace between the Allied and Associated Powers and Austria, Signed at Saint-Germain-en-Laye, 10 September 1919.

Treaty of Commerce and Navigation between Her Majesty and the King of Italy, 15 June 1883.

Treaty on Patents of Invention (Signed at Montevideo, 16 January 1889).

Payment of Various Serbian Loans Issued in France (France v Yugoslavia), Judgment, 1929 P.C.I.J. (ser. A) No. 20 (12 July 1929) para. 86.

PART 1

Versailles and Interwar Intellectual Property Relations

CHAPTER 1

Expropriation of German Patents under the Treaty of Versailles

Michael Blakeney

1 International Law on Confiscation Prior to the First World War

The international law on the confiscation of the assets of private persons, prior to the First World War has oscillated between the harshness of Roman law to a much more permissive attitude at the time of the Franco-Prussian War of 1870. The Roman law position as expressed by Gaius in his *Diurnal* was that "anything which is taken from the enemy immediately becomes by the Law of Nations the property of him who takes it".[1] In the Seventeenth Century Grotius conceded that tradition and practice allowed the complete confiscation of the property of enemies, but he condemned this practice arguing that it violated "the rules of piety and morality."[2] In the War of 1812 between the United States and Britain, the question of confiscation was considered by the US Supreme Court in *Brown v. United States*.[3] Chief Justice Marshall observed that "war gives to the sovereign full right to take the persons and confiscate the property of the enemy wherever found", but that "it is not believed that modern usage would sanction the seizure of the goods of an enemy on land, which were acquired in peace in the course of trade. Such a proceeding is rare, and would be deemed a harsh exercise of the rights of war".[4]

During the American Civil War the Confederate States in an Act of 1861 provided for the expropriation of "public stocks and securities." Lord Russell, speaking of this legislation, commented that " Whatever may have been the

1 See 'The Enactments of Justinian, The Digest or Pandects, Book XLI', In *The Civil Law, Including the Twelve Tables, The Institutes of Gaius, The Rules of Ulpian, The Opinions of Paulus, The Enactments of Justinian, and the Constrictions of Leo, Vols 1–7*, Samuel Scott, ed. (New York: AMS Press, 1973).

2 Grotius, Hugo. *De iure belli ac pacis* (On the Law of War and Peace) (1625) 4. Quoted in Littauer, Rudolf, 'Confiscation of the Property of Technical Enemies'. *Yale Law Journal* 52(4) (1943) 739–770, 743.

3 12 US 110 (1814).

4 Discussed in Turlington, Edgar, 'Treatment of Enemy Private Property in the United States before the World War'. *American Journal of International Law* 22(2) (1928) 270–290, 280.

 | DOI:10.1163/9789004714663_003

abstract rule of the Law of Nations in former times, the instances of its application in the manner contemplated in the Act of the Confederate Congress in modern and more civilized times are so rare and have been so generally condemned that it may almost be said to have become obsolete."[5] By way of comparison, the Union Acts of 1861 and 1862 were directed against property directly used in aid of the rebellion or against persons who treasonably aided the Confederate cause. So despite the savagery of the American Civil War there were not general confiscatory measures against enemy private property.[6]

European practice, after the depredations of Napoleon's armies,[7] was expressed by Kaiser Wilhelm I in 1870, who during the Franco-Prussian War, declared that, "I am at war with the French soldier and not with the citizens of France. The latter will, therefore, continue to enjoy the absolute security of their persons and property."[8] This liberalization was effectively expunged by the Great War. This article examines the changes in confiscation practice both during and after the War in relation to patents and explores some of the reasons for those changes. It considers the role of the Treaty of Versailles in dealing with the confiscation of industrial property and its influence on subsequent international law on the subject.

2 Intellectual Property Prior to the First World War

The development of an international intellectual property regime paralleled the industrial revolution. The first suggestions for the international protection for inventions was the suggestion of Prince Albert, Consort of Queen Victoria at the time of the Great Exhibition in London in 1851. This had not attracted much support outside Britain as the industrialising countries such as France, Italy the German States and the USA were more interested in imitation than protection. The first international conference devoted purely to the issue of patent protection was the Vienna Congress in 1873 which was a reaction to concerns of US inventors about inadequate industrial property protection,

5 Lord Russell to Acting Consul Cridland, quoted in Hall, William. *A Treatise on International Law*, 7th ed., (Oxford, Clarendon Press, 1917) 462.

6 See Hamilton, Daniel. *The Limits of Sovereignty Property Confiscation in the Union and the Confederacy During the Civil War* (Chicago: University of Chicago Press, 2007).

7 See e.g., Quynn, Dorothy, 'The Art Confiscations of the Napoleonic Wars'. *American Historical Review* 50(3) (1945) 437–460.

8 Quoted in Gibson, William. *Aliens and the Law* (Chapel Hill, University of North Carolina Press. 1940) 29.

who were reluctant to exhibit in Vienna.[9] These misgivings were resolved in 1883 with the promulgation of the Paris Convention on Industrial Property.[10] The principal industrialised states were now prepared to countenance international protection as they each had significant industrial property assets. The increasing internationalisation of trade was complicated by the different laws of other countries, calling forth efforts for industrial property harmonization, of which the Paris Convention was the first step.

Relevant to the wartime developments discussed below is the national treatment principle contained in Article 2(1) of the Paris Convention which stated that:

> Nationals of any country of the Union shall, as regards the protection of industrial property, enjoy in all the other countries of the Union the advantages that their respective laws now grant, or may hereafter grant, to nationals; all without prejudice to the rights specially provided for by this Convention. Consequently, they shall have the same protection as the latter, and the same legal remedy against any infringement of their rights, provided that the conditions and formalities imposed upon nationals are complied with.

The principal belligerents in the Great War were all signatories of the Paris Convention[11] but as we will see below, the denial of national treatment was an early casualty of the War.

2.1 *The First World War*

Like the Napoleonic wars the first World War was a contest of economic as well as military might. In this struggle industrial property rights were significant assets. The Germans had engaged in extensive patenting in relation to synthetic dyes.[12] Prior to World War I, Germany supplied nearly all the synthetic

9 Duncan, Louise, 'The Key Historical Influences Leading to the Paris Convention for the Protection of Industrial Property of 1883'. In *Intellectual Property and the Law of Nations, 1860–1920*, Morris, P. Sean, ed. (Leiden: Brill, 2022) 24.

10 See Ricketson, Sam. *The Paris Convention for the Protection of Industrial Property: A Commentary* (Oxford: Oxford University Press, 2015) ch.1.

11 Austria (January 1, 1909), France (July 7, 1884), Germany (May 1, 1903), UK (July 7, 1884), USA (May 30, 1887).

12 See Haber, Ludwig. *The Chemical Industry During the Nineteenth Century: A Century of the Economic Aspects of Applied Chemistry in Europe and North America* (Oxford: Clarendon Press, 1958); Beer, John. *The Emergence of the German Dye Industry* (Urbana: The University Illinois Press, 1959); Haber, Ludwig. *The Chemical Industry, 1900–1930: International Growth and Technological Change* (Oxford: Clarendon Press, 1971).

organic chemicals consumed in the USA. Some seventy percent of all US patents for synthetic organic compounds between 1900 and 1910 were granted to German firms.[13] On the eve of the war the United States imported from Germany 29,000 tons of synthetic dyes, about 90 percent of total consumption of dyes in the United States.[14] The American dependence on German synthetic organic chemicals became apparent with the outbreak of war with severe shortages and the expedient of transporting dyes and pharmaceuticals in 1916 by a German submarine, until the USA entered the War.[15] Thus at the beginning of the War Germany whose companies had been much more active in filing patents overseas than any of the other belligerents had the greatest desire to leave the industrial property system out of the conflict.[16] By the same token the Allied Powers progressively drew the confiscation of enemy country patents into their war measures.

The wartime legislation of the victorious allies relating to industrial property is outlined below.

2.2 *UK*

On 5 August 1914 Britain issued the Trading with the Enemy Proclamation which established that transactions with "subjects of, or resident or carrying on business in, a state for the time being at war with His Majesty" were unlawful. The Proclamation was then followed by a number of orders in council and by the Trading with the Enemy Act (TEA) of 18 September 1914 and the Trading with the Enemy Amendment Act of 27 November 1914. The TEA applied across the entire British empire, with Hong Kong's Alien Enemies Winding Up Ordinance of 27 October 1914, being the first colonial enactment in this area. Mulder noted that the chronology of the British economic warfare regime, in which construction (August 1914–February 1915) was followed by extension (throughout 1915) and then intensification (January 1916–summer 1918) was replicated in the USA.[17] An Advisory Committee of the Board of

13 Moser, Petra, and, Voena, Alessandra, 'Compulsory Licensing: Evidence from the Trading with the Enemy Act'. *American Economic Review* 102(1) (2012) 396–427, 300.

14 See Steen, Kathryn, 'Confiscated Commerce: American Importers of German Synthetic Organic Chemicals, 1914–1929'. *History and Technology: An International Journal* 12(3) (1995) 261–284.

15 Steen, ibid; Messimer, Dwight. *The Merchant U-Boat: Adventures of the Deutschland, 1916–1918* (Annapolis: Naval Institute Press, 1988) 48–73.

16 See Johnson, Philip, 'Mr Patent Goes to War! Industrial Property and the Breakdown of the International Order during World War'. In *Intellectual Property and the Law of Nations, 1860–1920*, Morris, P. Sean, ed. (Leiden: Brill, 2022) 151.

17 Mulder, Nicholas, 'The Trading with the Enemy Acts in the Age of Expropriation, 1914–49'. *Journal of Global History* 15(1) (2020) 81–99, 86.

Trade, established pursuant to the TEA, wound up companies which were considered to be associated with the enemy, unless they were profitable and could contribute to the war effort.[18]

A Patents, Designs, and Trade Marks Temporary Rules (Amendment) Act, 1914 provided for the suspension of the patent rights of enemy aliens. It granted the Board of Trade the authority to grant to other persons "licences to make, use, exercise or vend patented inventions". During the period of suspension. This power of the Board of Trade was tested in British Association of *Glass Bottle Manufacturers Ld. v. Forster & Sons Ld.*[19] In 1907 there had been formed in Germany an International Association for the purchase and exploitation of patents relating to machines for making glass bottles. This Association was composed of six national Associations, including the British association and the legal ownership of the patents was vested in a German trust company. On 17 September 1914 Forster applied to the Board of Trade for an order for the avoidance or suspension of the patents which was made on 19 May 1915 and by a deed of licence and agreement, the Board of Trade, in pursuance of the order, granted to Forster a licence to work the patents. The British Association failed in its application for a declaration that the order in favour of Foster was not properly granted.

The status of a German patentee during the war was considered by the Chancery Division of the High Court in *Mercedes Daimler Motor Company Ld v. Maudslay Motor Company Ld.*[20] Daimler was the co-owner, with a British company of a patent which had been granted in relation to a variable speed gear. In an action brought by the two companies for infringement of the patent, it was objected that Daimler was an alien enemy. By an agreement between the companies, it was declared that the British company should have the sole right of bringing actions to restrain infringement of the patent and on this basis the Court ruled that the will of the alien company was not relevant to the bringing of the action, and that it was maintainable by the British company alone. Warrington J. observed that had the action been brought by the German company it "would be open to the objection that an alien enemy, as the German Company is, cannot invoke the assistance of the Court and any action by him must be suspended during the continuance of the, war".[21]

18 See McDermott, John, 'Trading With the Enemy: British Business and the Law During the First World War'. *Canadian Journal of History* 32(2) (1997) 201–219.

19 (1917) 34 RPC 217.

20 (1915) 32 RPC 149.

21 Ibid., 155.

A similar approach was taken by the UK courts in relation to contractual rights. Typical of this is the House of Lords determination in *Dynamit Actien – Gesellschaft* (*Vormals Alfred Nobel & Co.*) *v. Rio Tinto Co., Ltd.*[22] This case concerned the enforceability of an ore supply contract. The House of Lords observed that the weight of previous authorities was that a state of war between the UK and another country "abrogates and puts an end to all executory contracts which for their further performance require … commercial intercourse between the one contracting party, subject of the King, and the other contracting party, an alien enemy, or anyone voluntarily residing in the enemy country."[23] Similarly in *Zinc Corporation Ltd. v. Hirsch*[24] The Court of Kings Bench declared that a supply contract for zinc concentrates "was hereby dissolved as from … 4th August 1914 by the existence of a state of war between Great Britain and Germany" and that the plaintiffs "as from the said time were and are released and absolved from any obligation at any time to supply to the defendants or their assigns any zinc concentrates."[25] By application of this reasoning a patent licence between a German company and a UK party would be unenforceable during the war.

By the autumn of 1915 the industrial property rights of Austrians and Germans had been suspended.[26] in January 1916 enemy patents to be granted to the public custodian[27] and permitting the seizure of enemy property, including industrial property. In June 1916 the Allies met at a conference in Paris where they sought to agree on how to deal with enemy subjects and enemy property for both the war period and the reconstruction and to facilitate the organization of their economic alliance on a permanent basis.[28] This had led to an increase in confiscations in the Allied countries. In Britain, by the end of the War in excess of 2000 enemy patents had been vested in the Public Custodian.[29]

22 [1918] UKHL 784.
23 Ibid., per Lord Dunedin.
24 [1916] 1 K.B., 541.
25 Ibid., 551.
26 Trading with the Enemy Amendment Act 1916 (5 & 6 Geo 5. c. 105).
27 Trading with the Enemy Amendment Act 1916 (5 & 6 Geo 5. c. 105), s. 6.
28 See Paris Economic Conference, Volume 85: Debated on Wednesday 2 August 1916, available at, https://hansard.parliament.uk/commons/1916-08-02/debates/760e160f-0673-43dd-b354-e019cc79b488/ParisEconomicConference, accessed 23 June 2023.
29 See 'Patent and Patent Applications Vested in Public Trustee' Notice (1918) 101 *Board of Trade Journal*, 575 and 'Enemy Interests in United Kingdom Patents', Official Journal (Patents), 13 November 1918.

2.3 *Germany*

The first significant economic measure against enemy combatants was an Ordinance of 4 September 1914. This empowered the Central State Authorities to place enemy or enemy-controlled undertakings under State supervision.[30] Further ordinances of 22 October, 26 November and 22 December 1914, established compulsory administration for British, French and Russian enterprises[31] Given that German overseas economic interests, including patents was more extensive than enemy investments and patents in Germany, at the beginning of the war the German approach towards enemy economic interests tended to be reactive in comparison with the confiscatory approach of British policy. Germany sought to preserve enemy owned businesses "as an asset for meeting the indemnities to be exacted from the enemy upon the termination of the war".[32] A turning point for Germany was the Paris Conference of 1916. The increase in Allied confiscations was met by an Ordinance of 31 July 1916 which launched the liquidation of British enemy property. Subsequently, confiscations were effected with rigour.[33]

2.4 *USA*

The USA entered into World War I in April 1917. On 6 October 1917, Congress passed the Trading with the Enemy Act (TWEA). This was intended to eliminate the influence of a German fifth column in the USA as well as to place all enemy property "beyond the control of influence of its former owners, where it cannot eventually yield aid or comfort to the enemy".[34] The Office of the Alien Property Custodian (APC) was established under the provisions of the TWEA and was responsible for the seizure of enemy owned businesses, financial assets and personal property, including patents and other forms of intellectual property. Section 10 of the Act permitted US firms to infringe enemy-owned patents if they contributed to the war effort.[35] Some 12,000 patents and a small

---

30 Caglioti, Daniela, 'Property Rights in Time of War: Sequestration and Liquidation of Enemy Aliens' Assets in Western Europe During the First World War'. *Journal of Modern European History* 12(4) (2014) 523–545, 532.

31 See Garner, James, 'Treatment of Enemy Aliens'. *American Journal of International Law* 12(4) (1918) 744–779, 754–55.

32 Armstrong, John. *War and Treaty Legislation: Affecting British Property in Germany and Austria, and Enemy Property in the United Kingdom* (London: Hutchinson, 1922) 8.

33 Garner, *Treatment of Enemy* (n 31) 757.

34 Alien Property Custodian, A Detailed Report by the Alien Property Custodian of All Proceedings Had by Him under the Trading with the Enemy Act during the Calendar Year 1918 and to the Close of Business on February 15, 1919 (Washington, DC: Government Printing Office, 1922), (hereinafter APC) 13–14.

35 12 USC § 95a.

number of patent applications were seized, of which about 5000 covered various chemistry-related inventions such as synthetic dyes, pharmaceuticals, munitions and explosives.[36]

With the continuation of the war the TWEA became progressively more punitive and one week before the Armistice, Congress amended the TWEA to confiscate all enemy-owned patents.

The TWEA empowered the Federal Trade Commission (FTC) to grant licences for drugs that were in critically short supply and urgently needed by the military and civilian medical authorities. The highest priority was Salvarsan (an anti- syphilitic), and Novocain (a dental anaesthetic), which were either imported from Germany or produced in the German- owned US plants.[37] The strategy for issuing licenses for the use of the patents covering Salvarsan and other pharmaceuticals was determined in a conference held on 30 October 1917.[38]

Major amendments to the TWEA were made in 1918 curtailing the power of the FTC over patents and granting the APC a general power of sale. The APC, A. Mitchell Palmer, explained that this change was to allow "the German industrial army on American soil" to be "captured and destroyed".[39] The confiscation and sale of German chemical patents was also the means by which the USA hoped to duplicate the success of the German chemical industry. In the 1920s, the APC was involved in a number of scandals involving bribery and fraud in the disposition of seized enemy property. The first of these involved the sale of approximately 4800 formerly German-owned patents to the Chemical Foundation, a private research and educational organization established in 1919 to promote the USA's organic chemical and dyestuff industry and to prevent German companies from re-establishing their "Teutonic Chemical Monopoly" in the US market.[40] Francis P. Garvan, who was the first president of the Chemical Foundation and the first Alien Property Custodian and A. Mitchell Palmer, the second APC, were accused of approving the sale of $10,000,000 worth of patents to the Foundation for a derisory $271,850.

36 White, Michael, 'US Alien Property Custodian Patent Documents: A Legacy Prior Art Collection from World War II – Part 1. History'. *World Patent Information* 29 (2007) 339–345, 340.

37 Steen, Kathryn, 'Patents, Patriotism, and "Skilled in the Art" USA v. The Chemical Foundation, Inc., 1923–1926'. *Isis* 92(1) (2001) 91–122, 96.

38 See Cooper, Dale, 'The Licensing of German Drug Patents Confiscated During World War I: Federal and Private Efforts to Maintain Control, Promote Production, and Protect Public Health'. *Pharmacy in History* 54(1) (2012) 3–32.

39 APC, Alien Property Custodian Report (Washington: Government Printing Office, 1919), 15.

40 See Steen (n 37).

The legality of the confiscation of German chemical patents and their assignment to the Chemical Foundation was considered by the Supreme Court in 1925 in *USA v. The Chemical Foundation, Inc.*[41] The complaint in the District Court for Delaware alleged that a number of domestic manufacturers as a result of war conditions had been able to combine and monopolize certain chemical industries in the USA and fearing that at the end of the war German competition would destroy their monopoly,

> they conspired to bring about transfers and sales of the patents at nominal prices to themselves or to a corporation controlled by them; that the patents so obtained would control the industries in question and perpetuate the monopoly; and that the sales were procured through the fraudulent deception of the President, the Alien Property Custodian, and other officials.[42]

The District Court dismissed the complaint[43] and its decree was affirmed by the Circuit Court of Appeals.[44] Both courts found that no unlawful scheme, combination, or conspiracy was shown, and that there was no deception or fraud. The Supreme Court denied certiorari, but the opinion of the Court delivered by Justice Butler outlined some useful background on the Chemical Foundation and on the patent confiscations. He explained that the certificate of incorporation of the chemical Foundation disclosed that it was created and empowered to purchase enemy-owned patents seized by the APC and to hold the "property and rights so acquired in a fiduciary capacity for the Americanization of such industries as may be affected thereby, for the exclusion or elimination of alien interest hostile or detrimental to the said industries, and for the advancement of chemical and allied science and industry in the United States"; to grant to the United States nonexclusive licenses to make, use, and sell the inventions covered by the patents, and also to grant like licenses, on equal terms and without advantage as between licensees, to American citizens and corporations under control of American citizens.[45]

The Court indicated that the considerations paid by the Foundation to the Custodian although amounting to $271,850.00 was confirmed by an executive order of the President on February 13, 1920, which was held by both courts

41 272 US 1 (1925).
42 Ibid., para.1.
43 294 F. 300 (1924).
44 5 F. (2d) 191 (1925).
45 272 US 1 (1925), para. 4.

below to constitute a ratification of the transactions. The Supreme Court agreed with the lower courts that the sales and transfers of the patents were ratified and confirmed by the President's order of February 13, 1920.[46]

The US also contended that the sales were void because made in violation of section 41 of the Criminal Code[47] and the rule of law forbidding sales by a public officer or fiduciary of trust property in his custody to himself or to a corporation of which he is the head. However, the Supreme Court ruled that "[n]either Mr. Garvan nor any of the others who acted for the United States had any financial interest in the Foundation, its profits or its contracts. All the corporate shares were subscribed and paid for by others-those interested in the chemical industries."[48]

Interestingly, the confiscation of the German patents concerning synthetic organic chemicals did not give the USA a significant industrial advantage, because in the 1920s it lacked scientists "skilled in the art" to interpret and apply those specifications.[49]

2.5 *France and Italy*

A French decree of 27 September 1914 forbade commercial relations with the enemy but, unlike Britain or the USA proceedings against enemy property and business enterprises were initiated, not by Parliament, but by the courts, giving effect to commercial decrees.[50] Judges and tribunals began to sequester and liquidate enemy firms and businesses on the pretext of rescuing and preserving the value and accountability of activities supposedly on the verge of bankruptcy because their owners had left the country in haste or had been interned.[51] Aristide Briand, the French Minister of Justice, in a speech of 2 April 1915 said that enemy property had to be considered an "economic hostage" until the end of the war, with a view to protecting the eventual rights of French creditors and those of the allies of France and of neutral countries, and also to prevent its being used to the prejudice of the national defence.[52] Insofar that German patents were confiscated, this would have been as a consequence

46 Ibid., para. 24.
47 35 Stat 1088, 1097.
48 272 US 1 (1925), para. 30.
49 Steen (n 14) 122.
50 Caglioti (n 30).
51 Garner (n 31) 747.
52 Quoted in Caglioti, Daniela, 'Property Rights and Economic Nationalism'. *International Encyclopaedia of the First World War,* 2014, available at https://encyclopedia.1914-1918-online.net/pdf/1914-1918-Online-property_rights_and_economic_nationalism-2014-10-08.pdf, accessed 3 April 2022.

of the seizure of German enterprises. In any event, French patent law at that time did not permit the patenting of medical pharmaceutical products.[53] Under the law of July 5, 1844 pharmaceutical inventions could not be patented. Legislation then evolved, keeping the prohibition for patenting products but allowing patents for processes. By an executive Order of February 4, 1959, and the law of January 2, 1966 introduced limited patents for pharmaceutical products in France, with the ban on patenting drugs being lifted only in 1978.[54]

Italian decrees of 8 and 10 August 1916 prohibited trade with the enemy and introduced the seizure of enemy businesses and industrial activities. These were followed by decrees concerning intellectual property issued between April and May 1917.

2.6 *British Empire*

The various British dominions and colonies enacted statutes emulating the UK wartime legislation. The Indian Enemy Trading Act 1916 permitted the Governor General in Council to vest in the Custodian established by the 1915 Enemy Trading Act "any property moveable or immoveable" held by or on behalf of a hostile foreigner, who could then sell, manage or otherwise deal with that property. Bayer had a wholly-owned subsidiary in India since 1896, which was expropriated.[55] Siemens conducted most of its business with India from Great Britain, where all its manufacturing facilities were also seized, bringing its India business to a complete halt and both companies lost their patents in India.[56]

Australia enacted a Trading with the Enemy Act 1914, which closely resembled the UK version. The High Court of Australia in *Hirsch v Zinc Corporation Ltd*[57] followed the UK decision between the same parties, observing that the Australian Act "may be regarded as substantially identical for the purposes of this case with the English Act of the same year".[58] Additionally, Australia had passed the *Enemy Contracts Annulment Act*, 1915, which annulled contractual

---

53 See Cassier, Maurice, 'Patents and Public Health in France. Pharmaceutical Patent Law in-the-making at the Patent Office between the Two World Wars'. *History and Technology: An International Journal* 24(2) (2008) 135–151.

54 Boldrin, Michele, and, Levine, David. *Against Intellectual Monopoly* (Cambridge: Cambridge University Press, 2008) ch 9.

55 Lubinski, Christina, Giacomin, Valeria, Schnitzer, Klara, 'Countering Political Risk in Colonial India: German Multinationals and the Challenge of Internment (1914–1947)'. Harvard Business School, Working Paper 18–090 (Cambridge: Harvard, 2018) 12.

56 Ibid.

57 (1917) 24 CLR 34.

58 Ibid., 45.

rights and obligations existing at the date it was passed (24th May 1915). The Australian Trading with the Enemy Act 1916 specifically addressed patents. Section 9K provided that patent applications made by enemies vested in the Public Trustee, who could dispose of it by sale or licence. The Australian Patents, Trade Marks and Designs Act 1914, emulated the UK Patents, Designs, and Trade Marks Temporary Rules (Amendment) Act, 1914, and in s.3 conferred upon the Governor General the power to make regulations

> (a) for avoiding or suspending in whole or in part any patent or licence the person entitled to the benefit of which is the subject of any State at war with the King;
> (b) for avoiding or suspending the registration, and all or any rights conferred by the registration, of any trade mark or design the proprietor whereof is a subject as aforesaid;
> (c) for avoiding or suspending any application made by any such person under any of -the Acts, referred to in this section; and
> (d) for enabling the Minister to grant, in favour of persons, other than such persons ... on such terms and conditions, and either for the whole term of the patent or registration or for such less period, as the Minister thinks fit, licences to make use, exercise or vend patented inventions.

In New Zealand the Trading with the Enemy Act, 1914 and its Patents, Designs, and Short Title, Trade-marks Amendment Act, 1914 were in identical terms to the Australian industrial property legislation dealing with confiscation.

In Ceylon (Sri Lanka), the Patents, Designs, and Trade Marks, Ordinance No. 10 of 1915 replicated the UK legislation to permit the privileges in respect of patents granted to subjects of enemy States to be suspended during the war and temporary grants to be made to other persons.[59]

Ordinance No. 16, of 1915 in the Straits Settlements, modelled on the UK legislation empowered the Governor in Council to avoid or suspend any patent to which the subject of an enemy State, or any person residing or trading in such State, or any company controlled by or wholly or mainly carried on for the benefit of subjects of any such State and "to grant a licence to any person other than the person so entitled to exercise the exclusive rights which, but for the war, would have been exercised by the person so entitled."[60]

59 Maartensz, L, Alabaster, C, de Mello, A, and Koenig, E, 'Review of Legislation, 1915, VI. "Eastern Colonies"'. *Journal of the Society of Comparative Legislation* 17 (1917) 140–160, 141.

60 Ibid., 153.

The Mauritius Patents, Designs, and Trade Marks (Temporary Rules) Ordinance (No. 3), 1915 was also modelled on the UK legislation.[61]

3 The Treaty of Versailles

At the end of the war the pace of confiscations by the victorious Allies had accelerated in anticipation of the property settlements of the forthcoming peace treaties.[62] The Treaty of Versailles concluded between Germany and the Allied and Associated Powers in 1919 sought to regularise the wartime sequestration and expropriation of German assets. These assets included industrial property rights. Articles 297 and 298 of Part X of the Treaty set up a mechanism to manage past and present expropriations and paragraph 18 of Annex II of Part VIII was an open-ended clause that enabled future appropriations to enforce the Treaty. Article 297(b) provided that

> Subject to any contrary stipulations which may be provided for in the present Treaty, the Allied and Associated Powers reserve the right to retain and liquidate all property, rights and interests belonging at the date of the coming into force of the present Treaty to German nationals, or companies controlled by them, within their territories, colonies, possessions and protectorates, ... The liquidation shall be carried out in accordance with the laws of the Allied or Associated State concerned, and the German owner shall not be able to dispose of such property, rights or interests nor to subject them to any charge without the consent of that State.

Paragraph 15 of Annex I provided that the provisions of Art. 297 and this Annex "apply to industrial, literary and artistic property which has been or will be dealt with in the liquidation of property, rights, interests, companies or businesses under war legislation by the Allied or Associated Powers, or in accordance with the stipulations of Article 297, paragraph (b)."

Article 306 of the Treaty made specific reference to industrial property and provided that all acts done by virtue of the special measures taken during the war under legislative, executive or administrative authority of any Allied or Associated Power in regard to the rights of German nationals in industrial

61 Ibid., 159.

62 Caglioti (n 50) 537.

property "shall remain in force and shall continue to maintain their full effect." It also provided that "[n]o claim shall be made or action brought by Germany or German nationals in respect of the use during the war by the Government of any Allied or Associated Power, or by any persons acting on behalf or with the assent of such Government, of any rights in industrial ... property, nor in respect of the sale, offering for sale, or use of any products, articles or apparatus whatsoever to which such rights applied."

Article 306 provided that each of the Allied or Associated Powers "reserves the right to treat as void and of no effect any transfer in whole or in part or other dealing with rights of or in respect of industrial ... property effected after August 1, 1914, or in the future, which would have the result of defeating the objects of the provisions of this Article." Finally, it provided that Article 306 did not apply to industrial property rights "which have been dealt with in the liquidation of businesses or companies under war legislation by the Allied or Associated Powers, or which may be so dealt with by virtue of Article 297, paragraph (b)".

Article 310 provided that licences in respect of industrial, literary or artistic property concluded before the war between nationals of the Allied or Associated Powers or persons residing in their territory or carrying on business therein and German nationals "shall be considered as cancelled as from the date of the declaration of war between Germany and the Allied or Associated Power."

Article 297(d) provided that

> As between the Allied and Associated Powers or their nationals on the one hand and Germany or her nationals on the other hand, all the exceptional war measures, or measures of transfer, or acts done or to be done in execution of such measures as defined in paragraphs 1 and 3 of the Annex hereto shall be considered as final and binding upon all persons except as regards the reservations laid down in the present Treaty.

Annex 1 to Article 297(d) confirmed the validity of "orders, directions, decisions or instructions of any court or any department of the Government of any of the High Contracting Parties made or given, or purporting to be made or given, in pursuance of war legislation with regard to enemy property, rights and interests". It also confirmed every action taken with regard to any property, including the sale or management of property, rights or interests, in pursuance of orders, directions, decisions, or instructions of any court or of any department of the Government of any of the High Contracting Parties, "made or given, or purporting to be made or given, in pursuance of war legislation with regard to enemy property, rights or interests".

Prior to the Treaty of Versailles, a distinction had been drawn between the property of a state, which was subject to confiscation and the property of its nationals, which was considered to be outside the scope of confiscation. However, as J.M Keynes asserted, this distinction had been rendered obsolescent by the broad economic impacts of the Great War.[63] However, he subsequently, commented that "The measures for the confiscation of private enemy property which were put into force during the late war" ... "represented a retrograde tendency and should not be imitated on future occasions" and that the older principles of international law regarding the non-confiscation of private property should be resumed.[64]

However, the genii had escaped from the bottle and the property transfer provisions of the Versailles Treaty "inaugurated a veritable international age of expropriation that marked the mid-century period from 1914 until the 1970s."[65] The commercial advantages which attended the confiscation of patents was probably a significant driver of the expropriation ethos.

3.1 *Did Patent Confiscation Promote National Industrial Development?*

A contemporary debate is whether the compulsory licensing of patents by countries is industrially beneficial in the confiscating country. This was the assumption underlying the confiscation of German patents in the First World War, particularly in the USA, where the confiscated patents were expected to stimulate the synthetic chemicals industry. This was not the case, however, as many companies did not have the technical capacity to exploit the patents which they had acquired. For example, the Winthrop Chemical Company, which had acquired Bayer's patents and all of its production machinery was unable to produce the 63 drugs that were its stock-in-trade.[66] Du Pont, having acquired BASF's patents for the manufacture of synthetic indigo, which would be used to dye military uniforms was unable to produce the required

63 Keynes, John (Maynard). *The Economic Consequences of the Peace* (London: MacMillan, 1919) 71–72.

64 Quoted in Mulder, Nicholas, '"A Retrograde Tendency": The Expropriation of German Property in the Versailles Treaty'. *Journal of the History of International Law* 22(4) (2020) 507–535, 530.

65 Ibid.

66 Mann, Charles, and Plummer, Mark. *The Aspirin Wars: Money, Medicine, and 100 Years of Rampant Competition* (Cambridge: Harvard Business School Press, 1991) 52–53.

blue colour.[67] Particular problem was that many of the patent specifications of the confiscated patents obscured the technological steps required to work the patents. For example, Haynes suggested that in relation to the Haber-Bosch process for the production of ammonia, BASF "effectively bulwarked its discovery with strong, broad patents which detailed meticulously the apparatus, temperatures and pressures, but cleverly avoided particulars as to the catalysts employed or their preparation."[68] Many German supervisors and chemists had been interned or deported removing those with the critical technical know-how for the development of the chemical industry.[69] In any event, the evolution of the industry in the USA required an extensive developmental process to understand the relationship between the chemical processes and the design and operation plant and machinery.[70] Compounding these difficulties was the post-War economic recession which cut into the funds available for research and development in the industry.[71]

Japan's experience with the confiscation of German chemical patents was similar to that of the USA. It had confiscated the patent for the Haber-Bosch process and assigned it to the Toyo Chisso Kumiai (Oriental Nitrogen Association), but no Japanese chemical firms had the knowledge to put this process to commercial use. At the end of the war an approach was unsuccessfully made to BASF in the hope of acquiring the necessary expertise, but it had responded with an unreasonably high fee indicating that it had no intention of offering a licence or technical cooperation.[72]

Studies of patent filings in the chemical industry confirm that the full effects of the confiscation of the German patents took several years to result in an increase in patenting by US firms. The effects of patent confiscation were mixed. Initially, the acquisition of the German patents undermined domestic research and development. Significant increases in domestic patenting were

67 Hounshell, David, and Smith, John. *Science and Corporate Strategy: Du Pont R and D, 1902–1980* (Cambridge: Cambridge University Press, 1989) 81.

68 Haynes, Williams. *American Chemical Industry – The World War I Period: 1912–1922* (New York: D. Van Nostrand Company, 1945) 86–87.

69 See Steen (n 14).

70 Haber, *The Chemical Industry* (n 12); Arora, Ashish, and, Rosenberg, Nathan. 'Chemicals: A US Success Story'. In *Chemicals and Long-Term Economic Growth: Insights from the Chemical Industry*, eds. Arora, Ashish, Rosenberg, Nathan, and Landau, Ralph (Hoboken, NJ: Wiley, 1998) 79.

71 See Hounshell and Smith (n 41) 89.

72 Kudo, Akira. 'Dominance Through Cooperation. I.G. Farben's Japan Strategy'. In *The German Chemical Industry in the Twentieth Century*, ed. John Lesch (Dordrecht: Kluwer, 2000) 243–278, 271.

noted from 1930.[73] Baten, Bianchi and Moser observed that in the fields where patents were confiscated in the USA there was a 28 percent increase in patenting by German inventors in 1918 compared with other fields of chemical invention.[74]

4 Expropriation of Industrial Property Rights in International Law after the First World War

Edwin M.Borchard had written, ten years after the beginning of the First World War that "[p]robably no rule of international law was regarded in 1914 as more firmly established than the rule that private property within the jurisdiction belonging to citizens of the enemy states is inviolable. The rule was not adopted in any sudden burst of humanitarian sentiment, but was the result of an evolution of centuries."[75] Articles 46 and 47 of the Hague Conventions of 1899 and 1907 expressly provided that "private property may not be confiscated" and "pillage is formally prohibited." At the end of the War in 1918, but prior to the Treaty of Versailles, the House of Lords had ruled that "It is not the law of this country [England] that the property of enemy subjects is confiscated. Until the restoration of peace the enemy can, of course, make no claim to have it delivered up to him, but when peace is restored he is considered as entitled to his property with any fruits it may have borne in the meantime."[76]

It came as some surprise when in the following year the Treaty of Versailles provided in Article 297 that

> Subject to any stipulations which may be provided for in the present treaty, the Allied and Associated Powers reserve the right to retain and liquidate all property, rights and interests belonging ... to German nationals, or companies controlled by them, within their territories, colonies, possessions and protectorates, including territories ceded to them by the present treaty.

---

73 Moser and Voena (n 8) 404.

74 Baten, Joerg, Bianchi, Nicola, and Moser, Petra, 'Compulsory Licensing and Innovation – Historical Evidence From German Patents After WWI'. *Journal of Development Economics* 126 (2017) 231–242.

75 Borchard, Edwin, 'Enemy Private Property'. *American Journal of International Law* 18(3) (1924) 523–532.

76 *Hugh Stevenson &. Sons v. Aktiengesellschaft fuir Cartonnagen-industrie* (H. L.) [1918] A. C. 239.

Borchard's comment on this provision was that "[f]or a temporary gain of a few millions within easy reach, the clock has been turned back several hundred years and there has been revived an ancient barbaric practice which is likely to do incalculable harm before a wiser generation will undo it."[77] He predicted that "few provisions of the treaties of peace are more ominous for the future than this measure for the confiscation of privately-owned enemy property within the jurisdiction."[78] The protection of property, which had hitherto been secured by international law and practice was now subject to the preponderance of force.

The confiscation of property effected by Article 297 had of course been anticipated by the confiscatory activities in the USA of the Alien Property Custodian. The sale of confiscated enemy patents was described as an excess of zeal, since the Custodian was meant to hold that property on trust for the enemy aliens until the termination of the war.[79] The danger of the confiscatory policy which had been followed both during and after the First World War was acknowledged by the US Secretary of State Charles Evans Hughes, who in an address on 23 November 1923 pointed out that

> A confiscatory policy strikes not only at the interests of particular individuals but at the foundations of international intercourse, for it is only on the basis of the security of property, validly possessed under the laws existing at the time of its acquisition, that the conduct of activities in helpful cooperation, is possible. … Rights acquired under its laws by citizens of another State, [the State] is under an international obligation appropriately to recognize. It is the policy of the United States to support these fundamental principles.[80]

The statement of Hughes implies that at least as far as US practice was concerned, the confiscation of property at large and industrial property specifically would no longer form part of US policy. The Office of the Alien Property Custodian, was abolished in 1934, however, within a few months of the USA's entry into the Second World War,[81] President Roosevelt re-established the office of Alien Property Custodian, authorizing the Custodian to take over various

77 Borchard (n 75) 526.

78 Ibid.

79 Moore, John. *International Law and Some Current Illusions*: *And Other Essays* (New York: Macmillan, 1924) 22.

80 Quoted in, Borchard (n 75) 531.

81 11 March 1942.

kinds of property of certain non-resident foreign nationals.[82] The Custodian seized more than 40,000 alien-owned patents and patent applications.[83]

In a report published by the Custodian in 1943 the Custodian explained that enemy patents would be made available to any legitimate American manufacturer on a non-exclusive basis, royalty free, and for the life of the patent and that they would remain "a permanent possession of the American people".[84] Among the assets held by the Alien Property Custodian in WWII was the copyright for Hitler's *Mein Kampf*, meaning that Hitler got none of the royalties from the book's sales in the USA amounting to US$ 20,580 by 1945.[85]

An indication of the US approach to asset confiscation after the First World War was the fact that in 1921, Congress, while adopting the *Joint Resolution Terminating the State of War Between the Imperial German Government and the United States of America and Between the Imperial and Royal Austro-Hungarian Government and the United States of America,* acknowledged that all property seized during the First World War, some $500 million of foreign assets, had remained in the United States ownership.[86] Also the Trading with the Enemy Act of 1917 was not terminated. After WWII the Alien Property Custodian was abolished in 1946 and its functions were transferred to the Office of Alien Property, Department of Justice. This survived until 1966 when most of the functions related to foreign assets control were passed to the Office of Foreign Assets Control (OFAC) in the United States Department of the Treasury.

From the international law perspective legal scholars were united in their condemnation of US confiscation policy,[87] but domestic agencies, such as the Alien Property Custodian, paid little attention to these principles. The

82 Executive Order No. 9095, 7 Fed. Reg. 1971 (1942), as amended by Executive Order No. 9193, 7 Fed. Reg. 5205 (1942), dated July 6, 1942.

83 Littauer, *Confiscation of the Property* (n.2).

84 U.S. Alien Property Custodian, Patents at Work, 1943, 11.

85 Plunder And Restitution: Findings and Recommendations of the Presidential Advisory Commission on Holocaust Assets in the United States and Staff Report, 2000 at 156 available at https://govinfo.library.unt.edu/pcha/PlunderRestitution.html/html/StaffChapter3.html, accessed 22 June 2023.

86 Gross, D.A., 'The US Confiscated Half a Billion Dollars in Private Property During WWI etc', *The Smithsonian*, July 28, 2014, available at https://www.smithsonianmag.com/history/us-confiscated-half-billion-dollars-private-property-during-wwi-180952144/, accessed 22 June 2023.

87 See Turlington, Edgar, 'Vesting Orders under the First War Powers Act, 1941'. *American Journal of International Law* 36(3) (1942) 460–465; Borchard, Edwin, 'Nationalization of Enemy Patents'. *American Journal of International Law* 37(1) (1943) 92–97; Sommerich, Otto, 'Recent Innovations in, Legal and Regulatory Concepts as to the Alien and His Property'. *American Journal of International Law* 37(1) (1943) 58–73.

confiscations of the First World War and their confirmation in the post War peace treaties is considered to be a watershed for the defence of property rights.[88] The economic war waged on private property went considerably beyond military objectives. For example, the confiscation of the German dye patents by the USA had little to do with strengthening military capacity.

The Versailles Treaty introduced principles of compensation and punishment which trumped the sanctity of private property which had preceded the war. The Versailles Treaty was also a response to the conviction that Germany had intended not merely to vanquish her enemies on the battlefield, but also to ruin them commercially, so that they could not be an economic threat after the cessation of hostilities.[89] As far as its departure from existing peace principles is concerned Prussia and Germany had set precedents with the Treaty of Frankfurt of May 1871 and the Treaty of Brest-Litovsk of March 1918, which imposed a draconian peace on France and Russia respectively.[90]

A confusing aspect of the role which the Versailles Treaty has had in revising the international law of confiscation is embedded in the nature of the Treaty. Maynard Keynes, in *The Economic Consequences of the Peace*[91] had pointed out that the armistice had not arisen as the result of unconditional surrender on the part of Germany, but, rather, "on agreed terms as to the general character of the peace".[92] It is questionable whether these "agreed terms" were reflected in the terms of the Versailles Treaty.[93]

The enduring significance of the Treaty is the way in which it signalled a decisive change in the status of private property, wrought by the First World War in which belligerent governments targeted the property of the civilians of enemy nationality who happened to live within the borders of their countries.[94] The assets of enemy nationals were confiscated on the ostensible

88 Caglioti (n 30).

89 See Shepley, Nick. *Britain, France and Germany and the Treaty of Versailles: How the Allies Built a Flawed Peace*, (2nd ed) (Luton: Andrews UK, 2011); *The Treaty of Versailles: A Reassessment After 75 Years*, Boemeke, Mandfred, Feldman, Gerald, and Glaser, Elisabeth, eds. (Cambridge: Cambridge University Press, 1998).

90 MacMillan, Margaret. *Paris 1919: Six Months that Changed the World* (New York, Random House, 2002) 161.

91 Keynes, *The Economic Consequences* (n 63).

92 Ibid., 35.

93 See Kristsiotis, Dino, 'Fourteen Ways of Looking Back at the Treaty of Versailles'. *London Review of International Law* 8(1) (2020) 43–88.

94 See Caglioti, Danielia, and, Brice, Catherine, 'Property Rights in Wartime – Sequestration, Confiscation and Restitution in Twentieth-century Europe: Introduction'. *European Review of History* 28(2) (2021) 163–175.

ground of nationality, subsequently, these grounds were economic nationalism and then ideology.

Bibliography

Secondary Sources

Armstrong, John. *War and Treaty Legislation: Affecting British Property in Germany and Austria, and Enemy Property in the United Kingdom* (London: Hutchinson, 1922).

Beer, John. *The Emergence of the German Dye Industry* (Urbana: The University Illinois Press, 1959).

Ashish, and Rosenberg, Nathan, 'Chemicals: A US Success Story'. In *Chemicals and Long-Term Economic Growth: Insights from the Chemical Industry,* eds. Arora, Ashish, Rosenberg, Nathan, and Landau, Ralph (Hoboken, NJ: Wiley, 1998).

Baten, Joerg, Bianchi, Nicola, and Moser, Petra, 'Compulsory Licensing and Innovation – Historical Evidence From German Patents After WWI'. *Journal of Development Economics* 126 (2017) 231–242.

Boemeke, Mandfred, Feldman, Gerald, and Glaser, Elisabeth, eds., *The Treaty of Versailles: A Reassessment After 75 Years* (Cambridge: Cambridge University Press, 1998).

Boldrin, Michele, and Levine, David. *Against Intellectual Monopoly* (Cambridge: Cambridge University Press, 2008).

Borchard, Edwin, 'Enemy Private Property'. *American Journal of International Law* 18(3) (1924) 523–532.

Borchard, Edwin, 'Nationalization of Enemy Patents'. *American Journal of International Law* 37(1) (1943) 92–97.

Caglioti, Daniela, 'Property Rights in Time of War: Sequestration and Liquidation of Enemy Aliens' Assets in Western Europe During the First World War'. *Journal of Modern European History* 12(4) (2014) 523–545.

Caglioti, Daniela, 'Property Rights and Economic Nationalism'. *International Encyclopaedia of the First World War,* 2014, available at https://encyclopedia.1914-1918-online.net/pdf/1914-1918-Online-property_rights_and_economic_nationalism-2014-10-08.pdf.

Caglioti, Danielia, and Brice, Catherine, 'Property Rights in Wartime – Sequestration, Confiscation and Restitution in Twentieth-century Europe: Introduction'. *European Review of History* 28(2) (2021) 163–175.

Cassier, Maurice, 'Patents and Public Health in France. Pharmaceutical Patent Law in-the-making at the Patent Office between the Two World Wars'. *History and Technology: An International Journal* 24(2) (2008) 135–151.

Cooper, Dale, 'The Licensing of German Drug Patents Confiscated During World War I: Federal and Private Efforts to Maintain Control, Promote Production, and Protect Public Health'. *Pharmacy in History* 54(1) (2012) 3–32.

Duncan, Louise, 'The Key Historical Influences Leading to the Paris Convention for the Protection of Industrial Property of 1883'. In *Intellectual Property and the Law of Nations, 1860–1920*, Morris, P. Sean, ed. (Leiden: Brill, 2022).

Gibson, William. *Aliens and the Law* (Chapel Hill: University of North Carolina Press, 1940) 29.

Gross, D.A., 'The US Confiscated Half a Billion Dollars in Private Property During WWI etc'. *The Smithsonian*, July 28, 2014.

Grotius, H. *De iure belli ac pacis* (On the Law of War and Peace) (1625).

Haber, Ludwig. *The Chemical Industry During the Nineteenth Century: A Century of the Economic Aspects of Applied Chemistry in Europe and North America* (Oxford: Clarendon Press, 1958).

Haber, Ludwig. *The Chemical Industry, 1900–1930: International Growth and Technological Change* (Oxford: Clarendon Press, 1971).

William. *A Treatise on International Law*, 7th ed., (Oxford: Clarendon Press, 1917).

Hamilton, Daniel. *The Limits of Sovereignty Property Confiscation in the Union and the Confederacy During the Civil War* (Chicago: University of Chicago Press, 2007).

Haynes, Williams. *American Chemical Industry – The World War I Period: 1912–1922* (New York: D. Van Nostrand Company, 1945).

Hounshell, David, and Smith, John. *Science and Corporate Strategy: Du Pont R and D, 1902–1980* (Cambridge: Cambridge University Press, 1989).

Johnson, Philip, 'Mr Patent Goes to War! Industrial Property and the Breakdown of the International Order during World War'. In *Intellectual Property and the Law of Nations, 1860–1920*, Morris, P. Sean, ed. (Leiden: Brill, 2022).

Keynes, John (Maynard). *The Economic Consequences of the Peace* (London: MacMillan, 1919).

Kristsiotis, Dino, 'Fourteen Ways of Looking Back at the Treaty of Versailles'. *London Review of International Law* 8(1) (2020) 43–88.

Kudo, Akira, 'Dominance Through Cooperation. I.G. Farben's Japan Strategy'. In *The German Chemical Industry in the Twentieth Century*, ed. John Lesch (Dordrecht: Kluwer, 2000) 243–278.

Littauer, Rudolf, 'Confiscation of the Property of Technical Enemies'. *Yale Law Journal* 52(4) (1943) 739–770.

Lubinski, Christina, Giacomin, Valeria, Schnitzer, Klara, 'Countering Political Risk in Colonial India: German Multinationals and the Challenge of Internment (1914–1947)'. Harvard Business School, Working Paper 18-090 (Cambridge: Harvard, 2018).

McDermott, John, 'Trading With the Enemy: British Business and the Law During the First World War'. *Canadian Journal of History* 32(2) (1997) 201–219.

MacMillan, Margaret. *Paris 1919: Six Months that Changed the World* (New York, Random House, 2002).

Maartensz, L., C. G. Alabaster, A. de Mello, and E. Koenig, "Review of Legislation, 1915, VI. Eastern Colonies". *Journal of the Society of Comparative Legislation* 17 (1917) 140–160.

Mann, Charles, and Plummer, Mark. *The Aspirin Wars: Money, Medicine, and 100 Years of Rampant Competition* (Cambridge: Harvard Business School Press, 1991).

Messimer, Dwight. *The Merchant U-Boat: Adventures of the Deutschland, 1916–1918* (Annapolis: Naval Institute Press, 1988).

Moore, John. *International Law and Some Current Illusions: And Other Essays* (New York: Macmillan, 1924).

Moser, Petra, and Voena, Alessandra, 'Compulsory Licensing: Evidence from the Trading with the Enemy Act'. *American Economic Review* 102(1) (2012) 396–427.

Mulder, Nicholas, '"A Retrograde Tendency": The Expropriation of German Property in the Versailles Treaty'. *Journal of the History of International Law* 22(4) (2020) 507–535.

Mulder, Nicholas, 'The Trading with the Enemy Acts in the Age of Expropriation, 1914–49'. *Journal of Global History* 15(1) (2020) 81–99.

Quynn, Dorothy, 'The Art Confiscations of the Napoleonic Wars'. *American Historical Review* 50(3) (1945) 437–460.

Ricketson, Sam. *The Paris Convention for the Protection of Industrial Property: A Commentary* (Oxford: Oxford University Press, 2015).

Scott, Samuel, ed, 'The Enactments of Justinian, The Digest or Pandects, Book XLI'. In *The Civil Law, Including the Twelve Tables, The Institutes of Gaius, The Rules of Ulpian, The Opinions of Paulus, The Enactments of Justinian, and the Constrictions of Leo, Vols 1–7* (New York: AMS Press, 1973).

Shepley, Nick. *Britain, France and Germany and the Treaty of Versailles: How the Allies Built a Flawed Peace*, (2nd ed) (Luton: Andrews UK, 2011).

Sommerich, Otto, 'Recent Innovations in, Legal and Regulatory Concepts as to the Alien and His Property'. *American Journal of International Law* 37(1) (1943) 58–73.

Steen, Kathryn, 'Patents, Patriotism, and "Skilled in the Art" USA v. The Chemical Foundation, Inc., 1923–1926'. *Isis* 92(1) (2001) 91–122.

Steen, Kathryn, 'Confiscated Commerce: American Importers of German Synthetic Organic Chemicals, 1914–1929'. *History and Technology: An International Journal* 12(3) (1995) 261–284.

Turlington, Edgar, 'Treatment of Enemy Private Property in the United States before the World War'. *American Journal of International Law* 22(2) (1928) 270–290.

Turlington, Edgar, 'Vesting Orders under the First War Powers Act, 1941'. *American Journal of International Law* 36(3) (1942) 460–465.

White, Michael, 'US Alien Property Custodian Patent Documents: A Legacy Prior Art Collection From World War II – Part 1. History'. *World Patent Information* 29 (2007) 339–345.

Government Reports

Alien Property Custodian Report, Washington: Government Printing Office, 1919.

'Enemy Interests in United Kingdom Patents', *Official Journal (Patents)*, 13 November 1918.

'Patent and Patent Applications Vested in Public Trustee, Notice' (1918) 101 *Board of Trade Journal*, 575.

Plunder And Restitution: Findings and Recommendations of the Presidential Advisory Commission on Holocaust Assets in the United States and Staff Report, 2000, available at https://govinfo.library.unt.edu/pcha/PlunderRestitution.html/html/StaffChapter3.html, accessed 22 June 2023.

US Alien Property Custodian, *Patents at Work*, Washington: Government Printing Office, 1943.

Cases

British Association of Glass Bottle Manufacturers Ld. v. Forster & Sons Ld. (1917) 34 RPC 217.

Dynamit Actien – Gesellschaft (Vormals Alfred Nobel & Co.) v. Rio Tinto Co., Ltd. [1918] UKHL 784.

Hirsch v Zinc Corporation Ltd (1917) 24 CLR 34.

Hugh *Stevenson* &. Sons *v. Aktiengesellschaft* fuir *Cartonnagen-industrie* (H. L.) [1918] A. C. 239.

Mercedes Daimler Motor Company Ld v. Maudslay Motor Company Ld (1915) 32 RPC 149.

USA v. The Chemical Foundation, Inc. 272 US 1 (1925).

CHAPTER 2

Industrial Property as War Policy Tool during and after World War 1

Enrico Bonadio, Anele Simon and Akshita Rohatgi

1 Introduction

Industrial property (IP) rights notoriously aim to promote innovation and regulate trade by giving inventors and entrepreneurs exclusive rights over their inventions and brands. These are all good and encouraging reasons to grant monopolistic rights in the form of patents and registered trademarks. What is less known is that IP regimes were once used in the furtherance of economic wars. Indeed, the World Wars which have ravaged the twentieth century were a battle of not just military strength but also economic resilience. And IP rights came to be used as a means to further economic warfare.

World War 1 (WW1) saw warring states like Germany and Britain openly flout their obligation of non-discrimination against protected property under the International Convention for the Protection of Industrial Property of 1883 (Paris Convention).[1] Britain, Germany, United States (US) and France all started discriminating against enemy property early during the war and later advanced to not granting at all any IP rights to enemies.[2] In Britain, 'enemy' applications for the grant of any trademark, patent or design were suspended before their publication in the initial stage of the war. Then, in 1916, Britain switched its strategy to suspend applications after publication to enable its public to benefit from the IP.[3] Even if IP rights were granted, an enemy could not sue against infringement in British courts as they had no standing anymore.[4] IP rights were essentially non-enforceable during wartime, violating the Paris Convention's guarantee of protection of rights under all circumstances.

1 Plasseraud, Yves, and, Savignon, Francois. *Paris 1883: Genèse du droit unioniste des brevets* (Paris: Lexis Nexis, 2000).

2 Johnson, Phillip, 'Mr Patent Goes to War! Industrial Property and the Breakdown of the International Order during World War'. In *Intellectual Property and the Law of Nations, 1860–1920* Morris, P. Sean, ed. (Boston: Brill, 2022).

3 Ibid., 157. 'Thirty-Third Report of the Comptroller 1916' (1916 HC Papers 58) Vol. 14, p. 463, p. 3.

4 Ibid.

 | DOI:10.1163/9789004714663_004

While belligerents enacted laws violating the requirement of non-discrimination and used IP as a means to further economic war, the patent order stayed resilient and was restored post-WW1.[5] The primary reason for this was the adoption of a strategy that separated the IP holder from their rights.[6] Britain was the first to adopt a mechanism that respected the patented property but not its proprietor and other belligerents followed soon after.[7] Private companies who owned IP in belligerent countries during armed conflicts such as WW1 lost the right to profit from patented protection in the enemy territory when war broke out. However, the property continued to be protected. In other words, warring countries denied and appropriated enemies' IP rights but continued to respect the patented property.[8] The IP owner thus could not profit off the IP in time of war but IP rights could be restored after the war ended.

This chapter looks at such IP law vicissitudes. It does so by focusing on the period between WW1 and World War 2 (WW2), particularly in Germany, Britain and the US. Sections 2, 3 and 4 of this chapter discuss the pre-WWI era during which states agreed to the protection and the promotion of IP rights via international treaties, especially the Paris and Berne Conventions. These sections also look at the US, British and German wartime legislations confiscating private, enemy-owned IP, particularly pharmaceutical patents. Section 5 then focuses on the impact of the Peace Treaty of Versailles on the IP assets of private, enemy-owned companies in the warring countries. Subsequently, Section 6 highlights the protection of foreign patents during the Interwar period – and compares the mechanisms employed by the ailing German pharmaceutical industry and the infant US and UK pharmaceutical industries. In this section we also expand on the use of ownership cloaking and cartelization in the pharmaceutical industry and how international technology transfers were being employed to mask IP ownership during the interwar period to the benefit of initially opposing sides. Section 7 concludes.

5 Chachereau, Nicolas, and Galvez-Behar, Gabriel, 'Patents, War and Peace. The Resilience of the International Patent Order Through the First World War'. *Journal of European Integration History* 29(2) (2023) 205–226.

6 Ibid., 152.

7 Ibid.

8 Mächtel, Forian. *Das Patentrecht im Krieg* (Tubingen: Mohr Siebeck, 2009) 244.

2 Pre-WWI International IP Law

IP protection in the 19th century was designed to cater to different priorities. In some jurisdictions it aimed to promote domestic innovation and in others it was intended to incentivise the inflow of foreign technology. Closer cooperation among the states produced a desire to promote mutual interests through international conventions, and this underpinned the adoption of the 1883 Paris Convention for the Protection of Industrial Property[9] (covering patents, trademarks, and industrial designs) and the 1886 Berne Convention Berne Convention for the Protection of Literary and Artistic Works (focusing on copyright).[10] Nations maintained the sovereignty to enact domestic IP laws but were obliged to grant IP owners of other signatory states the same protection afforded to nationals (national treatment clause). This is still the most important principle underlying both the Paris and Berne Conventions. As far as the former treaty is concerned, the right of priority was the other main principle:[11] it extended the protection to an applicant who filed a trademark or patent application in one country to all the other signatory states, provided they were the first to apply and the application adhered to prescribed time frames. At the outbreak of war, states did not abandon these treaties. They continued to accept international registrations of patents and trademarks under the Paris system; also, the US did not suspend its financial contributions towards the maintenance of the Convention's Bureau for the duration of WWI.[12]

Another treaty relevant for the purposes of this chapter is the Hague Convention of 1907 which was preceded by the Hague Convention of 1899 and largely reiterated the earlier Convention's principles.[13] It laid the groundwork for a new rules-based international legal order – and was ratified by all

9 Paris Convention for the Protection of Industrial Property of March 20, 1883, as revised at Brussels on December 14, 1900.

10 Berne Convention for the Protection of Literary and Artistic Works, 9 September 1886, 828 UNTS 221 (Berne Convention).

11 See also Sell, Susan, 'Intellectual Property and Public Policy in Historical Perspective: Contestation and Settlement'. *Loyola of Los Angeles Law Review* 38(2) (2004) 267–322.

12 Banerjee, Arpan, and Beldiman. Dana. 'International Trade mark Enforcement under the Versailles Treaty: A Case Study of Sanatogen.' In *Forgotten Intellectual Property Lore: Creativity, Entrepreneurship and Intellectual Property,* Ghosh, Shubha, ed. (Cheltenham: Edward Elgar, 2020) 361.

13 International Conferences (The Hague), Hague Convention (IV) Respecting the Laws and Customs of War on Land and Its Annex: Regulations Concerning the Laws and Customs of War on Land, 18 October 1907. https://oll.libertyfund.org/title/higgins-the-hague-peace-conferences-concerning-the-laws-and-usages-of-war.

the major powers of the time including Germany, France, UK and the US. A chief objective of the conference was the review of the policies regarding laws and customs of war including the regulation of the use of force.[14] More importantly, the Hague Convention affirmed that private property was to be respected during conflicts, and that looting, confiscation and arbitrary plunder of private property was formally prohibited during wars.[15] The inviolability of private property during war time was undoubtedly a mark of civilization, with international lawyers considering confiscation as archaic in the climate of liberal political systems, the advancement of international trade and the conventions which served to protect the property rights of states' nationals.[16] In other words, confiscation of private property during war was perceived as being akin to deliberate attacks on protected neutral persons like medical personnel.

3 Wartime Legislation in the UK and the US

The customary international law principle stating that private property belonging to citizens of enemy states within one's territory is inviolable emerged in international legal cooperation as part of a changing world order.[17] Yet, despite this principle and the above-mentioned Hague Convention, in response to the outbreak of the war in 1914, governments instituted policies aimed at depriving the enemy side of any resources that could aid them in their cause. This new trend was epitomized by the *Trading with the Enemy* laws, enacted by the UK and US in 1914 and 1917, respectively. Their purpose was to bring all property owned by enemies and their allies under government supervision in order to inhibit their contribution as economic weapons.

Take the example of pharmaceuticals. The manufacture of synthetic drugs developed as a by-product of Europe's dyestuffs and chemical industries which were taking shape in the late 19th century. German companies were dominating this market by the early 1900s, producing trademarked and patent-protected medicines such as anti-syphilitic drugs, local anaesthetics and

14 Ibid.

15 Article 46 of the Hague Conventions of 1899 and 1907 simply states that 'Private property cannot be confiscated' without any distinction between intangible and tangible property.

16 Caglioti, Daniela, 'Property Rights in Time of War: Sequestration and Liquidation of Enemy Aliens' Assets in Britain, Germany and France in the First World War'. *Journal of Modern European History* 12(4) (2014) 523–545, 525.

17 Borchard, Edwin, 'Enemy Private Property'. *American Journal of International Law* 18(3) (1924) 523–532.

making significant advancements in the development of synthetic alkaloids. The pre-1914 era was characterized by high receptivity to foreign business, particularly to German chemical brands, in both UK and US. In 1913 Germany produced more than 35% of the world's pharmaceutical exports followed by Britain which accounted for 25% and the US which claimed 15%.[18] The globalization of the pharmaceutical industry was reinforced by the implementation of the late 19th century international order in which the most important states pledged to uphold the reciprocal protection of foreign industrial and intellectual property.[19] Yet, the era of high receptivity to foreign business changed radically with the outbreak of WWI.

The Great War extended to the economic sphere and warring countries started ignoring the international law rule of not discriminating against foreign patentees and their trademarks, as mandated by the Paris Convention. Allies usurped numerous patents which belonged to privately-owned German companies. The dominance of "enemy" producers in the pharmaceutical market provoked striking legislative responses by both UK and US.[20] The US war legislation, i.e., the US *Trading with the Enemy Act*, was founded upon the earlier (and homonymous) British war legislation. The legislative terms "enemy" and "trade with an enemy" were based on each jurisdiction's public policy needs at the time. For example, a strategy for the compulsory licensing of enemy-owned patents was constructed *before* war legislation was enacted in UK, which suggests that the dependence on certain German inventions heavily informed the content of such legislation.[21] The British government evaluated the extent of its reliance on the German pharmaceutical industry, which prompted the UK to seek alternative sources for medicines including compulsory licences of the confiscated chemical patents in favour of British suppliers.[22] The US also amended its initial war legislation to allow compulsory licensing in favour of

---

18 Cramer, Tobias, 'Building the 'World's Pharmacy': The Rise of the German Pharmaceutical Industry, 1871–1914'. *The Business History Review* 89(1) (2015) 43–73, 46.

19 Berne Convention for the Protection of Literary and Artistic Works, 9 September 1886, 828 UNTS 221; Paris Convention for the Protection of Industrial Property, adopted 20 March 1883, 828 UNTS 305; Treaty of Frankfurt (1871).

20 Chachereau, Nicolas, and, Galvez-Behar, Gabriel, 'The International Patent System and the First World War'. *Digital Encyclopaedia of European History*. 06 August 2021. ISSN 2677–6588. https://ehne.fr/en/node/14180 [Accessed 30 April 2022].

21 Williams, Keith. British Pharmaceutical Industry, Synthetic Drug Manufacture and the Clinical Testing of Novel Drugs 1895 to 1939 (Unpublished, PhD, University of Manchester, 2005) 143–150. Williams notes that before the legislation was enacted, the British government set up 'The Committee on Drug Supply' to first decide which drugs and chemicals were a domestic necessity and to determine whether these could be produced in Britain.

22 Williams, British Pharmaceutical Industry, 143.

domestic pharmaceutical companies by granting them access to German IP to mitigate a number of public health emergencies.[23]

We first look at the UK scenario. The UK declared war on Germany on 4 August 1914. On 5 August 1914 the UK *Trading with the Enemy Proclamation* was adopted – it criminalized trade "with subjects or residents or the carrying on business in" enemy states for the entire duration of the war.[24] The British government suspended international relations between itself and enemy nations during the conflict. The Patents, Designs and Trade-Marks (Temporary Rules) Act (August 1914) passed on 27 August 1914 empowered the *Board of Trade*, a government institution, to wind up and liquidate enemy-owned companies – essentially eliminating the possibility of their revival after the war.[25] Indeed, German nationals owned lucrative chemical patents and trademarks in Britain, and the *Board of Trade* was also authorized to confiscate or cancel those registered titles. The *Trading with the Enemy Proclamation* progressed into the *Trading with the Enemy Act* (September 1914) and later the *Trading with the Enemy Amendment Act* (November 1914), which were the primary legislative measures that Britain enforced against alien enemy property on its territory and imposed penalties for trading with enemy aliens.[26]

It should be noted that in the early 20th century, German companies dominated the pharmaceutical industry to the point that there was a strong reliance on German drugs in Britain. The trade embargo exposed that weakness when some of those life-saving drugs became increasingly unavailable. One such drug was *Salvarsan*, a globally successful remedy for the prevalent sexually-transmitted disease syphilis. The UK Royal Commission on Venereal Disease reported that eight to twelve percent of British troops were infected with the often-fatal venereal disease[27] (syphilis' toll on public health was comparable to that of HIV in recent decades). The *Salvarsan* had been protected since 1910 by a UK patent owned by the German company Hoechst.[28] Initially a dyestuff

---

23 Cooper, Dale, 'The Trading with the Enemy Act of 1917 and Synthetic Drugs: Relieving Scarcity, Controlling Prices, and Establishing Pre-Marketing Licensing Controls.' *Pharmacy in History* 47(2) (2005) 47–61.

24 'A Proclamation Relating to Trading with the Enemy', Supplement to the London Gazette, 5 August 1914, Page 6166. https://www.thegazette.co.uk/London/issue/28862/supplement/6166/data.pdf [Accessed 10 March 2022].

25 Bird, John. *Control of Enemy Alien Civilians in Great Britain 1914–1918* (Abingdon: Routledge, 1986). The 1981 PhD thesis at the LSE is however used for citation purposes.

26 Ibid., 317.

27 Payne, E., 'The Battle Against Venereal Disease in Wartime Britain (1914–1918)'. April 2006. https://www.westernfrontassociation.com/world-war-i-articles/the-battle-against-venereal-disease-in-wartime-britain-1914-1918/.

28 Williams, British Pharmaceutical Industry (n 21) 157.

producer, Hoechst successfully diversified its business into pharmaceuticals and established subsidiaries outside of Germany, directly contributing to the globalization of the pharmaceutical industry. In October 1914, a local manufacturer, Burroughs Wellcome & Co., successfully applied for the suspension of Hoechst's *Salvarsan* patent and was granted a compulsory license to synthesize the drug for domestic use (their substitute was called *Kharsivan*).[29] Access to the *Salvarsan* patent marked a turning point for the development of the British drug trade. On the back of their success, Burroughs Wellcome & Co. were granted permission to synthesize other patent-protected German drugs including Bayer's aspirin.[30]

What about the US? Two months before the US joined the war, it unequivocally stated that it would under no circumstances exploit the war by seizing property protected by international conventions and American domestic laws. The US committed itself to upholding the international law principle of national treatment by treating the private rights of foreign nationals as it treated the private rights of its own citizens.[31] Yet, this valiant commitment to uphold the international law of the day did not survive the realities of war. The US enacted its own version of the *Trading with the Enemy Act* in October 1917, six months after declaring war on Germany. The *Act* authorised the placing of alien enemy property in the safekeeping of a government agency, the *Alien Property Custodian*, which would administer that property on behalf of its owners until the war against the enemy was over. In a complete departure from its pre-war assurance, congressional amendments to this Act empowered the *Alien Property Custodian* to violate and later trade all enemy-owned patents. Specifically, by 1919, 4,706 German-owned patents were expropriated and later made available for compulsory licensing to US companies by the Federal Trade Commission.[32] The seizure of IP belonging to private German companies was a blatant contrast to the US pre-war stance, disconnecting it from its international law obligations. We now briefly highlight how specific German companies were targeted by this law.

---

29 Ibid., 159.

30 Quirke, Viviane, 'Foreign Influences, National Styles, and the Creation of a Modern Pharmaceutical Industry in Britain and France'. *Pharmacy in History* 52(3/4) (2010) 134–147, 141.

31 Sommerich, Otto, 'A Brief Against Confiscation'. *Law and Contemporary Problems* 11(1) (1945) 152–165, 159.

32 Baten, Joerg, Bianchi, Nicola, and Moser, Petra, 'Compulsory Licensing and Innovation – Historical Evidence From German Patents After WWI'. *Journal of Development Economics* 126 (2017) 231–242.

3.1 *Bayer*

The *Alien Property Custodian* caused a colossal, recurring headache for the US subsidiary of the German pharmaceutical company Bayer AG. In 1897 the German company made a scientific breakthrough with its invention of an effective pain relief medicine that would later be known globally as *aspirin*. The drug's popularity soared beyond Germany and by the turn of the century Bayer's aspirin was the most popular drug in the world. The company was highly profitable in the US, had a wholly-US owned subsidiary by 1913 and called it *Bayer Co., Inc.* It also secured a US patent to protect aspirin since 1900, with the company trademarks – the word 'Bayer' and the logo incorporating such word inside a circle in a cross formation – having also been registered in the US.[33]

In January 1918, pursuant to provisions of the *Trading with the Enemy Act*, the US government classified *Bayer Co., Inc.* and other "enemy-owned" foreign private companies as being under enemy control of the German government and confiscated them. All the US subsidiary's assets including its IP rights, subsequently vested in the *Alien Property Custodian*. In December of that year, the US government agency publicly auctioned Bayer. It was eventually sold on the steps of its New York factory to the successful bid of the lesser-known American pharmaceutical company Sterling Drug, Inc. Due to the operation of the wartime legislation, the American company acquired the pharmaceutical giant as its subsidiary, and sold the dyestuff division of the company to the Grasselli Chemical Company. This would provide the Germans a fortuitous foot in the door in the future; in 1924 Grasselli Chemical Company would partner with Bayer AG and effectively revive their lost dyestuff business in the US. As we will see, the German parent company Bayer AG never recovered its American IP, not even under the *Versailles Treaty*, which multiplied its legal woes instead. In 1921 a US court ruled that Bayer's common law trademark 'aspirin' had become the generic name of the product, effectively allowing all other drug companies to use it.[34] Sterling Drug Inc remedied this by simply branding their painkiller "*Bayer aspirin*." The German parent company, although stripped of its assets by the war-induced *Trading with the Enemy Act*, did not benefit from the restoration of wartime confiscations provided for in the *Versailles Treaty*; this was because Germany had to make reparations for the war and thus the Allied countries retained the confiscated property of German private companies. Bayer AG faced decades of failed litigation and finally recovered the US

33 Farbenfabriken Bayer A.G. v. Sterling Drug, 307 F.2d 210, 212 (3d Cir. 1962).

34 Bayer Co. v. United Drug Co., 272 F. 505 (S.D.N.Y. 1921).

trademark 'Bayer Aspirin' by acquiring Sterling Winthrop (the successor in title of *Sterling Drug, Inc*) for $1 billion in 1994.[35]

3.2 *Hoechst*

The logistics of war and the subsequent shortfall of indispensable medications exposed the US dependency on German synthetic drugs just as it had in Britain. Two of Hoechst's products were prioritised for compulsory licensing: the already mentioned anti-syphilitic drug *Salvarsan* and the local anaesthetic *Novocain*.[36] Subsequent amendments to the legislation significantly strengthened the Federal Trade Commission's power to license enemy-owned patents in favour of US companies, and also gave the *Alien Property Custodian* the ability to dispose of the enemy-owned patents as though they were the agency's own property. As mentioned, the war exposed American dependence on German synthetic drugs but the *Trading with the Enemy Act* remedied this weakness twofold: it mitigated the scarcity of critical medications through licensing and stimulated the US drug production industry through access to German patented information.

3.3 *Beiersdorf*

Beiersdorf was another German chemical manufacturer that ventured into the US market in the late 19th century. The company licensed an American firm, Lehn & Fink, to manufacture its toothpaste *Pebeco* in the US. *Pebeco* soon became a successful product and before the war it accounted for nearly half of Beiersdorf's sales revenue.[37] Due to the application of the *Trading with the Enemy Act*, Beiersdorf was classified as enemy-owned business, and its trademarks were expropriated and sold to its former American partner Lehn & Fink. Accordingly, Beiersdorf's US business ceased to exist by the end of the war.[38]

---

35 Olmos, David, 'German Firm to Reclaim Bayer Aspirin Name: Drugs: It Will Acquire Sterling Winthrop's Over-The-Counter Business and Recover the Rights it Lost After WWI'. *Los Angeles Times*, 13 September 1994. https://www.latimes.com/archives/la-xpm-1994-09-13-fi-38019-story.html.

36 Cooper, Dale, 'The Licensing of German Drug Patents Confiscated During World War I: Federal and Private Efforts to Maintain Control, Promote Production, and Protect Public Health'. *Pharmacy in History* 54(1) (2012) 3–32.

37 Jones, Geoffrey, and, Lubinski, Christina, 'Managing Political Risk in Global Business: Beiersdorf 1914–1990'. *Enterprise and Society* 13(1)(2011) 85–119, 90.

38 Jones, and, Lubinski, 'Managing Political Risk in Global Business,' 1.

3.4 *Merck*

The American pharmaceutical company Merck & Co. was founded in the late 19th century as a subsidiary of the German pharmaceutical giant E. Merck Darmstadt. The Darmstadt-based pharmaceutical firm had entered the US market in 1891, expertly offering local anaesthetics such as cocaine, morphine, and the leading sedative on the US market, Veronal.[39] The latter was a powerful sedative whose effect could last up to two days – it was used for the treatment of paranoia, hysteria and other nervous conditions. It was also found to be effective in aiding the treatment of lung tuberculosis.[40] The *Alien Property Custodian* seized the German-owned portion of the US subsidiary (an 80% stake in that business), with the remainder shareholding being left to its American owner, George Merck. The American Merck family was subsequently able to reacquire a majority of the sequestered shares in 1919 on condition that Merck & Co. would sever all association with its German founder for a period of ten years. The reconstitution of the subsidiary resulted in loss of valuable business capacity as revenues plummeted from $8.15 million in 1917 to $4.36 million in 1921.[41] This unmasked the American company's reliance on the German parent's products and expertise.

•••

The *Trading with the Enemy* laws of Britain and the US were introduced as measures to merely prohibit the association with a hostile country during the war, but later the confiscations of enemy property were justified as retaliation for German actions of similar kind. The US affirmed that the elimination of German businesses from its markets was a positive outcome for its local industry.[42] The German chemical and pharmaceutical industries were at that time cutting-edge and therefore wartime compulsory licensing of German-owned patents allowed the US and British industries to gain competitive ground.

None of the warring States admitted having ignored obligations under international treaties, though. While Germany claimed their confiscations

39 Merck, E., 'E. Merck's Annual Report: Volume 17'. Library of the Ohio State University, (1904) 185.

40 Ibid.

41 Godley, Andrew, Joseph, Marissa, and, Leslie-Hughes, David, 'Technology Transfer in the Interwar US Pharmaceutical Sector: The Case of E. Merck of Darmstadt and Merck & Co., Rahway, New Jersey'. *Enterprise & Society* 20(3) (2019) 613–651.

42 Potterf, Rex, 'Treatment of Alien Enemy Property in War Time and After by the United States'. *Indiana Law Journal* 2(6) (1927) 453–472, 460.

were retaliatory (see the next section), the US government did not consider its *Trading with the Enemy Act* a violation or a departure from international law. The US maintained that countries reserved the sovereignty to determine what was to be regarded as unlawful trade with an enemy, and as mentioned did not renounce the relevant international conventions but in fact continued to contribute to the maintenance of the Paris Convention's International Bureau throughout the war.[43] On the other hand, Britain was suspected of using its international relations policy to confiscate privately-owned alien enemy property for reasons that were actually unrelated to the prosecution of WW1.[44]

4 Germany's Reaction

Germany's treatment of privately-owned British assets mirrored British treatment of German property on British soil during the war. The German government indeed retaliated by giving identical treatment to British alien property, with the German Property Custodian being established by an order of 19 April 1917, years after the British Proclamation of August 1914 prohibited commerce with Germany.[45] Germany kept the confiscated privately-owned British assets under the trusteeship of the German Alien Property Custodian and conducted the confiscated businesses profitably; this arrangement was similar to the UK and US alien property schemes.[46] Germany always maintained that their expropriation of enemy-owned property was retaliatory – and this was substantiated by Germany's retaliatory law being extended to include the confiscation of American property on 10 November 1917, just one month after the US' *Trading with the Enemy Act* came into effect.[47] As of 1 June 1920 the German Alien Property Custodian recorded that a smaller volume of US commercial businesses was on German soil while German operations were predominant in American territory – a ratio of 100 to 1 in favour of US.[48] This imbalance inevitably neutralised the severity of Germany's treatment of US alien property – thus

43 Banerjee and Beldiman, 'International Trade mark Enforcement Under the Versailles Treaty' (n 12) 360–361.

44 FCO. British Policy Towards Enemy Property During and after the Second World War. Foreign & Commonwealth Office (General Services Command, 1998) 2–3.

45 The Nation Newspaper. 'American Property in Germany'. February 16, 1921. Volume 112, No. 2902. https://babel.hathitrust.org/cgi/pt?id=umn.31951001355237y&view=1up&seq=336.

46 Potterf, 'Treatment of Alien Enemy Property' (n 42) 458.

47 Baten, Bianchi, and Moser, 'Compulsory Licensing' (n 32); Potterf, 'Treatment of Alien Enemy Property' (n 42).

48 Ibid.

Germany's reaction was cautious toward foreign economic interests because German economic interests abroad far outweighed enemy interests within its own territory.[49] After the Armistice which ended WW1, almost all US property seized by the German government, including IP rights, was returned to their owners.

What is also noteworthy is that British and US pharmaceutical and chemical companies did not patent at the volume of their more efficient German counterparts in the years preceding WW1. Also, despite US and UK compulsory licensing of German patents, many patented inventions could not be reproduced by the beneficiary firms because they lacked the professional expertise and skill that was necessary to work the inventions. Sterling Winthrop's acquisition of Bayer's IP did not trigger the expected reproduction and dissemination of drugs because Sterling Winthrop lacked the specialist knowledge and skill to operate Bayer's equipment. In some instances, the patents could not be exploited because German firms like Badische Anilin und Soda Fabrik (BASF) purposefully withheld or obscurely reported critical process information in their patent applications.[50] This is not to say however that UK and US businesses did not benefit from the appropriation of German IP. Britain had indeed relied on German dyes, chemicals and synthetic medicines for long time before WW1, and wartime access to key German patents helped avert a potentially perilous situation by strengthening the UK capacity to manufacture those products. Similarly, access to German patents via compulsory licensing stimulated the US synthetic organic chemicals industry – this is epitomized by a 20% surge in the registration of domestic chemical patents in the US in 1918.[51]

5 The Peace Treaty of Versailles

The 1919 Treaty of Versailles ended the war between the Allied Powers and Germany. The treaty was vague and ambiguous in that it legalised the wartime seizures by the Allies[52] but also provided for the restoration of warring nations' pre-war IP rights[53] while immunizing the Allied Nations for their unauthorised

49 Potterf, 'Treatment of Alien Enemy Property', 458. See particularly the discussion in footnote 51.

50 Moser, Petra, and Voena, Alessandra, 'Compulsory Licensing: Evidence from the Trading with the Enemy Act'. *American Economic Review* 102(1) (2012) 396–427.

51 Ibid., 11–12.

52 Article 297.

53 Article 306.

exploitation of enemy-owned (mainly German) IP assets.[54] The US ultimately was not a signatory of the treaty – yet it participated in negotiations regarding the handover of German dye stocks as war reparations to the Allied countries. The US did not bear a big financial cost of the war and thus did not need reparations of any other kind; interestingly, the US did however accept reparations in the form of German synthetic dye supplies.[55] The Versailles Treaty's undertaking of war reparations in the form of dyes was twofold: firstly, the victors claimed 50% of all available German dye supplies and secondly, they were entitled to an apportionment of 25% of German dye production for the following five years.[56] The only part of the Versailles Treaty that was accepted by the US was the German war reparations to be paid out in the form of synthetic dye supplies. This partial participation in the Versailles Treaty exhibited the US government's commitment to supporting its own domestic synthetic dye industry and the government's desire to propel the US synthetic dye sector to a global force.

The reparation clauses of the treaty maintained the 'economic warfare' between the Allies and Germany in the form of property seizure and compulsory transfer of rights.[57] Britain and the US indeed reserved the right to keep the confiscated IP of German private companies while Germany was expected to reimburse those companies for the wartime confiscations. This retention of enemy property clearly dishonoured the principle of the inviolability of foreign property rights and seemingly placed the blame of war on the shoulders of private companies.

The story around the German company Bauer Chemical, trading as Wülfing Bauer & Cie since the late 19th century and manufacturer of the food tonic *Sanatogen*, epitomises the war related tensions. The tonic in question aided in the enforcement of the daily diet of anaemic and convalescent patients of all ages, and received worldwide acclaim with commendations from many physicians and celebrities. It was extensively marketed as the best remedy for a multitude of illnesses and publicized as a "brain tonic". By the start of the 20th century *Sanatogen* was the preferred household brand available in the US, Europe, China and Australia, with a British newspaper advertising the

54 Article 309 of the Versailles Treaty. See also Banerjee (n 4) 363; Potterf (n 40) 469–470.

55 Steen, Kathryn. *The American Synthetic Organic Chemicals Industry: War and Politics, 1910–1930* (Chapel Hill, North Carolina: University of North Carolina Press, 2014) 190.

56 Ibid.

57 Glaser, Elisabeth, 'The Making of the Economic Peace.' In The Treaty of Versailles: A Reassessment after 75 Years, Boemeke, Manfred, Feldman, Gerald, and Glaser, Elisabeth, eds. (Washington, D.C.: German Historical Institute, 1998) 371–400.

product as "the greatest invention of modern medical science."[58] Its reputation stretched as far as India where the Times of India touted it as "the most powerful revitalizing and restorative agent known to the world".[59] *Sanatogen* was also heralded as the leading product for curing and preventing malaria. The Wülfing company invested heavily in the medicine's advertising and as a result of the product's popularity India became a highly profitable market for the German firm. The *Sanatogen* trademark was confidently associated with quality, and the German company in 1906 registered a British subsidiary, A Wülfing & Co., and began manufacturing the medicine in UK.

By the outbreak of the war in 1914, the *Sanatogen* retained its high demand despite the increasing anti-German sentiment as the war progressed. There was, after all, no initial prohibition against trading with German companies that were established in Britain as subsidiaries. Thus, the brand was safe – with the British subsidiary A Wülfing & Co even trying to distance itself from its German background. Yet, the entry into force of the *Trading with the Enemy Act* changed the fate of many German and other enemy-owned brands. Consequently, the name *Sanatogen* was removed from the UK Register of Trade Marks in October 1916 and subsequently the *Wülfing* subsidiary, including its goodwill, was sold to the UK firm Genatosan Limited. *Sanatogen* was then renamed *Genatosan* to further sanitise it of its German origins in Britain. From 1917 to 1923 the London owners, Genatosan Limited, continued to market its export as *Sanatogen* in India and other territories that did not harbour anti-German sentiments.

The German *Wülfing Bauer & Cie* also continued to produce, trade and export its medicine *Sanatogen* to India; the trademark had lost its distinctiveness due to other manufactures selling their products using the same name, including the British Genatosan Limited. When the war ended and the Treaty of Versailles restored IP protection, the original German owner of the *Sanatogen* trademark petitioned the Indian court for its reinstatement – and this resulted in a decision in the *AJ Von Wülfing v DH Jivandas* case on 19 December 1924.[60] Specifically, the Bombay High Court was tasked with deciding whether *Sanatogen* was a valid and protected trademark owned by the original German owner in India in the aftermath of the war and the

58 Banerjee, Arpan, and Beldiman. Dana. 'International Trade Mark Enforcement under the Versailles Treaty: A Case Study of Sanatogen.' In *Forgotten Intellectual Property Lore: Creativity, Entrepreneurship and Intellectual Property*, Ghosh, Shubha, ed. (Cheltenham: Edward Elgar, 2020).

59 Ibid.

60 A.J. Von Wulfing vs D.H. Jivandas And Co. (1926) 28 BOMLR 243.

Versailles Treaty. The registration had been cancelled in UK by British wartime legislation under *Trade with the Enemy Act*. This led to many firms in the UK selling their medicine under that popular name – yet India was not bound by the British legislation. The Bombay court held that the *Wülfing* company's *Sanatogen* trademark (despite not being a registered trademark in India) was entitled to the trademark protection rights that it had enjoyed before the war broke out, as restored by the *Versailles Treaty*. The court ruled that it was a trademark infringement for the defendants, the Indian company Jivandas, to sell their medicine in India using the name *Sanatogen*. This case shows how the *Versailles Treaty* was applied to actually restore IP rights expropriated or confiscated as a result of the war.

6 Interwar Period

After the war, the global importation and supply of critical German drugs and dyes resumed. Peace brought with it a new set of competition woes for the developing chemical and pharmaceutical industries of both UK and US. Export restrictions were removed, the demand to supply troops with pain medications diminished and due to the terms of the Versailles Treaty, there was an influx of competitive German products available. The Association of British Chemical Manufacturers heavily lobbied the UK government to shield Britain's bourgeoning industry from being supplanted by the resumption of trade of German products.[61] The collaboration between the government and the British pharmaceutical industry persisted during the interwar period, with protectionist trade policies being enforced as a temporary means to encourage British industry and firms to strengthen their competitive advantage against foreign firms. These policies included limiting market access through the introduction of standardisation requirements and the implementation of high import tariffs. The 1921 Safeguarding of Industry Act, for example, imposed a hefty 33.3% import tariff on foreign chemical products for a five-year period to allow the chemical industry to build competitiveness against robust import markets.[62]

American anti-German rhetoric also survived the war, with lobbyists in the US seeking the protection of US domestic production. The result of the lobbying was the Fordney-McCumber Tariff Act of 1922, imposing a hefty 60% tariff

61 Williams, 'British Pharmaceutical Industry' (n 21) 183.

62 Ibid., 215.

on imported synthetic dyes intentionally aimed at discouraging their importation.[63] By the end of that year the US synthetic organic chemicals industry had been legislatively supported to fend off the re-emergence of German firms. German producers realised that their chances of surviving the protectionist trade barriers and re-entering their former strongholds were poor and that their best response was to consolidate their firms in the form of industrial cartels.[64] Cartels in Germany at the end of the 19th and beginning of 20th century were not uncommon. In 1927 the German Reichsgericht (Supreme Court) held that "the pursuit of monopolistic position was nothing unlawful as long as permitted instruments were used and the purpose of the monopoly did not contravene morality."[65] Obviously, companies navigating declining industries were (and still are) more likely to form cartels than companies flourishing in expanding industries.[66] This observation perfectly encapsulates the German synthetic chemical industry and its response to its economic hardship during the interwar period.

Cartelisation was legalised in the German economy when a Supreme Court decision of February 4, 1897 made cartel agreements legally binding. The rapid emergence of business cartels in the interwar period was an industrial response to both political and economic uncertainty.[67] German chemical companies had suffered colossal financial losses because of the war, with the result that during the interwar years an unprecedented number of cartels began to form in several sectors including the ailing chemical industry (in the meantime Britain, France, and the US were investing in their own chemical industries to produce dyes, explosives and fertilisers, and passed protectionist measures to safeguard those developments). The rapid emergence of cartels in Germany precipitated the 1923 *Act to Prevent the Misuse of Economic Predominance* – an example of a German cartel regulation that was enacted to *inter alia* enable governmental action against cartels considered as compromising the economy. It also provided a withdrawal mechanism and a general prohibition on the intimidation

63 See Cooper (n 36).

64 Ibid.

65 Pahlow, Louis, 'Intellectual Property and Competition Policy: Patent Pooling and Industrial Concentration in Germany (1890–1930).' In *Expanding Intellectual Property: Copyrights and Patents in 20th Century Europe and Beyond* Siegrist, Hannes and, Dimou Augusta, eds. (Budapest: Central European University Press, 2017) 100.

66 Bouwens, Bram, and Dankers, Joost, 'Competition and Coordination: Reconsidering Economic Cooperation in Dutch Business, 1900–2000'. *Revue Économique* 64(6)(2013) 1105–1124, 1108.

67 Cramer, 'Building the 'World's Pharmacy'' (n 18) 36.

of non-cartel companies.[68] Despite this Act, cartels in Germany continued to thrive. The following examples are noteworthy.

6.1 *I.G Farben*

In 1925 six major firms including Bayer, BASF and Hoechst merged into the patent-pooling conglomerate *I.G Farben AG* – it came to be known as the 'dyestuff cartel'.[69] The chemical corporation boasted a prodigious research team. It employed 67,000 people of which 1,000 were chemists, and 36% of its sales were from dyestuff.[70] The cartel eradicated duplicate operations and modernised their dyes industry into a high-end dyes market,[71] seeking to use its combined dominance to penetrate international markets.

6.2 *Merck*

In 1920 E. Merck Darmstadt, the German former parent company of the American Merck & Co, joined a pharmaceutical manufacturers' profit-sharing cartel which consisted of German pharmaceutical companies Boehringer Mannheim and Knoll. The cartel popularly became known as the I.G Pharma, and agreed to pool their processes, expertise and to refrain from violating members' patents.[72] Around the same period, Merck & Co. dishonoured the reacquisition agreement between itself and the US government and tried to resuscitate a working relationship with its former German parent company, but this collaboration soon disintegrated.

6.3 *The European Hormone Cartel*

At that time, illnesses caused by hormone deficiency, such as recurrent miscarriages, were treated with synthetic sex hormones; the process patents for those hormones formed the basis of the 1937 hormone cartel comprised of primarily of Schering (German), Ciba (Swiss) and Organon (Dutch). Through exclusive cross licensing the cartel controlled the key patents relating to the synthesising of sex hormones, with such process patents including all possible methods of manufacturing sex steroids. The cartel parties negotiated export territorial divisions, restricted production of the synthetic hormones and initially barred

68 See Cooper (n 36).

69 Glaser-Schmidt, Elisabeth, 'Foreign Trade Strategies of I.G. Farben after World War I'. *Business and Economic History* 23(1) (1994) 201–211 (1994).

70 Morris, Peter, and Travis, Anthony, 'A History of the International Dyestuff Industry'. *American Dyestuff Reporter* 81(11) (1992) 59–108.

71 See Cooper (n 36).

72 Williams, 'British Pharmaceutical Industry' (n 21) 61–62.

cooperation with competitor pharmaceutical firms like the Merck companies.[73] The European hormone cartel is a prime example of cartelization based on anti-competitive and price collusion grounds during the interwar period.

•••

As mentioned, nationality played a fundamental role in the expropriation of enemy assets, including IP, during WW1. The political risk of expropriation and post-war anti-German attitudes resulted in many German companies protecting their businesses by 'cloaking'. Cloaking is the deliberate act of concealing the true ownership of a business, mainly from authorities.[74] The use of carefully constructed and sophisticated organizational structures enabled firms to obscure their German origins. A popular cloaking device was the use of a parent company's subsidiary established in a neutral territory to manage the operations of all subsidiaries in other territories thereby giving the impression that the controlling subsidiary was the parent company. The German Government's interests did not align with the business interests of companies trading with belligerent or unfriendly countries. As a result, companies tried to subvert IP policies that restricted trade with sanctioned entities using mechanisms like cloaking. Cloaking thus enabled private companies to adopt a different nationality and thus bypass the regulations of the host country. This strategy also served a secondary purpose for German companies when the anti-Semitic policies of the Nazi government targeted Jewish people and Jewish-owned businesses. We give below some examples of cloaking.

6.4 *Beiersdorf*

The surviving German business of the company *Beiersdorf* devised multiple strategies, including the use of cloaking devices, to protect itself from hostile economies and unfriendly sentiment. Cloaking facilitated the international movement of goods and capital, artfully dodging the stringent industrial policy restrictions during the interwar period. Beiersdorf's cloaking strategy was initially aimed at protecting the business from political risks which arose in foreign markets; but the company had Jewish ownership and its senior

---

73 United States Congress, Senate Committee on Military Affairs, 'Scientific and Technical Mobilization,' Hearing before a Subcommittee on Military Affairs, Seventy Eighth Congress Session on Section 702, March 30, 1943, 1132–1133.

74 Aalders, Gerard, and, Wiebes, Cees. *The Art of Cloaking Ownership: The Secret Collaboration and Protection of the German War Industry by the Neutrals: The Case of Sweden* (Amsterdam: Amsterdam University Press, 1996) 9.

management was largely Jewish. Cloaking its ownership from the anti-Semitic Nazi regime thus became imperative domestically too. The company relocated its Jewish employees to the subsidiaries it had established in neutral territories.

Also, in the Netherlands *Beiersdorf* camouflaged its business in a "Ring" formation consisting of two circles. While it had the German headquarters in Hamburg in one circle, the other circle consisted of its subsidiary in the Netherlands – i.e. the centre of the "Ring" managing from Amsterdam the operations of twelve other foreign subsidiaries.[75] Through the cloaking strategy Beiersdorf rebuilt its international business and repurchased confiscated international trademarks which German companies were otherwise barred from reacquiring. Protecting the company's pharmaceutical patents against political risk was a key concern of re-entering the international markets as a German-owned company.

6.5 *Schering AG*

Berlin-based Schering AG was one of Germany's largest companies before WWII. It owned a vast number of pharmaceutical patents – and licences under those patents were granted to its subsidiaries globally. Schering AG also owned a New York-based subsidiary named Schering Corporation which it had established in 1929. The subsidiary progressed from being a distributor of mainly bulk camphor to manufacturing its own pharmaceutical products including synthetic sex hormones. The German parent company insured the safety of its foreign assets by setting up a complex holding company structure based in Switzerland. This holding company operated the other foreign subsidiaries of Schering A.G. which jointly owned a Swiss company named Chemical & Pharmaceutical Enterprises, Ltd (Chepha) together with hormone cartel partners *Ciba* (49%) and the *Swiss Bank Corporation* (51%). Chepha in turn owned Schering Corporation in New York, effectively intensifying the camouflage of its true German ownership. In 1938 said NY-based subsidiary and Schering A.G. entered into a business agreement that involved the sharing of patents and a division of market territory. Schering Corporation was restricted to only trade within the US unless it had the express permission of Schering A.G. The German Schering agreed not to compete within the US market nor to supply any US entity apart from Schering Corporation.[76] The language in the

75 See Cooper (n 36).

76 See also, Cooper, Dale, 'The Licensing of German Drug Patents Confiscated During World War I: Federal and Private Efforts to Maintain Control, Promote Production, and Protect Public Health'. *Pharmacy in History* 54(1) (2012); Jones, Geoffrey, and, Lubinski, Christina, 'Managing Political Risk in Global Business: Beiersdorf 1914–1990'. *Enterprise and Society* 13(1)(2011) 85–119; Godley, Andrew, Joseph, Marissa, and, Leslie-Hughes, David,

agreement revealed the true relationship between the parent and its subsidiary company even though the ownership was cloaked as Swiss.

6.6 *I.G Farben*

German firms sometimes returned to the American industry with cloaking assistance from within the US. The Grasseli Chemical Co. had acquired Bayer's dyestuff division and all its patents from Sterling Products Co. In May and June 1924 Grasselli Chemical Co. and Bayer reached a series of agreements under which the two companies assigned all of their US dyestuff patents to a newly formed, jointly and equally owned company called Grasselli Dyestuff Corporation.[77] The following year the company's shareholding was altered. The US firm *Grasselli Chemical Co.* ended up owning a 35% interest in *Grasselli Dyestuff Corporation* and the German company *Bayer* a 30% interest; the remaining 35% shareholding belonged to an American trustee of Hoechst and an American sales representative of BASF.[78] Effectively, but not formally, the new corporation was owned by the I.G Farben conglomerate. A series of significant changes then followed: the restructured *Grasselli Dyestuff Corporation* became the sole selling agent of *I.G Farben's* dyestuff in the US and the company name was changed to *General Dyestuff Corp.* In 1928 *General Dyestuff Corp* was wholly acquired by a Swiss company called *I.G Chemie* through its US subsidiary and underwent another name change, this time to General Aniline Works.[79] As a New York company, the German owned (cloaked) subsidiary *General Aniline Works* was not only shielded from the high tariff walls of the 1922 Tariff Act, it also benefitted from the legislation because the Act excluded foreign dyestuff competitors from the US market.

None of the acquisitions and company restructuring were undertaken in vain. Shortly after WW1 the *Alien Property Custodian* sold more than 550

'Technology Transfer in the Interwar US Pharmaceutical Sector: The Case of E. Merck of Darmstadt and Merck & Co., Rahway, New Jersey'. *Enterprise & Society* 20(3) (2019) 613–651; Potterf, Rex, 'Treatment of Alien Enemy Property in War Time and After by the United States'. *Indiana Law Journal* 2(6) (1927) 453–472; Banerjee, Arpan, and Beldiman. Dana. 'International Trade mark Enforcement under the Versailles Treaty: A Case Study of Sanatogen.' In *Forgotten Intellectual Property Lore: Creativity, Entrepreneurship and Intellectual Property*, Ghosh, Shubha, ed. (Cheltenham: Edward Elgar, 2020).

77 United States v. General Dyestuff Corp., US District Court for the Southern District of New York – 57 F. Supp. 642 (S.D.N.Y. 1944), November 6, 1944.

78 Kronstein, Heinrich, 'The Dynamics of German Cartels and Patents. I'. *The University of Chicago Law Review* 9(4) (1942) 643–671, 667.

79 I.G Farben owned the Swiss holding company, I.G Chemie; the Swiss holding controlled a US firm called General Aniline & Film Corporation which acquired General Aniline Works as its subsidiary.

of *Bayer's* US patents as well as the dyestuff patents of other German firms because they were deemed enemy-owned. Experience is a great teacher and, in this case, German chemical firms were determined to protect their privately-owned IP rights through cloaking devices. This strategy not only allowed them to repurchase their old patents – it also protected, through *Americanization*, their present and future IP rights.

As mentioned, the cartels concealed their German ownership of US subsidiaries through cloaking. They also used contracts and patents to control their US subsidiaries by assigning only the US patent to the US subsidiary, and eventually gatekeep those US subsidiaries from operating outside of the US. If the US subsidiary supplied patented products to other territories without the permission of the German patent owner, for example in Latin America, then the US subsidiary would be in violation of both the contract and the patent. A practical illustration of this situation is given by the Schering Corporation. In 1939 the British Empire's naval blockade prevented German shipments from entering and supplying goods in Latin America. The blockade and blacklisting greatly affected Schering AG which was one of the main vendors of pharmaceutical products and synthetic sex hormones in Latin America.[80] In 1939–1941 the Swiss-owned, US-based Schering Corporation, which was not subject to any British blockades, was authorized by Schering AG to export pharmaceutical products to supply its Latin American subsidiaries. The leverage of patent power allowed the German firm to continue trade despite the embargo, and by extending the US subsidiary's license to include export to Latin America they were able to remain in business in a newly restricted market.

6.7 *E. Merck, Darmstadt*

Merck & Co's continuing loss of revenues in the US led it to a strategic merger with a formerly German-owned American fine chemicals producer, i.e., Powers-Weightman-Rosengarten.[81] The merger made Merck & Co. the biggest fine chemicals manufacturer in the US; the new prominence appealed to E. Merck, Darmstadt (the German former parent company of the American Merck & Co), and prompted it to revive their relations. The two firms entered into a comprehensive agreement which provided for technology transfers, the mutual rights to the Merck brand in various foreign markets, a restriction on the US business' export capabilities and a profit-sharing model for the German manufacturing processes. Although the contract limited Merck & Co's export

80 Berge, Wendell. *Cartels: Challenge to a Free World* (Washington DC, Beard Books, 2000) 59–70.

81 See Merck (n 39) 20.

prospects, it counteracted the limitation with a ground-breaking opportunity for Merck & Co to elevate the standard of its production processes through the technology transfer it would receive. The discovery of vitamins was one of the most cutting-edge pharmaceutical developments of the interwar era; while *E. Merck, Darmstadt* had already become a market leader in the production of vitamins A and C, the US *Merck* had no manufacturing experience in that field. A crown jewel of the contract was *Merck & Co's* prospect to manufacture vitamins in the US.[82]

The two *Mercks* were extensively sharing IP assets by 1934 but the lion's share of the technology transfer emanated from the Germans. More than 50% of patents filed by Merck & Co in the US, from the time that the contract was signed until 1940, belonged to E. Merck Darmstadt;[83] filing them through an American company would shield them from any future confiscation in the event of war. In contrast, no *Merck & Co* patents were filed in Germany during that same period. Access to E. Merck, Darmstadt's IP advanced the US firm's manufacturing processes above all other firms while the German former parent regained access to the US market without political red tape.[84]

7 Conclusion

This chapter has shown that IP assets have been used and treated as a war policy by belligerent countries during WW1 and the Interwar Period. IP laws were consciously used by governments to pursue specific policies aimed at weakening their war enemies. Call it *raison d'etat* – a way of justifying in the national interest a behaviour which is clearly against international law, in our case international IP law. At the same time, people and companies found mechanisms like cloaking to subvert such policies and pursue their business interests with partners from belligerent countries.

In exploring the wartime IP legislation of the interwar period, it is crucial to emphasize that this analysis neither sanctions nor romanticizes the actions of the Nazi regime. German private companies, driven by their own scientific ambitions, found themselves entangled in the tumultuous landscape of war, often using IP cloaking strategies to safeguard their assets from both Nazi seizures and foreign wartime legislation. Private companies typically operate independently of political agendas; the loss of their IP rights serves as a

82 Supra (n 39) 25–26.
83 Ibid.
84 Ibid., 26.

testament to the collateral damage inflicted upon businesses during times of conflict.

This kind of geo-political-economic scenario recently re-emerged after the Russian invasion of Ukraine. In March 2022 the Russian government issued a decree exempting Russian companies from the obligation to compensate "unfriendly countries" for patent infringement.[85] This is a slight deviation from WWI language of "enemy-owned property" but such suspension of IP rights during an armed conflict is the identical *modus operandi* from over a century ago. The "unfriendly countries" do not only include Ukraine, with whom Russia is presently at war, but extend to nations that have imposed economic sanctions on Russia for their attack on Ukraine such as the US and the UK. The consequence of the decree is that Russian companies can access and imitate patented inventions without the consent of patentees and without paying them any royalty.

History demonstrates that IP is not only essential for innovation and trade but also a strategic asset during conflicts. The WW1 era exemplifies how nations weaponized IP for economic gain. Russia's recent patent decree underscores that in the 21st century, IP continues to be a critical tool in the arsenal of nations in armed conflicts, influencing commerce and geopolitics alike. Time will tell if this is just an occasional 'history repeating', or whether IP battlegrounds will feature again in future armed conflicts.

Bibliography

Aalders, G., and Wiebes, C. *The Art of Cloaking Ownership: The Secret Collaboration and Protection of the German War Industry by the Neutrals: The Case of Sweden* (Amsterdam: Amsterdam University Press, 1996).

Banerjee, A., and Beldiman, D., 'International Trade Mark Enforcement under the Versailles Treaty: A Case Study of Sanatogen,' in Shubha Ghosh (Ed). *Forgotten Intellectual Property Lore: Creativity, Entrepreneurship and Intellectual Property* (Cheltenham: Edward Elgar, 2020).

Baten, J., Bianchi, N., and Moser, P., 'Compulsory Licensing and Innovation – Historical Evidence From German Patents After WWI'. *Journal of Development Economics* 126 231–242 (2017).

Berge, W. *Cartels: Challenge to a Free World.* (Washington DC: Beard Books, 2000).

85 Bonadio, Enrico, and, Trapova, Alina, 'How Russia is Using Intellectual Property as a War Tactic'. The Conversation, March 18, 2022. https://theconversation.com/how-russia-is-using-intellectual-property-as-a-war-tactic-179260.

Bird, J.C. Control of Enemy Alien Civilians in Great Britain 1914–1918. (PhD Thesis, London School of Economics and Political Science, 1981).

Bonadio, E., and Trapova, A., 'How Russia is Using Intellectual Property as a War Tactic'. *The Conversation*, March 18, 2022. https://theconversation.com/how-russia-is-using-intellectual-property-as-a-war-tactic-179260.

Borchard, E. M., 'Enemy Private Property'. *American Journal of International Law* 18(3) 523–532 (1924).

Bouwens, B., and Dankers, J., 'Competition and Coordination: Reconsidering Economic Cooperation in Dutch Business, 1900–2000'. *Revue Économique* 64(6) 1105–1124 (2013).

Burhop, C., 'The Transfer of Patents in Imperial Germany'. *The Journal of Economic History* 70(4) 921–939 (2010).

Caglioti, D.L., 'Property Rights in Time of War: Sequestration and Liquidation of Enemy Aliens' Assets in Britain, Germany and France in the First World War'. *Journal of Modern European History* 12(4) 523–545 (2014).

Chachereau, N., and Galvez-Behar, G., 'Patents, War and Peace. The Resilience of the International Patent Order through the First World War'. *Journal of European Integration History* 29(2) 205–226 (2023).

Cooper, D., 'The Trading with the Enemy Act of 1917 and Synthetic Drugs: Relieving Scarcity, Controlling Prices, and Establishing Pre-marketing Licensing Controls.' *Pharmacy in History* 47(2) 47–61 (2005).

Cooper, D., 'The Licensing of German Drug Patents Confiscated During World War I: Federal and Private Efforts to Maintain Control, Promote Production, and Protect Public Health'. *Pharmacy in History* 54(1) 3–32 (2012).

Cramer, T., 'Building the 'World's Pharmacy': The Rise of the German Pharmaceutical Industry, 1871–1914'. *The Business History Review* 89(1) 43–73 (2015).

Donges, A., and Selgert, F., 'Do Legal Differences Matter? A Comparison of German Patent Law Regimes before 1877'. *Economic History Yearbook* 60(1) 57–92 (2019).

FCO. *British Policy Towards Enemy Property During and after the Second World War.* (Foreign & Commonwealth Office, General Services Command, 1998).

Gilgen, D., 'Creating the Invisible Hand: The Construction of Property Rights and the Promotion of Economic Growth between State and Interest Groups in the First German Patent Law of 1877'. *Historical Social Research* 36(3) 99–111 (2011).

Glaser, E., 'The Making of the Economic Peace' in Boemeke, M., Feldman, G. and Glaser, E. (Eds.), *The Treaty of Versailles: A Reassessment after 75 Years* (Washington, D.C.: German Historical Institute, 1998).

Glaser-Schmidt, E., 'Foreign Trade Strategies of I.G. Farben after World War I'. *Business and Economic History* 23(1) 201–211 (1994).

Godley, A., Joseph, M., and Leslie-Hughes, D., 'Technology Transfer in the Interwar US Pharmaceutical Sector: The Case of E. Merck of Darmstadt and Merck & Co., Rahway, New Jersey'. *Enterprise & Society* 20(3) 613–651 (2019).

Homburg, E., Travis, A.S., and Schröter, H.G., (Eds.). *The Chemical Industry in Europe, 1850–1914: Industrial Growth, Pollution, and Professionalization* (Dordrecht: Springer, 1998).

Jones, G., and Lubinski, C., 'Managing Political Risk in Global Business: Beiersdorf 1914–1990'. *Enterprise and Society* 13(1) 85–119 (2011).

Johnson, P., 'Mr Patent Goes to War! Industrial Property and the Breakdown of the International Order during World War', in Morris, P. Sean. *Intellectual Property and the Law of Nations, 1860–1920* (Boston: Brill, 2022).

Kronstein, H., 'The Dynamics of German Cartels and Patents. I'. *The University of Chicago Law Review* 9(4) 643–671 (1942).

Mächtel, F. *Das Patentrecht im Krieg* (Tubingen: Mohr Siebeck, 2009).

Merck, E., 'E. Merck's Annual Report: Volume 17'. Library of the Ohio State University, 1904.

Morris, P., and Travis, A., 'A History of the International Dyestuff Industry'. *American Dyestuff Reporter* 81(11) 37–47 (1992).

Morris, P.T., 'Ambros, Reppe, and the Emergence of Heavy Organic Chemicals in Germany, 1925–1945,' in Travis, A.S., Schröter, H.G., Homburg, E., and Morris, P.T. (Eds.). *Determinants in the Evolution of the European Chemical Industry, 1900–1939: New Technologies, Political Frameworks, Markets and Companies* (Dordrecht: Springer, 1998).

Moser, P., and Voena, A., 'Compulsory Licensing: Evidence from the Trading with the Enemy Act'. *American Economic Review* 102(1) 396–427, 300 (2012).

Murmann, J. P., 'Knowledge and Competitive Advantage in the Synthetic Dye Industry, 1850—1914: The Coevolution of Firms, Technology, and National Institutions in Great Britain, Germany, and the United States'. *Enterprise & Society* 1(4) 699–704 (2000).

Olmos, D., 'German Firm to Reclaim Bayer Aspirin Name: Drugs: It Will Acquire Sterling Winthrop's Over-The-Counter Business and Recover the Rights it Lost After WWI'. *Los Angeles Times*, 13 September 1994. https://www.latimes.com/archives/la-xpm-1994-09-13-fi-38019-story.html.

Pahlow, L., 'Intellectual Property and Competition Policy: Patent Pooling and Industrial Concentration in Germany (1890–1930)' in Siegrist, H., and Dimou., (eds). *Expanding Intellectual Property: Copyrights and Patents in 20th Century Europe and beyond* (Budapest: Central European University Press, 2017).

Payne, E., 'The Battle against Venereal Disease in Wartime Britain (1914–1918)'. April 2006. https://www.westernfrontassociation.com/world-war-i-articles/the-battle-against-venereal-disease-in-wartime-britain-1914-1918/.

Plasseraud, Y., and Savignon, F. *Paris 1883: Genèse du droit unioniste des brevets* (Paris: Lexis Nexis, 2000).

Potterf, R.M., 'Treatment of Alien Enemy Property in War Time and After by the United States'. *Indiana Law Journal* 2(6) 453–472 (1927).

Quirke, V., 'Foreign influences, National Styles, and the Creation of a Modern Pharmaceutical Industry in Britain and France'. *Pharmacy in History* 52(3/4) 134–147 (2010).

Ritter, D.S., 'Switzerland's Patent Law History'. *Fordham Intellectual Property, Media & Entertainment Law Journal* 14 (2) 463–496 (2004).

Sell, S., 'Intellectual Property and Public Policy in Historical Perspective: Contestation and Settlement'. *Loyola of Los Angeles Law Review* 38(2) 267–322 (2004).

Sommerich, O.C., 'A Brief against Confiscation'. *Law and Contemporary Problems* 11(1) 152–165 (1945).

Steen, K. *The American Synthetic Organic Chemicals Industry: War and Politics, 1910–1930* (Chapel Hill, North Carolina: University of North Carolina Press, 2014).

Streb, J., Baten, J., and Yin, S., 'Technological and Geographical Knowledge Spillover in the German Empire 1877–1918'. *Economic History Review* 59(2) 347–373 (2006).

The Nation Newspaper, 'American Property in Germany'. February 16, 1921. Volume 112, No. 2902. https://babel.hathitrust.org/cgi/pt?id=umn.31951001355237y&view=1up&seq=336.

United States Congress, Senate Committee on Military Affairs, 'Scientific and Technical Mobilization,' Hearing before a Subcommittee on Military Affairs, Seventy Eighth Congress Session on Section 702, March 30, 1943.

Williams, J.J., British Pharmaceutical Industry, Synthetic Drug Manufacture and the Clinical Testing of Novel Drugs 1895 to 1939 (Unpublished, PhD, University of Manchester, 2005).

Case Law

A.J. Von Wulfing vs D.H. Jivandas And Co., (1926) 28 BOMLR 243.

Bayer Co. v. United Drug Co., 272 F. 505 (S.D.N.Y. 1921).

Farbenfabriken Bayer A.G. v. Sterling Drug, 307 F.2d 210 (3d Cir. 1962).

United States v. General Dyestuff Corp., US District Court for the Southern District of New York – 57 F. Supp. 642 (S.D.N.Y. 1944), November 6, 1944.

CHAPTER 3

The Birth of Inventor's Moral Rights: The 1934 London Conference on the Paris Convention for the Protection of Industrial Property

Phillip Johnson

1 Introduction[1]

The development of author's moral rights within municipal law was well established by the 1920s.[2] As the decade progressed it also became clear that the issue would be considered at the next revision of the Berne Convention for the Protection of Literary and Artistic Works which happened in Rome in 1928. By this point there was general support for protecting these rights[3] as part of the broader recognition that a copyright work is a representation of the personality of the author.[4] Ultimately, the Berne Convention included the right of attribution[5] in the following terms "the author shall have the right to claim authorship of the work".[6] This meant that the consideration of 'droit morale' for inventors was inevitable when the conference to revise the Paris Convention for the Protection of Industrial Property convened in 1934. The moral rights considered, however, were different. Like authors, there was the right to be identified

---

1 All BT 209 references are to the series of that number held in the United Kingdom National Archive.

2 Ricketson, Sam, and, Ginsburg, Jane. *International Copyright and Neighbouring Rights: The Berne Convention and Beyond, 3rd Ed* (Oxford: Oxford University Press, 2022) [10.13]. Moral right arguments had been used to justify new rights earlier: Lecomte, Georges. *Actes de la Conference, Réunie Berlin du 14 Octobre au 14 Novembre 1908* (Geneva: BIRPI, 1910) 246–7 (extensive comments in favour of moral rights). *Actes de la Conference Réunie a Rome*, 7 Mai – 2 Juin 1928 (Geneva: BIRPI, 1929) ('Berne Conference: Actes de Rome 1928'), 174 ('the same wishes have been repeated at more recent congresses; "Le mêmes vœux ont été répétés dans de congrès plus récents"').

3 *Berne Conference: Actes de Rome 1928*, 181–2 (Sub-Committee on Moral Rights; Sous-Commission pour Le Droit Moral).

4 *Berne Conference: Actes de Rome 1928*, 202.

5 It is traditionally called the paternity right.

6 Berne Convention for the Protection of Literary and Artistic Works, art 6*bis*(1). Article 6*bis*(1) also includes the integrity right, which has no parallel in patent law, and the rule the rights cannot be waived.

 | DOI:10.1163/9789004714663_005

but there was also consideration of a right for employed inventors to share the benefit of their patent and a right to communicate the invention more freely by way of a grace period. Only one of these rights was eventually protected and this was the one that was shared with authors.

2 Moral Rights at the International Labour Organisation

While author's moral rights were internationalised in the 1920s, the decade was also concerned with 'scientific property'[7] that is giving an economic right to those who made scientific developments or theoretical inventions.[8] The issue was even considered by the Bureaux Internationaux Réunis pour la Protection de la Propriété Intellectuelle (BIRPI)[9] with its Vice-Director, Professor George Gariel, arguing in favour of a such right.[10] Nevertheless, the consideration of scientific property at BIRPI was suspended indefinitely in the late 1920s,[11] yet Gariel's views regarding remunerating actual creators permeated elsewhere.

The first substantive step was not at BIRPI, but at the International Labour Organisation where two committees considered the issue of inventors' moral rights each doing so soon after their formation: the Advisory Committee on Professional Workers[12] and, three year later, the Committee on Salaried Employees.[13] While there was significant similarity between their conclusions

7 Miller, David, 'Intellectual Property and Narratives of Discovery/Invention: The League Of Nations' Draft Convention On 'Scientific Property' and Its Fate'. *History of Science* 46(3) (2008) 299–342; Ladas, Stephen, 'The Efforts for International Protection of Scientific Property'. *The American Journal of International Law* 23(3) (1929) 552–569.

8 Ilosvay, Thomas, 'Scientific Property'. *The American Journal of Comparative Law* 2(2)(1953) 178–197, 179. These things could not be protected under patent law.

9 BIRPI was the predecessor of the World Intellectual Property Organization (WIPO).

10 See 'Examen Critique du Probleme de la Propieté Scientifque' (1923) *Propriete Industrielle* 131.There were numerous other proposals considered during the period see Ladas, 'The Efforts for International Protection of Scientific Property', (n 7).

11 See 'La question de la propriété scientifique' (1927) *Propriété Industrielle*, 161, and 'Droit des auteurs de découvertes sur les applications industrielle de celles-ci (propriété scientifique)' (1928) *Propriété Industrielle*, 204.

12 This was originally the Committee of Intellectual Workers. The reasons and rationale for the Committee's creation can be found in *Minutes of 33rd Session of the Governing Body of the ILO* (Geneva 1926) 471–4; also see *Minutes of 34th Session* (Geneva 1927) 55–57; *Minutes of 35th Session* (Geneva 1927) 175–178; *Minutes of 38th Session* (Geneva 1928) 198–199; *Minutes of 41st Session* (Geneva 1928) 461.

13 The Salaried Workers Committee was set up in 1930 (see *Minutes of 43rd Session of the Governing Body of the ILO* (Geneva, 1928) 158) and consisted of 12 salaried employees, 3 members of the Governing body, and 2 employers representatives; but the employers representatives did not attend.

(that is resolutions), the latter committee was much more prescriptive.[14] The ILO Governing Body attempted to reconcile the views of the committees,[15] but ultimately both resolutions were circulated to governments but only the earlier Professional Workers resolution was published by BIRPI. And it was this which was a key source for moral rights at the London Conference:[16]

> *Resolution adopted by the Advisory Committee on Professional Workers at its Second Session (December 1929)*
> The Advisory Committee on Professional Workers, having taken note of the report submitted by the International Labour Office on the subject of the protection of inventions by wage earners, and having heard the views of Mr. Gariel in the capacity of an expert on the subject, is of the opinion that it is very desirable that the question of inventions made by wage earners should be regulated in as many countries as possible, in accordance with the following principles, the adoption of which would ensure for industry the fullest collaboration in connection with inventions of engineers, skilled workers, and others, while guaranteeing the latter suitable compensation for the efforts exerted. No recommendation is made with reference to inventions made by workers specially engaged in the research department conducted with a view to inventions, differences of opinion having arisen in the Committee on this subject:
> (1) All patents should mention the name of the inventor of inventors if they can be discovered. No agreement to the contrary should be allowed to deprive inventors of this right.
> (2) When an invention is made by a worker, either in a private undertaking or in a State undertaking, and the employer is granted a legal title to the patent, the employer shall be required, unless it is held that the worker has received fair remuneration, either in wages or otherwise, to compensate the worker in proportion to the value of the invention and the circumstances in which it was made. Any agreement to the contrary should be considered void.

---

14 See discussion, *Minutes of 62nd Session of the Governing Body of the ILO* (Geneva, 1933) 154; *Minutes of 43rd Session* (Geneva, 1929) 114.

15 *Minutes of 62nd Session of the Governing Body of the ILO* (Geneva, 1933) 154–60.

16 The Salaried Employee resolution had as paragraph (1): 'The inventor as author of creative intellectual work should be entitled to receive a patent and all other measures of industrial protection. If this right cannot at present be granted by national legislation, it is in any case necessary that the name of the inventor should be mentioned in all official documents concerning the protection of the inventor and on every occasion when such protection is mentioned'.

> Inventions made by workers specially employed in research departments remain to be dealt with.[17]

The resolution was followed by a request from the Committee to the ILO Governing Body: to ask the British Patent Office and BIRPI to include the proposal in the draft programme for the London Conference[18] (for which the British and BIRPI had joint responsibility).[19] However, the request had a bumpy ride. When it first went before the Governing Body there were concerns that the committee had not considered all types of workers,[20] that the proposal created potential issues with patents[21] and, more importantly, that the second proposition would lead to certain employees being compelled to take whatever was offered by employers.[22] Notwithstanding this caution, there still remained general support for the principles within the ILO and so it was unclear for sometime whether the proposition would be taken forward by BIRPI or by the ILO itself.[23] But as will become apparent, it would be BIRPI.

3 The Lead up to the Conference

The Paris Convention was signed in 1883 and subsequently revised in Brussels in 1900, in Washington in 1911 and in the Hague in 1925. At the end of the Hague Conference, it was agreed that the next revision conference would be held in 1933 and the British Government offered London as the venue[24] (although the

17 The *International Labour Code 1951* (Geneva, 1952) Vol. 2, 243–4 (English); *Propriete industrielle*, 1930, 44; reproduced Paris Convention: Actes de Londres, 90–91; it can also be found in *Minutes of 62nd Session of the Governing Body of the ILO* (Geneva, 1933) 197–198; *Minutes of 47th Session of the Governing Body of the ILO* (Geneva, 1930) 237–8 (notes of meeting). The additional two implementation paragraphs are omitted here.

18 Resolution, Implementation Paragraph (II).

19 Paris Convention (Hague Act), art 14.

20 See *Minutes of 49th Session of the Governing Body of ILO* (Geneva, June 1930) 515.

21 The consultation with Gariel was mentioned: *Minutes of 49th Session of the Governing Body of ILO* (Geneva, June 1930) 516.

22 *Minutes of 49th Session of the Governing Body of ILO* (Geneva, June 1930) Comments of Moore, 515.

23 *Minutes of 55th Session of the Governing Body of the ILO* (Geneva, 1931) 68–69.

24 *Actes de la Conférence Réunie a La Haye du 8 Octobre au 6 Novembre 1925*, 587–8. The British government tried, in conjunction with the United States government, to make English one of the official languages of the Convention (see the correspondence in BT 209/570). It also appears to have led to a heated discussion on the opening day: *Evening Standard*, 1 May 1934 'Australia Begins: Tower of Babel' (this article appears to be in a later

conference was delayed until 1934 due to the small number ratifications of the Hague text.[25]) As the organisers of the Conference, the British sought the views of its own stakeholders on the Draft Programme. The Chartered Institute of Patent Agents (CIPA),[26] the local branch of the International Association for the Protection of Intellectual Property (AIPPI),[27] and the Trade Mark, Patents and Designs Federation[28] formed a Joint Committee to consider the programme. The general mood of that Committee is clear from a resolution it carried on 20 March 1934:

> That this meeting feels that the Convention should deal with matters of international import and deprecates any attempt to use the Convention to interfere unduly with the details of domestic legislation and patent practice.[29]

This general mindset permeated its views long before this resolution was passed as will been seen below. The revision conference itself convened in Burlington Gardens, Mayfair on 1 May 1934. On the second day the conference broke up into Sub-Committees with the issue of moral rights being assigned to the Second Sub-Committee, which was chaired by Marcel Plaisant.[30] This Sub-Committee subsequently set up a Comité d'étude to consider particular issues and this reported back. Once the Sub-Committees had reached their conclusions, the Drafting Committee considered the issues raised and then the plenary reconvened on 31 May 1934. The Revised Convention being opened for signature on 2 June 1934. Thus, it was during the eighty meetings of the various Sub-Committees that most of the work took place[31] and of course delegations would often reconvene to compare notes and develop positions. The

edition than that retained by the British Library, but a cutting is in BT 209/768); also see *Paris Convention: Actes de Londres*, 322–323.

25 See inside cover of file in BT 209/742. The correspondence regarding the delay is included in BT 209/749. The notification is in *Actes de la Conference: Réunie a Londres du 1er Mai au 2 Juin 1934* (Geneva: BIRPI, 1934) ('Paris Convention: Actes de Londres') 40–41.

26 Now called the Chartered Institute of Patent Attorneys (CIPA).

27 Commonly known as AIPPI (*Association Internationale pour la Protection de la Propriété Intellectuelle*) was (and is) a non-governmental organisation seeking to develop and improve intellectual property laws around the world.

28 The organisation was set up in 1920 to represent the views of British industry in relation to intellectual property (it has now been renamed the IP Federation).

29 The minutes of the meeting are held in BT 209/754.

30 (1889–1940). French Senator of Cher (1929–1945) and heavily involved in Foreign Affairs.

31 *Paris Convention: Actes de Londres*, 5.

three aspects of *droit moral* considered during the conference will be looked at in turn.

4 Right to Be Identified

The right to be identified – now "commonly" called the "moral right" of the inventor[32] – was the only such right adopted at the London Conference. It began with the International Bureau sending a draft text (based on paragraph (1) of the Professional Workers resolution) to the British in January 1931.[33] However, the British explained in a meeting with Fritz Ostertag, the Director of the International Bureau, that domestic stakeholders believed that the proposal would unnecessarily complicate applications. This was because where the inventor-applicant did not indicate the name of the inventor and a dispute arose, it was not clear what would happen.[34] This objection largely resulted from the rule in British patent law that an importer of a new invention would be treated as its inventor[35] which was thought by some, such as the Glasgow Chamber of Commerce, to be incompatible with any right to be identified.[36] The view of the local Joint Committee was simply that such a right was "altogether too troublesome, and would involve harassing correspondence which time might not allow".[37]

This all meant that the British would not include the right in the draft programme.[38] Nevertheless once the draft was circulated to the contracting states, Norway, Finland, Sweden and Denmark all proposed reintroducing the BIRPI text into the programme.[39] This concerted action resulted from a meeting in

32 Bodenhausen, Georg. *Guide to the Application of the Paris Convention for the Protection of Industrial Property* (Geneva: World Intellectual Property Organization, 1969) 64; *Paris Convention: Actes de Londres*, 456: 'ce qu'on est convenu d'appeler le droit moral des inventeurs'.

33 The proposals were sent under a cover of Letter No 9, 5 January 1931 (BT 209/742).

34 Provisional Proposals of Industrial Property Department for Consideration (IP28382A), New Articles, p 1 (BT 209/744).

35 See *Plimpton v Malcolmson* (1876) LR 3 Ch D 531 at 555.

36 Comments from 'HCH', 10 Sep 1931 (BT 209/744).

37 Industrial Property Conference of London, 1933: Programme of Conference (Comments), Article 4*ter* (new) (p 18) (BT 209/744); also see Comments of the Joint Committee (BT 209/754).

38 'Reunion Consultative', 7–8 December 1931, p 4 (BT 209/742).

39 BIRPI, London Conference: Preliminary Documents; Summary of the Proposals, Counter-Proposals and Comments communicated by Countries of the Union: Series "A" (Berne, 1933) 13 (a copy is included in BT 209/754) (in English) ('Summary Series A'); BIRPI, London Conference: Preliminary Documents; Summary of the Proposals, Counter-Proposals and

August 1933 of the Inter-Scandinavian Assembly.[40] In addition, the Netherlands proposed the same draft with the addition of the phrase: "The Patent Office shall have the right to verify such information."[41] The revival of the proposal was also welcomed by Yugoslavia.[42] By the time the conference came around, the British position had softened towards the idea. The right to be identified was no longer seen as "important" even if it might cause some difficulties in practice.[43] Not only did the British "see no adequate reason for rejecting this proposal"[44] they also drew the link back to its literary origins:

> The grant of the Patent without any indication of inventorship is comparable with the publication of a book anonymously on the ground that the author has parted with all his rights.[45]

Once the programme had been agreed, the role of the British was less significant but some weight is always given to the views of the conference hosts. So once the British softened its position it is not surprising others followed suit. When the right was considered before the Sub-Committee there were supportive comments from the delegations of Japan, Sweden, the United States, Austria, Yugoslavia, Great Britain, Portugal, Poland, Spain, Germany, Mexico and Italy and another 14 countries voted in favour of the text proposed by the Dutch, which became the final text:[46]

> *Article 4ter*
> *Patents: Mention of the Inventor in the Patent*
> The inventor shall have the right to be mentioned as such in the patent.

Comments communicated by Countries of the Union: Series "B" (Berne, 1933) 12–3 (a copy is included in BT 209/754) (in English) ('Summary Series B'). A combined version of these documents is in *Paris Convention: Actes de Londres*, 371.

40 Summary Series B, 13.

41 Summary Series A, 13.

42 Summary Series A, 13.

43 See Instructions to British Delegation, 9: BT 209/756.

44 See 'JHM' Comments "Droit moral de l'inventor", 4 Mar 1932 (BT 209/748) (following Minute Sheet).

45 See 'JHM' Comments "Droit moral de l'inventor" (BT 209/748).

46 *Paris Convention: Actes de Londres*, 373 (abstention: Belgium, Danzig and Finland).

Critically, it can be seen that, as adopted in the Sub-Committee, there was nothing preventing the right to be mentioned being waived by contract.[47] This freedom remained despite attempts by Italy during the plenary session to reverse it.[48]

At first blush, the moral right granted to inventors appears quite different to that for authors. Authors have a right which is enforceable in the courts and which can lead to the payment of damages or the grant of injunctions.[49] Inventors have no right to a remedy other than their identification in documents. So as Nari Lee puts it, beyond recognition inventors do not have any "further right to control the outcome of their inventions"[50] and she goes on:[51]

> As a personal right, the inventor's moral right … is a relative right that works against other patent applicants or the patent proprietor only, and thus seems to be devoid of *erga omnes* effect. Moreover, the scope is limited to patent documents only, and it is not a right to be named as the inventor outside the granted patent document. Beyond the patent documents and registry, inventors do not have a right to claim their inventorship further, whereas the patent proprietor, for example, may claim their patent ownership in the products that embody their inventions.

However, the right to be identified in a patent is in many ways much more powerful than the moral rights of authors.[52] The patent register, and the patent itself, is issued by a public authority (a Patent Office) whereas a book (or other work) is published privately. In the usual course of things, a Patent Office can be trusted to name the right person when it becomes clear (whether initially or following a hearing) but the same cannot be said of a publisher at least without a court order. An author who was not identified can suffer harm because

47 Cf Article 6*bis*; The omission of this restriction meant that it was a matter of national law whether it could be waived or not: Bodenhausen, *Guide to the Application of the Paris Convention*, 64.

48 *Paris Convention: Actes de Londres*, 514.

49 See for instance, *Copyright Designs and Patents Act 1988*, s 103.

50 Lee, Nari, 'Inventor's Moral Right and Morality of Patents'. In *Research Handbook On Intellectual Property And Moral Rights,* Gendreau, Ysolde, ed. (Cheltenham: Edward Elgar, 2023).

51 Lee, 'Inventor's Moral Right and Morality of Patents' (the reference is to the European Patent Convention, art 62 but the comment is of general application).

52 For a contrary argument and a call for the introduction of a substantive moral right see Cross, John, 'An Attribution Right for Patented Inventions'. *University of Dayton Law Review* 37(2) (2012) 139–163 (albeit Cross does not mention Article 4*ter* at all).

improperly attributed books (or other works) will remain in circulation; it has long been the case that patents are corrected when republished and for those already in circulation the reattribution has been made by issuing correction slips.[53]

So while the right to be identified is often seen as procedural right or a mere formality to maintain the veracity of the legal system[54] this underplays the change that occurred. For as Bogsch says:

> any inventor has a natural pride in his intellectual creation and the world should know that the creation is his brainchild ... the mention is also useful for safeguarding the material interests of the inventor since it reduces the chances of fraudulent applications.[55]

The impact of the right to be identified would have paled into insignificance had a right been given to employed inventors to receive a share in the benefit of their inventions.

5 Employee Inventions

This second aspect of the proposed droit moral – employees sharing the benefit – also originated with the ILO Professional Workers Resolution. Like the right to be identified, the inclusion of benefit sharing in the draft programme was strongly resisted by the British.[56] The difference was that BIRPI had no desire to proceed with it either. This was because in the early 1930s only a few countries had addressed the question and each took a different approach.[57]

---

53 Some harm remains from the original misattribution now fully corrected, but this is difficult to compensate unless there was specific damage identified by it.

54 Lee, 'Inventor's Moral Right and Morality of Patents' (n 49).

55 Bogsch, Arpad, 'The First Hundred Years of the Paris Convention for the Protection of Industrial Property'. In WIPO, *The Paris Convention for the Protection of Industrial Property from 1883 to 1983* (Geneva: WIPO, 1983) 15, 32.

56 Draft of Conference Programme, 9*bis* (BT 209/742).

57 For some contemporary laws see, *Wet tot Regeling van het Octrooirecht voor Uitvindingen*, Stb. 1910, 313 (Dutch Patent Law 1910), art 10 (there is an English translation in, *Patents and Trade Marks Review* 16 (1917–18) 226); Japanese Patent Law 1921, art. 14 (*Law No. 96 on 29 April 1921*) (available in English in Becker, Joseph. *Japanese Laws and Ordinances concerning Patents, Trade-Marks, Designs and Utility Models* (London: Butterworths, 1930)); Relazione e Regio Decreto 13 settembre 1934, n. 1602. Privative industriali e marchi di fabbrica e di commercio, Gazzetta Ufficiale No. 240, 12 October 1934, p 4628 (The New Italian Law on Patents, Utility Models, Ornamental Designs and Trade Marks (Graziano & Borsatino

Furthermore, it was felt to be too closely connected with employment contracts to be within the scope of the Paris Convention.[58] This view is hardly surprising considering the proposal's origin being the ILO rather than the BIRPI. Once more, however, there were contracting states who did not follow this line with the Netherlands putting forward something very similar in effect to the 1929 Resolution:

> Article 4ter
> (1) An employee who has made an invention, while his employer is entitled to a patent for that invention, shall be granted equitable remuneration in accordance with the rules of the internal legislation of each of the countries of the Union.
> (2) Any agreement to the contrary is null and void.[59]

This largely reflected the requirement in Dutch law to give employed inventors a share of the benefit arising from the patent,[60] that is an equitable remuneration[61] having regard to the importance of the invention. The proposal, it was claimed by the Dutch, would balance the fact that an invention is the employee's personal creation with the commercial impossibility of allowing an employee to freely dispose of it. The Mexican delegation proposed an even more radical idea whereby: "The employee who has made an invention as well as his employer are entitled, in equal parts, to the patent obtained for this invention, which patent must be issued in the name of both."[62]

1934)), art 21 to 23 (this was not in force, but had been passed subject to Royal approval at the time of the Conference); Bundesgesetz vom 30. März 1911 betreffend die Ergänzung des Schweizerischen Zivilgesetzbuches (*Swiss Code of Obligations of 1911*), art 343; Bundesgesetz vom 2. Juli 1925 über die Abänderung und die Ergänzung von Bestimmungen des Patentgesetzes (Patentgesetznovelle 1925) Bundesgesetzblatt 1925 (No 219, p 847) (*Austrian Patents Amendment Act 1925*) which inserted a new s 5a-5n into the Patents Act. For some discussion of these provisions see Emanuel, Adler, 'Inventions of Employees and the Austrian Patents Act of 1925'. *International Labour Review* 13(1) (1926) 1–20.

58 Draft of Conference Programme, 9 (BT 209/742).

59 Article 4*ter* (1): 'Au salarié qui a fair une invention, tandis que son employeur a droit au brevet pour cette invention, une remuneration equitable doit être accordée d'après les règles de la legislation intérieure de chacun des pays de l'Union. (2) Toute convention contraire est nulle et non avenue': see *Paris Convention: Actes de Londres*, 370, fn (1).

60 *Dutch Patent Law 1910*, s 10.

61 This remuneration could come from salary or bonuses.

62 'Le salarié qui a fait une invention ainsi que son employeur ont droit, par parties égales, au brevet obtenu pour cette invention, lequel brevet doit être délivré au nom de tous les deux': *Paris Convention: Actes de Londres*, 371, fn (2).

The British delegation, like BIRPI, privately held the view that the matter should be left to national legislation.[63] The British also felt it to be acceptable for employees to assign all their inventions on payment of a nominal sum.[64] Something totally incompatible with the proposed benefit sharing. The Dutch proposal did not even get support from countries – like Japan – who already had something similar in domestic law.[65] And Germany, who a little under a decade later in the midst of war enacted something similar,[66] objected publicly; as did the British who took over forty years to adopt a comparable law.[67] The public justification for objecting being that the rule would improperly constrain contractual freedom.[68] Other delegations, such as the Belgians and Hungarians, thought the issue needed to mature before any international rule developed.[69] Ultimately, only seven delegations voted in favour,[70] eight voted against[71] and the remaining 14 delegations abstained.[72]

While some aspirational rights for inventors were subsequently included in multilateral human rights instruments, such as article 27(2) of the Universal Declaration of Human Rights ("Everyone has the right to the protection of the moral and material interests resulting from any scientific, literary or artistic production of which he is the author"[73]), a prescriptive (rather than aspirational) rule has never been adopted in any other instrument despite the matter being periodically reconsidered at the ILO.[74] This brings us to the third of the

63 See Instructions to British Delegation, 9 (BT 209/756); also see Observations on the Programme (BT 209/762).

64 Observations on Proposals set out in 'Troisieme fascicule (Série): Propositions et vous d'ordre general', 6 (BT 209/762).

65 *Japanese Patent Law* 1921, art 14.

66 *Verordnung über die Behandlung von Erfindungen von Gefolgschaftsmitgliedern* (Ordinance of 12 July 1942; Reichsgesetzblatt I 1942 S. 466); *Durchführungsverordnung zur Verordnung über die Behandlung von Erfindungen von Gefolgschaftsmitgliedern* (Ordinance 20 March 1943; Reichsgesetzblatt I 1943 S. 257).

67 *Patents Act 1977*, s 40 as to its origin see Johnson Phillip, 'From Banks to Shanks: the History of Employee Awards for Patented Inventions under the Patents Act 1977'. *QMJIP* 11 (2021) 124–157.

68 *Paris Convention: Actes de Londres*, 372.

69 *Paris Convention: Actes de Londres*, 372.

70 Austria, Spain, Italy, Netherlands, Poland, Czechoslovakia and Yugoslavia.

71 Australia, United States, Irish Free State, Japan, Liechtenstein, Mexico, Sweden and Switzerland.

72 *Paris Convention: Actes de Londres*, 372–3 (it appears that Mexico were initially in favour of the principle: 372).

73 Something similar is included in the *International Covenant on Economic, Social and Cultural Rights*, art 15(1).

74 See for instance, *The Protection of Salaried Authors and Inventors* (ILO, Geneva 1987); *Report of the Tripartite Meeting on Salaried Authors and Inventors* (TMSAI/1/1987/9)

moral rights, that is the inventor's right to communicate an invention during a grace period.

6 Grace Periods

From its inception the Paris Convention provided a grace period for inventions demonstrated at international exhibitions,[75] but the domestic law of some countries was more generous. For instance, the United States had a two-year general grace period in 1934 and Japan had only shortened it from two years to six months in 1921.[76] However, most countries did no more than international law required, which makes it surprising the extent to which the issue was debated at the London Conference. Initially, however, there was nothing in the draft programme, and, once more, it started with a Dutch proposal:[77]

> Article 4 quinquies: Communications or publications made by the author of an invention or by the applicant for a utility model, industrial design or model or trademark within six months before the complete filing will not constitute an obstacle to the grant of a patent to the author of the invention or to his successor in title, nor to the registration of a utility

---

(ILO: Geneva, 24 November to 2 December 1987): *Third Session, Geneva 1959, Record of Proceedings* (ILO 1960), Report of the Committee of Non-Manual Workers (Appendix X), 754–5 and 760; *The First Session of Advisory Committee on Salaried Employees and Professional Workers* (24–29 October 1949) thought it was an issue that needs to be considered; *Summary Record of Fourth Session of the Advisory Committee on Salaried Employees and Professional Workers* (1 to 13 April 1957) (1959) (Resolution No 40, 65); *Sixth Session of Advisory Committee on Salaried Employees and Professional Workers, Note of Proceedings* (Geneva, 4–14 December 1967) (CCETI/6/20) (Resolution No 64, 76–77); *Eighth Session of the Advisory Committee on Salaried Employees and Professional Workers* (13 to 22 January 1981) (GB.216/IA/2/4) (Geneva 1981) 6–7 (also see Resolution 86 (74–75)); *Ninth Session Advisory Committee on Salaried Employees and Professional Worker, Note on Proceeding* (17 to 25 April Geneva 1985) 108 (Resolution 95, 112): Neumeyer, Fredik, 'Employees' Rights in Their Inventions: A Comparison of National Laws'. *International Labour Review* 83/84(1) (1961) 36–105; Conditions of Work and Employment of Professional Workers (Geneva, 1977); Cornwell, Sally, 'Employee Rights in Innovative Works'. *International Labour Review* 119(3) (1980) 301–320.

75 Paris Convention, art 11.

76 There was a two year period under Law No 23 of 2 April 1909 art 5 (Translation into English: *Patents and Trade Marks Review* Vol 7 (1909) 2802). But under the Japanese Patent Act 1921, art 5 and 6 it was shorter and narrower (a 6 month grace period covered disclosures during experimental trials, against the inventors will or at international exhibitions).

77 Summary Series A, 13–4.

> model, an industrial design or model , of a trademark or trade mark to the applicant or his successor in title; they shall not diminish or invalidate the patent or the registration, provided that these communications or these publications are made by the author or by the depositor themselves and that the latter have expressly reserved their rights to protection.

It was justified by the Dutch on the four grounds: first, it was "common knowledge" that inventors suffered hardship by communicating their invention to others and so depriving themselves of a patent; secondly, the absence of a grace period meant that inventors were forced to file their patents before they had been perfected and this presented a risk that the original filing was inadequate;[78] thirdly, for certain types of invention the patent was of secondary importance to the inventor compared to communicating their ideas to others; finally, it was thought a general grace period could lead to the removal of the specific and existing grace period for exhibitions.[79] This link explains the suggested location in the Convention of the more generous Italian proposal:

> Article 11 bis – The author of an invention which has been the subject of a communication published in proceedings or journals of scientific academies or societies of one of the countries of the Union shall, for the purpose of effecting the deposit of an application for a patent relating to the said invention, enjoy a period of twelve months, during which the deposit effected by him shall not be invalidated by the fact of the said publication. The period shall commence from the date of the publication.[80]

The idea of some sort of grace period was hotly debated at the Diplomatic Conference.[81] The proposals being considered were often different from the proposer's own domestic law. For instance, the United States suggested a twelve-month grace period,[82] despite it lasting two years at

78 Summary Series A, 14; for a short introduction to some of the arguments put forward in contemporary debate see Johnson, Phillip, 'Patent Law: The Grace is On'. *New Law Journal* (2022) 15.

79 Summary Series A, 14; see *Paris Convention* (*Hague Act*), Article 11.

80 Summary Series A, 27.

81 *Paris Convention: Actes de Londres*, 260.

82 'Independently of the priority period provided for in Article 4 of this Convention, the author of an invention which has been the subject of a communication or publication shall enjoy, in each of the countries of the Union, the right to carry out the filing of a patent application relating to this invention, for a period of twelve months during which the application may not be affected or invalidated by said communication or publication. The period will begin to run from the date of the communication or publication'.

home;[83] and the Netherlands draft, set out above, was much more generous than its own law,[84] as was that for Italy.[85] Indeed, the Dutch were willing to go further still and accept the proposal from the United States.

It was therefore the United States who led the debate in favour of a grace period stating it was necessary "for reasons of justice for the inventor and to protect the general interests of the industry as too rigorous rules prevent useful patents."[86] In addition to Dutch and Italian support, the British also spoke to indicate it would be content to introduce some form of grace period[87] despite it to having to change its novelty rules.[88] But other countries were far less willing to move with strong dissent from Germany, Yugoslavia, Portugal, Hungary and Czechoslovakia precisely because a grace period would change their rules for novelty. This resistance led the Dutch to propose an alternative text and it along with the American proposal was sent to a Comité d'étude (Study Committee) with six member countries (and one other). The Comité agreed to little and from its six members came four different proposals.

In short, the French proposed a six month grace period for disclosures made orally or in writing within learned societies,[89] the Dutch went further excluding any disclosures made by the inventor within the six month grace period whereas the United States, who had started by proposing a grace period,

('Indépendamment du délai de priorité prévu par l'article 4 de la présente Convention, l'auteur d'une invention ayant fait l'objet d'une communication ou d'une puhlication jouira, dans chacun des pays de l'Union, pour effectuer le dépôt d'une demande de brevet portant sur cette invention, d'un délai de douze mois au cours duquel la demande ne pourra être ni affectée, ni invalidée par lesdites communication ou publication. Le délai commencera à courir de la date de la communication ou de la publication'.): *Paris Convention: Actes de Londres*, 372, fn (2).

83 The two year grace period was introduced in the US by An Act to revise, consolidate, and amend the statutes relating to patents and copyrights (Chapter 230; 16 Statues at Large 198), §24. It was reduced to one year by An Act to amend & c (Chapter 450; 53 Statutes at Large 1212), §1.

84 *Dutch Patent Law 1910*, art 8(1).

85 *Italian Patent Law 1934*, art 11 (twelve month grace period for exhibitions in Italy, but shorter where foreign countries offer only six months).

86 *Paris Convention: Actes de Londres*, 373: 'des raisons de justice à l'égard de l'inventeur, et d'intérêt général de l'industrie, que des dispositions trop rigoureuses privent souvent de brevets utiles'.

87 The Organisation for Intellectual Cooperation also spoke in favour: *Paris Convention: Actes de Londres*, 373.

88 There was no grace period under the *Patents and Designs Act 1907* which had effect in 1934, but a one year grace period was introduced by *Patents Act 1949*, s 51(3). There was no grace period under Italian law.

89 *Paris Convention: Actes de Londres*, 373–4.

actually took a different line and proposed a general rule of local novelty.[90] The United Kingdom divided the issue up and set out a draft excluding from the prior art any publication of the invention not authorised by the inventor[91] and any document read before a learned society.[92]

Back in the Sub-Committee none of the four approaches were acceptable.[93] The French, who had the narrowest approach, would accept nothing broader as they believed they were already derogating too much from their principle of novelty.[94] Yugoslavia preferred the local novelty rule put forward by the Americans but could also accept the Dutch proposal despite seeing it as too broad. The Japanese and Hungarians would accept the proposal for local novelty or one half of the British proposal but nothing more.[95] There was now some support from the Germans and Portuguese for the French proposal if it was extended from learned societies to include corporations and technical societies.[96] Following a final stand from the Americans with their bold claims that public opinion was in favour of some measure in favour of inventors[97] and the Italians trying to find a comprise, there was a vote on each proposal. None passed. The American proposal for local novelty received the highest number of votes (16 in favour; 5 against and 9 abstentions) and the modified French proposal received one fewer vote in favour and one more against.[98] The others failed more conclusively.

---

90 *Paris Convention: Actes de Londres*, 374: 'The public use and sale of an invention elsewhere than in the country where the patent application is filed shall not constitute an obstacle to the grant of the patent in any country of the Union'. ('L'emploi et la vente publics d'une invention ailleurs que dans le pays où la demande de brevet est déposée ne constitueront dans aucun pays de l'Union un obstacle à la délivrace du brevet'.).

91 Eg disclosed in breach of confidence: now see *Patents Act 1977*, s 2(4).

92 The British proposal left the period of grace to the 'requirements of international legislation'. It appears that a grace period was acceptable if it were six months and the rule was as established under domestic law: Instructions to British Delegation, 19 (BT 209/756); also see Observations on the Programme (BT 209/762).

93 Neither were related proposals put forward by Poland and the United States and Finland after the rejection of these initial four: *Paris Convention: Actes de Londres*, 376–7.

94 *Paris Convention: Actes de Londres*, 374. They later broadened their proposal.

95 *Paris Convention: Actes de Londres*, 374.

96 *Paris Convention: Actes de Londres*, 374 (the Germans said it was too narrow, and the Portuguese suggested it be extended). The broadening was accepted by the French.

97 *Paris Convention: Actes de Londres*, 375: 'elle fait un pressant appel aux délégués présents pour qu'une satisfaction soit donnée à l'opinion publique qui réclame instamment qu'une mesure de ce genre soit prise en faveur des inventeurs'.

98 *Paris Convention: Actes de Londres*, 376 and 457–8.

Even though nothing passed it was agreed by all that a record of the debates on grace periods should be maintained.[99] The issue was resurrected once more at the Lisbon Revision Conference in 1958,[100] but it too died. In Europe, the option was taken off the table by the Strasbourg Convention on the Unification of Certain Points of Substantive Law on Patents[101] with its narrow grace period and later the European Patent Convention.[102] More recently, there was an attempt in the failed Draft Substantive Patent Law Treaty[103] to adopt a grace period internationally. It now appears that free trade agreements[104] might actually lead to the grace periods being adopted widely enough for some rule to make it into an multilateral intellectual property treaty even if not the Paris Convention itself. If this happens it will have been a very long road from London in 1934.

7 Conclusions

The moral rights of inventor were a small part of the London Conference, but the issues raised and discussed in the Sub-Committee – the right to be identified as an inventor, the right of an inventor to share in the benefits of the invention and the right to disclosure during the grace period – were all controversial and struggled to even by considered in 1934. In the end only the most benign of the three rights was adopted but the other two proposed rights have remained on the international agenda ever since. The moves to introduce a multilateral rule on employed inventors returned to the International Labour Organisation,

99 *Paris Convention: Actes de Londres,* 458.

100 See *Actes de la conférence réunie à Lisbonne du 6 au 31 Octobre 1958* (Geneva: BIRPI, 1962); for a blunt assessment see Pfanner, Klaus, 'Vereinheitlichung des materiellen Patentrechts im Rahmen des Europarats'. *GRUR International* (1962) 545, 551.

101 (Strasbourg, 27.XI.1963), art 4 (ETS No 47); see Wadlow, Christopher, 'Strasbourg, the Forgotten Patent Convention, and the Origins of the European Patents Jurisdiction'. *IPQ* (2010) 123.

102 *European Patent Convention,* art 55; see Proceedings of 5th Meeting of Patents Working Group (EPC 1973 Trav Prep: Doc 3076/IV/62-E), 2-18 April 1962 and Preliminary Draft Convention (EPC 1973 Trav Prep: Doc 4488/IV/62-E).

103 Draft Substantive Patent Law Treaty, 14–19 May 2001 (WIPO Document SCP/5/2), art 10.

104 A grace period has been included in the following *US Free trade agreements: US-Australia,* art 17.19(9); *US-Bahrain,* art 14.8(8); *US-Canada-Mexico,* art 20.37; *US-Chile,* art 17.9(7); *US-Columbia,* art 16.9(7); *US-Korea,* art 18.8(7); *US-Morocco,* art 15.9(8); *US-CAFTA-DR* (Costa Rica, El Salvador, Guatemala, Honduras, Nicaragua, as well as the Dominican Republic), art 15.9(7); *US-Oman,* art 15.8(8); *US-Peru,* art 16.9(7); and more particularly, *CPTPP,* Article 18.38.

where it probably should have been all along, but even there little progress was made and the closest it has ever came to it being adopted may well have been in 1934. It also remains the case that there are no rules relating to the prior art and novelty in the Paris Convention or in any other similar instruments. Some controversies take a long time to pass. In both cases, however, the subsequent debates were rarely seen in the context of being the "moral" rights of inventors comparable to those for authors. That view was very much of its time.

Bibliography

Secondary Sources

Emanuel, Adler, 'Inventions of Employees and the Austrian Patents Act of 1925'. *International Labour Review* 13(1) (1926) 1–20.

Becker, Joseph. *Japanese Laws and Ordinances concerning Patents, Trade-Marks, Designs and Utility Models* (London: Butterworths, 1930).

Bogsch, Arpad, 'The First Hundred Years of the Paris Convention for the Protection of Industrial Property'. In WIPO, *The Paris Convention for the Protection of Industrial Property from 1883 to 1983* (Geneva: WIPO, 1983).

Bodenhausen, Georg. *Guide to the Application of the Paris Convention for the Protection of Industrial Property* (Geneva: World Intellectual Property Organization, 1969).

Cornwell, Sally, 'Employee Rights in Innovative Works'. *International Labour Review* 119(3) (1980) 301–320.

Cross, John, 'An Attribution Right for Patented Inventions'. *University of Dayton Law Review* 37(2) (2012) 139–163.

Ilosvay, Thomas, 'Scientific Property'. *The American Journal of Comparative Law* 2(2) (1953) 178–197.

Johnson, Phillip, 'From Banks to Shanks: the History of Employee Awards for Patented Inventions under the Patents Act 1977'. *QMJIP* 11 (2021) 124–157.

Ladas, Stephen, 'The Efforts for International Protection of Scientific Property'. *The American Journal of International Law* 23(3) (1929) 552–569.

Lee, Nari, 'Inventor's Moral Right and Morality of Patents'. In *Research Handbook On Intellectual Property And Moral Rights,* Gendreau, Ysolde, ed. (Cheltenham: Edward Elgar, 2023).

Miller, David, 'Intellectual Property and Narratives of Discovery/Invention: The League Of Nations' Draft Convention On 'Scientific Property' and Its Fate'. *History of Science* 46(3) (2008) 299–342.

Neumeyer, Fredik, 'Employees' Rights in Their Inventions: A Comparison of National Laws'. *International Labour Review* 83/84(1) (1961) 36–105.

Pfanner, Klaus, 'Vereinheitlichung des materiellen Patentrechts im Rahmen des Europarats'. GRUR *International* (1962) 545, 551.

Ricketson, Sam, and Ginsburg, Jane. *International Copyright and Neighbouring Rights: The Berne Convention and Beyond, 3rd Ed* (Oxford: Oxford University Press, 2022).

Wadlow, Christopher, 'Strasbourg, the Forgotten Patent Convention, and the Origins of the European Patents Jurisdiction'. *IPQ* (2010) 123.

Cases

Plimpton v Malcolmson (1876) LR 3 Ch D 531.

CHAPTER 4

A New Style of National Power: International IP Relations and Unfair Competition in the Interwar Years (1919–1939)

Laura Ford

"Modern law has its beginnings when Roman law became the rival of the law of the church and presently set itself free from clerical control."[1] So wrote Roscoe Pound, Dean Emeritus of Harvard Law School, in the first chapter of an extraordinary 3-volume compilation of essays, published in 1937, commissioned to celebrate "A Century of Progress" in law (1835–1935), as seen from NYU Law School.[2] Consistent, perhaps, with the attitude that Progressives tended to take toward intellectual property (they typically referred to "industrial" and "literary" property), patents, copyrights, trademarks, and trade secrets received relatively little attention in the essays.[3] But this relative rarity makes the points at which intellectual property did appear even more striking.

In a compilation of essays assessing the state of American law, looking back from the later end of the "Interwar Period" (1919–1939), developments in intellectual property law were noteworthy in reflections on two significant points of transformation in state power: (1) in international law, where intellectual property had been part of multilateral treaty frameworks since the Congress of Vienna in 1815, but with increasing prominence since the 1883 Union for the Protection of Industrial Property had been created by the International Convention signed at Paris, and (2) in the domestic merger between law and

1 Pound, Roscoe, 'A Hundred Years of American Law'. In *Law, a Century of Progress, 1835–1935: Contributions in Celebration of the 100th Anniversary of the Founding of the School of Law of New York University: in Three Volumes*, Vol. 1, Reppy, Alison ed. (New York: New York University Press 1937) 9.

2 Reppy, Alison, 'Editor's Note'. In *Law: A Century of Progress* (n 1) Vol. 1, VII; Sommer, Frank, 'Prefatory Note'. In *Law: A Century of Progress* (n 1) Vol. 1, 6–7.

3 On Progressive ambivalences with respect to intellectual property law generally, see the outstanding article, upon which I draw extensively in this contribution: Wilf, Steven, 'The Making of the Post-War Paradigm in American Intellectual Property Law'. *Columbia Journal of Law and Arts* 31(2) (2008) 139, 149–53. As Wilf emphasizes, the New Deal brought an altered perspective, but the changes were in occurring precisely in the Interwar Period.

 | DOI:10.1163/9789004714663_006

equity, which heightened the range of discretionary, "coercive" powers exercised by U.S. courts.[4]

The "Century of Progress" volumes serve as historical witnesses to a belief, on the part of at least some jurists, that a new era was dawning in the arena of state power. No essay illustrates this better than Harold Laski's on "The Crisis in the Theory of the State," which opened the second of the three volumes. Given the unchallengeable lucidity that he had come to see in a Marxist conception of the state, Laski claimed to speak for his generation of scholars when he confessed that "we are in a psychological condition comparable ... to the end of the feudal period, or to the epoch of the French Revolution, when men sought to reconstitute the foundations of society."[5]

The crisis, in Marxist terms, resulted from the class interests that rigidified the modern state, disabling it from responding adequately to the inevitable changes that were occurring in the relations of production. The market economy had become singular and global, while the legal structure of states remained anchored in the pluralist, bourgeois notions of state sovereignty, serving the interests of the owners, while feeding the ever-increasing pressures from rising new classes who would eventually refuse to serve those interests. To the elite jurists whose company he joined in writing his essay, Laski issued a solemn warning and clarion call:

> Our age is watching a debate in legal philosophy the intensity of which measures with some precision the degree to which the traditional conception of the state power is in jeopardy. As always in the past, a challenge to legal ideas is the harbinger of a revolutionary tune. The supreme problem for the jurists of this epoch is the need to awaken to the responsibilities of the issue they confront. For only a realistic awareness of what that issue fully implies can save us from the grim rigors of a new dark age.[6]

The ultimate question, for Laski, was the question of material distribution. The class struggle over state power was a struggle over the "authority to redefine, for new purposes, the legal postulates of society," and these legal postulates

4 Borchard, Edwin, 'A Century of International Law'. In *Law: A Century of Progress* (n 1) Vol. 2, 148, 151; Eder, Phanor, 'Law and Justice in Latin America'. In *Law: A Century of Progress*, Vol. 1, 65; Simons, Walter, 'One Hundred Years of German Law'. In *Law: A Century of Progress*, Vol. 1, 103; Walsh, William, 'The Growing Function of Equity in the Development of the Law'. In *Law: A Century of Progress*, Vol. 3, 173.

5 Laski, Harold, 'The Crisis in the Theory of the State'. In *Law: A Century of Progress*, Vol. 2, 6.

6 Ibid., 31.

"are always no more than principles which determine in what way the social product shall be determined."[7]

Given the commitment to serving class interests that he saw in contemporary jurisprudence, Laski was not sanguine about the possibilities for peaceful global coordination through the League of Nations. The League could only be successful if states relinquished their sovereignty, but states could never do this, so long as they served the interests of the owners of the means of production. Converted as he had been to a "Marxian" understanding of the problems of the emerging international order, Laski anticipated a revolutionary war that would ultimately destroy capitalist class relations and the state power that maintained them.[8] But he also recognized that the "capitalist system" might have "latent powers of recovery more profound than have yet been made apparent."[9] The success (or failure) of Soviet Russia's "experiment" in restructuring its class relations, and particularly Russia's capacity to "develop for its citizens a standard of living which compares favorably with that of capitalism," would provide vital lessons for jurists seeking to recraft the legal boundaries of state power within the broader international order.[10]

The war period that Laski looked back upon (World War I) had stimulated unrealistic hopes for democracy, which for Laski meant the capacity of citizens to use political power and the authority of the state to increase their material well-being. The modern state would only survive if it could find a way to adequately respond to the "concern of the masses" in material well-being that had been awakened by the Great War.[11]

As Laski was writing, however, New Deal programs were fundamentally reshaping the American state, a process that had begun with the Progressives around the turn of the century, with roots in Reconstruction.[12] And what would prove to be a century-long project in "Restating" American common law was well underway, with the Restatement of Contracts and the first installment of the Restatement of Torts having recently appeared.[13] Within the League of

7 Ibid.

8 Ibid., 14–26.

9 Ibid., 28.

10 Ibid.

11 Ibid., 15–26.

12 On the spirit of Progressivism and its historical context, see Hofstadter, Richard. *The Age of Reform* (New York: Vintage Books, 1955). For a recent treatment of Progressivism in law and politics, emphasizing continuities with the New Deal agenda and tactics, see Novak, William J. *New Democracy: The Creation of the Modern American State* (Cambridge, MA: Harvard University Press, 2022).

13 Lewis, William Draper. *Introduction to Restatement (First) of Torts* (Philadelphia: American Law Institute, 1934).

Nations, the Progressive project for which Wilson had fought so hard in Paris and Washington, seeds had been planted for a long-term project in "harmonizing" the international order of intellectual property law, which would bear fruit in the world that emerged in the wake of World War II, and in the United Nations.[14]

As Howard Laski's essay helps us to see, the Interwar Period was one in which influential jurists understood domestic problems of material distribution to be inevitably linked to structures of international cooperation, urging responsibility for radical reformation in consideration of that perception. This perspective lends an added dimension to Steven Wilf's persuasive argument that the Interwar Period was a time when intellectual property law, particularly trademark law, played a significant part in a broad-based reconstitution of American democracy, shifting it in nationalist and consumerist directions.[15] To be an American citizen was to have the opportunity of participating in what was just beginning to be called the "American Dream," and thereby to stake a claim in social-democratic power and prosperity.[16] Socio-legal foundations were being laid for what Michael Mann has called "consumer citizenship," and intellectual property, linked to understandings of international legal obligations, played an important part in the transformative drama.[17]

In this essay, I seek to explicate connections between developing structures of international legal cooperation and domestic U.S. developments in coalescing areas of intellectual property law, primarily unfair competition and trademark law. The essay unfolds in four parts. The first section presents the thesis that, all appearances to the contrary, the Interwar Period was one in which domestic U.S. intellectual property law took shape with explicit reference to international treaty-based obligations. Despite the isolationist turn in U.S. domestic politics during the Interwar Period, in other words, foundations were being laid for increased international cooperation in legal protections for knowledge-based assets. The second section of the essay goes backward in

14 Ford, Laura R., 'From Plato to WIPO: Old and New in Legal Harmonization'. In *Harmonizing Intellectual Property Law for a Trans-Atlantic Knowledge Economy,* Mezei, Péter, Pogácsás, Anett, and, Travis, Hannibal, eds., (Leiden: Brill, 2024) Ch. 1.

15 Wilf, 'Making of Post-War Paradigm' (n 3) 146–49, 153–74, 206–7.

16 As detailed in a recent cultural history, the concept of the American dream was popularized during our period, see Churchwell, Sarah. *Behold America: The Entangled History of America First and the American Dream* (New York: Basic Books, 2018).

17 Mann, Michael, *The Sources of Social Power, Volume 4: Globalizations, 1945–2011* (Cambridge, UK: Cambridge University Press, 2013) 322–60; Ford, Laura R., *The Intellectual Property of Nations: Sociological and Historical Perspectives on a Modern Legal Institution* (Cambridge, UK: Cambridge University Press 2021) 373–4.

time to the negotiations in Paris leading to the Treaty of Versailles, highlighting the subtle part that intellectual property-related priorities played in that fateful drama, and emphasizing the new style of moral rhetoric deployed in those negotiations.

This new style of moral rhetoric, I argue, was reflected in U.S. legal discussions about "fairness" in competition. The third section of the essay explicates this argument. I seek to show that the confluence of cultural, social, and legal developments coalescing in U.S. unfair competition and trademark law during the Interwar Period manifested a new style of national state power. In the Conclusion I highlight the extent to which this new style of national state power, reinforced by intellectual property law, relied upon a post-Christian deployment of Christian moral conceptions.[18]

1 The International Connection for U.S. Intellectual Property Law in the Interwar Years

The Interwar Period is often presented as a time of isolationism in U.S. politics. From the rejection of President Wilson's League of Nations to President Roosevelt's domestically-focused "New Deal," the years 1919–1939 can hardly be presented as a high point in U.S. commitments to constructive internationalism.[19] And yet, while the characterization of U.S. politics as isolationist during Interwar Period may be a fair generalization, like all generalizations, it is only partially true. In fact, U.S. jurists participated in a dramatic reshaping of U.S. domestic law during the Interwar Period, with explicit reference to international treaty-based obligations. A focus on intellectual property law helps to make this apparent.

The linkage between developments in international and domestic intellectual property law, seen from an American perspective, starts to become evident when we focus on trademark law, which at this time was part of a broader, rapidly developing law of "unfair competition."[20] In this rapidly growing area

18 I am using 'post-Christian' in this essay similarly to Mark Thomas Edwards, whose recent biography of Walter Lippmann defines it as 'an imaginary, common among the Progressives and their pragmatist successors like Lippmann, that assumed the utility of Christian ideas, ethics, and institutions to promote mental health and social order.' Edwards, Mark Thomas, *Walter Lippmann: American Skeptic, American Pastor* (Oxford: Oxford University Press, 2023) 208.

19 See Kennedy, David M. *Freedom From Fear: The American People in Depression and War, 1929–1945* (Oxford: Oxford University Press, 1999).

20 The points asserted here are explicated in Section III below.

of law, the merger between law and equity, which had been largely carried out over the course of the "Century of Progress," was responsible for a set of moralistic legal conceptions within which "business rights and interests" should be recognized.[21] This conceptual framework for "fair competition" was grafted into the U.S. common law of torts, recognized by the American Law Institute (ALI) in the second and third installments of the Restatement (First) of Torts (1938 and 1939). At the same time, this framework was being energetically elaborated through international diplomacy and academic scholarship.[22]

The recognition of "business rights and interests" in "fair competition" – a competition that was conceived to extend not only to other businessmen but also between employers and unionized employees – is characteristic of reformatory, Progressive jurisprudence.[23] Competition was valorized, but it was to be rendered ethical, according to the newly ascendant social sciences. "Interests" were to be legally recognized and allowed the fullest room to operate, bounded by the point at which they violated an implicitly Kantian categorical imperative.[24] The "jurisprudence of interests" that Roscoe Pound had so effectively advocated over the course of his scholarly career, had arrived, embraced in the ALI's Restatement of Torts. At the core of this jurisprudence was a faith in social science, guided by Progressive legal philosophy.

Dean Pound's honorary opening essay for the NYU celebration of a "Century of Progress" in law was emblematic of this jurisprudential style. "Law" was effectively defined as the secular ideology of legal professionals. And the task set for these legal professionals was to adjust the "measure" of justice for a brave new world of business in a rapidly urbanizing, national economy. The new era of legal creativity that Pound saw dawning would be especially the province of law professors, given their social conditions of work, but their task would be most effectively carried out through cooperation with practicing lawyers and judges, a "conscious cooperation" facilitated by organizations like the ALI and the American Bar Association (ABA).[25]

---

21 Walsh, 'Growing Function of Equity' (n 4) 167.

22 Ladas, Stephen P. *The International Protection of Trade Marks by the American Republics* (Cambridge, MA: Harvard University Press, 1929); Ladas, Stephen P. *The International Protection of Industrial Property* (Cambridge, MA: Harvard University Press, 1930); Langner, Lawrence. *The Magic Curtain: The Story of a Life in Two Fields, Theatre and Invention* (New York: E.P. Dutton & Company, 1951) 344–45.

23 Hofstadter, *Age of Reform* (n 12).

24 Walsh, 'Growing Function of Equity' (n 4) 169.

25 Pound, 'Hundred Years' (n 1) 8–9, 15, 24–6. See also, Crane, Frederick, 'A Century of New York University School of Law'. In *Law: A Century of Progress* (n 1) Vol. 1, 3.

The crafting of a new, national legal framework for the protection of "trademarks" fitted Dean Pound's vision of legal creativity, pursued through cooperative organization alongside the ALI's common law restatements. In the ABA's 1920 Annual Meeting the skilled practitioner and legal scholar, Edward Sidney Rogers, gave an invited speech to the section on Patent, Trademark and Copyright law, calling for reform of trademark law and for better conformity to international obligations in the area of unfair competition law.[26] This marked the first step along a path that can be seen, in hindsight, as leading to the federal law that governs trademark protection in the U.S. today: the Lanham Act. As Rogers would later testify in Congress, a significant and explicit goal of the Act was to bring the U.S. domestic law of trademarks and unfair competition into conformity with U.S. treaty-based obligations.[27]

Looking back on the Interwar Period in the wake of the enactment of the Lanham Act in 1946, Stephen Ladas, a lawyer and scholar who published extensively on the international frameworks relevant to industrial and literary property, credited the efforts of Edward Rogers to bring U.S. trademark law into closer conformity with the commitments of international conventions, even while advocating further steps in this direction.[28] Article IX of the Lanham Act, Ladas noted, had been included "with a view to carrying out as fully as possible the commitments of our country under international conventions for the protection of trade-marks and trade names and for the suppression of unfair competition."[29] Despite the imperfections of the existing framework, interpreted from the perspective of U.S. businesses seeking protection for their trademarks in "foreign" markets, the Lanham Act had marked a milestone toward legal protections for fair competition, securing its protection, both domestically and internationally.

The dramatic international backdrop for Rogers' 1920 speech at the ABA Annual Meeting had been, of course, the Treaty of Versailles, together with the storm of controversy over the role that President Woodrow Wilson had played in the Paris negotiations. In 1920, the picture did not look rosy for American internationalists, including those internationalists, like Stephen Ladas, who

---

26 Litman, Jessica, 'Edward S. Rogers, The Lanham Act, and the Common Law'. In *Research Handbook on the History of Trademark Law,* Bone, Robert, and Bently, Lionel, eds. (Cheltenham: Edward Elgar, 2024).

27 Trade-Marks: Hearings before the Committee on Patents, Subcommittee on Trade-Marks, House of Representatives, Seventy-Fifth Congress, Third Session on H.R. 9041, March 15–18, 1938 (Washington, D.C.: Government Printing Office), 11–14.

28 Ladas, Stephen, 'The Lanham Act and International Trade'. *Law and Contemporary Problems* 14 (1949) 269.

29 Ibid., 270.

focused on the globalizing world of intellectual property protection. But by the end of the Interwar Period, the picture was rapidly changing, and the settlements after World War II would cement the transformation.

2 The League of Nations and the New Style of National Power

Intellectual property was not a primary focus for the League of Nations, or for Wilson's "Covenant" articulating foundational principles and ideals for the League. The primary focus for strategic negotiations among the post-War "principals" involved military pacification, territorial acquisition, colonial (and post-colonial) settlements, and spheres of influence. But intellectual property did play a subtle and suggestive role. This is ascertainable from a remarkable three-volume work written by the Progressive legal scholar and journalist, Ray Stannard Baker, who served as an informally-inaugurated Press Secretary for Woodrow Wilson in the Paris negotiations leading to the Treaty of Versailles.[30] According to Baker's record of the negotiations, based on a rare degree of access to Wilson's private notes, protections for intellectual property came up at several discrete points. Interestingly, it was not an American proposal that initiated the discussion, but French proposals, anchored in the backdrop of the Concert of Vienna's treaty-based settlement of the Napoleonic Wars.[31]

On December 2, 1918, as the President was preparing to leave for his historic trip to Paris, a set of materials was transmitted to him by Frank Polk, "Counsellor of the State Department," together with a cover letter from Polk and a letter from the French Ambassador, Jean-Jules Jusserand.[32] The package contained an English translation of the French proposal for the plan of procedure to be followed in the peace talks. The proposal is significant in specifying the historical precedents for the talks (the Congresses of Vienna (1814–15), Paris (1856), and Berlin (1878)), and in its framework for principles upon which the "Society of Nations" was to be organized after the more immediate settlements of the peace. Going forward, the French plan contemplated creation of an international economic regime, consistent with Wilson's "Fourteen

30 Baker, Ray Stannard. *Woodrow Wilson and World Settlement, Written from his Unpublished and Personal Material*, 3 Vols. (Garden City: Doubleday, Page & Co., 1922).

31 On IP-related provisions in the Concert of Vienna, *see, e.g.*, Ford, *Intellectual Property of Nations*, 387–90.

32 On Jean-Jules Jusserand, see Young, Robert J. *An American by Degrees: The Extraordinary Lives of French Ambassador Jules Jusserand* (Montreal: McGill-Queen's University Press, 2009).

Points" speech (3rd proposition), and, to that end, a set of committees would be established to study conditions and make ongoing proposals. One of these committees would offer studies and proposals with respect to the "law relative to patents and trademarks."[33]

Consistent with this initial proposal, the French also proposed, as part of their official plan for the League of Nations, that the League be given sanctioning powers, in order to protect the stability and efficacy of the new, global legal framework. One sanctioning power that the French contemplated would operate by penalizing a state's citizens, exerting a beneficent, national pressure for compliance: the mechanism was suspension of conventions relating to protection of literary and industrial property.[34] Businessmen whose patents and trademarks were not being protected in the international arena would presumably become motivated to write (or call) their political representatives to complain, pressuring the state into compliance with the League.

And further, in an undated memo submitted to the Economic Commission working busily at Paris, the French proposed that the "new economic state" in process of formation should ensure protection for trademarks and indications of origin. Heightened international cooperation to ensure effective protection for trademarks and indications of origin would "safeguard" the integrity and morality of commercial transactions, contributing to the global insurance for material prosperity that was to be a fundamental priority for international cooperation, going forward.[35]

These notices of IP-related proposals are consistent with a broader "spirit" of the Paris negotiations, which Baker highlighted as the dimension that was most significant about the new world inaugurated through the negotiations at Paris. This new world was rooted in a "new style" of diplomatic settlement. The new style of normative settlement, Baker emphasized, involved a profound distrust of politics and a new faith in social scientific expertise to determine what the rules of world cooperation should be. For Wilson, Baker tells us early in his narrative,

> this was to be a peace conference in which arrangements could not be made in the old style. And the problem of the Conference – he referred

33 Baker, *World Settlement* (n 30) Vol 3, 62. The third of Wilson's 'Fourteen Points' proposed, as a basis for world settlement, 'The removal, so far as possible, of all economic barriers and the establishment of an equality of trade conditions among all the nations consenting to the peace and associating themselves for its maintenance.' Ibid., 43.

34 Ibid., 155.

35 Ibid., 415–16; also 421.

> particularly to the question of German indemnity – must not be left "in purely political hands," but must be studied by commissions. He made a frank appeal to the experts.[36]

This theme of social scientific expertise, as the new foundation for settlement of the world's intractable problems – problems so pathetically on display in letters sent to Wilson by representatives of national groups from around the world – was a leitmotif for Baker's account of Wilson's heroic and insufficiently appreciated efforts at Paris.

Faith in social science provided essential support for Wilson's reformatory program, formulated as he was sailing to Paris. As Baker saw it, there were "two great central ideas" in Wilson's program, "both American in their origin." These central ideals were to constitute nothing less than a revolutionary change in the foundations of the "rights and liberties of human kind," on the one hand, corresponding to a transformation in the foundations of duty and obligation, on the other. The basis for human rights was to rest in the social-democratic right of "self determination" of "peoples," which Baker equated to a principle of "consent of the governed." The revolution in duty and obligation was to be found in the new covenantal order that would establish a league of nations – the obligation to cooperate in "a world association for mutual aid and protection."[37] Quoting Wilson's Mount Vernon speech of July 4, 1918, Baker distilled the two "great ideas" into a unitary legal program: "What we seek is the reign of law, based upon the consent of the governed, and sustained by the organized opinion of mankind."[38] American-style democracy would come to the rescue of a world torn apart by war, conducted on a scale hitherto unseen.

Baker recognized the voices of skepticism, but he could not really sympathize with them or present them as worthy of moral consideration. For him they were simply the counterpart, on the international stage, of the Southern Confederacy in U.S. history: they were a kind of "states' rights" party in international affairs, selfishly concerned with maintaining national sovereignty at the expense of world peace.[39] For Harold Laski, too, although he put his point quite differently, there was nothing to be said for the "leadership in the Senate," which opposed Wilson, namely the position articulated by Henry Cabot Lodge and his allies. The inevitable way forward for the world was organized

36 Baker, *World Settlement* (n 30) Vol 1, 10.

37 Ibid., 11.

38 Ibid.

39 Ibid., 15.

cooperation, led by social scientific (especially economic) expertise. The forces of reaction could only delay this, not prevent it.

From within an American Progressive frame of reference, the project of scientifically enlightened global cooperation might seem like an inevitable outcome of world history, shaped teleologically by a post-Christian faith in social democracy or orthodox Marxism. But Baker also recognized an alternative perspective, offered by the Italian Prime Minister in a 1919 speech at Rome. For Minister Orlando, the American stance was actually supremely rhetorical and political, representing a new kind of *noblesse oblige* to the European world that effectively "checkmated" German imperialism. Rather than the "might makes right" of power politics, Wilson was proposing to structure the world according to the "duty of the strongest," thereby placing "the authority of the moral law above the might of the United States."[40]

This rhetorical style of legal arrangements for the world, as articulated by Baker, projected "social justice" as the moral framework for American world leadership.[41] It was a new style of diplomacy, but also a new style of rhetoric within which to anchor legal principles.

> The new way so boldly launched at Paris (so ineffectively carried out!) was, first, to start with certain general principles of justice, such as those laid down by President Wilson and accepted by all the world; and, second, to have those principles applied, not by diplomats and politicians each eager to serve his own interests, but by dispassionate scientists – geographers, ethnologists, economists – who had made studies of the problems involved. It has often been charged that Wilson had no programme: this *was* his programme.[42]

40 Ibid., 19, also 262–5, 282–3.

41 As can be seen with the help of Google Ngram, the language of 'social justice' was used to increasingly dramatic effect in the decade preceding World War I, and again in the decade preceding World War II. It was an important symbolic dimension of Progressive reform, as seen, for example in President Wilson's 1913 State of the Union address: 'We ought to devote ourselves to meeting pressing demands of plain justice like this [Workmen's Compensation laws to protect railroad employees] as earnestly as to the accomplishment of political and economic reforms. Social justice comes first. Law is the machinery for its realization and is vital only as it expresses and embodies it.' *The American Presidency Project*, UC Santa Barbara, First Annual Message of Woodrow Wilson, December 2, 1913, available at https://www.presidency.ucsb.edu/documents/first-annual-message-18 (accessed Dec. 29, 22).

42 Baker, *World Settlement* (n 30) Vol. 1, 112; also 187.

A primary target for this "new style of diplomacy," as Baker presented it, was diplomatic secrecy, epitomized in the pervasive secret treaties of old style diplomacy. Indeed, Baker tells us that we cannot understand what happened at Paris unless we understand the character of these treaties, together with the diplomatic culture they fostered.[43] A world in which the relationships between nations are protected as secrets is a world given to deep distrust and fearful overreaction.[44]

It was in the context of his efforts to work through this atmosphere of deep distrust fostered by secret treaties that Wilson, through Baker, turned to the press. In his Fourteen Points speech of January 1918, Wilson proclaimed a set of ideals for transparent, purposive diplomacy going forward, including a principle of "open covenants of peace openly arrived at, after which there shall be no private international understandings of any kind."[45] Article XVIII of the Covenant negotiated at Paris accordingly required that treaties be registered with the secretariat of the League before they could have binding effect. Drawing perhaps on Theodore Roosevelt's earlier example,[46] Wilson understood that transparency and openness, in constant communication with the press, offered the opportunity to influence public opinion, which was becoming an ever more powerful force in national and world politics.

Comparing the diplomatic world of Paris in 1919 with that of Vienna in 1815, Baker observed:

> Mechanical invention had changed the whole world since Vienna, it had forced men into irritable contact as never before; popular education had awakened the under groups of the people to a new self-consciousness; a popular press and world-wide cheap communication had laid the foundations of a new world public opinion.[47]

This "new world public opinion" provided a source of social power that could be wielded against the retrograde forces of the "old diplomacy," and no one understood "the possibilities of the power so exerted" better than President Wilson.[48]

---

43 Ibid., 26.

44 Ibid., 27. On the connections between this aspect of Wilson's international diplomacy and his domestic political agenda, see Hofstadter, *Age of Reform* (n 12) Chapter 6.

45 Baker, *World Settlement* (n 30) Vol. 1, 46.

46 Goodwin, Doris Kearns. *The Bully Pulpit: Theodore Roosevelt, William Howard Taft, and the Golden Age of Journalism* (New York: Simon & Schuster, 2013).

47 Baker, *World Settlement* (n 30) Vol. 1, 103.

48 Ibid.

The Concert of Vienna was, strikingly, a constant point of reference for Baker, in his account of the Paris negotiations. And while he insistently stressed the differences between the realities with which the diplomats had to deal in these two architectonic congresses, there was perhaps no greater difference than the role of the press. And it is natural that this should have been the case for Baker, himself a journalist with solid "muckraking" credentials from his days at McClure's magazine, tasked now by President Wilson with overseeing the American press corps at Paris in 1919. It was through their organized press leadership that Wilson and Baker sought to respond to the dizzying array of interest-group demands pressed with such urgency at Paris. The Progressive Americans had an advantage over their sophisticated old-world brethren here, because the "whole technique of ... dealing with publics in the matter of foreign affairs was fire-new."[49]

The perils of this brave new world were great, but so were the possibilities. Nothing less than the "shaping" of world opinion was now possible.[50] And the substance of that shaping, Baker stresses repeatedly, was increasingly economic in character.[51] Wilson turned constantly to economists and other "scientific experts," who were busily producing reports to inform the negotiations.[52] His basic vision for achieving lasting peace, through a "new moral purpose" that would lift the world onto a "higher plane" involved fundamental trust in "dispassionate scientific inquiry," guaranteed by "positive responsibility."[53] In keeping with Wilson's vision, Baker himself implemented, with Wilson's approval, a program of education for the American press corps, so naïve in matters of world politics, providing factual background statements, prepared by the omnipresent and omniscient experts, enabling the journalists to understand the historical, political, and geographic stakes of the negotiations taking place, upon which they were to report.[54]

The implications of this "schooling" of press technique, with its pregnant possibilities for shaping public opinion in service of socio-economic purposes, went well beyond Paris, as Baker saw. The spirit of aggressive interrogation in service of progressive, social-democratic liberalism for world politics was one that the journalists would take home with them, "shaping the public opinion of the next quarter century in knowledge of world affairs and in the

49 Ibid., 117.

50 Ibid., 121.

51 Ibid., 79, 105, 113–4, 133, 137, 187–88.

52 Ibid., 113–14, 187–88, 199.

53 Ibid., 181, 176, 184–5, 187–88.

54 Ibid., 129–30.

understanding of other peoples."[55] In Paris, Wilson sought to use this power in service of his tactical struggles for achieving the "concert" of world power that would underpin world peace, going forward.[56]

Baker tells us straightforwardly that the "most vital struggle" of the Paris Peace Conference, at least from President Wilson's perspective, was to "bring into being a league of nations," and to "relate" that league "definitely" to the peace treaty.[57] At the time he was writing (1922), Baker noted, the League was functioning and fifty-one nations had joined it, despite the holdouts of the United States, Germany, and Russia.[58] But as Wilson was struggling to secure a place for his League-founding Covenant – this "constitution of the whole world" – amidst the old-world-style wrangling for colonial possessions, the possibilities at times seemed very dim.[59] Nonetheless, as of February 1919, when Wilson was preparing to return to America, it seemed that he had won, and that the Covenant for the League of Nations would serve as a cornerstone for a "concert of power," in service of peace, that would stabilize the world.[60] "A living thing is born … a definite guarantee by word against aggression," the President proclaimed to a plenary session on February 14, 1919.[61]

Nearly 20 years later, however, the League seemed more like something still-born to the American jurists looking back on that Century of Progress through which NYU law school had cultivated new generations of lawyers and legal scholars. While the League of Nations was too fragile to merit much celebratory self-congratulation, however, the new era of "cooperative effort" exemplified in organizations like the ALI and the ABA, as in rapidly progressing urbanization, was well worth celebrating.[62]

There was a new grandiosity of social power emerging in American legal consciousness, justifying new consolidations of social force and functionalism in the law, and American jurists were urged to overcome the small-town prejudices that might worry them about all this. As Dean Emeritus Pound himself put the point:

55 Ibid., 122.
56 Ibid., 196.
57 Ibid., 213, 235–49, 276.
58 Ibid., 213.
59 Ibid., 273.
60 Ibid., 285–6, 193.
61 Ibid., 285.
62 Goodrich, Herbert, 'Cooperative Effort in the Law'. In *Law: A Century of Progress* (n 1) Vol. 1, 191–206.

> Our traditional measure of law is this small-townism. We have become big, but we like to picture ourselves as small. We have become economically unified, but we like to think of ourselves as a congeries of economically self-sufficient small neighborhood towns. We seek to try and to value the manifold human claims with which administration of justice has to do in great urban communities by the measure of the small town, the citizen of the small town, and the life in the small town of our formative era. Let us not fear bigness. Whether we will or not, we live in a country of big things on every hand .... Such things call for a changed measure, and the finding and application of that measure disturb for a time law and politics, as the finding of a changed measure when we shifted from a colonial to a national regime disturbed the law and politics of the generation after the Revolution.[63]

Dean Pound acknowledged that the rapid development of city-based populations in the U.S. was causing some disturbances to the social order. There was perhaps "some retrogression" in the urbanizing population, but his sense was that any negative repercussions from such rapid social changes was only temporary, a blip on the larger screen of social Progress, which would bring with it the inevitable calls for more and better laws. This would mean more "law" of the type that his essay celebrated: secular, professional, expert legal knowledge.[64]

> Urban development may very likely go further still with further conquests of the external conditions of life and of physical nature, and with it will go the call for more laws and so for more law. As the lawyers of one hundred years ago were struggling with problems of adaptation of law to a new country, we must be struggling to adapt it to a big country with all manner of unforeseen questions inherent in its very bigness. Let our law schools see to it that these problems are approached with courage, with intelligence, with enlightenment. The result will be a creative era no less glorious in legal history than that in which this school was founded.[65]

The legal scholars assembled in NYU's "Century of Progress" volumes made no reference to the fact that confiscations of German intellectual property on an industrial scale – patents and trademarks, in particular – had supported the

63 Pound, 'One Hundred Years' (n 1) 25.

64 Ibid., 25–6, 8–9.

65 Ibid., 25–6.

rapid post-war development of the U.S. pharmaceutical industry, under the watchful eyes of federal regulators who had overseen the transfer.[66] But they did concentrate attention on transformations in international and domestic law that were taking place in conjunction with developments they saw as being significant in the broader international arena of "industrial property."

3 International Moralism, Unfair Competition, and a National Trademark Law

In his contributions to the second of the three "Century of Progress" volumes, Professor Edwin Borchard of Yale Law School looked back on "a century's development in international law," noting the novelty of developments in commercial treaties during this period, and the fact that such treaties came to embrace subjects, "such as patents, trademarks, and copyright, unknown to earlier centuries."[67] These developments, taking place in the third quarter of the nineteenth century, exemplified a broader theme of Professor Borchard's essay, the establishment of "international administrative unions" and the embrace of global social power through pragmatic cooperation.[68] Although he did not see the century as one of unqualified progress, particularly with regard to the "institution of war," Professor Borchard nonetheless viewed "the development of arbitration as an institution" as distinctly positive, exemplified partly in the pragmatic unions of the commercial law treaties.[69]

Genuine progress had also been made, Professor Borchard argued, in the conceptions of political theory and sovereignty, in relation to international law. It was now understood, he believed, that "no State can posit its freedom from the rules of international law."[70] While states did not always comply with international law, and while there were genuine weaknesses in the capacity of the international state system to enforce its legal order, the fact that states no longer professed their freedom from the rules of international law demonstrated a real, positive change. But alongside the heightened powers of the international system, he saw dangers in the emergence of new ideologies, closely associated with the League of Nations.[71]

66 U.S. v. Chemical Foundation, 272 U.S. 1 (1926); Steen, Kathryn, 'Patents, Patriots, and "Skilled in the Art": USA v The Chemical Foundation, Inc., 1923–1926'. *ISIS* (2001) 91–122.

67 Borchard, 'Century of International Law' (n 4) 151.

68 Ibid., 146, 148.

69 Ibid., 149, 151, 154.

70 Ibid., 154.

71 Ibid., 152–56.

Professor Borchard discerned, in the new League of Nations, a naïve form of mechanistic thinking, according to which the positing of a new system of "collective security" justified dispensing with the old, hard ambiguities of international relations. The moral absolutism in this new ideology was particularly dangerous and regressive in its condemnation of state neutrality. In place of the old model of studied neutrality, the ideologists of the new system were substituting schemes to "enforce" peace against "aggressor" nations through armed blockades and embargoes. The "postulate of a holy crusade" had carried over from the Great War into this new period of enforced peace. Under the cover of a "cloak of romantic uplift" an "astronomic increase in armaments" was taking place, and public opinion was blinded by a "world-wide and especially American campaign to discredit neutrality as a thing of the past, and to discountenance the very philosophy of neutrality as immoral, impractical, and iniquitous."[72]

Twenty years earlier, in lectures given near the end of his life, Max Weber had also pointed to the dangers and hypocrisies of moral absolutes, projected onto the world stage at the end of the Great War. It was not just that economic realities tended always to compromise the most "otherworldly" of professions, as the history of Christianity and American political parties (among many other examples) had tended to show. It was also that genuine moral commitment required spiritual discernment, the capacity to recognize with clarity what a particular moral commitment entailed, and where it was being compromised by competing values and priorities. Those who claimed most stridently to be pursuing a path of "social justice" often failed to honestly grapple with the implications of their avowals. They refused to acknowledge the realities of power and violence that they either consciously or unconsciously deployed. With respect to absolutist moral frameworks in general, Weber borrowed a colloquial quip made earlier about the principle of causality in science: "it is not a hired cab which one may stop at will and climb into or out of as one sees fit."[73]

In 1930, Talcott Parsons published his English translation of Max Weber's essays on *The Protestant Ethic and the Spirit of Capitalism*, essays written originally in 1904–1905, examining the spiritual legacies of radical Protestantism for the socio-economic transformations of the modern world.[74] Max Weber

72 Ibid., 158–9.

73 Weber, Max, 'The Vocation of Politics'. In *The Essential Weber* Whimster, Sam, ed (New York: Routledge 2004) 260–61, 265–66; Weber, Max, 'The Profession and Vocation of Politics'. In *Weber: Political Writings Politics* Lassman, Peter, and Speirs, Ronald, eds. (Cambridge, UK: Cambridge University Press, 1994) 309–69.

74 Swedberg, Richard, ed. *The Protestant Ethic and the Spirit of Capitalism* (New York: w.w. Norton, 2009).

became, through the translation efforts of Talcott parsons, one of the "founding fathers" of U.S. sociology, which, under the leadership of Parsons, focused analytical attention on the social and economic functions of institutions.[75]

Max Weber had shared with Karl Marx and Friedrich Engels the sense that the economic conditions of a particular activity (whether this be politics, journalism, or science) tended to shape the values according to which that activity was morally justified. At the same time, however, Weber criticized the reductivism in historical materialism, focusing his analytical attention on the "spiritual" potential for difference-making power in value-commitments ("vocations"), as well as the organizing, direction-giving power of shared conceptions lending social meaning to "interests." While interests (particularly economic interests) tended to have the largest aggregate effects on social action and institutions, ideals and values gave meaningful shape and direction to those interests, and could sometimes, in human history, shift them in new directions.[76]

The history of law was no exception to this broader pattern, and Weber recognized his time as one in which popular, post-Christian moralities of various pedigrees were displacing old conceptual formalities rooted in Roman law and naturalized Christian theology. It was an age in which new prophets, proclaiming new moralities to give coherence to the ordering forces of law, might arise, with effects analogous to the railroad switch-man, directing even the most conservative of institutions, like the state, down new tracks.[77]

The Progressive proclaimers of "social justice," as the organizing framework for legal reform, did sometimes conceive themselves in prophetic terms, as is documented by N.E.H. Hull in her historical treatment of American legal realism.[78] And one important arena in which the Progressive legal realists focused their efforts during the Interwar Period was business law, particularly in legal concepts and legislative efforts defining "fairness" in competition. In both international and domestic law, "unfair" forms of competition were being legally proscribed as part of a broader moral project to reform society, particularly its economic dimensions. As one of the self-appointed prophets of this movement, Stephen Ladas, put the point in 1929:

---

75 Coser, Lewis. *Masters of Sociological Thought: Ideas in Historical and Social Context*, 2d ed. (Long Grove, IL: Waveland Press, 1977) 561–65; Max Weber, *The Theory of Social and Economic Organization*, Parsons, Talcott, ed. (New York: Oxford University Press, 1947).

76 Max Weber, 'Introduction to the Economic Ethics of the World Religions'. In *The Essential Weber* (n 73) 55–80.

77 Ibid., 69; Rheinstein, Max, ed., *Max Weber on Law in Economy and Society* (New York: Simon & Schuster 1954) 301–21.

78 Hull, NEH, Roscoe Pound and Karl Llewellyn: Searching for an American Jurisprudence. *Searching for an American Jurisprudence* (Chicago: University of Chicago Press, 1997).

> In recent years a great development of the law of unfair competition has been accomplished. In [all the countries described in his book] earnest efforts are being made to protect the business relations of competing manufacturers or traders without destroying competition, and to defeat the frauds committed by business parasites. In an increasing number of countries, it was found that commercial affairs moved and changed too rapidly to await the slow process of the growth of law by court decisions through experience and development by logical deduction, and that the interests clamoring for protection should be satisfied by special legislation reaching all known and foreseen acts of unfair competition. This is also, perhaps, one of the phases of the general faith in the efficacy of conscious effort to improve law and to improve society through law, which constitutes one of the chief characteristics of twentieth century legal history.[79]

Following up in 1930, Ladas detailed the rapid globalization of trademark law, which he conceived as the center-point in a broader framework of "unfair competition" law.[80] In 1937, he added a two-volume work to address the globalization of legal protections for literary and artistic property, as a companion to his earlier treatments of industrial property.[81]

Ladas conceived the law of unfair competition as a general law, encompassing the infringement of industrial property, but extending more broadly to "all inequitable acts of competition to the injury of a competitor and of fair dealing."[82] In a more restricted sense this law pertained to the "repression" of "acts contrary to honest practices in trade" that were not addressed by specific laws governing industrial property.[83] In common law countries the law had been "worked out by the courts," but in an unduly restrictive way, limited to cases of "passing off," where a defendant falsely represented his goods as being those of another.[84] Through his advocacy and scholarship, Ladas hoped to move lawmakers toward a more informed understanding of the value of industrial property, both in regulating domestic competition and in enabling profitable

79 Ladas, *The International Protection of Trade Marks* (22) 47–48.

80 Ibid.; Ladas, Stephen. *The International Protection of Industrial Property* (Cambridge, MA: Harvard University Press, 1930).

81 Ladas, Stephen. *The International Protection of Literary and Artistic Property in Two Volumes* (New York: The MacMillan Company, 1938).

82 Ladas, *International Protection of Industrial Property*, 51.

83 Ibid.

84 Ibid.

business activity in foreign countries. It troubled him that the subject of industrial property had not received "systematic exposition" by U.S. scholars, as compared to their European counterparts, either with respect to international or domestic law.[85]

Tracing the "Growing Function of Equity in the Development of the Law" for NYU's "Century of Progress" volumes, William F. Walsh agreed with the judgment of Stephen Ladas that the law of "unfair competition" was new, and he also argued that it was largely attributable to the exercise of equity powers by U.S. courts. The emergence of this new area of law was the "most significant and most important development of the law of torts during the last hundred years," and it had occurred "almost exclusively in equity."[86] The story of unfair competition law, the law developed to protect against interferences with a person's "right to make a living," was, according to Walsh, part of the broader, extraordinary story about the "growth of law accomplished by equity in modern times."[87] Here was a second phase of equity's contribution to the system of U.S. tort law, following the phase in which equitable maxims were drawn upon to construct the basic framework of general negligence law, during the age of conceptualist "legal science."[88]

The equitable regulation provided by this new body of law extended, according to William Walsh, not only to the relationship between competing businesses, but to the relations between "capital and labor."[89] Indeed, Walsh considered the accomplishments of unfair competition law in this particular arena to be the "most striking illustration" of the way in which equity had contributed to legal developments over the preceding century.

> Competition between an employer and his employees involves the well-established right of labor to organize and to strike or threaten to strike in order to secure better wages and conditions of labor, and the equally well-established right of the employer to hire and discharge employees as he pleases and to lay down the terms of employment. In this competition each must act within the limits of what is reasonable and fair.[90]

85 Ibid., VII.
86 Walsh, 'Growing Function of Equity' (n 4) 167.
87 Ibid., 169.
88 White, G. Edward. *Tort Law in America: An Intellectual History* (Oxford: Oxford University Press, 2003) Chapter 1.
89 Walsh, 'Growing Function of Equity' (n 4) 169.
90 Ibid.

As in the areas of negligence and nuisance law, the test of the reasonably prudent person, or "average man," provided the basic standard by which to determine what is reasonable and fair. "So long as each side acts within the limits of reasonable and fair competition as determined by this standard he commits no legal wrong no matter how serious the resulting damage may be to the other's right to carry on his business or to earn wages."[91] Equitably constituted unfair competition law, in other words, supplied the basic regulating principles according to which the economic relations of competition, both between businesses and between employers and employees, could be rendered just and lawful.

In 1938 and 1939, just after the Century of Progress volumes were published, the ALI approved the third and fourth volumes of the Restatement of Torts, bringing that important restatement project to conclusion.[92] Division Nine, stretching across volumes three and four, addressed wrongs committed through acts that interfered with "business relations," with chapters 35 and 36 addressed to unfair competition and related "miscellaneous" actions, essentially what we consider today the arenas of trademark and trade secrecy law. Preceding these two chapters, providing a general framework for the law of business relations, was chapter 34, titled "The Privilege to Engage in Business," laying down a basic principle of "good faith," as the criterion of liability. So long as a businessman acted in good faith, he would not be liable for losses of business or occupation to another.[93] In 1995, these chapters were refashioned into the Restatement (Third) of Unfair Competition, which abandoned the orienting framework of "good faith."[94]

One of the prophets of "law and economics" for our own age, Richard Posner, has powerfully critiqued the facile moralism that a phrase like "good faith" can carry.[95] But the moralism in the concept of "good faith," as described in the Restatement (First) of Torts, was not quite what Judge Posner seemed to assume. Commentary in the definitional section of the Restatement elaborated on the notion of "good faith" by defining it intentionally.[96] The purpose of a person entering into business in good faith was "engaging in the business in a business way," *i.e.* with the intent of making profits and remaining in the business so long as it is profitable.

91 Ibid., 170.

92 Lewis, *Introduction to Restatement* (n 13) (1934, 1938, 1939).

93 Restatement (First) of Torts § 708 (1938).

94 Restatement (Third) of Unfair Competition §1 (1995).

95 Market Street Associates Limited Partnership v. Frey (7th Cir. 1991).

96 Comment c, § 708.

This "good faith" entry into business could include limited situations where a profit was not expected, at least in the short term. "For example, a building contractor may open a real estate agency with the intention of operating it only until the slump in building activity passes. Or a young man may open a gasoline filling station with the intention of operating it only until he saves enough money to enable him to go to law school." These were instances of "good faith" business activity. What was excluded however, was the situation in which a person entered a business for the exclusive purpose of "injuring or destroying the business of another." Good faith, as defined for purposes of unfair competition law, simply proscribed the forms of cut-throat competition that were mainly possible for monopolistic entities, such as the large and infamous trusts against which the muckrakers had campaigned so effectively.

In reality, the rule of good faith operated to define a "privilege to engage in business," protecting the business person acting in good faith against tort liability for damage caused to the business of another.[97] The theory underlying the privilege, as explained in the commentary, was that "in the long run, competition promotes efficiency and economic general welfare and that to subject a person to liability merely for competing would result in preventing competition."[98] The privilege defined through the concept of good faith was intended to reassure potential competitors that they would not face liability merely for mistakes in judgment, or because they entered into business knowing that they would probably drive another person out of business. This privilege was "a basic assumption in the law of unfair competition, as it is, in an even broader form, in the economics of free enterprise and in the politics of individualism."[99]

An introductory note, probably written by the reporter, Francis Bohlen, offers a revealing glimpse into the Progressive goals driving the restatement of common law principles in this particular area of business relations.[100] The note clarified that "legal protection of interests in commercial transactions" was provided by contract and property law, alongside tort law, and that other chapters of the torts restatement addressed themselves, similarly, to the "interest in commercial advantages." What set chapters 35 and 36 apart was the type of business-related conduct that they proscribed, the characteristically bad faith "trade practices … calculated to cause business loss to another." The law addressed to these bad faith practices was "the law of Trade-mark

97 Title of chapter 34 and comment b, § 708.

98 Comment d, § 708.

99 Comment c, § 708.

100 Introduction, Chapter 35, *Restatement (First) of Torts* (American Law Institute 1938).

Infringement and Unfair Competition," which should be better described as the law of "unfair trade practices," since "trade-mark infringement is but one form of unfair competition," with "competition" broadly understood as the "struggle for commercial advantage," extending beyond direct competition to the relations of business generally.[101]

The introductory note described the historical development of this field of law, locating its origins in common law actions for "deceit" and fraudulent "passing off," but noting that the framework had shifted rapidly in subtler directions, such that "liability is now imposed for methods of appropriating, or causing harm to, another's trade values." The law was in an extraordinarily rapid process of development and remained somewhat eclectic and inchoate. But the firm impetus for the law's development was moral progress: "the tendency of the law, both legislative and common, has been in the direction of enforcing increasingly higher standards of fairness or commercial morality in trade."[102]

Among the "special features" of this rapidly developing area of tort law, perhaps the most important was its anchoring in the equity jurisdiction of courts. The remedy was typically equitable, "and it is in the equity courts rather than in the law courts that this branch of the law has received its largest development." Partly because of the equitable discretion that typically addressed the trade practices at issue, alongside rapid changes in business methods and morality, "the scope of liability in this field is constantly expanding." The easy recourse to injunctions "facilitates the condemnation as illegal of practices which were not previously so regarded and thus aids the development of this branch of the law."[103]

It would be difficult to find a franker acknowledgement of the role that equitable jurisdiction and Progressive morality were playing, in conjunction, to shape trademark and trade secret law during the Interwar Period. And, while no mention was made in this Introductory Note of the role that international IP relations were playing in shaping the developments, such acknowledgments can readily be found elsewhere, in the books of Stephen Ladas, for example, and in Congress.

For it was in the same year, 1938, that the U.S. House of Representatives' Subcommittee on Trademarks, chaired by Fritz Lanham of Texas, began its

101 Ibid.

102 Ibid.

103 Ibid.

hearings on the bill, H.R. 9041,[104] which would finally be enacted after World War II as the Trademark Act of 1946, known since the time of its enactment as the Lanham Act.[105] The first to testify was Edward Sidney Rogers, the drafter of the bill. Opening his testimony with a description of the background to the bill, Rogers modestly described himself as an editor, receiving input from members of the ABA and "groups in foreign countries," meeting every couple of years under the aegis of the International Chamber of Commerce's "industrial property commission" and the Inter-American commission that had facilitated "Pan-American" treaties pertaining to industrial and literary property.[106] These various inputs had gone into a previous bill debated in Congress, the "Vestal Bill," without resulting in final legislation. But Rogers described a new urgency for federal legislation, to respond to activism on the part of state legislatures and the potential for multiple, conflicting trademark regimes operating on the national level.

Jessica Litman has recently unearthed fascinating new insights into the life and legacy of Edward Rogers, providing at the same time a valuable synthesis of the broader historical context, and the series of events leading to passage of the Lanham Act. We learn from her about Rogers' social network, anchored in his Chicago-based partnership with Frank Fremont Reed, the first specialized lecturer in copyright law at University of Michigan law school.[107] Rogers brought a developing specialization in trademark law to the partnership, and the list of important clients for their services expanded over the years to include such recognizable names as Coca Cola, West Publishing, Standard Oil, and McIlhenny Tabasco.[108] A less recognizable name today, but one that is significant in regard to the themes of this article, was their early and longstanding client, Sterling Remedy, maker of the "patent medicine" Cascarets Candy Cathartic laxative tablets.[109] In 1917, Sterling had been a major beneficiary of the U.S. confiscation of German industrial property, acquiring Bayer Aspirin, Luminal (phenobarbital), and Novocain.[110]

104 Trade-Marks: Hearings before the Committee on Patents, Subcommittee on Trade-Marks, House of Representatives, Seventy-Fifth Congress, Third Session on H.R. 9041, March 15–18, 1938.

105 Public Law No. 79–489, 60 Stat. 427, as amended through 2022. On the proprieties of citation format, see Horton, Paul, 'A Plea for the Proper Citation of the Lanham Act'. *Trademark Reporter* 106 (2016) 754.

106 Trade-Marks: Hearings, 11.

107 Litman, 'Edward S. Rogers' (n 26) 6.

108 Ibid, 7.

109 Ibid.

110 Ibid, 8–9; see also (n 66) and accompanying text.

In 1938, in his testimony before Congress, Rogers stressed the urgent need for federal legislation because commerce had become "Nation-wide." As important, valuable identifying instrumentalities for commerce, trade-marks should also operate on a national scale. Congress should exercise the full extent of its commerce clause powers, under the U.S. constitution, to protect trademarks at the national level, and, notably, this would bring U.S. law into better conformity with its international treaty obligations.

> The preliminary question and the primary question, as I see it, is whether we should have a single statute which makes trade-mark property more secure, to the full extent of the congressional power over it, and which will, incidentally, carry out some of our treaty obligations that we are not now observing.[111]

While Rogers did not overly stress the international dimension, in his testimony before Congress, it was clear both from that testimony, and from the bill itself, that Rogers considered the international dimension important.

And it was no surprise that he should, given the important role he had played, alongside Stephen Ladas, in negotiating the Pan-American Trademark Convention of 1929.[112] This trademark framework for the Americas had come into existence in 1889, and had gone through several iterations prior to 1929, when it was renegotiated and renewed in Washington, D.C. The treaty was ultimately signed by 19 American countries, including the U.S., and 10 countries later ratified it. A primary goal of the treaty, from the U.S. perspective, was to ensure the possibility for trademark protection in external American markets. As Christine Haight Farley has pointed out, the treaty remains in effect, and it is self-executing, meaning that it is valid U.S. law even in the absence of implementing legislation.[113]

Looking back on his efforts to secure federal legal protections for national trademarks, in a 1949 article published posthumously in Duke Law School's journal, *Law and Contemporary Problems*, Rogers modestly disclaimed any notion that the Lanham Act was his own brainchild, elevating it instead to a collective product of cooperative effort by the best and brightest of the

---

111 Trade-Marks: Hearings, 13.

112 Farley, Christine Haight, 'The Pan-American Trademark Convention of 1929: A Bold Vision of Extraterritorial Meets Current Realities'. In *Trademark Protections and Territoriality Challenges in a Global Economy* Caboldi, Irene, and Lee, Edward, (Cheltenham: Edward Elgar 2014) 57–76.

113 Ibid.

U.S. legal and business communities.[114] Rogers' article on the "Social Function of Trade-marks" may, however, be seen as a testimony to the moral framework through which he regarded trademark law, at the end of a lifetime in IP-related legal practice. The arguments he made in 1949 were very similar to those that he had published in 1914, in a book written for a popular audience: *Good Will, Trade-Marks and Unfair Trading*. Both publications extolled the "social values" implicit in trademarks, carefully distinguishing them from monopolies and explaining the importance of Good Will for businesses.

> The whole idea of free enterprise, as we understand it in this country, is based on the importance of identity and personal responsibility of the producer for the goods he sells, which are evidenced by his trade-marks, names, and brands. If that is the sort of an economy we are to have in this country – and I sincerely hope it is, because we have had it for a good many years and it has worked – then trade-marks and brands should be protected so that an incentive will be given to all manufacturers to produce the best goods they know how and take pride in them – and not merely comply with minimum government specifications. You can't have competition unless you can distinguish the competing goods and choose between them. Trade-marks make this distinction and this choice possible. Without them there could be none.[115]

Trademark law, as Steven Wilf has argued, serves here as the centerpiece for a national framework of vigorous, but fair, competition, tied to the global framework for international IP relations that Rogers had helped to build, alongside Stephen Ladas, and Ladas' partner, Lawrence Langner, who had assisted in negotiating the industrial property provisions in the Treaty of Versailles, on behalf of the U.S.[116] This national framework was envisioned in moralizing terms, but the morality was ambivalent, pragmatically stressing the values of

114 Rogers, Edward, 'The Lanham Act and the Social Function of Trade-Marks'. *Law and Contemporary Problems* 14 (1949) 173. This was a symposium issue on 'Trademarks in Transition' featuring an introduction from Brainerd Currie, alongside articles by Stephen Ladas and Edward Rogers, among others. A footnote to Rogers' article noted 'with deep regret' that Rogers had died shortly before the symposium issue was published. The editors described Rogers as a beloved and respect 'dean of the trade-mark bar,' and registered the honor of publishing this final product of Rogers' 'rich experience and his intimate leadership of the long struggle to revise the statutory law of trade-marks.'

115 Rogers, 'Social Function' 180.

116 Langer, Lawrence. *The Magic Curtain: The Story of a Life in Two Fields, Theatre and Invention* (Dutton: New York, 1951) 344–45.

free enterprise, personal responsibility, and competition, alongside ambiguous concepts of good faith and good will.

Although Rogers' life extended beyond the Interwar Period, his efforts between 1914 and 1938 helped to cement a legal framework for trademark and unfair competition law that connected U.S. national protections to international treaty-based obligations. Indeed the linkages between international and domestic frameworks for IP protection, seen in the activities and social network of Edward Rogers, seem particularly close during the Interwar Period. And likewise, the easy, moral resonances of concepts like "good will," to which Edward Rogers devoted so much of his scholarship, point to the significance of post-Christian moral rhetoric in offering an ethical coloring to the broader projects of legal Progressivism.

4 Conclusion: A New Style of National Power

Good will and good faith. These were Christian concepts used for post-Christian purposes in the Progressive reshaping of law, society, and democracy during the Interwar Period. We might see them as emblems for a new style of national power, both furthering, and being furthered by, developments in intellectual property law. New federal legislation to unify trademark law on a national level was introduced in the U.S. Congress, justified partly by the need to better conform domestic law to international obligations, while equitable powers in U.S. courts enabled rapid, judicially directed development of unfair competition law. Meanwhile, the ALI's project in restating the basic principles of U.S. common law supported these developments through its recognition of trademark and unfair competition law as elements of U.S. tort law. Good faith and good will became anchors, so to speak, in an expanding legal ethos for fair competition, elements of the broader Progressive effort to reform commercial morality in the service of beneficent social power. Trademark and unfair competition law functioned as instruments in the broader, Progressive project of social-democratic reform, culminating in the New Deal. Industrial property law, in short, became an instrument of social-democratic, national power.

In their seminal *Introduction to Comparative Law*, Zweigert and Kötz identified five factors characterizing the distinctive styles of legal families: (1) historical background and development, (2) predominant and characteristic mode of legal thought, (3) distinctive institutions, (4) the kind of legal sources acknowledged, and the mode of handling them, and (5) ideology, which they defined as the "religious or political conception of how social or economic life should be organized."[117] Noting that they were borrowing the concept from the study of culture, particularly the literary and fine arts, Zweigert and Kötz extolled the usefulness of a notion of "legal style" to capture the multifaceted ways in which legal systems may be related to one another comparatively.[118] Extending their concept only slightly, we might use it to evaluate the multifaceted ways in which legal institutions contribute to national organization and culture.

In this essay, I have argued that the Interwar Period marked an important shift in the U.S. legal framework for intellectual property law, focusing on developments in national trademark law and unfair competition. I have presented these developments as culminations of a broader set of Progressive projects, rooted in the quarter century following the U.S. Civil War, linking domestic protection of fairness in competition with international IP relations, and framing the connection within a broader embrace of social-democratic reforms and post-Christian moral rhetoric.

Looking back on these developments a century later, the moral agenda of Progressivism is in some ways eerily familiar, and in some ways strikingly different from the moral agendas of our own age. But as much difference as we might see between their concept of "social justice" and ours, their agenda shaped our world, and it is still with us.

For the Progressives, protections for industrial and literary property were justified as elements in a broader moral framework for "fair competition." The justification was unapologetically instrumentalist, in keeping with the functionalist frameworks of the emerging social sciences, which were embraced as "measures" for justice by the Progressives. Law was a means, never an end, and the ends that law was to serve were social-democratic ends, both domestic and international.[119]

The new style of national power that they inaugurated was indeed supported by a "predominant and characteristic mode of legal thought," which drew on the popular literature of the day in conceiving itself as "realist." The label of "legal realism" had been embraced by Roscoe Pound in 1914, and it would be increasingly used to describe the new generation of legal reformers whose ideological commitments to social democracy made themselves felt in the legislation of the New Deal, in the exercise of equitable powers by U.S. courts, in the "restatements" of U.S. common law, and in international diplomacy.[120]

---

117 Zweigert, Konrad, and Kötz, Hein. *An Introduction to Comparative Law* (3rd ed., translated by Tony Weir, Oxford: Clarendon Press 1998) 72.

118 Ibid 67.

119 Hull, Roscoe Pound & Karl Llewellyn (n 78) 67.

120 Ibid., 91.

While many have argued that the coherence of U.S. legal realism has been overstated, there is little question that it was basically reformist and social-democratic, treating law as a malleable, ever-changing instrument for the achievement of a complex constellation of social and economic ends. Leon Green's conclusion to his essay on "One Hundred Years of Tort Law," written to celebrate NYU Law School's place in a "Century of Progress," illustrates the point perfectly.

> Few are bold enough to treat the stuff we dignify as law as nothing more nor less than the intellectual mechanisms through which lawyers exercise the power society has entrusted to them to serve the ends of government. It is only they who seem to know that, aside from statement, even if there, certainty and uniformity in law are merely the "pot of gold at the end of the governmental rainbow." Any one who visualizes the development of law during the last century must know that if we continue invention, industry, trade, and scientific methods generally, as we surely shall, the flux of the law will of necessity continue. Thus it is not a stabilization of processes for which we must hope, but their constant revision, as has been in large part carried on during the last century through the work of the courts.[121]

Given this reality of law as an ever-changing instrument of state power, Green advocated that law professors should serve as the inventors and refiners of "formulas," offering these to the courts and other agents of government, then leaving the results, "as must be done in all governmental processes, to the intelligence and good faith of those who administer them."[122]

In this essay I have concentrated on the roots of IP-related legal reforms in U.S. Progressivism, downplaying the contrasts that are sometimes drawn between the earlier Progressive era and the New Deal. While it is true that rhetorical tone of the earlier Progressive period could sound naïve to later generations, hardened as they were by the experiences of the Great War and then later of World War II, the continuities of method are ultimately more significant than the differences in rhetoric: the earlier Progressives, too, were determined to embrace social power in a "realistic" and "rational" way, so that it might be effectively deployed for beneficent, national purposes.

---

121 Green, Leon, 'One Hundred Years of Tort Law'. In *Law: A Century of Progress* (n 1) Vol. 3, 66–67.

122 Ibid., 67.

In the first decade of the twentieth century, the Progressives were much more heavy-handed in their use of Christian rhetoric, as can been seen, for example, in Edward Ross's *Sin and Society: An Analysis of Latter-Day Iniquity* (1907). Like so many of the founding generation of U.S. sociologists, Ross had been raised in an evangelical, Christian environment, knowing the power of Christian rhetoric well, then finding a substitute in the positivist faith of Auguste Comte.[123] The language of Christianity became thereafter, for Ross as for others, a rhetorical instrument to be deployed for post-Christian, social reform purposes.

For Ross, as for others, early experiences with the "delusions" of evangelical Christianity resulted in a severe commitment to realism and rationalism, traits that evidently impressed Oliver Wendel Holmes, Jr. and Theodore Roosevelt, whose endorsement prefaced *Sin and Society*. As Ross noted in his own preface:

> In praising or blaming each of us exerts a power over his fellows. When the praises or blames of many men run together, they become a torrent no one can withstand. Why let this moral power run to waste? Why not use this public opinion to protect our dearest possessions?[124]

In order to become fit for purpose, however, public opinion must be rationalized, modernized, and brought to recognize that "sin evolves along with society."[125] Properly educated, public opinion could be molded into an effective instrument of social power, "a flaming sword guarding the sacred interests of society."[126] As we have seen, Woodrow Wilson brought this new style of Progressive, post-Christian rhetoric to his diplomacy in the post-war settlements of Paris and Versailles. And in a much more moderate way, it leavened the Restatements of U.S. common law, with their developing legal framework for protecting fairness in competition.

The Progressives saw the great problem of their times as a multifaceted problem of social power.[127] The proper response, as they saw it, was to rationally, realistically, and systematically embrace social power.[128] "Sinful" social powers,

---

123 Harp, Gillis J. *Positivist Republic: Auguste Comte and the Reconstruction of American Liberalism, 1865–1920* (University Park: Pennsylvania State University Press, 1995); Ross, Edward Alsworth. *Sin and Society: An Analysis of Latter-Day Iniquity* (Boston: Houghton Mifflin Company, 1907).

124 Ross, *Sin and Society*, VII.

125 Ibid.

126 Ibid., VII–VIII.

127 Hofstadter, *Age of Reform* (n 12).

128 Ibid.

conceived in modern rational terms, could be counteracted by righteous social power, with righteousness defined in post-Christian, social-democratic terms. In the writings of Herbert Croly, echoed by Theodore Roosevelt and others, this basic project was presented as a "new economic nationalism."[129] Legal realism served as the jurisprudential counterpart to this Progressive ideology, treating law as an ever-malleable instrument in the modern, rational project of social-democratic reform.

In this essay, I have viewed U.S. trademark law, with its proprietary legal protections of goodwill, together with the broader framework of unfair competition law and economic "good faith," as culminations of this Progressivism, coming to fruition in the Interwar Period and the New Deal. Linking domestic U.S. protections for fair competition more closely to international treaty-based obligations, industrial property law became part of a broader effort to deepen social democracy while building a powerful, national economy.

Intellectual property, more than ever before, became an instrument for social power, an instrument by which national wealth could be accumulated and distributed, an instrument for national uplift, to be shared as gospel with the world.

References

Baker, Ray Stannard. 1922. *Woodrow Wilson and World Settlement: Written from his Unpublished and Personal Material.* Garden City: Doubleday, Page & Co.

Churchwell, Sarah. 2018. *Behold America: The Entangled History of America First and the American Dream.* New York: Basic Books.

Cooper, Dale. 2012. "The Licensing of German Drug Patents Confiscated in World War I." *Pharmacy in History* Volume 54, Issue 1, 3–32.

Coser, Lewis. 2003. *Masters of Sociological Thought, 2d ed.* Long Grove, IL: Waveland Press.

Croly, Herbert. 1915. *Progressive Democracy.* New York: The Macmillan Company.

Edwards, Mark Thomas. 2023. *Walter Lippmann: American Skeptic, American Pastor* (Oxford: Oxford University Press).

Ford, Laura R. 2021. *The Intellectual Property of Nations: Sociological and Historical Perspectives on a Modern Legal Institution.* Cambridge, UK: Cambridge University Press.

129 Croly, Herbert. *Progressive Democracy* (New York: The MacMillan Company, 1915).

Ford, Laura R. Forthcoming. "From Plato to WIPO: Old and New in Legal Harmonization," in Péter Mezei, Anett Pogácsás and Hannibal Travis, eds., *Harmonizing Intellectual Property Law for a Trans-Atlantic Knowledge Economy* (Leiden: Brill).

Goodwin, Doris Kearns. 2013. *The Bully Pulpit: Theodore Roosevelt, William Howard Taft, and the Golden Age of Journalism.* New York: Simon & Schuster.

Harp, Gillis S. 1995. *Positivist Republic: Auguste Comte and the Reconstruction of American Liberalism, 1865–1920.* Philadelphia: Pennsylvania University Press.

Hofstadter, Richard. 1955. *The Age of Reform.* New York: Vintage Books.

Hull, N.E.H. 1997. *Roscoe Pound & Karl Llewellyn: Searching for an American Jurisprudence.* Chicago: University of Chicago Press.

Kennedy, David M. 1999. *Freedom From Fear: The American People in Depression and War, 1929–1945* (Oxford: Oxford University Press).

Ladas, Stephen P. 1929. *The International Protection of Trade Marks by the American Republics.* Cambridge, UK: Harvard University Press.

Ladas, Stephen P. 1930. *The International Protection of Industrial Property.* Cambridge, MA: Harvard University Press.

Ladas, Stephen P. 1938. *The International Protection of Literary and Artistic Property in Two Volumes.* New York: The Macmillan Company.

Ladas, Stephen P. 1949. "The Lanham Act and International Trade." *Law & Contemporary Problems* Volume 14, Issue 2, 269–87.

Langner, Lawrence. 1951. *The Magic Curtain: The Story of a Life in Two Fields, Theatre and Invention.* New York: E.P. Dutton & Company.

Lassmann, Peter and Ronald Speirs. 1994. *Weber: Political Writings.* Cambridge, UK: Cambridge University Press.

Mann, Michael. 2012. *The Sources of Social Power Volume 1: A History of Power from the Beginning to AD 1760, 2d ed.* Cambridge: Cambridge University Press.

Mann, Michael. 2013. *The Sources of Social Power Volume 4: Globalizations, 1945–2011.* Cambridge, MA: Cambridge University Press.

Novak, William J. 2022. *New Democracy: The Making of the Modern American State.* Cambridge, MA: Harvard University Press.

Reppy, Alison (ed.). 1937. *Law: A Century of Progress (1835–1935).* New York: New York University Press.

Rheinstein, Max (ed.). 1954. *Max Weber on Law in Economy and Society.* Edited by Max Rheinstein. Translated by Edward Shils. New York: Simon and Schuster.

Rogers, Edward S. 1909. "Comments on the Modern Law of Unfair Trade." *Illinois Law Review* 551–64.

Rogers, Edward S. 1914. *Good Will, Trade-Marks and Unfair Trading.* Chicago: A.W. Shaw Company.

Rogers, Edward S. 1949. "The Lanham Act and the Social Function of Trade-Marks." *Law & Contemporary Problems* 173–84.

Ross, Edward Alsworth. 1907. *Sin and Society: An Analysis of Latter-Day Iniquity.* Boston: Houghton Mifflin Company.

Ross, Edward Alsworth. 1936. *Seventy Years of It: An Autobiography.* New York: D. Appleton-Century Company.

Steen, Kathryn. 2001. "Patents, Patriots, and "Skilled in the Art": USA v The Chemical Foundation, Inc., 1923–1926." *ISIS* 91–122.

Weber, Max. 1947. *The Theory of Social and Economic Organization.* Edited by Talcott Parsons. Translated by A.M. Henderson. New York: Oxford University Press.

Weber, Max. 2009. *The Protestant Ethic and the Spirit of Capitalism.* Edited by Richard Swedberg. Translated by Talcott Parsons. New York: W.W. Norton & Co.

Weber, Max. 2013 [1968]. *Economy and Society.* Edited by Guenther Roth and Claus Wittich. Translated by Ephraim Fischoff et al. 2 vols. Berkeley: University of California Press.

Whimster, Sam (ed.). 2004. *The Essential Weber.* Oxford: Routledge.

White, G. Edward. 2003. *Tort Law in America: An Intellectual History.* Oxford: Oxford University Press.

Wilf, Steven. 2008. "The Making of the Post-War Paradigm in American Intellectual Property Law." *Columbia Journal of Law & the Arts* Volume 31, Issue 2, 139–207.

Zweigert, K. and H. Koetz. 1998. *An Introduction to Comparative Law, 3rd ed.* Oxford: Oxford University Press.

PART 2

Copyright Fascism, Plunder in Europe and American Trademark Markets

CHAPTER 5

Furthering Interests Abroad: Advancing Trademark Rights in the Americas in the First Decades of the Twentieth Century

Christine Haight Farley

1 Introduction

The 1929 General Inter-American Convention for Trademarks and Commercial Protection ("Pan-American Convention")[1] provided pioneering protection of trademarks and prohibitions on unfair competition in its day, and, as it is remains in force, still offers protections that are novel as compared to other treaties covering trademarks. The convention's unfair competition provisions are the most comprehensive treatment on the subject in any international instrument to date, the geographical indication ("GI")[2] protections were the most extensive at the time the convention became effective, and the convention provides a mechanism to protect foreign marks from preemptive local registration that has never been seen before or since. It is surprising then, that this convention remains somewhat enigmatic given few scholars or lawyers are even aware of it.

An analysis of the substantive provisions of the convention prompts the questions of how and why the drafters devised such an innovative text. This question is especially perplexing considering both the time and region. The Pan-American Convention was drafted just five years after the 1925 Hague revision[3] of the Paris Convention for the Protection of Industrial Property (Paris

1 General Inter-American Convention for Trade-mark and Commercial Protection, Feb. 20, 1929, 46 Stat. 2907, 124 L.N.T.S. 357 [hereinafter Pan-American Convention]. The convention is referred to as the 'Pan American Convention,' the 'Inter-American Convention,' and the 'Washington Convention' depending the country of the speaker. The convention entered into force in the United States on February 17, 1931.

2 For convenience, I will refer to these protections as 'GI' protections even though they do not perfectly correspond to that legal category as we understand it in the TRIPS Agreement.

3 International Convention for the Protection of Industrial Property, art. 10*bis*, Nov. 6, 1925, 47 Stat. 1789 (modified at The Hague); International Convention for the Protection of Industrial Property, art. 10*bis*, June 2, 1934, 53 Stat. 1748. The 1925 Hague revision was the third revision and the first revision to bind member states. Bodenhausen, Georg, *Guide to the Application*

 | DOI:10.1163/9789004714663_007

Convention).[4] The Hague revision introduced Article 6*bis*, which provides protection for well-known marks, revised article 10*bis* by providing a definition and examples of acts of unfair competition,[5] and revised Article 1 to include "indications of source or appellations of origin" among the various subjects of protected intellectual property. It is surprising then that the Pan-American Convention did not simply copy the Paris Convention text or even use it as a model, but instead created an entirely new set of provisions. In doing so, the Pan-American Convention leapfrogged the Paris Convention in several respects by offering broader and stronger protections. When the Pan-American Convention was drafted, the Paris Convention had only 37 member states[6] with just five coming from the Americas.[7] The Pan-American Convention was an ambitious project with aspirations to rival the Paris Convention and serve as an alternative approach to the protection of trademarks in the Americas.

2 History of the Pan-American Trademark Convention

The 1929 Pan-American Convention was an outgrowth of several preceding Pan-American conferences—a forty-year-long effort to create a Pan-American Union for trade in the Americas. This series of conferences grew out of the Pan-Americanism movement in the United States (U.S.) in the early twentieth century, whose objectives included replacing Europe as the dominant power in the region, using institutionalism as an alternative to U.S. territorial expansionism and military interventions, and cultivating Latin America as a commercial marketplace for goods manufactured in the U.S. The ambitions of the union even included the creation of a common customs union, a cross-continent railway

of the Paris Convention for the Protection of Industrial Property: As Revised at Stockholm in 1967 (Geneva: BIRPI, 1968) 9.

4 Paris Convention for the Protection of Industrial Property, Mar. 20, 1883, *as revised* July 14, 1967, 21 U.S.T. 1583, 828 U.N.T.S. 305.

5 Bodenhausen, 'Guide to the Application of the Paris Convention for the Protection of Industrial Property: As Revised at Stockholm in 1967', 142.

6 Bodenhausen, 'Guide to the Application of the Paris Convention for the Protection of Industrial Property: As Revised at Stockholm in 1967', 117.

7 Brazil, Cuba, the Dominican Republic, Mexico, and the United States were contracting parties to the Paris Convention by 1929. 'Contracting Parties: Paris Convention,' WIPO. https://www.wipo.int/wipolex/en/treaties/ShowResults?search_what=C&treaty_id=2. Although a member of the Paris Convention, Canada was not eligible to ratify the Pan-American Convention.

system, and a common currency.[8] A harmonized intellectual property system was just one aspect of the larger objective of creating a regional market. The movement's importance to the U.S. warranted a grand building in Washington D.C. near the White House. President Theodore Roosevelt commemorated the opening of an architecturally magnificent building, which many considered to be among the most beautiful in the U.S. capitol.

While Pan Americanism promised a transnational partnership of equals, the imperialist actions of the U.S. that both preceded and followed this period made that goal suspect. Unquestionably, the most important moment in the history of U.S. relations with Latin America had been the "Monroe Doctrine." In his State of the Union address, President Monroe unambiguously stated a new U.S. policy that any further efforts by European nations to colonize land or interfere with states in North or South America would be viewed as acts of aggression, requiring U.S. intervention. Implicit in this pronouncement was an assertion that the New World and the Old World were to remain distinctly separate spheres of influence, for they were composed of entirely separate and independent nations. The policy became deeply resented by Latin American nations for its overt interventionism and perceived imperialism.

The "Big Brother" policy was an extension of the Monroe Doctrine formulated by Secretary of State James G. Blaine in the 1880s. As a promoter of free trade and tariff reciprocity, he envisioned a strengthened relationship between the U.S. and Latin America as a way of supplying the increasingly industrialized North with the raw materials of its Southern neighbors and with a new market in which to sell the resultant products.[9] The objective of this policy was to solidify the idea of the "Western Hemisphere" and rally Latin American nations behind U.S. leadership. Blaine also thought that increased trade with Latin America was an effective tactic to prevent Britain from dominating the region.

---

8 *Fifth International Conference of American States, Special Handbook for the Use of the Delegates* (1922) 6 (listing the topics the Conference was called upon to consider: '1. To preserve the peace and promote the prosperity of the American states. 2. Formation of an American customs union. 3. Establishment of regular and frequent communication between the American States. 4. Establishment of a uniform system of customs regulations. 5. Adoption of a uniform system of weights and measures, and laws to protect patents, copyrights, and trade-marks. 6. Adoption of a common silver coin. 7. Agreement upon the recommendation for adoption to their Governments of a definite plan of arbitration. 8. Consideration of other matters relating to the welfare of the several countries, which may be presented at the Conference.').

9 Crapol, Edward. *James G. Blaine: Architect of Empire. Biographies in American Foreign Policy* (Delaware: Scholarly Resources, 2000) 4; Muzzey, David Saville. *James G. Blaine: A Political Idol of Other Days* (New York: Dodd, Mead, and Company, 1934).

Blaine's idea of an international conference of the nations of the Western Hemisphere resulted in the First International Conference of American States, which met in Washington in 1889. Blaine said publicly that his only interest was in "annexation of trade," not annexation of territory.[10] Nevertheless, some of the other nations were wary of deepening ties with the U.S. to the exclusion of European powers.

Latin American envoys to the 1889 Congress, as well as all other Pan American Union meetings, engaged with U.S. diplomats as equals in the organization's diplomatic activities. Commenting on the 1919 Conference, the Director General of the Pan American Union stated that "the interests of Latin America, just as much as those of the U.S., have been frankly considered and discussed by the most eminent and skilled authorities of both North and South America."[11] The Cuban nationalist José Martí, who attended the 1889 Congress as a journalist, had a different viewpoint. He reported that the U.S. only invited the other American nations to join a union because it was "glutted with unsaleable merchandise and determined to extend its dominions in America."[12]

The conference ultimately achieved none of Blaine's goals in the short-term. It did, however, lead to further diplomatic meetings and what would eventually become the Organization of American States.

The objective of harmonizing intellectual property protection in the Americas was present from the beginning. These efforts produced seven different Pan-American conventions that covered trademarks,[13] but those prior to 1929 proved to be substantively deficient. At first, these conventions covered all areas of intellectual property, but over time separate conventions dealt exclusively with patents, copyrights, and trademarks respectively.

The first Pan-American convention was ratified in 1889 just three years after the Berne Convention and six years after the first Paris Convention of 1883,[14]

---

10 Wilgus, Curtis, 'James G. Blaine and the Pan American Movement'. *Hispanic American Historical Review* 5 (1922): 622.

11 'Sees New Epoch of the Americas.' *New York Times,* June 7, 1919. 750 representatives attended the five day meetings in 1919.

12 Martí, José, 'On the Inter-American Congress'. *La Nación,* December 19–20, 1889. Likewise, in an interview published in the New York Times, the U.S. envoy honestly revealed: 'We disregard the merits of our Southern neighbors, both as peoples and as customers for our commodities.' Marshall, Edward, 'Fight for South America's Great Trade'. *New York Times,* December 4, 1910.

13 The six conventions were ratified in 1889, 1902, 1906, 1910, 1923, and 1929.

14 Ladas, Stephen. *The International Protection of Trade Marks by the American Republics* (Cambridge: Harvard University Press, 1929) 11. The contracting countries of this convention were Argentina, Bolivia, Chile, Paraguay, Peru, and Uruguay. Bolivia and Chile did

the first multilateral treaty devoted to industrial property. As the large majority of Latin American states were not members of the Paris Union,[15] one of the primary objectives would have been to provide national treatment within the new union and to create a more harmonized system for the protection of foreign trademarks. The main feature of the 1889 convention was to secure reciprocal national treatment for trademark owners in the contracting countries. Later Pan-American conventions in 1902, 1906, 1910, and 1923 would offer a number of important new features including a priority right.[16] The central objective of the 1923 convention appears to be to create for the Americas a centralized registration regime modeled on the 1891 Madrid Agreement.[17] Since none of these conventions succeeded in securing widespread adoption in the region,[18] a final attempt was made that would become the pivotal 1929 Convention.

The 1929 convention included nineteen signatory countries,[19] but only ten states ultimately ratified the convention: Colombia, Cuba, Guatemala, Haiti,

---

not ratify. A corollary patent treaty was also adopted that gave patent owners a one-year priority.

15 Only Brazil, Cuba and Mexico became members of the Paris Union by 1929. Brazil ratified the Paris Convention in 1883, Mexico ratified in 1903, and Cuba ratified in 1904. The U.S. ratified the Paris Convention in 1887. A few other Latin American states ratified the Paris Convention only to denounce the treaty shortly thereafter. For instance, the Dominican Republic ratified in 1884, but denounced in 1888. Likewise, Guatemala ratified in 1883, but denounced in 1894. Ecuador denounced in 1885. During the 1929 Pan-American conference it was stated that Brazil and Cuba intended to withdraw from the Paris Convention. *Pan American Trademark Conference, Minutes of the Plenary Sessions and of the Committees of the Conferences* (1929) 5. Brazil, Cuba, and Mexico were also members of the Madrid Agreement of 1891.

In 1906 Argentina invited the USTA to comment on its domestic trademark law. Similarly, in 1908, Ecuador asked the USTA to propose a trademark law which was to become the model for other Latin American countries. 'About INTA History.' International Trademark Association, www.inta.org/history/pages/history.aspx.

16 Ladas, *The International Protection of Trade Marks by the American Republics*, 20, 29. The Pan-American convention of 1923 remains in effect between Brazil, Chile, Cuba, the Dominican Republic, Guatemala, Haiti, Paraguay, and the United States.

17 Ladas, *The International Protection of Trade Marks by the American Republics*, 13.

18 Ladas, Stephen. *Patents, Trademarks, and Related Rights: National and International Protection* (Cambridge: Harvard University Press, 1975) 1752. Stating that despite repeated attempts for more than 40 years to create an American union for the protection of industrial property, the American states had yet to arrive at a workable resolution, acceptable to all states.

19 Chile, Colombia, Costa Rica, Cuba, the Dominican Republic, Ecuador, Guatemala, Haiti, Honduras, Mexico, Nicaragua, Panama, Paraguay, Peru, the United States, Uruguay, and Venezuela. *General Inter-American Convention for Trade-mark and Commercial Protection.*

Honduras, Nicaragua, Panama, Paraguay, Peru, and the U.S. The convention entered into force on April 2, 1930, and remains in force today in every one of the original member states.[20]

3 The Unequal Bargain

As the Pan-American Convention was negotiated between the U.S. and various Latin American states, it can be contrasted with the Paris Convention, which was essentially negotiated by the U.S. and various European states. In terms of negotiating power, substantive expertise, and defined objectives, the parties to the U.S. and European states were not so different. However, in the case of the Pan-American Convention, the U.S. occupied quite a different position from the other Latin American States.

Put simply, the Pan-American convention was not drafted for the equal benefit of all member states. The protections contained in the convention were primarily designed with the interest of U.S. business operating in Latin America in mind. The primary objective of U.S. negotiators was to provide these businesses with trademark protections in advance expansion into one of the contracting states.

During the negotiations, the U.S. not only had the clearest objective, but it also had the most expertise. While the delegates from Latin America were knowledgeable and distinguished diplomats, none had substantive expertise in trademark law. In the early 1900s, there was not a vibrant trademark practice in any of the Latin American states involved in the Pan-American Conferences. As a result, some of the negotiators lamented the lack of expertise they were able to bring to the table.[21]

In contrast were the negotiators representing the U.S. One of the three U.S. delegates was Edward S. Rogers, one of the foremost experts in U.S. trademark law in the first half of the twentieth century.[22] In the 1920s, Rogers was

20 'Contracting Parties/Signatories: General Inter-American Convention for Trade-Mark and Commercial Protection.' WIPO. http://www.wipo.int/wipolex/en/other_treaties/parties.jsp?treaty_id=353&group_id=21.

21 Ladas, *Patents, Trademarks, and Related Rights: National and International Protection*, 1753.

22 Alexander, Miles, '100th Anniversary Issue: Reflections of Former Editors-in-Chief'. *The Trademark Reporter* 101 (2011): 7, 9; Chafee, Zechariah, 'Unfair Competition.' *Harvard Law Review* 53 (1940): 1289; Bone, Robert, 'Hunting Goodwill: A History of the Concept of Goodwill in Trademark Law'. *Boston University Law Review* 86 (2006): 119. At the time of his death, Rogers was so well regarded in U.S. trademark law that *The Trademark Reporter*

known as the "Dean of the Trademark Bar,"[23] later he became known as the "father"[24] of the U.S. trademark act. It was not surprising that Rogers would have been chosen by the U.S. to lead its delegation in drafting a new trademark treaty for the Americas.[25]

In addition, playing a behind the scenes role was Stephen P. Ladas, a distinguished intellectual property practitioner, scholar, and diplomat. He published numerous books and articles on the international protection of trademarks and was later a U.S. delegate to the 1958 revision of the Paris Convention.[26] Ladas's law firm, which eventually became known as Ladas & Parry, was initially focused on seeking protection for American inventions and trademarks in foreign countries.

Both Rogers and Ladas approached this treaty with a keen sense of what protections major U.S. trademark holders desired and the various ways that U.S. trademarks owners were vulnerable internationally.[27] In his book anticipating the 1929 Pan-American Conference, Ladas stated that "[w]hat [U.S] manufacturers and traders ... need especially today is ... more effective and complete protection."[28]

In addition to the vulnerability of U.S. trademark rights in Latin America, U.S. manufacturers complained that goods produced in Latin America were being sold there as American-made. It is likely for this reason that unfair

---

devoted an entire volume to his legacy. 'In Memoriam, Edward S. Rogers Memorial Edition'. *The Trademark Reporter* 62 (1972): 175–265.

23 Pattishall, Beverly, 'Trademarks and the Monopoly Phobia'. *Michigan Law Review* 50 (1952): 967; Lunsford, Julius, 'Foreword'. *The Trademark Reporter* 62 (1972): IV.

24 Alexander, '100th Anniversary Issue: Reflections of Former Editors-in-Chief,' 9–10.

25 By 1929, Rogers already had years of experience drafting the U.S. trademark act, which work he began in 1921 in preparation for the ABA committee meeting. McCarthy, J. Thomas. *McCarthy on Trademarks and Unfair Competition,* 5th ed. (West Publishing: St. Paul, Minnesota, 2019) § 5:4. In 1937, Representative Lanham, who was then Chairman of the House Patent Committee, invited Rogers to share his personal draft act based on the Vestal Bill. This draft became the basis of the Trademark Act of 1946. The Vestal Bill, H.R. 7118, 72d Cong. (1st Sess. 1931); Levine, Sondra, 'Part One: The Common Law, the States, and Historical perspectives: The Origins of the Lanham Act'. *Journal of Contemporary Legal Issues* 19 (2010): 24–25.

26 'Dr. Stephen Ladas, Patent Lawyer, 77'. *New York Times,* March 15, 1976.

27 At an international conference in 1930, Rogers described 'a prevailing sport' in other countries where 'two or three people ... get together and start a company under the name of Coca Cola. Then the Coca Cola firm gets into that country and finds a company under that name already there, with the result that the firm has either to change the name or buy the company.' Katz, Hanna, 'An International Aspect of the Pending Trade-Mark Bill'. *The Trademark Reporter* 35 (1945): 148.

28 Ladas, *The International Protection of Trade Marks by the American Republics,* 34.

competition and GI style protections were included in the convention, and that the title of the convention went beyond trademarks to include "Commercial Protection." After the convention was finalized, but before it was ratified, the U.S. delegation produced a public relations document entitled "The Advantages Accruing to American Citizens from the General Convention for Trademark and Commercial Protection." One of the advantages highlighted relates to GIs: "if American-made goods acquire a reputation in Latin America, this chapter will prevent goods originating elsewhere from masquerading directly or indirectly as American-made."[29] It also highlights protections against unfair competition, stating that the convention "extends through Latin America common law principles of honest trading which have been enforced in the U.S. for forty years under the elastic jurisdiction of our equity courts."[30]

In contrast to the benefits for U.S. firms conducting business in Latin America, almost nothing in the convention would have benefited Latin American firms then. At the time, the chance that any of the rights contained in the convention would be asserted by a Latin American party in a U.S. court were simply nonexistent. The problems of preemptive trademark registration and falsely indicating geographic origin appear to have been only occurring in Latin America. Moreover, it does not appear that Latin American trademark owners had any interest in protecting their marks in the U.S. at that time. Ladas admitted as much when he noted that Latin American "countries rarely register any trademarks in U.S., and the problem of protection of their trademarks is hardly existing."[31]

One may wonder why Latin American states would ratify the convention as it addressed only the concerns of U.S. businesses. Much like so many north-south IP treaty negotiations, perhaps these Latin American states thought that by providing these rights, they would be successful in attracting U.S. businesses to the region. At the time, the dominant economic interest in Latin America, which was largely comprised of raw material exporters, was commercial trade with the U.S.[32]

---

29 Press Release, U.S. Delegation to the Inter-American Convention, *The Advantages Accruing to American Citizens from the General Convention for Trademark and Commercial Protection* (February 11, 1929) 2.

30 Press Release, U.S. Delegation to the Inter-American Convention, *The Advantages Accruing to American Citizens from the General Convention for Trademark and Commercial Protection* (February 11, 1929) 2.

31 Ladas, *The International Protection of Trade Marks by the American Republics*, 32.

32 Donghi, Tulio Halperin. *The Contemporary History of Latin America* (Durham: Duke University Press, 1993) 159; Cardenas, Enrique, Ocampo Jose Antonio, and Thorp,

Rogers and Ladas later stated that the protections achieved in the Pan-American Convention were superior to those achieved in the Paris Convention.[33] It is not surprising that they would have exceeded the Paris Convention protections. The freedom they had to create new protections whole cloth in the Pan-American Convention was unparalleled. Rogers and Ladas were not constrained by the need to reconcile conflicting legal standards across jurisdictions. They instead were working from a blank slate; the other states had no laws pertaining to unfair competition or GIs, and they had rudimentary trademark laws.[34] They were also operating without the normal constraints in treaty negotiation since the Latin American delegates were diplomats, not trademark experts. In addition, the environment was hospitable to creativity. Previous Pan-American Conventions had already served as a creative space for the development of new solutions for trademark owners, such as the creation of a Pan-American trademark registration and priority based on protection in another member state.[35] The convention provided Rogers and Ladas nearly unrestricted freedom to draft an ambitious set of protections with concern solely for U.S. traders.

4 The Convention's Innovative Text

Several provisions of the Pan-American Convention distinguish it from other international treaties, domestic trademark laws, and even the preceding Pan-American conventions. Not only do many provisions go beyond the scope of then existing international and domestic law, but they also forge new approaches and introduce new concepts to intellectual property law.

Because the text of this convention is so inventive, its origins must be called into question. Intriguingly, the drafting of the Pan-American Convention did not follow the prescribed procedure. Officially, the delegates were to meet in Washington D.C. in 1929 to discuss a draft text that was to be prepared by an

---

Rosemary. *An Economic History of Twentieth-Century Latin America: Volume 1 The Export Age* (London: Palgrave Macmillan, 2000) 4.

33 Rogers, Edward S. and, Ladas, Stephen P., 'Proposal for Uniform Trademark Laws.' *The Trademark Reporter* 40(1) (1950) 14.

34 Rogers and Ladas, 'Proposal for Uniform Trademark Laws,' 14; Ladas, *Patents, Trademarks, and Related Rights National and International Protection*, 52.

35 *Convention for the Protection of Commercial, Industrial and Agricultural Trade Marks and Commercial Names*, April 28, 1923. 44 Stat. 2494; *Convention for the Protection of Trade Marks*, August 20, 1910. 39 Stat. 1675.

appointed committee.[36] That committee consisted of three Latin American diplomats, none of whom were trademark experts.[37] The draft the committee produced was, like the previous Pan-American convention, preoccupied with creating a registration-based system for the Americas as an alternative to the Madrid Arrangement.

Just prior to the conference, however, Ladas published a book titled *The International Protection of Trade Marks by the American Republics*.[38] Ladas explicitly stated that the objective of his book was to facilitate the 1929 convention.[39] In the book, he sharply criticized the committee's draft as inadequate and, presumptuously, offered his own proposal as a substitute. Ladas's proposal was radically different from the committee's draft.

However, neither the committee's draft nor Ladas's proposal ended up serving as the basis for the conference negotiations. Instead, when the delegates assembled in Washington D.C. on February 11, 1929, a Cuban delegate proposed that a new draft text serve as the basis of the negotiations. This new draft, ostensibly prepared by the Cuban delegation, was modelled on Ladas's proposal and not the committee's draft.

It seems implausible that the substitute draft text was the work of the two Cuban delegates alone, especially as it was to supersede the committee's draft, which was the work of another Cuban diplomat.[40] Ladas later acknowledged that this new draft text was prepared "with the cooperation of the

36 A resolution was made at the previous conference held in Havana a year earlier to appoint a special committee of the governing board of the Pan American Union to draft a text for the delegates to consider at the Washington conference. A draft was thus prepared by a committee composed of the Cuban Ambassador to United States and ministers from Ecuador and Uruguay and submitted to the conference on November 23, 1928. Pan American Trademark Conference, *Preparatory Data for the Pan American Trade Mark Conference: Report of the Committee of the Governing Board of the Pan American Union*, February 11, 1929. The governments were requested to send to the Pan American Union any 'suggestions and observations that may be utilized in the formation of the bases of a project that shall be prepared by the Pan American Union and that shall serve as a basis of discussion when the conference convenes.' Ladas, *Pan American Conventions on Industrial Property*, 803.

37 Ladas, 'Pan American Conventions on Industrial Property,' 803. The delegates were Dr. Orestes Ferrara, Cuban Ambassador to the U.S. and former Speaker of the House of Representatives in Cuba, Dr. Adrian Recinos, a historian and diplomat from Guatemala, and Gonzalo Zaldumbide, a writer and diplomat from Ecuador.

38 Ladas, *The International Protection of Trade Marks by the American Republics*, 53.

39 Ladas, *The International Protection of Trade Marks by the American Republics*, 53.

40 The Cuban delegates were Dr. Gustavo Gutierrez and Dr. Alfredo Bufill.

U.S. delegation,"[41] which may underestimate the role of the U.S. delegation, and Rogers in particular.

After agreeing to accept this new draft text as the basis of negotiations, the conference then agreed to appoint four committees. One committee was devoted to "Unfair Competition and False Indication of Origin," which were topics never previously addressed by any Pan-American convention. Another committee served as the "drafting committee" and its membership consisted Rogers and just four other delegates.[42]

5 The Substantive Provisions of the Convention

5.1 *The Convention's Protection of Unfair Competition*

The 1929 convention was the first to include specific protections against unfair competition and it devoted an entire chapter to the topic. The importance of unfair competition protection can also be seen in the preamble of the convention, which states that the contracting states were "animated by the desire to reconcile the different juridical systems which prevail in the several American Republics" and resolved to negotiate the convention "for the protection of trade marks, trade names, and for the repression of unfair competition and false indications of geographical origin."[43]

Chapter 4, titled "Repression of Unfair Competition," sets out both broad and detailed protections against acts of unfair competition that went well beyond the then existing protection under U.S. common law, statutory law in any of the member states, and international convention.

The chapter is noteworthy for indicating specific acts that are "declared to be acts of unfair competition" and therefore "prohibited."[44] These include: "Acts calculated directly or indirectly to represent that the goods or business of a manufacturer, industrialist, merchant or agriculturist are the goods or business of another ... of any of the other Contracting States, whether such representation be made by the appropriation or simulation of trade marks, symbols, distinctive names, the imitation of labels, wrappers, containers, commercial names, or other means of identification."[45]

---

41 Ladas, *Patents, Trademarks, and Related Rights National and International Protection*, 1755.

42 *Minutes of the Plenary Sessions*, 3.

43 *Final Act, General Inter-American Convention for Trade-mark and Commercial Protection*, February 20, 1929, 46 Stat. 2907, 124 L.N.T.S. 357.

44 *General Inter-American Convention for Trade-mark and Commercial Protection.*

45 *General Inter-American Convention for Trade-mark and Commercial Protection.*

Though based on passing off, this prohibition is formulated more expansively. Actionable conduct includes misrepresentation of the origin of goods "indirectly." There appears to be no requirement of direct competition, economic injury, or proof of a likelihood of consumer confusion. The protection applies not only to goods, but also to a trader's "business" and may therefore reach services. Protection is not limited to devices that would constitute protectable unregistered marks or trade dress. The only "means of identification" that is qualified by "distinctive," is "names." Presumably, other means of identification could be descriptive and yet still be protected.

In addition to the Pan-American Convention and Protocol, the 1929 Pan-American Trademark Convention adopted 12 resolutions, which were annexed to the Final Act. The Seventh Resolution was a "Declaration of Principles on Unfair Trade Practices," stating:

> That every act including breach of contract without just cause or which discredits the products or methods of a competitor; commercial bribery; enticing employees of a competitor to obtain confidential information with respect to his activities; false use of testimonials, warrant and appointments and false statements of membership in associations; and in general every act which tends to secure the patronage of a competitor through intimidation or coercion, is declared unfair and fraudulent. [46]

According to this resolution, the delegates' view of unfair competition was expansive and extended beyond the acts typically addressed in trademark law.

The convention remains the strongest commitment to unfair competition protection in international law to date. The specificity and breadth of protections against unfair competition contained in the Pan-American Convention distinguish it from other international agreements. The Paris Convention provides that "[a]ll acts contrary to honest usage in industrial or commercial matters" and "[a]cts of any kind whatsoever tending in any way to create confusion with the merchandise or products of a competitor" constitute unfair competition.[47] Thus, actionable conduct must be dishonest as per industry practice,[48]

---

46 *General Inter-American Convention for Trade-mark and Commercial Protection.*

47 *General Inter-American Convention for Trade-mark and Commercial Protection*, art. 10.

48 Compare the Paris Convention's insistence on dishonesty with the Pan-American Convention's language: 'contrary to commercial good faith or to the normal and honorable development of industrial or business activities.' *General Inter-American Convention for Trade-mark and Commercial Protection*, art. 20. Even though the French phrase 'concurrence déloyal' was translated into 'unfair competition,' 'déloyale' is more accurately translated as 'fraudulent' than 'unfair,' which might suggest a higher threshold. Wadlow,

between competitors, and cause consumer confusion. Intriguingly, none of these limitations are included in the Pan-American Convention drafted four years later. Although Article 10*bis* of the Paris Convention was subsequently revised in 1934 and 1958, these limitations persist.[49]

5.2 *The Convention's Protection of Geographical Indications*

The Pan-American Convention's protections for GIs was pioneering. Since there were not many treaty protections or domestic laws that preceded it, its attempt to define protections in the GI area was without many models. In addition to devoting an entire chapter to GI protection, the convention addresses the subject in its preamble, as was mentioned. The breadth and depth of the protections in the convention is remarkable for the period.

The convention uses the phrase "indication of geographical origin or source." "Geographical" was inserted into the phrase "indications of origin or source" at the suggestion of Rogers.[50] Although the concept is not defined in the Pan-American Convention, indications of source generally do not demand a link to the geographical area, nor do they demand a reputation of the area for the goods. Therefore, this Chapter can be understood to address the false use of geographic terms generally. As a result, it offers protection to a broader category of geographical terms than the protection offered to GIs under the Agreement on Trade Related Aspects to Intellectual Property Rights (TRIPS Agreement).[51]

Article 23 provides that indications of geographical origin that do not actually correspond to the product's origin "shall be considered fraudulent and illegal, and therefore prohibited." This provision is devoid of any requirement that the use be misleading. Thus, Article 23 of the Pan-American Convention mirrors the strict standard of Article 23 of the TRIPS Agreement, but is not limited

---

Christopher. *The Law of Passing-Off: Unfair Competition by Misrepresentation*, 3rd ed. (London: Sweet & Maxwell, 2004).

49 Art. 10*bis* presently provides the following example of an act of unfair competition: 'all acts of such a nature as to create confusion by any means whatever with the establishment, the goods, or the industrial or commercial activities, of a competitor.' *International Convention for the Protection of Industrial Property*, Article 10*bis*, March 20, 1883. 828 U.N.T.S. 107, 139. An attempt to remove the restriction of the protection to competitors was defeated at the 1958 Lisbon Conference. Wadlow, *The Law of Passing-Off: Unfair Competition by Misrepresentation*, 60.

50 *Minutes of the Plenary Sessions*, 62.

51 *Agreement on Trade-Related Aspects of Intellectual Property Rights*. Articles 22–24, April 15, 1994. Marrakesh Agreement Establishing the World Trade Organization, Annex 1C, 1869 U.N.T.S. 299.

to wines and spirits. Here the convention text departs from Ladas's proposal, which conditioned protection on uses that were misleading. Moreover, since it does not appear from this article that the falsehood need be believable or material to be actionable, arbitrary uses of geographic names also appear to be prohibited.

Subsequent articles offer some qualifications of the broad protection suggested by Article 23. Article 27 exempts generic terms[52] with a special exemption for "regional indication of origins of industrial or agricultural products, the quality and reputation of which, to the consuming public, depends on the production of origin." This article also indicates that "industrial" products are protected along with "agricultural products."

The convention also limits the acquisition of trademark rights over geographical terms. Article 25 flatly states that "geographical names are not susceptible to individual appropriation." Depending on the interpretation given to "geographical names," this restriction may prohibit any geographical term from being protected as a trademark in any of the member states.

> Article 24 provides:
>
> For the purposes of this Convention the place of geographical origin or source shall be considered as indicated when the geographical name of a definite locality, region, country or nation, either expressly and directly, or indirectly, appears on any trade mark, label, cover, packing or wrapping, of any article, product or merchandise, directly or indirectly thereon, provided that said geographical name serves as a basis for or is the dominant element of the sentences, words or expressions used.

In the conference, Rogers stated that this article deals only with cases of deception and should be drafted to clearly indicate this limitation.[53] The last phrase of this article was added by Rogers to make this point. His original formulation was as follows: "provided that said geographical name serves as a basis or motive for the sentences, words or expressions employed."[54] Article 24 also makes clear that GIs are protected even when used indirectly, that is, not just when used in trademarks, but in other areas of the label or packaging.

52 Interestingly, the original draft had limitations on the use of generic terms within Article 23. Somewhere along the way the qualification was removed and now only appears in Article 27.

53 *Minutes of the Plenary Sessions*, 87.

54 *Minutes of the Plenary Sessions*, 87.

An indirect reference to a geographical origin could be graphic, and it thus appears that such a use would be covered.

Later in his career, Ladas pointedly referred to the GI chapter in the Pan-American Convention as an "amelioration" of the Madrid Agreement,[55] which was revised in 1925 just four years prior to the Pan-American Convention. Perhaps, Ladas had in mind Article 4 of the Madrid Agreement, which prescribed protection for products of the vine according to the country of origin. In contrast, the Pan-American Convention did not privilege wines and spirits, or even agricultural products.

5.3 *The Convention's Protection of Foreign Marks*

A major discordance between the U.S. and the other Latin American states was over the source of trademark rights. In the U.S., the common law creates trademark rights based on use of the mark; registration is merely evidence of that right.[56] In contrast, throughout Latin America, registration created the right, and until registration, the mark was available for use by anyone. Moreover, registration created an incontestable right. U.S. trademark owners believed that the different system existing in Latin America left their trademarks vulnerable to adoption by others.[57]

A unique feature of the Pan-American Convention is its mechanism to deal with the problem of foreign preemptive registration. As with the well-known marks protection in Article 6*bis* of the Paris Convention, it was desired that in some instances foreign trademark owners should have the right to priority over a local conflicting mark even in cases in which the foreign mark was neither registered nor used in that jurisdiction. Such protection enables trademark owners in any member state to prevent intermeddlers in another member state from preempting the foreign owner's access to protections in the member state by establishing priority. Under the Pan-American Convention, this extraordinary protection hinges not on whether the mark is well-known, but instead on whether the local party had knowledge of the foreign trademark rights.

---

55 Ladas, *Patents, Trademarks, and Related Rights National and International Protection*, 1754.

56 Rogers, Edward, 'Some Suggestions Concerning a Trademark Registration Act'. *Annual Report A.B.A.* 43 (1920) 412, 413.

57 A 1920 article written for the ABA by Edward Rogers mentions 'much loose talk condemnatory' of the Latin American trademark system, and '[h]orrible examples [] cited where valuable marks owned … by American citizens, have been pirated and appropriated by foreigners for their own benefit.' Rogers, 'Some Suggestions Concerning a Trademark Registration.'

These protections are found in Articles 7 and 8 of the convention. Article 7 provides foreign mark owners the right to challenge any application or use of an interfering mark, and Article 8 provides foreign mark owners the right to cancel the registration of an interfering mark. Of the two articles, the rights contained in Article 7 are more unusual. This article entitles the foreign mark owner to "the preferential right to use [the] mark ... or priority to register [it]."

The required elements of a claim under Article 7 are that: 1) the foreign mark is protected in one of the member states; 2) the local party is either using, applying to register, or has registered an interfering mark for goods of the same class; and 3) the local party had knowledge of "the existence and continuous use" of the claimant's mark in another member state. The required elements of a claim under Article 8 are that: 1) the claimant's application for registration in the member state has been refused because of the prior registration of the conflicting mark; 2) the foreign mark has been protected in another member state from a date prior to the local application; and 3) either the local filer had knowledge of the existence of the foreign mark for the same goods, or the claimant has "traded" in that member state and its goods have "circulated" there.

Such rights had never existed in any previous Pan-American convention, but appeared for the first time in the "Cuban draft" that was presented at the 1929 Washington.[58] Articles 7 and 8 were novel at the time and remain unique in international trademark law today. They are unlike the Paris Convention's "well-known marks" protection in that the senior user does not have to prove fame in the country in which it seeks protection, but may merely show that the junior user was aware of senior user's rights in any member country. Furthermore, until 1958, Paris Convention Article 6*bis* offered only a means to cancel or refuse the registration of an interfering mark, whereas since 1929, the Pan-American Convention has also prohibited the *use* the of mark in the foreign state. Moreover because of the knowledge requirement, these articles do not create a trap for the "innocent filer" as the Paris Convention priority

---

58 *Minutes of the Plenary Sessions*. Article 5 of that draft provided that the 'owner of a mark legally protected in' a member state has the right to challenge the use, application, or registration of 'a mark substantially the same as his or likely to cause confusion' upon proof that the other party 'had knowledge of the existence and use of the marks' in any of the contracting States ... and may claim for himself the right to use his mark preferentially.' Similarly, Article 6 in that draft provided that 'the owner of a mark' has the right to cancel a conflicting registration if his mark enjoyed legal protection in a contracting state at the filing date, and the registrant had knowledge of the use or registration in a contracting state for the same goods, or that his goods have circulated in the country of registration by the filing date.

right does.[59] Finally, unlike the Paris Convention's priority right, Articles 7 and 8 are not time limited.

These provisions introduce to trademark law the element of knowledge of rights in another country. Significantly, there is no requirement of bad faith, just knowledge. During the negotiations, Rogers stated the knowledge requirement could be met with either actual or constructive knowledge and that to require actual knowledge would be unnecessarily burdensome. The Cuban delegate who authored the draft text pushed back just a bit and reminded Mr. Rogers of the great stretch it was for Latin American States to recognize use, but quickly accepted the proposal.[60] This knowledge standard provides a novel alternative approach to the protection of well-known marks.

5.4 *Enforcement of the Convention's Provisions*

In addition to providing stronger and more detailed protections than was provided by the Paris Convention against unfair competition, the misuse of GIs, and the appropriation of foreign trademarks, the Pan-American Convention also resolved one of the most vexing issues for treaty beneficiaries by providing them with an effective means of enforcing the rights granted in the treaty. Although the Pan-American Convention resembles the other treaties in obligating member states to enact domestic laws where necessary to ensure the rights granted by the treaty will be given effect in each contracting state, it goes further.

It anticipates member states' dereliction in Article 21, which provides that "unless otherwise effectively dealt with under the domestic laws of the Contracting States," acts of unfair competition "shall be repressed under the provisions of this Convention." Furthermore, Article 22 states that "[t]he Contracting States which may not yet have enacted legislation repressing the acts of unfair competition …, shall apply to such acts the penalties contained in their legislation on trade marks … and shall grant relief by way of injunction against the continuance of said acts at the request of any party injured; those causing such injury shall also be answerable in damages to the injured party." Likewise Article 28 states that "[i]n the absence of any special remedies ensuring the repression of false indications of geographical origin or source, remedies provided by the domestic sanitary laws, laws dealing with misbranding and the laws relating to trade marks or trade names, shall be applicable in the Contracting States." These provisions establish that the unfair competition

59 SCM Corp. v. Langis Foods Ltd., 539 F.2d 196 (D.C. Cir. 1976).
60 *Minutes of the Plenary Sessions*, 65.

protections are to be given immediate effect even in the absence of relevant domestic legislation. The protections against unfair competition are thus framed as self-executing. The prohibited acts are sufficiently described in the convention and the remedies provided in existing trademark legislation shall be available.

In addition, the convention includes an "answerable in damages" clause in Article 22. This provision mandates a civil remedy; something not required by the Paris Convention.[61] The convention was prescient and pragmatic. With the exception of the U.S., all of the member states were civil law countries that depend on a code to provide rights.

Sometimes treaties contain language indicating that they are not self-executing. There is no language in the Inter-American Convention suggesting that it is not self-executing. In addition, in most cases, the rights are so specific and detailed that legislative implementation is unnecessary. Indeed, the Pan-American Convention explicitly states that it is meant to be a self-executing treaty in Article 35: "The provisions of this Convention shall have the force of law in those States in which international treaties possess that character, as soon as they are ratified by their constitutional organs."

The U.S. Supreme Court has held that the Inter-American Convention is a self-executing treaty, and thus became law in the United States without the necessity for implementing legislation: "This treaty on ratification became a part of our law. No special legislation in the United States was necessary to make it effective."[62] Coincidentally, Edward Rogers, the U.S. delegate to the Pan American Conference, represented the petitioner who successfully asserted a claim under the Inter-American Convention in the Supreme Court case.

A recent 2023 case in the United States applies the convention precisely as it was intended. In *Industria De Alimentos Zenú S.A.S. v. Latinfood U.S. Corp.*, the court ruled in favor of a trademark holder in Columbia who asserted claims under Articles 7 and 8 of the convention, among others.[63] This decision represents the first time a federal court has applied provisions of the convention on the merits. Prior to this case, the tribunal within United States Patent and Trademark Office with jurisdiction over the registration process had consistently applied the convention beginning in 2000.[64] In an earlier decision in *Industria De Alimentos Zenú*, the court determined that "[b]eyond the general principle that it is 'self-executing,' the [Pan-American Convention] manifests a

61 Wadlow, *The Law of Passing-Off: Unfair Competition by Misrepresentation*, 59.

62 *Bacardi v Domench* 311 U.S. 150, 162–163 (1940).

63 2023 U.S. Dist. Lexis 110317.

64 British-American Tobacco Co. v. Philip Morris, 55 U.S.P.Q.2d 1585 (T.T.A.B. 2000).

specific intent to confer a private right of action on individuals."[65] With regard to the particular provisions at issue in the case, the court concluded "that their language strongly supports a finding of intent to create a private cause of action."[66]

Perhaps this case harkens a new era in which U.S. courts will adhere to the convention. Until the late 1990s, no U.S. court had had reason to consider the convention. This put the convention's applicability in the U.S. in sharp contrast with a few member states in Latin America where the convention consistently fulfills its objectives on behalf of U.S. trademark owners who make strategic use of its provisions abroad.[67]

---

65 Industria De Alimentos Zenu S.A.S. v. Latinfood U.S. Corp., 2017 U.S. Dist. LEXIS 213338 at 38.

66 2017 U.S. Dist. Lexis 213338 at 35.

67 Superintendency of Industry and Commerce of Colombia. Resolution of October 11, 2011 (cancelling Colombian registration for CROSS FIT under the convention based on registration in the U.S.); Superintendency of Industry and Commerce of Colombia, Resolution No. 4328 of February 20, 2001 (cancelling Colombian registration for HAWAIIAN TROPIC under the convention since the mark was previously registered in member state Ecuador and registrant had knowledge); Exclusividades Finas, Sociedad Anónima v. Inversiones San Agustin, Sociedad Anónima, Case 59–94, Supreme Court of Justice (1994) (cancelling Guatemalan registration for OSHKOSH B'GOSH as contravening the convention due to the prior registration by Oshkosh B'Gosh Inc. in the United States); Midas International Corporation v. Jorge Oswaldo Urrutia Lamas. Case 69–95. Supreme Court of Justice (1995) (cancelling Guatemalan registration for MIDAS as contravening the convention due to the existence of prior rights in the United States); Antonio Malouf Gabriel v. Calvin Klein. Supreme Court of Justice (1999) (cancelling Guatemalan registration for CALVIN KLEIN as contravening the Convention based on prior rights in the United States); Nicaragua. Decision No. 94, 10:45 AM, July 12, 1996 (unpublished) (cancelling Nicaraguan registration for SUR under the convention based on prior registration in member state Panama); Panama. Appeal from Resolution No. 106 of December 16, 1993, of the General Directorate of Interior Commerce of the Ministry of Commerce. Supreme Court of Justice, September 9, 1994 (cancelling Panamanian registration for FOOT LOCKER under the convention based on prior U.S. registration for the identical mark for the same goods and the notoriousness of the mark); Saks & Company v. Saks Zona Libre, S.A., Ministry of Commerce, Resolution 39 of June 2, 1995 (cancelling Panamanian registration for SAKS FIFTH AVENUE under the convention based Saks & Company's prior registration of the mark in the U.S.); Resolution No. 94, June 8, 1994 (cancelling Panamanian registration for VOGUE under the convention based on prior registration in member state Colombia); Resolution No. 147, August 9, 1994 (cancelling Panamanian registration for LAMBORGHINI under the convention based on prior registration in the United States); Resolution No. 147, August 9, 1994 (cancelling Panamanian registration for CREAMETTE under the convention based on prior registration in the United States); Resolution No. 147, August 9, 1994 (cancelling Panamanian registration for JAGUAR under the convention based on prior registration in the United States); Resolution No. 69, April 20, 1994 (cancelling Panamanian registration for GAP under the convention based on prior registration in the United States).

6 Conclusion: The Forgotten Trademark Treaty

The Pan-American Convention developed international protections for trademarks, including unfair competition law and unfair competition that exceeded the then-existing protections. It did so in novel and creative ways. The drafters had a degree of freedom to formulate new protections that did exist in other multilateral fora. The dearth constraints on the drafters was due to the uneven bargaining power between the U.S. and the other Latin American states, as well as the minimal development of trademark law in Latin America.

However, for the most part these innovative protections were not taken up in other treaties. Indeed, they may not have even been implemented in domestic law in the member states. Moreover in litigation, it is primarily only Articles 7 and 8 that have continued to be asserted in Latin American member states and more recently in the U.S. As a result, the fullness of the protections of this convention reside exclusively in its text despite the fact that the convention remains in force in all of the original member states.[68] Perhaps such an expeditious advance in trademark protections was objectionable in other fora. Likely for these reasons, the Pan-American Convention is neglected in the literature on intellectual property law.

The Pan-American Convention is, however, illuminating as an early example of a regional approach to IP protection. Interestingly, this early twentieth century attempt at regionalism in the Americas, much like more recent regional agreements, was motivated in part by a strategy of forum shifting. The Pan-American Convention was an attempt by the U.S. to create a regional alternative to the Paris Convention, which at that time was dominated by European countries with few Latin American signatories.[69] Also in common with more recent examples of Free Trade Agreements, we see in the Pan-American Convention one country imposing its interests on the others, whose economies have a greater need for foreign trade than more developed intellectual property protections.

---

68 The United States did, however, formally renounce the convention's Protocol on the Inter-American Registration of Trade-marks in 1945. Ladas, 'The Lanham Act and International Trade,' 269–271.

69 Ladas, *The International Protection of Trade Marks by the American Republics*, 11. In addition to addressing the meager participation of Latin American states in the Paris Union, it appears that the drafters of the Pan-American Convention were interested in dealing with the perceived issues in the region with greater focus.

Acknowledgments

I am grateful for the excellent research assistance provided by Jaclyn Bell and Aasees Kaur. This chapter is based partially on Farley, Christine Haight, 'The Lost Unfair Competition Law.' *The Trademark Reporter* 110 (2020): 739.

Bibliography

Alexander, Miles, '100th Anniversary Issue: Reflections of Former Editors-in-Chief.' *The Trademark Reporter* 9 (2011) 101.

Bodenhausen, Georg. *Guide to the Application of the Paris Convention for the Protection of Industrial Property: As Revised at Stockholm in 1967* (Geneva: BIRPI, 1968).

Bone, Robert G., 'Hunting Goodwill: A History of the Concept of Goodwill in Trademark Law.' *Boston University Law Review* 86 (2006) 119.

Chafee, Jr., Zechariah, 'Unfair Competition.' *Harvard Law Review* 53 (1940): 1289.

Crapol, Edward P. *James G. Blaine: Architect of Empire. Biographies in American Foreign Policy* (Delaware: Scholarly Resources, 2000).

Donghi, Tulio Halperin. *The Contemporary History of Latin America* (Durham: Duke University Press, 1993).

'Dr. Stephen Ladas, Patent Lawyer, 77.' *New York Times*. March 15, 1976.

Cardenas, Enrique, Jose Antonio Ocampo and Thorp, Rosemary. *An Economic History of Twentieth-Century Latin America: Volume 1 The Export Age* (London: Palgrave Macmillan, 2000).

Fifth International Conference of American States, Special Handbook for the Use of the Delegates. 1922.

Katz, Hanna, 'An International Aspect of the Pending Trade-Mark Bill.' *The Trademark Reporter* 35 (1945): 146.

Ladas, Stephen, 'Pan American Conventions on Industrial Property.' *American Journal of International Law* 22 (1928): 803–821.

Ladas, Stephen P. *Patents, Trademarks, and Related Rights: National and International Protection* (Cambridge: Harvard University Press, 1975).

Ladas, Stephen P. *The International Protection of Industrial Property* (Cambridge: Harvard University Press, 1930).

Ladas, Stephen P. *The International Protection of Trade Marks by the American Republics* (Cambridge: Harvard University Press, 1929).

Ladas, Stephen P., 'The Lanham Act and International Trade.' *Law & Contemporary Problems* 14 (1949): 269–287.

Levine, Sondra, 'Part One: The Common Law, the States, and Historical Perspectives: The Origins of the Lanham Act.' *Journal of Contemporary Legal Issues* 19 (2010) 22.

Lunsford, Julius, 'Foreword.' *The Trademark Reporter* 62 (1972): IV.

Marshall, Edward, 'Fight for South America's Great Trade.' *New York Times*, December 4, 1910.

Martí, José, 'On the Inter-American Congress.' *La Nación*, December 19-20, 1889.

Muzzey, David Saville. *James G. Blaine: A Political Idol of Other Days* (New York: Dodd, Mead, and Company, 1934).

Pan American Trademark Conference, Minutes of the Plenary Sessions and of the Committees of the Conferences. 1929.

Pan American Trademark Conference, Preparatory Data for the Pan American Trade Mark Conference: Report of the Committee of the Governing Board of the Pan American Union. February 11, 1929.

Pattishall, Beverly W., 'Trademarks and the Monopoly Phobia.' *Michigan Law Review* 50 (1952) 967.

Press Release, U.S. Delegation to the Inter-American Convention, *The Advantages Accruing to American Citizens from the General Convention for Trademark and Commercial Protection*. February 11, 1929.

Rogers, Edward S., 'Some Suggestions Concerning a Trademark Registration Act.' *Annual Report A.B.A.* 43 (1920): 412.

Rogers, Edward S. and Ladas, Stephen P., 'Proposal for Uniform Trademark Laws.' *The Trademark Reporter* 40, no. 1 (1950): 14.

Wadlow, Christopher. *The Law of Passing-Off: Unfair Competition by Misrepresentation 3rd ed.* (London: Sweet & Maxwell, 2004).

Wilgus, A. Curtis, 'James G. Blaine and the Pan American Movement.' *Hispanic American Historical Review* 5 (1922): 622.

CHAPTER 6

When Politics Met Intellectual Property Cooperation in the Pan-American Union

Patricia Covarrubia

1 The Nature of Latin America Intellectual Property in the Interwar Period, and the Linkage to Broader International Legal Developments

During the late nineteenth and early twentieth centuries, Latin America saw the expansion of the intellectual property system, which was linked to the internationalisation of national systems. The national intellectual property systems were based on treaties signed in the regional inter-American system, some of which mirrored international intellectual property conventions.[1]

The Paris Convention was a development in the internationalisation and protection of intellectual property rights that included provisions on "national treatment".[2] The convention established basic intellectual property principles, and while mainly Europe and the United States engaged in the debates that started formally in Vienna in 1873, only a few Latin American countries were signatories to the Paris Convention. Before the interwar period, Brazil, Cuba, the Dominican Republic, Ecuador, El Salvador, Guatemala, Mexico, and the United States adhered to the Paris Convention, but later Ecuador,[3] El Salvador,[4] and Guatemala[5] exited the convention.[6]

1 Pedro Roffe, "Evolución e Importancia del Sistema de la Propiedad Intelectual," *Comercio Exterior* 37, no. 12 (1985): 1039, 1042.

2 Roffe, "Evolución e Importancia del Sistema de la Propiedad Intelectual," 1043.

3 Accession to the Paris Convention: 21 December 1883; entry into force: 7 July 1884; denunciation: 26 December 1886; accession: 22 March 1999; entry into force: 22 June 1999.

4 Signature of the Paris Convention: 20 March 1883; ratification: 6 June 1884; entry into force: 7 July 1884; denunciation: 17 August 1887; accession: 18 November 1993; entry into force: 19 February 1994.

5 Signature of the Paris Convention: 20 March 1883; ratification: 6 June 1884; entry into force: 7 July 1884; denunciation: 8 November 1895; accession: 18 May 1998; entry into force: 18 August 1998.

6 See Roffe (fn. 1), 1041; Stephen P. Ladas, "Pan American Conventions on Industrial Property," *American Journal of International Law* 22, no. 4 (1928): 803, 820.

 | DOI:10.1163/9789004714663_008

During the interwar period (1919–1939) per se, no Latin American country joined the Convention. Nevertheless, the majority of national laws regarding the intellectual property system were developed late in the nineteenth century and at the start of the twentieth century, but this was not led by any international obligation[7] other than a will and an effort to be part of the "civilised nations".[8] By 2023, most Latin American countries[9] are signatories of the Paris Convention, which has served as a model for the formulation of national laws, even for those that are not part of it.[10]

During the interwar period, laws seemed to be more open on the rights of exploitation of patents and more restrictive on copyrights, focusing on the rights of the authors, especially in Latin American countries.[11] Although it is observed that as of today there are only 15 Latin American countries that are signatories to the Berne Convention of 1886, the first signatory from the region and the only member during the interwar timeframe was Brazil (signed in 1922).

Regarding trademarks, the General Inter-American Convention for Trademark and Commercial Protection 1929 followed the normative structure of the Paris Convention. Generally, it seemed that although the region was not fully committing to international intellectual property conventions, indirectly it was on track to have a harmonised intellectual property system, certainly observing the relationship between the few international intellectual property treaties.[12] Furthermore, during the interwar period, there were regionally few Pan-American Conferences where intellectual property engagement was noticeable.

During the interwar period, the major conventions on intellectual property were: the Convention of Santiago de Chile 1923 and the Convention of Washington 1929, both of which provided harmonised protection in trademarks

---

7 Ladas, "Pan American Conventions on Industrial Property," 803, 820; Fabrício Bertini Pasquot Polido and Mônica Steffen Guide Rosina, "The Emergence and Development of Intellectual Property Law in South America," in *The Oxford Handbook of Intellectual property Law*, ed. Rochelle Dreyfuss and Justine Pila (Oxford: OUP, 2018), 432.

8 For further observations, see P. Sean Morris, "Innovation Diplomacy: International Exhibitions and the Rise of Innovation in the Law of Nations, " in *Intellectual Property and the Law of Nations, 1860–1920*, ed. P. Sean Morris (Nijhoff: Brill, 2022), 115.

9 It includes Mexico, Central America, the Caribbean, and South America. World Atlas, "Latin American Countries" (World Atlas), accessed 18 April 2023, <https://www.worldatlas.com/geography/latin-american-countries.html>.

10 Roffe (fn. 1), 1041.

11 Roffe (fn. 1), 1041.

12 Polido and Rosina (fn. 7), 432.

and commercial names; and the Treaty of Montevideo on Intellectual Property of 1939,[13] which notes the recognition and force of intellectual property rights and their exercise. Scholarly writers such as Polido and Rosina observe that the letter of the conventions contains a "diversity of instruments that are perceived, even today, as relevant international legal sources within the framework of Inter-American law".[14]

Aside from these Pan-American intellectual property-specific conventions, there was the Havana Treaty on Private International Law 1928 (Bustamante Code), which has two articles covering intellectual property matters.[15] However, many of the Pan-American conventions did not enter into force due to a lack of ratification.[16] While this may seem like a failure, it shows the effort made by the region to engage in a harmonised intellectual property system and shape it regionally.

There is a noticeable division in the region, on one hand, between *industrial property* covering patents, trademarks, and industrial designs and, on the other, authors' rights, that is, *copyright* covering literary and artistic works. This was inspired by the separation drawn by the Paris Convention and the Berne Convention.[17]

2 The Pan-American Conventions: International Relations and Politics

The Pan-American conventions (reconstituted as the Organization of American States since 1948) aimed to bring together the general interests of the American countries. The suggestion made by the United States Secretary of State back in 1881, mainly based on preventing war between the nations of the Americas,[18] brought many conventions in the region into fruitful international law.[19] The first of these conferences took place in Washington in 1889;

13 Roffe (fn. 1), 1042; Polido and Rosina (fn. 7), 434.

14 Polido and Rosina (fn. 7), 435.

15 The Treaty is known as the Bustamante Code, as Juris Dr Antonio Sánchez de Bustamante y Sirvén drafted this project of a Code of Private International Law, aiming to regulate the relations among the "Republics of America".

16 Polido and Rosina (fn. 7), 434.

17 Polido and Rosina (fn. 7), 436–37.

18 James Brown Scott, "Editorial Comment: The Fifth International Conference of American States," *American Journal of International Law* 17, no. 3 (1923): 518–19.

19 Alejandro Alvarez, "Latin America and International Law," *American Journal of International Law* 3, no. 2 (1909): 269.

the second in Mexico City in 1901; the third in Rio de Janeiro in 1906; and the fourth in Buenos Aires in 1910.

During the beginning of World War I (the Great War), the American Institute of International Law examined two matters: the future of the Pan-American community and a new basis of international law aiming at compliance.[20] The rest of the discussion in this chapter covers the conferences, meetings, and discussions from the Fifth Conference (Santiago, Chile, 1923) onwards. References to early conferences and conventions are noted to establish backgrounds and to document international relations and politics as well as to examine the changes in intellectual property law.

2.1 *The Fifth International Conference of the Pan-American Countries (Santiago, 1923)*

The Fifth Conference was expected to be a turning point. First, it was taking place after major global upheavals after the last conference, the Buenos Aires Convention in 1910. Secondly, most countries were just recovering from the Great War. Moreover, the relationship between the United States and Latin American countries was tense even where Latin America supplied most of the raw material for the global economy.[21] The Mexican Revolution (1910–1920) affected relations with the United States, and the rest of the Latin American countries were mindful of the many interventions undertaken by the military forces of the United States.[22]

There was always a complexity in the meetings, mainly based on different points of view: on one hand, the Anglo-American and, on the other, the Latin; this resulted in a lack of leadership. Moreover, according to scholars such as Scarfi and Preuss, the United States always showed a dominant presence.[23] However, after World War I, the United States was not comfortable engaging in any political debate, especially attempts for an association of

20 Alejandro Alvarez, "Pan-Americanism as a Working Program," *Proceedings of the Academy of Political Science in the City of New York* 7, no. 2 (1917): 303, 307.

21 Demand for food and raw materials due to the war placed Latin America in the world economy. See Stephen P. Duggan, "Latin America, the League, and the United States," Foreign Affairs 12, no. 2 (1934): 281.

22 The United States controlled Haiti (1915–1934), the Dominic Republic (1916–1924), and Central America. See Samuel G. Inman, "Obstacles to Pan-American Concord," *Current History* 17, no. 5 (1923): 789.

23 Ori Preuss and Juan Pablo Scarfi, "Relaciones Internacionales, Identidades Colectivas y Vida Intellectual en Sudamérica, 1810–1945," *Revista Complutense de Historia de América* 39 (2013): 15–16.

American nations, such as an American League of Nations, as first proposed by (Uruguayan) President Brum in 1919.[24]

At the international level, the League of Nations was established in Geneva and provided a forum for resolving international disputes. The Latin American countries were major actors and great supporters of the League of Nations,[25] and occupied a good position in international affairs, holding, during the years to come, the presidency,[26] the chairman position of the League's Assembly, and judge positions in the League's World Court of Justice.[27] The United States did not join, and this was seen by the Latin American countries as a "moral betrayal".[28] Consequently, in the Fifth Pan-American Conference, they felt equal to the United States.[29] The conference was aimed to enhance "friendship and cooperation",[30] where not only commercial debates and agreements over trademarks and patents should take place, but also it was possible to "settle disputes, to guarantee international justice".[31] Each government was represented in each sub-committee, and some of the committees were held with open doors.[32] However, the Fifth Conference was criticised for lacking a "common mind", even though it accomplished some of the points in the program, as a few of the committees had practical agendas that got results.[33]

A crucial point during the Fifth Conference was the Monroe Doctrine. Some delegations led by Colombia requested a definition of the doctrine.[34] The head of the United States delegation observed that such a doctrine was unilateral and, as such, they were the responsible party.[35] This was not taken lightly by its

---

24 Samuel Guy Inman, "Pan American Conferences and their Results," *The Southwestern Political and Social Science Quarterly* 4 (1924): 341, 354; Duggan (fn. 21), 291.

25 Eighteen Latin American countries joined, which represented one-third of the total membership. See Duggan (fn. 21), 283; Inman, "Pan American Conferences and their Results," 342.

26 During the interwar period, there were Chile (1922–1923), Cuba (1923–1924), El Salvador (1929–1930), Mexico (1934–1935), Argentina (1936–1937).

27 Inman, "Obstacles to Pan-American Concord," 791. Note that the League of Nations and its court ceased to exist in 1946. They were replaced by the United Nations and the International Court of Justice, respectively.

28 Duggan (fn. 21), 282.

29 Inman, "Pan American Conferences and their Results" (fn. 24), 343.

30 Inman, "Pan American Conferences and their Results" (fn. 24), 343.

31 Inman, "Obstacles to Pan-American Concord" (fn. 22), 789.

32 Education, political, juridical and disbarment committees were held behind closed doors. See Inman, "Pan American Conferences and their Results" (fn. 24), 344.

33 Inman, "Pan American Conferences and their Results" (fn. 24), 345.

34 Inman, "Pan American Conferences and their Results" (fn. 24), 354.

35 Inman, "Pan American Conferences and their Results" (fn. 24), 354.

counterparts, as the policy, although proclaimed by the United States President Monroe in 1823, is a principle of American International law.

The Monroe Doctrine is based on the right to independence, opposing European colonialism in the Americas[36] or any other attempt from Africa or Asia.[37] Its aim is to maintain the independence of the American continent.[38] As noted by jurist and scholar Jose Ingenieros, the United States was gradually imposing a right to intervene in Latin American affairs, and it had expanded its control over some of the Latin American countries, impinging on their political independence.[39] This view and sentiment were also explicit in the Sixth Conference (Havana, 1928), where the Argentinian delegation openly challenged the United States' military intervention in Latin America.[40]

Therefore, one of the mottos of the Fifth Conference was that "American disputes [were] to be settled by Americans".[41] This was based on policies by the League of Nations that disputes in the region would preferably settled among its countries, in that case, via the Pan-American conferences.[42] Finally, the discussion of a codification of American International Law and the setup of an American Court of Justice was resumed by a special commission discussed during the Fifth Conference (Santiago, 1923) and finally formed in Rio de Janeiro in 1925. These debates started during the Second Conference (Mexico, 1901) and continued in the years to come, but were interrupted by the war.

The code was to collate principles of the Monroe Doctrine, the right of foreigners, arbitration, and other principles.[43] Therefore, the Fifth Conference (Santiago, 1923) laid the foundation for the movement towards American unity.[44] It had the key subject of "disarmament", but did not result in a

36 Alvarez, "Pan-Americanism as a Working Program" (fn. 20), 304; Duggan (fn. 21), 282.

37 James Brown Scott, "The Seventh International Conference of American States," American Journal of International Law 28, no. 2 (1934): 219, 224.

38 Scott, "Editorial Comment: The Fifth International Conference of American States" (fn. 18), 518.

39 Jose Ingenieros cited in Inman, "Obstacles to Pan-American Concord" (fn. 22), 798.

40 Daniel Sheinin, "Argentina and the United States at the Sixth Pan American Conference (Havana 1928)," ISA Research Papers (1991), 1.

41 Scott, "Editorial Comment: The Fifth International Conference of American States" (fn. 18), 519.

42 Duggan (fn. 21), 284, 291. For instance, this is noticeable in the Chaco case, where a dispute arose over territory between Bolivia and Paraguay.

43 Inman, "Pan American Conferences and their Results" (fn. 24), 355.

44 Inman, "Pan American Conferences and their Results" (fn. 24), 356. The codification of international law has been one of the important topics acknowledged in the Americas since the Congress of Panama (1826) called by Simon Bolivar. See Manuel S. Canyes, "The Pan American Union and Comparative Law Studies in the Americas," *Bulletin of the Pan American Union* 76, no. 12 (1942): 681–82.

definitive agreement; still, the idea of inter-American peace was adopted and actioned.[45] Consequently, the Gondra Treaty, framed to prevent and avoid conflicts among the American States, was adopted during the Fifth Conference. However, this treaty was limited to investigation with no provisions to report a possible settlement.[46]

In addition, American journalist and scholar George Howland Cox observed that other resolutions were adopted during the Fifth Conference that helped the region's relationships; among these resolutions, there were a judicial settlement of disputes, sanitary safeguarding of national frontiers, and arbitration of commercial disputes.[47] The Fifth Conference reorganised the International Commission of American Jurists (the first official body created at the Third International Conference in 1906).[48] This body contributed to the formation of conventions and treaties in the Americas (e.g. the Bustamante Code).

2.2 *The Sixth International Pan-American Conference (Havana, 1928)*

The mood at the conference included a desire to settle doubts and clarify any misunderstandings regarding political authority that the Union may have. A declaration was adopted that none of the institutions shall exercise functions of a political character.[49] The latter was based on the principles of "cementing the bonds of economic, social, and cultural unions between the nations".[50] Howland regards the Sixth Conference as stormy and perhaps bitter, since at that time United States Marines were stationed in Nicaragua and Haiti.[51] Yet, conversations and debates were uplifted by tactics, such as the New York governor (later to become president) Franklin Roosevelt promising that as long as he remained president, there would be no "interventions".[52]

The Sixth Conference adopted a resolution on the methods of codification. To this effect, the National Commission for the Codification of International

45 See Inman, "Pan American Conferences and their Results" (fn. 24), 356.

46 Charles G Fenwick, "The Coordination of Inter-American Peace Agreements," *American Journal of International Law* 38, no. 1 (1944): 4, 9.

47 George Howland Cox, "Was the Seventh Pan American Conference a Success?," *World Affairs* 97, no. 1 (1934): 38, 40.

48 Canyes, "The Pan American Union and Comparative Law Studies in the Americas" (fn. 44), 682.

49 William Manger, "The Pan American Union at the Sixth International Conference of American States," *American Journal of International Law* 22, no. 4 (1928): 764, 769.

50 Manger, "The Pan American Union at the Sixth International Conference of American States," 764.

51 Cox (fn. 47), 40.

52 Cox (fn. 47), 40.

Law was created, and its proposals were to be reviewed by three Permanent Committees (adopted at the time): one Permanent Committee in Rio de Janeiro on public international law; a Second Permanent Committee in Montevideo on conflict of laws; and a Third Permanent Committee in Havana on comparative legislation.[53] Edwin Borchard (1884–1951), a prominent American jurist and scholar at Yale University, observed that this structure did not work well due to, among other reasons, few countries appointing their National Committees; thus, in the Permanent Committees, the members did not have the "necessary prestige for continental persuasion".[54]

Mostly, the Sixth Conference at Havana adopted the projects presented by the American Institute of International Law and codified seven subjects of international law.[55]

2.3 *The Seventh International Pan-American Conference (Montevideo, 1933)*

According to William Sanders, the conference was seen as an "effort to organize and maintain world peace" by eliminating barriers and expanding "international protection of the products of the human mind and spirit".[56] At the conference, six conventions and one protocol were drafted, and the members signed an "intention to subscribe the pacts for the settlement of international conflicts by pacific means".[57] Multilateral American peace treaties developed up to this year by the Union were: the Gondra Treaty (Santiago, 1923),[58] the Convention of Inter-American Conciliation (Washington, D.C., 1929),[59] and the Inter-American Arbitration Conciliation (Washington, D.C., 1929);[60] the latter

53 Canyes, "The Pan American Union and Comparative Law Studies in the Americas" (fn. 44), 683; Edwin Borchard, "The Committee of Experts at the Lima Conference," *American Journal of International Law* 33, no. 2 (1939): 269–270.

54 Borchard (fn. 53), 269–270.

55 Manger (fn. 49), 775.

56 William Sanders, "International Copyright Protection: The Present Status," *Bulletin of the Pan American Union* 73, no. 7 (1939): 419, 428.

57 There were a few multilateral American peace treaties that were still not ratified by some of the members. Report of the Delegates of the United States of America to the Seventh International Conference of American States, Montevideo, Uruguay, 3–26 December 1933 (U.S. Government Printing Office, 1934), 6.

58 Unratified by Argentina and Bolivia.

59 Unratified by Argentina, Bolivia, Colombia, Costa Rica, Honduras, Paraguay, Perú, Uruguay, and Venezuela.

60 Unratified by Argentina, Bolivia, Colombia, Costa Rica, Ecuador, Honduras, Paraguay, Perú, and Uruguay. The United States ratified it in 1935. The General Convention of Inter-American Conciliation 1929 supplements the Gondra Treaty by giving the commission of

two supplement the Gondra Treaty.[61] Many of the members had also taken further steps and ratified international pacts of peace, such as the General Treaty for Renunciation of War 1928 (the Kellogg-Briand Pact or Pact of Paris). One author observed that these agreements and treaties covered "all of the generally accepted procedures, except that of judicial settlement", referring to a permanent court aside from an arbitral tribunal.[62]

During the Seventh Conference, there was pressure on delegates to sign the peace treaties, because generally there was a failure by many to ratify the various treaties and agreements.[63] The pressure to sign such agreements and treaties was based on the conditions in the region: Cuba was undergoing a social revolution; there were still American Marines stationed in Haiti; the United States was not recognising El Salvador's president; Argentina had issues with the United States over tariff restrictions; there were differences between Colombia and Peru; and Bolivia and Paraguay were at war.[64] Therefore, at the conference, the unified voice was that the nations needed to ratify the peace treaties. Moreover, although the Chaco conflict between Bolivia and Paraguay was not on the agenda, delegates took the opportunity to address the matter and put forward views to arrive at a solution.[65] Several presidents sent telegrams, which were read at the Seventh Conference, urging the promotion of an amicable solution to the Chaco conflict.[66] A truce was signed between Bolivia and Paraguay (19 December 1933), and the League of the Nations Commission formally expressed its gratitude to the Pan-American Conference meeting in Montevideo.[67]

In 1933, on Pan-American Day (12 April), U.S. President Roosevelt addressed the Pan-American Union. He stated: "This celebration commemorates a movement based upon the policy of fraternal cooperation. In my inaugural address

---

inquiry a "conciliatory function" rather than just doing a mere investigation. Fenwick (fn. 46), 9.

61 Leo Stanton Rowe, "The Significance of the Seventh International Conference of American States," *America Society of International Law Proceedings* 28 (1934): 34, 36.

62 Fenwick (fn. 46), 4.

63 Fenwick (fn. 46), 4.

64 George Howland Cox, "Was the Seventh Pan American Conference a Success?," *World Affairs* 97, no. 1 (1934): 38, 41; Rowe (fn. 61), 34.

65 Report of the Delegates of the United States of America to the Seventh International Conference of American States, Montevideo, Uruguay, 3–26 December 1933 (U.S. Government Printing Office, 1934), 12; Rowe (fn. 61), 35.

66 Report of the Delegates of the United States of America to the Seventh International Conference of American States (fn. 65), 13.

67 Report of the Delegates of the United States of America to the Seventh International Conference of American States (fn. 65), 13.

I stated that I would "dedicate this nation to the policy of the *good neighbor'*."[68] The American jurist and legal scholar James Brown Scott (1866–1943), an authority in international law, evaluated the speech. He noted the use of the keyword "friendship" as well as the way President Roosevelt defined Pan-Americanism as a quality of "mutual understanding". Accordingly, the speech covered the "fears and criticism at the United States by [the] Latin American countrymen".[69] There is also the declaration made by Roosevelt that "the definite policy of the United States from now on is one opposed to armed intervention". However, while the speech and the president's drive sounded "friendly" and praised "mutual understanding", the United States did not sign the Convention on Rights and Duties of States[70] during the Seventh Conference.

The Convention on Rights and Duties of States contains the following articles:

a) Article 9 states that "foreigners may not claim rights other or more extensive rights than those of the nationals", that is, equality theory.[71] Many Latin American nations' constitutions based on the Chilean Civil Code (1855, drafted by Andres Bello) granted equality of civil rights.[72] However, this was a contentious issue, as Borchard attested, because there are some minimum rights that every country should extend based on the Convention of the Rights of Man (1929).[73]
b) Article 11 incorporated Article 2 of the Anti-War Treaty of Non-aggression and Conciliation (Rio de Janeiro, October 1933). The Anti-War Treaty incorporated the principles of the Stimson Doctrine based on the principle of "non-recognition" of states due to aggression.[74] The Anti-War Treaty laid down provisions for the creation of conciliation commissions.[75] However, on 26 December 1933, the creation of commissions

68 Emphasis mine.
69 Scott, "The Seventh International Conference of American States" (fn. 37), 225.
70 It was signed and ratified by 10 countries: Brazil, Costa Rica, Ecuador, Haiti, Honduras, Mexico, Nicaragua, Panama, and Venezuela. The Convention on Rights and Duties of States addresses the definition of "state" (Article 1) and the primary "interest" of the state (Article 3).
71 Article 9, Convention on Rights and Duties of States. See Borchard (fn. 53), 269–77.
72 John Ward Cutler, "The Treatment of Foreigners: In Relation to the Draft Convention and Conference of 1929," *The American Journal of International Law* 27, no. 2 (1933): 225, 229.
73 See Borchard (fn. 53), 278.
74 Article 11, Convention on Rights and Duties of States, reads: "The contracting States definitely establish as the rule of their conduct the precise obligation not to recognize territorial acquisitions or special advantages which have been obtained by force…" See John Trone, "The Stimson Doctrine of Non-recognitions of Territorial Conquest", 160, 161–62.
75 Fenwick (fn. 46), 15.

was abandoned by the Additional Protocol to the General Convention of Inter-American Conciliation.

On one hand, the conference adopted an important international law prepared by the Executive Council of the America Institute of International Law. These topics were, among others, nationality, extradition, political asylum, the teaching of history, a resolution to establish the Inter-American Labor Institution, the Convention of the Nationality of Women, and, as previously noted, the Convention on the Rights and Duties of States.[76] On the other hand, it abolished the three Permanent Committees (Rio de Janeiro, Montevideo, and Havana) and created a Committee of Experts to initiate questionnaires and drafts of codes that were to be submitted to the National Commission for comments, and the revised draft to be submitted for adoption to the government at International Conferences.[77] The conference also produced some recommendations, which were later drafted as a declaration (Juridical Personality of Foreign Companies, June 1936) and a protocol (Uniformity of Powers of Attorney, February 1940).[78]

Other important steps taken by the conference were: first, a resolution authorising the Pan-American Union to draft a paper that aimed to include the ideas voiced by Simón Bolivar and expressed by congresses, jurisconsults, and others on the creation of an American League of Nations with a Permanent American Tribunal of International Justice;[79] secondly, a resolution that established ways for the future work of codifying international law, which latter maintained the International Commission of American Jurists;[80] and lastly, a Peace Code introduced by the Mexican delegation with novel provisions coordinating in one single instrument all principles and procedures. The Peace Code was referred to the American Government for their attention.[81] A version of the Peace Code was also referred to the Committee

76 See Rowe (fn. 61), 37–38; Herbert Wright, "The Montevideo conference and organization for peace," *World Affairs* 97, no. 2 (1934): 100–103, 101.

77 Numeral 1 and 2, Seventh International Conference of American States, Resolution No XLVIII. See Borchard (fn. 53), 270.

78 The Seventh International Conference of American States, Resolution No XLVIII. See Canyes, "The Pan American Union and Comparative Law Studies in the Americas" (fn. 44), 685.

79 *Las Ideas de Bolívar* (Séptima Conferencia Internacional Americana, Montevideo 1933), approved 22 December 1933. See William Manger, "The Pan American Union and the Conclusions of the Seventh International Conference of American States," *Bulletin of the Pan American Union* 669, no. 2 (1935): 77, 90.

80 Manger, "The Pan American Union and the Conclusions of the Seventh International Conference of American States," 90.

81 Fenwick (fn. 46), 5.

of Experts for the Codification of International Law to present to the Lima (Eighth) Conference.[82] Finally, the Seventh Conference re-established the three Permanent Committees and adopted a new method of codification.[83] Consequently, the Seventh Conference is noted as a positive one in international law, as it saw the codification of the Convention on Rights and Duties of States and supported the United States president's claim for a "good neighbour" policy.

In the interim before the next conference, there was a Special Conference for the Maintenance of Peace (Buenos Aires Conference of 1936),[84] where the Mexican delegation presented a revised text that adopted the Treaty of Prevention of Controversies presented by the Chilean Delegation;[85] the Convention for the Maintenance, Preservation and Re-establishment of Peace; the Convention to Coordinate, Extend and Assure the Fulfilment of the Existing Treaties; the Inter-American Treaty on Goods Offices and Mediation; and the Declaration of Principles of Inter-American Solidarity and Cooperation.[86]

2.4 *The Eighth International Pan-American Conference (Lima, 1938)*

All delegates of the American Nations attended the conference. Apart from studying political, juridical, and economic matters, the agenda envisioned guaranteeing the maintenance of peace on the American continent.[87] This vision was stated by the Peruvian Minister of Foreign Affairs in his letter of invitation to all governments of the American nations. In the reply to the invitation, the United States Secretary of State remarked on the recent problems of the world and the importance of the Eighth Conference, as it would be seen as "an opportunity to set an example to the world through the creation of new bonds of solidarity and friendship".[88] Accepting the invitation, he asserted

82 *Métodos de Codificación del Derecho Internacional* (Séptima Conferencia Internacional Americana, Montevideo, 1933). See Fenwick (fn. 46), 5.

83 Borchard (fn. 53), 270.

84 Fenwick (fn. 46), 5.

85 The Treaty was signed on 23 December 1936. It was ratified by Colombia, Chile, the Dominican Republic, Ecuador, El Salvador, Guatemala, Honduras, and Mexico, with reservations from Costa Rica, Haiti, Nicaragua, and Panama. See United Nations, *United Nations – Treaty Series* (UN-iLibrary, 1994), 413–14.

86 The conventions can be found in Borchard (fn. 53), n12.

87 Union of American Republics, "The Eighth International Conference of American States," 617, 618–19. See also George A Finch, "Eighth International Conference of American States," *American Journal of International Law* 34, no. 4 (1940): 714.

88 Union of American Republics, "The Eighth International Conference of American States"(fn. 86), 617–18.

that this was an opportunity to collaborate for the "common good" based on "respect" for each other "independence, sovereignty and political equality".[89] There was, according to George Finch, who was a member of the advisory committee on research in international law at Harvard Law School (1928–1940), a determination "to keep the ravages of war away from the shores of the Western Hemisphere".[90]

The agenda focused on the six topics referred by the Committee of Experts who met in the Buenos Aires Conference for the Maintenance of Peace, 1936, plus a topic on Methods of Codification.[91] However, no treaties or conventions were adopted but declarations, resolutions, and recommendations were abundant. Resolutions were on the topics of reduction of barriers to international trade; defence of human rights; non-recognition of the acquisition of territory by force; on foreign minorities; the political activities of foreigners; to revise the procedure for the codification of international law;[92] and a resolution providing for the establishment of a Permanent Committee of Jurists represented by both Anglo-American and Latin juridical systems.[93] Declarations were on the topic of solidarity and cooperation, that is, the Declaration of Lima; improvements in the procedure of consultation; the firm purpose of establishing an Inter-American Court of International Justice; condemning persecution for racial or religious motives.[94] A report on the matter of sanctions and the definition of "aggressor", which was prepared by the Committee of Experts, was left to the International Conference of American Jurists that were to meet in Rio de Janeiro in 1942.[95]

Aside from the Peace Code, the conference also discussed the Treaty of Consolidation of American Peace Agreements presented by the United States delegation. However, there was no conclusion about the general substance of the Code of Peace or any other submission introduced on the same topic. The matter was referred to the International Conference of American Jurists,

89 Union of American Republics, "The Eighth International Conference of American States"(fn. 86), 619.

90 Finch (fn. 86), 714.

91 The six topics covered were: pecuniary claims; the coordination of the peace instrument or Peace Code; definition of "sanctions and aggressor"; coordination of investigation, conciliation, and arbitration treaties; immunity of government-owned vessels; and nationality. See Borchard (fn. 53), 269.

92 Finch (fn. 86), 716.

93 Canyes, "The Pan American Union and Comparative Law Studies in the Americas" (fn. 44), 685.

94 Finch (fn. 86), 716.

95 Finch (fn. 86), 715.

who were instructed to present a report on the matter and submit it to the next conference.[96] Additionally, the Inter-American Judicial Committee was called upon to prepare and submit a "coordinated peace agreement" to the American Governments for observation and comments before the Conference of American Jurists.[97] The conference also reemphasised that all existing agencies were active, including the Permanent Committees (which were enlarged), and resurrected the International Commission of Jurists, which was to be called the International Conference of American Jurists.[98] The latter body was to be composed of two delegates from each country, which would have one vote.[99] Other facts during the Eighth Conference were that it permanently established the Inter-American Commission of Women. By 1939 and close of the interwar period, there was the creation of the Inter-American Neutrality Committee,[100] which looked into the codification of international law (public and private).[101]

To end this section, the discussion of all conferences and several meetings between conferences saw the collaboration between nations. However, one needs to recognise that some of the drafts that were later codified (public and private international law) were prepared (by request of the Pan-American Union or the Pan-American Conference), in the interim of conferences, by private organisations, professional associations, and individuals who did so voluntarily.[102] They all assisted in the shape of international treaties.

3 The Work of the Fifth, Sixth, Seventh, and Eighth Pan-American Conferences in the Intellectual Property Field

During the interwar period (1919–1939), there were several meetings of the American States and Pan-American Conferences, but only a few covered

---

96 Some of the provisions contained in the code were controversial. See Fenwick (fn. 46), 5. The next meeting was organised in Rio de Janeiro, Brazil in January 1942 due to the United States' entry into World War II.

97 Fenwick (fn. 46), 6.

98 Borchard (fn. 53), 269–71; Canyes, "The Pan American Union and Comparative Law Studies in the Americas" (fn. 44), 682.

99 Borchard (fn. 53), 269–72.

100 This body was transformed in 1942 into the Inter-American Juridical Committee, which still exists (2023). See A.A. Cançado Trindade, "The Inter-American Juridical Committee: An Overview," The World Today 38, no. 11 (1982): 437.

101 Canyes, "The Pan American Union and Comparative Law Studies in the Americas" (fn. 44), 683.

102 Canyes, "The Pan American Union and Comparative Law Studies in the Americas" (fn. 44), 681.

intellectual property rights. Around the patent system, no regional development occurred during the interwar period; the main regional conventions, which were signed before the interwar period, are in place even today. These are the Inter-American Convention for the Protection of Inventions, Designs, and Industrial Models, signed in Buenos Aires on 20 August 1910 and ratified by many countries, including the United States.[103] It adopted the principles of national treatment, right of priority, and independence of patents, and defined what a patentable invention is. Argentina and Peru did not sign; therefore, the Montevideo Convention on Patents (1889) remains in effect between these two countries.[104] There is also the Bolivia Patent Convention (Agreement on Patents and Privileges of Invention), signed at Caracas on 18 July 1911 between Bolivia, Colombia, Ecuador, Peru, and Venezuela. The section on the intellectual property field will be examined by intellectual property subject matter, excluding patents, and follows a chronological structure.

3.1 *Fifth Conference (Santiago, 1923)*

The conference was scheduled to be in 1914, but because of World War I, it was postponed.[105] Mexico was absent, as its government refused to attend as a consequence of not being recognised by the United States; thus, it was considered to have no voice in the Pan-American Union.[106]

The Fifth Conference contained eight committees: political, juridical, hygiene, communications, commerce, agriculture, limitation of armaments, and education.[107] According to Inman, the commerce committee was the one to achieve the most progress, especially around trademarks.[108] In fact, during the conference, there were four conventions signed, one of which refers to intellectual property, specifically trademarks.[109]

The Fifth Conference and the previous one in 1910 suggested a separate Pan-American Treaty on matters of intellectual property. This was never approved, and some delegates as well as the International Chamber of Commerce suggested adhering to the Paris Convention and the Protocol of Madrid. Specifically, the Argentinian delegate recommended abandoning the idea of a

---

103 Ladas, "Pan American Conventions on Industrial Property" (fn. 6), 808.
104 Ladas, "Pan American Conventions on Industrial Property" (fn. 6), 817.
105 Inman, "Pan American Conferences and their Results" (fn. 24), 342.
106 Inman, "Pan American Conferences and their Results" (fn. 24), 350.
107 *Acta General* (Quinta Conferencia Internacional Americana, Santiago 1923). See Inman, "Pan American Conferences and their Results" (fn. 24), 343.
108 Inman, "Pan American Conferences and their Results" (fn. 24), 346.
109 *Convención para la Protección de Marcas de Fábrica, Comercio y Agricultura y Nombres Comerciales* (Quinta Conferencia Internacional Americana, Santiago 1923).

Pan-American Treaty, making the recommendation that nations should adhere to the Paris Convention and the Protocol of Madrid instead. Additionally, a proposed draft convention for the protection of trademarks and commercial names was introduced by the United States and drafted by the Inter-American High Commission's Central Executive Council assisted by United States' trademarks experts before the Fifth Conference.[110]

According to Ladas, while the Latin American counterparts did not provide any assistance with the drafting, all signed the convention apart from Bolivia, Mexico, and Peru.[111] In the end, only eight countries ratified the Convention for the Protection of Trademarks and Commercial Names 1923. In principle, the convention was divided into two parts: a Protocol for the Inter-American Registration of Trademarks and the General Inter-American Convention for Trademarks and Commercial Protection. While it is considered more like a revision of the one adopted at the Fourth Conference (Buenos Aires, 1910), there were some changes from the previous conventions, such as removing the wording "all persons", set up in the Convention of 1910, which permitted everyone to benefit from it. On the contrary, the Convention of 1923 noted that only "persons domiciled in any of the contracting countries" could benefit from it.[112] This is partly in line with the Madrid Agreement of 1891, as it applies to a person or business that has a connection with the contracting party, be it by nationality or domicile.

Another change established is that once an application is received by the Bureau, each country determines, per its domestic law, if the application is granted.[113] Moreover, once registration is granted in one country, it provides rights over the mark for all other countries, that is, a "priority right", without a fixed period.[114] Regarding the time frame for the process, the wording "as soon as possible"[115] differentiates it from the Madrid Agreement, as the latter requires a period of 12 to 18 months.[116]

110 Ladas, "Pan American Conventions on Industrial Property" (fn. 6), 811.

111 Ladas, "Pan American Conventions on Industrial Property" (fn. 6), 811.

112 Article I, Section 1, Convention for the Protection of Trademarks and Commercial Names 1923.

113 Article I, Section 1, Convention for the Protection of Trademarks and Commercial Names 1923.

114 Article II, Convention for the Protection of Trademarks and Commercial Names 1923.

115 Article III, Convention for the Protection of Trademarks and Commercial Names 1923.

116 Patricia Covarrubia, "The Madrid Protocol in Latin America: Is Colombia Changing Business Strategies or Acting as a Guinea Pig? European Intellectual Property Review 35, no. 1 (2013): 1, 19.

Additionally, it notes the "cancellation right", granting such right just to proprietors of a mark claiming recognition and seeking cancellation of previously registered marks in some circumstances.[117] This was taken from the previous convention but added a numeral which, according to Ladas, seemed to specify that "the good faith of [an applicant] is immaterial"; this is applicable only in cases where the marks registered by another is identical, rather than the mark making any resembling or creating confusion.[118] Additionally, no uniform term of protection was granted,[119] while the Madrid Agreement set up that marks will be registered for a period of 10 years. Regarding the protection of trade names (Article 1, Section 4), it followed the previous convention and mirrored Article 8 of the Paris Convention; that is, they are protected whether or not they form part of a trademark in accordance with the domestic law of each state.

Finally, in the matter of trademarks, the Inter-American Trademark Registration Bureau of Havana started to fully operate in 1919. In its first year, the United States was the only country that used it, with 80 registrations in total.[120] Regarding copyright, the committee of education did not have much (or any at all) development on the topic, but just offered a recommendation to the members (even if they had not signed the Buenos Aires Convention of 1910) to incorporate in their legislation arrangements to register authors' rights in the respective offices and to adopt effective legal procedures in cases of infringements.[121]

3.2 *Sixth Conference (Havana, 1928)*

A resolution proposed by the Argentine delegation was passed. It recommended to the governing body of the Pan-American Union to call a special conference to only deal with the topic of industrial property. This special conference took place in Washington in 1929, and its results were to be considered by the different governments without the need to present them to the Seventh International Conference of American States.[122]

---

117 Article V, Section 2, Convention for the Protection of Trademarks and Commercial Names 1923.

118 Ladas, "Pan American Conventions on Industrial Property" (fn. 6), 814–15.

119 Article V, Section 2, Convention for the Protection of Trademarks and Commercial Names 1923.

120 See Ladas, "Pan American Conventions on Industrial Property" (fn. 6), 811. According to Article IX, Convention for the Protection of Trademarks and Commercial Names 1923, there were 12 countries to use the Havana Bureau.

121 Propiedad Literaria y Artística (Quinta Conferencia Internacional Americana, Santiago, 1923), numerals 1 and 2.

122 Ladas, "Pan American Conventions on Industrial Property" (fn. 6), 804.

The results of this special conference were the drafting of two instruments: a Protocol for the Inter-American Registration of Trademarks and the General Inter-American Convention for Trademarks and Commercial Protection. Previous conventions on trademarks covered both registration and subject matter in one instrument. The departure from this practice was based on providing the choice to the countries to independently sign and ratify the General Convention, and not the inter-American registrations, which many states in the region were hesitant to do.[123]

The Sixth Conference revisited the Pan-American Trademark Treaty set up in Santiago in 1923. The Argentinian delegate presented a report on trademarks, noting that this topic had been on the agenda for the last 40 years. Previous conferences focused on political matters and in attendance were diplomats instead of trademark experts, who were competent in the topic. The delegate called for a conference dedicated to trademarks and attended by delegates who were trademark experts.[124]

Consequently, the Sixth Conference determined that there shall be a "special conference" attended by trademark representatives of all American nations and that they should consider international problems of inter-American trademarks.[125] This recommendation was passed to the governing board of the Pan-American Union, which was to meet in 1929 in Washington. A few of the important issues the conference considered during the drafting and amendment stages were:

a) To strike Article 1, Section 1. This section set up the formalities and conditions required to register a trademark, which was to be governed by the domestic law of each American nation. Likewise, amendments to Paragraph b) were proposed.[126] This section referred to fees, in which one part was to be retained by the Inter-American Bureau and the other part to be distributed among the signatory nations. Section 2 was to be revised noting the term of protection to be established by domestic law but not to exceed 20 years.[127]

b) Amendments were proposed to Article 2 regarding ownership of a mark. This extended to protect not only marks where ownership is acquired

123 Arthur D Herrick, "Denunciation of the Protocol for Inter-American Registration of Trade-Marks" *Trademark Report* 35 (1945): 39.

124 Karl Fenning, "Trade Marks in Pan America as Affected by the Havana Conference 1928," *Journal of the Patent Office Society* 10 (1928), 483.

125 Fenning, "Trade Marks in Pan America as Affected by the Havana Conference 1928," 484.

126 Fenning, "Trade Marks in Pan America as Affected by the Havana Conference 1928," 484.

127 Fenning, "Trade Marks in Pan America as Affected by the Havana Conference 1928," 485.

through registration but also to provide full protection to trademark users in any of the signatory nations.[128] The Article also touched upon the date of filing, clarifying that it is the date of "filing of the application for registration" in the country of origin.[129]

c) Article 3, Section 1, was to be included, adding grounds of refusal and/or invalidation, including marks contrary to morality or public policy. In Section 3, a new disclaimer was noted, covering the time frame for processes. It refers to a speedy response to acknowledge the application and to be considered registered if a response is not given within four months.[130]

d) Article 4 amendments were on the table to cover the "equal recognition" in each of the signatories' states of a mark registered or deposited in any of the countries and registered in any of the Inter-American Bureaus.[131]

e) Article 5 presided over unfair competition. The wording mirrors the Paris Convention Article 10*bis*, that is, that all contracting parties shall assure all nationals of the signatory states protection against unfair competition.[132]

The rationale of the amendments and additions were based on the reservations expressed by the United States at the Fifth Conference.[133] The drafting, according to Farley, mirrors the Madrid Agreement, although it neither covers the principle of "national treatment" nor the "priority right".[134] Concerning copyright, and thus involving literary and artistic works, the Pan-American conferences and meetings developed six copyright conventions in total.[135]

128 See the Report of the Delegates of the United States of America to the Fifth International Conference of American States, held in Santiago, Chile, 25 March to 3 May 1923 (U.S. Government Printing Office, 1923), 17, accessed 26 August 2022, https://archive.org/details/reportofdelegate00unit_0/page/n3/mode/2up?ref=ol&view=theater.

129 Fenning (fn. 123), 486.

130 Fenning (fn. 123), 487.

131 Fenning (fn. 123), 487.

132 Fenning (fn. 123), 487.

133 Fenning (fn. 123), 489.

134 Christine Haight Farley, "The Pan-American Trademark Convention of 1929: A bold vision of extraterritorial meets current realities" in *Trademark Protection and Territoriality Challenges in a Global Economy*, ed. Irene Calboli and Edward Lee (Cheltenham: Edward Elgar, 2014), 60.

135 Harry G Henn, "Interrelation between the Universal Copyright Convention and the Pan-American Copyright Convention," *Bulletin of the Copyright Society of the U.S.A.* 2, no. 4 (1955): 110; see the Report of the Delegates of the United States of America to the Fifth International Conference of American States, held in Santiago, Chile, 25 March to 3 May 1923 (U.S. Government Printing Office, 1923), 27.

Scholars regard the Buenos Aires Convention as the most important and successful as it was signed by the majority of the Union members including the United States.[136] Towards the end of the Sixth Conference, the Buenos Aires Convention was amended but only ratified by a few.[137]

Ladas noted that some matters dealt with by the Havana Convention that amended the Buenos Aires Convention were:

a) The retention of the "notice of copyright", to be affixed to each copy of the work, reserving the author's rights, including foreign works. The Havana Convention added to the "All Rights Reserved" requirement, to complement the name of the person in whose favour the right is registered the country of origin and the year of first publication.

b) The "deposit and registration" condition, which remained from the Buenos Aires Convention. These formalities or any others are not present in the International Berne Convention, which provides for automatic protection to the creation of the work in party's country.[138] Some of the earlier Pan-American Conventions did not mention the requirement of formalities.[139] While the Havana Convention extended the definition noted in the Buenos Aires Convention, adding other works and including "arts applied to any human activity",[140] it still did not protect unpublished works.[141]

c) The author's rights,[142] which retained the principle of *lex fori* (the laws of the country where the protection is sought) but used the principle of *lex loci* (the laws of the country of origin) for the rights not covered under the convention.[143] For the first time, it recognised the moral right of integrity where an author has the right to oppose the reproduction or public exhibition of the work in an "altered, mutilated or revised form"; moral rights were set up to be inalienable.[144]

---

136 Henn (fn. 134), 111; Stephen P. Ladas, "Inter-American Copyright," *University of Pittsburgh Law Review* 7, no. 4 (1941): 283, 285.

137 Ladas, "Inter-American Copyright," 282, 285.

138 Ladas, "Inter-American Copyright," 288.

139 Sanders (fn. 56), 421.

140 Article 2, Havana Convention; Ladas, "Inter-American Copyright," 288.

141 Alfred L. Rinaldo, Jr, "Scope of Copyright Protection in the United States under Existing Inter-American Relations: Abrogation of the Need for U.S. Protection under the Buenos Aires Convention by Reliance upon the UCC," *Bulletin of the Copyright Society of the U.S.A.* 22, no. 6 (1975): 417, 423.

142 Rinaldo, Jr, "Scope of Copyright Protection in the United States under Existing Inter-American Relations," 419; Ladas, "Inter-American Copyright" (fn. 136), 293.

143 Sanders (fn. 56), 422; Rinaldo (fn. 141), 422.

144 Article 13, Havana Convention.

d) The term of protection, extending to fifty years from the death of the creator; if not all countries were to adopt it, *lex fori* would apply.[145]

At the time, the American nations were acquainted with the Berne Convention, which did not and does not provide a definition of "author"; this gave flexibility to both sides, the Latin American countries based on the concept of the "author's right" (*droit d'auteur*), the works of the mind being seen as an expression of the personality of their creator, and the Anglo-American based on "copyright". Although early Pan-American legislation followed the Anglo-American concept regarding authorship granted by the state, it seems that the system was to be a hybrid one.

In 1928, the delegation of Brazil (the only member of the Berne Convention at the time) together with the French delegation discussed at the Berne Revision Conference in Rome the desire to merge the Berne Convention with the Inter-American copyright agreements in existence.[146] The International Committee on Intellectual Cooperation created by the General Assembly of the League of Nations took the responsibility to harmonise both the Berne Convention and the Pan-American Union agreements on copyright.[147]

Concerning the whole intellectual property system, the Havana Treaty on Private International Law 1928 (Bustamante Code) was signed during the conference.[148] This Treaty included two intellectual property provisions, as follows:

a) Chapter I titled "classification of goods", Article 108 sets the applicable law, that is, the "law of the place" for industrial and intellectual property, asserting that it is where such property has been registered.
b) The chapter titled "of property", Article 115 sets that industrial and intellectual property shall be governed by the existing (or adopted in the future) international conventions. In absence of these rules, it sets that the law that shall govern is the national law where the right has been granted.

145 Article 6, Havana Convention.

146 Isabella Löhr, "Intellectual Cooperation in Transnational Networks: The League of Nations and the Globalization of Intellectual Property Rights" in *Transnational Political Spaces: Agents – Structures – Encounters* (*History of Political Communication*), 2nd edition, ed. Mathias Albert et al. (Chicago: University of Chicago Press, 2009), 66.

147 Löhr, "Intellectual Cooperation in Transnational Networks," 69–71.

148 The Code was ratified without reservations by six Latin American countries and in part by nine others.

3.2.1 The General Inter-American Convention for Trademark and Commercial Protection 1929 (the Washington Convention)

The Washington Convention was ratified by 10 nations, although signed by 19 countries, and adopted following the Sixth Conference. According to Farley, the focus of the Pan-American Conventions was to "provide national treatment" within the region and to "create a uniform system for the protection of foreign trademarks".[149]

The Washington Convention remains valid and in force today among the contracting parties[150] and replaces, as between contracting parties, the Convention of 1910 and the Convention of 1923.[151] Some of the matters covered in the Washington Convention are:[152]

a) The "national treatment" and "priority right", which follows the normative structure of the Paris Convention.[153] Consequently, the convention establishes a set of substantive rights for trademark owners.[154] Additionally, the Washington Convention regulates the "principle of independence" of filings and registrations. Note that the "dependency rule" noted in the Madrid Agreement is not followed by the Washington Convention, nor does it need to.[155]
b) The addition of the "ground of refusal" (Article 3). This is mentioned in both the Paris Convention and the Madrid Agreement.
c) A discussion on "ownership" continued to be discussed. Yet, based on the foundations, it vastly differs between the United States and its counterparts. On one hand, the United States is based on common law, which created the right of the mark "by use", while the Latin American counterpart is based on the principle of registration.[156] The Washington

149 Farley, "The Pan-American Trademark Convention of 1929" (fn. 133), 59.

150 WIPO, "IP Treaties Collection: General Inter-American Convention for Trade Mark and Commercial Protection"(WIPO), accessed 2 June 2023, https://www.wipo.int/wipolex/en/treaties/parties/353.

151 The United States Department of State, "Treaties in Force"(2020), accessed 5 September 2022, https://www.state.gov/treaties-in-force/. Brazil, the Dominican Republic, and Uruguay are not parties but ratified the Convention of 1923. Likewise, Bolivia and Ecuador signed neither the Convention of 1923 nor the Convention of 1929 but are a party of the Convention of 1920.

152 For more information, see the chapter "Furthering interest abroad: Advancing trademark rights in the Americas in the first decades of the twentieth century" by Christine Haight Farley, in this volume.

153 Farley, "The Pan-American Trademark Convention of 1929" (fn. 133), 60.

154 Polido and Rosina (fn. 7), 43.

155 Article 6(3), Madrid Agreement. See Covarrubia (fn. 113), 21.

156 Farley, "The Pan-American Trademark Convention of 1929" (fn. 133), 61.

Convention, therefore, merges the two practices: on one hand, the common law of unfair competition and, on the other, the Latin American registration-based system.[157]

d) The priority right (Article 7). This "priority right" negotiated by the United States is without limitation in time (distinct from the Paris Convention) and is seen as "novel" and "unique" in international trademark law. This involves the right to challenge the use, registration, or deposit of a mark in another contracting country upon proof that such a third party knew of the existence and continued use of the mark in compliance with the domestic legislation in the country where the action took place.[158] This entailed asserting four matters, two made by the claimant and the remaining by the defendant. The claimant is the owner of a mark which is protected, having complied with the domestic law in both countries; the defendant is using or seeks to register an "interfering mark", and has knowledge of the use of the prior mark in the same class.[159]

e) The "right to cancel" (Article 8). Cancelling a conflicting registration consequently extends the "priority right". Both require "knowledge", which differs from the Paris Convention, which does not require this for the priority right, protecting the "unaware" applicant or user.[160] This part of the Washington Convention was debated, as the Cuban delegate believed that the Latin American states were at a "great stretch" first to recognise the "use" as a right and then to require "knowledge" to avoid liabilities upon them.[161]

f) Article 12 covers the "right of the owner", whose right has been acquired by another contracting party, to cancel or refuse any registration or pending application by a third party.

g) The protection of "trade names or commercial names", be it the surname of individuals or name of business, without the need for registration and whether the name forms part of the trademarks as such.[162]

Aside from the topic of trademarks and trade names, the Washington Convention for the first time covered the topic of geographical indications

157 Christine Haight Farley, "The Protection of Geographical Indications in the Inter-American Convention," *The WIPO Journal* 6, no. 1 (2014): 52–53.

158 Article 7, General Inter-American Convention for Trademark and Commercial Protection 1929.

159 Farley, "The Pan-American Trademark Convention of 1929" (fn. 133), 64.

160 Farley, "The Pan-American Trademark Convention of 1929" (fn. 133), 66.

161 Farley, "The Pan-American Trademark Convention of 1929" (fn. 133), 76.

162 Chapter 3, Protection of Commercial Names General Inter-American Convention for Trademark and Commercial Protection.

(GI). This was seen as pioneering because before 1929 there were no plurilateral agreements that protected GIs as extensively as this convention. For instance, the Paris Convention of 1883 acknowledges indications of source and appellation of origin but does not define the terms, just the fact that they are protected areas of intellectual property. On the same topic, there is also the Madrid Agreement of 1891, which refers to "indication of sources" and its protection against false indication and/or deceptive indications, but no definition is provided. Therefore, the Washington Convention pioneered by presenting a broad GI chapter and setting up extensive protection.[163]

Chapter 5, titled "Repression of false indications of geographical origin or source", contains six articles. It uses the term "indication of geographical origin or source" and prohibits the use of them when false (but not when misleading) and extends to indirect protection not only to protect when used as a trademark or in labels but also when used in "packing or wrapping".[164] It notes in Article 25 that GIs are not subject to individual appropriation, and Article 26 demands for GIs to be used "exactly to the place in which the product" comes from. Another original article is Article 28, which directly addresses remedies "in the absence of" the nation not having a GI system in their domestic law.[165]

To sum up, while there were just a few countries signatory to the Paris Convention, indirectly the region was on track to have not only a harmonised intellectual property system among itself but also internationally.

3.3 *Seventh Conference (Montevideo, 1933)*

The governments of the American countries were to appoint representatives to serve at the Inter-American Commission on Industrial Property. This Commission was to elaborate a project of a convention on this specific topic, that is, intellectual property. The Committee IV on Economic and Financial Problems annotated in the program the "Inter-American Protection of Patents of Invention". However, many of the agenda topics annotated under this committee were thought to be "highly technical" and needed study by experts beforehand and thus should not be considered during the conference. For

---

163 Farley, "The Protection of Geographical Indications in the Inter-American Convention" (fn. 157), 54.

164 Articles 23 and 24, General Inter-American Convention for Trademark and Commercial Protection. See Farley, "The Protection of Geographical Indications in the Inter-American Convention" (fn. 157), 58.

165 Article 28, General Inter-American Convention for Trademark and Commercial Protection, notes that the laws "dealing with misbranding and the laws relating to trade marks or trade names" in domestic law shall apply instead.

instance, the Cuban delegation presented a draft convention on patents which was not discussed.[166] Therefore, the conference required the establishing of special conferences and congresses and the appointing of technical commissions.[167] The terms of the resolution urged to appoint representatives for the coming Inter-American Commission on Industrial Property and for the latter to draw up a project to be submitted to the Third Pan-American Financial Conference or a special one convened for this subject.[168] Added to this, there was a call for the creation of a commission to prepare a preliminary draft convention on copyright.[169]

At the Seventh Conference at Montevideo in 1933, the program pinned the "possibility of reconciling the Buenos-Havana and Berne-Rome Conventions".[170] The proposal was to adopt an Additional Protocol to the Conciliation Convention having the good practices of Havana and removing any discrepancies and ambiguities of the same.[171]

3.4 *Eighth Conference (Lima, 1938)*

The Eighth Conference at Lima in 1938 considered the project drafted in Montevideo, which was resolute to send delegates to the Diplomatic Conference in 1939 and for the delegates to consider the Montevideo draft.[172] This was followed by a draft resolution and a draft protocol to the Buenos Aires Convention by the United States to be submitted to the governments of the Pan-American Union, and for the Pan-American Union to prepare a definitive draft once the governments replied to the protocol.[173] This final draft was to be discussed during the Ninth Conference.[174] Resolution XXXIX "Inter-American Copyright" was put forward, which provided a convocation of the Conference of Experts on Copyright with 48 delegates from all member states.

---

166 *Report of the Delegates of the United States of America to the Seventh International Conference of American States*, Montevideo, Uruguay, 3–26 December 1933 (U.S. Government Printing Office, 1934), 33.

167 Manger, "The Pan American Union and the Conclusions of the Seventh International Conference of American States" (fn. 78), 79.

168 Manger, "The Pan American Union and the Conclusions of the Seventh International Conference of American States" (fn. 78), 83.

169 Manger, "The Pan American Union and the Conclusions of the Seventh International Conference of American States" (fn. 78), 84. See numeral 1, Inter-American Protection of Intellectual Property (Seventh Conference, Montevideo, 1933).

170 See Sanders (fn. 56).

171 Sanders (fn. 56), 426.

172 Sanders (fn. 56), 419.

173 Articles 1 and 2, Inter-American Intellectual Property (Eighth Conference, Lima, 1938).

174 Article 3, Inter-American Intellectual Property (Eighth Conference, Lima, 1938).

The Conference of Experts took place in 1946 in Washington as the war disrupted the aspirations to have it earlier.[175]

The Eight Conference in Lima did not adopt any resolution or protocol, and it was taken as the time for the American nations to come together and reemphasise the importance of working together under the same ethos.

3.4.1 Treaty of Montevideo on Intellectual Property of 1939

The conference was organised by the government of Argentina and Uruguay and a few countries attended with their delegates.[176] The aim was a re-examination of the treaties of Montevideo, and the results were the introduction of eight treaties and a protocol, ratified by Paraguay and Uruguay only. One of the said treaties was the Treaty on Intellectual Property of August 1939, which improved the protection of literary and artistic property and specified the categories of protected rights. Although it is named with a broad title, the treaty covers only copyright; no other intellectual property rights, such as trademarks, patents, and designs, are stated.[177]

The treaty contains 19 articles; Article 2 provides a non-exhaustive list of works (e.g. books, brochures, conferences, school or university lessons, speeches, addresses, sermons; musical compositions, with or without words, dramatic, dramatic-musical, choreographic, pantomimic, drawings, painting, sculpture, architectural composition, engraving, lithography, photography; cartographic, among others), in general, "an intellectual creation that is likely to be published or reproduced by any means". A missed opportunity to harmonise the term of protection is seen in Article 7, as it regulates that time is delimited by the country of origin and as such, "[no] State shall be obliged to recognize the right to literary or artistic property for a longer period than it applies to authors who obtain that right within". Besides, Article 9 asserts that speeches that are delivered at assemblies in front of Courts of Justice or public meetings do not need authorisation to be published by the press. While the treaty recognises the rights and limitations of copyright, Article 14 goes further to set up that for works that are considered contrary to public order or

---

175 Manuel S. Canyes, "Inter-American Conference of Experts on Copyright" *Bulletin of the Pan American Union* 80, no. 9 (1946): 501.

176 Argentina, Bolivia, Chile, Paraguay, Perú, and Uruguay. See further Ana Delić, "The Birth of Modern Private International Law: The Treaties of Montevideo (1889, amended 1940)" in *Oxford Public International Law* (online resources), accessed 13 October 2022, https://opil.ouplaw.com/page/Treaties-Montevideo.

177 James E. Ritch, Jr, "Codification of the Private International Law of the American Countries," *Inter-American Law Review* 7, no. 2 (1965): 395, 401.

morality, a state can prohibit the publication, reproduction, and circulation of such work. Finally, another article in line with the Berne Convention is the recognition of moral rights. Consequently, Article 15 sets up that regardless of economic rights, authors retain moral rights, including the paternity right, and the right to oppose mutilation or any kind of modification or deformation that may be considered harmful to the author's honour or reputation. The Treaty provides amendments that give clear protection to literal and artistic works.

4 A Dream That Did (Not) Come True

Latin America was looking for common aims in the region and the Pan-American Union launched in 1889 started this initiative. Within the Union, intellectual property negotiations were led by the United States, which was seeking recognition of its intellectual property rights. Mainly, during 1919–1939 the national intellectual property legislation in the region was based on both continental European intellectual property laws, due to their influence in their old colonies, and the regional intellectual property system based on the Pan-American conventions examined in this chapter.[178]

Based on the works of scholars who studied the period, the Pan-American conventions failed due to different reasons. Some have identified the costs of running the centralised Inter-American Bureaus in two different locations: Havana and Rio de Janeiro. The bureaus were established at the Third Conference (Rio de Janeiro, 1906). Another reasons for the failure of the early conventions, they argue, was the lack of an authentic IP system. Thirdly, they cite the increasing nationalistic attitude of states that favoured domestic rules.[179] Other scholars, such as Ladas, explained that that the United States was only developing its industry at the expense of other countries in the region, which incidentally had an abundant supply of raw material.[180] Therefore, it would appear that the United States' goal of promoting innovation was linked to markets, materials, and the protection of inventions and authors' privileges. At the same time, the other countries in the region looked outward, or at least the extent of innovation and market access was a form of direct foreign investment.[181] Additionally, the conventions neither offer consistency in the

178 Polido and Rosina (fn. 7), 433–34.

179 Polido and Rosina (fn. 7), 441.

180 Stephen Ladas, *The International Protection of Industrial Property* (Cambridge, MA: Harvard University Press 1930), 80.

181 Polido and Rosina (fn. 7), 444.

TABLE 6.1 Intellectual property legislation in place during the interwar period (1919–1939)

Pan-American countries	**Paris Convention**	**Berne Convention**	**Montevideo Convention on Patents 1889**	**Buenos Aires Convention on Literary and Artistic Copyright 1910**	**Inter-American Convention for the Protection of Inventions, Designs, and Industrial Models 1910**	**Bolivia Patent Convention (Agreement on Patents and Privileges of Invention) 1911**
Argentina			•	Signed (ratified in 1950)		
Bolivia				•	•	•
Brazil	•	•		•	•	
Chile				•		
Colombia				•		•
Costa Rica				•	•	
Cuba	•			Signed but not ratified		
Dominican Republic	•			•	•	
Ecuador				•	•	•
El Salvador				Signed but not ratified		
Guatemala				•	•	
Haiti				•	•	
Honduras				•	•	
Nicaragua				•	•	
Mexico	•			•		
Panama				•	•	
Paraguay				•	•	
Peru			•	•		•
Uruguay				•		
United States of America	•			•	•	
Venezuela						•

The 'dot' represents ratification.

SOURCE: THE WORLD INTELLECTUAL PROPERTY ORGANIZATION AND THE ORGANIZATION OF AMERICAN S

Caracas Convention 1911	Santiago de Chile Convention for the Protection of Commercial, Industrial, and Agricultural Trademarks and Commercial Names 1923	Havana Treaty on Private International Law 1928 (aka Bustamante Code)	Havana Convention revising the Buenos Aires Convention 1928	General Inter-American Convention for Trademark and Commercial Protection 1929 (aka the Washington Convention)	Treaty of Montevideo on Intellectual Property of 1939
		Signed but not ratified			
		•		Signed but not ratified	
	•	•		Signed but not ratified	
	•	•		Signed but not ratified	
		Signed but not ratified		•	
		•	•	Signed but not ratified	
	•	•		•	
	•	•		Signed but not ratified	
		•	•	Signed but not ratified	
		•			
	•	•	•	•	
	•	•		•	
		•		•	
		•	•	•	
		Signed but not ratified		Signed but not ratified	
		•	•	•	
	•	Signed but not ratified		•	•
		•	•	•	
		Signed but not ratified		Signed but not ratified	•
	•		•	•	
		•		Signed but not ratified	

minimum rights granted nor uniformity in intellectual property principles.[182] Nevertheless, the conferences during the interwar period promoted peace in the region and the sense of a "good neighbour" for some countries. The Monroe Doctrine also had a long-lasting impression, and the ideas and thoughts of Simon Bolivar persisted, that is, the unification of Latin America.[183]

5 The Re-alignment of Intellectual Property Rights

The relevant Inter-American and international conventions regarding intellectual property applicable in the region during the interwar period (1919–1939) are found in Table 6.1. This shows that the Pan-American Conferences developed a few conventions, treaties, resolutions, and protocols, trying to harmonise the law with the international intellectual property conventions which had not yet been signed by most states. Yet, it is noteworthy that only a few Pan-American Union members ratified and implemented the Pan-American conventions and treaties.

6 Conclusion

The interwar period (1919–1939) in the American nations was rather active in relation to the development of rules and norms for intellectual property and the desires for a harmonised and codified body of international law (public and private) of intellectual property. The Pan-American Union and the corresponding conferences provided a forum to discuss internal matters which were affecting many, and they were used as a good practice to learn about each other's experiences while establishing common policy. From the Fifth to the Eighth International Pan-American Conferences, together with the interim meetings between conferences, the American nations built closer relations. While there were some heated discussions and an interest for countries to preserve their own political agendas, the Pan-American forum provided a place to strengthen relations, aside from the attempt to create an American League of Nations. The cooperation and collaboration, however, were not only seen between governments, that is, an intergovernmental relationship; they also

182 Polido and Rosina (fn. 7), 441.

183 Carolina Pizarro Cortés, "The Decentring of the Historical Subject in the Contemporary Imaginary of the Independence Process," *Journal of Latin American Cultural Studies* 20, no. 4 (2011), 323.

included participation of professional associations and experts as well as private organisations. Attempts were made to address cross-border trade in commerce, and for copyright the aim was to align with the Berne Convention and to join its initiatives.

As a final remark, the Pan-American Union can be said to have been a political infrastructure for international cooperation that was continuous and reliable. The continuous conferences and the revision of projects as well as the interim meetings guaranteed the permanency of the Pan-American Union over the years.

Acknowledgments

I would like to thank Professor Christine H. Farley for her helpful comments on the draft chapter.

Bibliography

Alvarez, Alejandro. 'Latin America and International Law'. *American Journal of International Law* 3(2) 269–353 (1909).

Alvarez, Alejandro. 'Pan-Americanism as a Working Program'. *Proceedings of the Academy of Political Science in the City of New York* 7(2) 303–309 (1917).

Borchard, Edwin. 'The Committee of Experts at the Lima Conference'. *American Journal of International Law* 33(2) 269–282 (1939).

Canyes, Manuel S. 'The Pan American Union and Comparative Law Studies in the Americas'. *Bulletin of the Pan American Union* 76(12) 681–689 (1942).

Canyes, Manuel S. 'Inter-American Conference of Experts on Copyright'. *Bulletin of the Pan American Union* 80(9) 501–506 (1946).

Covarrubia, Patricia. 'The Madrid Protocol in Latin America: Is Colombia Changing Business Strategies or Acting as a Guinea Pig?' *European Intellectual Property Review* 35(1) 15–24 (2013).

Cox, George Howland. 'Was the Seventh Pan American Conference a Success?' *World Affairs* 97(1) 38–44 (1934).

Cutler, John Ward. 'The Treatment of Foreigners: in Relation to the Draft Convention and Conference of 1929'. *The American Journal of International Law* 27(2) 225–246 (1933).

Delić, Ana. 'The Birth of Modern Private International Law: The Treaties of Montevideo (1889, amended 1940)' in *Oxford Public International Law* (online resource) at https://opil.ouplaw.com/page/Treaties-Montevideo.

Duggan, Stephen P. 'Latin America, the League, and the United States'. *Foreign Affairs* 12(2) 281–293 (1934).

Farley, Christine Haight. 'The Pan-American Trademark Convention of 1929: A Bold Vision of Extraterritorial Meets Current Realities' in Irene Calboli and Edward Lee (eds), *Trademark Protection and Territoriality Challenges in a Global Economy* (Cheltelham: Edward Elgar, 2014).

Farley, Christine Haight. 'The Protection of Geographical Indications in the Inter-American Convention'. *The WIPO Journal* 6(1) 52–62 (2014).

Fenning, Karl. 'Trade Marks in Pan America as affected by the Havana Conference 1928'. *Journal of the Patent Office Society* 10(1) 483–489 (1928).

Fenwick, Charles G. 'The Coordination of Inter-American Peace Agreements'. *American Journal of International Law* 38(1) 4–19 (1944).

Finch, George A. 'Eighth International Conference of American States'. *American Journal of International Law* 34(4) 714–716 (1940).

Henn, Harry G. 'Interrelation between the Universal Copyright Convention and the Pan-American Copyright Convention'. *Bulletin of the Copyright Society of the U.S.A.* 2(4) 110–112 (1955).

Herrick, Arthur D. 'Denunciation of the Protocol for Inter-American Registration of Trade-Marks'. *Trademark Reporter* 35(1) 39–43 (1945).

Inman, Samuel G. 'Obstacles to Pan-American Concord'. *Current History* 17(5) 789–799 (1923).

Inman, Samuel G. 'Pan American Conference and their Results'. *The Southwestern Political and Social Science Quarterly* 4(4) 341–373(1924).

Ladas, Stephen. 'Pan American Conventions on Industrial Property'. *American Journal of International Law* 22(4) 803–821 (1928).

Ladas, Stephen. *The International Protection of Industrial Property* (Harvard University Press, 1930).

Ladas, Stephen. 'Inter-American Copyright'. *University of Pittsburgh Law Review* 7(4) 283–297 (1941).

Löhr, Isabella. 'Intellectual Cooperation in Transnational Networks: The League of Nations and the Globalization of Intellectual Property Rights' in Mathias Albert et al (eds), *Transnational Political Spaces: Agents – Structures – Encounters (History of Political Communication)* (University of Chicago Press, 2nd edn, 2009).

Manger, William. 'The Pan American Union at the Sixth International Conference of American States'. *American Journal of International Law* 22(4) 764–775 (1928).

Manger, William. 'The Pan American Union and the Conclusions of the Seventh International Conference of American States'. *Bulletin of the Pan American Union* 669(2) 77–94 (1935).

Morris, P Sean. 'Innovation Diplomacy: International Exhibitions and the Rise of Innovation in the Law of Nations' in P Sean Morris (eds), *Intellectual Property and the Law of Nations, 1860–1920* (Brill Nijhoff, 2022).

Pizarro Cortés, Carolina. 'The Decentring of the Historical Subject in the Contemporary Imaginary of the Independence Process'. *Journal of Latin American Cultural Studies* 20(4) 323–342 (2011).

Polido F B P and Rosina M S G. 'The Emergence and Development of Intellectual property Law in South America' in Rochelle Dreyfuss and Justine Pila (eds), *The Oxford Handbook of Intellectual property Law* (Oxford: OUP, 2018).

Preuss, Ori and Scarfi, Juan Pablo. 'Relaciones Internacionales, Identidades Colectivas y Vida Intellectual en Sudamérica, 1810–1945'. *Revista Complutense de Historia de América* 39(1) 15–21 (2013).

Report of the Delegates of the United States of America to the Fifth International Conference of American States, Santiago, Chile, March 25 to May 3, 1923 (U.S. Government Printing Office 1923).

Report of the Delegates of the United States of America to the Seventh International Conference of American States, Montevideo, Uruguay, December 3-26, 1933 (U.S. Government Printing Office, 1934).

Ritch Jr, James E. 'Codification of the Private International Law of the American Countries'. *Inter-American Law Review* 7(2) 395–418 (1965).

Rinaldo Jr, Alfred L. 'Scope of Copyright Protection in the United States under Existing Inter-American Relations: Abrogation of the Need for U.S. Protection under the Buenos Aires Convention by Reliance upon the UCC'. *Bulletin of the Copyright Society of the U.S.A.* 22(6) 417–436 (1975).

Roffe, Pedro. 'Evolución e importancia del Sistema de la propiedad intelectual'. *Comercio Exterior* 137(12) 039–1045 (1985).

Rowe, Leo Stanton. 'The Significance of the Seventh International Conference of American States'. *American Society of International Law Proceedings* 28(1) 34–40 (1934).

Rowe, Leo Stanton. 'The Eighth International Conference of American States'. *Bulletin of the Pan American Union* 72(11) 617–619 (1938).

Scott, James Brown. 'Editorial Comment: The Fifth International Conference of American States'. *American Journal of International Law* 17(3) 518–521 (1923).

Scott, James Brown. 'The Seventh International Conference of American States'. *American Journal of International Law* 28(2) 219–230 (1934).

Trindade, A A Cançado. 'The Inter-American Juridical Committee; an Overview'. *The World Today* 38(11) 437–442 (1982).

Trone, John. 'The Stimson Doctrine of Non-recognitions of Territorial Conquest'. *The University of Queensland Law Journal* 19(1) 160–164 (1996).

Sanders, William. 'International Copyright Protection: The Present Status'. *Bulletin of the Pan American Union* 73(7) 418–428 (1939).

Sheinin, Daniel. 'Argentina and the United States at the Sixth Pan American Conference (Havana 1928)'. *ISA Research Papers* 1 (1991).

Union of American Republics. 'The Eighth International Conference of American States'. *Bulletin of the Pan American Union* 72(11) 617–619 (1938).

Vasyliev, Ie O. 'The Beginning of International Legal Protection of Intellectual Property in the XIX Century'. BBC 94 Z 40 95–107 (2021).

Wright, Herbert. 'The Montevideo conference and organization for peace'. 97(2) *World Affairs* 100–103 (1934).

CHAPTER 7

Intellectual Property Rights in Fascist Italy: "Modernisation" and Continuity under Dictatorship

Giacomo Gabbuti, Caterina Sganga and Alessandro Nuvolari

1 Introduction: Continuity and Modernisation in Fascist Italy

Mussolini's Fascism promoted a new kind of autocratic regime, whose ideology aimed to combine "traditional", openly reactionary, and conservative policies and rhetoric. These included the realm of family and gender roles, in opposition to urbanism, and more broadly, in a celebration of the "irrational" in politics, a truly "modernistic" tendency towards future and change – and possibly its own peculiar "myth of science".[1] This is exemplified by the rationalist architecture characterising most public buildings.[2] Fascist rhetoric, and Mussolini's own expressions of it, could thus at the same time glorify the traditional virtues of frugal, rural Italy – such as the very important "habit", in times of crisis, of not eating too much, or many times per day, contrary to the vicious Anglo-Saxons,[3] and the novelties and gadgets produced by science and economic progress. Of course, this contradictory rhetoric evolved over time: while the Great Depression prompted a more "anti-capitalistic" turn, the collapse of the international economy – with both the "old" and "new" leading economies, the US and the UK, abandoning the Gold Standard between 1931 and 1933, and moving towards protectionism[4] – led the regime to depict "autarky"

1 L. Benadusi, "Il mito della scienza", *Storia d'Italia – Annali 16: Scienze e cultura dell'Italia unita*, ed. F. Cassata and C. Pogliano (Turin: Einaudi, 2011), 157.

2 G. Lucaroni, *Architetture di Storia. Fascismo, storicità, cultura architettonica italiana* (Rome: Viella, 2022).

3 A. Gagliardi, "Il mercato e i limiti dello Stato fascista", *Annali Fondazione Feltrinelli* LVI (2022), 74–75.

4 Most notably, with the Smoot-Hawley Tariff Act of 1930, and the "Imperial Preference" approved at the Ottawa conference of 1932, respectively; see D. Irwin, *Trade Policy Disaster: Lessons from the 1930s* (Cambridge, MA: MIT Press, 2011).

 | DOI:10.1163/9789004714663_009

as a necessary, largely externally induced policy for preserving the equilibrium of the balance of payments.[5]

Fascist autarky, recently "downgraded" by economic historians to something akin to a rhetoric form of industrial policy, was not built around meticulous planning and authoritative prescriptions for firms by the central government. These measures were instead implemented through mechanisms like tax breaks and comparable incentives, whose detail was actually significantly shaped by the strategies of major corporations – an approach described as "co-determined".[6] This is also proven by the key role played by "Corporatist" institutions, which were consolidated since the mid-1920s and became the sounding board through which the most significant social groups (especially firms and professionals) tried to shape public policies.[7]

Indeed, historians of interwar Italy have to deal with what has been described as a "recurring reality of the fascist *ventennio*", that is, "the gulf between words and facts, between programmes and realizations".[8] This is particularly true when examining the degree of actual "modernisation" of Italian society, culture, and economy – an aspect highlighted by some historians since the late 1960s under the influence of sociologists such as Barrington Moore and, in Italy, Gino Germani.[9] As Bruno Settis explained, the recent emphasis on the modernisation features of the fascist regime was somehow prompted by the traditional interpretations of Fascism as a "parenthesis" in Italian history.[10]

Writing in the 1970s, Ester Fano Damascelli observed that most anti-fascists, while rejecting this simplistic – and, most of all, self-absolving – interpretation of a regime that had been supported by many on anti-socialist, nationalistic, and opportunistic grounds ended up accepting this interpretation for

5 R. Petri, *Storia economica d'Italia. Dalla Grande guerra al miracolo economico (1918–1963)* (Bologna: il Mulino, 2002), 34–35.

6 M. Bertilorenzi, V. Cerretano, and M. Perugini, "Between Constraints and Opportunities: Big Italia Business and Autarky, 1934–1943", *Rivista di storia economica / Italian Review of Economic History* 38, no. 3 (2022): 303–36.

7 In light of the emphasis given by Fascism to the concept, a different word was (and is) used in Italian, *corporativismo*, to distinguish the Fascist sense from the broader *corporatismo* ("corporatism"); see L. Cerasi, "Corporatismo/corporativismo e storia d'Italia. Un percorso di lettura", *Contemporanea* 4, no. 2 (2001): 367–77. This distinction is lost in translation. For a discussion of Fascist corporatism between "myth" and practical consequences, see A. Gagliardi, *Il corporativismo fascista* (Rome-Bari: Laterza, 2010).

8 Gagliardi, *Il corporativismo fascista*, VII.

9 B. Settis, "Fascist economy: Private powers and State intervention", in *Rethinking the History of Italian Fascism*, ed. G. Albanese (London: Routledge, 2022), 104–31, 135–36.

10 Settis, "Fascist economy", 135–36.

economic doctrines and policies.[11] By virtue of the proliferation of monopolies and rents granted to backward agrarian and industrial élites, the Italian economy and society stagnated and isolated itself, in effect wasting two full decades, postponing its development until the post-WWII period. In fact, recent research in economic and social history has by and large confirmed Fano Damascelli's judgment, showing that the picture of deep stagnation covering the entire duration of the fascist regime is unwarranted. Gianni Toniolo has shown that while it is impossible to speak of a "developmental dictatorship"[12] or anything like a "fascist economy", this historical phase witnessed periods of relatively fast growth, as well as a "successful" increase of industrial output.[13] Furthermore, allegedly "fascist" policies were actually adaptations of broader trends developed by transnational circles, a result confirmed by global historians even in the case of the more interventionist economic policies of the 1930s.[14]

More generally, and beyond pure economic and industrial policies, the Fascist regime was ready to adopt "modernity" to strengthen its control on Italian society. Fascist reforms passed through intensive waves of new legislation.[15] In the domain of fundamental freedoms and civil and political rights, the "fascistisation" of Italian society was clearly reflected in controversial

11 E. Fano-Damascelli, "La 'restaurazione antifascista liberista': ristagno e sviluppo economico durante il fascismo", *Il movimento di liberazione in Italia* 104 (1971), 47–99.

12 G. Toniolo, *Economia dell'Italia fascista* (Rome-Bari: Laterza, 1980). The expression and the concept have been developed by A. James Gregor. For a discussion of this and similar interpretations, see the classic article by J.S. Cohen, "Was Italian Fascism a Developmental Dictatorship? Some Evidence to the Contrary", *Economic History Review* 41, no. 1 (1988): 95–113.

13 For an English survey of the recent economic history of the period, see G. Gabbuti, "'When We Were Worse off': The Economy, Living Standards and Inequality in Fascist Italy", *Rivista di storia economica / Italian Review of Economic History* 36, no. 3 (2020): 253–98.

14 See K.K. Patel, *The New Deal: A Global History* (Princeton: Princeton University Press, 2016). An exemplary case is the welfare state, which developed precisely in those decades. However, in Fascist Italy it had poorer results than elsewhere, being mostly guided by the intent of increasing social control; see C. Giorgi and I. Pavan, *Storia dello stato sociale in Italia* (Bologna: Il Mulino, 2021). While the regime claimed to have realised the "most modern welfare state in the world", the Fascist welfare provided only limited economic support to poor Italians, which was not enough to prevent a dramatic worsening of their living standards; see G. Gabbuti, "Those Who Were Better Off: Capital and Top Incomes in Fascist Italy", LEM Working Paper Series 2022/31, https://www.lem.sssup.it/WPLem/2022-31.html, 276–86. As stressed by Giorgi and Pavan, such drivers implied lasting, detrimental consequences for countries that developed welfare systems under similar conditions.

15 See M.A. Livingstone, P.G. Monateri, and F. Parisi, *The Italian Legal System* (Stanford: Stanford University Press, 2015), 33.

fascist laws. These eventually transformed fascist doctrines into blackletter law provisions; soon becoming flagships of the new regime, they reinforced its rhetorically autarkic message towards fellow European countries and the international community.[16] In economic and industrial policies, and even in substantial systemic reforms like the overhaul of the Italian Civil Code in 1942 and the Italian Criminal Code in 1939,[17] the array of measures implemented during the interwar decades displayed remarkably "moderate" characteristics. There existed a prevailing conservative disposition, evident in the weaker link between fascist declarations and the resulting legal regulations, so that in reality the observed continuity surpassed the anticipated change conveyed in the rhetoric. De Cecco and Migone noted that despite its nationalist and interventionist stances, for the whole of the 1920s and even the first part of the 1930s, Fascist Italy contributed to the attempt to restore the international economic order.[18] It was only after the definitive collapse of this order, in the aftermath of the Great Depression, that alternative routes were actually pursued.

Legal historians have often highlighted the relative independence that surrounded the work of the drafters of fascist reforms, and the powerful impact that the Pandectist legal scholarship had on them, as opposed to fascist doctrines.[19] In addition, the fascist regime did not refrain from abandoning autarky or self-isolation regarding specific economic matters, confirming, for instance, the participation of Italy in international treaties and conventions that established national treatment, principles of mutual recognition, and/or other forms of cooperation mechanisms between states in such sectors as intellectual property rights.[20] In this context, the fascist regime enacted a brand new

16 Among the most iconic (and, at least on paper, all-encompassing) examples of Fascist demographic policies, see C. Ipsen, "The Organization of Demographic Totalitarianism: Early Population Policy in Fascist Italy", *Social Science History* 17, no. 1 (1993): 71–108, ranging from fiscal and in-kind incentives to large family and special surtaxes on unmarried adult males, to the creation of institutions such as the ONMI devoted to the welfare of mothers and infants; see M.S. Quine, *Italy's Social Revolution: Charity and Welfare from Liberalism to Fascism* (Basingstoke: Palgrave, 2002).

17 R.D. 19 October 1930, no. 1398, Approvazione del testo definitivo del Codice penale, Official Gazette, no. 251, 26 October 1930; R.D. 16 March 1942, no. 262, Appovazione del testo definitvo del codice civile, Official Gazette no. 79, 4 April 1942.

18 M. De Cecco and G.G. Migone, "La collocazione internazionale dell'economia italiana", in *La politica estera italiana, 1860–1985*, ed. R. Bosworth and S. Romano (Bologna: il Mulino, 1991), 171–73.

19 Livingstone, Monateri, and Parisi, *The Italian Legal System*, 34.

20 V. Roghi, "Il dibattito sul diritto d'autore e la proprietà intellettuale nell'Italia fascista", *Studi Storici* 48, no. 1 (2007): 208.

patent act in 1939, followed by a reform of copyright law in 1941 – that is, in the most "fascist", autarkic moment of the interwar period.[21]

Little attention has been paid by scholars to the attitude of the fascist government vis-à-vis the international intellectual property system and foreign authors and inventors. Similarly, only a few contributions offer some hints on the real impact of fascist economic doctrines on the new patent and copyright systems, both in terms of internal policies and in terms of the positioning of Italy in the international arena.[22] This neglect is particularly striking if one only considers the role that patent law plays in the implementation of innovation and industrial policies (even more in an autarkic setting), and the impact that copyright law can exert on the development of national, cultural (and social) identities. Moreover, the power of the State to shape and control old and new media – a field in which clearly Italian Fascists were innovators, according to some historians[23] – has also been underexplored.

To fill this gap (and in the spirit of the edited collection to which this chapter is contributing), the following discussion aims to assess whether and to what extent Mussolini's economic agenda and views effectively influenced the drafting of copyright and patent legislation and the articulation of Italy's international intellectual property policies. In this context, the research will try to unveil eventual correlations between the degree of influence exerted by Fascism on copyright vis-à-vis patent law, and how copyright, as opposed to patents, differed in relevance for the Italian economy and the political agenda of the regime. After an introduction to the state of the art of intellectual property rights in Liberal Italy (that is, from the unification of the country in 1861 to the March on Rome in 1922), we will first discuss copyright law, as well as the key importance Mussolini attributed to the emergence and consolidation of a "fascist art and literature", both in old and new media, for the possibility this gave to consolidate the middle classes' support of Fascism and to use these media for propaganda. Then, in discussing the reforms of patent law, particular emphasis will be put on the interplay between patent policies and the economic and technological backwardness of a country traditionally "characterized by limited investments in scientific research and innovative activities".[24]

---

21 Indeed, even in this period the Fascist regime did not discourage multinational enterprises from operating in Italy, to the point of involving them in autarkic plans; see M. Bertilorenzi, "Un Nazionalismo immaginario? Multinazionali in Italia durante il fascismo", *Studi Storici* 61, no. 4 (2020): 935–58.

22 Roghi (fn. 20).

23 P.V. Cannistraro, *La macchina del consenso. Fascismo e mass media* (Rome-Bari: Laterza, 1975).

24 A. Nuvolari and M. Vasta, "The Ghost in the Attic? Italian National Innovation System in Historical Perspective, 1861–2011", *Enterprise & Society* 16, no. 2 (2015): 270.

This will also help to shed light on the role that the fascist regime wanted to – and did play – in international law-making around intellectual property, and the reasons underlining such a policy choice and its coherence vis-à-vis the fascist doctrine of economic autarky, and the impact of this position on national intellectual property law reforms.

2 The Background: Copyright and Patent Law in Liberal Italy

The roots of Italian copyright law can be traced back to the second half of the 1820s, when the Kingdom of Sardinia – the precursor of the Kingdom of Italy – began transitioning towards the governance principles of a modern constitutional state. This transformation process culminated in the Albertine Statute of 1848 and transformed the Kingdom into a constitutional monarchy, albeit with traits of the *ancien regime.* Censorship, for instance, was still exercised through the concession of letter patents to publishers in 1833.[25] The Royal Patents Act 1899/1825, for instance, removed authors' rights from letter patents. Although the act still regulated in detail the privileges granted to publishers by the king, its last provision exempted from the general regulation "authors of books and drawings, which will be published in our States [...], to whom it will be granted the exclusive right to print and sell their work for 15 years", with a right that was not gently conceded by the Court but stemming *ex lege* from the creation of the work. The shift was later reinforced by the new criminal code of 1839, which also offered protection to musical works and paintings.[26]

The law granted protection only to authors who published their works in the kingdom, with the clear aim to incentivise the local publishing industry. Exclusive rights were still those granted under the traditional privilege system, but the criminal code extended them to imports, and subsequent bilateral and international treaties progressively broadened their range. Moral rights were still just embryonic, being limited to an indirect protection of paternity through censorship rules, which required the mention of the author and publisher on every published work already from 1729.[27] This choice was confirmed by the Albertine Civil Code, enacted in 1838, which defined products of the human mind as the "property" of their authors, with a radical change compared to other codes of that age, which either did not mention authors' rights, such

25 Regie Lettere e Patenti (1833), 101.

26 L.C. Ubertazzi, "I Savoia e gli autori", *Quaderni di AIDA*, no. 3l (Giuffrè, 2000): 30.

27 Ubertazzi, "I Savoia e gli autori", 31.

as the Code Napoleon of 1803, or regulated them as work-for-hire contracts.[28] The Explanatory Memorandum to the Code explicitly justified the choice with the need to provide authors with a fully-fledged right, not a mere concession/privilege, to gain adequate remuneration for their works.[29]

In 1844, guilds were abolished, including those of the printing industry.[30] In 1848, state censorship was abolished and the press became free.[31] Between 1848 and 1860, Piedmont began to slowly industrialise, and in 1855 the first modern patent and trademark acts were enacted.[32] In this context, authors' rights played a pioneering role for the development of modern Italian intellectual property law. In fact, both interventions were inspired by liberal principles, and aimed at putting authors at the centre, emphasising their roles as independent thinkers for the construction of the national cultural milieu, in line with the moderate liberalism of the age.

From 1826 on, the development of copyright law in the Kingdom of Sardinia passed through bilateral treaties. The Savoy had a long tradition of diplomatic relations with other States, and they did not hesitate to use it to conclude treaties on literary property, which had a strong economic and political relevance for the kingdom. They did not enjoy uniform protection across countries or very often offer protection for foreign authors. This was also the case for pre-unitary Italian States – a circumstance that, due to the common spoken language, enormously facilitated literary piracy. In the two following decades (1830s–1850s), the Kingdom of Sardinia had a dense net of bilateral conventions,[33] the most important of which was the Austro-Sardinian Treaty (AST) of 1840, which stands out as a prime example of the approach embraced by the Piedmontese government.

28 ABGB, 1811.

29 "Motivi dei codici per gli Stati sardi", vol. II (Genova: Tipografia della Gazzetta dei Tribunali, 1856), XI.

30 "Regie Lettere Patenti con le quali S.M. sopprime le Università o Corporazioni di arti e mestieri, e ne abolisce gli statuti o regolamenti, conservando agli individui addetti ad una medesima arte la facoltà di esercitare in comune atti di religione e di carità e beneficenza", 14 August 1844, in *Raccolta degli atti del governo di S.M. il Re di Sardegna,* vol. XII (Torino: Stamperia Reale, n.d.), 153ff.

31 Editto sulla stampa, 26 March 1848, no. 695, in *Raccolta degli atti del governo di S.M. il Re di Sardegna,* vol. XVI (Torino: Stamperia Reale, n.d.), 233ff.

32 Law of 12 March 1855, no. 782 on patents; law of 13 March 1855, no. 836, reported by L. Franchi, Leggi e convenzioni sulle privative industriali, disegni e modelli di fabbrica, marchi di fabbrica e di commercio. Legislazione italiana, legislazioni straniere, convenzioni esistenti fra l'Italia e gli altri stati (Hoepli, 1904).

33 After the one with Austria (1840), the Savoy entered into bilateral agreements with France (1843, 1846, 1850), Belgium (1859), Spain (1860), and the UK (1860).

The AST protected literary and artistic works published in the two states, regardless of the citizenship of their authors. The subject matter also included theatrical pieces and translations, while exclusive rights covered reproduction and public performances but not translation and rearrangements; their duration was prolonged to 30 years *post mortem auctoris.* Dedicated rules covered specific types of works, and the Treaty also included provisions regulating enforcement (compensation, seizure and destruction of counterfeited goods, etc.) and exceptions. Overall, it ruled over all the main pillars of copyright law, using language that was more similar to the style of a domestic law, with directly applicable rules, than that of an international convention. Despite Article 25, in which the AST requested the two signatories to notify each other regarding the enactment of new laws in application of the Treaty, the governments and courts of the Kingdom of Savoy and of the other pre-unitary Italian States started using the AST as if it was directly applicable.[34] In fact, the Treaty was meant to protect foreigners against unauthorised reprinting of their works. However, most Italian commentators and courts viewed it as an instrument of uniform substantial law, particularly since Articles 1–24 of the AST never distinguished between authors on the basis of their nationality. Furthermore, preparatory works confirmed that the aim of the act was "to favour and protect arts and sciences, by guaranteeing [...] the property over their literary and artistic works", also in order to consolidate the reputation of the two contracting states vis-à-vis authors and the *classes eclairées*.[35]

In this way, the AST slowly substituted those Sardinian provisions still in force and regulating authors' rights, with the exception of the formalities requested by Article 18 of the Royal Patents of 1826, the definition of literary "property" offered by Article 440 of the Albertin Code, which allowed the application of general property law to copyright matters, and the sanctions introduced by the criminal code in 1839, declared unprejudiced by the AST.

Most publishers were not happy with the Code of Commerce of 1842, which did not consider at all the publishing industry and its particular features. This was especially the situation after the guilds were abolished. In fact, the relationship between authors/creators and publishers long remained unregulated,

34 In Tuscany, for instance, the AST was applied to solve the controversy between Manzoni and Le Monnier, while in Milan this was the case for the case of Ricordi/Sonzogno. See P. Esperson, *De' diritto di autore sulle opera dell'ingegno ne' rapporti internazionali. Studio di legislazioen comparata e di diritto internazionale convenzionale* (Unione Tipografico Editrice, 1899), 35.

35 A. Rabbeno, *Nuova legge e regolamento sui diritti degli autori delle opere d'ingegno* (Sonzogno, 1865), 19.

being anchored to a view of cultural creations as material products, the ownership of which (and thus the right for publishers to dispose of them) passed through a sale.[36] At the same time, censorship kept being intertwined with the regulation of authors' rights, backing the maintenance of rules that protected, for example, paternity and integrity (to guarantee the traceability of works and the fact that they were not modified after they were first cleared), or requested certain formalities for the protection to be granted (registration and deposit of a copy of every work published). However, the AST clearly brought within range of the copyright system of all pre-unitary Italian States key liberalist elements, such as the emphasis put on a broader notion of creative workers, and the need to grant them a fair remuneration over the exploitation of their works for them to be independent and contribute to the development of a national cultural milieu, in line with Illuminist views.

A similar development characterised the evolution of patent laws. The patent laws of the pre-unitary states, even if sometimes echoing the French patent law of 1791, may be regarded as an *ancien regime* system of "privileges" since they retained a strong examination component, which allowed significant discretionary power on the part of the state in the granting of patent rights.[37] In 1855, Piedmont enacted a completely new patent law drafted by the famous economist Antonio Scialoja, who undertook a thorough examination of the existing patent laws of other European countries. In the end, the Piedmont patent law of 1855 (revised in 1859) by and large adopted the French model. The law established a straightforward registration procedure, without examination. Following the French model, the law contemplated a duration of fifteen years with a flexible yearly fee structure, which provided the inventor the option to take a patent for any duration between one and fifteen years (in the French system, the inventor could opt for a duration of 5, 10, or 15 years). The higher degree of flexibility of the Piedmont law had the purpose of also making the system accessible to independent inventors with limited financial resources.[38] In general terms, the patent reform of 1855–1859 was important because it marked the definitive transition of the Italian patent system "from privilege to property".[39]

---

36 As it was still defined in a Turin court decision on 17 April 1848, reported in Rabbeno, *Nuova legge e regolamento sui diritti degli autori delle opere d'ingegno*, 99.

37 A. Nuvolari and M. Vasta, "The Italian Patent System during the long nineteenth century: From privileges to property in a latecomer industrializing country", *Patent Cultures. Diversity and Harmonization in Historical Perspective*, ed. G. Gooday and S. Wilf (Cambridge, UK: Cambridge University Press, 2020), 147–65.

38 Nuvolari and Vasta (fn. 37).

39 Nuvolari and Vasta (fn. 37).

After the unification of Italy in 1861, Sardinian laws were extended to all the new territories, with a process that was completed in 1870. The first unitary copyright law was introduced with Annex G of law of 2 April 1865 (no. 2215). Albeit being innovative in certain traits, it was quickly drafted, like many other laws of that time, and shaped on the basis of existing Sardinian provisions. Thus, privileges and censorship were no longer required, but the combination of the AST and Albertine Code. The Albertine Code, with its liberalist traits (the notion of literary "property"), the centrality of authors, and their freedom, a different interplay between authors and publishers/producers became the ultimate regulatory framework.

In 1864, the new unitary Kingdom of Italy instituted the *Ufficio della proprietà intellettuale* ("Office for intellectual property"), which had the task to grant intellectual property rights, and also operated as a physical place where creative works to be protected under copyright could be deposited and registered. Interestingly, the Office was initially anchored within the Ministry of Agriculture, Industry, and Commerce, where it remained until 1916,[40] indicating the inherent lack of a conceptual distinction between industrial property rights and authors' rights.

With the advent of the Berne Convention of 1886 – to which Italy was among the first signatories – and its first modification in Berlin in 1908, which introduced a new, independent definition of authors' rights that excluded the requirement of formalities of registration and provided for the national treatment and country of origin principles,[41] the need for a radical revision of the Italian copyright system could no longer be avoided.

A similar pattern also characterised the evolution of patent law. The Piedmont patent law was extended to the entire country in 1864.[42] The cheap fee structure made the system very accessible to independent inventors with limited financial resources, but also to foreign inventors. Overall, the Italian patent system was characterised by a significant "degree of openness" even before the Paris Convention. In 1864–1865, the share of foreign residents in total patenting was 50.7%, and by 1883 it increased to 63.8%.[43] Indeed, the Italian patent law of 1864 did not contain particular discriminatory norms against foreign inventors. As a result, the Paris Convention, which established the principle of national treatment (i.e. the right of foreign inventors to be treated as domestic inventors) and the "right of priority" (i.e. the right of foreign inventors to file

40 Roghi (fn. 20).

41 S. Ricketson and J. Ginsburg, *International Copyright and Neighbouring Rights: The Berne Convention and Beyond* (New York: Oxford University Press, 2022).

42 Law no. 1657, 31 January 1864.

43 Nuvolari and Vasta (fn. 37).

for a patent within six months from the date of the first application in their own country), did not represent a major discontinuity; accordingly, the share of foreign patents remained stable, slightly above 60%, until 1914.[44]

Against this background, it is now time to discuss the "fascist" nature of the reforms enacted by Mussolini's government in the interwar decades, starting with copyright.

3 How "Fascist" Was the Reform of Copyright Law?

In the field of copyright – the one on which historians have focused the most, due to its more obvious relationship with the fascist attempt to mobilise intellectuals for its propaganda – the regime faced a real "problem of definitions",[45] as well as systematisation of the entire discipline, which largely lagged behind international standards.[46] At the same time, authors and their unions had long been claiming an independent standing as a class – and later, in fascist terms, as a corporation – vis-à-vis the legal system.[47] Neglected artists, such as playwrights, composers, and independent writers, and later other creators – comprising part of the broader and heterogeneous "middle classes" that represented the backbone of fascist mass support[48] – demanded recognition of their rights against the powers of producers and publishers.[49] In the political

44 Nuvolari and Vasta (fn. 24; fn. 37).

45 P. Beneduce, "Privilegi e diritti dell'autore nel pensiero economico-giuridico della prima metà dell'Ottocento in Italia", in *Das Priliveg im Europeischen Vergleich*, ed. B. Dölemeyer and H. Mohnhaupt (Frankfurt am Main: Klostermann, 1999), 425.

46 Beneduce, "Privilegi e diritti dell'autore nel pensiero economico-giuridico della prima metà dell'Ottocento in Italia", 425.

47 See, for instance, R. Liguori (ed.), L'ordinamento sindacale fascista degli autori e scrittori. Raccolta di leggi, dati e scritti di Luigi Monelli, Corrado Govoni, Renato Liguori, Lorenz Ruggi ed Ettore Valerio (Rome: Cuggiani, 1942), VII. This notes the introduction by the head of the authors' Fascist Union (*Sindacato Nazionale Fascista degli Autori e degli Scrittori*) to a collection of laws and writings on this matter. On the professionals' Fascist trade unionism and its origins, see G. Turi, *Libere professioni e fascismo* (Milan: Franco Angeli, 1994).

48 On Fascism and the middle classes, see, among many, M. Salvati, "Da piccola borghesia a ceti medi. Fascismo e ceti medi nelle interpretazioni dei contemporanei e degli storici", *Italia Contemporanea* 194 (1994): 65–84; T. Baris, "Consent, Mobilization and Participation: The Rise of the Middle Class and Its Support for the Fascist Regime", in *In the Society of Fascists. Acclamation, Acquiescence, and Agency in Mussolini's Italy*, ed. R. Pergher and G. Albanese (London: PalgraveMacmillan, 2012), 69–85.

49 M.I. Palazzolo, "Un editore francese in lingua italiana: Louis Claude Baudry", *Studi Storici* 28 (1987): 206.

debate of the early years of the fascist regime, authors started acquiring a public status as "creative workers", whose efforts deserved the same protection as the material work they produced.[50] The great war did accelerate the "nationalisation" of many professional and intellectual categories,[51] and contributed to the separate analysis and treatment of heavy industry and technologies from the rising cultural industry, and thus between patents and copyright.

The first effects of these claims were the scholarly definition of authors' rights as personality rights; these reflected the numerous plagiarism claims filed in court by composers and musicians who did not find any other ground to protect their sheet music, adaptations, and performances.[52] Moreover, draft legislations in the early 1920s were aimed at expanding the subject matter of copyright to cover cinematographic and photographic works, and regulating publishing contracts and the relationship between authors and publishers of musical works.[53]

The fascist regime leveraged the debate on the mobilisation of intellectuals to build social consensus around its doctrines,[54] and it fully supported the constitution of the *Confederazione dei professionisti e degli artisti* ("Corporation for professionals and artists", or CPA) in 1923. The latter was used to aggregate all categories of intellectual workers as a tool to channel their claims,[55] and particularly those of authors, to support fascist cultural policies.[56] When the institutional and legal bases of the totalitarian regime were laid down in 1925, and the Manifesto of Fascist Intellectuals was published, collecting all the most important names of the Italian cultural milieu of that age, Mussolini decided to target all the remaining layers of intellectual "workers" by first organising

---

50 E. Piola Caselli, "Il diritto morale d'autore. Un rivolgimento costituzionale nella tutela delle opere di ingegno", *Diritto d'autore. Rivista giuridica trimestrale della società italiana degli autori ed editori* 1 (1930): 4.

51 See the various chapters in Turi (fn. 47) for the most representative groups, such as lawyers and engineers; on the field of scientific research, see R. Maiocchi, *Gli scienziati del duce. Il ruolo dei ricercatori e del CNR nella politica autarchica del fascismo* (Rome: Carocci, 2003).

52 A.G. Mantelli, *L'oggetto del diritto d'autore nella creazione musicale* (Rome: Athenum, 1930).

53 The bill was drafted by the IV Commission appointed by Ministerial Decree on 17 April 1917. The rapporteur was the famous copyright scholar Nicola Stolfi, and the bill was tabled by the Minister of Industry Belotti in 1921 before the Senate. See also Atti Parlamentari (1921), 317.

54 L. Mangoni, *L'interventismo della cultura* (Rome-Bari: Laterza, 1974).

55 See Turi (fn. 47). For a "live" account from a leader of Fascist unionism deeply involved with intellectual property rights, see G. Di Giacomo, *Intellettuali e Fascismo. Dieci anni di sindacalismo fascista tra professionisti e artisti* (Rome: Libreria del Littorio, 1932).

56 N. Tranfaglia and A. Vittoria, *Storia degli editori italiani dall'Unità agli anni Sessanta* (Rome-Bari: Laterza, 2000), 229.

regular meetings with them in theatres and other circles[57] and then engaging in a reform of Italian copyright law.

The Decree of 7 November 1925 (no. 1950) defined the object and content of authors' rights (all scientific, literary, artistic, and didactic works and their rearrangement, representations, and reproductions), their duration (50 years *post mortem auctoris*), and their protection via civil and criminal sanctions. The first unitary law from 1865 did not contain any list of protected works, while the new decree provided more concrete examples, fully in line with Article 2 of the Berne Convention, also including works such as engineering projects, drawings, and industrial designs. The reform also introduced provisions related to expropriation for public utility, alienation, and other forms of transfers, publicity, and State or other public ownership of works published with public funds (20 years). Rights of photographic works were limited to 20 years, while authors of scientific publications could retain their translation rights for 10 years. The government also took the opportunity to approve the Additional Protocol to the Berne Convention, which granted to every State member of the Berne Union the power to deny protection to authors from countries that did not grant enough reciprocal protection, unless such authors were domiciled in a country of the Union.[58] The decree was made into law on 18 March 1926, with few amendments that were still not enough to fill an important lacunae on the regulation of new technologies, such as the lack of protection of authors in the case of radio transmissions and the superficial definition of rights holders of cinematographic works.[59]

Most commentators praised the new law, skipping over its shortcomings and highlighting instead the landmark nature of the reform. One influential voice at the time was Eduardo Piola Caselli,[60] who advocated for the abandonment of the proprietary conception of rights of works, which privileged the position of publishers and producers, in favour of a greater centrality of moral rights. Authors were the most important, original rights holders, without need for any bureaucratic formality, independently of their political beliefs.[61]

57 One of these was the famous meeting at the Teatro Argentina. See R. Forges Davanzati, "Mussolini parla agli scrittori", *Nuova Antologia* LXVIII, fasc. 1468 (1933), 187.

58 Atti Parlamentari (1922), 321.

59 A. Giannini, "Il diritto dell'artista esecutore", Diritto d'autore, *Rivista giuridica trimestrale della società italiana degli autori ed editori* 2, no. 2 (1932): 163.

60 On the figure of Piola Caselli, see C. Melloni, "Eduardo Piola Caselli, magistrato e giurista", *Le Carte e la Storia* 2 (2008): 128–48.

61 E. Piola Caselli, "Il nuovo regolamento interno ed internazionale del diritto esclusivo di traduzione secondo la legge 12 giugno 1931, n.774, di approvazione della Convenzione di

Interestingly, studies on the history of Italian publishing industry do not discuss the 1926 law at length, but instead analyse the effects of censorship and control over cultural outputs. The reason is quite simple. In the words of the secretary of the Fascist Association of Italian Publishers, the reform of copyright law did not "revolutionize the subject [...], the evolution of which is slow with regard to its fundamental principles [...], but updated its rules in line with forty years of progress, and coordinated them with those of other States and with international conventions".[62] This "un-exceptionalism" vis-à-vis other European democracies made commentators believe that the copyright reform was only one among the numerous acts drafted by conservative scholars under the influence of liberal ideologies, and thus they were not relevant for the construction of social consensus and the new regime.[63] In fact, as pointed out by Vanessa Roghi[64] the rhetoric surrounding the broadening of protected authors and their new centrality in the system[65] showed how much the key pillars of the 1926 copyright reform were an integral part of the "consensus mechanism" deployed by the regime, and anticipated the corporatist idea of the new society that the fascist regime wanted to build. This is well substantiated by Article 35 of the new copyright act, which conferred significant annual funding "to encourage authors, entities and institutions which have produced or promoted works of particular quality and importance for culture and industry". This also entailed funding their membership in the Italian Society of Authors and Publishers (SIAE), and thus in the National Confederation of Fascist Unions of intellectual workers and artists. The 1926 act also modified the status of the SIAE, transforming it into a public law entity, in line with its corporatist policies, and stripping away from members their right to elect the SIAE's governing bodies, which became subject to political appointment.[66] When the Ministry of Corporations was set up in 1926, the new copyright act also moved the Office for Intellectual Property under its jurisdiction, confirming the full integration of fundamental aspects of the copyright system, such as the granting of rights and authors' remuneration, within the tangles of the new corporatist society.

Roma, 2 giugno 1928", *Diritto d'autore, Rivista giuridica trimestrale della società italiana degli autori ed editori* 2 (Roma: 1931), 37.

62 C. Marrubini, "Le nuove disposizioni sul diritto d'autore", *L'Italia che scrive* 9, no. 1 (1926): 1.

63 G. Turi, *Il fascismo e il consenso degli intellettuali* (Bologna: Il Mulino, 1980).

64 Roghi (fn. 20), 216.

65 See, for instance, the emphasis put by Augusto Turati (1926) – at the time, just appointed Secretary of the National Fascist Party – on the importance of the new copyright act for the production of quality literature for the benefit of "Italians at home and abroad".

66 Tranfaglia and Vittoria (fn. 56), 139.

The mid-1920s marked a decisive shift in economic policies from a laissez-faire attitude towards protectionism. In line with insights by observers[67] at the Rome Conference of 1928, which was convened to amend the Berne Convention, the fascist regime sought to present itself as the government that introduced the most advanced copyright legislation. In doing so, it took full credit from the international status of scholars, such as Piola Caselli; this was fully consistent with the pre-fascist, liberal doctrine but still aimed at introducing into the Convention ameliorations also inspired by other national laws. And even more strikingly, it advocated for the protection of individual authors across borders and without discrimination, as opposed to radically protectionist approaches such as those advanced by the French government, which instead pointed to the need to protect their national intellectual property rights, particularly against the "invasion" of US works.[68] Fascist Italy tried, at least in the 1920s, to gain credit abroad by adhering to the restoration and improvement of an international economy, of which agreed-upon standards of property rights were a crucial component, rather than revolutionising them or isolating Italy into autarky.

Remarkable innovations by the Rome text were, inter alia, Article 2*bis* on the power of the state to exclude protection of political speeches and speeches delivered in the course of legal proceedings; Article 6, on the possibility of restricting protection in the case of works made by nationals of certain non-Union countries; Article 6*bis*, on the protection of moral rights of paternity and integrity, which left out the right of divulgation; and Article 11*bis*, introducing rights of broadcasting and leaving to Member States the possibility to submit those to compulsory licenses, without prejudice to moral rights and under the payment of a fair remuneration. In line with its announced positions, the Italian government played a key role in the introduction of the two latter provisions – moral rights on the basis of its own legislation and the emphasis put on them by the fascist rhetoric, and the rights of broadcasting as a response to the national debate on the lacunae of the current legislation.

In the 1930s, other laws introduced in the copyright act a number of changes which were required by specific stakeholders, such as the extension of the term of protection for rights of display and the performance of artistic works, or the shift from automatic resolution to the author's right to terminate a publishing contract when the publisher did not publish, reproduce, or represent the work by the term fixed by the court. However, one of the hardest points to solve was

---

67 De Cecco and Migone (fn. 18).

68 E. Valerio, *Disposizioni sul diritto d'autore. Conferenza internazionale di Roma sul diritto d'autore 7 maggio–2 giugno 1928* (Rome: Libreria del Littorio, 1930), 113–14.

the regulation of rights of public performance vis-à-vis radio broadcasting, and even more the determination of the fair compensation to be paid for the performance of musical works by orchestras and radios in public places. In 1938, Royal Decree no. 2151 transformed into a mere remuneration right the rights of radio broadcasting of new musical works by State-authorised entities, on the basis of the principle of expropriation for public utility and of the superior interest of the State in disseminating such works of authorship to any social class in any part of the national territory.[69]

Significantly, the ratification of the Rome text of the Berne Convention also led to the equalisation of translation rights and authors' rights in terms of duration. Since Italy did not sign the Berlin reform of the Berne Convention, Article 27 of its 1926 law could still provide for a limited term of protection for the former (10 years). In this way, Italian authors enjoyed a stronger protection than foreign authors, since their translation rights were protected as long as author rights in most of the countries of the Berne Union, while foreign authors enjoyed their translation rights in Italy for a much shorter time. Despite the positive effect of such discrimination for the national cultural milieu, for the broader possibility to translate for free and disseminate foreign works in Italy the fascist government still maintained its non-discriminative and open approach during the Rome Conference, and accepted and implemented the new provision and its negative trade-off, circumscribing the shorter duration of translation rights to scientific works only.[70]

The real turn in the approach to the function of copyright and the role of authors for the Fascist State came only in 1936, with the establishment of the Ministry of Popular Culture (Minculpop),[71] which was entrusted with the power of coordinating, controlling, and directing all media (press, theatres, cinema, radio) in order to align them with the political and educational needs of the regime. The Ministry also coordinated all funding initiatives for single authors, who could also be commissioned to produce articles, scripts, and sheet music by the government; in 1936, it got assigned all the functions in the field of copyright covered by the Office for Intellectual Property, and also the monitoring of the SIAE.

The reaction of publishers was to rely less and less on public funding and turn to "commercial" funds to maintain their independence. Their historical clash with authors was thus solved not by corporatism – as the regime wanted – but

---

69 E. Santoro, "L'evoluzione legislativa in materia di radiodiffusioni circolari: notizie e spunti", Il diritto delle radiodiffusioni e delle telecomunicazioni I (1969), 3–52.

70 Piola Caselli (fn. 61), 2.

71 P.V. Cannistraro, *La macchina del consenso. Fascismo e mass media* (Rome-Bari: Laterza, 1975).

by the need to cooperate on market strategies. As a response, the Minculpop reacted by instituting a commission to initiate a reform again the Italian copyright act, with the aim not only to update it vis-à-vis new technologies and to ameliorate enforcement measures but also (and especially) to introduce new rules to regulate the relationship between producers, publishers, and authors in line with the principles of the corporatist State.[72] The commission, constituted by a restricted group of fascist scholars (inter alia, Valerio De Sanctis, legal counsel of the SIAE, and the aforementioned Carlo Marrubini, director of the Fascist Federation of Publishers), was explicitly asked to tilt the internal balance of the copyright system back towards publishers. This turn cracked the strong link between authors and the regime, already severely hurt by the decision to subordinate the possibility to exercise intellectual professions to the membership of related corporations. At the same time, it did not bring any idyllic relationship with publishers, since in parallel to it, the Minculpop also instituted a commission for "books cleansing", which strengthened to the maximum extent possible the grip over independent editors.

The change in the approach of the fascist regime to copyright and to its role in regulating cultural production and the interplay between its main actors (authors, other creators, performers, publishers, producers, and other commercial players), inspired by the corporatist doctrine, went hand in hand with a number of protectionist measures taken to incentivise national cinema and literature against foreign "products". Mussolini wanted the new copyright system to become "a strategic field for the fascist legislative policy", where the imprinting on the new regime could be seen in the "maintenance and consolidation of the protection of intellectual work [...], coordinating it to the objectives of the State, and complemented by the corporatist legal order".[73] At the same time, the main seat of the Italian Society of Authors – now called the Italian Society of Authors and Publishers (SIAE) – was moved from Milan, the economic heart of Italy, to Rome, its political centre. The SIAE statute was amended in 1927 and in 1931 to strip from members the possibility to elect the management, a competence that was entrusted to the Italian Confederation of Fascist Trade Unions.[74] The first issue of the SIAE's Bulletin, which was transformed from a journal collecting authors' instances and views into a law review led by authoritative fascist legal scholars, became influential.[75] In its first Introduction, its

---

72 Roghi (fn. 20), 236.

73 E. Piola Caselli, "Autore (diritto di), in Dizionario di politica, a cura del Pnf", vol. I, A-D (Treccani, 1940), 254.

74 M.I. Palazzolo, *La nascita del diritto d'autore in Italia. Concetti, interessi, controversie giudiziarie (1840–1941)* (Roma: Viella, 2013), 188–89.

75 SIAE (1930).

new director highlighted that achieving a real and full protection of authors could have not been possible before Mussolini had tackled the issue "within the broader framework of the corporativist legal order, so that the interests of authors and publishers could be balanced, subordinating both to the general national interest".[76]

This was the background in which the new reform of the copyright act, introduced in 1941 with Royal Decree no. 633 as a *legge fascistissima* ("the most fascist law", a term used to identify those acts which could be understood as flagships of the regime in its last years) was built. The new Italian copyright statute did not intervene in the basic pillars of the 1925 act but adapted them to include new technologies (mostly phonograms and radio). Its main goals were to reinforce copyright enforcement with more articulated civil and criminal sanctions, and to introduce new provisions to regulate the relationship between authors, producers, and publishers[77] with a particularly detailed definition of rights and obligations of the new "contratto di edizione" (publishing contract, art. 118–135). Most of the rules were declared mandatory and could not be overridden by a contract, and a key role was attributed to the Minculpop, which substituted the judicial authority in solving conflicts between rights holders. The Minculpop also became responsible for the enforcement of moral rights in the public interest (art.23 l.aut.), for the selection of authors and performers for the attribution of cultural prizes, and for the designation of the president of the Italian Entity for Authors' Rights, which replaced the SIAE from 1942.[78]

4 The Reform of Patent Law: A Real Autarky in the Making?

As in the case of copyright protection, throughout the Liberal period there was a strong call for the reform of the patenting system inherited from the Kingdom of Piedmont. Some have noted[79] that a first commission to reform the patenting system had been appointed in 1906, but the resulting report, presented to Parliament in 1908, was never discussed. Moreover, a new commission,

76 G. Bottai, "Parole introduttive", in "Il diritto d'autore. Rivista giuridica trimestrale della SIAE", I (1930), III.

77 E. Piola Caselli, "Il contratto di edizione", in Enciclopedia Italiana, vol. XIII (Milano: Treves-Treccani-Tumminelli, 1932), 475ff.

78 E. Valerio and Z. Algardi, *Il diritto d'autore. Commento teorico-pratico alla nuova legge italiana 22 aprile 1941*, no. 633 (Milano: Giuffré, 1942), 411ff.

79 M. Vasta, "Capitale umano e ricerca scientifica e tecnologica", *Storia d'Italia. Annali 15. L'industria*, ed. F. Amatori, D. Bigazzi, R. Giannetti, and L. Segreto (Turin: Einaudi, 1999), 1108.

appointed in 1917, also ended up in no actual reform. After the March on Rome, the Minister for the National Economy, the liberal physicist Orso Mario Corbino, who was involved in the development of hydroelectric energy in Italy,[80] presented his proposal in 1924. However, according to Vasta, the government withdrew the project because "it did not introduce fundamental changes to the 1859 law".[81] After signing the Hague Agreement on 6 November 1925, the government, at the request of the associations of industrialists, "extended to Italian citizens and subjects all benefits in terms of industrial [intellectual] property granted and about to be granted to foreigners in Italy by any international agreement".[82] In 1926, after a project drafted by the Italian delegates to the Hague international conference resulted in a new stalemate, the Parliament instructed the government to reform the patent law.[83] At this time, the minister responsible for the matter was the engineer Giuseppe Belluzzo, an author of important works and inventions involving steam turbines.[84] However, the reform of patenting rights did not become a central issue for the fascist government. In the late 1920s, a major fascist unionist and protagonist of the copyright debate, Giacomo Di Giacomo, increased his calls for actions "on the important issue of inventors and inventions".[85] While expressing their wishes for a quick resolution of the matter, however, industrialists showed all their concern for the "practical difficulties in implementing the new institute" of a novelty test, like the ones adopted in other States, and noted:

80 E. Amaldi and L. Segreto, "CORBINO, Orso Mario", Dizionario Biografico degli Italiani, Vol. 28 (1983), https://www.treccani.it/enciclopedia/orso-mario-corbino_(Dizionario-Biografico)/.

81 Vasta (fn. 79).

82 *Assonime* (1927), 231. Since the early twentieth century, *Assonime* was the association of Italian listed companies; while technically different from *Confindustria*, created in the same year as the federation of industrial and tertiary enterprises, the two associations lobbied together on technical issues such as intellectual property rights, and even merged their technical offices in the interwar period.

83 Legge 25 novembre 1926, no. 2032. Delega al Governo di emanare norme legislative di riforma delle disposizioni vigenti sulla proprietà industriale, GU no. 285, 11 December 1926.

84 Belluzzo's appointment at the National Economy, together with Giuseppe Volpi as Finance Minister, was regarded by contemporaries, as well as by most historians, as a sign of the increasing political weight of electricity producers. See R. Maiocchi, "Il ruolo delle scienze nello sviluppo industriale italiano", in *Storia d'Italia. Annali 3. Scienza e Tecnica*, ed. G. Micheli (Turin: Einaudi, 1980), 1938; M. Minesso, *Giuseppe Belluzzo. Tecnico e politico nella storia d'Italia 1876–1952* (Milan: Franco Angeli, 2013).

85 "I diritti degli inventori", *Il Lavoro d'Italia*, 29 November 29, 1928, reproduced in Di Giacomo (fn. 55), 199–203.

> while not excluding, *a priori*, the gradual creation of a suitable and well organised administrative body, we strongly believe this should not be improvised, and to proceed with the reform, once admitted the principle, with great caution, to balance the need of an immediate protection of inventions and their economic exploitation, with the longer investigations on its novelty.[86]

It was only in 1930 that a new commission was appointed.[87] In the following years it worked on a proposal that incorporated the major request of a new, pugnacious association.

Indeed, among the most vocal proponents of a "fascist", radical reform of intellectual property rights were the "inventors", and especially Artemio Ferrario, the first and only secretary of the *Associazione Nazionale Fascista degli Inventori* ("National Fascist Association of Inventors", or ANFI). The ANFI was launched in 1931, within the CPA, which had been responsible for organising the various unions of authors and professionals since the early 1920s.[88] Contrary to other professions, this small group and its official organisation do not seem to have attracted historians' attention; however, its own existence was linked to the necessity of introducing some sort of State control on patent quality and innovative content, making them a relevant actor in the evolution of their legal protection in interwar Italy.

The matter of an "invention" and an "inventor" became a heated discussion in one of the first issues of *Le professioni e le arti* – the CPA "monthly bulletin".[89] For instance, it has been noted that the difficult definition of what constitutes an "invention" – and thus an inventor – was not easily defined.[90] As a result of a "linguistic, rather than interpretative, difficulty", according to their secretary, the inventors "happen to be in a position of quarantine and exile, with respect

86 See *Assonime* (1927), 233.

87 Vasta (fn. 79), 1109.

88 As reported by Di Giacomo (fn. 55), 41, "inventors" were listed since 1924 as the last of the thirteen "categories of professionals and intellectuals" organised "in National, Provincial and Municipal Unions" by the CPA.

89 The magazine was issued from December 1931, initially under the direction of Emilio Bodrero, undersecretary for education in 1926–1928 and 1941, and then by the high-ranking Fascist Alessandro Pavolini; its editorial board featured notable figures, such as the futurist author Filippo Tommaso Marinetti – who wrote a short article on copyright in the first issue; see F.T. Marinetti, "Verso un diritto d'autore perpetuo", *Le professioni e le arti – Bollettino mensile della confederazione nazionale professionisti e artisti* 1, no. 1 (1931): 10.

90 A. Ferrario, "L'inquadramento Sindacale degli inventori", *Le professioni e le arti – Bollettino mensile della confederazione nazionale professionisti e artisti* 1, no. 1 (1931a): 13–14.

of all other intellectual producers"; this led to a paradoxical, "painful condition of inferiority with respect to all other intellectuals".[91] While representing three categories of associates (patent holders; those "employed in industrial firms", whose contractual obligation to the employees implied inventive activities; and those who, "while not holding patents yet, study, make practice and experiences, in order to do so"), one of the ANFI's major objectives was to elevate the social and economic status of genuine inventors by "eliminating" those responsible for their dubious reputation – "the plagiarisers, deceived, fanatics, and those acting in bad faith". Not surprisingly, one year later, at the first national conference of fascist inventors,[92] it was stressed that the ANFI "placed technical examination of applications at the foundation of its whole action". This was at odds with the aforementioned fears by industrialists, who in 1930 stressed their preference for the "English system" of novelty testing, "particularly suited for our country current conditions, balancing a relative simplicity with a satisfactory completeness".[93] Fascist inventors required not only an examination of "novelty" but also one of "merit", aimed at "determining whether the inventive production has practical value, and how much".[94] Similar examinations were necessary, first of all, to overcome the "barrier of diffidence and misunderstanding" erected "between inventors and the general public" by "bureaucracy, finance and industry" in their "grim and hasty" examination of innovations. Moreover, the creation of the ANFI, with its "programme of support and protection" of associates, made it necessary to scrutinise applicants to select those genuinely deserving support.

In the following, we will draw on Ferrario's writings and, more broadly, on the official outlets of both the ANFI[95] and the CPA, to integrate and enrich the historical appraisal of the debate on patent reform in 1930s Italy, and intended to make links with the necessities of the Italian economy in this period. In stark contrast with the very limited attention devoted to the issue by the fascist political press,[96] as well as major economic journals, a scrutiny of these

91 Ferrario, "L'inquadramento Sindacale degli inventori", 13–14.

92 A. Ferrario, "La commissione centrale per l'esame delle invenzioni", *L'inventore italiano – Rivista mensile dell'Associazione nazionale fascista inventori* 2, nos. 9–10 (1932b): 197–202.

93 *Confindustria* (1930), 440.

94 A. Ferrario, "Giudizi ed indagini sulle invenzioni", *Le professioni e le arti – Bollettino mensile della confederazione nazionale professionisti e artisti* 2, no. 7 (1932): 2–5.

95 First launched in 1931 as *L'inventore italiano* ("The Italian inventor") and from its fourth volume relabelled as *Le attualità scientifiche* ("Scientific Latest News"), and eventually from 1937 to 1942 as *Ingegni e congegni* ("Whizzes and Devices"), the monthly maintained throughout the years a progressive numeration of issues under Ferrario's direction.

96 Especially in the later "autarkic" years, it is hard to find mention to patent rights reforms, or peculiar Fascist views on the matter, in the table of contents of major Fascist political

magazines makes it possible to understand the motivations behind the reform proposals, and to understand their continuous postponement and eventual failure. As noted by Turi,[97] the "corporatist" nature of this form of "professional press", inevitably attempting to exert political pressure on legislators to improve the position of its associates, reveals conflicts between professions, pressure groups, and the like behind the official statements.

In June 1932, a draft proposal[98] that incorporated the ANFI's major requests – the introduction of novelty and merit exams, and the moral rights of the inventor working as an employee – was discussed by the National Council of Corporations.[99] Some of the debates on the draft were captured in the magazine of the CPA.[100] Notably, after the introduction of the author of the proposal – the President of Rome's Court of Appeals (at the time, the first president), among the organisers of the first "Fascist Law Congress"[101] – the founder and General Secretary of the *Confindustria* association, MP Gino Olivetti, was the first to speak. While stressing the "importance, also political" of the reform, Olivetti "proposed not to state any deadline for the application of the law", postponing that to the "preparation of the necessary technical staff", and not to distinguish in a first phase between "foreign and Italian inventions", making both subject to the preventive examination.[102] "Naturally", *Confindustria* also opposed the idea of rewarding the inventions made by employees of industrial firms (the second type of ANFI members). This has been a long-standing position by Italian industrialists, where three principles have been identified.[103] The three are:

reviews, such as *Gerarchia*, founded in January 1922 and directed by Mussolini himself, or *Critica Fascista*, directed by Giuseppe Bottai, one of the major figures of the debate and practice of corporatism, and thus heavily involved with economic matters.

97 Turi (no. 47), 35.

98 D. Faggella, "Relazione e disegno di legge per la protezione della proprietà industriale", Atti della Assemblea generale del Consiglio Nazionale delle Corporazioni 1 (Rome, 1932).

99 Established by royal decrees number 1131 (2 July 1926) and 1347 (14 July 1927) but inaugurated only in 1930, the National Council of Corporations was, in Mussolini's own words, "to the Italian economy what the Staff is in the Armed Forces – the thinking brain which prepares and coordinates"; see B. Mussolini, "Per il Consiglio Nazionale delle Corporazioni", 21 aprile 1930, *Opera Omnia, Vol. XXIV: Dagli accordi del Laterano al dodicesimo anniversario della fondazione dei Fasci (12 febbraio 1929– 23 marzo 1931)*, ed. E. Susmel and D. Susmel (Roma: La Fenice, 1930).

100 "Il Consiglio Generale delle Corporazioni. La prima seduta inaugurate dal Capo del Governo", *Le professioni e le arti* 2, no. 6: 22–31.

101 "Il Congresso Giuridico Fascista", *Le professioni e le arti* 2, no. 5: 56.

102 "Il Congresso Giuridico Fascista", 22.

103 *Confindustria* (1930), 440.

> a) when the invention is part of the customary duties of the employee, the patent should belong to the employer, possibly mentioning the inventor's name and granting him an appropriate reward when it has relevant value; b) when the invention, not part of the employee's usual activity, is in the employer's field of activity and some relation with the employee's activity in the firm, the employer should have pre-emption rights; c) when the invention is obtained through the means or contracts of the employer, the patent should go to the employee, but the employer should receive an appropriate compensation.[104]

But as the reports from the council meeting indicated, Grisostomi-Marini[105] (along with other founding members of fascist lawyers' associations), while "applauding the overall spirit of the project", was more sensible to the firms' positions, stressing how "the same industrial world will be able of discriminating against inventions with no practical use". Indeed, the technical office[106] had "carefully analysed the proposal" and sent a "memorandum" to the Minister of Corporations, with "the apprehensions raised by the proposal in the industrial world". In the ANFI's magazine, as argued by one writer,[107] the point was that "Italian inventors" faced hurdles in the absence of such exams, and the Italian patent "has no value", apart from "establishing a date for eventual property claims", to the point that "investors always look for the German patent, considered by the public the most serious and authoritative". In line with its 1859 rationale, the Italian law merely had the "valid and positive" value of "effectively extending to Italy the protection granted by foreign patents obtained

---

104 *Confindustria* (1930), 440. Later was added the possibility of leaving this matter to private contracts, such that the law should intervene only in absence of specific clauses. Another point of *Assonime* and *Confindustria* was opposition to the intellectual protection of "scientific invention", a matter considered "not yet ready for legislation"; see *Assonime* (1928), 68. In both these matters, the positions of Italian industrialists actually advocated changes in law and jurisprudence that had already taken place in more technological advanced countries. For a detailed study on the regulation and jurisprudence concerning inventors-employees in the US in the period 1870–1930, see C. Fisk, *Working Knowledge: Employee Innovation and the Rise of Corporate Intellectual Property, 1800–1930* (Chapel Hill, NC: The University of North Carolina Press, 2009). Note that in 1936, only 13% of Italian patents were taken by firms, while the corresponding share for foreign inventors was 36%; see G. Domini, "Innovation and business performance in Italy, 1913–1936", *Rivista di storia economica/Italian Review of Economic History* 39, no. 3 (2023): 287–330.

105 Di Giacomo (fn. 55), 31.

106 *Confindustria* (1932), 407.

107 A. Ferrario, "Gli inventori davanti ai loro giudici", *L'inventore italiano – Rivista mensile dell'Associazione nazionale fascista inventori* 2, no. 5 (1932): 85.

through novelty examination", resulting in the "countless factories that in our country work using foreign procedures and patents". Leaning on a quintessential argument of fascist and nationalist rhetoric – that is, Italians' "innate ingenuity"[108] – the "qualitative and quantitative insufficiency of Italian inventions" had to be explained by "admitting an extraordinary, depressive influence of our law on industrial property".

Against these proposals, the influential, former Minister Belluzzo[109] suggested a much milder update of the existing laws to avoid "printing patent grants with no rhyme or reason, with badly designed text, full of errors".[110] For Di Marzio, this was in stark contrast with the spirit of the mandate he had asked for and received as a Minister, finally with the more recent entrustment of an authoritative commission. Industrial owners did not like all invention, because some of them, by transforming the production, "disturb the periodic amortisation of plants and machineries", whose cost was increasing as a result of "serial production".[111] Thus, the opposite could happen with workers, displaced by automation. For this reason, Fascist Italy's corporatism was necessary to "equally represent" and balance the interests of all categories.

Despite the opposition of industrialists – who actually expressed their "great satisfaction" for the significant improvements to Faggella's draft, due to the 1926–1927 proposals and, more broadly, for the great attention devoted by the Ministry to their requests[112] – the resulting law, issued in late 1934,[113] maintained some of the original traits. Hence, it was notable[114] that in one of the few articles devoted to the issue by the bulletin of the Engineers' Fascist Union, the new law "sanctioned the protection of the inventor's moral right, in line with my own proposals". Also in this case, while bringing Italy to the frontier of intellectual property rights protection, the reform was "a general sentiment

108 This myth, also promoted by the regime by appointing a charismatic figure such as Guglielmo Marconi as head of the National Research Council, constituted an intrinsic limitation in the Fascist approach to scientific research, sacrificing organisation and, most of all, appropriate funding; see Maiocchi (fn. 51).

109 C. Di Marzio, "Sulla proprietà industriale", *Le professioni e le arti – Bollettino mensile della confederazione nazionale professionisti e artisti* 1, no. 4 (1932): 1–2.

110 Di Marzio, "Sulla proprietà Industriale", 1–2.

111 A. Ferrario, "Giudizi ed indagini sulle invenzioni", *Le professioni e le arti – Bollettino mensile della confederazione nazionale professionisti e artisti* 2, no. 7 (1932): 2–5.

112 *Confindustria* (1932), 407.

113 Royal Decree 13 September 1934, no. 1602, Privative industriali e marchi di fabbrica e di commercio, GU no. 240 of 12 October 1934.

114 E. Piola Caselli, "Gli interessi materiali e morali degli inventori", *L'Ingegnere – Rivista tecnica e sindacale, Sindacato Nazionale Fascista Ingegneri* 8, no. 23 (1934): 1094–95.

and development in all civil countries". In other cases, it has been noted[115] that the new law also extended the maximum protection from 15 to 18 years: "however, it never came into effect".[116] The government, in fact, did not issue the implementing decree, in order to introduce some changes. While the circumstances of the commission appointed by the Ministry approved "most of their proposals",[117] little was left to the imagination whether or not the resulting decree "was not published". Lamenting the resulting "uncertainty", industrialists proposed to first put in practice the "parts of the reform that did not need the profound, radical reorganisation" that was needed to apply the novelty test.

It would take a new decree in June 1939 and its corresponding rules the following February to have an actual reform of the Italian patent system of 1859.[118] In substance, it had not "introduced any radical innovation" to the previous norms, adapting them to a radically changed economic and social reality but "postponing *sine die* the great reform sketched in the 1934 decree, because some of its provisions were considered too dangerous to be applied".[119] In this field also, Fascism "did not manage to elaborate and put in practice its own intellectual property law, but only kept to a natural process of adaptation of Liberal legislation".[120] The only, modest incentive was represented by the "assistance" provided by the ANFI to the invention that passed the examination of the Central Commission for the Examination of Invention, instituted within the National Research Council;[121] while there was a need for more research, it seems to have left few traces outside the ANFI's publications.

Paradoxically, a more radical reform was definitely abandoned by fascists precisely when the autarky made it more necessary – or at least reinforced its supporting rhetoric. Not only more and more magazine contributors[122] but

115 Vasta (fn. 79).

116 Ibid.

117 *Associazione fra le Società Italiane per Azioni (Assonime) (1937). Relazione sull'attività dell'Associazione nel campo della legislazione e consulenza commerciale, tributaria, finanziaria ed amministrativa nel biennio 1935–1936* (Rome: Castaldi, 1936), 30.

118 Respectively, Royal Decree no. 1127 of 29 June 1939, Testo delle disposizioni legislative in materia di brevetti per invenzioni industriali, GU no. 189 of 14 August 1939; Royal Decree 5 February 1940, no. 244, Testo delle disposizioni regolamentari in materia di brevetti per invenzioni industriali, GU no. 94 of 20 April 1940.

119 Vasta (fn. 79), 1110.

120 Vasta (fn. 79), 1110.

121 A. Ferrario, "Le opere assistenziali a favore degli Inventori", *Ingegni e congegni: rassegna mensile dell'Associazione nazionale fascista inventori* 7, no. 2 (1937): 1–2.

122 Notably, Ferrario mentioned "colour cinematography" among the most promising fields of autarkic research, despite "pressure" by "Italian industrialists and speculators" to buy foreign patents, and the fact that all Italian investments "are not even one thousandth of

also corporatist economists increasingly asked for the protection of Italian, autarkic patents against foreign ones,[123] "within the limits imposed by logics and convenience"; this was something that Ferrario had been advocating for almost ten years.[124] On paper, similar measures were introduced in the application of the law of 9 January 1939 (no. 189), which reinforced the "preference to national products", stressing how it meant to "promote Italian genius and promote research", recognised as "one of the most powerful and appropriate tools to reach autarky".[125] Thus, *ceteris paribus*, preference should be given "to firms with their own research offices" and for "Italian products not requiring, to be produced, any payment or credit abroad" due to intellectual property. Once again, an important supporter of autarkic policies (such as Belluzzo) showed in practice for Italian industrialists this side of autarky – the one more clearly demanding investments, and possibly to disrupt existing machinery – came very last on the priority list. In the collection of his popular writings on autarky, patents were barely mentioned. The only substantial occurrence, when Italy's options were dramatically restricted by the inevitable trade deficits,[126] discussed the "six major holes in our balance of payment that must be closed or reduced". The "intelligence imported as designs, patents, consultancies not always needed" came last – and once again, the "preparatory" legislative work "had already been down: it's now time for concrete action".[127]

Against this background, one is indeed left to wonder what the reasons were for such a hiatus between words and action and, ultimately, what the actual impact of such reforms were – if any – on the Italian economy, particularly when compared to their declared aims and vis-à-vis the standing of Italy as an autarkic State. The task is clearly arduous, and no direct causal inference can be drawn on the basis of the current state of knowledge. It is nonetheless interesting to analyse trends in patents and other innovating activities within the broader economic performance of Fascist Italy, to see if it is possible to infer

---

what a single foreign firm invest". See A. Ferrario, "Autarchia e invenzioni", *Economia – Rivista di economia corporativa e d i scienze sociali* 25, no. 3 (1940): 35–42.

123 L. Fabbrini, "Spunti di economia autarchica al II Convegno Nazionale dell' I. S. C. A.", *Economia – Rivista di economia corporativa e d i scienze sociali* 25, no. 4 (1940): 307–21.

124 A. Ferrario, "Brevetti e Marchi di Importazione", *Le professioni e le arti – Bollettino mensile della confederazione nazionale professionisti e artisti* 1, no. 4 (1932): 3–4.

125 "Legislazione economica e finanziaria – Preferenza ai prodotti nazionali", *Economia* 25 (1940): 71–72.

126 E. Berbenni, "External devaluation and trade balance in 1930s Italy", *Structural Change and Economic Dynamics* 57 (2021): 93–107.

127 "Ai margini dell'autarchia", *Gazzetta del Popolo*, November 1937, in G. Belluzzo, *L'autarchia italiana vista da un ingegnere* (Milan: Hoepli, 1940), 295–307.

any positive contributions from the regime's policies regarding intellectual property rights. First of all, it is important to note that the aggregate macroeconomic picture offered by the renewed national accounts is different from "classic" interpretations.[128] In particular, it is now evident how the interwar decades were all but "stagnant". After a period of fast economic growth in the 1920s, and before the declaration in 1926 of the so-called "Quota 90", when Italy returned to the Gold Standard at the 1922 parity of 90 lire per British pound,[129] there was a shift from a "laissez-faire" attitude to a progressively more interventionist style of economic policy.[130] The new series show a more important contraction of the economy after the Great Depression. In particular, industrial output[131] showed that in 1929, for the first time since unification had reached agriculture in terms of value added to the economy. But the economy contracted in the early 1920s by almost a quarter. On the other hand, the rest of the decade now show more sustained growth. More importantly,[132] in the 1930s the share of so-called "modern" sectors – metalmaking, engineering, and chemicals – increased by ten percentage points, reaching almost half of the overall industrial output. Overall,[133] it is possible to talk about a "success story". Especially considering the troubled period, this was especially dramatic for a small, open, and transformative economy dependent on global trade. The Italian industrial output outperformed most countries, continuing its convergence towards the "core" and most of all building the "preconditions" for the post-war economic miracle[134] in terms of a more modern and variegated industrial base.

When the evidence on real industrial productivity is examined, the optimistic view will gradually change, however. For instance, it was noted[135] that after

128 Toniolo (fn. 12); Petri (fn. 5). For a more extensive discussion on the recent quantitative economic history literature on Fascist Italy, see Gabbuti (fn. 13).

129 J.S. Cohen, "The 1927 Revaluation of the Lira: A Study in Political Economy", *Economic History Review* 25, no. 1 (1972): 642–54.

130 C. Giordano and F. Giugliano, "A Tale of Two Fascisms: Labour Productivity Growth and Competition Policy in Italy, 1911–1951", *Explorations in Economic History* 55, no. 1 (2015): 25–38.

131 E. Felice and A. Carreras, "When Did Modernization Begin? Italy's Industrial Growth Reconsidered in Light of New Value-Added Series, 1911–1951", *Explorations in Economic History* 49, no. 1 (2012): 443–60.

132 M. Gomellini and G. Toniolo, "The Industrialization of Italy, 1861–1971", in *The Spread of Modern Industry to the Periphery Since 1871*, ed. K.H. O'Rourke and J.G. Williamson (Oxford: Oxford University Press, 2017), 115–141.

133 Felice and Carreras (fn. 130).

134 Petri (fn. 5).

135 Giordano and Giugliano (fn. 129).

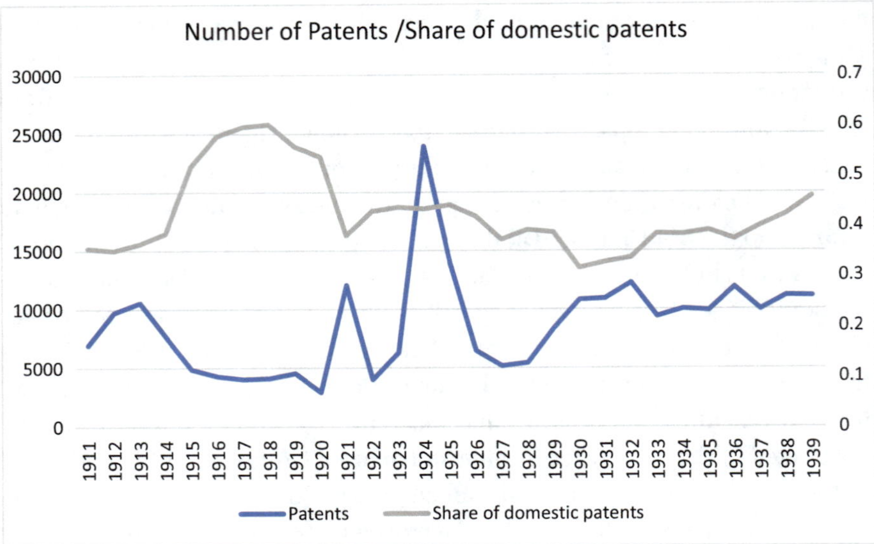

FIGURE 7.1 Italian Patents, 1911–1939
SOURCE: THIS IS BASED ON OUR INTERPRETATION AND DATA PRODUCED IN FEDERICO (1964).

the deflationary shift of the mid-1920s, labour productivity growth in Italy was even negative. The increase in industrial output would thus have depended exclusively on the increasing labour and capital input. The truly fascist, peculiar aspect of Italian economic policy – the suppression of workers' wages, allowed first by open repression of free trade unions and then by the celebrated Corporatist system of industrial relations,[136] granted industrial owners high profit rates, resulting in stable rates of investment and capital accumulation.[137] As highlighted by labour historians, even in the organisation of production Italian industrialists mostly limited themselves to the application of more intensive systems of labour organisation, such as the Bedaux system, rather than transitioning to the Fordist models of mass production. Against this background, it is instructive to consider the evolution of patent activities.[138]

136 Toniolo (fn. 12).
137 Gabbuti (fn. 14).
138 On the connection between patent systems and inventive activities, see the recent survey by C. MacLeod and A. Nuvolari, "Inventive Activities, Patents and Early Industrialisation: A Synthesis of Research Issues", *Rivista di storia economica / Italian Review of Economic History* 32, no. 1 (2016): 77–108.

In Figure 7.1, we show the total number of patents granted in Italy between 1911 and 1939, together with the share of domestic patents. Despite the growth of Italian industry and more modern sectors within it (together with the increase in population), the total of patents granted in Italy was at the outbreak of WWII in line with the one just before the Great War, as it had remained stable for the whole of the 1930s, despite the efforts of Ferrario's ANFI. Apart from the late 1910s, the same can be said about the share of Italian patentees within this total. This indicator can be interpreted as a proxy of technological dependence from abroad: even in the dramatic context of the 1930s, in which the Italian economic policy was severely constrained by the persistent precariousness of the country balance of payments,[139] patenting activities in Italy were dominated by foreign inventors. Interestingly, it was observed that the "very indicative evidence" of the deficit was implied by the fact that "of the 10 thousands of patent applications every year, 6,700 come from foreign citizens".[140] This already remarkable figure was even worse considering that Italian applicants included people who should not be considered truly inventors, but crooks who tried to take advantage of the absence of any novelty check.[141]

Indeed, according to Ferrario, more than 4,000 of the patents granted to foreigners actually "enter every year industrial productive cycles", compared to "330, at the most, Italian ones".[142] As explained two years later,[143] this figure was attributed to the fact that "foreign patents arrived to Italy already fiercely selected". The 1937 Report of the *Giunta Generale del Bilancio*, presented to the Chamber of Deputies and republished by the ANFI's magazine *Ingegni e congegni*,[144] noted that in terms of patents Italy was in a "disadvantaged" position. According to the report, it was well known that the low share of domestic patents was at odds with the experience of "industrially important" other States,

139 Berbenni (fn. 125).

140 A. Ferrario, "Il «prodotto italiano» con riguardo alla provenienza dei suoi elementi inventivi", *Le professioni e le arti – Bollettino mensile della confederazione nazionale professionisti e artisti* V, no. 9 (1935): 30–31.

141 This picture of patenting activity dominated by independent inventors with mostly incremental, if not trifling innovations is supported by Domini (fn. 104), who shows that most firms took patents sporadically, especially in traditional sectors. The most persistent innovators to make systematic use of the patent system in 1936 were a limited number of firms active on the scale, being intensive and specialised supplier sectors.

142 Ferrario (fn. 139).

143 A. Ferrario, "La seconda mostra nazionale delle invenzioni e della indipendenza economica", *Ingegni e congegni: le attualità scientifiche: rassegna mensile dell'Associazione nazionale fascista inventori* VII, no. 1 (1937): 1–4.

144 G. Bruni, "Brevetti d'invenzione, modelli e marchi", *Ingegni e congegni : le attualità scientifiche: rassegna mensile dell'Associazione nazionale fascista inventori* 7, no. 5 (1937): 6–9.

and it was not going to improve any soon. The report's author presented data on the longer average duration of foreign patents: of 100 new patents, 40% of foreign-owned patents reached 5 years, 16% celebrated 10, and 4% reached 15 years, compared to 14%, 5%, and 1% for their "autarkic" competitors. As a result, the increase in maximum protection included in the 1934 reform was paradoxically going to disproportionally benefit foreign inventors and increase their relative share (which, considering the different duration, could be already proxied at 80%).

He also presented a tentative estimate of the mismatch in bilateral "trade" of patents with Germany, France, the UK, and Switzerland: for each, he presented ratios of the most recent number of patents granted to Italian inventors in that country, compared to the number of patents granted in Italy to citizens of those countries. While this ratio was between 35 and 45% for France and UK – two countries without rigorous patent examinations – it fell to less than 10% with Germany and, even more disappointingly, 15–24% with Switzerland. A more positive note was the aforementioned cooperation between the ANFI and the National Research Council: according to the report's author, in 1936 the joint commissions examined 811 inventions and approved 104 of them (even though we do not know if and how they were supported in practice). In line with this picture,[145] this period in Italy did not match that of more advanced countries in its capacity of technical innovation (lagging even behind Spain). Rather, it improved its ability of imitating and diffusing existing innovation – in line with the aforementioned literature on multinationals in Fascist Italy – that continued to play a crucial role in transferring technology.[146]

In Figure 7.2, we then track another commonly adopted indicator of innovative capability, that is, the number and relative share of Italian patents registered in the USA. In the 1930s, both absolute and relative figures decreased. This result has been already discussed by other writers,[147] according to whom the interwar period represented a "period of relative decline" compared to the liberal period.[148] For these authors, the innovative performance in the autarkic period was particularly disappointing, given that the share of Italian patents

145 R. Giannetti, *Tecnologia e sviluppo economico italiano, 1870–1990* (Bologna: il Mulino, 1999), 42–45.

146 A. Colli, "Multinationals and economic development in Italy during the Twentieth century", *Business History Review* 88 (2014): 303–327.

147 Vasta (fn. 79), 1120; Nuvolari and Vasta (fn. 153), 276.

148 F. Barbiellini Amidei, J. Cantwell, and A. Spadavecchia, "Innovation and Foreign Technology", in *The Oxford Handbook of the Italian Economy Since Unification*, ed. G. Toniolo (New York: Oxford University Press, 2013), 378–416.

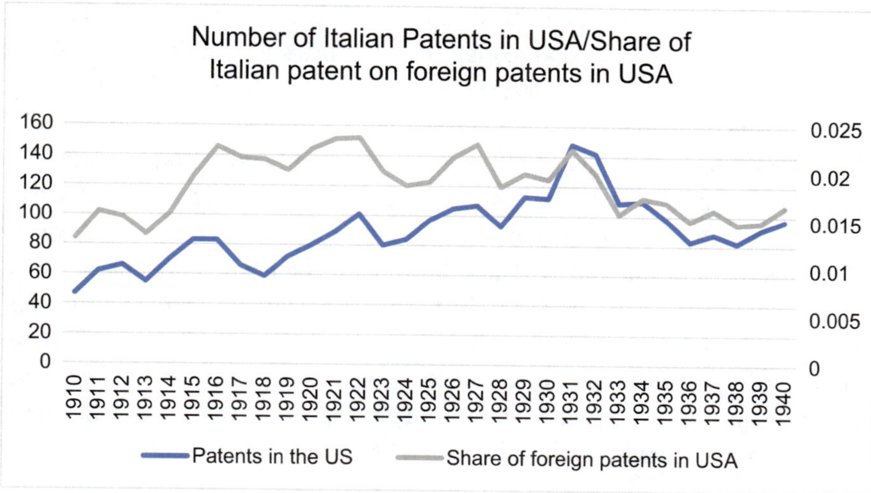

FIGURE 7.2 Italian Patents in the USA, 1910–1940
SOURCE: THIS ASSESSMENT IS BASED ON OUR ANALYSIS OF DATA TAKEN FROM USPTO (US PATENT AND TRADEMARK OFFICE), *TECHNOLOGY ASSESSMENT AND FORECAST, SEVENTH REPORT* (1977).

declined in "all modern sectors", except for rubber.[149] While economists and historians are well aware that similar indicators provide an informative but rough proxy of innovative performance,[150] it is interesting that attributions were made based on the "prodigious industrial and economic progresses" of the United States and their ability to "honour and encourage inventors, who benefit from unextinguishable incentives".[151] In fact, modern scholarship suggests that patent systems alone cannot solely propel innovation; rather, they must align with other components of the national innovation system, such as the education and university system, competition laws, industrial policies, and more.[152] The patent reforms undertaken in the 1930s lacked this comprehensive approach, so that even the positive advancements were unlikely to yield significant effects.

According to the preliminary analysis of this section, Ferrario's (not so autarkic) objective of imitating the US model of innovation through the import and corporatist adaptation of a German-style examination of patent merit can be

149 Barbiellini Amidei, Cantwell, and Spadavecchia, "Innovation and Foreign Technology", 534.

150 MacLeod and Nuvolari (fn. 137).

151 A. Ferrario, "Vecchi episodi e propositi nuovi per gli inventori", *Le professioni e le arti – Bollettino mensile della confederazione nazionale professionisti e artisti* 1, no. 2 (1931): 5.

152 J. Streb, "Patent law and economic performance", *Rivista di Storia Economica/Italian Review of Economic History*, 39, no. 1 (2023): 3–26.

considered a failure. As others have observed,[153] the interwar decades, and in particular the autarkic period, constituted the basis for the later, post-WWII Miracle. This basis reinforced lasting, negative features of the Italian economy, "a country characterized by limited investments in research and innovation"[154] that, at least until the 1960s, built its competitive advantage on low wages[155] rather than innovation. From Fascism and corporatism, Italian industrialists enjoyed the repression of workers' independent unionism. Only in a few sectors (most notably chemicals,[156] and in some of the firms reorganised by the State holding IRI)[157] did Italian industry aim at creating technological innovation; instead, it continued to rely on transfers from abroad. Outside mere patent policy, even the creation of the National Research Council, while representing an improvement, was not pursued consistently, and it lacked the financial resources necessary to close the gap with more advanced economies.[158]

5 Conclusions

In general terms, notwithstanding the rhetoric on the development of the national economy, neither the earlier "Corporatist" nor the later "autarkic" suggestions exerted a major role in shaping intellectual property legislation during the fascist regime. Intellectual property legislation remained consistent with international standards, and the introduction of discriminatory regulations against foreigners was limited.

Within this general framework, it is possible to notice interesting differences between copyright and patents. In the first case, the regime was particularly active in promoting reforms, insisting on modernisation of the laws and regulations inherited from the Liberal state. The "Fascist" laws adhered to international standards, while at the same time they tried to "mobilise" support for

153 Petri (fn. 5).

154 A. Nuvolari and M. Vasta, "The Ghost in the Attic? Italian National Innovation System in Historical Perspective, 1861–2011", *Enterprise & Society* 16, no. 2 (2015): 270.

155 V. Zamagni, "La dinamica dei salari nel settore industriale, 1921–1939", *Quaderni storici* 10 (1975): 530–49.

156 R. Petri, "Technical change in the Italian chemical industry: Markets, firms and State intervention", *Determinants in the evolution of the European Chemical Industry, 1900–1939*, ed. A. Travis, H. Schröter, E. Homburg, and P.J.T. Morris (Dordrecht: Springer, 1998), 275–300.

157 S. Gasperin, "Lessons from the past for 21st century systems of state-owned enterprises: The case of Italy's IRI in the 1930s", *Structural Change and Economic Dynamics* 62, no. 1 (2022): 599–612.

158 Maiocchi (fn. 51).

the regime of authors and intellectuals within the "corporatist" institutional set-up. Only later did the fascist regime reinforce its grip on the Italian cultural milieu, to this purpose favouring publishers over authors and centralising the governmental control over the publishing sector and the management of authors' moral and economic rights. This very short turn towards autarky and against the international trends, however, represented only the very last years of the fascist era (1941–1943).

The development of patent laws followed a different trajectory. Notwithstanding the pleadings for patent reform voiced by engineers and inventors, the regime was rather slow in taking up the matter. The patent reform finally introduced did not contemplate major shifts. In the end, the regime opted for simple procedures that kept access to the patent system relatively easy for both small independent inventors and foreign companies. Most notably, there was no introduction of a compulsory examination procedure, following the German model: the examination process carried on by the ANFI and National Research Council was voluntary, and while it deserves more research, it arguably was too little, too late, to reduce the foreign dependency on technology and raw materials at a time when both the collapse of world trade and the sanctions induced by Italy's imperialistic foreign policy made some "autarky" inevitable. In sum, the twenty-year regime did very little to improve the technological dependence of the Italian economy, both in theory and in practice.

What could explain the difference between these two domains? While the question deserves more research, the material covered in this chapter allows us to stress the different kinds of interest groups involved in the legislative process. Both "authors" and "inventors" were part of the "intellectual professions", to which fascist propaganda assigned a peculiar role within the Corporatist state. According to the President of the Corporation of Professionals and Artists, to which both groups contributed, this corporation was the only one that did not need to contend with owners' and trade unions; its relevance would rather come from being "the technical element, the intermediary between owners and workers, between which they realise their role of moderator, the herald of the social and spiritual values of the productive forces of the Nation".[159] Indeed, as we can see in the words of fascist unionists such as Di Giacomo (1932), within their broader attempt at luring the middle classes, fascists did pay great attention to the organisation of these groups.[160] In the case

159 Report by Di Marzio, 23 April 23 1940, quoted in A. Vittoria, "DI MARZIO, Cornelio", *Dizionario Biografico degli Italiani* 40, https://www.treccani.it/enciclopedia/cornelio-di-marzio_%28Dizionario-Biografico%29/.

160 Baris (fn. 48).

of inventors, however, the "technical element" could conflict with the much less "spiritual" interests of business leaders – and as far as we can tell from this story, in similar cases, Mussolini's regime ended up favouring the latter.

Acknowledgements

Throughout the chapter, unless otherwise indicated, translations of quotes from non-English references are our own.

References

Amaldi, E., and L. Segreto (1983), "CORBINO, Orso Mario", *Dizionario Biografico degli Italiani,* Vol. 28, https://www.treccani.it/enciclopedia/orso-mario-corbino_(Dizionario-Biografico)/.

Amar, M. (1874), *Dei diritti degli autori di opere dell'ingegno. Studi teorico-pratici sulla legislazione italiana in rapporto colle leggi delle altre Nazioni, coi Trattati internazionali e colle Decisioni dei Magistrati italiani e stranieri,* Turin, Fratelli Bocca.

Associazione fra le Società Italiane per Azioni (*Assonime*) (1927), *Sedici anni di attività della Associazione fra le società italiane per azioni: 1911–1927*, Rome, Castaldi.

Associazione fra le Società Italiane per Azioni (*Assonime*) (1928). *Relazione sull'attività dell'Associazione nell'anno 1927 in materia di legislazione, consulenza e assistenza tributaria, commerciale e amministrativa*, Rome, Castaldi.

Associazione fra le Società Italiane per Azioni (*Assonime*) (1937), *Relazione sull'attività dell'Associazione nel campo della legislazione e consulenza commerciale, tributaria, finanziaria ed amministrativa nel biennio 1935–1936*, Rome, Castaldi.

Atti Parlamentari (1921–24), XXVI legislatura, Indice.

Baffigi, A. (2013), "National accounts, 1861–2011", in G. Toniolo (ed.), *The Oxford handbook of the Italian economy since Unification*, New York, Oxford University Press, pp. 157–186.

Baffigi, A. (2015), *Il PIL per la storia d'Italia: Istruzioni per l'uso*, Venice, Marsilio.

Barbiellini Amidei, F., Cantwell, J., and Spadavecchia, A. (2013), "Innovation and Foreign Technology", in G. Toniolo (Ed.), *The Oxford Handbook of the Italian Economy since Unification,* New York, Oxford University Press, pp. 378–416.

Baris, T. (2012), "Consent, Mobilization and Participation. The Rise of the Middle Class and Its Support for the Fascist Regime", in R. Pergher and G. Albanese (Eds.), *In the Society of Fascists. Acclamation, Acquiescence, and Agency in Mussolini's Italy*, London, Palgrave Macmillan pp. 69–85.

Belluzzo, G. (1940), *L'autarchia italiana vista da un ingegnere*, Milan, Hoepli.

Benadusi, L. (2011), "Il mito della scienza", in F. Cassata and C. Pogliano (Eds.), *Storia d'Italia – Annali 16: Scienze e cultura dell'Italia unita*, Turin, Einaudi, pp. 157–176.

Beneduce, P. (1999), "Privilegi e diritti dell'autore nel pensiero economico-giuridico della prima metà dell'Ottocento in Italia", in *Das Priliveg im Europeischen Vergleich*, Klostermann, pp. 401–418.

Berbenni, E. (2021), "External devaluation and trade balance in 1930s Italy", *Structural Change and Economic Dynamics*, 57, pp. 93–107.

Bertilorenzi, M. (2020a), "Un Nazionalismo immaginario? Multinazionali in Italia durante il fascismo", *Studi Storici*, 61, n. 4, pp. 935–958.

Bertilorenzi, M. (2020b) "Introduzione: autarchia e multinazionali", *Ricerche Storiche*, 50, n. 1, pp. 5–16.

Bertilorenzi, M., V. Cerretano and M. Perugini (2022), "Between Constraints and Opportunities: Big Italia Business and Autarky, 1934–1943", *Rivista di storia economica / Italian Review of Economic History*, 38, n. 3, pp. 303–336.

Bottai, G. (1930), Parole introduttive, in "Il diritto d'autore. Rivista giuridica trimestrale della SIAE", I, pp. I–III.

Bruni, G. (1937), "Brevetti d'invenzione, modelli e marchi", *Ingegni e congegni : le attualità scientifiche : rassegna mensile dell'Associazione nazionale fascista inventori*, 7, n. 5, pp. 6–9.

Cannistraro, P.V. (1975), *La macchina del consenso. Fascismo e mass media*, Rome-Bari, Laterza.

Cerasi, L. (2001), "Corporatismo/corporativismo e storia d'Italia. Un percorso di lettura", *Contemporanea*, 4, n. 2, pp. 367–77.

Cohen, J.S. (1972), 'The 1927 Revaluation of the Lira: A Study in Political Economy', *Economic History Review*, 25, pp. 642–654.

Cohen, J.S. (1988), "Was Italian Fascism a Developmental Dictatorship? Some Evidence to the Contrary", *Economic History Review*, 41, pp. 95–113.

Colli, A. (2014), "Multinationals and economic development in Italy during the Twentieth century", *Business History Review*, 88, pp. 303–327.

Confederazione Generale Fascista dell'Industria Italiana (*Confindustria*) (1930), *Annuario 1930–VIII*, Rome, Castaldi.

Confederazione Generale Fascista dell'Industria Italiana (*Confindustria*) (1932), *Annuario 1932–X*, Rome, Castaldi.

De Cecco, M., and G. G. Migone (1991), "La collocazione internazionale dell'economia italiana", in R. Bosworth and S. Romano (Eds.), *La politica estera italiana, 1860–1985*, Bologna, il Mulino, pp. 147–196.

Di Giacomo, G. (1932), *Intellettuali e Fascismo. Dieci anni di sindacalismo fascista tra professionisti e artisti*, Rome, Libreria del Littorio.

Di Marzio, C. (1932), "Sulla proprietà industriale", *Le professioni e le arti – Bollettino mensile della confederazione nazionale professionisti e artisti*, 1, n. 4, pp. 1–2.

Domini, G. (2023), "Innovation and business performance in Italy, 1913–1936", *Rivista di storia economica/Italian Review of Economic History*, 39, n. 3, pp. 287–330.

Esperson, P. (1899), *De' diritto di autore sulle opera dell'ingegno ne' rapporti internazionali. Studio di legislazioen comparata e di diritto internazionale convenzionale*, Unione Tipografico Editrice.

Fabbrini, L. (1940), "Spunti di economia autarchica al II Convegno Nazionale dell' I. S. C. A", *Economia – Rivista di economia corporativa e d i scienze sociali*, 25, n. 4, pp. 307–321.

Faggella, D. (1932), "Relazione e disegno di legge per la protezione della proprietà industriale", *Atti della Assemblea generale del Consiglio Nazionale delle Corporazioni*, 1, Rome.

Fano-Damascelli, E. (1971), "La "restaurazione antifascista liberista": ristagno e sviluppo economico durante il fascismo", *Il movimento di liberazione in Italia*, n. 104, pp. 47–99.

Federico, P. (1964), 'Historical patent statistics', *Journal of the Patent Office Society*, vol. 76, pp. 89–171.

Felice, E. and Carreras, A. (2012), "When Did Modernization Begin? Italy's Industrial Growth Reconsidered in Light of New Value-Added Series, 1911–1951", *Explorations in Economic History*, Vol. 49, pp. 443–460.

Ferrario, A. (1931a), "L'inquadramento Sindacale degli inventori", *Le professioni e le arti – Bollettino mensile della confederazione nazionale professionisti e artisti*, 1, n. 1, pp. 13–14.

Ferrario, A. (1931b), "Vecchi episodi e propositi nuovi per gli inventori", *Le professioni e le arti – Bollettino mensile della confederazione nazionale professionisti e artisti*, 1, n. 2, pp. 4–5.

Ferrario, A. (1932a), "Giudizi ed indagini sulle invenzioni", *Le professioni e le arti – Bollettino mensile della confederazione nazionale professionisti e artisti*, 2, n. 7, pp. 2–5.

Ferrario, A. (1932b), "La commissione centrale per l'esame delle invenzioni", *L'inventore italiano – Rivista mensile dell'Associazione nazionale fascista inventori*, 2, n. 9–10, pp. 197–202.

Ferrario, A. (1932c), "Gli inventori davanti ai loro giudici", *L'inventore italiano – Rivista mensile dell'Associazione nazionale fascista inventori*, 2, n. 5, pp. 85

Ferrario, A. (1932d), "Brevetti e Marchi di Importazione", *Le professioni e le arti – Bollettino mensile della confederazione nazionale professionisti e artisti*, 1, n. 4, pp. 3–4.

Ferrario, A. (1935a), "Il «prodotto italiano» con riguardo alla provenienza dei suoi elementi inventivi", *Le professioni e le arti – Bollettino mensile della confederazione nazionale professionisti e artisti*, V, n. 9, pp. 30–31.

Ferrario, A. (1935b), "Contro i brevetti stranieri", *Tecnica fascista*, 1 novembre.

Ferrario, A. (1937a), "La seconda mostra nazionale delle invenzioni e della indipendenza economica", *Ingegni e congegni: le attualità scientifiche: rassegna mensile dell'Associazione nazionale fascista inventori*, VII, n. 1, pp. 1–4.

Ferrario, A. (1937b), "Le opere assistenziali a favore degli Inventori", *Ingegni e congegni: rassegna mensile dell'Associazione nazionale fascista inventori*, 7, n. 2, pp. 1–2.

Ferrario, A. (1938), "Anno XVII", *Ingegni e congegni: le attualità scientifiche: rassegna mensile dell'Associazione nazionale fascista inventori*, IX, n. 1, pp. 1–2.

Ferrario, A. (1940), "Autarchia e invenzioni", *Economia – Rivista di economia corporativa e d i scienze sociali*, 25, n. 3, pp-35–42.

Fisk, C. (2009), *Working Knowledge. Employee Innovation and the Rise of Corporate Intellectual Property, 1800–1930*, Chapel Hill, NC, The University of North Carolina Press.

Forges Davanzati, R. (1933), "Mussolini parla agli scrittori", *Nuova Antologia*, LXVIII, fasc. 1468.

Franchi, L. (1904), Leggi e convenzioni sulle privative industriali, disegni e modelli di fabbrica, marchi di fabbrica e di commercio. Legislazione italiana, legislazioni straniere, convenzioni esistenti fra l'Italia e gli altri stati, Hoepli.

Gabbuti, G. (2020), "«When We Were Worse off». The Economy, Living Standards and Inequality in Fascist Italy", *Rivista di storia economica / Italian Review of Economic History*, 36, n. 3, pp. 253–298.

Gabbuti, G. (2022), "Those Who Were Better Off: Capital and Top Incomes in Fascist Italy", *LEM Working Paper Series* 2022/31, https://www.lem.sssup.it/WPLem/2022-31.html.

Gagliardi, A. (2010), *Il corporativismo fascista*, Rome-Bari, Laterza.

Gagliardi, A. (2016), "The corporatism of Fascist Italy between words and reality", *Estudos Ibero-Americanos*, 42, pp. 409–429.

Gagliardi, A. (2022), "Il mercato e i limiti dello Stato fascista", *Annali Fondazione Feltrinelli*, LVI, pp. 137–162.

Gasperin, S. (2022), "Lessons from the past for 21st century systems of state-owned enterprises The case of Italy's IRI in the 1930s", *Structural Change and Economic Dynamics*, 62, pp. 599–612.

Giannetti, R. (1999), *Tecnologia e sviluppo economico italiano, 1870–1990*, Bologna, il Mulino.

Giannini, A. (1931), "Il diritto dell'artista esecutore", *Diritto d'autore. Rivista giuridica trimestrale della società italiana degli autori ed editori*, 2, n. 2, pp.161–175.

Giordano, C. and Giugliano, F. (2015), "A Tale of Two Fascisms: Labour Productivity Growth and Competition Policy in Italy, 1911–1951", *Explorations in Economic History*, 55, pp. 25–38.

Giorgi, C. and I. Pavan (2021), *Storia dello stato sociale in Italia.* Bologna, Il Mulino.

Gomellini, M. and Toniolo, G. (2017), "The Industrialization of Italy, 1861–1971", in K.H. O'Rourke and J.G. Williamson (eds.), *The Spread of Modern Industry to the Periphery Since 1871*, Oxford, Oxford University Press, pp. 115–141.

Ipsen, C. (1993), "The Organization of Demographic Totalitarianism: Early Population Policy in Fascist Italy", *Social Science History*, 17, 1993, pp. 71–108.

Irwin, D. (2011), *Trade Policy Disaster: Lessons from the 1930s*, Cambridge (MA), MIT Press.

Liguori, R. (Ed.) (1942), *L'ordinamento sindacale fascista degli autori e scrittori. Raccolta di leggi, dati e scritti di Luigi Monelli, Corrado Govoni, Renato Liguori, Lorenz Ruggi ed Ettore Valerio*, Rome, Cuggiani.

Livingstone, M.A., Monateri, P.G. and Parisi, F. (2015), *The Italian Legal System*, Stanford University Press.

Lucaroni, G. (2022), *Architetture di Storia. Fascismo, storicità, cultura architettonica italiana*, Rome, Viella.

MacLeod, C., and Nuvolari, A. (2016), "Inventive Activities, Patents and Early Industrialisation: A Synthesis of Research Issues", *Rivista di storia economica / Italian Review of Economic History*, 32, n. 1, pp. 77–108.

Maiocchi, R. (1980), "Il ruolo delle scienze nello sviluppo industriale italiano", in G. Micheli (Ed.), *Storia d'Italia. Annali 3. Scienza e Tecnica*, Turin, Einaudi, pp. 863–999.

Maiocchi, R. (2003), *Gli scienziati del duce. Il ruolo dei ricercatori e del CNR nella politica autarchica del fascismo*, Rome, Carocci.

Mangoni, L. (1974), *L'interventismo della cultura*, Rome-Bari, Laterza.

Mantelli, A.G. (1930), *L'oggetto del diritto d'autore nella creazione musicale*, Athenum.

Marinetti, F.T. (1931), "Verso un diritto d'autore perpetuo", *Le professioni e le arti – Bollettino mensile della confederazione nazionale professionisti e artisti*, 1, n. 1, p. 10.

Marrubini, C. (1926), "Le nuove disposizioni sul diritto d'autore", L'Italia che scrive, 9, n.1, p.1.

Melloni, C. (2008), "Eduardo Piola Caselli, magistrato e giurista", *Le Carte e la Storia*, n. 2, pp. 128–148.

Minesso, M. (2013), *Giuseppe Belluzzo. Tecnico e politico nella storia d'Italia 1876–1952*, Milan, Franco Angeli.

Mussolini, B. (1930), "Per il Consiglio Nazionale delle Corporazioni", 21 aprile 1930, now in Id. (1957), *Opera Omnia, Vol. XXIV: Dagli accordi del Laterano al dodicesimo anniversario della fondazione dei Fasci: (12 febbraio 1929–23 marzo 1931)*, edited by E. and D. Susmel, La Fenice, Roma.

Nuvolari, A. and M. Vasta (2015), "The Ghost in the Attic? Italian National Innovation System in Historical Perspective, 1861–2011", *Enterprise & Society*, 16, n. 2, pp. 270–290.

Nuvolari, A. and M. Vasta (2020), "The Italian Patent System during the long nineteenth century: from privileges to property in a latecomer industrialie country" in G.

Gooday and S. Wilf (eds.), *Patent Cultures. Diversity and Harmonization in Historical Perspective*, Cambridge, Cambridge University Press, pp. 147–165.

OTAF [Office of Technology Assessment and Forecast, US Department of Commerce, Patent Trademark Office] (1977), *Technology Assessment and Forecast 7th Report*

Palazzolo, M.I (1987), "Un editore francese in lingua italiana: Louis Claude Baudry", *Studi Storici*, 28, pp. 203–224.

Palazzolo, M.I. (2013), *La nascita del diritto d'autore in Italia. Concetti, interessi, controversie giudiziarie (1840–1941)*, Roma, Viella.

Patel, K.K. (2016), *The New Deal: A Global History*. Princeton, Princeton University Press.

Petri, R. (1998), "Technical change in the Italian chemical industry. Markets, firms and State intervention", in A. Travis, H. Schröter, E. Homburg and P.J.T. Morris (Eds.), *Determinants in the evolution of the European Chemical Industry, 1900–1939*, Dordrecht, Springer, pp. 275–300.

Petri, R. (2002), *Storia economica d'Italia. Dalla Grande guerra al miracolo economico (1918–1963)*, Bologna, il Mulino.

Piola Caselli, E. (1930), "Il diritto morale d'autore. Un rivolgimento costituzionale nella tutela delle opere di ingegno", *Diritto d'autore. Rivista giuridica trimestrale della società italiana degli autori ed editori*, 1, pp.3–41.

Piola Caselli, E. (1931), "Il nuovo regolamento interno ed internazionale del diritto esclusivo di traduzione secondo la legge 12 giugno 1931, n.774, di approvazione della Convenzione di Roma, 2 giugno 1928", *Diritto d'autore. Rivista giuridica trimestrale della società italiana degli autori ed editori*, 2.

Piola Caselli, E. (1932), "Il contratto di edizione", in *Enciclopedia Italiana*, vol.XIII, Milano, Treves-Treccani-Tumminelli, pp.474–476.

Piola Caselli, E. (1934), "Gli interessi materiali e morali degli inventori", *L'Ingegnere – Rivista tecnica e sindacale, Sindacato Nazionale Fascista Ingegneri*, 8, n. 23, pp. 1094–1095.

Piola Caselli, E. (1940), Autore (diritto di), in *Dizionario di politica*, a cura del Pnf, vol I, A-D, Treccani, pp.254.

Quine, M.S. (2002), *Italy's Social Revolution: Charity and Welfare from Liberalism to Fascism*, Basingstoke, Palgrave.

Rabbeno, A. (1865), *Nuova legge e regolamento sui diritti degli autori delle opere d'ingegno*, Sonzogno.

Regie Lettere e Patenti (1833), colle quali S.M. stabilisce alcune sanzioni penali intorno all'introduzione clandestina ne' Regii Stati di libri, giornali, ed altri scritti ivi specificati, 20 May 1833, in *Raccolta degli atti del governo di S.M. il Re di Sardegna*, I, Stamperia Reale, pp.101 ss.

Ricketson, S. and Ginsburg, J. (2022), *International copyright and neighboring rights. The Berne Convention and beyond*, New York, Oxford University Press.

Roghi, V. (2007), "Il dibattito sul diritto d'autore e la proprietà intellettuale nell'Italia fascista", *Studi Storici*, 48 (1), pp. 203–240.

Salvati, M. (1994), "Da piccola borghesia a ceti medi. Fascismo e ceti medi nelle interpretazioni dei contemporanei e degli storici", *Italia Contemporanea*, 194, pp. 65–84.

Santoro, E. (1969), "L'evoluzione legislativa in materia di radiodiffusioni circolari: notizie e spunti", *Il diritto delle radiodiffusioni e delle telecomunicazioni*, I, 1969, pp-3–52.

Sapelli, G. (1976), "Organizzazione 'scientifica' del lavoro e innovazione tecnologica durante il fascismo", *Italia contemporanea*, 125, pp. 3–27.

Serra, R. (1918), *Le lettere (ristampa), con aggiunta dei Frammenti inediti del secondo volume e di un indice onomastico*, La Voce, pp. 16–17.

Settis, B. (2022), "Fascist economy. Private powers and State intervention", in G. Albanese (Ed.), *Rethinking the History of Italian Fascism*, Routledge, pp. 104–131.

SIAE (1930), Il diritto di autore. Rivista giuridica trimestrale della SIAE, I.

Stolfi, N. (1915), *La proprietà intellettuale*, Turin, UTET.

Streb, J. (2023), "Patent law and economic performance", *Rivista di Storia Economica/ Italian Review of Economic History*, 39, n. 1, pp. 3–26.

Toniolo, G. (1980). *Economia dell'Italia fascista*, Rome-Bari, Laterza.

Tranfaglia, N, Vittoria, A. (2000), *Storia degli editori italiani dall'Unità agli anni Sessanta*, Rome-Bari, Laterza.

Turati, A. (1926), "La Libreria del Littorio", *Bibliografia fascista*, I, 30 November 1926, n.9.

Turi, G. (1980), *Il fascismo e il consenso degli intellettuali*, Bologna, Il Mulino.

Turi, G. (Ed.) (1994), *Libere professioni e fascismo*, Milan, Franco Angeli.

Ubertazzi, L.C. (2000), "I Savoia e gli autori", *Quaderni di AIDA*, n.3, Giuffrè.

Valerio, E. (1930), *Disposizioni sul diritto d'autore. Conferenza internazionale di Roma sul diritto d'autore 7 maggio-2 giugno 1928*, Rome, Libreria del Littorio.

Valerio, E. and Algardi, Z. (1942), *Il diritto d'autore. Commento teorico-pratico alla nuova legge italiana 22 aprile 1941, n.633*, Milano, Giuffré.

Vasta, M. (1999), "Capitale umano e ricerca scientifica e tecnologica", in F. Amatori, D. Bigazzi, R. Giannetti and L. Segreto, (Eds.), *Storia d'Italia. Annali 15. L'industria*, Turin, Einaudi, pp. 1043–1124.

Vittoria, A. (1991), "DI MARZIO, Cornelio", *Dizionario Biografico degli Italiani*, Vol. 40, https://www.treccani.it/enciclopedia/cornelio-di-marzio_%28Dizionario-Biografico%29/.

Zamagni, V. (1975), "La dinamica dei salari nel settore industriale, 1921–1939", *Quaderni storici*, Vol. 10, pp. 530–549.

CHAPTER 8

Copyright Aryanization

Lior Zemer and Anat Lior

1 Introduction

Shortly after the Nazi party gained power in Germany in 1933, the phenomenon of "Nazi plunder" emerged. The term Nazi plunder refers to the massive theft of art and other significant cultural items stolen by the Nazi party as part of an organized looting scheme across Europe. This plunder was carried out by military units of the German army known as *Kunstschutz*, which ironically means "art protection." In 1935, along with the Nuremberg Laws depriving Jews of their German citizenship,[1] Nazi Germany enacted a new law, which required Jews to register their domestic and foreign property and assets.[2] The Nazis pushed to "Aryanize" all Jewish businesses. By the end of 1938, approximately two-thirds of Jewish-owned businesses had been sold to Germans at a fixed price below market value. On October 3, 1938, a decree ordered the confiscation of Jewish-owned property and its immediate transfer to non-Jewish hands.

A different form of Nazi plunder also took place during those years leading up to the war. This plunder was not of physical property, but rather a spiritual one of protected artworks authored by Jewish authors. The Nazis published artworks created by Jews under different names and plagiarized their work in an attempt to Aryanize Jewish works. A prominent example is that of Alice Urbach's cookbook. Her book, *So kocht man in Wien!* (This Is How We Cook in Vienna!), was a massive success in German-speaking countries in the 1930s. Urbach was recognized as the author of the book in the edition published in 1938, but despite the fact the cover of the book and the vast majority of its content were identical in every other way, the edition in 1939 was published under the name of Rudolf Rösch. Urbach, who fled to England in 1938 and died in 1983, never got her rights in her cookbook back. She was not the only victim. Other non-fiction publishers used this method to Aryanize books authored

1 Gesetz zum Schutze des deutschen Blutes und der deutschen Ehre (Law for the Protection of German Blood and German Honor), § 1–5. Reichsgesetzblatt. Vom 15. September, 1935, Nr. 125, S. 1333f.

2 Verordnung über die Anmeldung des Vermögens von Juden (Regulation on the Registration of Jewish Property), § 1. Reichsgesetzblatt, Vom 26. April 1938, Teil I – Inneres, Nr. 56, 414–415.

 | DOI:10.1163/9789004714663_010

by Jewish writers. Another example is that of Ludwig Reiners who plagiarized Jewish writer Eduard Engel for his bestseller *Stilkunst* (Art of Style). Only a handful of cases of this practice have come to light so far.

This form of Nazi plunder has failed to receive the scholarly attention it deserves. This Chapter aims to amend this wrong. It focuses on the underexplored works created by Jewish authors which were soon Aryanized following the rise of Nazis to power. It argues that this practice denies and confiscates authorial identity. The public has the right to know the authentic truth embedded within these works, which is directly linked to the origin and identity of an artwork. Aryanizing Jewish works essentially denies the public of its valuable right. This right relates to the set of moral rights copyright laws recognized and protected. Moral rights protect authorial integrity, allow viewers of the works to know, if possible, who is the original author, and safeguard the authentic message and meaning they project. Plagiarizing one's spiritual work violates individual and collective moral rights. Moral rights in the case of plagiarized Jewish work, we claim, maintain fairness for both authors and the public. This Chapter calls for a global endeavor to ensure that similar to physical property that was looted during the years before the war, stolen intellectual property will also be restituted to its rightful owners and their heirs.

2 Copyright Protection of Jewish Artworks in Nazi Germany

Germany signed the Berne Convention in 1886,[3] and was thus obligated by its core principles of protecting "literary and artistic works."[4] The latter refers to "every production in the literary, scientific and artistic domain, whatever may be the mode or form of its expression."[5] However, in complete violation of these obligations, the Nazi regime in the interwar period (mostly from 1933 to 1939) slowly transferred copyright protected artworks created by Jews to Nazi authors and individuals,[6] in a process known as

3 Berne Convention for the Protection of Literary and Artistic Works art. 2(6), Sept. 9, 1886, S. Treaty Doc. NO. 99–27 [hereinafter Berne Convention]; *WIPO-Administered Treaties: Contracting Parties >Berne Convention (Total Contracting Parties: 179)*, WIPO, www.wipo.int/treaties/en/ShowResults.jsp?treaty_id=15.

4 Berne Convention, ibid., art. 2(1).

5 Ibid.

6 It is important to note that the Berne Convention creates a minimum standard of protection within, as well as outside, the signatory country. This is to ensure that foreign authors will know their rights in countries that signed the convention. Domestically, the convention creates minimum standards and doesn't apply only to foreigner authors. The

'Aryanization'.[7] The Holocaust Encyclopedia of the United States Holocaust Memorial Museum defines 'Aryanization' as "the transfer of Jewish-owned property to non-Jews in Nazi Germany" starting from 1933.[8] The common narrative of the 'Aryanization' process focuses entirely on physical property and its economic effects in the interwar period. However, this process also took place with regard to intellectual property which was forcefully transferred from Jewish authors to non-Jews individuals in Nazi Germany.

On August 17, 1938,[9] the Nazi regime issued an executive order obligating all Jewish men to add "Israel" as an additional name, and all Jewish women to add "Sara."[10] As a result, Nazi officials were better able to identify Jewish applicants and deny them the ability to register or renew the registration of their intellectual property via the Nazi IP system.[11] Even though written IP legislation in Nazi Germany did not include specific exclusions for Jewish applicants and authors, in practice, they were excluded by administrative measures alone rather than legal ordinances.[12] This is in light of the Nazi regime's desire to

---

Berne convention does affect domestic authors as these countries cannot provide less than the minimum standards of protection as stated in the convention (except for Article 7(8) regarding the duration of the protection of the artwork). On a personal note, the Berne Convention was signed and agreed upon in times of peace when countries discussed creating reciprocal standards aimed at protecting authors and artists. It is apparent that the Nazi regime has been found unlawful and as a result, the Aryanization laws were unlawful.

7 Gesetz zum Schutze des deutschen Blutes und der deutschen Ehre (Law for the Protection of German Blood and German Honor), § 1–4. Reichsgesetzblatt. Vom 15. September, 1935, Nr. 125, S. 1333f.

Verordnung über die Anmeldung des Vermögens von Juden (Regulation on the Registration of Jewish Property), § 1. Reichsgesetzblatt, Vom 26. April 1938, Teil I – Inneres, Nr. 56, 414–415.

8 'Aryanization'. HOLOCAUST ENCYCLOPEDIA, encyclopedia.ushmm.org/content/en/article/aryanization.

9 Zweite Verordnung zur Durchführung des Gesetzes über die Änderung von Familiennamen und Vornamen (Second Decree for the Enforcement of the Name Law), § 2(1) Reichsgesetzblatt. Vom 17 August 1938 I S. 1044.

10 'Law on Alteration of Family and Personal Names'. TIMELINE OF EVENTS, UNITED STATES HOLOCAUST MEMORIAL MUSEUM, www.ushmm.org/learn/timeline-of-events/1933-1938/law-on-alteration-of-family-and-personal-names.

11 Barner, Lida. '"Aryanization" Expanded? Patent Rights of Jews under the Nazi Regime'. In *Expanding Intellectual Property: Copyrights and Patents in 20th Century Europe and Beyond*, Siegrist, Hannes, and, Dimou, Augusta, ed. (Budapest: Central European University Press, 2017) 127; Andreadis, Steve. 'The Seizure of Jewish Intellectual Property Ahead of World War II'. LIBRARY OF CONGRESS (Apr. 28, 2022), https://blogs.loc.gov/copyright/2022/04/the-seizure-of-jewish-intellectual-property-ahead-of-world-war-ii/.

12 Barner, '"Aryanization" Expanded?' 132.

avoid any negative international appearances and to maintain their income from German patents used abroad.[13]

The systematic anti-Jewish legislation in the interwar period created an aggregated stigma against Jewish authors and innovators which essentially sidelined them and their ability to take a proactive part in the cultural and artistic sphere of Nazi Germany. As a result, some Jewish coauthors agreed to omit their names from research or other artistic works to enable its dissemination into the market. For example, the work of the inventor Otto Eppenstein of the Zeiss factory was never acknowledged as he agreed to forgo his economic and moral rights to ensure his work will be registered via the Nazi IP system.[14]

Furthermore, a Nazi decree which went into effect in 1933 prohibited Jews from being members of the Reich Chamber of Culture. Thus, Jews were excluded from working in radio, and theaters as well as lost their ability to sell their art.[15] On top of that, an unimaginable number of books written by Jewish novelists, or which had Jewish elements in them, were burned in massive bonfires in 1933.[16]

The new legislation of the Nazi regime deprived Jewish authors of the economic and moral rights associated with their intellectual property. Their creative works were fundamentally criminalized, and they lacked the genuine ability to create new artworks in light of the aggregated restrictions imposed on them. A prominent part of this Aryanization process by law focused on artworks that were already in existence and registered under Jewish authors. We turn below to discuss this process and the implications it had on the moral and economic rights of Jewish authors in the years leading to World War II and the Holocaust.

3 Aryanization of Patents, Music and Books, Authored by Jews

The interwar period provided the perfect opportunity for the Nazi regime to proactively confiscate, misappropriate or aggressively edit artworks authored

13 However, in 1941 an official decree was issued aiming to deprive Jewish inventors of being named in public, ibid., 133.

14 Barner, '"Aryanization" Expanded?' 135.

15 Reichskulturkammergesetz (Reich Chamber of Culture Law) vom 22. September 1933, ergänzt durch Ergänzungsgesetz vom 15. Mai 1934 (RGBl. I. S. 413), Reichsgesetzblatt 1933 I S. 661; Nazi Germany and Anti-Jewish Policy, ADL (March 6, 2017), www.adl.org/resources/backgrounders/nazi-germany-and-anti-jewish-policy.

16 'Book Burning'. Timeline of Events, United States Holocaust Memorial Museum, www.ushmm.org/learn/timeline-of-events/1933-1938/book-burning.

by Jewish authors. As we have seen, this Aryanization process had a strong influence on physical property, depriving Jews of their homes, businesses, and physical property in an effort to outlaw their mere existence and erect a barrier preventing them from participating in Germany's commercial life. Another important aspect of this process was a spiritual one, in which Jews were excluded from creative spheres and were deprived of their intellectual protection. Their rights in artistic works and patents were confiscated and misappropriated under authors, or plain names, who were more in line with the Nazi propaganda agenda.

A couple of examples have been exposed in recent years, though the scope of this phenomenon remains unknown. In the field of patent law, Jewish inventors who survived the Holocaust and filed restitution claims for patent loss present a grim picture of vast and deep patent appropriation.[17] The majority of Jewish patent holders lost their patent rights as a result of persecution which made it impossible for them to "continue exploiting their patents"[18] and the economic rights attached to them. In some instances, their social exclusion forced them to sell their rights far under their market value, and in other instances in the process of fleeing or being deported from their homes, they left behind patent documents that were either stolen or destroyed.[19] The circumstances surrounding their continued persecution prevented them from paying their patent fees, which ultimately led to the lapse of their protection.

Despite the fact no official legal decree was ever issued concerning the Aryanization of patents of Jewish inventors, after a discussion with Hitler, Göring clarified that "Jewish patents are property values and as such are to be Aryanized as well."[20] This led to the broad transfer of patents owned by Jewish businesses to non-Jewish hands, and to pressuring Jewish owner of patent rights into forced sales of their patents.[21]

In the musical realm,[22] Levi noted that in the years leading up to the war the Nazi regime "scanned the whole literature of music with the sole intention of rooting out all traces of Judaic influence."[23] In 1938, the Nazi regime issued

17 Barner, '"Aryanization" Expanded?' 134.

18 Ibid.

19 Ibid., 135.

20 'Additional Information on Some Details of Hitler's Oral Orders, 28 December 1938' in Norbert Kampe, ed., *Emigration and Expulsion of German Jews, 1933–1945: A Documentary* History (New York: KG: Saur, 1992) 469.

21 Barner, '"Aryanization" Expanded?' 144.

22 See generally Levi, Erik. *Music in the Third Reich* (Basingstoke: MacMillan, 1994) 70.

23 Levi, Erik, 'The Aryanization of Music in Nazi Germany'. *The Musical Times* 131 (1763) (1990) 19–23.

an official decree banning music publishers and recording companies to perform music authored by Jewish artists.[24] This greatly affected the performance of Jewish composers, such as Felix Mendellsohn, whose name was constantly smeared by the Nazi regime, and the public performance of his works was outlawed or simply replaced by non-Jewish works.[25]

Hermann Levi, a German Jewish orchestral conductor who worked in Germany between 1850–1900,[26] translated Mozart's and Da Ponte's Così fan Tutte, Le Nozze di Figaro, and Don Giovanni.[27] In this case, the Nazi regime opted to avoid completely banning these works given the renowned identity of Mozart,[28] and instead, they were retranslated by Siegfried Anheisser and used in seventy-six German theaters.[29]

As mentioned, when the Nazis rose to power, books that were considered "un-German" were burnt. However, another category of non-fiction books presented a different type of challenge. Those books' content was apolitical, they were extremely popular, loved, useful, and deeply entrenched within German culture. They were considered a part of its identity, regardless of the identity of the author of the artwork. The only problem was that they were authored by Jews.[30] This led their publishers, who were usually implicated with the Nazi regime, to Aryanize them by maintaining the vast majority of the content but republishing under a non-Jew name. Mendellsohn's work was more easily excluded as it wasn't entrenched in the German culture, unlike Levi and other authors which will be discussed below.

In the field of medical scholarship, Dr. Josef Löbel, an Austrian Jewish medical practitioner, was the author of 'Knaurs Gesundheitslexikon', a popular

24 Verordnung zur Ausschaltung der Juden aus dem deutschen Wirtschaftsleben (Decree on the Elimination of Jews from German Economic Life), § 2. Reichsgesetzblatt, vom 12. November 1938, I 1938, 1580.

25 Ibid.,; Levitin, Micahel, 'Rescuing Mendellsohn from the Nazi Smear Campaign'. Newsweek (May 29, 2009), www.newsweek.com/rescuing-mendelssohn-nazi-smear-campaign-80229.

26 Hermann Levi (1839–1900), Schumann Netzwerk, www.schumann-portal.de/hermann-levi-1359.html.

27 Levi, 'The Aryanization of Music in Nazi Germany', 21.

28 For more on Mozart and the Nazi regime see generally, Levi, Erik. *Mozart and the Nazis: How the Third Reich Abused a Cultural Icon* (New Haven: Yale University Press, 2010).

29 He also claimed that 'Hermann Levi initiated a massive conspiracy in which the Jews were engaged in appropriating Mozart for themselves'. Levi, 'The Aryanization of Music in Nazi Germany', 21.

30 Wilson, Bee, 'Alice's Book by Karina Urbach – the Recipes Stolen by the Nazis'. *Financial Times* (May 5, 2022), www.ft.com/content/ee4f7456-f617-4b33-981f-d682bd7d4b20.

health encyclopedia that was published in 1930.[31] This book was translated into sixteen languages and was published under the Jewish publishing house of Otto Liebmann. Once this publishing house was taken over by the Nazi publisher, C.H. Beck, Löbel's bestseller was still published but under the name of Peter Hiron, the pseudonym of the German physician Herbert Volkmann.[32] Moreover, Volkmann edited 'Knaurs Gesundheitslexikon' to include new material in line with the Nazi agenda on subjects such as "race, homosexuality, prison psychosis and megalomania."[33] Similarly, Volkmann also usurped Dr. Walter Guttmann's book "Medizinische Terminologie – Medical Terminology" starting from its 29th edition onwards. Guttmann's book on the terminology of medicine was first published in 1902 under his name. Until 1937 there have been 28 new editions published under Dr. Guttmann's name. In July 1939, the 29th edition of Gutmann's book was republished under the name Herbert Volkman. Up until that point, the book was titled 'Guttmann's Terminologie' but the publishing house changed it by deleting Guttman's name from the title.[34] Löbel and Guttmann lost everything once the Nazi regime rose into power and confiscated their lives' work.

In the legal domain, a short commentary on the German Civil Code (BGB) named the Grüneberg (until the 80th edition in 2021 when it was renamed 'Palandt') was originally based on Otto Libemann's 'pocket and short commentaries' edited by Liebmann's publishing house.[35] As mentioned, in 1933 Liebmann was forced to sell his publishing house, including his series 'Short Comments', to the Nazi-supporting publishing house, CH Beck. The reference to Liebmann was removed from the works he founded, and his property was gradually confiscated by German authorities.[36] Liebmann died in 1942, penniless and socially isolated. Despite calls to rename this commentary after Libemann, it was eventually decided in 2021 that its new name would be Palandt, the name of one of the current contributors to this commentary.

---

31 Weiss, Ruth, 'Aryanization of Jewish Writer's Intellectual Property'. *Ruth Weis Blog*, ruthweiss.net/blog/aryanization-of-jewish-writers-intellectual-property/.

32 Ibid.

33 Ibid.

34 Voswinckel, Peter, 'Um das Lebenswerk betrogen: Walter Guttmann (1873–1941) und seine Medizinische Terminologie'. *Medizinhistorisches Journal* 32 (3/4) (1997) 321–354, 321–325.

35 Allison, Jennifer, 'Great News From Germany: Legal Publisher Beck Verlag is Renaming the Palandt Civil Code Commentary'. https://etseq.law.harvard.edu/2021/07/great-news-from-germany-legal-publisher-beck-verlag-is-renaming-the-palandt-civil-code-commentary/.

36 Rebenich, Stefan. *C.H. Beck, 1763–2013 der kulturwissenschaftliche Verlag und seine Geschichte* (München: CH Beck, 2013) 376.

Perhaps the most well-known instance of copyright Aryanization during the interwar period is that of Alice Urbach's cookbook, which was first published in 1935.[37] In 1938 Urbach was forced to transfer the rights to her more than 500-page cookbook, *So kocht man in Wien!* (This is How We Cook in Vienna!), which was republished under the name Rudolf Rösch. The plagiarized version altered or completely removed about 40% of the original texts but it still included photos showing Alice's hands demonstrating how to make different dishes. However, elements celebrating Vienna's diversity were removed.[38] The manager of the publishing company maintained his stance until 1974, that Rösch simply 'modernized' the original publication.[39]

Returning to Austria after fleeing to England when the Nazis rose to power, Urbach found the revised version of her cookbook at a local Viennese bookshop in 1949.[40] She then attempted to have her rights in the cookbook returned to her by writing to the publisher, but to no avail. Her request was never granted, and she denied an offer to be written as co-author of the book with Rösch. After she died in 1983, at the age of 97, her granddaughter, historian Dr. Katarina Urbach, conducted extensive research into her grandmother's story and published the story of her grandmother's copyright theft.[41] Only in 2020, 85 years after the book came out, 40 years after her death, and after a persistent public battle conducted by her granddaughter, the publisher agreed to restore Alice's copyright in her book.[42]

The case of Alice Urbach's cookbook perfectly illustrates why even in the post-war period, copyright could not have been 'reclaimed' or just recognized.[43] An extremely strong resistance within Germany after the war, which even lingers today, still sets significant barriers for survivors and heirs to be

37 Urbach, Karina. *Alice's Book: How the Nazis Stole My Grandmother's Cookbook* (London: Macelehose Press, 2022).

38 Corke, Sophie, 'Nazi Aryanisation of Intellectual Property – and Contemporary Efforts to Restore It'. IPKAT (Jan. 18, 2021), ipkitten.blogspot.com/2021/01/nazi-aryanisation-of-intellectual.html.

39 Ibid., See also, Felder, Tracey, 'Alice Urbach's Stolen Cookbook'. Leo Beck Institute, www.lbi.org/collections/Mahlzeit/alice-urbachs-stolen-cookbook/.

40 Felder, ibid.

41 Urbach, *Alice's Book*.

42 'How The Nazis Stole a Cookbook'. *Learn German*, learngerman.dw.com/en/how-the-nazis-stole-a-cookbook/a-55434703.

43 See e.g., in the physical artworks context, Hickley, Catherine, 'She Tracked Nazi-Looted Art. She Quit When No One Returned It'. *The New York Times*, (March 17, 2020), www.nytimes.com/2020/03/17/arts/design/georg-schafer-museum-nazi-looted-art.html. This is even more difficult to achieve in the context of copyright.

recognized.[44] Combined with the severe lack of evidence and bureaucracy hurdles these heirs have to deal with lead to the conclusion that invoking these rights, including a post-war attribution right,[45] is almost an impossible redress to utilize.

4 Moral Rights and Authenticity Considerations

Copyright, as defined in this Chapter, involves "duties to the public as well as rights in the work."[46] Authors of creative works created in the interwar period have exclusive property rights in their intangible expressions. These rights allow them to control the economic and social future of their artworks. No user can interfere with or eliminate these rights. At the same time, however, these works, because of their historical and social value, cannot be presented to the public under false authorial identity. As dialogical properties,[47] the public has a right to know the authentic truth embedded within these works, including the true identity of those who authored them.[48] This truth is one of the major vessels by which to spread accurate information about the years leading to Nazi Germany and Nazi occupation, to teach the lessons, and to promote the messages from which all generations must learn. Accuracy on these terms is less a matter of the economic rights vested in the works, to which the authors have exclusivity, but more related to the set of moral rights copyright laws recognize and protect. These rights protect authorial integrity, allow viewers of the works to know who the original author is, and safeguard the authentic

---

44 See e.g., the story of Dina Babit who painted for Josef Mengele and fought her entire life to receive copyright over her artworks, Ostalowska, Lidia. *Watercolours: A Story from Auschwitz* (Sean Gasper Bye trans., 2016) (New Delhi: Zubaan, 2011).

45 This right colossally failed in the context of tangibles goods and even more so in the context of copyright protection. See, Zemer & Lior, 'Art and Copyright in Ghettos and Concentration Camps', *infra* note 94, at 828 (discussing efforts to return looted artworks after WWII).

46 Kwall, Roberta Rosenthal, 'The Author as Steward "For Limited Times": A Review of 'The Idea of Authorship in Copyright'. (https://papers.ssrn.com/sol3/papers.cfm?abstract_id=1095047) *Boston University Law Review* 88(3) (2008) 685–708, 704.

47 For more on this see Zemer, Lior, 'Dialogical Transactions'. *Oregon Law Review* 95(1) (2016) 141–222.

48 This is not a general claim as we acknowledge the value of anonymously, pseudonymously and consent to other attribution ('ghost authorship'). This claim is specific to the field of Holocaust art where the identity of the author is of great value and the circumstances of the creation of the artwork render a different theoretical approach.

message and meaning they project. Moral rights in the case of Aryanized art, we claim, maintain fairness for both authors and the public.

The right of attribution and the right of integrity are the two most prominently recognized moral rights.[49] The former safeguards the author's right to be recognized as the author of the work, while the latter guarantees that the author's work truly represents his creative personality, free of distortions and mutilations amounting to misrepresentation of his creative vision and uniquely personal experiences. As Kwall explained, both rights are intended to "safeguard the author's meaning and message, and thus are designed to increase an author's ability to safeguard the integrity of her texts."[50] Safeguarding integrity as a goal of moral rights requires striking a balance between authors and the public: "From the creator's perspective, to receive credit for what one does

---

49 Continental countries often recognize additional moral rights – e.g., the right of disclosure and the right of withdrawal and repentance. The former recognizes the author as the ultimate judge of when and under what conditions a work can be disseminated, and the latter provides the author with the power to withdraw the work from the public, even after publication, if it no longer reflects his convictions. See, e.g., Adeney, Elizabeth, 'The Moral Right of Integrity: The Past and Future of "Honour"'. *Intellectual Property Quarterly* 2005(2) 111–134. Interestingly, the European Union has not, to date, harmonized moral rights protection, although all member states have such provisions. The Wittem Project Report, however, which introduces a copyright code for Europe, suggests thorough harmonization of moral rights. The Report recognizes the following three moral rights: the right of divulgation, the right of attribution and the right of integrity. *The Wittem Project, European Copyright Code* 11–17 (2010); see also Rosati, Eleonora, 'The Wittem Group and the European Copyright Code'. *Journal of Intellectual Property Law and Practice* 5(12) (2010) 862–868, 865–66 (explaining the *European Copyright Code*'s integration of moral rights); Hugenholtz, Bernt, 'The Wittem Group's European Copyright Code', In *Codification of European Copyright Law: Challenges and Perspectives,* Synodinou, Tatiana-Heleni, ed. (Alphen aan den Rijn: Kluwer, 2012) 339.

50 Kwall, Roberta Rosenthal. *The Soul of Creativity: Forging a Moral Rights Law for the United States* (Stanford: Stanford Law Books, 2010) 6. Certain legal systems provide strong moral rights protection to authors similar in strength to the set of economic rights. 'In contrast, American copyright law rewards economic incentives almost exclusively and lacks adequate moral rights protections'. Ibid., XIII. In the 1990s, the United States has joined the group of countries protecting moral rights, but chose a more restrictive application of moral rights. The Visual Artists Rights Act (VARA) was passed two years after the United States joined the Berne Convention for the Protection of Literary and Artistic Works. Visual Artists Rights Act of 1990, Pub. L. No. 101–650, tit. VI, 104 Stat. 5128 (codified in scattered sections of title 17 of the U.S.C.). Enacting VARA was meant to accommodate the obligations imposed on the United States by Article 6*bis* of the Berne Convention, which requires all signatory states to provide at least some protection for the moral rights of authors. In essence, VARA imported 'a limited version of the civil-law concept of the "moral rights of the artist" into our intellectual-property law'. *Kelley v. Chicago Park District*, No. 08-3701 & 08-3712, slip op. at 2 (7th Cir. Feb. 15, 2011).

(and to have credit not falsely attributed) and from the audience's perspective, to be able to identify the source of material with which one engages."[51] In contemporary times, the need to identify the source is more acute, as "traditional publishers play less of a role in distributing, and thus controlling the quality of, material disseminated to audiences."[52] The unique author-work relations depicted in Aryanized art require a sensitive understanding of how far the public's right to know may interfere with individual proprietary aspirations.

If we consider copyright law to possess a "communicative impact"[53] on society and see it as the source for a variety of discursive activities, being exposed to the exact original message and meaning of authorial works is crucial. Preservation of the original meaning emphasizes the special connection between authors and their copyrightable "spiritual children,"[54] while also defining access as a public right.[55] As Mira Sundara Rajan writes, moral rights were created in order to avoid "false attribution …; inaccurate and inappropriate translations; misleading representations of the poet's personality; and erroneous statements about his life and works."[56] In this way, moral rights impact cultural integrity. Governments have a duty to protect "national culture for its own prestige and for the benefit of the public."[57] Works created in the interwar period and then Aryanized by the Nazi regime are representations of the Jewish culture, in the shape of non-fiction artworks as well as innovating scientific developments Jewish scientists contributed via patents, that once thrived on European soil. Any misattribution, manipulation, distortion of information, or illegitimate claims of rights in these works is a public wrong. Thus, we claim that moral rights are sacrosanct entitlements to authors of these works but are also imperative to the public itself.

We wish to step outside of the scope of this Chapter on German anti-Semitic crime in the 1930s and into copyright laws in the U.S. We do this to show the

---

51 Heymann, Laura, 'Naming, Identity, and Trademark Law'. *Indiana Law Journal* 86(2) (2011) 381–446, 382.

52 Ibid.

53 Kwall, *The Soul of Creativity,* 61 (internal quotations omitted).

54 Zemer, Lior, 'Moral Rights: Limited Edition'. *Boston University Law Review* 91(4) (2011) 1519–1568, 1528.

55 Shifting the focus from authors to the benefit for society in general can also be found in the rhetoric preferred by the new trademark-style consumer protectionists. See, e.g., Lastowka, Greg, 'The Trademark Function of Authorship'. *Boston University Law Review* 85(4) (2005) 1171–1242, 1175–1176.

56 Rajan, Mira T. Sundara, 'Moral Rights in the Public Domain: Copyright Matters in the Works of Indian Poet C. Subramania Bharati'. *Singapore Journal of Legal Studies* (2001) 161–195, 167.

57 Ibid., 181.

importance of protecting moral rights and its theoretical framework, despite the physical and jurisprudent distance from the events standing at the heart of this Chapter. In *Bilski v. Kappos*, the United States Supreme Court stated that "certain things are free for all to use."[58] Art created in the interwar period and then Aryanized by the Nazi regime has valuable historical and cultural value and thus must remain one of these "certain things." From a social perspective, we argue that limiting the dual goal of moral rights, both to the author and the public, amounts to a violation of an authorship norm. Moral rights are not only vehicles that afford fairness to authors. The right of attribution, for example, is a "moral obligation."[59] True, the right has an "obvious utility in protecting artists from theft of the reputation they have cultivated."[60] But this is not its only goal – the right of attribution exists to protect "the public at large from being misled":[61] "[T]here is more at stake than the concern of the artist ... There is also the interests of others in seeing, or preserving the opportunity to see, the work as the artist intended it, undistorted ... We yearn for the authentic, for contact with the work in its true version."[62] As Kwall emphasized, if the intention of the framers of the Copyright Clause of the U.S. Constitution[63] was to "stimulate an open culture steeped in knowledge and education,"[64] then "through a legal framework that promotes the public's interest in knowing the original

58 See *Bilski*, 561 U.S. at 622 (internal quotation marks omitted) (quoting Bonito Boats, Inc. v. Thunder Craft Boats, Inc., 489 U.S. 141, 151 (1989)).

59 Green, Stuart, 'Plagiarism, Norms, and the Limits of Theft Law: Some Observations on the Use of Criminal Sanctions in Enforcing Intellectual Property Rights'. *Hastings Law Journal* 54(1) (2002) 167–242, 175 (aarguing that attribution norms are moral obligations).

60 Hansmann, Henry, and, Santilli, Marina, 'Authors' and Artists' Moral Rights: A Comparative Legal and Economic Analysis'. *The Journal of Legal Studies* 26(1) (1997) 95–143, 130; see also Lastowka, Greg, 'Digital Attribution: Copyright and the Right to Credit'. *Boston University Law Review* 87(1) (2007) 41–90, 78 (remarking that the right of attribution is important in order to 'promote the smooth functioning of reputation economies').

61 Hansmann and Santilli, 'Authors' and Artists', 131.

62 Merryman, John Henry, 'The Refrigerator of Bernard Buffet'. *Hastings Law Journal* 27(5) (1976) 1023–1050, 1041. Praising the public interest in the right of integrity, Hansmann and Santilli remark: '[W]orks of art often become important elements in a community's culture: other works of art are created in response to them, and they become common reference points ... The loss or alteration of such works would therefore be costly to the community at large, depriving that community ... of a widely used part of its previously shared vocabulary'. Hansmann & Santilli, 'Authors' and Artists', 106.

63 'To promote the Progress of Science and useful Arts, by securing for limited Times to Authors and Inventors the exclusive Right to their respective Writings and Discoveries'. U. S. Constitution, art. I, § 8, cl. 8.

64 Kwall, *The Soul of Creativity*, 57.

source of a work and understanding it in the context of the author's original meaning and message,"[65] the objectives of the Clause can be maintained.

A crucial question relating to moral rights and the public's right not to be misled is whether moral rights ought to have an expiration date. If the author retains a "right to inform the public about the original nature of her artistic message and the meaning of her work,"[66] why should Picasso's moral rights end in 2043? Or, for that matter, why should Alice's moral rights end in 2053?[67] An expiration date means that personalities die. Once the human brain stops operating, the personality ceases too. However, works of creative content – embodying their author's personality – never cease to exist even when destroyed, and the public right to be informed continues along with it.

Aryanized artworks are strong candidates for perpetual moral rights protection in order to protect the public interest and reinforce the public's perpetual duty to respect and never forget, to learn from history and pass on the lessons to future generations. In other words, ownership, when applied to authorial and artistic commodities, cannot be interpreted solely through the lens of economic benefits and rewards. This argument especially applies in the context of Aryanized art, where economic benefits were bluntly deprived as soon as the Nazis rose to power.[68] Kwall urges us to rethink the anatomy of copyright and criticizes the hegemony of economic justifications for human creativity, defining "works of authorship as fungible commodities."[69] These justifications protect only one convenient subset of the creative process. Translating this line of reasoning into a workable legal standard requires a redefinition of the rigid set of time limitations to which moral rights are subjected to reward the author for his human capital and cater to the public interest and the public's role as the entity that eventually takes the work in new directions. Practically, accommodating these concerns can be achieved by a limited-in-time actionable right for authors to infringement on their moral rights, lasting as long as economic rights do. Once the actionable right expires, the public's unlimited right to be informed begins. The right of the public can be secured by implementing a system of perpetual mandatory disclaimers. These will require a user of an

65 Ibid.

66 Ibid., 151.

67 She died in California in 1983. See Sara Tor, Sara, 'Family's Fight for Cookbook 'Aryanised' by the Nazis'. *The Times* (Jan. 11, 2021), www.thetimes.co.uk/article/family-s-victory-over-nazi-theft-of-cookbook-g2xfnjmfs.

68 Verordnung zur Ausschaltung der Juden aus dem deutschen Wirtschaftsleben (Decree on the Elimination of Jews from German Economic Life), § 1–3. Reichsgesetzblatt, vom 12. November 1938, I 1938, 1580.

69 Ibid., 24.

original work, for which copyright has expired and moral rights are no longer actionable, to provide sufficient attribution to the author who was deprived of their spiritual work.

This offer focuses on the moral rights aspect of copyright, not the economic one. This requirement is urgent in the context of Aryanized artworks. This derives from the unique history surrounding the circumstances that led to these types of Aryanization of artworks and the extensive human rights deprivation the Jewish community suffered from in the years leading to WWII. In these works, the names of the original authors were deliberately and intentionally erased from their lives work in a continuous attempt to completely remove any trace of Jewish identity from the artistic world. Providing this attribution will strive to make amends and ensure those authors' rights will be restituted, thus, giving them and their heirs a piece of their identity and history back. This suggestion focuses on Germany and Austria as the Aryanization process took place predominantly on this territory. Nonetheless, it will require international cooperation to reinstate the names of the true authors and inventors over their artworks and patents as their fruits of labor were disseminated across the globe following the chaos of WWII.

Finally, it is important to note that the perpetual right solution mainly focuses on copyright-protected artworks. Patents and trademarks present a different set of challenges that are outside of the scope of this Chapter. They deserve a separate set of solutions given their different features, scope, and protection periods. We do believe that patents that were Aryanized should be reinstated under the name of the original Jewish inventor for the historical record, but they cannot belong to them perpetually. Trademarks present an extremely difficult challenge that we cannot properly address in this chapter.[70]

70 For example, if a Jewish trademark was taken by a German company back in 1933 should it be returned? If so, for Germany alone? For any spread of the German company overseas (e.g. a French sister mark)? If it is just a German company still does it lose its investment in the brand over the last 90 years? What if it has been brought by a post-war German company? And in any event, what use is a trademark to the decedent of the original owner 90 years ago? Or should money be paid for the appropriation, but how would it be valued? And in any event, as goodwill is so closely linked to marks, what about restitution for seized Jewish businesses (i.e. are trademarks anyway different?).

5 IP Restitution

Restitution has been an important remedy in the years following the war with regard to physical looted artworks. Restitution is a legal remedy that enables a victim to receive an amount of recovery based on the gains of the wrongdoer rather than the actual loss of the victim. This remedy is associated with unjust enrichment cases in which a wrongdoer is enriched at the expense of the victim in circumstances that are considered legally unjust (e.g., breach of contract or in the process of committing a crime). Thus, plagiarism of Jewish artworks by the Nazis presents an impeccable example of incidents where a wrongdoer makes a profit via an act that is utterly unjust and unfair to the true author of the artwork.

In this sense, restitution is an important remedy that can be used by victims of Aryanized artworks to ensure they will be compensated for the economic value of their work which was manipulated and abused by the Nazis. Thus, one can consider the solution of restitution as an IP instrument to install 'peace' and remedy the harms caused to Jewish authors during the interwar period.

In the physical property context, art restitution refers to situations in which a wrongdoer returns an object, artifact, or collectible to its rightful owner or heir. However, this has proven to be extremely difficult in the years following World War II. When the Eastern Bloc dissolved in 1990, the East German government passed legislation to return property that the previous communist regime had nationalized.[71] This legislation covered Jewish-owned property that was sold under duress after 1933 or subject to Nazi confiscation and allowed survivors and heirs to file claims for property in former East Germany.[72] However, these restitution agreements had limitations and strict conditions.[73] For example, the German government declared December 31, 1992, as the application deadline for real estate claims and June 30, 1993, as the deadline for movable property claims.[74] In light of the vast information and evidence required to prove

71 See 'The Successor Organization'. *Claims of Conference on Jewish Material Claims Against Germany*, https://www.claimscon.org/our-work/successor/ [https://perma.cc/U998-EMJZ] (last visited Jan. 27, 2021).

72 Ibid.

73 See Shingleton, Bradley, Ahrens, Volker, and, Ries, Peter, 'Property Rights in Eastern Germany: An Overview of the Amended Property Law'. *Georgia Journal of International and Comparative Law* 21(3) (1991) 345–358, 346.

74 *Claims of Conference on Jewish Material Claims against Germany. 2007 Annual Report with 2008 Highlights* 42 (2008), http://www.claimscon.org/forms/CC_AR_2007.pdf.

ownership, such deadlines essentially rendered the obtained restitution agreements impractical.[75]

Even though some looted items were eventually recovered, many artworks are still missing today, more than seventy years after the liberation of the ghettos and concentration camps. International endeavors have been carried out for decades to identify unaccounted for items to return them to their rightful owners or heirs. These efforts included, *inter alia*: international conferences such as the Washington Conference;[76] U.S. legislation, such as the Holocaust Victims Redress Act[77] and the "Holocaust Expropriated Art Recovery Act of 2016";[78] and international declarations, such as the "Terezin Declaration on Holocaust Era and Related Issues."[79] Research has shown that the property of over nine million Jews in Europe was looted, confiscated, or destroyed before,

75 See *In re* Holocaust Victim Assets Litig., 105 F. Supp. 2d 139, 142, 159 (E.D.N.Y. 2000); Federal Ministry of Finance – Compensation for National Socialist Injustice: Indemnifications Provisions 21 (2019), https://www.bundesfinanzministerium.de/Content/EN/Standardartikel/Press_Room/Publications/Brochures/2018-08-15-entschaedigung-ns-unrecht-engl.html.

76 The Washington Conference produced a document titled 'Principles on Nazi-Confiscated Art', which is comprised of eleven non-binding principles that, *inter alia*, expressly declare the importance of identifying such artwork and returning such works to their rightful owners. See 'Washington Conference Principles on Nazi-Confiscated Art'. U.S. Department of State, 2001–2009.state.gov/p/eur/rt/hlcst/23231.htm. See also Elie, Samantha, 'Why Wait So Long: The Cornelius Gurlitt Collection and the Need for Clear ADR Mechanisms in the Restitution of Looted Art'. *Cardozo Journal of Conflict Resolution* 18(2) (2016) 363–390, 369; Meaney, Jillian, 'From Platitudes to the Passage of the Hear Act: How Procedural Obstacles in U.S. Courts Have Prevented the Restitution of Nazi-Expropriated Art and Congress's Efforts to Provide a Resolution'. *University of Florida Journal of Law and Public Policy* 28(2) (2017) 371–IV, 375.

77 Holocaust Victims Redress Act, P.L. § 105–158, 112 Stat. 15 (1998). This Act stated that all governments should take measures to facilitate the return of private and public property that was looted by the Nazis.

78 For more on this Act see Kreder, Jennifer Anglim, 'Analysis of the Holocaust Expropriated Art Recovery Act of 2016'. *Chapman Law Review* 20(1) (2017) 1–24; Barnes, Jason, 'Holocaust Expropriated Art Recovery (Hear) Act of 2016: A Federal Reform to State Statutes of Limitations for Art Restitution Claims'. *Columbia Journal of Transnational Law* 56(3) (2017) 593–635. See also Caravello, Scott, 'The Role of the Doctrine of Laches in Undermining the Holocaust Expropriated Art Recovery Act'. *Virginia Law Review* 106(8) (2020) 1769–1818 (arguing that the doctrine of laches undermines the effectiveness of this Act and thus must be precluded as an available defense); Zuckerman v. Metro. Museum of Art, 307 F. Supp. 3d 304 (S.D.N.Y. 2018) (discussing the laches defense in a restitution claim under the Act).

79 Prague Holocaust Era Assets Conference, *The Terezín Declaration* (Jun. 30, 2009). This declaration was signed by 46 states. For the complete declaration see wjro.org.il/our-work/international-declarations-resolutions/terezin-declaration/ at WJR.

during, and shortly after the Holocaust.[80] Most looted property was owned by individuals and families. It is estimated that no more than 20% of Jewish properties (private and communal) have been restituted to their rightful owners since the war ended.[81] New Jewish communities that arose from the ashes in Europe received only a small portion of property that had belonged to their predecessors. Legislation was enacted across Europe in an attempt to restitute Jewish property, but these were rarely enforced by local authorities.[82]

Similar to the U.S. Holocaust Expropriated Art Recovery Act of 2016, Israel legislated a designated restitution law, the Israeli Restitution Act.[83] The Act established the Holocaust Restitution Company of Israel (*Hashava*),[84] and it defined two main goals for the company: (1) to encourage locating assets in Israel in cases where the assets' owners died in the Holocaust, locate heirs and other rightful owners, and restitute the misappropriated assets; and (2) to ensure that assets for which heirs or other rightful holders could not be found are used to assist Holocaust survivors.[85] Similar to the U.S. law, the Israeli Restitution Act has limitations. It applies only within Israel's domestic territory, and the law was enacted in 2006, more than sixty years after the end of World War II.[86] The law's limited reach and late enactment cast doubt on its ability to locate and restitute assets.

Globally, nongovernmental organizations and programs played an important role in fighting for the restitution of looted art – one example is the Claims Conference, an international body that operates for the welfare of Holocaust survivors.[87] The objective of this organization is to negotiate compensation

80 Mizrahi, Shelly, 'Restitution Victims of the Holocaust – Comparative Review'. Knesset Research Center (May 23, 2010).

81 Ibid.

82 Vinbaum, Lorens, 'Defrosting History: Restitution of Jewish Property in Eastern Europe'. *Beshvil Hazicaron* 31 (1999) 4.

83 See Assets of Holocaust Victims Law (Restitution and Dedication to Aid and Commemoration), 5766–2006, SH No. 2049 p. 202–29 (Isr.) [hereinafter Israeli Restitution Act]. Israel also enacted corresponding regulations to facilitate the Israeli Restitution Act's execution and enforcement. See Regulations for Assets of Holocaust Victims (Inheritance Issues), 5769–2008, KT 6732 p. 226 (Isr.).

84 See Israeli Restitution Act, ibid., 203–04; 'Types of Assets'. Hashava: Holocaust Restitution Company Israel (Dec. 31, 2017), https://www.hashava.info/template/default.aspx?catId=37&pageId=358#.X5123YhKjIV [https://perma.cc/X584-Y4CA].

85 See Israeli Restitution Act, 202.

86 Ibid.

87 'What We Do'. Claims Conference on Jewish Material Claims Against Germany, https://www.claimscon.org/our-work/ [https://perma.cc/A33H-6Q6N] (last visited Jan. 29, 2021).

payments for Holocaust victims from the German government.[88] The Claims Conference has reached numerous important agreements regarding compensation payments by German and other European governments.[89] Another important organization working in this sphere is the World Jewish Restoration Organization (WJRO).[90] The WJRO's main objective is to negotiate the restitution of private and public property in all countries (except for Germany and Austria).[91] The WJRO is considered the legal and moral representative of the Jewish people in all matters related to the restitution of assets belonging to Jews in Europe during the interwar period.[92]

Despite the challenges entrenched in restitution, when enforced properly and with global collaboration, it can act as an important remedy in the realm of Aryanized artworks, especially in light of today's global connectivity enabling enforcement agencies around the world to locate and restitute artworks which were Aryanized during the interwar period. Furthermore, unlike physical property, claimers have a greater array of ways to prove ownership over artworks thus it should be feasible to prove intellectual property ownership which was plagiarized by the Nazis when they first rose to power. It is important to acknowledge evidentiary issues are still a significant hurdle as

88 Ibid.

89 Ibid., see also 'The Successor Organization', ('In the absence of a claim from an entitled heir, if the Claims Conference filed a claim and successfully proves the original Jewish ownership of the property, it is entitled to recover property').

90 See 'About Us / Our Mission'. World Jewish Restitution Organization, https://wjro.org.il/about-wjro/about-us-our-mission [https://perma.cc/Y92W-GG35] (last visited Jan. 29, 2021).

91 Ibid.

92 Ibid., In 1993, WJRO signed an agreement with the government of Israel establishing principles of cooperation and coordination. See Cashman, Greer, 'Israel, WJRO to Work to Retrieve Assets from Holocaust Era'. *Jerusalem Post* (May 5, 2017, 5:18 AM), https://www.jpost.com/israel-news/israel-wjro-to-work-to-retrieve-assets-from-holocaust-era-489843; see also *Claims Conference on Jewish Material Claims Against Germany and World Jewish Restitution Organization Holocaust-Era Judaica and Jewish Cultural Property: A World-Wide Overview*, at IV. 2 (2009) (hereinafter 'Claims Conference and WJRO World-Wide Overview') (discussing the WJRO's efforts concerning the restitution of Judaica). Some countries tried to return Judaica artifacts to Jewish communities and individuals after the war, but others deposited such artifacts in governmental institutions, such as the Jewish Historical Institute in Warsaw, Poland; libraries in Minsk; and the *Osobyi Arkhiv* (Special Archive) in Moscow, Russia, which is now part of the Russian State Military Archive. See Claims Conference on Jewish Material Claims Against Germany and WJRO Descriptive Catalogue of Looted Judaica 9–33 (2016) (discussing restitution attempts of looted or ruined Judaica). Looted Judaica artifacts can be found today in many countries around the world. The Claims Conference has published a summary report about the restitution attempts of Judaica artifacts in more than fifty countries. Ibid., IV. 5–26.

documents proving ownership over patents and trademarks, for example, have been lost or destroyed prior to and during the war. With regards to these works, challenges are still fierce once one attempts to prove ownership for the purpose of restitution, similar to today's difficulties of heirs proving their ancestries property was looted.[93]

When discussing artworks protected by copyright, however, it seems that some evidentiary hurdles could be overcome via originals or copies of the original artwork that were smuggled out of Germany and protected over the years. As the case of Urbach's cookbook demonstrates, the road to achieving restitution is not an easy path. Many attempt to bury the past by simply ignoring or even deliberately distorting the devastating impact the Nazi regime had during the interwar period. Nonetheless, public pressure along with public awareness of these issues have become a valuable instrument to push back against this norm of denial and fight for the restitution of copyright of Jewish authors and their heirs. Considering this, restitution should always be kept in mind as an important intellectual property remedy. Restitution ensures that those who have been wronged in the past will have the opportunity to demand and achieve justice today and that their name will be rightfully reinstated upon their fruits of labor.

Governments have an important role in guaranteeing these restitution remedies are available and effective. They can ensure that by creating mechanisms for adequate enforcement; establishing extended statutes of limitations once artworks created in the interwar periods are involved; setting lenient evidentiary standards to acknowledge the difficulties involved in collecting evidence regarding artworks Aryanized by the Nazis etc. Restitution is an important tool, but it cannot be a stand-alone solution to the multifaced challenge presented by works that were Aryanized during the interwar period. Only with active engagement of regulators around the world the heirs of these Jewish authors will receive the justice their forefathers deserve.

6 Conclusion

Incidents of Aryanized artworks during the interwar period remain a severely underexplore field in the current vast literature discussing Holocaust art and intellectual property protection. It is safe to assume that vast amounts of

93 See e.g., Graham Bowley, Graham, 'Court Rules for Germany in Nazi-Era Dispute Over the Guelph Treasure'. *The New York Times*, (Aug. 31, 2022), www.nytimes.com/2022/08/31/arts/design/germany-nazi-era-dispute-guelph-treasure.html.

patents, trademarks and artworks created and authored by Jewish inventors, businessman and authors were republished and rebranded under Nazi names in the years leading up to World War II. The extensive media coverage of the intellectual theft of Urbach's cookbook has brought some attention to these types of cases, but there is still much more to explore. Our aim at the moment should be to pursue justice for Jewish authors who lost their "spiritual children" for the sole reason of being Jewish.

This Chapter aims to take the first step in this direction and shine a much-needed spotlight on plagiarized Jewish artworks in the interwar period. Similar to extensive restitution attempts conducted throughout the years in an attempt to restitute physical property that was stolen by the Nazis,[94] there lays an important international interest to strive to provide the same justice to Jewish authors whose artworks were Aryanized. This effort will require international coordination, but it is necessary to ensure that moral rights are protected, and society at large has access to authentic works of art manifesting the remarkable Jewish community that once flourished throughout Europe.

Acknowledgments

Lior Zemer, Professor of Law, Dean, Harry Radzyner School of Law, Reichman University (IDC); Anat Lior, Assistant Professor at Drexel University's Thomas R. Kline School of Law. The authors would like to thank Phillip Johnson, Michael Blakeney, Roberta Rosenthal Kwall, and P. Sean Morris for their helpful comments and to Yochai Rosnerfor, Shelbi Wasser and Or Morag for superb research assistance. This Chapter is partially based on our previous work. See Zemer, Lior & Anat, Lior, 'Inhuman Copyright Scene: The Forgotten Law of Art in the Holocaust'. *Utah Law Review* 2022(2) 353–412; and Zemer, Lior & Anat, Lior, 'Art and Copyright in Ghettos and Concentration Camps: A Manifesto of Third Generation Holocaust Survivors'. *Georgetown Law Journal* 109(4) (2011) 818–878.

94 Lior Zemer & Lior Anat, 'Art and Copyright in Ghettos and Concentration Camps: A Manifesto of Third Generation Holocaust Survivors'. Georgetown Law Journal 109(4) (2021) L.J. 813–877, 828.

Bibliography

Secondary sources

Adeney, Elizabeth, 'The Moral Right of Integrity: The Past and Future of "Honour"'. *Intellectual Property Quarterly* 2005 (2) 111–134.

Barnes, Jason, 'Holocaust Expropriated Art Recovery (Hear) Act of 2016: A Federal Reform to State Statutes of Limitations for Art Restitution Claims'. *Columbia Journal of Transnational Law* 56(3) (2017) 593–635.

Barner, Lida, '"Aryanization" Expanded? Patent Rights of Jews under the Nazi Regime'. In *Expanding Intellectual Property: Copyrights and Patents in 20th Century Europe and Beyond*, Siegrist, Hannes, and Dimou, Augusta, ed. (Budapest: Central European University Press, 2017).

Caravello, Scott, 'The Role of the Doctrine of Laches in Undermining the Holocaust Expropriated Art Recovery Act'. *Virginia Law Review* 106(8) (2020) 1769–1818.

Elie, Samantha, 'Why Wait So Long: The Cornelius Gurlitt Collection and the Need for Clear ADR Mechanisms in the Restitution of Looted Art'. *Cardozo Journal of Conflict Resolution* 18(2) (2016) 363–390.

Green, Stuart, 'Plagiarism, Norms, and the Limits of Theft Law: Some Observations on the Use of Criminal Sanctions in Enforcing Intellectual Property Rights'. *Hastings Law Journal* 54(1) (2002) 167–242.

Hansmann, Henry, and Santilli, Marina, 'Authors' and Artists' Moral Rights: A Comparative Legal and Economic Analysis'. *The Journal of Legal Studies* 26(1) (1997) 95–143.

Heymann, Laura, 'Naming, Identity, and Trademark Law'. *Indiana Law Journal* 86(2) (2011) 381–446.

Hugenholtz, Bernt, 'The Wittem Group's European Copyright Code', In *Codification of European Copyright Law: Challenges and Perspectives*, Synodinou, Tatiana-Heleni, ed. (Alphen aan den Rijn: Kluwer, 2012).

Kreder, Jennifer Anglim, 'Analysis of the Holocaust Expropriated Art Recovery Act of 2016'. *Chapman Law Review* 20(1) (2017) 1–24.

Kwall, Roberta Rosenthal, The Author as Steward 'For Limited Times': A Review of 'The Idea of Authorship in Copyright'. *Boston University Law Review* 88(3) (2008) 685–708.

Kwall, Roberta Rosenthal. *The Soul of Creativity: Forging a Moral Rights Law for the United States* (Stanford: Stanford Law Books, 2010).

Lastowka, Greg, 'The Trademark Function of Authorship'. *Boston University Law Review* 85(4) (2005) 1171–1242.

Lastowka, Greg, 'Digital Attribution: Copyright and the Right to Credit'. *Boston University Law Review* 87(1) (2007) 41–90.

Levi, Erik, 'The Aryanization of Music in Nazi Germany'. *The Musical Times* 131 (1763) (1990) 19–23.

Levi, Erik. *Music in the Third Reich* (Basingstoke: Macmillan, 1994).

Levi, Erik. *Mozart and the Nazis: How the Third Reich Abused a Cultural Icon* (Yale University Press, 2010).

Meaney, Jillian E., 'From Platitudes to the Passage of the Hear Act: How Procedural Obstacles in U.S. Courts Have Prevented the Restitution of Nazi-Expropriated Art and Congress's Efforts to Provide a Resolution'. *University of Florida Journal of Law and Public Policy* 28(2) (2017) 371–IV.

Merryman, John Henry, 'The Refrigerator of Bernard Buffet'. *Hastings Law Journal* 27(5) (1976) 1023–1050.

Ostalowska, Lidia. *Watercolours: A Story from Auschwitz* (Sean Gasper Bye trans., 2016) (New Delhi: Zubaan, 2011).

Rajan, Mira T. Sundara, 'Moral Rights in the Public Domain: Copyright Matters in the Works of Indian Poet C. Subramania Bharati'. *Singapore Journal of Legal Studies* (2001) 161–195.

Rebenich, Stefan. *C.H. Beck, 1763–2013 der kulturwissenschaftliche Verlag und seine Geschichte* (München: CH Beck, 2013).

Rosati, Eleonora, 'The Wittem Group and the European Copyright Code'. *Journal of Intellectual Property Law and Practice* 5(12) (2010) 862–868.

Shingleton, Bradley, A., Ahrens, Volker, and Ries, Peter, 'Property Rights in Eastern Germany: An Overview of the Amended Property Law'. *Georgia Journal of International and Comparative Law* 21(3) (1991) 345–358.

Urbach, Karina. *Alice's Book: How the Nazis Stole My Grandmother's Cookbook* (London: Maclehose Press, 2022).

Voswinckel, Peter, 'Um das Lebenswerk betrogen: Walter Guttmann (1873–1941) und seine Medizinische Terminologie'. *Medizinhistorisches Journal* 32 (3/4) (1997) 321–354.

Zemer, Lior and Anat, Lior, 'Art and Copyright in Ghettos and Concentration Camps: A Manifesto of Third Generation Holocaust Survivors'. *Georgetown Law Journal* 109(4) (2021) 818–878.

Zemer, Lior and Anat, Lior, 'Inhuman Copyright Scene: The Forgotten Law of Art in the Holocaust'. *Utah Law Review* 2022(2) 353–412.

Legislations and Cases

Reichskulturkammergesetz (Reich Chamber of Culture Law) vom 22. September 1933, ergänzt durch Ergänzungsgesetz vom 15. Mai 1934 (RGBl. I. S. 413), Reichsgesetzblatt 1933 I S. 661.

Verordnung zur Ausschaltung der Juden aus dem deutschen Wirtschaftsleben (Decree on the Elimination of Jews from German Economic Life), § 2. Reichsgesetzblatt, vom 12. November 1938, I 1938, 1580.

Verordnung zur Ausschaltung der Juden aus dem deutschen Wirtschaftsleben (Decree on the Elimination of Jews from German Economic Life), § 1–3. Reichsgesetzblatt, vom 12. November 1938, I 1938, 1580.

Gesetz zum Schutze des deutschen Blutes und der deutschen Ehre (Law for the Protection of German Blood and German Honor), § 1–5. Reichsgesetzblatt. Vom 15. September, 1935, Nr. 125, S. 1333f.

Verordnung über die Anmeldung des Vermögens von Juden (Regulation on the Registration of Jewish Property), § 1. Reichsgesetzblatt, Vom 26. April 1938, Teil I – Inneres, Nr. 56, pp. 414–415.

Gesetz zum Schutze des deutschen Blutes und der deutschen Ehre (Law for the Protection of German Blood and German Honor), § 1–4. Reichsgesetzblatt. Vom 15. September, 1935, Nr. 125, S. 1333f.

Verordnung über die Anmeldung des Vermögens von Juden (Regulation on the Registration of Jewish Property), § 1. Reichsgesetzblatt, Vom 26. April 1938, Teil I – Inneres, Nr. 56, pp. 414–415.

Zweite Verordnung zur Durchführung des Gesetzes über die Änderung von Familiennamen und Vornamen (Second Decree for the Enforcement of the Name Law), § 2(1) Reichsgesetzblatt. Vom 17 August 1938 I S. 1044.

Assets of Holocaust Victims Law (Restitution and Dedication to Aid and Commemoration), 5766–2006, SH No. 2049 p. 202–29 (Isr.).

Regulations for Assets of Holocaust Victims (Inheritance Issues), 5769–2008, KT 6732 p. 226 (Isr.).

In re Holocaust Victim Assets Litig., 105 F. Supp. 2d 139, 142, 159 (E.D.N.Y. 2000).

Holocaust Victims Redress Act, P.L. § 105–158, 112 Stat. 15 (1998).

Zuckerman v. Metro. Museum of Art, 307 F. Supp. 3d 304 (S.D.N.Y. 2018).

Kelley v. Chicago Park District, No. 08-3701 & 08-3712, slip op. at 2 (7th Cir. Feb. 15, 2011).

Bilski v. Kappos, 561 U.S 593 (2010).

Other Documents and Internet Resources

Additional Information on Some Details of Hitler's Oral Orders, 28 December 1938, quoted in Emigration and Expulsion of German Jews, 1933–1945: A Documentary History 469 (Norbert Kampe, ed., 1992).

Shelly Mizrahi, *Restitution Victims of the Holocaust – Comparative Review*, Knesset Research Center (May 23, 2010).

Claims Conference on Jewish Material Claims Against Ger. & World Jewish Restitution Org., Holocaust-Era Judaica and Jewish Cultural Property: A World-Wide Overview, at IV. 2 (2009).

Claims Conference on Jewish Material Claims Against Ger. & World Jewish Restitution Org., Descriptive Catalogue of Looted Judaica 9–33 (2016).

Claims Conference on Jewish Material Claims Against Ger., 2007 Annual Report with 2008 Highlights 42 (2008), http://www.claimscon.org/forms/CC_AR_2007.pdf [https://perma.cc/69QJ-6DMH].

The Wittem Project, European Copyright Code 17–18 (2010).

"Aryanization", Holocaust Encyclopedia, encyclopedia.ushmm.org/content/en/article/aryanization.

Jennifer Allison, Great News From Germany: Legal Publisher Beck Verlag is Renaming the Palandt Civil Code Commentary, https://etseq.law.harvard.edu/2021/07/great-news-from-germany-legal-publisher-beck-verlag-is-renaming-the-palandt-civil-code-commentary/.

Michael Levitin, *Rescuing Mendellsohn from the Nazi Smear Campaign*, Newsweek (May 29, 2009), www.newsweek.com/rescuing-mendelssohn-nazi-smear-campaign-80229.

Catherine Hickley, *She Tracked Nazi-Looted Art. She Quit When No One Returned It*, The New York Times (Mar. 17, 2020), www.nytimes.com/2020/03/17/arts/design/georg-schafer-museum-nazi-looted-art.html.

Graham Bowley, *Court Rules for Germany in Nazi-Era Dispute Over the Guelph Treasure*, The New York Times (Aug. 31, 2022), www.nytimes.com/2022/08/31/arts/design/germany-nazi-era-dispute-guelph-treasure.html.

Sara Tor, *Family's Fight for Cookbook 'Aryanised' by the Nazis*, The Times (Jan. 11, 2021), www.thetimes.co.uk/article/family-s-victory-over-nazi-theft-of-cookbook-g2xfnjmfs.

Steve Andreadis, *The Seizure of Jewish Intellectual Property Ahead of World War II*, Library of Congress (Apr. 28, 2022), blogs.loc.gov/copyright/2022/04/the-seizure-of-jewish-intellectual-property-ahead-of-world-war-ii/

Washington Conference Principles on Nazi-Confiscated Art, U.S. Department of State, 2001-2009.state.gov/p/eur/rt/hlcst/23231.htm

Prague Holocaust Era Assets Conference, *The Terezín Declaration* (Jun. 30, 2009) wjro.org.il/our-work/international-declarations-resolutions/terezin-declaration/.

Fed. Ministry of Fin., Compensation for National Socialist Injustice: Indemnification Provisions 21 (2019), https://www.bundesfinanzministerium.de/Content/EN/Standardartikel/Press_Room/Publications/Brochures/2018-08-15-entschaedigungns-unrecht-engl.html

Nazi Germany and Anti-Jewish Policy, ADL (Mar. 6, 2017), www.adl.org/resources/backgrounders/nazi-germany-and-anti-jewish-policy.

Types of Assets, HASHAVA: Holocaust Restitution Company Isr. (Dec. 31, 2017), https://www.hashava.info/template/default.aspx?catId=37&pageId=358#.X5123YhKjIV.

Greer Fay Cashman, *Israel, WJRO to Work to Retrieve Assets from Holocaust Era*, Jerusalem Post (May 5, 2017, 5:18 AM), https://www.jpost.com/israel-news/israel-wjro-to-work-to-retrieve-assets-from-holocaust-era-489843.

Law on Alteration of Family and Personal Names, Timeline of Events, United States Holocaust Memorial Museum, www.ushmm.org/learn/timeline-of-events/1933-1938/law-on-alteration-of-family-and-personal-names.

The Successor Organization, Claims Conf. on Jewish Material Claims Against Ger., https://www.claimscon.org/our-work/successor/.

Hermann Levi (1839–1900), Schumann Netzwerk, www.schumann-portal.de/hermann-levi-1359.html.

Bee Wilson, *Alice's Book by Karina Urbach – the Recipes Stolen by the Nazis*, Financial Times (May 5, 2022), www.ft.com/content/ee4f7456-f617-4b33-981f-d682bd7d4b20.

Ruth Weiss, *Aryanization of Jewish Writer's Intellectual Property*, Ruth Weiss Blog, ruth-weiss.net/blog/aryanization-of-jewish-writers-intellectual-property/.

Sophie Corke, *Nazi Aryanisation of Intellectual Property – and Contemporary Efforts to Restore It*, IPKat (Jan. 18, 2021), ipkitten.blogspot.com/2021/01/nazi-aryanisation-of-intellectual.html.

Tracey Felder, *Alice Urbach's Stolen Cookbook*, Leo Beck Institute, www.lbi.org/collections/Mahlzeit/alice-urbachs-stolen-cookbook/.

How The Nazis Stole a Cookbook, Learn German, learngerman.dw.com/en/how-the-nazis-stole-a-cookbook/a-55434703.

Book Burning, Timeline of Events, United States Holocaust Memorial Museum, www.ushmm.org/learn/timeline-of-events/1933-1938/book-burning.

What We Do, Claims Conf. on Jewish Material Claims Against Ger., https://www.claimscon.org/our-work/successor/ [https://perma.cc/A33H-6Q6N] (last visited Jan. 29, 2021).

About Us / Our Mission, World Jewish Restitution Org., https://wjro.org.il/about-wjro/about-us-our-mission [https://perma.cc/Y92W-GG35] (last visited Jan. 29, 2021).

PART 3

The Interwar Global World of Intellectual Property Internationalism

CHAPTER 9

Multinational Enterprises and the Protection of Trademarks in Colonial Nigeria during the Interwar Years

Emmanuel Kolawole Oke

1 Introduction

As a colony of the United Kingdom, colonial Nigeria was not a party to the Paris Convention for the Protection of Industrial Property when it was adopted. The colonial authorities however introduced the legal framework for the protection of trademarks in colonial Nigeria via various Proclamations and Ordinances. Moreover, both registered and unregistered trademarks could be protected in colonial Nigeria through the tort of passing off. At the time, trademarks were the only type of industrial property rights that could be registered in the country.[1] This was no coincidence as the economic model adopted by the colonial authorities was based on the extraction and exportation of raw materials from Nigeria and the importation of luxurious goods into the country for sale to the local colonial subjects.[2] During the period that is the focus of this chapter, i.e. the interwar years between 1919 and 1939, and also for most of the colonial period in Nigeria, the corporate sector within colonial Nigeria was dominated by foreign multinational enterprises with a keen interest in the protection of their trademarks in the country.[3]

Interestingly, in interpreting and applying the colonial trademark law, the colonial courts in Nigeria developed an approach of adapting the principles of English trademark law and the common law tort of passing off to the peculiar local conditions in Nigeria. Thus, in determining the likelihood of confusion or

1 Shyllon, Folarin. *Intellectual Property Law in Nigeria* (Munich: CH Beck, 2003) 191 (observing that: 'The first legislation on trade mark registration in Nigeria was the Trade Marks Registration Ordinance of 1914 … While this ordinance allowed local registration of trade marks, other industrial property ordinances for patents and designs … did not.').

2 Falola, Toyin, and, Heaton, Matthew. *A History of Nigeria* (Cambridge: Cambridge University Press, 2008) 111.

3 Burns, Alan. *History of Nigeria*, 5th edn. (London: Allen and Unwin, 1955) 288; Shyllon, *Intellectual Property Law in Nigeria*, 191.

 | DOI:10.1163/9789004714663_011

deception in trademark and passing off disputes, these colonial courts drew a distinction between literate and illiterate consumers and they typically found a likelihood of confusion or deception in disputes involving marks that they thought might be confusing to illiterate consumers. This approach, which was developed at the start of the twentieth century prior to the interwar years, was continuously followed during the interwar period.[4] The adoption of this approach by the colonial courts has long bewildered Nigerian legal scholars with some of them contending that this approach seemingly conflates literacy with intelligence.[5]

The approach adopted by the colonial courts in Nigeria in trademark cases during this period seems to have been influenced by the doctrine of instruments of fraud (also known as the doctrine of instruments of deception). As described by Carty, the doctrine 'imposes liability where the defendant is responsible for so marking or getting-up goods that they are "inherently likely to deceive" ultimate customers [and] liability can be imposed where the defendant makes "through the medium of another person, a false representation that his goods are the goods of another person"'.[6] In such cases, the defendant is not allowed to rely on the defence that 'the middleman/retailers of the inherently deceptive products supplied by the defendant would not be deceived.'[7] As Bently points out, the 'primary function of the doctrine was to remove any possibility of a defence merely because the initial purchaser was

4 In this regard, there are eight such relevant cases that were reported in the *Nigerian Law Reports* during the interwar years: *John Walkden & Co. Ltd. v. Jacob Akiyemi Oshodi and John Radcliffe, Ltd*, (1923) 4 Nigerian Law Reports 105; *G.B. Ollivant & Co. Ltd. v. John Christian, Trading as J. Christian & Co*, (1925) 6 Nigerian Law Reports 102; *Ferris George v. John Walkden & Co. Ltd.*, (1926) 7 Nigerian Law Reports 64; *Alcoholfabriek & Co. v. Netherlands Distilleries*, (1928) 8 Nigerian Law Reports 48; *The United Kingdom Tobacco Co. Ltd. v. Carreras Ltd.*, (1931) 16 Nigerian Law Reports 1; *John Sinclair Ltd. v. British American Tobacco Company*, (1932) 11 Nigerian Law Reports 45; *In Re Henkes' Distilleerdery*, (1933) 11 Nigerian Law Reports 76; and *Savage v. Allen*, (1936) 13 Nigerian Law Reports 34. As discussed in Part 4 below, out of the eight cases, it is only in the last case where the court chose not to follow the approach that was adopted in previous cases.

5 See Elias, Taslim, *Groundwork of Nigerian Law* (London: Routledge & Kegan Paul, 1954) 263; Nwogugu, E.I., 'An Examination of the Position of Illiterates in Nigerian Law'. *Journal of African Law* 12(1) (1968) 32, 50; Babafemi, F.O.B. 'Trade Marks and the Illiterate: A Critique of the Judicial Attitude'. *Journal of African Law* (18(2) 1974) 180, 181; Shyllon, *Intellectual Property Law in Nigeria*, 217.

6 Carty, Hazel, 'Passing Off and Instruments of Deception: The Need for Clarity'. *European Intellectual Property Review* 25(4) (2003) 188.

7 Ibid., 189.

not deceived.'[8] Among other functions, 'the doctrine offered a mechanism for finding liability in relation to international supply chains in circumstances where purchasers might not be deceived through sales in Britain, but those who purchased the goods abroad would be.'[9]

A case that demonstrates the function of the doctrine of instruments of fraud in the context of international supply chains is *Johnston v. Orr-Ewing*.[10] In this case, the dispute centred around the use of the images of two elephants on labels for yarns sold by both parties to consignees in Bombay and Aden. While the plaintiffs were the first to use two elephants on their label, the defendants subsequently did the same although with noticeable differences. Nevertheless, even though no purchaser had actually been misled, the trial court, the Court of Appeal, and the House of Lords all held that the defendants should be restrained by injunction. The courts were primarily concerned that illiterate purchasers further down the supply chain may be deceived by the defendants' use of two elephants on their label.[11] As Lord Selborne L.C. pointed out in the House of Lords:

> although the mere appearance of these two tickets could not lead anyone to mistake one of them for the other, it might easily happen that they might both be taken by natives of Aden or of India unable to read and understand the English language as equally symbolical of the plaintiffs' goods … here the use of two elephants in the upper corners, with an inscribed cloth or banner depending between them, was in my judgment enough for the [purposes of deception]. It is true that deception in fact is not in this case proved; but there is a large body of trustworthy evidence to the effect that such deception would be liable, and very likely, to occur, at all events with the more ignorant class of consumers, particularly in the up-country districts; and with this evidence my own judgment concurs.[12]

As Bently rightly observes, the effect of the decision in *Johnston v. Orr-Ewing* 'was close to conferring a trade mark monopoly over a concept'.[13] The decision

8 Bently, Lionel, 'The Doctrine of Instruments of Fraud in Historical Perspective'. In *The Cambridge Handbook of International and Comparative Trademark Law,* Calboli, Irene, and, Ginsburg, Jane, eds. (Cambridge: Cambridge University Press, 2020) 468, 474.

9 Ibid., 476.

10 (1882) LR 7 HL 219.

11 Bently, 'The Doctrine of Instruments of Fraud in Historical Perspective', 476.

12 *Johnston v. Orr-Ewing*, (1882) LR 7 HL 219, 225–226.

13 Bently, 'The Doctrine of Instruments of Fraud in Historical Perspective', 476.

also reveals the paternalistic attitude of English judges towards British colonial subjects they considered to be illiterates and ignorant. According to Bently:

> Extending the geographical reach of English trade mark law carried with it a clear tendency to extend the breadth of protection. This was, in part, a result of sensitivity to the practices of foreign consumers, but the effect was often that the adoption of marks which would not be regarded as "deceptively similar" to English operators would be enjoined in relation to foreign markets. Sometimes evidence was produced of the methods of consumption in foreign markets, but the proceedings also betray a ready willingness on English witnesses and courts to portray some foreign purchasers as ignorant or easily beguiled.[14]

In this regard, it is instructive to note that reference was made to the decision in *Johnston v. Orr-Ewing* in one of the early reported trademark cases decided by the colonial courts in Nigeria. Thus, in *MacIver & Co. Ltd. v. Compagnie Francaise de L'Afrique Occidentale* (CFAO)[15] which was decided in 1917, Weber J. cited *Johnston v. Orr-Ewing* and noted that it was held in that case that 'ordinary purchasers' should be 'construed with reference to the degree of intelligence and experience of people who are the ultimate purchasers'.[16] Although the case of *MacIver* was decided prior to the interwar years, it had a significant influence on the decisions of other Nigerian colonial judges in the subsequent trademark cases that were decided during the interwar years.

---

14 Ibid 480. The decision of the House of Lords in *Johnston v. Orr-Ewing* can be contrasted with a subsequent decision of the House of Lords in *Hennessy & Co. v. Keating*, (1908) 25(12) *Reports of Patent, Design and Trade Mark Cases* 361. In this case, involving Irish consumers and purchasers, the House of Lords affirmed the decision of the Court of Appeal in Ireland to refuse the grant of an injunction. While noting that the respondent's label resembled that of the appellants' label in some respects, it was held that there were many points of dissimilarity. It was also held that the features of the respondent's label that resembled that of the appellants' label were in common use in the trade and were not likely to mislead any person of ordinary intelligence.

15 *MacIver & Co. Ltd. v. Compagnie Francaise de L'Afrique Occidentale* (CFAO), (1917) 3 Nigerian Law Reports 18.

16 Ibid 20. It should be noted that, in context, Weber J. was in fact citing an earlier 1903 decision by another Nigerian colonial judge which is unreported and is simply referred to in the law report as the *Ibadan case*. In that earlier case, the colonial judge, Acting Chief Justice Speed (as he then was), had referred to both *Seixo v Provezende* (1865–66) LR 1 Ch App 192 and *Johnston v. Orr-Ewing*. Thus, the ordinary purchasers that Acting Chief Justice Speed had in mind in the *Ibadan case* was the native population of Ibadan.

This chapter revisits the decisions of Nigerian colonial courts in trademark cases during the interwar years from a new angle. Specifically, it explores the link between the paternalistic attitude of the colonial courts towards illiterate consumers in trademark cases and the economic interests of the colonial authorities in colonial Nigeria during the interwar period. By lowering the standard to establish a likelihood of confusion or deception using the excuse of the need to protect illiterate consumers, these colonial courts more or less introduced an indirect 'anti-dilution' standard that would have made it more difficult for third parties to compete with established firms during the colonial period. This in turn would have helped to preserve the dominance of some established firms in the Nigerian market during the interwar years. At a time when there was a global economic depression, some competition in the market would have been beneficial to (both literate and illiterate) consumers in colonial Nigeria.

The chapter is structured into three main parts. Part 2 briefly examines the protection of trademarks under international law during the interwar years. It equally briefly examines the historical development of trademark law in colonial Nigeria during the interwar years. Part 3 thereafter situates the discussion in this chapter within the legal and economic context of colonial Nigeria during the interwar years. Crucially, it highlights how colonial courts engaged in local exceptionalism and colonial difference and it shows how all of these is linked to preserving the economic interests of the colonial authorities in their colonies. Building on this, Part 4 demonstrates how the paternalistic attitude of colonial courts in trademark disputes during the interwar period is best explained through the lens of local exceptionalism and colonial difference. Importantly, by protecting the commercial interests of those multinational enterprises that were regarded as pioneers of trade in colonial Nigeria, the colonial courts were also safeguarding the economic interests of the colonial authorities in colonial Nigeria.

2 International Trademark Law and the Protection of Trademarks in Colonial Nigeria during the Interwar Years

The focus of this chapter is on the protection of trademarks in colonial Nigeria during the interwar years. However, it is helpful to consider, if only briefly, the legal framework for the protection of trademarks at the international level during this period. The starting point in that regard is the Paris Convention for the Protection of Industrial Property (Paris Convention) which was signed by 11 states in 1883 and subsequently ratified in 1884.[17] It is noteworthy that the United Kingdom was not part of the 11 states that initially signed the Paris Convention as it only acceded to the Convention in 1884.[18]

The Paris Convention was revised a number of times prior to the interwar years. It was equally revised twice during the interwar years, at The Hague in 1925 and in London in 1934.[19] It should be mentioned here that Article 1(2) of the Paris Convention which defines the object of the protection of industrial property under the Convention was introduced at the 1925 Revision Conference at The Hague.[20] Article 1(2) of the Paris Convention currently provides that: 'The protection of industrial property has as its object patents, utility models, industrial designs, trademarks, service marks, trade names, indications of source or appellations of origin, and the repression of unfair competition.'[21]

Prior to its accession to the Paris Convention in 1884, the United Kingdom enacted its first 'modern' trademark law, the Trade Marks Registration Act, in 1875.[22] This Act was amended in both 1876 and 1877 before being incorporated into the Patents, Designs and Trade Marks Act of 1883. In 1905, trademarks regained its own separate statutory framework via the Trade Marks Act of 1905. Thereafter, in 1919, the trademarks register was divided into two parts i.e. 'Parts A and B' via the Trade Marks Act of 1919. In 1938, another Trade Marks Act was enacted (consolidating both the 1905 and 1919 Acts) and this Act remained in force until it was replaced by the Trade Marks Act of 1994.

Obviously, as a colony of the United Kingdom, Nigeria was not a party to the Paris Convention during this period. Nevertheless, British trademark law was extended to Nigeria via Proclamations and Ordinances and this provided

17 Bodenhausen, Georg. *Guide to the Application of the Paris Convention for the Protection of Industrial Property* (Geneva: United International Bureaux for the Protection of Intellectual Property, 1969) 9.

18 Ibid.

19 Ibid.

20 Ibid., 21.

21 As Bodenhausen points out, 'The earlier Acts of the Paris Convention, although they mentioned several subjects of industrial property, did not contain a definition of this notion as such. This definition was introduced at the Revision Conference of The Hague in 1925. It was afterwards modified only as to form, except that at the Revision Conference of Lisbon in 1958 the subject of service marks was added to the definition.' Ibid., 21.

22 Bently, Lionel, 'The Making of Modern Trade Mark Law: The Construction of the Legal Concept of Trade Mark (1860–1880)'. In *Trade Marks and Brands: An Interdisciplinary Critique,* Bently, Lionel, Davis, Jennifer, and, Ginsburg, Jane, eds. (Cambridge University Press, 2008) 3. See also, Sherman, Brad, and Bently, Lionel. *The Making of Modern Intellectual Property Law: The British Experience, 1760–1911* (Cambridge: Cambridge University Press, 1999).

a means for businesses to protect their trademarks in Nigeria during the interwar years. Indeed, it is worth highlighting the fact that, of the various types of intellectual property rights, the colonial authorities in Nigeria prioritized the development of trademark law in colonial Nigeria during this period in order to facilitate trade within the colony.[23] In essence, the development of trademark law in Nigeria during this period provided a means for various multinational enterprises to protect their trademarks in the country even though Nigeria was not a party to the Paris Convention at the time.[24]

In this regard, the first trademark law in Nigeria was the Trademark Proclamation of 1900 which made the British Act of 1883 applicable to the then Protectorate of Southern Nigeria.[25] This was subsequently replaced by the Trademarks Ordinance of 1910 (also only applicable to Southern Nigeria). After the amalgamation of the Northern and Southern Protectorates of Nigeria in 1914, the Trademarks Ordinance of 1914 was introduced and this applied to the whole of Nigeria.[26] Thus, in a technical sense, the Trademarks Ordinance of 1914 is actually the first Nigerian trademark law as it was the first trademark law that was applicable to the entire country. Between 1920 and 1926, three Trademarks Ordinances were introduced by the colonial authorities in Nigeria i.e. the Trademarks Ordinance of 1920, the Trademarks Ordinance of 1923, and the Trademarks Ordinance of 1926.[27] The last colonial trademark law in Nigeria was the Trademarks Ordinance of 1958 which was subsequently replaced after Nigeria gained independence in 1960 by the Trademarks Act of 1965.

3 The Economic and Legal Context of Colonial Nigeria during the Interwar Period

The objective behind the British colonial project in Africa in general and in Nigeria in particular is best encapsulated in the words of Lord Lugard (who also served as the first Governor-General of (the amalgamated) colonial Nigeria between 1914 and 1919). According to Lugard, British imperialism and colonialism had a 'dual mandate' that was aimed at the mutual benefit of both the coloniser and the colonised: for the colonised, the goal was to help them

---

23 Shyllon, *Intellectual Property Law in Nigeria*, 27.

24 Ibid., 191.

25 Oyewunmi, Adejoke. *Nigerian Law of Intellectual Property* (University of Lagos Press, 2015) 234.

26 Elias, *Groundwork of Nigerian Law*, 259.

27 Oyewunmi, *Nigerian Law of Intellectual Property*, 234.

'progress to a higher plane' i.e. become more 'civilised'; for the coloniser, the goal was to ensure that the imperial enterprise was beneficial to the industrial classes of the empire.[28]

There is therefore a clear connection between the colonial project in Africa and the economic interests of the colonisers. In fact, from Lugard's point of view, Europe had a 'right' to the resources in Africa and it needed those resources to improve the well-being of Europeans (although he tried to delink this from capitalist greed).[29] Essentially, commerce (and, in this context, securing the commercial interests of European companies) was regarded by the colonisers as an agent of civilisation.[30]

As will be shown in Part 4 below, the 'dual mandate', especially the need to preserve and safeguard the commercial interests of British and other foreign firms in the colonies,[31] also informed the approach of Nigerian colonial courts to resolving trademark disputes (particularly where the trademark belonged to a multinational enterprise). The colonial courts were clearly concerned about adopting any approach that would upset the flow and distribution of manufactured goods from Europe to the colonial subjects in Nigeria. In sum, from an economic perspective, the 'dual mandate' was designed for the benefit of the imperialists although it was coated with the aim of 'civilising' the natives whom the colonisers regarded as inferior to themselves.[32] Thus, the 'dual mandate' helped to ensure that African colonies remained mainly exporters of raw materials and importers of goods manufactured by European multinational enterprises.[33] The 'dual mandate' philosophy that was articulated by Lugard in the early 1920s was maintained and followed by the colonial authorities in Nigeria during the interwar years.[34]

---

28 Lugard, Frederick. *The Dual Mandate in British Tropical Africa* (London: William Blackwood & Sons, 1922) 617.

29 Ibid., 615.

30 Morel, Edmund. *Affairs of West Africa* (London: William Heinemann, 1902) 21.

31 Nwaubani, Ebere, 'The British Labour Party, the "Dual Mandate" and Africa 1945–1951'. *Transafrican Journal of History* 21(1992) 93, 94.

32 Falola and Heaton, *A History of Nigeria,* 129; Nwaubani, 'The British Labour Party, the "Dual Mandate" and Africa 1945–1951', 106. See also Mars, J, 'Extra-Territorial Enterprises'. In *The Economics of a Tropical Dependency Volume 2: Mining, Commerce, and Finance in Nigeria* Perham, Margery, ed. (London: Faber & Faber, 1948) 136.

33 Nwaubani, 'The British Labour Party, the "Dual Mandate" and Africa 1945–1951', 107.

34 See Korieh, Chima. *Nigeria and World War II: Colonialism, Empire, and Global Conflict* (Cambridge: Cambridge University Press, 2020) 37; Falola and Heaton, *A History of Nigeria,* 111; Meredith, David, 'The British Government and Colonial Economic Policy, 1919–39'. *The Economic History Review* 28(3) (1975) 484, 498–499.

Apart from the economic context of colonial Nigeria during this period, it is also necessary to examine the legal context with a specific focus on Nigerian colonial courts. In this regard, the focus of this chapter will be on the colonial Nigerian Supreme Court which was the site of the reported trademark disputes considered in this chapter. After the amalgamation of Northern and Southern Nigeria in 1914, the posts of Chief Justice for both the Northern and Southern protectorates and their respective Supreme Courts were abolished and replaced with a single Supreme Court and one Chief Justice for the whole country.[35] The colonial Supreme Court was made up of both a lower Divisional Court (the equivalent of a High Court) and a higher Full Court (the equivalent of a Court of Appeal).[36]

In his work on British imperial courts of appeal in African colonies, Ibhawoh has argued that these courts struggled with the tension between 'the homogenizing impulses of English law' and 'the imperatives of maintaining colonial difference'.[37] In other words, British imperial courts sought to manage 'the tensions between native exceptionalism and imperial universalism.'[38] Focusing specifically on the Judicial Committee of the Privy Council and the colonial regional West African Court of Appeal (WACA) and the East African Court of Appeal (EACA), Ibhawoh contends that:

> The 'civilizing' and modernizing mission of British justice could only truly be achieved through the recognition of local exceptionality and difference. Natives who appealed to the Courts of Empire were entitled to the same standards of justice as their 'civilized' colonists, yet the boundaries of racial, ethnic, and cultural difference somehow had to be recognized and maintained.[39]

According to Ibhawoh, the maintenance of 'colonial difference in the realm of law-making and administration of justice was essential to sustaining Empire' because a 'uniform rule of law would have profoundly threatened the power dynamic that distinguished colonizer from the colonized, and abrogated the

35 Lugard, Frederick, 'Report on the Amalgamation of Northern and Southern Nigeria, and Administration, 1912–1919'. Cmd. 468, (1920) para 33.

36 Elias, *Groundwork of Nigerian Law*, 124; Elias, Taslim, 'Colonial Courts and the Doctrine of Judicial Precedent'. *Modern Law Review* 18 (1955) 356, 357.

37 Ibhawoh, Bonny. *Imperial Justice: Africans in Empire's Court* (Oxford: Oxford University Press, 2013) 4.

38 Ibid., 9.

39 Ibid., 4.

very foundations of the imperial project.'[40] Thus, just like with Lugard's dual mandate, imperial courts worked to secure and preserve the interests of the colonisers by relying on local exceptionalism where necessary and convenient, although this was invariably equally coated with the goal of universalising British conceptions of law and justice.[41]

Drawing on Ibhawoh's analysis, this chapter will make the case that attempts to manage the tension between native (or local) exceptionalism and imperial universalism did not just occur at the appellate level (i.e. at the Privy Council, WACA, or EACA). In fact, during the interwar years, the colonial Nigerian Supreme Court also attempted to manage this tension while it was resolving trademark disputes involving multinational enterprises. Crucially, and as will be further demonstrated in Part 4 below, it is contended here that the need to maintain 'colonial difference' best explains why the colonial Nigerian Supreme Court lowered the standard to establish a likelihood of confusion or deception in trademark disputes under the guise of the need to protect illiterate consumers. The analysis in Part 4 will show that the colonial courts consistently used the excuse of native exceptionalism to maintain a clear distinction between the coloniser and the colonised and that this was ultimately done to preserve the interests of multinational enterprises rather than out of real concern for the Nigerian consumers.

Moreover, apart from the dual mandate ideology and colonial difference, another crucial factor that should not be overlooked in this regard is the fact that there was no real separation of powers between the executive and the judiciary during the colonial period in Nigeria. In fact, it has been noted that most of the colonial judges were also administrators.[42] It is therefore perhaps unsurprising that the colonial judges applied the principle of local exceptionalism and strived to maintain colonial difference in their decisions as doing so would have been in line with the ideology of the dual mandate underpinning colonialism in Africa. The lack of separation of powers also probably explains why the colonial judges did not adopt decisions that could potentially undermine the commercial interests of multinational enterprises operating in the

40 Ibid., 9. See also, Chatterjee, Partha, *The Nation and Its Fragments: Colonial and Postcolonial Histories* (New Jersey: Princeton University Press, 1993) 9–10; Kolsky, Elizabeth, 'Codification and the Rule of Colonial Difference: Criminal Procedure in British India'. *Law and History Review* 23(3) (2005) 631, 636.

41 Ibhawoh, *Imperial Justice*, 11.

42 Taiwo, Olufemi. *How Colonialism Preempted Modernity in Africa* (Indianapolis: Indiana University Press, 2010) 192–193 citing Omoniyi Adewoye, 'One Hundred Years of the Legal Profession in Nigeria,' Seminar Paper presented to the History Department, University of Ibadan, Nigeria, (1986) 4–5.

colonies as that would have ultimately undermined the economic interests of the colonial authorities. As will be shown below in Part 4, this attitude of safeguarding the interests of multinational enterprises and colonial authorities was also demonstrated in the resolution of trademark disputes during the interwar years in colonial Nigeria.

4 Local Exceptionalism and the Maintenance of Colonial Difference by Nigerian Colonial Courts in Trademark Disputes during the Interwar Years

4.1 *Osborne C.J. and the Origins of Colonial Difference and Local Exceptionalism in Trademark Disputes in Colonial Nigeria*

In order to fully understand the origins of local exceptionalism and colonial difference in trademark disputes in colonial Nigeria during the interwar period, it is necessary to go back to some years prior to 1919. The seeds of local exceptionalism and colonial difference appear to have been sown in two early unreported trademark cases decided in 1901 and 1903 respectively.[43] However, the clear articulation of local exceptionalism and colonial difference in the context of trademark disputes in colonial Nigeria can be traced to Algernon Willoughby Osborne who served as the Chief Justice of Southern Nigeria between 1908 and 1913. Osborne essentially lost his job due to the amalgamation of Northern Nigeria and Southern Nigeria as his colleague, Edwin Speed, who was then Chief Justice of Northern Nigeria, became the Chief Justice of the whole of Nigeria after the amalgamation in 1914.[44] Osborne died a year later in 1915.

---

43 The first case in this regard is *The Lagos Stores, Ltd. v. Blackstock & Co.*, unreported, decided in 1901 by an unnamed colonial judge. This case was discussed by Weber J. in *MacIver & Co. Ltd. v. Compagnie Francaise de L'Afrique Occidentale* (CFAO), (1917) 3 Nigerian Law Reports 18, 20 where he notes that this 'was an infringement case, and the Judge said the question was whether the two labels were so similar as to be likely to be mistaken by "an ordinary native."' The second case is the *Ibadan case*, unreported, decided in 1903. Again, this case was discussed by Weber J. in *MacIver* and he notes that it was decided by Acting Chief Justice Speed. Among other things, Weber J. notes that, in the *Ibadan case*, Acting Chief Justice Speed referred to the case of *Johnston v. Orr-Ewing* to the effect that 'ordinary purchasers' was 'construed with reference to the degree of intelligence and experience of people who are the ultimate purchasers – in that case the native population of Ibadan.'

44 See the response of Lewis Harcourt MP (then Secretary of State for the Colonies) in the British House of Commons to a question regarding the grounds on which Willoughby Osborne was relieved of his duties as Chief Justice of Southern Nigeria. According to Harcourt, 'On the amalgamation of Northern and Southern Nigeria the two Supreme

In a line of trademark cases decided between 1909 and 1912, Osborne as Chief Justice of Southern Nigeria developed the idea that marks which are unlikely to deceive or confuse educated people may be deceptive or confusing to illiterate natives.[45] Thus, in *John Holt & Co. Ltd. v. Peters & Co.*, which was decided in 1909 but unreported, he held that the representation of a dingo dog was capable of being confused with the representation of a pointer dog with a bird in its mouth. Although the case is not reported, the ruling of Osborne C.J. was obviously influential as it was cited in subsequent trademark cases by other colonial judges and these citations provide a glimpse into the thinking of Osborne C.J. in this regard.

Crucially, in the case of *MacIver & Co. Ltd. v. Compagnie Francaise de L'Afrique Occidentale* (CFAO),[46] (decided in 1917), Weber J. cited with approval the decision of Osborne C.J. in the *John Holt* case and he noted that:

> In the *John Holt* case decided in 1909 trade marks were registered by Messrs. John Holt & Co., containing representations of a dingo dog. Messrs. Peters had already registered at Calabar, trade marks containing among other features, the representations of a pointer dog with the addition of a bird in his mouth. Osborne, C.J., said "It is too much to expect an illiterate native to appreciate such differences; he sees the dog, which he associates with the name of Peters and cannot read anything on the label. The standard of a more civilised community does not apply in his case, and he is in greater need of protection in matters of this nature than a European who is supposed to be able to read and write."[47]

Similarly, in *Houtman & Co. v. Hoytema & Co.* which was decided in 1912, Osborne C.J. followed his earlier approach in the *John Holt* case. The *Houtman*

Courts were to be replaced by one, and Sir Edwin Speed (hitherto Chief Justice of Northern Nigeria) having been selected for the post of Chief Justice of the new Supreme Court, it became necessary to retire the other Chief Justice (Mr. Osborne) on pension.' UK Parliament, Oral Answers to Questions, Volume 60: debated on Wednesday, 25 March 1914, Column 353, Hansard, (1914).

45 There is anecdotal evidence that Osborne regarded Africans to be inferior. In response to the trial of his wife in England for cruelty towards an African girl residing in their marital home in 1908, Osborne reportedly stated that 'the only way to correct black people was to flog them'. See Green, Jeffrey. *Black Edwardians: Black People in Britain 1901–1914* (London: Frank Cass, 1998) 44–45.

46 *MacIver & Co. Ltd. v. Compagnie Francaise de L'Afrique Occidentale* (CFAO), (1917) 3 Nigerian Law Reports 18.

47 Ibid., 20.

case, which was also unreported, involved a mark consisting of two anchors emerging from a crown which he held as likely to be confused with another mark that contained only one anchor. Fortunately, again, Weber J. in *MacIver* cited Osborne C.J.'s decision in *Houtman* with approval:

> In the *Houtman* case decided in 1912 the design of the applicant consisted of two anchors emerging from under a crown and a representation of two gold medals. Messrs. Van Hoytema & Co. had already registered the trade mark of an anchor. Osborne, C.J., held, and rightly too in my opinion, that the applicant's mark was calculated to deceive and in the course of his judgment said – "It cannot be too clearly understood by those who desire to register new Trade Marks in this Colony that the Court will view with suspicion and scrutinise most carefully any application brought before it which attempt to utilise any feature of a registered mark which has acquired an established reputation in any part of Southern Nigeria, and also that the standard of similarity and comparison is vastly different here from what it is in Europe."[48]

Osborne C.J.'s decision in *Houtman* also provides an insight into the rationale behind his introduction of local exceptionalism and colonial difference into the context of trademark disputes. This was done 'with a view to protecting not only a vast illiterate population little acquainted with pictorial representations, but also the pioneers of trade who have earned a reputation among these illiterate folk by the quality of goods associated with some recognised mark such as a particular bird, animal, tree or other object.'[49] In essence, for Osborne C.J., once any foreign firm had established a reputation through the use of a mark that consisted of an essential feature, such as an animal or an object, then no other firm (whether foreign or local) was permitted to use that essential feature (even in a modified form) to sell any product.

Even though Lugard did not articulate the dual mandate philosophy until about 10 years later, Osborne C.J. was clearly thinking along the same lines. For Osborne, maintaining colonial difference in this regard was essential not just for the protection of the illiterate natives who he perceived as been ill-equipped to distinguish between different pictures but also, perhaps more importantly, it was necessary to protect the 'pioneers of trade'. In other words, just like the dual mandate, this was another means of safeguarding the commercial

48 Ibid., 20.

49 Ibid., 19 (as quoted by Weber J in *MacIver*).

interests of multinational enterprises operating in colonial Nigeria. Thus, it was crucial to maintain colonial difference in this regard to prevent undermining the commercial interests of these foreign firms in the country.

The fact that Osborne's perception of the level of intelligence of Nigerians played a role in his application of colonial difference in this case is shown in another case that he decided in 1912 i.e. *Compagnie Francaise de L'Afrique Occidentale* (*CFAO*) *v. Miller Brothers, Ltd* (also unreported). In this case, Miller Brothers had registered a guinea fowl as a trademark for certain classes of goods and CFAO had applied to register a mark consisting of a turkey for other classes of goods. Even though CFAO sought to register a mark consisting of a different bird for different classes of goods other than those for which Miller Brothers' mark was registered, Osborne C.J., following his approach in *John Holt*, ruled that the turkey mark was likely to be confused with the guinea fowl mark by the natives of Nigeria. While this case is unreported, it was cited with approval in the case of *Ferris George v. John Walkden & Co. Ltd.*[50] (decided in 1926) where Tew J. noted that Osborne C.J. had stated in *CFAO* that:

> In my judgment, the Trade Marks Ordinance should be construed and administered with due regard to local conditions and peculiarities of trade, and with due allowance for the fact that *the average standard of intelligence* of the British public is not found, and *cannot be expected*, in the purchasing public of southern Nigeria. Both Millers and the French Company are general merchants dealing in all classes of goods … Millers have registered in several widely different classes the guinea fowl mark, which was at once identified as "Millers" by one of the native witnesses called by the Applicants, and to a certain extent has become identified with Millers goods, and I have no doubt that a large number of southern Nigeria natives, who have ordinary sight and ordinary minds, would be confused between that mark and the French Company's turkey. It follows that such natives might easily purchase goods with the turkey mark in the belief that they were the goods of the firm with the guinea fowl mark, precisely the state of affairs which Trade Mark laws are designed to prevent. I hold that in these circumstances, it would be contrary to the spirit, and would defeat the object, of the Ordinance if the Court were to allow the registration of this particular deceptive turkey mark in any class of goods sold by Millers, even though the guinea fowl mark has not been registered in such class.[51]

50 *Ferris George v. John Walkden & Co. Ltd.*, (1926) 7 Nigerian Law Reports 64.

51 Ibid., 67–68 (emphasis added).

Thus, in this case, the focus was not on *literacy* but on *intelligence*. It is also striking that, while Osborne C.J. noted that one of the native witnesses recognised the guinea fowl mark as belonging to Miller Brothers, he did not state that any particular native witness said they would confuse the guinea fowl mark with the turkey mark. Osborne C.J. essentially came to the conclusion that the natives would be deceived by the turkey mark based on his own mistaken perception regarding the level of intelligence of native Nigerians.

In the case of *MacIver & Co. Ltd. v. Compagnie Francaise de L'Afrique Occidentale* (*CFAO*),[52] (decided in 1917 as noted above), MacIver & Co. (the applicants) had applied to register a trademark consisting of a design of a puncheon standing on end on the ground with men in the act of coopering it. CFAO opposed this application as they had previously registered a trademark that consisted of a native rolling a puncheon on the ground. The lower Divisional Court allowed the registration of the applicants' mark and CFAO appealed against this decision to the Full Court of the Supreme Court. The Full Court (consisting of Weber J., Ross J., and Speed C.J.) reversed the decision of the Divisional Court. In essence, according to the Full Court, because the essential feature of both trademarks was a puncheon, MacIver & Co.'s mark was calculated to deceive and should therefore be refused registration.[53]

The decision of the Full Court in *MacIver* was clearly influenced by its adoption of local exceptionalism and colonial difference as can be seen from the leading judgment of Weber J. who drew inspiration from the decision of Osborne C.J. in the *Houtman* case:

> To the trained eye of a civilised community there is undoubtedly a considerable difference in the two designs set side by side and the one would hardly be likely to be mistaken for the other, but while the broad principles laid down in English cases should be applied, the Trade Marks laws of this country should be administered with due regard to local conditions and, as stated by Osborne, Chief Justice, in the *Houtman* case, "with a view to protecting not only a vast illiterate population little acquainted with pictorial representation, but also the pioneers of trade who have earned a reputation among these illiterate folk by the quality of goods associated with some recognised mark such as a particular bird, animal, tree or other object." Judges of the Supreme Court of this Colony have consistently administered these laws with due regard to local conditions

52 *MacIver & Co. Ltd. v. Compagnie Francaise de L'Afrique Occidentale* (*CFAO*), (1917) 3 Nigerian Law Reports 18.

53 Ibid.

> and I think we should embrace this opportunity of expressing our unqualified approval of their decisions.[54]

In his application of the law (as encapsulated in *John Holt* and *Houtman*) to the facts before him, Weber J. concluded that:

> In this case before us the main and essential feature is the cask or puncheon. To the illiterate there is no other feature connected with this particular class of goods which this mark is intended to represent, and whether the cask or puncheon is being rolled by one man, or being coopered by three men, no difference is discernible by the illiterate native. It is the cask by which he associates a particular seller with his particular class of goods, the other minor features and differences he will not appreciate.[55]

For his own part, Ross J. agreed with Weber J. While noting that 'when both the trade marks are looked at together there would appear to be no similarity between them, generally speaking', Ross J. stressed that in 'a highly intelligent and civilised community' he would 'have no hesitation in saying that the likelihood of confusing the two marks is so very negligible that no one could reasonably say that the respondents' mark is calculated to deceive'.[56] He could not however overlook the fact that 'attention must be paid to surrounding circumstances and local conditions' because 'the percentage of persons who can read and write, and especially of those to whom the class of goods are concerned are sold, is extremely small.'[57] Thus, Ross J. clearly conflated literacy with intelligence. For him, the problem was not just the fact that the natives of colonial Nigeria were mostly illiterate, it was also because colonial Nigeria was not, according to him, 'a highly intelligent and civilised community'. This theme of conflating literacy with intelligence also reoccurs in subsequent cases during this period.

However, Edwin Speed C.J., the first Chief Justice after the amalgamation of Nigeria, had some reservations regarding the approach adopted by his colleagues although he was not in principle opposed to applying the principle of local exceptionalism. While acknowledging the need to have regard to local conditions, Speed C.J. was also concerned about the 'danger of unduly

54 Ibid., 19.
55 Ibid., 21.
56 Ibid., 21.
57 Ibid., 21–22.

restricting the field from which trade marks may be chosen.'[58] Ultimately, however, he equally agreed that the decision of the lower court should be set aside.[59]

4.2 *The Maintenance of Colonial Difference in Trademark Disputes in Colonial Nigeria during the Interwar Years*

While the quartet of *John Holt, Houtman, CFAO*, and *MacIver* were decided prior to the interwar years, they constitute the foundation on which other colonial judges built on in the subsequent trademark cases that were decided during the interwar years. As will be shown below, out of the eight reported trademark and passing off cases during this period, it was only in one case that the colonial judge chose not to follow the practice of local exceptionalism and colonial difference that had been developed in the previous cases.

The first case that will be considered in this regard is that of *John Walkden & Co. Ltd. v. Jacob Akiyemi Oshodi and John Radcliffe, Ltd*[60] which was decided by Van der Meulen J. of the Divisional Court at Lagos in 1923. In this case, for a number of years, the plaintiffs had been marketing in Nigeria cotton piece goods with a trademark consisting of a single fish but the trademark had not been registered in Nigeria. The plaintiffs subsequently noticed that the defendants were selling cotton piece goods with a single fish similar to that of the plaintiffs. The plaintiffs therefore brought an action to restrain the use of their marks by the defendants and also to restrain the defendants from passing off their own goods as those of the plaintiffs. The court held that, as the trademark was not registered, there could be no injunction to restrain the infringement of the trademark but an injunction could be granted to restrain the passing off by the defendants of their goods as those of the plaintiffs.[61] The court also rejected the defendants' argument that the plaintiffs had lost the right to the exclusive use of their mark containing a single fish because they had acquiesced to the use by another company of a mark containing three fishes for the marketing of similar goods.[62]

Interestingly, at the start of the proceedings, Mr Ajasa (a Nigerian), the counsel for the defendants stated his intention to contend that native traders and customers would not mistake the mark used by the defendants for the

58 Ibid., 22.

59 Ibid., 23.

60 *John Walkden & Co. Ltd. v. Jacob Akiyemi Oshodi and John Radcliffe, Ltd*, (1923) 4 Nigerian Law Reports 105.

61 Ibid.

62 Ibid.

mark belonging to the plaintiffs.[63] Ajasa contended that 'illiterate natives were much more sophisticated than was commonly thought.'[64] Curiously, however, when the hearings resumed, Ajasa abandoned this line of defence and instead chose to argue that there could be no infringement because the plaintiffs' mark was unregistered and that there was no exclusive right to use the mark because the plaintiffs had acquiesced to the use of a mark consisting of three fishes by another company.[65] While the court agreed that the plaintiffs could not succeed in an action for trademark infringement because the mark was unregistered, the court said that this does not mean that the plaintiffs could not succeed in an action for passing off.[66]

In this regard, in resolving the passing off claim, the court followed *MacIver* and applied the principle of local exceptionalism. According to Van der Meulen J., there could be no 'doubt that illiterate natives would mistake cotton piece goods bearing upon them the Defendants' fish mark of a single fish for the goods of the Plaintiffs.'[67] Concerning the claim that the plaintiffs had no exclusive rights to their mark because they had acquiesced in the use by another company of a mark containing three fishes, the defendants' counsel ironically and surprisingly tried to rely on local exceptionalism to contend that 'illiterate native traders and dealers when buying goods do not look at or at all closely examine the trade mark by which such goods are known … and that it is quite immaterial to them whether such goods have upon them a mark consisting of one fish or of several fishes.'[68] Coming from a Nigerian lawyer, this was quite a remarkable argument bearing in mind the initial plan of the same lawyer to contend that native traders and customers would not mistake the mark used by the defendants for the mark belonging to the plaintiff. While still relying on the principle of local exceptionalism and drawing on *MacIver*, even the colonial judge found it incredible to believe that illiterate natives would confuse a mark consisting of one fish with another mark consisting of three fishes:

> although, applying the principles laid down in *McIver & Co. v. Compagnie Francaise,* it is in the highest degree improbable that illiterate natives would be able to distinguish between similar goods each bearing a mark consisting of a design of a single very ordinary fish of almost identical

63 Ibid., 107.
64 Ibid.
65 Ibid.
66 Ibid., 108.
67 Ibid.
68 Ibid., 109.

> shape and size, it is almost incredible that such persons would not be able to distinguish between such goods and these having another trade mark consisting of three or more fishes. I am therefore of the opinion that the use in Nigeria of another trade mark consisting of a design of three or more fishes does not constitute a common use of the Plaintiffs' trade mark of a single fish.[69]

One could however argue that, in this case, it was unnecessary for the court to resort to the principle of local exceptionalism. Obviously, it is ridiculous to suggest that Nigerians (whether literate or illiterate) would be unable to distinguish between a mark consisting of one fish and another mark consisting of three fishes. At the same time, a mark consisting of one fish could arguably confuse both a literate and an illiterate person especially where both marks are almost identical in terms of shape and size. As Van der Meulen J. also noted, 'other firms who have in the past applied a trade mark consisting of a single fish to similar goods, have desisted from the use of such trade marks when representations have been made to them by the Plaintiffs.'[70] Thus, there was really no need to rely on local exceptionalism and colonial difference to resolve this dispute.

The next reported trademark dispute is that of *G.B. Ollivant & Co. Ltd. v. John Christian, Trading as J. Christian & Co.*[71] Like the previous case analysed above, this was also decided by Van der Meulen J. sitting as a judge of the Divisional Court in 1925. In this case, the plaintiffs were the owners of a registered trademark that consisted of a man mounted on a horse with a spear pointed at an animal on the ground. In 1923, the defendant started to sell cotton piece goods bearing a mark consisting of a horse on which a man was balanced on one foot. This led the plaintiffs to launch an action to restrain the defendant from passing off his own goods as those of the plaintiffs. Once again, relying on local exceptionalism and colonial difference, the court held that, as the defendant's mark was likely to mislead illiterate natives, the plaintiffs were entitled to an injunction.[72] Citing both *Houtman* and *MacIver*, Van der Meulen J. stated that: 'to the eye of the educated and discriminating person the differences between the two marks are so pronounced as to leave little room for confusion.

69 Ibid.

70 Ibid., 110.

71 *G.B. Ollivant & Co. Ltd. v. John Christian, Trading as J. Christian & Co*, (1925) 6 Nigerian Law Reports 102.

72 Ibid.

In this country however the standards by which such matters must be judged are entirely different.'[73] As he further explained:

> I do not think that the class of native to whom I have referred, and who would doubtless form the bulk of the purchasers of the goods in question, would be impressed by the fact that in the one case the rider is seated and in the other he is maintaining his equilibrium upon one foot; so long as he received goods bearing a device of a horse with a man upon it, I do not doubt he would think that he had got goods of the well known "horseman" brand in respect of which the plaintiffs have established a reputation.[74]

It is unclear why Van der Meulen J. thought that illiterate natives would not be able to draw a distinction between a mark consisting of a man seated on a horse and another mark consisting of a man standing on a horse. One plausible explanation for this reliance on local exceptionalism and colonial difference was probably the need to protect the status of G.B. Ollivant as (in the words of Osborne C.J. in *Houtman*) one of the 'pioneers of trade' in Nigeria. As Van der Meulen J. noted at the beginning of his judgment, the plaintiffs' registered trademark 'has been used by them for very many years in conjunction with cotton piece goods and has established a very general reputation.'[75]

In the subsequent case of *Ferris George v. John Walkden & Co. Ltd.*,[76] decided in 1926 by Tew J. of the Divisional Court, the applicant (George) sought to register a mark consisting of a ram for wool and perfumery products but the opponents (Walkden & Co.) objected to this on the ground that they had already registered a similar mark for other classes of goods. Tew J. admitted that the 'two marks are by no means identical, for the opponents' ram does not resemble the other closely and is further distinguished by the addition of an Ashanti stool on the off hind quarter of the animal' and that 'one would not be likely to be mistaken for the other by members of a civilised community.'[77] However, since he did not regard colonial Nigeria to be a 'civilised community', he went further to apply local exceptionalism and noted that, in Nigeria, 'different considerations prevail.'[78] In deciding the case, Tew J. considered that he was bound

73 Ibid., 103.
74 Ibid., 104.
75 Ibid., 102.
76 *Ferris George v. John Walkden & Co. Ltd.*, (1926) 7 Nigerian Law Reports 64.
77 Ibid., 65–66.
78 Ibid., 66.

by Osborne C.J.'s earlier decision in *CFAO* (1912) and he ruled that the applicant's mark should not be registered.[79] According to him:

> I consider that I am bound by this decision [i.e. *CFAO*], against which there has been no appeal ... [The opponents] have shown by their evidence that the "ram" is widely known as their trade mark in respect of certain goods, including goods which come under [the classes for which the applicant is seeking registration], and the principle laid down by the learned Chief Justice must be applied to this case ... I agree that in a community in which the *standard of intelligence* is higher, the principle could not be stated in such wide terms: but the learned Chief Justice laid stress on the fact that he was deciding the question with special reference to local conditions.[80]

Thus, it seems that like Osborne C.J. (in *CFAO*) and Ross J. (in *MacIver*), Tew J. also thought that native Nigerians had a lower standard of intelligence. This was therefore not simply about the protection of illiterates but a misconception about the intelligence of the natives by these colonial judges.

In 1928, there was another reported decision of the Full Court of the Supreme Court in the case of *Alcoholfabriek & Co. v. Netherlands Distilleries*.[81] This time around the Full Court was composed of Combe C.J., Tew J., and Maxwell J. The facts of the case are simple and relatively straightforward. Alcoholfabriek (the applicants) had sought to register a mark consisting of a parrot in a class of goods in respect of which Netherlands Distilleries (the opponents) had already registered a mark consisting of a toucan. Netherlands Distilleries were therefore opposed to the registration of Alcoholfabriek's mark. The lower Divisional Court held that Alcoholfabriek's mark could be registered as it was not calculated to deceive. This decision was however reversed on appeal by the Full Court.[82]

It is particularly striking that, for Combe C.J., even the evidence that illiterate Nigerians would not be misled by any similarity in the two marks was not sufficient to dissuade him from applying local exceptionalism and colonial difference in this case. According to Combe C.J.:

79 Ibid., 68.

80 Ibid (emphasis added).

81 *Alcoholfabriek & Co. v. Netherlands Distilleries*, (1928) 8 Nigerian Law Reports 48.

82 Ibid.

> It is not suggested that any educated African would be misled by any similarity between the applicants' mark, which represents a parrot, and the opponents' mark, which purports to represent a toucan. The question of fact is whether, if the applicants' mark is registered, some illiterate Africans who are capable of recognising that both the opponents' registered trade mark and the mark which the applicants desire to register depict birds may be misled by the similarity of the two marks into accepting a bottle of the applicants' gin when they think that they are purchasing a bottle of the opponents' gin.
>
> …
>
> The conclusion at which I should have arrived on the question as to whether the similarity of the two marks is calculated to deceive the ultimate purchasers of gin in this country, if no witnesses had been called in the Court below, is not altered by the evidence of the witnesses called by the applicant, notwithstanding that I recognise that the third witness, who states in effect that his customers would not be misled by any similarity in the two marks, is in a better position to answer that question than I am, since he has been selling goods for years to illiterate Africans who recognise the goods they want by the trade mark on them.
>
> …
>
> The second witness is a trader of some forty years experience in selling cotton goods. On being shown the two marks he stated "… I myself can tell the difference. If I had been selling one brand of gin with a parrot on it and I offered the customers the one with a toucan on it they would not accept". This witness it seems has had experience in trying to pass off on his customers goods which are not goods which the customers wish to buy, and he gives an example of a case in which he had difficulty in deceiving his customers … This is exactly what I am satisfied would happen if the applicants' mark is registered … It is, I conceive, the duty of the Court to protect those customers who would be deceived, and for this reason I consider that the appeal should be allowed and that the Registrar should be directed not to proceed with the registration of the applicants' mark.[83]

Unsurprisingly, Tew J. was more concerned about the level of intelligence of native Nigerians and not literacy (as he was in *Ferris George v. John Walkden*

83 Ibid., 48–50.

& Co discussed above). Citing both *Houtman* and *MacIver* with approval, he noted that:

> the question as to likelihood of deception must be decided entirely on the comparison of one bird with the other, having regard to the *standard of intelligence* of the ultimate consumer ... Looking then at these two marks, and having considered the evidence, for what it is worth, and using my own experience, extending over a period of more than twenty years, of *the mentality of the primitive African*, I ask myself what would happen in the case of such a person who had bought and enjoyed a bottle of gin bearing the trade mark of the parrot. Would he, when anxious to buy more gin of the same brand, be satisfied with a bottle on which the mark of the toucan was displayed? I think there is no doubt that he would. He would look for a bird of about the same size and would go no further than that; the fact that the second bird had a much larger bill would not affect his choice.[84]

Maxwell J.'s opinion was quite similar to Tew J's view on the matter. According to him, the main question was whether the proposed trademark of the applicants is 'likely to deceive and confuse the ultimate retail buyer of their and their opponents' goods, *viz.*, the *unsophisticated bush native* of the hinterland?'[85] Citing Ross J.'s judgement in *MacIver*, Maxwell J. concluded that an average uneducated native would not be able to 'remember the difference between these two pictured birds'.[86]

The situation is not different with regard to the trademark cases decided in the early 1930s. Thus, in *The United Kingdom Tobacco Co. Ltd. v. Carreras Ltd.*,[87] a passing off case which was decided by Butler Lloyd J. in 1931, the plaintiffs (United Kingdom Tobacco Co.) were the owners of a brand of cigarettes called 'Bandmaster' which had the picture of a white man in the uniform of a bandmaster. The defendants (Carreras) started to put on the market a new brand of cigarettes called 'Barrister' which had the picture of a white man in the robe of a barrister. The plaintiffs claimed that the get-up of the defendants' cigarettes was likely to deceive purchasers and sought to restrain the defendants from importing and selling the 'Barrister' cigarettes.

84 Ibid., 52 (emphasis added).

85 Ibid., 53 (emphasis added).

86 Ibid., 54.

87 *The United Kingdom Tobacco Co. Ltd. v. Carreras Ltd.*, (1931) 16 Nigerian Law Reports 1.

The plaintiffs' main contention was that the defendants' get-up was likely to mislead an illiterate purchaser.[88] The defendants however highlighted a number of differences between both brands and contended that 'even an illiterate native is perfectly capable of discriminating between a picture of a white man in military uniform and one in a barrister's wig and gown.'[89] Following the approach adopted in earlier cases and applying the principle of local exceptionalism, the court ruled in favour of the plaintiffs.[90] In this regard, Butler Lloyd J. appears to have conflated literacy with intelligence:

> It is a well established principle, not only in this country, that the likelihood of deception varies with the *intelligence and education* of the consumers and in accordance with this principle this Court has repeatedly held to be likely to deceive illiterate natives marks which would certainly not have been likely to deceive an educated European. This divergence between English and local decisions will no doubt tend to disappear as the local standard of *education and intelligence* improves; but the illiterate native is and must for a long time yet remain a factor for the Court to consider in arriving at a decision in this class of case.[91]

In another tobacco-related dispute decided in 1932, the same approach was followed by Weber, now acting Chief Justice, sitting as a judge of the Divisional Court. Thus, in *John Sinclair Ltd. v. British American Tobacco Company*,[92] the applicants (Sinclair) sought to register a trademark consisting of a castle with three turrets and the words 'Old Castle' written above it. The opponents (British American Tobacco Company) opposed the registration of this mark on the ground that it resembled their own trademark of 'Three Castles' and that it was calculated to mislead illiterate natives. It should come as no surprise that Weber, Acting C.J., ruled in favour of the opponents and, applying local exceptionalism, held that the applicants' mark should be refused registration.[93] Recalling his earlier opinion in *MacIver*, Weber, Acting C.J., stated that:

> In dealing with the question of deception, this Court has by various decisions laid down an established principle that the likelihood of

88 Ibid., 3.
89 Ibid.
90 Ibid.
91 Ibid., 2 (emphasis added).
92 *John Sinclair Ltd. v. British American Tobacco Company*, (1932) 11 Nigerian Law Reports 45.
93 Ibid.

> deception varies with the *intelligence and education* of the consumers and it has repeatedly held that a mark which would certainly not be likely to deceive an educated European may nevertheless be likely to deceive illiterate natives. I am clearly of opinion that the adoption of the words "Old Castle" and the general appearance of the applied for trade mark bear such a close resemblance to the opponents' registered trade mark as to be calculated to deceive.[94]

The Full Court of the Supreme Court had a chance to revisit this issue in 1933 in the case of *Re Henkes' Distilleerdery*.[95] This time around, the Full Court was composed of new judges i.e. Sir Donald Kingdon C.J. (who delivered the court's judgment), Yates J., and Carey J. In this case, Henkes Distillery had applied to register a trademark which was opposed by Netherlands Distilleries. At the trial, the judge of the lower Divisional Court declined to take into account the possibility of the mark of Henkes Distillery being used in the same colours as that of Netherlands Distilleries and had allowed the mark to be registered. On appeal to the Full Court, it was held that the trial judge was wrong in declining to consider the possibility that the mark could be used in the same colours as that of Netherlands Distilleries. The Full Court ruled that the mark of Henkes Distillery should be refused registration because it had not shown that its mark was not calculated to deceive.[96]

In this case, it is interesting to note that both parties called witnesses to support their claims in this regard. Henkes Distillery called three witnesses to show that its marks were not calculated to deceive (including to show that illiterate natives would not be confused) while Netherlands Distilleries called a single witness to show the opposite but the court chose to believe the witness called by Netherlands Distilleries. As Kingdon C.J. noted in his judgment:

> The third witness [called by Henkes Distillery], Karimu Kotun, does give valuable evidence. He is a trader of Lagos and says:-
>
> > "I sell spirits. I don't know opponents' mark. Looking at it I should notice the E.K. mainly. I should not confuse it with applicants' mark. I sell to illiterates. They would not confuse either."
>
> and in cross-examination:-

94 Ibid., 46 (emphasis added).

95 *In Re Henkes' Distilleerdery*, (1933) 11 Nigerian Law Reports 76.

96 Ibid.

> "I am a Mohammedan. I think a bush native would know the difference although he cannot read the letters. I have designed trade marks myself."
>
> and in re-examination:-
>
> "I have known a native bring on the label to show what he wants."
>
> Against this the opponents [Netherlands Distilleries] call only one witness. His name is Gilbert Idowu and he is also a Lagos Trader and says:-
>
> "I handle gin. I know opponents marks … Natives would describe any of applicants's [sic] mark as *Olowo* and would not be able to distinguish them from opponents."
>
> In my view this evidence [by Gilbert Idowu] has a more convincing ring than that for the applicants.[97]

Ultimately, the Full Court did not depart from the precedent set in previous cases. Citing with approval previous cases such as *Houtman*, *Ferris George*, and *Alocoholfabriek*, Kingdon C.J. equally applied the principle of local exceptionalism and he came to the conclusion that the applicants' proposed marks so nearly resemble the Netherlands Distilleries' mark as to be calculated to deceive.[98]

4.3 *Graham Paul J. and the Refusal to Maintain Colonial Difference*

The only reported trademark dispute during the interwar period where a colonial judge refused to apply local exceptionalism and colonial difference is the last reported case during this period. This was the case of *Savage v. Allen*[99] which was decided by Graham Paul J. at the Divisional Court in 1936. In this case, the plaintiff (Savage) sought, inter alia, an injunction to restrain the defendant (Allen) from infringing his registered marks and also from passing off his goods as those of the plaintiff. The plaintiff's mark was a composite mark consisting of the word 'Yaro', a Hausa word meaning 'baby boy', and the picture of a baby. The defendant's mark was also a composite mark consisting of the word 'Yiola', a Yoruba word meaning 'it will live', and the picture of a baby.

Both parties used their respective marks to sell medicines for babies. The only similarity between both pictures was that they both contained the picture of a baby and it was established by the court that it was common practice in Lagos for medicines for babies to have the picture of a baby. The court ruled

97 Ibid., 79–80.

98 Ibid., 81.

99 *Savage v. Allen*, (1936) 13 Nigerian Law Reports 34.

in favour of the defendant and it held that, due to the established practice of using pictures of babies on medicines for babies and the difference between the pictures of both parties, there was no trademark infringement or any evidence of passing off.[100]

The plaintiff attempted to use local exceptionalism and he called two natives as witnesses to support his claim in this regard. Graham Paul J. was however unimpressed with both witnesses and he noted that the natives could tell the difference between the products of both parties. Commenting on the evidence of the two witnesses, he noted that:

> Neither of these witnesses impressed me as reliable or truthful in the oral evidence they gave or in the way they gave it. There was, however while they were in the witness box, a certain amount of real evidence which impressed me most forcibly. Neither of them had the slightest difficulty in distinguishing between the "Yiola Fluid" Carton and the "Yaro" Carton – at a glance, without hesitation or mistake, though *illiterate*, they could tell which was which of the two cartons … I preferred that ocular demonstration to their most unconvincing oral evidence that they couldn't tell the difference between the two cartons.[101]

Graham Paul J. was equally satisfied that both literate and illiterate persons would not be confused by both words.[102] In relation to the pictures, he observed that both baby photographs were remarkably different from each other.[103] He also rightly noted that the implication of holding that the defendant's baby picture infringed the plaintiff's baby picture would be that the plaintiff would be 'the only person allowed to put a representation of a baby on a carton of baby medicine for sale in Lagos.'[104]

Interestingly, in resolving this dispute, Graham Paul J. did not cite or discuss any of the previous cases decided before or during the interwar years in this regard. Unlike other colonial judges, he did not conflate literacy with intelligence and he seemed uninterested in applying local exceptionalism and colonial difference. As he notes in his judgment:

100 Ibid.
101 Ibid., 35–36 (emphasis added).
102 Ibid., 36.
103 Ibid.
104 Ibid.

> As I have said I am satisfied that the two illiterate mothers who were called by the plaintiff had no difficulty whatever in distinguishing between the two babies. And I am doing the plaintiff no injustice in taking his two chosen specimens as typical of illiterate mothers in Lagos. One must remember in this connection that this class of goods is designed to catch the eyes of mothers of young babies; and whatever her *race or colour*, and even if she be *illiterate*, a mother of a young baby has a very keen and appraising eye for this kind of picture. These marks being in my view distinguishable even by the *illiterate* customers, am I then to hold that by virtue of his registration of one particular baby the plaintiff is to be the only person allowed to use a pictorial representation of a baby on baby medicines? I think not.[105]

The approach adopted by Graham Paul J. in this case is the correct approach which should have been followed all along in the previous cases decided during this period. One could argue that it was easier for Graham Paul to refuse to maintain colonial difference in this case because none of the parties were multinational enterprises. It is also noteworthy that Graham Paul, unlike most colonial judges, was not a colonial administrator whilst serving as a judge.[106] Nevertheless, the judgement of Graham Paul J in this case indicates that perhaps not all the colonial judges shared the same misconception regarding the intelligence of the colonial subjects and the mistaken conflation of literacy with intelligence.

5 Conclusion

This chapter has examined how trademark disputes were resolved by colonial judges and courts in Nigeria during the interwar years. In determining the likelihood of confusion and deception in trademark and passing off disputes, these colonial courts drew a distinction between literate and illiterate consumers and they typically found a likelihood of confusion or deception in disputes involving marks that they thought might be confusing to illiterate consumers. This chapter contends that this approach to resolving trademark disputes during the interwar years is best explained by the reliance on the principle of local exceptionalism and the perceived need of the colonial courts to maintain

105 Ibid., (emphasis added).
106 Taiwo, *How Colonialism Preempted Modernity in Africa*, 193.

colonial difference. In line with the philosophy of the dual mandate articulated by Lugard, the reliance on local exceptionalism and the maintenance of colonial difference in this regard by colonial judges (who were also in most cases doubling as colonial administrators) was essential to safeguarding the commercial interests of multinational enterprises that were regarded as pioneers of trade in colonial Nigeria and, by necessary implication, the protection of the economic interests of the colonial authorities in Nigeria.

Acknowledgment

The author is grateful to Temitope Coker for providing excellent research assistance with regard to locating the court decisions discussed in this chapter.

Bibliography

Books

Bently, Lionel, 'The Making of Modern Trade Mark Law: The Construction of the Legal Concept of Trade Mark (1860–1880)'. In *Trade Marks and Brands: An Interdisciplinary Critique*, Bently, Lionel, Davis, Jennifer, and Ginsburg, Jane, eds. (Cambridge University Press, 2008).

Bodenhausen, Georg. *Guide to the Application of the Paris Convention for the Protection of Industrial Property* (Geneva: United International Bureaux for the Protection of Intellectual Property, 1969).

Burns, Alan. *History of Nigeria*, 5th edn. (London: Allen and Unwin, 1955).

Chatterjee, Partha, *The Nation and Its Fragments: Colonial and Postcolonial Histories* (New Jersey: Princeton University Press, 1993).

Elias, Taslim, *Groundwork of Nigerian Law* (London: Routledge & Kegan Paul, 1954).

Falola, Toyin, and Heaton, Matthew. *A History of Nigeria* (Cambridge: Cambridge University Press, 2008).

Green, Jeffrey. *Black Edwardians: Black People in Britain 1901–1914* (London: Frank Cass, 1998).

Ibhawoh, Bonny. *Imperial Justice: Africans in Empire's Court* (Oxford: Oxford University Press, 2013).

See Korieh, Chima. *Nigeria and World War II: Colonialism, Empire, and Global Conflict* (Cambridge: Cambridge University Press, 2020).

Lugard, Frederick. *The Dual Mandate in British Tropical Africa* (London: William Blackwood & Sons, 1922).

Mars, J. 'Extra-Territorial Enterprises'. In *The Economics of a Tropical Dependency Volume 2: Mining, Commerce, and Finance in Nigeria* Perham, Margery, ed. (London: Faber & Faber, 1948).

Morel, Edmund. *Affairs of West Africa* (London: William Heinemann, 1902).

Oyewunmi, Adejoke. *Nigerian Law of Intellectual Property* (Lagos: University of Lagos Press, 2015).

Sherman, Brad, and Bently, Lionel. *The Making of Modern Intellectual Property Law: The British Experience, 1760–1911* (Cambridge: Cambridge University Press, 1999).

Shyllon, Folarin. *Intellectual Property Law in Nigeria* (Munich: CH Beck, 2003).

Taiwo, Olufemi. *How Colonialism Preempted Modernity in Africa* (Indianapolis: Indiana University Press, 2010).

Articles

Babafemi, F.O.B. 'Trade Marks and the Illiterate: A Critique of the Judicial Attitude'. *Journal of African Law* 18(2) (1974) 180.

Carty, Hazel, 'Passing Off and Instruments of Deception: The Need for Clarity'. *European Intellectual Property Review* 25(4) (2003) 188.

Elias, Taslim, 'Colonial Courts and the Doctrine of Judicial Precedent'. *Modern Law Review* 18 (1955) 356, 357.

Kolsky, Elizabeth, 'Codification and the Rule of Colonial Difference: Criminal Procedure in British India'. *Law and History Review* 23(3) (2005) 631.

Meredith, David, 'The British Government and Colonial Economic Policy, 1919–39'. *The Economic History Review* 28(3) (1975) 484.

Nwaubani, Ebere, 'The British Labour Party, the "Dual Mandate" and Africa 1945–1951'. *Transafrican Journal of History* 21(1992) 93.

Nwogugu, E.I., 'An Examination of the Position of Illiterates in Nigerian Law'. *Journal of African Law* 12(1) (1968) 32.

Chapters in Edited Books

Bently, Lionel, 'The Doctrine of Instruments of Fraud in Historical Perspective'. In *The Cambridge Handbook of International and Comparative Trademark Law,* Calboli, Irene, and Ginsburg, Jane, eds. (Cambridge: Cambridge University Press, 2020) 468.

Papers and Reports

Adewoye, O., 'One Hundred Years of the Legal Profession in Nigeria,' Seminar Paper presented to the History Department, University of Ibadan, Nigeria, (1986).

Lugard, F.D., 'Report on the Amalgamation of Northern and Southern Nigeria, and Administration, 1912–1919', Cmd. 468, (1920).

UK Parliament, Oral Answers to Questions, Volume 60: debated on Wednesday, 25 March 1914, Column 353, Hansard, (1914).

CHAPTER 10

Intellectual Property Rights in Belgium and in the Congo: Between Internationalism and Colonialism

Véronique Pouillard

1 Introduction

Belgium was among the first signatories of both the Paris Convention for the Protection of Industrial Property of 1883 (signed by Belgium in 1884) and the Berne Convention for the Protection of Literary and Artistic Works (in 1886). At this point in its history, Belgium was among the most industrialized countries in the world and an epicenter for the arts and literature, where artists and politicians had developed a strong commitment to internationalism. This internationalism has been the topic of studies addressing the history of political socialism, peace activism, artistic exchanges, and scientific networks.[1] Two prominent figures of progressive peace activism were Paul Otlet and Henri La Fontaine (the latter a recipient of the Nobel Peace Prize in 1913), founders of the Mundaneum, who aimed to make the availability of the entirety of the world's knowledge a peace-building tool.[2]

During this era, Belgium was the center of a colonial empire founded by Leopold II during the Scramble for Africa. It was widely expected in the Belgian parliament that colonizing the Congo would cost large sums of money. Facing opposition, Leopold II decided to pursue the colonization of the Congo as a private enterprise and made the Congo his personal colony, which remains unparalleled in the history of nineteenth-century colonization.[3] Following several enquiries that brought to light the atrocities perpetrated in the Congo Free State, notably in support of the extraction of wild rubber, Leopold II was

1 Laqua, Daniel, *Age of internationalism and Belgium, 1880–1930: Peace, Progress and Prestige* (Manchester: Manchester University Press, 2015) 9–12.

2 Levie, Françoise, *L'homme qui voulait classer le monde: Paul Otlet et le Mundaneum* (Brussels: Les Impressions Nouvelles, 2006 [2020]); Wright, Alex, *Cataloging the World: Paul Otlet and the Birth of the Information Age* (Oxford: Oxford University Press, 2014).

3 Hochschild, Adam, 'Introduction'. In *Lord Leverhulme's Ghosts: Colonial Exploitation in the Congo*, Jules Marchal, ed. (New York: Verso Books, 2017), xi.

forced to cede the colony to Belgium, and in 1908 it became the Belgian Congo. Two territories resulting from losses incurred by Germany during World War I were subsequently added to the Congo: Rwanda and Burundi, first under military occupation from 1916 to 1922, then as the mandates of Ruanda-Urundi, which gained independence two years after the Congo, in 1962. In practice, the mandates were managed under the same rule as the colony.

Focusing on the interwar period, this chapter examines Belgium's system of intellectual property, examining both the harmonization of intellectual property at the international level and the extension of intellectual property to Belgium's colony.[4] It examines the work of Belgian lawyers including Albert Guislain, Henri La Fontaine, Paul Otlet, and Jules Destrée, who worked in the international organizations that pursued the goal of unifying intellectual property, and Théodore Smolders, Daniel Coppieters, and Paul Vander Haeghen, who wrote the decrees and laws implemented in the Congo. By bringing together the international and the colonial dimensions of intellectual property, the chapter discusses Belgium's extension of its regime internationally.[5]

Were there any links between the Belgian intellectuals who traveled and discussed internationalist conceptions of intellectual property, and the situation in the Congo? In his book on Paul Otlet, Alex Wright has shown that Otlet had personal ties to the colony and that he viewed the colonization of the Congo as a civilizing mission. Recent works show more complex facets of Otlet's links to the Congo. For example, he had a long-term intellectual relationship and correspondence with one of the pioneering intellectuals in Belgian Congo, Paul Panda Farnana, who was also one of the earliest supporters of the further extension of rights to intermediary levels of government in the colony, a vision he came to defend in Brussels.[6] Furthermore, the legal works cited here were written by lawyers who were acquainted with the situation of the colony in various matters, and who entertained different views on colonialism. I have tried to indicate these views when they resulted in remarkable observations and comments, even though this is not the central theme of this chapter.

Two understandings of intellectual property – an internationalist one and a colonialist one – were already present during the late nineteenth century

4 Ricketson, Sam, and, Ginsburg, Jane, 'The Berne Convention: Historical and Institutional Aspects'. In *International Intellectual Property: A Handbook of Contemporary Research*, Gervais, Daniel, ed. (London: Edward Elgar Publishing, 2015).

5 Bonyi, Mukadi, dir. *Cinquante ans de législation postcoloniale au Congo-Zaïre: quel bilan?* (Brussels: Centre de Recherche de Droit Social, 2010).

6 Kongolo, Antoine Tshitungu. *Visages de Paul Panda Farnana: Nationaliste, Panafricaniste* (Paris: L'Harmattan, 2011) 23–25; Wright, *Cataloging the World*, 50–55.

and matured during the interwar period.[7] Protection of industrial design, for example, was strengthened in order to address the commercialization of artistic forms, with changes at both the international and the colonial level. An important development that took place during the interwar period was the writing of the customary laws of the people of the Congo into the colonial legal system of the Congo and the mandates of Ruanda-Urundi. This was intended to reinforce indirect rule in governing the colony, but created some difficulties for its subjects, who were compelled to try to make two cultures coexist.[8] At the international level, the 1928 revision of the Berne Treaty in Rome and the preparations for the Brussels Conference, initially planned during the 1930s, resulted in productive exchanges in the international legal milieu, even though the Brussels meeting was eventually postponed to 1948.

The chapter starts with an examination of the involvement of Belgian experts in the international intellectual property organizations. The following sections are organized according to the varieties of intellectual property rights in the colony, outlining the relations between the legal systems of the metropole and of the colony in the fields of patents, trademarks, and country-of-origin labels, industrial designs, copyrights, and trade secrets. The research in this chapter is based on primary sources kept at the Bibliothèque Royale Albert Ier in Brussels, and at the Africa Museum in Tervueren, in the archives of the League of Nations (SDN) kept in digitalized repositories by the United Nations Educational, Scientific and Cultural Organization (UNESCO), and in the archives of lawyers (Albert Guislain in particular) kept at the Archives Générales du Royaume (AGR) in Brussels.

2 Belgian Experts and the Internationalization of Intellectual Property

Paul Otlet and Henri La Fontaine had a formative role in the creation of two important institutions for intellectual property: the International Committee on Intellectual Cooperation (hereafter ICIC) in 1922, and the International Institute of Intellectual Cooperation in 1926.[9] La Fontaine's role as an

7 Wirtén, Eva Hemmungs, 'Colonial Copyright, Postcolonial Publics: The Berne Convention and the 1967 Stockholm Diplomatic Conference Revisited'. *SCRIPTed* 7 (3) (2010) 532.

8 Ncube, Caroline, 'Three Centuries and Counting: The Emergence and Development of Intellectual Property Law in Africa'. In *The Oxford Handbook of Intellectual Property Law* Dreyfuss, Rochelle, and Pila, Justine, eds. (Oxford: Oxford University Press, 2016) 411.

9 UNESCO Archives, Paris, digitalized funds, FR PUNES AG 1-IICI-E 1927-1931-33; Extrait d'un Rapport présenté en juillet 1927, par l'IICI, à la Sous-Commission des Droits Intellectuels

avant-garde pacifist made him a president of the Bureau International de la Paix.[10] Indeed, during the interwar period Otlet's and La Fontaine's roles centered increasingly on peace building. Among the Belgian politicians and intellectuals involved in the ICIC, Jules Destrée, a Walloon lawyer and socialist politican, distinguished himself by his activity, including numerous interventions on intellectual property matters. Destrée was the Belgian Minister for Sciences and Arts in 1919–1921 and then worked on the ICIC until his death in 1936, when he was replaced by the Flemish intellectual Auguste Vermeylen. A major chapter of Destrée's work was dedicated to the Rome Conference for the revision of the Berne Convention of 1928,[11] for which he prepared the text presented by the ICIC. The main Italian delegate Eduardo Piola-Caselli penned the text adopted in Rome as the final revision of the Berne Convention, but Destrée's text was strongly influential in shaping the international future of intellectual property.

The Rome conference gathered 69 countries, of which 39 were, at that time, members of the Berne Union, the others being observers. Destrée and Piola-Caselli defended measures in favor of strong moral rights of the author, aligned with the French and Belgian laws that defined authors' right as the moral right of the author over his or her work, rather than a right based on a utilitarian definition of public access to the work. Both Destrée and Piola-Caselli defended the integrity of the work after the death of the author, and the representatives of three member countries, France, Belgium, and Czechoslovakia, insisted on the importance of granting copyright revenue after the death of the author to the heirs.[12] Destrée had written the Belgian law of 20 August 1921 on the *droit de suite*, itself inspired by the French law signed the previous year. Destrée's ongoing concern, noted some of his contemporary critics, was to secure rights

de la SDN, sur les premiers résultats d'une enquête relative au Statut des Associations Internationales (Proposition de M. le Sénateur Lafontaine), 1928 (Création), E.33.1920; Laqua, *Age of internationalism*, 194–195.

10 Thyssens, Jeffrey, 'Henri Lafontaine et l'idée de paix internationale'. In *Cent ans de l'office international de bibliographie,* Despy-Meyer, Andrée, *et al.* ed. (Mons: Editions du Mundaneum, 1995) 106–108.

11 UNESCO Archives, Paris, digitalized funds, FR PUNES AG 1-IICI-E 1927-1931-36, Convention de Berne pour la Protection des Œuvres Littéraires et Artistiques du 9 Septembre 1886 révisée à Berlin le 13 Novembre 1908 et à Rome le 2 Juin 1928, 1928.

12 UNESCO Archives, Paris, digitalized funds, FR PUNES AG 1-IICI-E 1927-1931-40, « Aperçu sur les travaux de la Conférence Diplomatique de Rome pour la Protection des Œuvres Littéraires et Artistiques (Révision de la Convention de Berne, Mai 1928) Présenté à la Réunion des Délégués d'Etats du 19 Décembre 1928 par M. Raymond Weiss, ... » , 1929, Société des Nations. Institut International de Coopération Intellectuelle, 1–2.

for the artists that took precedence over the socialist vision of the redistribution of wealth.[13]

Lively discussions in Rome were duly transcribed in reports that show the issues at stake for intellectual property. Among them was the right of reservation, which some countries could require for specific parts of the Berne Convention. The Rome participants preferred to reduce the right of reservation as much as possible, but it was agreed to keep it for translations, after a delegate of the Kingdom of Siam (now Thailand) mentioned problems of access to works for distant countries.[14]

Another thorny issue was raised by press articles, over which the extension of intellectual property remained a subject of debate. Some conference participants argued for the widespread character of the medium and others for the need to keep access to information open in a democratic context. Among further challenging questions was that of radio performance. The medium was very recent and raised numerous questions. It seemed logical that artists broadcasting their works on the radio should be compensated by the collection of fees for intellectual property rights in radio just as in concert halls, but on this topic, too, some conference members argued for the importance of the medium in providing information, especially in distant countries. A New Zealand delegate noted that the radio was vital for information in remote regions and that it was daunting to seek permissions from artists and composers who lived in sometimes very distant countries. The discussion that took place in Rome on the topic thus showed important contradictions posed by the medium of radio, a new technology that challenged the boundaries between creativity and dissemination. In these debates, the need to compensate composers and performers was regularly pitted against the desire to make popular culture accessible to the masses. The revised version of the Berne Convention tried to reconcile these points of tension by affirming the principle of exclusivity of the author over his or her works and by ensuring the payment of the authors and composers through obligatory licenses.[15]

---

13 Dumont, Georges-Henri, 'Le Ministre des Sciences et des Arts'. In *Jules Destrée le multiple,* Trousson, Raymond, ed. (Brussels: Académie de Langue et de Littérature Françaises, 1995) 71.

14 UNESCO Archives, Paris, digitalized funds, FR PUNES AG 1-IICI-E 1927-1931-40, Aperçu sur les travaux de la Conférence Diplomatique de Rome, 4.

15 UNESCO Archives, Paris, digitalized funds, FR PUNES AG 1-IICI-E 1927-1931-40, Aperçu sur les travaux de la Conférence Diplomatique de Rome, 5–6; Archives Générales du Royaume, Brussels, Fonds Albert Guislain, nr. 2700, Rapports de l'Institut International de Coopération Intellectuelle, Berne. Rapport sur le droit d'auteur et la presse.

The topic of the rights of mechanical reproduction was treated again at a Congress in Vienna in 1932. There the ICIC developed a collaboration with the Federation for the Rights on Mechanical Reproduction, the latter being integrated in the French Société des Auteurs, Compositeurs et Editeurs de Musique (SACEM). The Belgians also participated in the Vienna Congress, sending delegates of the Société des Auteurs belges – Belgisch Auteurs Maatschappij (SABAM), a collective management society founded in 1922 on the model of the SACEM. The SABAM would play an important role in Congolese music authorship during the postwar era.[16]

The influence of technological change on intellectual property was a connecting thread between several topics discussed in Rome. Initially, as the reports from Rome reminds us, the Berne Convention protects artistic and literary works. Creations considered to be mixed products of arts and inventions enjoyed only industrial protection, as per provisions in the Paris Convention. This meant that industrial designs needed to be registered with the relevant bureau (nationally or internationally) for protection. In Rome, the ICIC defended the idea that arts and crafts should be protected under both industrial design and copyright regimes, in line with the thesis of the unity of the art that supported the idea of similar rights for the high arts and for industrial arts, but the Italian and Japanese delegations opposed the thesis of the unity of the art. The signatories of the Berne Convention were, as a consequence, left to choose their own manner of protection, to be implemented nationally.[17] France and Belgium decided to grant the double protection of industrial design and copyright to the arts and crafts. As we will see below, industrial design remains interesting, as the regimes of protection offered in the metropole and in the colony diverged.

The rights over the resale of artistic works, the *droit de suite*, was one of Destrée's particular preoccupations. An issue of debate in Rome was the disparity in the lengths of protection granted to works after the death of their author. Destrée supported a 50-year term of protection, but the British system allowed only half of this. In the end, the 50-year protection was maintained, but without becoming an obligation for all the signatories of the Berne convention;[18] however, the ICIC planned to revisit this discussion at the next

16 UNESCO Archives, Paris, digitalized funds, FR PUNES AG 1-IICI-CFCE-B-A-8.45, Congrès de la Confédération internationale des sociétés d'auteurs et compositeurs dramatiques, Vienne, 6–12 juin 1932, 'Au Congrès de Vienne', in *L'Ecran*, 18 juin 1932, 4.

17 UNESCO Archives, Paris, digitalized funds, FR PUNES AG 1-IICI-E 1927-1931-40, Aperçu sur les travaux de la Conférence Diplomatique de Rome, 6–7.

18 UNESCO Archives, Paris, digitalized funds, FR PUNES AG 1-IICI-E 1927-1931-40, Aperçu sur les travaux de la Conférence Diplomatique de Rome, 5–6.

revision conference in Brussels. More generally, during that era, the ICIC asked the International Labor Organization (ILO) to conduct a broad enquiry into intellectuals' labor and careers. Destrée was one of the supporters of this enquiry, denoting his general interest in the revenue of the intellectual professions beyond the question of copyright revenue.[19]

Another proposal, made by the Swedish and the Norwegian delegations to the Rome Conference, was for the establishment of an international court for the treatment of cases of infringement of intellectual property rights. The issue of infringements across national borders was a long-standing problem that motivated the organization of conferences on intellectual property in the nineteenth century. But the motion proposed by Sweden and Norway enjoyed very little support in Rome. It was put aside, where it has remained until the present day.[20]

Overall, the results of the Rome Conference were quite limited.[21] Destrée was active in promoting the Belgian view, which aligned with the French, of strong authors' rights, rather than an utilitarian understanding of copyright.[22] The moral right of the author was, according to Destrée, to be defined as an inalienable right, which ensured that the author would retain great control over his or her work in the long term, including resale rights and the right to protect the integrity of the work after the death of the author. In Belgium, Destrée founded a national representation of the ICIC in 1923 that gathered prominent Belgian academics and politicians: Ernest Mahaim, Henri Pirenne, Paulin Ladeuze, Henri La Fontaine, Prosper Poullet, and Paul Hymans. At the international level, Destrée was among the ten most-mentioned names in the files of the ICIC; in other words, he was one of the most active members of the organization.[23]

---

19 UNESCO Archives, Paris, digitalized funds, FR PUNES AG 1-IICI-E 1927.1931.35.d (Point 5 de l'ordre du jour), Rapport à la Sous-Commission des Droits Intellectuels sur la Condition Juridique et Sociale des Travailleurs Intellectuels, 1928, 1–2.

20 UNESCO Archives, Paris, digitalized funds, FR PUNES AG 1-IICI-E 1927-1931-40, Aperçu sur les travaux de la Conférence Diplomatique de Rome, 8–9.

21 Dommann, Monika, *Authors and Apparatus: A Media History of Copyright* (Ithaca NY: Cornell University Press, 2019) 109; Ladas, Stephen, *Patents, Trademarks, and Related Rights: National and International Protection*, vol. 1 (Cambridge MA: Harvard University Press, 1975) 834.

22 Ngombé, Laurier Yvon, *Le droit d'auteur en Afrique* (Paris: L'Harmattan, 2009) 19–20.

23 Grandjean, Martin. Les réseaux de coopération intellectuelle. La Société des Nations comme actrice des échanges scientifiques et culturels dans l'entre-deux-guerres. (PhD thesis, Université de Lausanne, 2018) 62, 231.

The ICIC worked on a variety of topics during the following years. Discussions of the incentives given to scientific work were taken up in Belgium, and in 1928 a National Fund for Scientific Research was created.[24] An idea widespread among the members of the ICIC was the need to equally protect scientific research with intellectual property along the same lines of protection afforded to the arts, literary works or inventions.[25] Historian Gabriel Galvez Behar has discussed two rival understandings of intellectual property in the scientific domain, one promoted by the Confédération des Travailleurs Intellectuels (CTI), which saw property rights as pertaining to individual scientists, and another promoted by Paul Langevin, which made intellectual property a collective right of the scientists to demand funding by the industry.[26] The ICIC members considered that the domain of the authors' rights was more advanced than other domains of intellectual production, such as patents, in protecting rights at the international level. The Belgian delegates to the international congresses for intellectual property kept insisting on a strong moral right of the author, rather than for example on more utilitarianist views on intellectual property rights, during the whole interwar period.[27]

24 UNESCO Archives, Paris, digitalized funds, Fonds IICI, 1921–1954, FR PUNES AG 1-IICI-E 1927-1931-35.b (Point 2 de l'ordre du jour), Rapport sur l'Etat Actuel des Travaux concernant le Droit à accorder aux Savants sur l'utilisation lucrative de leurs découvertes. Rapport soumis à la Sous-Commission des Droits intellectuels, 1928, 4.

25 UNESCO Archives, Paris, digitalized funds, FR PUNES AG 1-IICI-E 1927-1931-44, Résumé d'un Exposé Verbal présenté par M. Raymond Weiss, chef du Service Juridique de l'IICI, sur l'Aspect International de la Protection des Droits Intellectuels. (Sous-Commission des Droits d'Auteur de la Chambre des Députés) Séance du mercredi 26 Juin 1929, 1929, 2.

26 Galvez-Behar, Gabriel, 'L'impossible institutionnalisation de la propriété scientifique, 1919–1939', *L'échelle des régulations politiques, XVIIIe–XXIe siècles: L'histoire et les sciences sociales aux prises avec les normes, les acteurs et les institutions* (Lille: Presses Universitaires du Septentrion, 2019) 9.

27 UNESCO Archives, Paris, digitalized funds, FR PUNES AG 1-IICI-E 1927-1931-44, Résumé d'un Exposé Verbal présenté par M. Raymond Weiss, chef du Service Juridique de l'IICI, sur l'Aspect International de la Protection des Droits Intellectuels. (Sous-Commission des Droits d'Auteur de la Chambre des Députés) Séance du mercredi 26 Juin 1929, 1929, 2–4; Löhr, Isabella, *Die Globalisierung geistiger Eigentumsrechte: neue Strukturen internationaler Zusammenarbeit, 1886–1952*, Kritische Studien zur Geschichtswissenschaft (Göttingen: Vandenhoeck & Ruprecht, 2010), 43; Löhr, Isabella, *Auf dem Weg zu einer global governance kultureller Güter: die Globalisierung geistiger Eigentumsrechte in neuten Strukturen internationaler Zusammenarbeit (1886–1952)* (Leipzig: Universität Leipzig, 2008); Demeulenaere, Pascale, *L'Organisation internationale de coopération intellectuelle et la Belgique, 1922–1939* (Louvain: Université catholique de Louvain, 1994).

3 Convergences and Divergences in the Law between Belgium and Its Colonies

Belgium adhered to the Paris Convention for the protection of industrial property of 1883, and to the Madrid arrangement of 1891 on the international registration of trademarks. The Congo Free State did not adhere to these agreements. Lawyers were unsure at first whether these laws and regulations were applicable to the Congo and, after 1908, Belgium did not immediately specify whether its colony would become a signatory of those treaties.[28]

According to the lawyer Daniel Coppieters, the law stipulated that, in these domains, there was no difference between the Belgians, the Congolese, and people of other nationalities living in the Congo.[29] The laws of the Congo were modified to reflect more colonial forms of governance.[30] For Belgian jurists the coexistence of colonial laws and the customary laws of the Congo attributed to the Congolese people who often preferred the customary practices while colonial administration were thinking in forms of legal governance as per the laws of Belgium.[31] The colonial courts could intervene in cases that contradicted the colonial order – for instance, those involving acts of sorcery,[32] and those on property. Such issues were particularly important as far as landed property was concerned.[33]

The applicable law to Belgians, other foreigners, and registered Congolese in civil and commercial matters was the Belgian Civil Code. In any event, only few Congolese obtained registration rights equivalent to the Europeans (the matriculated status, called the *immatriculés*). Most Congolese were instead ruled by the customs that were especially significant in terms of the status of

28 Coppieters, Daniel, *Le régime de la propriété industrielle au Congo belge* (Brussels: Etablissements Emile Bruylant, 1909) 13.

29 Coppieters. *Le régime de la propriété industrielle au Congo belge*, 14.

30 Congolese intellectuals Paul Panda Farnana and Stefano Kaoze promoted in Belgium the inclusion of intermediary levels in Congolese government in the colony and the development of the customary courts needs to be analyzed from this perspective. Kongolo, Antoine Tshitungu. *Visages de Paul Panda Farnana: Nationaliste, Panafricaniste* (Paris: L'Harmattan, 2011) 28–32.

31 Tousignant, Nathalie, 'The Belgian colonial experience and legal journals (1908–1960): an overview', *C@hiers du CRHiDI. Histoire, droit, institutions, société* 37 (2015) 1–16.

32 Verstraete, Maurice. *Aperçu de droit civil du Congo belge, de la condition de ses habitants et des personnes morales, conflits coloniaux* (Antwerp: Editions coloniales Zaïre, 1946) 9–10.

33 Clément, Piet. 'The Land Tenure System in the Congo, 1885–1960. Actors, Motivations, and Consequences'. In *Colonial Exploitation and Economic Development: The Belgian Congo and the Netherlands Indies Compared,* Frankema, Ewout, and Buelens, Frans, eds. (Abingdon: Routledge, 2013) 88–108.

the people, their family relations, and questions of property, liability, and contracts. Some domains of intellectual property were included in the customary laws, such as traditional know-how and the prerogative to engage in certain arts and crafts, such as making music instruments, which could be a privilege reserved, for example, to a specific gender.[34] This meant that in practice, traditional cultural expressions remained mostly protected *sui generis*, that is, negatively, during the colonial period.[35] Following in the footsteps of the French jurists Arthur Girault, author of the *Principes de colonisation et de législation coloniale*, and Henry Solus, author of a *Traité de la condition des indigènes en droit privé*, Maurice Verstraete, a lawyer active in the courts of the colony, wrote that applying the same law to all in the colony was unrealistic.[36] The customs were applicable only when they were compatible with colonial law and respect for public order.[37]

The Colonial Charter of 18 October 1908 was modelled to some extent on the Belgian Constitution, aside from the principles of constitutional monarchy and representative democracy. The colony was ruled by the Ministry of the Colonies in Brussels and the Governor General in the Congo. The fundamental freedoms of the press, association, education, and religion were not transferred from the Constitution to the Colonial Charter.[38] The colony was governed by decrees, legal dispositions to be applied by the courts as the law. The courts applied the decrees so far as they did not contradict the Belgian law. The Colonial Charter provisioned a double guarantee for the decrees: they were proposed and counter-signed by the Minister of the Colonies and examined by the consultative Council of Congo (*Conseil du Congo*). In difficult cases, the Minister of the Colonies could consult with the Council of State – the supreme administrative court of Belgium – and with the Governor General of the Congo.[39]

A significant difference between the organisation of the colony and of the metropole was the status of the soil and of property. Part of the land of the Congo was reserved to the indigenous people, who had an inalienable right to it. And yet, the Congolese could not, during the interwar period, own land in

34 Verstraete, *Aperçu de droit civil*, 10.

35 Nwauche, Enyinna. *The Protection of Traditional Cultural Expressions in Africa* (New York: Springer, 2017) 2.

36 Verstraete, *Aperçu de droit civil*, 49.

37 Paulus, Jean-Pierre. *Droit public du Congo belge* (Brussels: Institut de Sociologie Solvay, 1959) 141–142.

38 Paulus, *Droit public du Congo belge*, 12, 23.

39 Paulus, *Droit public du Congo belge*, 137–138.

the same manner as codified in the Belgian Civil Code; the ownership of the so-called indigenous land was collective. Pierre Ryckmans, who was Governor of the Congo from 1934 until 1946, argued in the mid-1930s that it was time to grant the Congolese access to property. Ryckmans considered that this access would be challenging in terms of the writing and transmission of contracts. To some extent the Compulsory Cultivation System implemented by the colonial authority aimed to encourage privatization of small land plots for farmers, but it was two more decades of hesitation from the colonial government before property was granted to the Congolese, which came about during the 1950s.[40]

The differences of status in the colony, according to Verstraete, were not morally equivalent to those observed during the absolutist regimes of pre-revolutionary Europe. The difference in the law as applied to the colonized and the colonizers was, he argued, a product of the respect for the traditions of the colonized.[41] But other jurists wrote that it was the "situation" (in their own words) of the Congolese that demanded a special legal regime to govern their everyday lives.[42]

The Belgian jurists who wrote about the legal regime of the Congo observed that, even though it seemed crucial to adapt Belgian laws to the colony, judgments followed the case law of the metropole.[43] The judges in the Congo studied in Belgium and were considered to be part of the Belgian judiciary staff. Most of them took periodical leaves in Belgium, which reinforced the relations between the legal systems of the metropole and the colony.[44]

3.1 *Writing Patent Laws for Belgium and Its Colonies*

The Belgian patent law provided the model for the king's decree on patents for the Congo, dated 29 October 1886, that stated that any discovery or improvement that industry or commerce could exploit could be the subject of a patent. Patents in the Congo were granted without a preliminary examination, at the risks and perils of the patentees, with no guarantee of the merit of the patent, the quality of the description, or the absence of prejudice to third parties. This decree, observed the Belgian lawyer Théodore Smolders, was rudimentary, and

40 Ryckmans, Pierre. *Allo! Congo! Chroniques radiophoniques par Pierre Ryckmans* (Brussels: L'Edition Universelle, 1935) 15–18; Vinez, Margaux, 'Division of the Commons and Access to Land on The Frontier: Lessons from The Colonial Legacy in The Democratic Republic of Congo', Working Paper, World Bank, (2017) 7–9.

41 Verstraete, *Aperçu de droit civil*, 9, 11.

42 Paulus, *Droit public du Congo belge*, 23.

43 *Annales parlementaires, Chambre des Représentants*, 1907, 358; Paulus, *Droit public du Congo belge*, 24.

44 Paulus, *Droit public du Congo belge*, 23–24.

for this reason it was acceptable to use Belgian law as a supplement to the colonial decree.[45]

Belgian and Congolese legislation organized patents within three categories: invention, import, and perfecting (or improvement) patents, all of which were protected for a maximum of 20 years. Anyone could file a patent without limits on the age, gender, or status of the patentee,[46] although, in fact, the filing fee was a deterrent to impecunious innovators; the overwhelming majority of patentees were international firms. The objects of a patent could be material or immaterial, in the form of products, results, proceeds, or series of operations.[47] The decree of 27 June 1913 summed up the conditions for filing a patent, which included the delivery of a patent description in three copies on paper and appendixes in the form of texts, drawings, or samples. The copies had to be delivered to the Ministry of the Colonies in Brussels or to the Governor general in the Congo. The request needed to include the names, profession, and address of the inventor and, in the case of an import patent, the country of registration of the original patent, its date, and duration.[48] The physical description that constituted the patent needed to include the request for patenting, the description of the patent, and, if relevant, drawings, diagrams, or samples. The mention of an object in the patent title was insufficient to file a patent.[49] Upon registration, the person requesting a patent had to pay a fee of 3,000 Belgian francs.[50]

As we have seen earlier, the colonial decree on patents did not include a patent review procedure. The form of the patent demanded created clear restrictions on the filing of patents to begin with. The requirements were stricter for the metropole than in the colony, but in this case, again, the law of the metropole could be used in the colony. Reading the greater restrictions to patent in the metropole as an encouragement to patenting in the colony may therefore be premature.[51]

There were certain restrictions on patenting in the colony which means only few inventions or innovations were eligible for patenting. Raw materials

---

45 Smolders, Théodore, *Droit civil du Congo belge* (Brussels: F. Larcier, 1956) 8.

46 Coppieters, *Le régime de la propriété industrielle*, 17.

47 Smolders, *Droit civil du Congo belge*, 7–10; Coppieters, *Le régime de la propriété industrielle*, 17.

48 *Législation Commerciale du Congo Belge* (Brussels: Librairie Falk et Fils, 1930), 68; Smolders, *Droit civil du Congo belge*, 27.

49 Smolders, *Droit civil du Congo belge*, 11–12.

50 Smolders, *Droit civil du Congo belge*, 27.

51 Caroline Ncube mentions that the relation between a robust IP framework and development is controversial, and that relation between such a framework and FDI (Foreign Direct Investments) is to be nuanced. Ncube, 'Three Centuries and Counting', 430.

were not eligible for a patent, according to Belgian law, which would effectively rule out, for example, the patenting of untreated plants or minerals, such as the controversial and eventually abandoned idea of patenting turmeric in India.[52] Patents were limited in duration to 20 years, but also by the principle of the common good. Coppieters had, already at the time of the retrocession of the Congo to Belgium, cited article 2 of the Congo decree of 29 October 1886 that mentioned that filing patents should be done without prejudice to third parties (*sans préjudice des droits des tiers*). Patents, added Coppieters, should therefore not be taken out for previously patented inventions that were now within the public domain, since the patentee would then be pretending to have exclusive rights on a common good.[53]

To be patentable, wrote the Belgian jurist Théodore Smolders, a discovery could not, as stated in the legal treaties, be taken out for *immoral* inventions. Thus, for example, patents for unproven remedies[54] that purported to be medicines were rejected. Raw materials were not patentable, as mentioned above, although, as we will see below, mining prospection was subject to special protections in the Congo. Patents also could only be attributed to original innovations, defined as non-similar to previous patents. In the case of patents seeking to improve an invention, a new combination of procedures was considered sufficient to grant a new patent.[55]

Belgian law allowed the voiding of a patent in cases of proven anteriority (state of art) of the exploitation or description. Although trade secrecy could be evoked as an argument in intellectual property cases in Belgian and colonial courts, keeping the secret on an innovation had no value in the courts to prove anteriority, which indicates clear trade-offs in using trade secrets.[56] Should a patentee wish to cede a patent, he or she was required to notify the Ministry of Foreign Affairs. Belgian case law, also applicable in the Congo, was also detailed about the difficulties that could arise when an entrepreneur filed a patent for an invention made by one of his employees. The presumption of ownership, wrote the Belgian jurist Smolders, was in favor of the inventor, but Belgian case law, also in force in the Congo, confirmed that if the employee had

---

52 Kumar, Sanjay, 'India Wins Battle with USA over Turmeric Patent'. *The Lancet*, 350 (9079) (1997), 724.

53 Coppieters, *Le régime de la propriété industrielle au Congo belge*, 16.

54 Pouillard, Véronique. *La publicité en Belgique, 1850–1975: Des courtiers aux agences internationales* (Brussels: Académie Royale de Belgique, Classe des Lettres et des Sciences Morales et Politiques, 2005) 76–77.

55 Smolders, *Droit civil du Congo belge*, 13–15.

56 Smolders, *Droit civil du Congo belge*, 19.

made the discovery in the framework of his work assignments then the innovation belonged to his boss. Belgian law further stipulated that the employee was supposed to bring his entire capabilities to the workplace.[57]

The unjustified use of the word "patented" to advertise an object or a product that was not patented was subject to restriction (*censure*) in the colony.[58] The courts of first instance in the Congo were in charge of civil and commercial cases, including counterfeiting lawsuits.[59] As far as the repression of counterfeits was concerned, Congolese law was more vague than Belgian law about the nature of counterfeits. In Congolese law, there was an insistence that counterfeits should be interpreted with regard to their similarities to the originals. The seizing of objects suspected of being counterfeit was authorized in Belgium, but the decrees for the Congo did not mention this action, which was thus ruled out in the legal treaties. However, other reasons, especially illicit or unfair competition, were accepted in counterfeiting lawsuits in colonial law. In the eventuality that counterfeiting was proved, both Belgian law and Congolese decrees allowed for damages to be claimed by the plaintiff.[60]

3.2 *Brands and Trademarks in the Metropole and in the Colony*

The creation and use of trademarks and brands in Belgian Congo was strictly modelled on the law of the metropole. Article 1 of the colonial decree of 26 April 1888 reproduced the first article of the Belgian law of 1 April 1879.[61] In principle, any sign or name of a person or of an object could serve as a brand. It was left up to case law to decide whether signs and names were appropriate or not. Some signs, such as the Red Cross, were protected and could not be used as trademarks, and some banal signs could not be registered as brands.[62] Any sign or name adopted as a brand needed to differ from already existing brands.

The product categories permitted to use trademarking, wrote Coppieters, could include all the products of agriculture and minerals for commerce[63] – indicating the specificities of the colonial economy. During the interwar period, an active policy developed towards the trademarking of coffees from the Congo and the mandate over Rwanda.[64] In the case of the Congo, Belgian jurists underlined

57 Smolders, *Droit civil du Congo belge*, 29.
58 Smolders, *Droit civil du Congo belge*, 236.
59 Coppieters, *Le régime de la propriété industrielle*, 21.
60 Smolders, *Droit civil du Congo belge*, 32, 35.
61 Coppieters, *Le régime de la propriété industrielle*, 23–24.
62 Smolders, *Les droits intellectuels au Congo belge*, 45.
63 Coppieters, *Le régime de la propriété industrielle*, 23–24.
64 Melkebeke, Sven Van. *Dissimilar Coffee Frontiers: Mobilizing Labor and Land in the Lake Kivu Region, Congo and Rwanda (1918–1960/62)* (Leiden: Brill, 2020) 50; Mosselmans, Paul.

the importance of origins labeling of quality products.[65] Besides trademarks, country-of-origin labels were an important medium for informing consumers about the quality of products. Such collective labels have played an important role in trade, and their regulation by law has a long history. In the case of the Congo, the question of labels of origins was raised in 1909 by Paul Mosselmans, who theorized on advertising, trademarks, and patents in Belgian Congo. During the interwar period, Governor Pierre Ryckmans noted the importance of creating labels specific to quality products from the colony. Ryckmans evoked in particular the example of the coffees produced in the Belgian colony and mandates.[66] And yet, in their case, the purpose was to strengthen the quality of products that would eventually be advertised as hailing from the colonies of Belgium, reinforcing the image of the metropole.[67] In Belgium and its colonies, the law required that signboards, packaging, and tags were original, without borrowing from other producers' brand names. In addition to these rules, Belgian law provided protection to specific country-of-origin labels, such as on regional alcohols, wines, and water products. This protection for regional labels, however, did not exist in the Congo.[68]

Trademark or brand protection belonged to the first user of the brand, but in order to enjoy brand protection entrepreneurs were asked to register their brand, as codified in the Belgian law of 1 April 1879 and, in the Congo, in the Decree of 26 April 1888, modeled on the Belgian law. There was no need to renew the registration of brands.[69] The person who decided to register a brand for the Congo had to file three copies, including a picture of the trademark, to the Ministry of the Colonies in Brussels, the General Secretary in Léopoldville (today Kinshasa), and the Direction of the Economic Affairs in Elisabethville (today Lumumbashi). A small fee was required upon registration.[70]

La Publicité Coloniale. Simple Essai (Brussels: Editions commerciales et industrielles, 1910) 10–15; Pouillard, *La Publicité en Belgique*, 120–4 ; Pierre Ryckmans, *Allo! Congo!*, 97–99.

65 Smolders, *Les droits intellectuels au Congo belge*, 43.

66 Van Melkebeke, *Dissimilar Coffee Frontiers*, 50–55.

67 Stanziani, Alessandro, 'Wine Reputation and Quality Controls: The Origin of the AOCs in 19th century France'. *European Journal of Law and Economics*, 18(2) (2004) 149–167; Guy, Kolleen. *When Champagne became French: Wine and the Making of a National Identity* (Baltimore MD: Johns Hopkins University Press, 2007); Mosselmans, *La Publicité Coloniale*, 5–15; Ryckmans, *Allo! Congo!*, 97–99.

68 Smolders, *Droit civil du Congo belge*, 224, 228.

69 Coppieters, *Le régime de la propriété industrielle*, 24–26; Smolders, *Les droits intellectuels au Congo belge*, 51 sq.

70 *Législation Commerciale du Congo Belge*, 'Dessins et modèles industriels'.

In the eventuality of brand counterfeiting, the Belgian law of 1 April 1879 and the Congolese decree of 27 April 1888 allowed the judge to require the confiscation of the counterfeited products and the publication of the judgments. The Belgian law also allowed the destruction of merchandise judged to be counterfeits, but the colonial decree did not.[71] In the Congo, the law was meant to be applied to the same way for Belgians, Congolese, and foreign merchants, who constituted an important group in the business activities of the colony.[72]

3.3 *The Registration and the Protection of Industrial Designs* (*Dessins et Modèles*)

At the beginning of the interwar period there was no specific law organizing the protection of industrial design in Belgian Congo. Coppieters felt that it was necessary to urgently address this gap in the law, especially so in the case of the importers of printed fabrics – a popular type of consumer good in the Congo – who wished to protect the designs that they imported.[73] Indeed, some importers of wax printed fabrics sued counterfeiters in the courts.[74]

This lack of protection of industrial designs was remedied by the decree of 24 April 1922 that organized the registration of designs and industrial models. Innovators could register designs in the form of a sample or a sketch in a sealed and signed envelope for one, three or five years, or perpetuity, at the Ministry of the Colonies in Brussels, at the General Secretariat in Léopoldville, or at the Directorate for Economic Affairs in Elisabethville. The amount of the registration fee varied.[75]

During the interwar period, the law on the ownership of design was a topic of debate, much of which resulted from problems in defining the contours of arts and industry. Numerous products, such as fashionable garments and interior designs, found themselves, as coined by Dreyfuss and Ginsburg, *at the edge* of art and commerce. Some nations accepted these products as arts, and adapted their law accordingly; in Belgium and France, for example, designs could be protected both by industrial design law and by authors' rights law. But in other countries, such as the United States, fashion designs could not be copyrighted. Belgium protected all designs under authors' rights legislation in 1935, but colonial decrees did not follow suit. Designs thus remained under a weaker regime of protection in the Congo, until a new colonial decree modified

71 Coppieters, *Le régime de la propriété industrielle*, 28–29.

72 Smolders, *Les droits intellectuels au Congo belge*, 75–76, 80.

73 Coppieters, *Le régime de la propriété industrielle*, 10–14.

74 Grosfilley, Anne. *African Wax Print Textiles* (Munich: Prestel, 2018) 101–112.

75 *Législation Commerciale du Congo Belge*, 'Dessins et modèles industriels'.

this state of affairs in 1948.[76] This aligns with what we have seen earlier about the Conference of Rome in 1928, where a stronger protection for the arts and crafts was discussed without immediate results in terms of the international unification of the law.

Despite this state of affairs, during the interwar period protection of industrial designs was provided to entrepreneurs who registered their innovations either in Brussels or in the Congo. Design registrations were of particular interest to the trade of novelty products, such as printed fabrics. The entrepreneurs who protected their wax fabrics, for example, were often international businesspeople who had commercial operations in the Congo, where they sold fabrics produced by the textile industry based in the colony, but also overseas, in, for example, Asia, where a significant part of the wax production was centered. The case law was mostly from Belgium during the interwar period.[77] Building on a growing corpus of case law, a number of cases relating to the counterfeiting of industrial design were judged in the courts of the Congo during the postwar era.

3.4 *Asserting the Moral Right of the Author in the Metropole and in the Colony*

In the realm of authors' rights, the Congo and the mandates of Ruanda-Urundi aligned on Belgium in most matters. In the broader context, Belgium was, like France, a proponent of a protective law composed of two elements: a patrimonial (or pecuniary) right, and a moral right to authorship, the latter being an unalienable right.[78] The definition of the law thus emphasized the moral right of the author and, to some extent, its preeminence over a more utilitarian view that, especially in the Anglo-Saxon realm, tended to emphasize the importance of the audiences.[79] The law on authors' rights in the Congo had, as in other domains of intellectual property rights, to a large extent assimilated to Belgian law, and yet the Belgian jurists who examined the case of the Congo agreed that it presented a lacuna in comparison with the laws in effect in the metropole. Belgium signed neither the Berne Convention nor the revisions of Berlin in 1908 and Rome in 1928 on behalf of the Congo and Ruanda-Urundi,

76 Dreyfuss, Rochelle, and, Ginsburg, Jane, eds. *Intellectual Property at the Edge: The Contested Contours of IP* (Cambridge: Cambridge University Press, 2014); Smolders, *Droit civil du Congo belge*, 89.

77 Haeghen, Paul Vander. *Répertoire des Droits Intellectuels en Belgique et au Congo* (Brussels: L'Ingénieur-Conseil, 1924) 131.

78 Smolders, *Droit civil du Congo belge*, 118.

79 Smolders, *Droit civil du Congo belge*, 113 ; Ngombé, *Le droit d'auteur en Afrique*, 19–20.

and Théodore Smolders commented that he wished a colonial decree would acknowledge the adoption of the Berne Convention and its subsequent revisions, in order for the Congo to participate in international scientific and artistic life and to protect its authors.

This decree was eventually passed in 1948, and contributed to make Congo's intellectual property rights system one of the most extensive on the African continent. During the interwar years, Congo's reliance on Belgian intellectual property law meant that there were few differences between the colony and the metropole,[80] reinforced by the principle written in the Berne Convention that foreigners were assimilated with nationals as far as copyright was concerned (national treatment) – or, in line with the Belgian legislation on authors' rights. Berne's principle of assimilation of the foreigner to the national resulted in a similarity of intellectual property rights between the colonizers and the colonized.[81] This was coherent with the universalism professed by the Belgians intellectuals who participated in the field of international intellectual property rights.

But the apparent symmetry between colonizers and colonized that resulted from the Berne system was not the whole of the existing system of intellectual property. In the colony and mandates the customary courts delivered judgments to the Congolese that were not registered (or matriculated, *immatriculés*). The adoption of the Universal Copyright Convention of 6 September 1952 in Geneva aimed to create a system that reflected more accurately the needs of non-Western cultures, yet, this time, Belgium would not be among its first signatories. It was not until 1960, just after Congo's independence, that Belgium signed this convention.[82]

3.5 *Unfair Competition as a Part of the Belgian System of Intellectual Property*

During the interwar period and afterwards, the treaties that outlined the contours of intellectual property for Belgium and its colonies usually included a few pages on unfair competition. Contemporary international experts on intellectual property tend to propose limits to the intersections between unfair competition and intellectual property.[83] During the interwar period, however,

80 Smolders, *Droit civil du Congo belge*, 113.

81 Smolders, *Droit civil du Congo belge*, 116.

82 Smolders, *Droit civil du Congo belge*, 114.

83 Maggiolino, Mariateresa, and, Zoboli, Laura, 'The Intersection Between Intellectual Property and Antitrust Law'. In *Handbook of Intellectual Property Research. Lenses, Methods, Perspectives,* Calboli, Irene, and Montagnani, Maria Lillà, eds. (Oxford: Oxford University Press, 2021) 121–134.

the legal treaties for the Belgian colonies considered that unfair competition was part of the domain of intellectual property. In the case of the colony, the laws on unfair competition show some peculiarities, notably in regulating the work and the employment of the indigenous populations.

As discussed above, the freedom of the press was not acknowledged in the Belgian colony. The case law for the Belgian Congo contains a series of lawsuits for defamation, a matter taken seriously by the colonial authority, which considered that defamation could stir opposition and revolts. The colonial laws considered attacks to reputation to be a relevant cause for pursuits in cases of unfair competition.[84] Unfair competition cases could also apply to improper or fraudulent labeling of merchandise, relating to, for example, the quality of foodstuffs – despite the absence, as discussed above, of protection for country-of-origin labels in the Congo.[85]

In certain parts of the colonial economy the regulation of competition, especially in terms of the tasks and duties of both the workforce and employers, took on a particular significance. This was the case with the special provisions that the colonial decrees laid out for the mining industries. These rules were different from the laws in force in the metropole, and had been purposefully organized in order to protect the activity of the mining industries in the colony. A decree of 4 October 1930 that regulated the rights of mining labor and research can, in that sense, be considered a complement to the protection of trade secrets.[86] Another decree dated 24 September 1937 regulated the mining regime of the colony, confirming the principle of state ownership property over the mines, with a reservation for the rights that might have been acquired by the Congolese people. The decree stipulated that a prospection permit was required to search for mining fields in any geographical domain. The exploitation of mineral resources was subject to both obtaining a concession permit and administrative authorization.[87] A specific point in regard to authors' rights is complementary to the question of access to research on mineral resources in the Congo:[88] in the case of colonial Congo and Ruanda-Urundi, geographical maps were the object of a specific measure forbidding illegal reproductions.[89]

84 *Les Novelles, Droit colonial*, t. 1, nr. 237.

85 Smolders, *Droit civil du Congo belge*, 181.

86 Institut Royal Colonial Belge, *Bulletin des séances*, IX, 1938, 3, Extrait, Fernand Dellicour, *Un aspect du Droit public et du Droit administratif au Congo belge* (Brussels: Imprimeur de l'Académie Royale, 1938), 603.

87 Verstraete, Maurice. *Aperçu de droit civil du Congo belge, de la condition de ses habitants et des personnes morales, conflits coloniaux* (Antwerp: Editions coloniales Zaïre, 1946) 18.

88 Smolders, *Droit civil du Congo belge*, 143.

89 Smolders, *Droit civil du Congo belge*, 143.

In some regions of the Congo, the colonial administration had supplemented rights on mining with further provisions. For example, the Special Committee for the Katanga controlled mining prospection on its territories, and the mining rights of the National Committee of the Kivu were the object of a convention approved by the decree of 8 May 1928. The Committee retained exclusive control over the exploitation of the mines in that region until 1948.[90]

According to Belgian legal experts, the interwar period was characterized by mounting legal interventionism in the Congo. This observation is coherent with the project of making the Congo a model colony in terms of the management of its resources, the enforcement of health care measures, and the implementation of order and security.[91] Numerous decrees were passed during the interwar period regulating a myriad of aspects of life in the colony. Only some of these decrees were relevant to the theme of this chapter, especially in the domain of the regulation of labor, professions, and employment, which was an important theme of administrative regulations. Questions of (un)fair competition were relevant to the management of some colonial firms. The Belgian legislator aimed to regulate employment, to stabilize the workforce in businesses in the colony, to regulate the relations between leaders and employees, and to protect knowledge and know-how from industrial espionage. The regulation of relations between workers and entrepreneurs received particular attention, with one of the goals of these measures being to control competition and transfers of knowledge.[92]

Following a decree of 31 October 1931, an employer in the Congo could forbid his former employees, for a duration of three years after their departure, from exploiting a mining operation on their own, from acquiring the rights to mine, and from associating with others with an intention to mine, if the activity was to be pursued within a distance of 25 kilometers from the areas where the former employer was exercising his mining rights and exploitation. The case law in both Belgium and the Congo followed these rules. Several cases served to sum up other situations. For example, in the case of the wife of a former mining employee who wanted to engage in her turn in mining operations, the clauses mentioned above did not apply, according to a case judged in the courts of Elisabethville at the very end of the interwar period.[93] The mining

---

90 Paulus, *Droit public du Congo belge*, 121–123, 131.

91 Institut Royal colonial belge, *Bulletin des séances*, IX, 1938, 3, Dellicour, 602; Stengers, Jean. *Congo: Mythes et réalités* (Brussels: Racine Lannoo, 2007); Reybrouck, David Van. *Congo: The Epic History of a People* (Amsterdam: De Bezige Bij, 2014).

92 Institut Royal colonial belge, *Bulletin des séances*, IX, 1938, 3, Dellicour, 601–606.

93 Smolders, *Droit civil du Congo belge*, 194–197.

law thus extended protective rights over the sites prospected by international firms. It also reserved some exceptions, for example for family members of previous employees, in this case wives or widows, with the objective of extending the rights of one mining entrepreneur to his family.

4 Epilogue

This examination of the status of intellectual property law in Belgium's colonial empire has shown that the colonial administration aimed to organize a comprehensive legal framework for the colony. This included supplementary attention to specific points in the law that mattered to the colonial economy, such as the proper labelling of consumer goods, the extension of patent protection to international firms and innovators present in the Congo, and measures aimed at controlling the dissemination of know-how in specific sectors such as the mining industry.

During the interwar period colonial Congo's intellectual property law was on the way to becoming one of the most complete systems of intellectual property on the African continent, a situation that would be reached at the Brussels revision conference of the Berne Treaty in 1948. The files kept in the archive of Albert Guislain, a Belgian lawyer and a vice-president of the ALAI (International Literary and Artistic Association) during the interwar period, show that Belgian intellectual property specialists put great efforts into preparation for the Brussels conference. The expert committee for the universal status of authors' rights held a preparatory meeting in Brussels on 19 and 20 October 1938, which aimed to lobby newer countries in signing the Berne Convention. The Brussels conference was eventually postponed, however, not only because of the mounting political difficulties during the interwar years but also because it appeared premature to hold a new revision meeting so soon after the 1928 Rome conference if more countries had not yet joined as signatories of Berne.[94] A much scrutinized case was the United States, which would not join until 1989.

Works by Caroline Ncube and Daniel Acquah have demonstrated that intellectual property laws were imposed from the outside on African populations, who had no choice but to accept legal frameworks that rested upon definitions

94 Archives Générales du Royaume, Brussels, Fonds Guislain, 2701: documents préparatoires pour une Conférence diplomatique pour la préparation d'une Convention Universelle sur le Droit d'Auteur, Brussels, 1938.

of innovation decided by the colonizers.[95] A systematical examination of the patents taken out in the colony of the Congo, for example, confirms this point: an overwhelming majority of patentees were colonizers and international firms. In an important article, Eva Hemmungs Wirtén has also shown the enduring limitations that the copyright system posed for countries such as the Congo, where the ever insufficient adaptation of copyrights to the question of translations, for example, contributed to limiting the dissemination of books and of literacy.[96] In that respect, the decisions taken under the aegis of international experts on intellectual property, including Jules Destrée, to keep a right of reservation to member countries in the realm of translation was a relevant decision.

The interwar period was a decisive time for the legislator of colonial Congo, which, in addition to the imposition of a legal framework directly imported from the metropole, formalized in writing the activity of the customary courts. This chapter has traced the broad contours of the activity of these courts to show that some aspects of the protection of innovation and inventions were already covered by the customary law and that the customary laws were mediated by the colonial authority.

This chapter has also shown that intellectual property occupied a specific place amidst the broader legal framework that governed the colony. A contrast appears between the absence of rights for the colonial *subjects*, who had no voting rights and no democratic freedoms, and the framework for intellectual property that was increasingly developed during the interwar period. The Congolese could not vote, but they could, at least on paper, take out a patent for an innovation, register an industrial design for a fabric, and receive copyright fees for writing literary texts or music. Intellectual property was a domain where greater access to citizenship was granted to the subjects of the colony, than was the case in other domains.[97] The principle of reciprocity set out in the Berne convention was coherent with this generalization of the framework for intellectual property rights in the colony.

This situation raises the question of whether the Belgian legislator considered the conditions of innovation for the Congolese. During the interwar period, this may have been the case only in a limited number of instances.

---

95 Acquah, Daniel Opoku, 'The Unusual Extension of Imperial Intellectual Property Laws to Colonies in Africa'. In *Intellectual Property and the Law of Nations, 1860–1920,* Morris, P. Sean, ed. (Leiden: Brill Nijhoff, 2022) 291–331; Ncube, 'Three centuries and counting', 409–430.

96 Wirtén, 'Colonial Copyright, Postcolonial Publics', 532.

97 Cooper, Frederick. *Colonialism in Question: Theory, Knowledge, History* (Berkeley: University of California Press, 2005).

The colonial authority aimed to protect firms against unwanted transfer of knowledge, for example in the mining industry. Trade secrecy and unfair competition laws in the colony were designed to protect the entrepreneurs. Furthermore, the patent records show that patents were taken out in the Congo by multinationals and Western innovators,[98] while the role of the Congolese in innovation was limited to areas where the colonizers acknowledged the creativity of the colonized populations. In 1935, the colonial authority in Belgium created a commission for the protection of the so-called indigenous arts and professions (Commission pour la Protection des Arts et des Métiers Indigènes, COPAMI) that aimed to preserve and support the activities of the colonized in these domains. The COPAMI did not include any Congolese in its ranks. It was not directly involved in creating protective legislation, but discussed the topic occasionally and worked on the creation of stamps for the collective trademarking of Congolese artistic productions.[99] The areas where the Congolese were effectively able to support and promote invention remained limited. During the postwar era, the colonized populations of the Congo found some possibilities in the intellectual property rights framework, in, for example, protecting textiles and receiving intellectual property revenue from their musical compositions. The latter became especially effective after the creation of a local branch of the Belgian collective management organization SABAM in Congo and Ruanda-Urundi in 1949.[100]

The legal treaties examined in this chapter show a concern for interests in the resources of the colony, whether they be the products of agriculture, such as coffee, or of mining. In this respect, intellectual property was one of the tools in the arsenal of economic protectionism,[101] and in the trademark, patenting, and unfair competition laws the mining industry appeared as a source of interest and concern. The registered innovations however show a preeminence of Westerners among innovators. This can signify a short-term policy in terms of development, and thus a mitigated conclusion as to the contribution of such a protective system to FDI.[102] This point also aligns with the broader history of the colony, that shows that the colonizer succeeded in educational

98 *Bulletin administratif du Congo belge*, 1920–1939.

99 Beurden, Sarah Van. *Authentically African: Arts and the Transnational Politics of Congolese Culture* (Athens, OH: Ohio University Press, 2015).

100 *Bulletin administratif du Congo belge*, 25 November 1949, n. 18, 803; 25 May 1951, 906–907.

101 Hesse, Carla, 'The Rise of Intellectual Property, 700 BC–AD 2000: An Idea in the Balance', *Daedalus*, 131(2) (2002) 26–45.

102 Ncube, 'Three centuries and counting', 409–430.

efforts at the level of primary school, but did too little and too late to educate local elites for a postcolonial future.[103]

At the international level, the Belgians pursued the tasks they had started during the nineteenth century. Otlet and La Fontaine pursued their pacifist interests, which intersected less with questions of intellectual property, and new experts took over, such as Destrée, who became very active in questions of the unification of intellectual property internationally. His main concern was to secure revenue for the artistic professions, and the internationalism that he pursued was composed of elites. The legal regime of the colony aligned to the Berne principle of reciprocity, creating a framework that was protective of creativity. The internationalization of intellectual property had the potential to be rather insensitive to local differences and needs, showing the limits of a universally imposed system of property rights. The experts sought to mitigate this by organizing a space for the customary laws. The Belgian legal experts remained active in the international conferences for intellectual property. Their work continued the ideas from the previous period of internationalism, socialism, and interest in the arts, pursuing the concept that the arts were an important element in fostering peace between people.

Acknowledgments

I would like to thank the anonymous referees for their helpful comments on this chapter. My thanks also go to the participants of the Creative IPR Workshop 5 at the Norwegian Center in Athens, for helpful comments on an earlier version of this text. Research for this chapter has received funding from the European Research Council (ERC) under the European Union's Horizon 2020 research and innovation program: Creative IPR: The History of Intellectual Property Rights in the Creative Industries, ERC CoG Grant agreement No. 818523.

Bibliography

Acquah, Daniel Opoku, 'The Unusual Extension of Imperial Intellectual Property Laws to Colonies in Africa'. In *Intellectual Property and the Law of Nations, 1860–1920*, Morris, P. Sean, ed. (Leiden: Brill Nijhoff, 2022).

103 Nzongola-Ntalaja, Georges. *The Congo from Leopold to Kabila. A People's History* (London, Zed Books, 2003) 88–89, 122–123.

Annales parlementaires, Chambre des Représentants, Belgium, 1907.

Bonyi, Mukadi, dir. *Cinquante ans de législation postcoloniale au Congo-Zaïre: quel bilan?* (Brussels: Centre de Recherche de Droit Social, 2010).

Bulletin administratif du Congo belge, 1920–1951.

Clément, Piet, 'The Land Tenure System in the Congo, 1885–1960. Actors, Motivations, and Consequences'. In *Colonial Exploitation and Economic Development: The Belgian Congo and the Netherlands Indies Compared,* Frankema, Ewout, and Buelens, Frans, eds. (Abingdon: Routledge, 2013).

Cooper, Frederick. *Colonialism in Question: Theory, Knowledge, History* (Berkeley: University of California Press, 2005).

Coppieters, Daniel, *Le régime de la propriété industrielle au Congo belge* (Brussels: Etablissements Emile Bruylant, 1909).

Demeulenaere, Pascale, *L'Organisation internationale de coopération intellectuelle et la Belgique, 1922–1939* (Louvain: Université catholique de Louvain, 1994).

Dommann, Monika. *Authors and Apparatus: A Media History of Copyright* (Ithaca NY: Cornell University Press, 2019).

Dreyfuss, Rochelle, and Ginsburg, Jane, eds. *Intellectual Property at the Edge: The Contested Contours of IP* (Cambridge: Cambridge University Press, 2014).

Dumont, Georges-Henri, 'Le Ministre des Sciences et des Arts'. In *Jules Destrée le multiple,* Trousson, Raymond, ed. (Brussels: Académie de Langue et de Littérature Françaises, 1995).

Galvez-Behar, Gabriel, 'L'impossible institutionnalisation de la propriété scientifique, 1919–1939', *L'échelle des régulations politiques, XVIIIe–XXIe siècles: L'histoire et les sciences sociales aux prises avec les normes, les acteurs et les institutions* (Lille: Presses Universitaires du Septentrion, 2019).

Grandjean, Martin. Les réseaux de coopération intellectuelle. La Société des Nations comme actrice des échanges scientifiques et culturels dans l'entre-deux-guerres. (PhD thesis, Université de Lausanne, 2018).

Grosfilley, Anne. *African Wax Print Textiles* (Munich: Prestel, 2018).

Guy, Kolleen. *When Champagne became French: Wine and the Making of a National Identity* (Baltimore MD: Johns Hopkins University Press, 2007).

Hesse, Carla, 'The Rise of Intellectual Property, 700 BC–AD 2000: An Idea in the Balance', *Daedalus*, 131(2) (2002).

Hochschild, Adam, 'Introduction'. In *Lord Leverhulme's Ghosts: Colonial Exploitation in the Congo,* Jules Marchal, ed. (New York: Verso Books, 2017).

Institut Royal Colonial Belge. *Bulletin des séances*, IX, 1938, 3, Extrait, Fernand Dellicour, *Un aspect du Droit public et du Droit administratif au Congo belge* (Brussels: Imprimeur de l'Académie Royale, 1938).

Kongolo, Antoine Tshitungu. *Visages de Paul Panda Farnana: Nationaliste, Panafricaniste* (Paris: L'Harmattan, 2011).

Kumar, Sanjay, 'India Wins Battle with USA over Turmeric Patent'. *The Lancet*, 350 (9079) (1997).

Ladas, Stephen P. *Patents, Trademarks, and Related Rights: National and International Protection* (reprinted, Cambridge MA: Harvard University Press, 1975).

Laqua, Daniel. *Age of Internationalism and Belgium, 1880–1930: Peace, Progress and Prestige* (Manchester: Manchester University Press, 2015).

Législation Commerciale du Congo Belge (Brussels: Librairie Falk et Fils, 1930).

Les Novelles, Droit colonial.

Levie, Françoise. *L'homme qui voulait classer le monde: Paul Otlet et le Mundaneum* (Brussels: Les Impressions Nouvelles, 2006 [2020]).

Löhr, Isabella. *Auf dem Weg zu einer global governance kultureller Güter: die Globalisierung geistiger Eigentumsrechte in neuten Strukturen internationaler Zusammenarbeit (1886–1952)* (Leipzig: Universität Leipzig, 2008).

Löhr, Isabella. *Die Globalisierung geistiger Eigentumsrechte: neue Strukturen internationaler Zusammenarbeit, 1886–1952* (Kritische Studien zur Geschichtswissenschaft, Göttingen: Vandenhoeck & Ruprecht, 2010).

Maggiolino, Mariateresa, and Zoboli, Laura, 'The Intersection Between Intellectual Property and Antitrust Law'. In *Handbook of Intellectual Property Research. Lenses, Methods, Perspectives,* Calboli, Irene, and Montagnani, Maria Lillà, eds. (Oxford: Oxford University Press, 2021).

Mosselmans, Paul. *La Publicité Coloniale. Simple Essai* (Brussels: Editions commerciales et industrielles, 1910).

Ncube, Caroline, 'Three Centuries and Counting: The Emergence and Development of Intellectual Property Law in Africa'. In *The Oxford Handbook of Intellectual Property Law* Dreyfuss, Rochelle, and Pila, Justine, eds. (Oxford: Oxford University Press, 2016).

Ngombé, Laurier Yvon. *Le droit d'auteur en Afrique* (Paris: L'Harmattan, 2009).

Nwauche, Enyinna. *The Protection of Traditional Cultural Expressions in Africa* (New York: Springer, 2017).

Nzongola-Ntalaja, Georges. *The Congo from Leopold to Kabila. A People's History* (London: Zed Books, 2003).

Paulus, Jean-Pierre. *Droit public du Congo belge* (Brussels: Institut de Sociologie Solvay, 1959).

Pouillard, Véronique. *La publicité en Belgique, 1850–1975: Des courtiers aux agences internationales* (Brussels: Académie Royale de Belgique, Classe des Lettres et des Sciences Morales et Politiques, 2005).

Ricketson, Sam, and Ginsburg, Jane, 'The Berne Convention: Historical and Institutional Aspects'. In *International Intellectual Property: A Handbook of Contemporary Research,* Gervais, Daniel, ed. (London: Edward Elgar Publishing, 2015).

Ryckmans, Pierre. *Allo! Congo! Chroniques radiophoniques par Pierre Ryckmans* (Brussels: L'Edition Universelle, 1935).

Smolders, Théodore. *Droit civil du Congo belge* (Brussels: F. Larcier, 1956).

Stanziani, Alessandro, 'Wine Reputation and Quality Controls: The Origin of the AOCs in 19th century France'. *European Journal of Law and Economics*, 18(2) (2004) 149–167.

Stengers, Jean. *Congo: Mythes et réalités* (Brussels: Racine Lannoo, 2007).

Thyssens, Jeffrey, 'Henri Lafontaine et l'idée de paix internationale'. In *Cent ans de l'office international de bibliographie*, Despy-Meyer, Andrée, et al., ed. (Mons: Editions du Mundaneum, 1995).

Tousignant, Nathalie, 'The Belgian Colonial Experience and Legal Journals (1908–1960): An Overview'. *C@hiers du CRHiDI. Histoire, droit, institutions, société* 37 (2015) 1:16.

Van Beurden, Sarah. *Authentically African: Arts and the Transnational Politics of Congolese Culture* (Athens, OH: Ohio University Press, 2015).

Van Melkebeke, Sven. *Dissimilar Coffee Frontiers: Mobilizing Labor and Land in the Lake Kivu Region, Congo and Rwanda (1918–1960/62)* (Leiden: Brill, 2020).

Van Reybrouck, David. *Congo: The Epic History of a People* (Amsterdam: De Bezige Bij, 2014).

Vander Haeghen, Paul. *Répertoire des Droit Intellectuels en Belgique et au Congo* (Brussels: L'Ingénieur-Conseil, 1924).

Verstraete, Maurice. *Aperçu de droit civil du Congo belge, de la condition de ses habitants et des personnes morales, conflits coloniaux* (Antwerp: Editions coloniales Zaïre, 1946).

Vinez, Margaux. 'Division of the Commons and Access to Land on The Frontier: Lessons from The Colonial Legacy in The Democratic Republic of Congo'. (Working Paper, World Bank, 2017).

Wirtén, Eva Hemmungs, 'Colonial Copyright, Postcolonial Publics: The Berne Convention and the 1967 Stockholm Diplomatic Conference Revisited'. *SCRIPTed*, 7(3) (2010) 532.

Wright, Alex. *Cataloging the World: Paul Otlet and the Birth of the Information Age* (Oxford: Oxford University Press, 2014).

Archives

Archives Générales du Royaume, Brussels, Fonds Albert Guislain.

UNESCO Archives, Paris, digitalized funds, FR PUNES.

CHAPTER 11

Accession to the Berne Convention in 1931 and the Development of Copyright Law in Thailand

Noppanun Supasiripongchai

1 Interwar Internationalism and Copyright Law in Thailand

The emergence of interwar internationalism at the end of World War I brought with it hopes for a new international order dominated by democracy, international cooperation, and global trade, so that with the influence of interwar internationalism, many countries would learn to coexist in a more peaceful environment of mutual prosperity regulated by law.[1] Although interwar internationalism focused on the promotion of peace, its true basis also emphasised the peaceful effects of trade and the growing interdependence of the world through increased international trade.[2] In line with this development, copyright played the role of a silent peacemaker in the interwar period by allowing many countries to cooperate and continue to recognise the protection of copyrights through the Berlin Act 1908 of the Berne Convention and the Berne Additional Protocol of 1914. This is important, given that Thailand acceded to the Berne Act 1908 in 1931.[3]

Regarding Thailand's relationship with the world during 1919–1939, the nation acceded to the Berlin Act 1908 of the Berne Convention, when many countries, including Thailand itself, was faced with a global financial crisis.[4]

1 Hjalmar Falk, "Carl Schmitt and the Challenges of Interwar Internationalism: Against Weimar – Geneva – Versailles," *Global Intellectual History* 7, no. 4 (2020): 766.

2 John Thompson, "American Power and Interwar internationalism," *The Historical Journal* 61, no. 4 (2018): 1147; Steve Witt, "Interwar Internationalism and the Rebuilding of the Catholic University of Louvain Library," *Libraries: Culture, History, and Society* 4, no. 1 (2020): 1; Waqar Zaidi, "Liberal Internationalism and the Search for International Peace," in *The Routledge History of World Peace Since 1750*, ed. Christian Peterson, William Knoblauch, and Michael Loadenthal (Oxon and New York: Routledge, 2019), 61–62.

3 The Berne Convention for the Protection of Literary and Artistic Works in 1886 has had two Additions and five Revisions, as follows: the Paris Additional Act 1896, the Berlin Act 1908, the Berne Additional Protocol of 1914, the Rome Act 1928, Brussels Act 1948, the Stockholm Act 1967 and the current Paris Act 1971 of the Berne Convention. It can be said that the level of protection in the Berne Convention has increased gradually since 1886.

4 Barend Terwiel, *A Window on Thai History* (Bangkok: Editions Duang Kamol, 1989), 21–25.

 | DOI:10.1163/9789004714663_013

The drought of 1920 caused a decline in rice exports as well as other economic havoc for the country.[5] With these problems, Thailand's economic position in the world at that time seemed weaker than ever and its international reserves were dwindling.[6]

In order to solve this crisis, more moderate economic and legal reforms were introduced and the Thai government attempted to promote investment in local industry.[7] Although copyright was mainly intended to encourage creativity by rewarding creative activity, its main consequence was to promote trade and investment in industries, such as the book industry.[8]

One of the significant reforms introduced by the Thai government was the reform of copyright law to meet the international standard of the Berlin Act 1908 of the Berne Convention and the Berne Additional Protocol of 1914, to which Thailand became a signatory country in 1931.[9] As a result of this obligation, PLAWA 1931 was enacted in order to comply with the Berlin Act 1908 and the Berne Additional Protocol of 1914. Considered the first Thai copyright law based on international standards, it contained several provisions on international copyright protection that provided protection for foreign copyright works.

For example, PLAWA 1931 recognised the principle of national treatment for the first time in Thailand, which ensured that if Thailand provides certain rights to its own citizens, then it should also provide equivalent rights to foreigners.[10] On the other hand, the principle of giving foreign rights holders the same treatment as Thai rights holders prevented the latter from having an unfair advantage.[11] This principle can be seen in Section 28 of PLAWA 1931, which prescribed that the provisions of PLAWA 1931 shall apply to literary and artistic works of authors who are citizens of other member countries of the Berne Convention in the same way that they apply to the works of authors who are citizens of Thailand.[12]

---

5 Terwiel, *A Window on Thai History*, 22.

6 Terwiel, *A Window on Thai History*, 22.

7 Terwiel, *A Window on Thai History*, 25.

8 William Landes and Richard Posner, "An Economic Analysis of Copyright Law," *Journal of Legal Studies* 18, no. 2 (1989), 325.

9 World Intellectual Property Organization, "Contracting Parties: Berne Convention Berlin Act 1908" (2022), accessed 5 November 2023, https://wipolex.wipo.int/en/treaties/ShowResults?search_what=A&act_id=44.

10 Noppanun Supasiripongchai, *Intellectual Property Law for the Protection of Plant Varieties* (Chiang Mai: Nuntapun Printing, 2022), 29–30, 49.

11 Supasiripongchai, *Intellectual Property Law for the Protection of Plant Varieties*, 20–24.

12 Protection of Literary and Artistic Works Act 1931, Section 28.

The Thai government attempted to use the provisions on international copyright protection and the principle of national treatment to eliminate domestic barriers to foreign copyright protection in order to promote trade and investment in the book industry. The introduction in PLAWA 1931 of the provisions on international copyright protection and the principle of national treatment helped foreign rights holders get a better economic return from their investment, because without such provisions, any person could reproduce, translate, adapt or exploit foreign literary works in Thailand without prior authorisation of the foreign rights holder.

With PLAWA 1931, Thailand could cooperate with other countries and continue to recognise the protection of foreign copyright through the Berlin Act 1908 of the Berne Convention and the Berne Additional Protocol of 1914. Thus, the copyright law at that time played the role of a peacemaker. Even after PLAWA 1931 was replaced by the Copyright Act 1978, the Thai government was still in favour of the provisions on international copyright protection and the principle of national treatment, inserting them into the Copyright Act 1978 and the current Copyright Act 1994, even though the details of such provisions were different.

2 Copyright Protection in Thailand before the Accession to the Berlin Act 1908 of the Berne Convention

There were two copyright laws before Thailand's accession to the Berlin Act 1908 of the Berne Convention. The first was the Royal Announcement of the Vachirayan Library in 1892 (hereinafter called Royal Announcement 1892). Established in 1881, the Vachirayan Library was under the administration of a library committee called the "Kamma-Sampathika-Sapa".[13] In 1888, this committee reached a resolution that the reproduction or publication by others of any articles or any parts published in books of the Vachirayan Library called "Vachirayanvises Books" should be prohibited, unless they were authorised by the library committee.[14] Then, the resolution was passed to King Rama V of the Chakri dynasty for his approval. After the resolution had been approved, Royal Announcement 1892 was issued and it came into force in on 29 August 1892.[15]

13 Dhajjai Subhapholsiri, *Copyright Law: The Copyright Act B.E. 2537*, 3rd edition (Bangkok: Nititham Publishing House, 2001) 4.

14 Subhapholsiri, *Copyright Law.*

15 Royal Announcement of the Vachirayan Library 1892, Paragraph 2.

The Royal Announcement 1892 stipulated that any person shall not take the articles or any parts that had been published in the Vachirayanvises Books and shall not publish them as a book of any kind, unless such person obtained permission from the library committee.[16] There were two reasons for such a prohibition. The first was that articles published in the Vachirayanvises Books were written and bought for the purpose of entertaining the members of the library only. Secondly, the library had spent large sums of money buying those articles and it followed that if they had commercial values for publication, then the library should be the only one to publish them and gain the benefits from selling them.[17]

Although the Royal Announcement 1892 had not been influenced by any international copyright laws, the scope of copyright protection under the Royal Announcement 1892 was very narrow since it only protected the articles published in the Vachirayanvises Books, so the articles published in other books in Thailand at that time would not be protected under Royal Announcement 1892. Also, there was no copyright exception in Royal Announcement 1892 and the publication of articles contained in the Vachirayanvises Books could be made only when prior permission had been granted from the library committee.[18]

Further, Royal Announcement 1892 provided no legal penalty for violating its provisions and it did not include the notion of a national treatment for modern copyright. However, it could be considered as the first law that provided copyright protection in Thailand, because the official administration and legal system in Thailand at that time comprised an absolute monarchy; with such system, a royal announcement of the King was generally applied to all people as a law.[19]

Also, since the Royal Announcement of 1892 prohibited a person from publishing the articles or any part of the Vachirayanvises Books and gave the authority to the library committee to grant the permission for such publication, it was consistent with copyright principles that recognise the exclusive

---

16 Royal Announcement of the Vachirayan Library 1892, Paragraph 2.

17 Royal Announcement of the Vachirayan Library 1892, Paragraph 1.

18 Noppanun Supasiripongchai, "The Development of the Copyright Exception in Thailand: Where Has It Come From, Where is It Now Under the Thai Copyright Amendment Act 2015, and Where is It Heading?," *European Intellectual Property Review* 38, no. 10 (2016): 620–632, 621.

19 Chaiyos Hemaratchata, *Copyright Law*, 4th edition (Bangkok: Nititham Publishing House, 2006), 10; Chaiyos Hemaratchata, *Problems of Copyright Law* (Bangkok: Niti Bannakan Publishing, 1985), 9.

right of the copyright owner in authorising the publication and reproduction of a copyright work.[20]

The second copyright law was the Ownership of Authors Act 1901 (hereinafter called OAA 1901) and the Amendment of Ownership of Authors Act 1914 (hereinafter called AOAA 1914). OAA 1901 had been enacted by the government of King Rama V for two reasons. First, the unauthorised reproduction or publication of the books at that time seemed to occur on a regular basis. Especially, if such books were best-selling books, there were often people who arbitrarily took such books to print and then sold them without permission or authorisation of the author. In order to protect the rights and interests of the author, who wrote a book with his own wisdom and knowledge, it was necessary to enact OAA 1901.[21] Second, most developed countries at that time had a law to prohibit others from copying or publishing books without authorisation of the author, and therefore it was important for Thailand to have such a law to protect their interests.[22]

OAA 1901 extended the scope of protection to cover all books by granting the ownership rights for authors to print, reproduce, and translate into other languages, and sell their books as well as the right to prohibit other persons from publication, reproduction, or translation of the books without prior authorisation from their authors.[23] It required that in order to obtain ownership rights and acquire protection under OAA 1901, such books must be printed in Thailand and must be sold for the first time in Thailand.[24]

This was different from the scope of protection under Royal Announcement 1892, which was limited to only the articles published by the Vachirayanvises Books, so it could not protect articles published in other books. Although there were no criminal sanctions in OAA 1901, the provision on civil remedies for copyright infringement, such as damage, was inserted into Section 16 of OAA 1901.

This provision prevented any person from copying, translating, or selling the books which were protected under OAA 1901 without the authorisation of the rights holder. It also stated that in circumstances of a person violating this provision, the rights holder shall bring the case to the Court and claim damages or remunerations.[25]

---

20 Dhajjai Subhapholsiri, *Copyright Law: The Copyright Act B.E. 2537*, 3rd edition (Bangkok: Nititham Publishing House 2001) 5.

21 Ownership of Authors Act 1901, Preamble.

22 Ownership of Authors Act 1901, Preamble.

23 Ownership of Authors Act 1901, Section 4.

24 Ownership of Authors Act 1901, Section 7.

25 Ownership of Authors Act 1901, Section 16.

In addition, OAA 1901 also provided that the ownership rights in a book should endure for the natural life of the author and for the further term of seven years commencing at the time of their death, but if the said term of seven years had expired before the end of forty-two years from the date of obtaining the ownership rights, then the ownership rights in a book shall endure for the term of forty-two years.[26] Also, it required the rights holder of the books to send copies to the Royal Library, the Vachirayan Library, and the Buddhasasanasangaha Library.[27] Further, it prescribed that all books which were entitled to ownership rights under OAA 1901 must be printed and the author must bring the book to the officer for registration within 12 months of the first publication, or if the author of the book died before receiving the ownership rights, then the estate of the author must apply for registration within 12 months of their death.[28] It also stipulated that in order for the book to be registered for ownership rights, the applicant must send one copy of the book to the officer[29] and the officer must have a Book of Registry to register every book requested for ownership rights, and when any book was registered, both the applicant and the officer must sign their name in the Book of Registry and in a copy of the book that the applicant had sent to the officer.[30] If there was an assignment of ownership rights, then the evidence that the ownership rights had been assigned must be shown to the officer in order to register the assignment of ownership rights, and after such registration, the assignee would have the right of ownership under OAA 1901.[31]

OAA 1901 was amended by AOAA 1914, which stipulated that all infringing copies of the books that were held by the infringer must become the property of the rights holder.[32] Also, AOAA 1914 improved the registration methods by requiring more details, such as the name of the book, the date of the first publication, the name of the publisher, and the name and address of the rights holder, to be given to the officers.[33] Some amendments were made in order to improve the provisions of OAA 1901 and make them easier to enforce in practice. For example, OAA 1901 provided no definition of the term "book";

26 Ownership of Authors Act 1901, Section 5.

27 Ownership of Authors Act 1901, Section 15. The Royal Library was demolished, but the Vachirayan Library and the Buddhasasanasangaha Library later became part of the National Library of Thailand.

28 Ownership of Authors Act 1901, Section 10.

29 Ownership of Authors Act 1901, Section 12.

30 Ownership of Authors Act 1901, Section 13.

31 Ownership of Authors Act 1901, Section 14.

32 Amendment of the Ownership of the Authors Act 1914, Section 20.

33 Amendment of the Ownership of the Authors Act 1914, Section 4.

therefore, it was unclear about the scope of protection. In contrast, AOAA 1914 made it clearer by defining the term "book". At the same time it extended the term to cover all written works, but other types of copyright works were still not protected under both OAA 1901 and AOAA 1914. Moreover, AOAA 1914 provided that the plaintiff could request an order from the Court to stop others from selling their books without any need to prove to the Court that damage had actually occurred.[34] It also granted more advantages to the plaintiff. For example, in the case where there was infringement of the rights of ownership, the plaintiff did not need to prove the malicious intent of the infringer, since it was presumed that the infringer had a malicious intent to inflict damage on the plaintiff.[35]

AOAA 1914 also prevented some types of works from obtaining rights of ownership. Pursuant to Section 15, a book containing obscene works, a work that insulted religion, or a work that opposed public order could not obtain rights of ownership, and any book containing false information could not obtain rights of ownership.[36] This was the first and last time that Thai Copyright law prohibited the granting of copyright on these types of works. Although the equivalent provision to Section 15 of AOAA 1914 could not be found in PLAWA 1931 and the Copyright Act 1987, the Thai Court still hold the same position as in Section 15 that such obscene works could not obtain copyright, since it could not be considered as copyright work.[37] However, OAA 1901 provided no copyright exception, and even though OAA 1901 was amended by AOAA 1914, the amendment did not insert any copyright exceptions into OAA 1901.[38] Both OAA 1901 and AOAA 1914 had not been influenced by the Berne Convention or any international copyright laws.

34 Amendment of the Ownership of the Authors Act 1914, Section 20.

35 Amendment of the Ownership of the Authors Act 1914, Section 21.

36 Amendment of the Ownership of the Authors Act 1914, Section 15.

37 Supreme Court Decision No. 3705/2530 (1987), System for Searching Judgments, Orders, Petitions and Rulings of the Supreme Court, Information Technology and Communication Center of the Supreme Court of Thailand, accessed 5 November 2023, http://deka.supremecourt.or.th/.

38 Supasiripongchai, "The Development of the Copyright Exception in Thailand," 621.

3 Copyright Protection in Thailand after the Accession to the Berlin Act 1908 of the Berne Convention

OAA 1901 and AOAA 1914 were replaced by PLAWA 1931 in order to comply with Thailand's obligation under the Berlin Act 1908 of the Berne Convention and the Berne Additional Protocol of 1914. Section 2 stipulated that PLAWA 1931 shall come into force from the date of publication in the Government Gazette.[39] PLAWA 1931 was published in the Government Gazette on 21 June 1931, so it came into force on 21 June 1931.[40] However, Thailand acceded to the Berlin Act 1908 of the Berne Convention and the Berne Additional Protocol of 1914 with six reservations. Under these reservations, some provisions of the Berlin Act 1908 would not be implemented, since Thailand would choose to implement some provisions of the Berne Convention of 1886 and the Paris Additional Act 1896 instead.[41] Although there were six reservations, the Berlin Act 1908 of the Berne Convention and the Berne Additional Protocol of 1914 still played an important role of silent peacemaker by allowing Thailand and other Member States of the Berne Convention to cooperate and continue to recognise the protection of copyrights. This can be seen from the provisions of PLAWA 1931.

This section will be divided into two subsections. The first will consider the changes and improvements in PLAWA 1931, which were better than the provisions of OAA 1901 and AOAA 1914. The second will consider the changes and improvements in PLAWA 1931, which were influenced by the Berlin Act 1908 of the Berne Convention and the Berne Additional Protocol of 1914.

3.1 *Significant Changes and Improvements in PLAWA 1931*

There were several legal changes and improvements in PLAWA 1931. For example, PLAWA 1931 was the first copyright law in Thailand to define the term "copyright" as exclusive rights in literary and artistic works. It stipulated that "copyright" means the exclusive right to produce or reproduce the work or any

39 Protection of Literary and Artistic Works Act 1931, Section 2.

40 Protection of Literary and Artistic Works Act 1931, PLAWA 1931 was published in the Government Gazette, accessed 5 November 2023, http://www.ratchakitcha.soc.go.th/DATA/PDF/2474/A/127.PDF.

41 It is important to note that even when PLAWA 1931 was replaced by the Copyright Act 1978, some of the six reservations to the Berlin Act 1908, which Thailand had joined since 1931, were still implemented through the Copyright Act 1978 and the Royal Decree of 1983, which was issued under the Copyright Act 1978. However, these six reservations to the Berlin Act 1908 are now unenforceable, since Thailand formally changed its obligation to Paris Act 1971 of the Berne Convention of 1971 in September 1995, which is currently implemented through the Copyright Act 1994.

substantial part of literary and artistic works in any material form whatsoever, to perform, or in the case of a lecture, to deliver, the work or any substantial part in public, and if the work is unpublished, to publish the work or any substantial part.[42] According to the 1931 Act, copyright included exclusive rights which gave permission: (a) to produce or reproduce literary and artistic works, perform dramatic work, or publish any translation of the literary work; (b) in the case of a dramatic work, to convert it into a novel or other non-dramatic work; (c) in the case of a novel or other non-dramatic work, or an artistic work, to convert it into a dramatic work by way of performance in public or otherwise; and (d) in the case of a literary, dramatic, or musical work, to make any record, perforated roll, cinematograph film, or other contrivance by means of which the work may be mechanically performed, and to authorise any such acts as aforesaid.[43]

Further, PLAWA 1931 was the first copyright law in Thailand that contained provisions on copyright exceptions, making clear which actions could be exempted from infringement of copyright. The copyright exceptions were regulated in Section 20 of PLAWA 1931, which stipulated that copyright of a work shall be deemed to be infringed without the consent of the copyright owner.[44] However, there were four exceptions that ensured that certain acts did not constitute the infringement of a copyright. First, it provided that any fair dealing with any work for the purposes of private study, research, criticism, review, or a newspaper summary shall not constitute infringement of copyright.[45] It was the first time that the use of copyright works for the purpose of research and study was recognised as a permitted act under Thai copyright law. However, this provision was the only fair dealing provision to ever appear in the history of Thai copyright law because, after the replacement of PLAWA 1931 by the Thai Copyright Act 1978, the term "fair dealing" never appeared in the Thai copyright system again, including in the current Thai Copyright Act 1994.[46] Second, it prescribed that the making or publishing of paintings, drawings, engravings, or photographs of a work of sculpture or artistic craftsmanship, if permanently situated in a public place, or building, or the making or publishing of paintings, drawings, engravings, or photographs of any architectural work of art, should not constitute infringement of copyright.[47] Third, it

42 Protection of Literary and Artistic Works Act 1931, Section 4, Paragraph 2.

43 Protection of Literary and Artistic Works Act 1931, Section 4, Paragraph 3.

44 Protection of Literary and Artistic Works Act 1931, Section 20.

45 Protection of Literary and Artistic Works Act 1931, Section 20(1).

46 Supasiripongchai, "The Development of the Copyright Exception in Thailand," 622.

47 Protection of Literary and Artistic Works Act 1931, Section 20(2).

stipulated that the publication of short passages from published literary works in a collection for the benefit of education, science, or literary meetings shall not constitute infringement of copyright, provided that the source from which such passages are taken is acknowledged.[48] Fourth, it prescribed that the publication in a newspaper of reports of lectures or sermons delivered in public shall not constitute infringement of copyright.[49] This exception only applied to publication in a newspaper, giving the author exclusive rights to authorise the publication of the reports of lectures or sermons by any other means.[50]

In addition, PLAWA 1931 was the first copyright law to contain provisions on copyright infringement with civil and criminal remedies. In this instance, PLAWA 1931 listed actions considered an infringement of copyright by stipulating that copyright in a work shall be deemed to be infringed by any person who (a) sells or lets for hire, or by way of trade exposes or offers for sale or hire; (b) distributes for the purposes of trade; (c) by way of trade exhibits in public; or (d) imports for sale or hire of literary and artistic works made by infringing copyright in Thailand.[51] It also contained the provision on civil remedies in Section 22, which provided that in the case of copyright infringement, the copyright owners can take civil action in order to prevent such infringement and claim for damages.[52] This provision was similar to Section 16 of the previous OAA 1901, which allowed the rights holder to bring the case to the Court and claim for damages in case of copyright infringement.[53]

Nevertheless, PLAWA 1931 further stated that in any action for infringement of copyright, the literary work or artistic work shall be presumed to be a work in which copyright subsists and the plaintiff shall be presumed to be the copyright owner, unless the defendant puts in question the existence of the copyright or the title of the plaintiff.[54] In the case where any such question is in question, then (a) if a name purporting to be that of the author of the work is printed or otherwise indicated in the usual manner, the person whose name is so printed or indicated shall be presumed to be the author of the work; or (b) if no name is so printed or indicated, or if the name so printed or indicated is not the author's true name or the name by which they are commonly known, and a name purporting to be that of the publisher or proprietor of the work is

48 Protection of Literary and Artistic Works Act 1931, Section 20(3).
49 Protection of Literary and Artistic Works Act 1931, Section 20(4).
50 Protection of Literary and Artistic Works Act 1931, Section 20(4).
51 Protection of Literary and Artistic Works Act 1931, Section 21(a), (b), (c), and (d).
52 Protection of Literary and Artistic Works Act 1931, Section 22, Paragraph 1.
53 Ownership of Authors Act 1901, Section 16.
54 Protection of Literary and Artistic Works Act 1931, Section 22, Paragraph 2.

printed or otherwise indicated in the usual manner, the person whose name is so printed or indicated shall, unless the contrary is proved, be presumed to be the owner of the copyright of the work for the purposes of proceedings in respect to the infringement of copyright.[55] These presumptions did not appear in OAA 1901 and AOAA 1914. AOAA 1914 only provided one clause that in the case where there was an infringement, it would be presumed that the infringer had a malicious intent to inflict damage on the plaintiff.[56] This presumption was removed from PLAWA 1931. Moreover, PLAWA 1931 stipulated that all infringing copies of any work in which copyright subsists, or of any substantial part, and all plates used or intended to be used for the production of such infringing copies, shall be deemed to be the property of the owner of the copyright, who accordingly may engage in proceedings for the recovery of the possession of such property.[57] It also prescribed that an action in respect to infringement of copyright shall not be commenced after the expiration of three years from the day of the infringement.[58]

PLAWA 1931 also provided for criminal sanctions for copyright infringement for the first time in Thailand. It prescribed that any person shall be guilty of an offence and be liable to a fine not exceeding fifty baht for every copy, but not exceeding five hundred baht in respect to the same transaction if such person knowingly (a) makes for sale or hire any infringing copy of a work in which copyright subsists; (b) sells or lets for hire, or by way of trade, exposes or offers for sale or hire any infringing copy of any such work; (c) distributes infringing copies of any such work for the purposes of trade; or (d) by way of trade exhibits in public any infringing copy of any such work, or imports for sale or hire into Thailand any infringing copy of any such work.[59] It also indicated that if any person knowingly makes or has in their possession any plate for the purpose of making infringing copies of any work for which copyright subsists, or knowingly and for his private profit causes any such work to be performed in public without the consent of the copyright owner, they shall be guilty of an offence and be liable to a fine not exceeding five hundred baht.[60] In addition, it provided that any person who has committed an offence and subsequently commits an offence under this provision within five years shall be liable to

55 Protection of Literary and Artistic Works Act 1931, Section 22, Paragraph 2(a) and (b).

56 Amendment of the Ownership of the Authors Act 1914, Section 21.

57 Protection of Literary and Artistic Works Act 1931, Section 23.

58 Protection of Literary and Artistic Works Act 1931, Section 24.

59 Protection of Literary and Artistic Works Act 1931, Section 25, Paragraph 1(a)–(d) and Paragraph 2.

60 Protection of Literary and Artistic Works Act 1931, Section 25, Paragraph 3.

the highest penalty as prescribed for the offence.[61] These provisions on copyright infringement with civil and criminal remedies of PLAWA 1931 seemed to be more effective in protecting the interests of the copyright owner than the previous OAA 1901 and AOAA 1914. Also, since foreign copyright works could be protected under PLAWA 1931, the foreign copyright owners could also benefit from these provisions. This issue will be discussed in the next section.

3.2 *Changes and Improvements with the Influences of the Berne Convention*

Some legal changes and improvements in PLAWA 1931 were influenced by the Berlin Act 1908 of the Berne Convention and the Berne Additional Protocol of 1914. Such influences can be seen from the scope of protection; the term of copyright protection; provisions on international copyright protection and principles of national treatment; and other provisions of PLAWA 1931.

3.2.1 Scope of Protection

The scope of protection under PLAWA 1931 was extended to cover all literary and artistic works, so it was broader than the scope of protection under the previous OAA 1901 and AOAA 1914, which only provided protection for books. This change was based on Thailand's obligation under the Berlin Act 1908 of the Berne Convention, since Thailand incorporated the definition of the term "literary and artistic works" in Paragraph 1 of Article 2 of the Berlin Act 1908 into Section 4 of PLAWA 1931. This can be seen from Section 4 of PLAWA 1931, which stated, in similar language as Paragraph 1 of Article 2 of the Berlin Act 1908, that "literary and artistic works" shall include, inter alia, any work in the literary, scientific, or artistic domain in whatever may be the mode or form of its expression.[62]

However, Thailand's accession to the Berlin Act 1908 of the Berne Convention was subject to six reservations. The first reservation was also related to the scope of protection, and it stated that Paragraph 4 of Article 2 of the Berlin Act 1908 is replaced by Article 4 of the Berne Convention of 1886 with respect to the protection of works of art applied for industrial purposes.[63] Pursuant to Paragraph 4 of Article 2 of the Berlin Act 1908, works of art applied to industrial

61 Protection of Literary and Artistic Works Act 1931, Section 25, Paragraph 4.

62 Protection of Literary and Artistic Works Act 1931, Section 4, Paragraph 5; Berlin Act 1908 of the Berne Convention, Article 2, Paragraph 1.

63 World Intellectual Property Organization, "General information: States Which Have Stipulated Reservations to Berlin Act: Thailand" (2023), accessed 5 November 2023, https://www.wipo.int/edocs/pubdocs/en/wipo_pub_berne_birpi.

purposes must be protected so far as the domestic legislation of each country allows.[64] Thailand did not implement this provision, but it relied on the approach in Article 4 of the Berne Convention of 1886, which did not mention works of art applied for industrial purposes.[65] This can be seen from the definition of the term "literary and artistic works" in Section 4 of PLAWA 1931, which did not include works of art applied for industrial purposes. There was also no provision in PLAWA 1931 that provided protection for works of art applied for industrial purposes. Even though PLAWA 1931 did not provide protection for works of art applied for industrial purpose, since it relied on the first reservation and did not implement Paragraph 4 of Article 2 of the Berlin Act 1908, the scope of protection under PLAWA 1931 was still consistent with the Berlin Act 1908 of the Berne Convention, since Thailand used Paragraph 1 of Article 2 of the Berlin Act 1908 as a model for the definition of the term "literary and artistic works" in PLAWA 1931.

3.2.2 Term of Copyright Protection

Paragraph 1 of Article 7 of the Berlin Act 1908 provided that the term of protection shall include the life of the author and fifty years after their death.[66] Nevertheless, Paragraph 2 of Article 7 further stated that in the case such term of protection should not be uniformly adopted by all contracting countries, then such term shall be regulated by the law of the country where protection is claimed and must not exceed the term fixed in the country of origin of the work, so the contracting countries should only be bound to apply the provisions of Paragraph 1 insofar as such provisions are consistent with their domestic laws.[67] With this provision, the term of protection should include the life of the author and fifty years after their death, but if the term of protection could not be uniformly adopted by all countries, the different term of protection could be regulated by law of the contracting country where the copyright protection is claimed.

Thailand relied on the provision in Paragraph 2 of Article 7 in order to have a different term of protection from the term prescribed by Paragraph 1 of Article 7. This can be seen from Section 14 of PLAWA 1931, which provided that copyright protection shall subsist for the life of the author and thirty years after their death and if the author died before the publication of the works, then

64 Berlin Act 1908 of the Berne Convention, Article 2, Paragraph 4.
65 Berne Convention 1886, Article 4.
66 Berlin Act 1908 of the Berne Convention, Article 7, Paragraph 1.
67 Berlin Act 1908 of the Berne Convention, Article 7, Paragraph 2.

copyright shall subsist for thirty years from the date of publication.[68] Although the life of the author plus a thirty-year term of protection in Section 14 of PLAWA 1931 was shorter than the uniform standard in Paragraph 1 of Article 7 of the Berlin Act 1908, which required the life of the author plus a fifty-year term of protection, it was still better than the term of protection in Section 5 of the previous OAA 1901, which provided that ownership of a book should endure for the life of the author plus seven years.[69]

Furthermore, Paragraph 3 of Article 7 provided that for photographic works and works produced by a process analogous to photography, the term of protection shall be regulated by the law of the country where protection is claimed, provided that the said term should not exceed the term fixed in the country of origin of the work.[70] This provision allowed the term of protection to be regulated by the law of the contracting country, so Thailand relied on this provision in order to regulate the term of protection in Section 16 of PLAWA 1931, which provided that copyright of photographic work and works produced by a process analogous to photography shall subsist for thirty years from the date of shooting or making such work.[71] These provisions of PLAWA 1931 had been influenced by the Berlin Act 1908 of the Berne Convention.

In addition, some provisions relating to the term of protection were inserted into PLAWA 1931 for the first time. For example, Section 15 provided that in the case of a work of joint authorship, copyright subsists for the life of joint authors and continues to subsist for thirty years from the death of the last surviving joint author.[72] Moreover, Section 17 indicated that copyright of a gramophone record, perforated roll, or any other record capable of being replayed with equipment shall subsist for thirty years from the date of making the original gramophone record or making any other record.[73] Section 18 stipulated that copyright of a cinematograph film shall subsist for thirty years from the date of making such work,[74] while Section 19 prescribed that copyright of newspapers shall subsist for thirty years from the date of publication and the right of the

---

68 Protection of Literary and Artistic Works Act 1931, Section 14, Paragraphs 1 and 2.

69 Ownership of Authors Act 1901, Section 5. Although the life of the author plus a fifty-year term of protection under Article 7, Paragraph 1 of the Berlin Act 1908 had not been accepted in PLAWA 1931, it was later accepted in Thailand with the introduction of the Copyright Act 1978; Section 16 of the Thai Copyright Act 1978 clearly provided that copyright protection shall subsist for the life of the author and fifty years after their death.

70 Berlin Act 1908 of the Berne Convention, Article 7, Paragraph 3.

71 Protection of Literary and Artistic Works Act 1931, Section 16.

72 Protection of Literary and Artistic Works Act 1931, Section 15.

73 Protection of Literary and Artistic Works Act 1931, Section 17.

74 Protection of Literary and Artistic Works Act 1931, Section 18.

author of articles published in the newspapers or periodicals shall be under the term of protection in Section 14 of PLAWA 1931.[75] These provisions relating to the term of protection in Sections 14 to 19 of PLAWA 1931 applied to Thai copyright works, but the term of protection of the foreign copyright works may be subject to certain conditions, which will be discussed in the next section.

3.2.3 Provisions on International Copyright Protection and Principles of National Treatment

In order to comply with the Berlin Act 1908 of the Berne Convention, PLAWA 1931 provided copyright protection for foreign works for the first time in its "Chapter 2 international copyright" (Sections 28 to 31). Section 31 stated that the provisions of "Chapter 2 international copyright" shall apply from the date with which the government of His Majesty has become a contracting party to the Berne Convention for the Protection of Literary and Artistic Works of September 1886, as amended at Berlin on 13 November 1908 and completed by the Additional Protocol signed at Berne on 20 March 1914.[76] In 1931, Thailand became a contracting party to the Berlin Act 1908 of the Berne Convention and the Berne Additional Protocol of 1914, so the provisions of "Chapter 2 international copyright" of PLAWA 1931, which applied to foreign copyright works, came into force in 1931.

The Berlin Act 1908 of the Berne Convention played the important role of peacemaker since it allowed Thailand and other countries to cooperate and continue to recognise the protection of copyright. The role of copyright as a peacemaker can be seen from the principle of national treatment in Article 5 of the Berlin Act 1908, which stipulated that the authors being subjects or citizens of one of the countries of the Union who first publish their works in another country of the Union shall have in the latter country the same rights as native authors.[77]

This provision ensured that works originating in one of the contracting countries must be given the same protection in each of the other contracting countries as the latter grants to the works of its own nationals. This principle is a rule of non-discrimination, which is based on the legal ideal that all men are equal before the law, regardless of whether they are nationals or foreigners, so foreign copyright owners can enjoy their rights in a protecting country with at least the same treatment as the protecting country gives to its own

75 Protection of Literary and Artistic Works Act 1931, Section 19, Paragraphs 1–2.
76 Protection of Literary and Artistic Works Act 1931, Section 31.
77 Berlin Act 1908 of the Berne Convention, Article 5.

nationals, regardless of how foreign copyright owners are treated in their own countries.[78]

Thailand adopted the principle of national treatment in Section 28 of PLAWA 1931, which stipulated that the provisions of PLAWA 1931 shall apply to literary and artistic works published in other member countries of the Union in the same way as they apply to works published for the first time in Thailand, and also such provisions shall apply to the literary and artistic works of authors who are subjects or citizens of one of the countries of the Union in the same way as they apply to the works of authors who are subjects or citizens of Thailand.[79] PLAWA 1931 was the first copyright law in Thailand to recognise the principle of national treatment and provide protection for foreign copyright works.

Nevertheless, there were some limitations on the principle of national treatment. These came from the second reservation of Thailand to the Berlin Act 1908, which indicated that Paragraph 2 of Article 4 of the Berlin Act 1908 is replaced by Paragraph 2 of Article 2 of the Berne Convention of 1886, in respect to compliance with the conditions and formalities required by the law of the country of origin of the work.[80]

Pursuant to Paragraph 2 of Article 4 of the Berlin Act 1908, the enjoyment and the exercise of the rights must not be subject to any formality, but such enjoyment and exercise are independent of the existence of protection in the country of origin of the work.[81] This provision was based on the principle of independent protection, which required the contracting countries to protect the literary and artistic works of other contracting countries without considering whether or not such works are fully protected under the national law in their country of origin.[82]

---

78 Supasiripongchai, *Intellectual Property Law for the Protection of Plant Varieties*, 29–30, 49. The principle of national treatment was embodied in the first Berne Convention of 1886 and can still be found in the current Berne Convention Paris Revision of 1971 as well as in the TRIPS Agreement.

79 Protection of Literary and Artistic Works Act 1931, Section 28.

80 World Intellectual Property Organization, "General information: States Which Have Stipulated Reservations to Berlin Act: Thailand" (2023), accessed 5 November 2002, https://www.wipo.int/edocs/pubdocs/en/wipo_pub_berne_birpi.

81 Berlin Act 1908 of the Berne Convention, Article 4, Paragraph 2. The principle of independent protection was first embodied in Article 4, Paragraph 2 of the Berlin Act 1908. Since then, it continued to be embodied in the Berne Convention until the current Paris Act 1971.

82 Although the principle of independent protection was first embodied in Article 4, Paragraph 2 of the Berlin Act 1908, it was not recognised by PLAWA 1931. This principle was later recognised in Thailand with the introduction of Royal Decree 1993, which

However, Thailand did not implement this provision. Instead it chose to implement Paragraph 2 of Article 2 of the Berne Convention of 1886, which provided that enjoyment of rights be subject to the accomplishment of the conditions and formalities prescribed by law in the country of origin of the work and cannot exceed in other countries the term of protection granted in the country of origin.[83]

This provision contained two conditions which can be regarded as limitations to the principle of national treatment, since they applied to foreign literary and artistic works but not to Thai literary and artistic works. First, it allowed the contracting countries to set the requirement that the foreign copyright work be protected only if they meet the conditions and formalities prescribed by law in the country of origin of the work. This condition was incorporated into Section 29 of PLAWA 1931, which stipulated that literary and artistic works that are not conditionally and formally protected by law in their country of origin shall not be protected under PLAWA 1931.[84]

Second, it allowed the contracting countries to set the requirement that the protection for foreign copyright works not exceed the term of protection granted in the country of origin. This condition was incorporated into Section 28 of PLAWA 1931, which stipulated that the term of copyright protection in Thailand could not exceed the term of protection granted in the country of origin.[85] As a result of this provision, even though Section 14 of PLAWA 1931 guaranteed that copyright protection shall subsist for the life of the author and thirty years after their death,[86] such a term of protection in Section 14 could not exceed the term of protection granted in the country of origin. For instance, if the term of protection in Thailand was 30 years after the death of the author and the term of protection in India, which was also a contracting party to the Berlin Act 1908, was 25 years after the death of the author, then the Indian copyright works would be protected in Thailand for only 25 years after the death of the author, which was the same as the term of protection in India. If India wanted its copyright works to be protected in Thailand for 30 years after the death of the author, then India must extend its term of protection from 25 years after the death of the author to 30 years after the death

---

was issued under the Copyright Act 1978. This principle is now embodied in the current Copyright Act 1994 as well.

83 Berne Convention of 1886, Article 2, Paragraph 2.

84 Protection of Literary and Artistic Works Act 1931, Section 29(A).

85 Protection of Literary and Artistic Works Act 1931, Section 29(A) and Section 28.

86 Protection of Literary and Artistic Works Act 1931, Section 14, Paragraphs 1 and 2.

of the author. This was the limitation to the principle of national treatment in Thailand at that time.

However, although this second reservation allowed Thailand to implement Paragraph 2 of Article 2 of the Berne Convention of 1886 as a substitute for Paragraph 2 of Article 4 of the Berlin Act 1908, Thailand only relied on this reservation and imposed some limitations on foreign copyright works. However, Thailand still followed the principle of automatic protection without formality in Paragraph 2 of Article 4 of the Berlin Act 1908, which indicated that the enjoyment and the exercise of the rights must not be subject to any formality. This principle prohibited the imposition of any formalities as preconditions for copyright protection, such as registration or recording of copyright works, or deposit of copyright works.[87] With this principle, the registration of copyright works as a requirement for copyright protection and a requirement for deposit of copyright works at the libraries under OAA 1901 and AOAA 1914 were removed from PLAWA 1931, so the literary and artistic works were protected under PLAWA 1931 without the need for registration or deposit of copyright works.

In addition to second reservation, there was also another limitation to the principle of national treatment in respect of foreign copyright works. This limitation came from the third reservation, which allowed Thailand to limit copyright protection to the condition that the copyright owner of literary and dramatic works must translate their work into Thai language within ten years from the date of the first publication of the original work. This reservation stated that Article 8 of the Berlin Act 1908 is replaced by Article 5 of the Berne Convention of 1886, as amended by Article 1, Number 3 of the Paris Additional Act 1896, in respect to the exclusive right of authors to make or to authorise translation of their works.[88]

Pursuant to Article 8 of the Berlin Act 1908, the authors of published works, being subjects or citizens of one of the countries of the Union, and the authors of works first published in one of those countries, should enjoy the exclusive right of making or authorising a translation of their works in the other countries of the Union during the whole term of the rights in the original work.[89]

87 Noppanun Supasiripongchai, "Intellectual Property Law in Thailand," *International Encyclopaedia of Laws: Intellectual Property*, ed. Hendrik Vanhees (Deventer: Kluwer Law International, 2022), 35.

88 World Intellectual Property Organization, "General information: States Which Have Stipulated Reservations to Berlin Act: Thailand" (2023), accessed 5 November 2003, https://www.wipo.int/edocs/pubdocs/en/wipo_pub_berne_birpi.

89 Berlin Act 1908 of the Berne Convention, Article 8.

Thailand did not implement this provision but chose to implement Article 5 of the Berne Convention of 1886, as amended by Article 1, Number 3 of the Paris Additional Act 1896, which stipulated that the authors belonging to any one of the countries of the Union should enjoy in the other countries the exclusive right of making or authorising the translation of their works during the entire period of their rights over the original work.[90]

However, this provision further stated that such exclusive rights of translation will cease to exist if the author shall not have availed themself of it, during a period of ten years from the date of the first publication of the original work, by publishing or causing to be published in one of the countries of the Union, a translation in the language for which protection is to be claimed.[91] This provision was inserted into Section 29 of PLAWA 1931, which provided that in case of literary and dramatic works, the exclusive rights of copyright owner to prevent reproduction and authorise a translation can be maintained only if the copyright owner authorises a translation into the language that they want to claim protection within a period of ten years from the date of the first publication of the original works.[92] Under this provision, even though copyright in the foreign works had not yet expired, the exclusive rights to make or authorise a translation of the foreign copyright owner could not be maintained if the foreign copyright owner did not translate their work into Thai language within ten years from the date of the first publication of the original work.[93]

3.2.4 Other Influences of the Berne Convention on PLAWA 1931

In addition to the first to the third reservations discussed in the previous sections, there were other reservations embodied in PLAWA 1931. For example, the fourth reservation allowed Thailand to limit copyright protection on the condition that the articles published in newspapers or periodicals could be reproduced with acknowledgment of the source, unless there was a clear prohibition. This reservation stated that Article 9 of the Berlin Act 1908 would be

90 Berne Convention of 1886, Article 5, as amended by Paris Additional Act 1896, Article 1, Number 3.

91 Berne Convention of 1886, Article 5, as amended by Paris Additional Act 1896, Article 1, Number 3.

92 Protection of Literary and Artistic Works Act 1931, Section 29(B).

93 This limitation to the principle of national treatment was later removed in 1993, when PLAWA 1931 was replaced by the Copyright Act 1978 and its Royal Decree of 1983, which cancelled this condition. After the Royal Decree of 1993 cancelled this condition, foreign authors who did not translate or authorise a translation into Thai within such a period would still obtain copyright protection for their works in Thailand and no one could translate their works into Thai without their authorisation.

replaced by Article 7 of the Berne Convention of 1886, as amended by Article 1, Number 4 of the Paris Additional Act 1896, in respect to the reproduction of articles published in newspapers or periodicals.[94] In this vein, Article 9 of the Berlin Act 1908 stipulated that serial stories, tales, and all other works, whether literary, scientific, or artistic, whatever their object, published in the newspapers or periodicals of one of the countries of the Union may not be reproduced in the other countries without the consent of the authors.[95] However, Thailand did not implement this provision, but chose to implement Article 7 of the Berne Convention of 1886, as amended by Article 1, Number 4 of the Paris Additional Act 1896, which indicated that serial stories, including tales, published in the newspapers or periodicals of one of the countries of the Union may not be reproduced in the other countries without the permission of the authors.[96] This provision was held to apply equally to other articles in newspapers or periodicals when the authors or editors expressly declared in the newspaper or periodical itself in which they were published that the right of reproduction was prohibited, but in the case of periodicals it sufficed if such a prohibition was indicated in general terms at the beginning of each number.[97] In the absence of such prohibition, articles could be reproduced on the condition that the source was acknowledged.[98] These provisions of Article 7 were incorporated into Section 7 of PLAWA 1931.[99] The main difference is that Article 9 of the Berlin Act 1908 did not allow articles published in newspapers or periodicals to be reproduced in other countries without the consent of the authors, regardless of whether or not there was a clear prohibition, while Article 7 of the Berne Convention of 1886, as amended by Article 1, Number 4 of the Paris Additional Act 1896, allowed articles published in newspapers or periodicals to be reproduced with acknowledgment of the source, unless there was a clear prohibition.

Similarly, the fifth reservation allowed Thailand to limit copyright protection with the condition that the musical works can be protected from public

94 World Intellectual Property Organization, "General information: States Which Have Stipulated Reservations to Berlin Act: Thailand" (2023), accessed 5 November 2023, https://www.wipo.int/edocs/pubdocs/en/wipo_pub_berne_birpi.

95 Berlin Act 1908 of the Berne Convention, Article 9, Paragraph 1.

96 Berne Convention of 1886, Article 7, Paragraph 1, as amended by the Paris Additional Act 1896, Article 1, Number 4.

97 Berne Convention of 1886, Article 7, Paragraph 2, as amended by the Paris Additional Act 1896, Article 1, Number 4.

98 Berne Convention of 1886, Article 7, Paragraph 3, as amended by the Paris Additional Act 1896, Article 1, Number 4.

99 Protection of Literary and Artistic Works Act 1931, Section 7, Paragraphs 1–3.

performance only if the author has clearly stated on the title page or commencement of the work that they prohibit that. This reservation stated that Article 11 of the Berlin Act 1908 was replaced by Article 9 of the Berne Convention of 1886 and Number 2 of the Final Protocol of the Berne Convention of 1886, in respect to the right of public performance of dramatic, dramatic-musical, and musical works.[100] Pursuant to Article 11 of the Berlin Act 1908, the stipulations of the present Convention was held to apply to the public representation of dramatic or dramatic-musical works and to the public performance of musical works, whether such works were published or not.[101] However, Thailand did not implement this provision, but chose to implement Article 9 of the Berne Convention of 1886, which provided that copyright protection must apply to the public representation of dramatic or dramatic-musical work, whether such works were published or not.[102] It also stated that copyright protection must apply equally to the public performance of unpublished musical works or published works in which the author expressly declared on the title page or commencement of the work that they forbade public performance.[103] The second provision of the Final Protocol of the Berne Convention of 1886 extended the scope of protection of Article 9 to include choreographic works among dramatic-musical works.[104] These provisions were incorporated into Section 8 of PLAWA 1931, which provided the authors with the exclusive right of public performance of dramatic, dramatico-musical, and musical works.[105] Article 9 of the Berne Convention of 1886 was different from Article 11 of the Berlin Act 1908 because Article 9 contained the condition that musical works must be protected from public performance only if the author has clearly stated on the title page or commencement of the work that they prohibit public performance. This condition also appeared in Paragraph 3 of Section 8 of PLAWA 1931.

Finally, the sixth reservation limited copyright protection to literary and artistic works that had not fallen into the public domain within the country of origin. This reservation stated that Article 18 of the Berlin Act 1908 was replaced by Article 14 of the Berne Convention of 1886, and Number 4 of the Final Protocol of the Berne Convention of 1886, as amended by Article 2, Number 2 of the Paris Additional Act 1896.[106] Pursuant to Article 18 of the Berlin Act

100 World Intellectual Property Organization, "General information."
101 Berlin Act 1908 of the Berne Convention, Article 11, Paragraph 1.
102 Berne Convention of 1886, Article 9, Paragraph 1 and Article 2.
103 Berne Convention of 1886, Article 9, Paragraph 3.
104 Final Protocol of the Berne Convention of 1886, Number 2.
105 Protection of Literary and Artistic Works Act 1931, Section 8, Paragraphs 1–3.
106 World Intellectual Property Organization, "General information."

1908, this Convention was held to apply to all works which at the moment of its coming into force had not yet fallen into the public domain in the country of origin through the expiration of the term of protection, but if, through the expiration of the term of protection which was previously granted, a work had fallen into the public domain of the country where protection was claimed, then such work would not be protected anew in that country.[107] Thailand did not implement this provision but chose to implement Article 14 of the Berne Convention of 1886, which stipulated that under the reserves and conditions to be determined by common agreement, this Convention would apply to all works which at the moment of its coming into force had not yet fallen into the public domain in the country of origin.[108] This provision provided broader ground for Thailand to deny the protection of works that had fallen into the public domain within the country of origin at the time when these provisions came into force, regardless of whether or not such work had fallen into the public domain in Thailand. In terms of the wording, Article 14 of the Berne Convention of 1886 seemed to be more flexible than that of Article 18 of the Berlin Act 1908, since it contained the phase "under the reserves and conditions to be determined by common agreement". The term "common agreement" was described in Number 4 of the Final Protocol of the Berne Convention of 1886, as amended by Article 2, Number 2 of the Paris Additional Act 1896. The common agreement contemplated in Article 14 of the Berne Convention was its to works which had not fallen into the public domain within the country of origin at the time when these engagements came into force must take effect according to the relevant stipulations contained in special Conventions existing or to be concluded to this effect.[109] In the absence of such stipulations between the countries of the Union, the contracting countries could regulate by domestic legislation in the manner in which the principle contained in Article 14 was to be applied.[110] Thailand would benefit from this reservation because there was no stipulation between Thailand and other contracting countries, and thus Thailand could regulate the protection of the literary and artistic works that had fallen into public domain in its domestic law at its discretion. This approach was embodied in Section 32, which provided that PLAWA 1931 shall apply to all literary and artistic works, which at the moment of PLAWA 1931

107 Berlin Act 1908 of the Berne Convention, Article 18, Paragraphs 1 and 2.

108 Berne Convention of 1886, Article 14.

109 Final Protocol of the Berne Convention of 1886, Number 4, Paragraph 1, as amended by the Paris Additional Act 1896, Article 2, Number 2.

110 Final Protocol of the Berne Convention of 1886, Number 4, Paragraph 2, as amended by the Paris Additional Act 1896, Article 2, Number 2.

coming into force, had not yet fallen into the public domain because of the expiration of the term of protection under PLAWA 1931.[111] This provision functioned together with Section 28 of PLAWA 1931, which provided that the term of protection in Thailand could not exceed the term of protection granted in the country of origin. Hence, only those literary and artistic works that had not yet fallen into the public domain in both Thailand and the country of origin could be protected under PLAWA 1931.

4 Conclusion

At the time of global economic crisis in the interwar period, the Berlin Act 1908 of the Berne Convention and the Berne Additional Protocol of 1914 played the role of silent peacemaker, since they allowed Thailand and other contracting countries to cooperate and continue to recognise the protection of copyrights. The role of copyright as peacemaker can be seen from the provision on the principle of national treatment of the Berlin Act 1908, which ensured that works originating in one contracting country must be given the same protection in another contracting country as the latter granted to the works of its own nationals. PLAWA 1931 adopted the principle of national treatment of the Berlin Act 1908 in order to provide protection for works originating in other contracting countries in the same way as works of Thai copyright owners were protected. Although there were some limitations to the principle of national treatment in PLAWA 1931, it was the first copyright law in Thailand to provide protection for foreign copyright works.

Under PLAWA 1931, the scope of copyright protection was extended to cover all literary and artistic works, and this was much broader than the scope of protection under OAA 1901 and AOAA 1914, which only provided protection for books. Some provisions that made the enforcement of copyright law more effective had been inserted into PLAWA 1931, such as the provisions on copyright infringement with both civil and criminal remedies. Some provisions were strongly influenced by the Berlin Act 1908, such as the provisions on international copyright protection. All these changes in PLAWA 1931 could be considered as the realignment of copyright after the accession to the Berlin Act 1908. PLAWA 1931 had been in effect for forty-seven years without any amendment, until it was finally repealed and replaced by the Thai Copyright Act 1978.

---

111 Protection of Literary and Artistic Works Act 1931, Section 32, Paragraph 1.

Acknowledgments

I deeply thank Professor Hector MacQueen at the University of Edinburgh and P. Sean Morris at the University of Helsinki for providing helpful comments, but I alone am responsible for any errors of fact, law and opinion contained within it. I can be reached by email at noppanun.su@up.ac.th or noppanun@hotmail.com.

Bibliography

Falk, Hjalmar, 'Carl Schmitt and the Challenges of Interwar Internationalism: Against Weimar – Geneva – Versailles'. *Global Intellectual History* 7(4) 765–783 (2020).

Hemaratchata, Chaiyos. *Problems of Copyright Law* (Bangkok: Niti Bannakan Publishing, 1985).

Hemaratchata, Chaiyos. *Copyright Law,* 4th edn. (Bangkok: Nititham Publishing House, 2006).

Landes, William and Posner, Richard, 'An Economic Analysis of Copyright Law'. *Journal of Legal Studies* 18(2) 325–363 (1989).

Subhapholsiri, Dhajjai. *Copyright Law: The Copyright Act B.E. 2537,* 3rd edn. (Bangkok: Nititham Publishing House, 2001).

Supasiripongchai, Noppanun. *Intellectual Property Law for the Protection of Plant Varieties* (Chiang Mai: Nuntapun Printing, 2022).

Supasiripongchai, Noppanun, 'Intellectual Property Law in Thailand' in Hendrik Vanhees (Ed). *International Encyclopaedia of Laws: Intellectual Property* (Deventer: Kluwer Law International, 2022).

Supasiripongchai, Noppanun, 'The Development of the Copyright Exception in Thailand: Where Has It Come From, Where is It Now Under the Thai Copyright Amendment Act 2015, and Where is It Heading?'. *European Intellectual Property Review* 38 (10) 620–632 (2016).

Terwiel, Barend. *A Window on Thai history* (Bangkok: Duangkamol Publishing, 1989).

Thompson, John, 'American Power and Interwar internationalism'. *The Historical Journal* 61(4) 1137–1148 (2018).

Witt, Steve, 'Interwar Internationalism and the Rebuilding of the Catholic University of Louvain Library'. *Libraries: Culture, History, and Society* 4(1) 1–28 (2020).

Zaidi, Waqar, 'Liberal Internationalism and the Search for International Peace', in Christian Peterson, William Knoblauch, Michael Loadenthal, (eds). *The Routledge History of World Peace Since 1750* (CRC Press, 2018).

Internet Resources

World Intellectual Property Organization, 'Contracting Parties: Berne Convention Berlin Act 1908' (2022) <https://wipolex.wipo.int/en/treaties/ShowResults?search_what=A&act_id=44> accessed 2 October 2022.

World Intellectual Property Organization, 'General information: States Which Have Stipulated Reservations to Berlin Act: Thailand' <https://www.wipo.int/edocs/pubdocs/en/wipo_pub_berne_birpi.

CHAPTER 12

Internationalism to Nationalism: Interwar Japan Observed through the Lens of Copyright Enforcement

Masabumi Suzuki

1 Introduction

This chapter examines copyright-related developments in Japan during the interwar period as an example of the significance of the intellectual property system to the formation or disruption of the international order. During the interwar period, Japan drastically shifted its stance from cooperation to hostility toward the international order. An analysis of the Japanese experience at that time will be meaningful from the perspective of this book as a whole.

Since the latter half of the 19th century, Japan strived to become a modern nation on par with the major Western countries, and to achieve this goal, Japan made efforts to establish domestic systems consistent with the international order. By the beginning of the 20th century, Japan had reached its goal and participated in World War I as the Allied Powers side with Britain, France, and other countries. Even after the war, it took a stance of emphasizing international cooperation. However, Japan gradually expanded its territory in Asia, became more nationalistic at home, and finally formed a military alliance with Germany and Italy to fight in World War II (the Sino-Japanese War and the Pacific War from the viewpoint of Japan).

During the interwar period, Japan's attitude toward the international order was directly reflected in its policy on copyright. In the first half of the interwar period, the copyright system was developed in an internationally coordinated manner as a means of internationalizing Japan's legal system and society. However, in the latter half of the interwar period, exclusionary domestic measures were taken with regard to the copyright system. It should not be forgotten, however, that even in the latter half of the interwar period, Japan maintained its policy of remaining a member of the Berne Convention on copyright, despite its policy of distancing itself from the global international order, as symbolized by its withdrawal from the League of Nations (1931).

This chapter will proceed in the following order.

 | DOI:10.1163/9789004714663_014

First, we review the development of the copyright system in the period leading up to the interwar period. Specifically, first, the development of the Berne Convention, an international institutional framework for copyright protection, will be reviewed. Second, the development of the copyright system in Japan will be reviewed.

Then, the international situation surrounding Japan during the interwar period will be reviewed. The developments related to the Berne Convention during the interwar period will also be explained.

Next, the trends of the copyright system in Japan during the interwar period will be reviewed. The period will be divided into two parts, with the second half starting around 1930. For the first half, it will be explained that efforts were made to establish a copyright system consistent with the Berne Convention. In the second half, the so-called Plage Whirlwind, a turmoil caused by a German agent Wilhelm Plage exercising copyright by proxy, and the exclusionary measures adopted, as a result, will be explained.

Finally, the chapter will conclude by presenting an analysis based on the above.

2 Prehistory: Development of the Copyright System in the World and Japan before World War I

2.1 *Development of the Berne Convention*

This section looks at the developments of international law relating to copyright to the extent that it is relevant to the theme of this chapter. In addition, an overview of Japan's involvement in these developments is also presented.

The first and, to date the most fundamental multilateral treaty on the copyright system is the Berne Convention. The Berne Convention was adopted at a diplomatic conference in 1886 and entered into force on December 5, 1887.[1] Japan had no intention of joining the Berne Convention at the time, but participated as an observer at the diplomatic conference.

The Berne Convention was subsequently revised in 1896 at the Paris Revision Conference in the form of the Additional Act.[2] As Professors Ricketson and

1 The original signatories were Belgium, France, Germany, Great Britain, Haiti, Italy, Liberia, Spain, Switzerland and Tunis. It should be noted that the signature of France, Great Britain and Spain included all of their colonies and possessions. *See* Seville, Catherine. *The Internationalisation of Copyright Law* (Cambridge: Cambridge University Press, 2006) 5.

2 The revised versions of the Berne Convention are officially called "Acts" (e.g., the "Paris Additional Act" and the "Berlin Act"). However, in order to avoid confusion with domestic

Ginsburg describe, "[t]he amendments agreed by the Conference were of a relatively limited nature, and affected only a small number of articles."[3] However, the inclusion of amendments related to translation rights was of great significance to Japan. The Berne Convention of 1886 used to stipulate that the right of translation would expire in ten years. But the Paris Revision of the Berne Convention provided that the right of translation would continue for the same period as other rights (although it lacked specific provisions regarding the terms of protection of other rights) and subjected it to the condition that if an authorized translation was not done within ten years of the publication of the original work, the right would expire.

As we will see in the next section, it became necessary for Japan to join the Berne Convention in order to revise the unequal bilateral treaties. Specifically, in the Protocols to the Treaties of Commerce and Navigation concluded with Britain, Italy, France, and Germany between 1894 and 1896, Japan promised to join the Berne Convention prior to the abolition of consular jurisdiction for those countries in Japan. However, there were solid domestic opinions that it was too early to join, including voices of concern about the impact of granting translation rights on the publishing industry and academic research. Nevertheless, in 1899, Japan acceded to the Berne Convention (the Berne Convention of 1886 Act and the Paris Revision of the Convention).

The Berne Convention was revised again in 1908 at the Berlin Conference. The revision contained major changes and additions which, in retrospect, made it the most extensive revision of the Berne Convention to date.[4] Namely, the Berlin Revision of the Berne Convention included amendments concerning works protected, persons protected, independence of protection, absence of formality, duration of protection, translation rights, newspaper and periodical articles, public performance rights, indirect appropriations and mechanical reproduction rights, and cinematographic works.

Particularly noteworthy in relation to the theme of this chapter are the amendments related to, first, translation rights, second, public performance rights, and third, the rights of musical copyright owners with regard to the use of their works with instruments capable of reproducing them mechanically.

First, the Berlin Revision of the Berne Convention deleted the Paris Revision's provision providing an exception to the duration of translation rights, making

---

acts, they are referred to as "Revisions" (e.g., the "Paris Revision" and the "Berlin Revision" of the Berne Convention) in this chapter.

3 Ricketson, Sam, and, Ginsburg, Jane. *International Copyright and Neighbouring Rights: The Berne Convention and Beyond. 3rd ed.* (Oxford: Oxford University Press, 2022) 80.

4 Ibid., 75.

the translation rights equal to the other rights in terms of the duration period (the Berlin Revision, Article 8). Japan advanced a proposal to the effect that translations into the Japanese language should be free, but this proposal was not accepted.[5] Japan believed that learning the science, technology, and culture of the West was essential for the modernization of Japan, and since the literacy rate of its citizens was high enough due to its efforts to promote public education, it was an extremely important national issue to allow free translation of Western works.

Second, with regard to public performance rights, the Berne Convention of 1886 required authors to reserve their rights in advance of the performance of their works by indicating so on the published musical score in order to get the protection of the rights (Article 9(3)). This requirement was abolished in the Berlin Revision.

Third, the Berlin Revision recognized the exclusive rights of musical copyright owners in relation to the adaptation of their works to instruments capable of reproducing them mechanically (phonograph recordings, piano rolls, etc.), as well as the public performance of those works by means of these instruments (Article 13. The provision recognizing these rights was deleted later in the 1967 Stockholm Revision as the latter Revision introduced a general article for reproduction rights (Article 9), and the public performance rights had already been provided in Article 11.). At the same time, the article for the above rights (Article 13) allowed Union members to determine "reservations and conditions" by domestic legislation. This meant a system of compulsory licensing for the benefit of recording interests.[6]

At the 1908 Berlin Conference, Japan made reservations concerning translation rights and public performance rights. Specifically, Japan declared that it would continue to be governed by the Berne Convention of 1886 and the Paris Revision on these issues.[7]

In 1914, the Additional Protocol was signed in Berne. It permitted Union members to restrict protection in the case of authors from non-Union countries that failed to protect the authors from the Union member in an adequate manner. The purpose was to admit a countermeasure to Union member

---

5 Ibid., 88; Japanese Society for Rights of Authors, Composers and Publishers (JASRAC), ed. *Nihon Ongaku Chosakuken shi* (*History of Japanese Music Copyright*) Vol. 1 (Tokyo: JASRAC, 1990) 15–37 (quoting a report by Mr. Rentarō Mizuno, the head of the Japanese delegation to the Berlin Conference).

6 Ricketson and Ginsburg, *International Copyright* (n 3) 90.

7 JASRAC, *History of Japanese Musical Copyright* (n 5) 114–16.

countries against non-Union countries that enjoyed the benefit of the Berne Convention.[8]

2.2 *Early Years of the Copyright System of Japan*

2.2.1 Background: Modernization of Japan

Let us briefly review the history of the development of the copyright system in Japan up to the interwar period. In a nutshell, the Japanese copyright system during this period was developed not only to protect authors and copyright holders, but also as a means of establishing Japan's international status, i.e., on an equal footing with major Western countries.

Japan's modernization began in the 1860s. In the history of Japan, the period from 1600 to 1868 is called the Tokugawa period, a period dominated by military rulers with the Tokugawa family at the top.[9] According to Professor Kitaoka, the Tokugawa political system, or the *bakuhan* system, contained elements of both feudalism and patrimonialism, but it was clearly closer to the latter.[10]

During the Tokugawa period, Japan's foreign policy was strictly controlled, and exchange with only a limited number of countries (e.g., the Netherlands, Korea, and the Qing Dynasty) was allowed in limited areas and through limited routes. Japan's foreign policy at that time is called "Sakoku" (isolationism).[11]

One of the main factors that shook the Tokugawa political system was foreign pressure, such as the visit of "black ships" led by Commodore Matthew Perry of the United States in 1853.[12] Other Western nations, such as Britain and France, also began to push for strengthening trade and other relations with Japan. As a result, Japan concluded treaties with the United States, Britain, Russia, the Netherlands, and France promising to initiate diplomatic relations,

8 The Berne Convention gives protection to authors of non-Union countries who first publish their works in a Union member country. Taking advantage of this mechanism, authors of the United States, a non-Union country, often published their works in Canada and Britain, both Union countries, as well as in the United States, and enjoyed the protection under the Convention. However, authors of Canada and Britain had to abide by the requirements under U.S. law in order to have their works protected in the United States. There were complaints among Canadian and British authors about such an imbalance in protection.

9 Gordon, Andrew. *A Modern History of Japan: From Tokugawa Times to the Present. 4th ed* (New York: Oxford University Press, 2020) 11.

10 Kitaoka, Shinichi. *The Political History of Modern Japan: Foreign Relations and Domestic Politics*. Translated by Robert D. Eldridge and Graham Leonard (Abingdon, Oxon: Routledge, 2018) 4.

11 In recent years, this concept of "Sakoku" has been the subject of much debate. Ibid., 10.

12 The main purpose of Perry's visit was to start and expand trade with Japan, and to force Japan to provide ports to U.S. vessels including U.S. whaling ships.

permit port calls to certain ports, and initiate further commercial relations.[13] However, these bilateral treaties with Western countries concluded in the mid-19th century were unequal to Japan, especially in terms of accepting consular jurisdiction and not recognizing tariff autonomy.[14]

The Tokugawa political system ended in 1868, and within a few years, Japan transitioned to a modern political system, a centralized system under the Emperor. This transition process is called the "Meiji Restoration" and is understood to have been a kind of revolution. From this point on, Japan moved forward with the formation of a modern nation. The challenges for Japan at that time were establishing a domestic system and developing foreign relations.[15] From the legal system's perspective, the main goals of these tasks were the establishment of the Constitution (leading to its enactment in 1889) and the revision of unequal treaties with the major Western countries. With regard to the latter, as mentioned above, the treaties that Japan concluded with Western countries in the mid-19th century were disadvantageous to Japan, especially in terms of allowing consular jurisdiction and the one-sided tariff system, and Japan sought to amend them to allow it an equal footing with the Western countries.[16]

2.2.2 Establishment and Early Development of the Copyright System of Japan

In 1869, the newly established Japanese government enacted the Newspaper Ordinance and the Publication Ordinance to control publishing. The Publication Ordinance, revised in 1875, included a provision allowing the right to monopolize the sale of books, granted by government license, for a period of 30 years, which was the germ of the copyright system.

---

13 The treaties concluded in this period were: the bilateral Treaties of Peace and Amity between Japan and the United States (1854), Britain (1854), Russia (1855), and the Netherlands (1856); and the bilateral Treaties of Amity and Trade between Japan and the United States, the Netherlands, Russia, Britain, and France respectively (1858). These treaties did not mention intellectual property specifically.

14 Ibid., 53–55; Gordon, *A Modern History of Japan* (n 9) 51; Fuess, Harald, 'Unequal Treaties, Consular Jurisdiction, and Treaty Port Society.' *In Routledge Handbook of Modern Japanese History*, Saaler, Sven and Szpilman, Christopher, eds, (Abingdon, Oxon: Routledge, 2020) 47–61.

15 Kitaoka, *The Political History of Modern Japan* (n 10) 34.

16 Ibid., 54 (stating '[r]evision of the unequal domestic treaties was thus absolutely necessary to Japan for reasons of national honor, income security, stability, and the promotion of domestic industry').

After that, during negotiations to revise the unequal treaties with Western countries, the Japanese government became increasingly aware of the need to improve the copyright system. Therefore, it proceeded to investigate Western copyright systems and sent a diplomat as an observer to the diplomatic conference for the creation of the Berne Convention in 1886. In 1887, Japan enacted the Ordinance on Copyright, under which the exclusive right to publish literally works and drawings was changed from a licensing system to a registration system. It also established penalties for infringement of moral rights. In the same year, the Ordinance on Scripts and Musical Scores and the Ordinance on Photographs and Copyrights was also enacted, granting exclusive rights for the publication and performance of dramatic scripts and musical scores, and for the publication of photographs, respectively. Thus, a legal framework similar to the copyright system was established. Still, the protection was only for Japanese works and did not reach the level of protection required by the Berne Convention with its principle of national treatment.

On the other hand, the European countries with whom Japan negotiated the treaty revision explicitly demanded that Japan join the Berne Convention. As a result, from 1894 to 1896, Japan concluded the Treaties of Commerce and Navigation with countries including Britain, Italy, France, and Germany, and won the abolition of consular jurisdiction for those countries. In the Protocol attached to the treaties, Japan promised to join the Berne Convention prior to the abolition of consular jurisdiction.[17]

In 1899, Japan acceded to the Berne Convention and enacted the Copyright Act (now called the old Copyright Act in Japan, as opposed to the current law enacted in 1970). With the enactment of the Copyright Act of 1899, Japan established a copyright system consistent with the Berne Convention for the first time. However, the primary motivation was to establish Japan's position in the international community, including the revision of unequal treaties, and not so much to meet the growing domestic demand for copyright protection.

---

17 Editing Committee on Centennial History of Copyright Law of Japan, *Chosakuken-hō Hyakunen Shi* (*Centennial History of Copyright Law of Japan*) (Tokyo: Chosakuken Joho Center (Copyright Research and Information Center), 2000), 88–91; JASRAC, *History of Japanese Musical Copyright* (n 5) 71. Since the United States had not acceded to the Berne Convention, the Treaty of Commerce and Navigation between the U.S. and Japan concluded in 1894 only provided for national treatment regarding industrial property rights. In 1905, after Japan joined the Berne Convention, it concluded a bilateral treaty with the United States on copyright protection. (It is interesting to note that the U.S.-Japan Copyright Treaty allowed freedom of translation, which gives a glimpse into the thinking of the two countries regarding translation.).

The Copyright Act of Japan was subsequently amended in 1910. The amendment was mainly in response to the Berlin Revision of the Berne Convention in 1908. For example, architecture was added to the list of examples of works, and adaptations to cinematographic works were made subject to copyright. However, with respect to two of the matters implemented in the Berlin Revision of the Berne Convention, namely the protection of translation rights on par with ordinary copyright and the elimination of the special requirement for the protection of public performance rights (i.e., the prohibition must be clearly stated before performance), Japan made reservations in the ratification of the Berlin Revision and these matters were not incorporated in the 1910 amendment of the Copyright Act. Also, with regard to the rights of musical copyright owners related to mechanical instruments such as phonograph recordings, which were newly stipulated in Article 13 of the Berlin Revision, the Copyright Act did not recognize these rights in the 1910 amendment. The rights of performance and musical copyright owners were incorporated into Japanese law during the interwar period, and this change in the legal system triggered the Plage Whirlwind, which will be discussed later.

2.2.3 World War I and Japan's Intellectual Property System during the War

Japan declared war on Germany in August 1914 and participated in World War I. Thereafter, Japan severed diplomatic relations with Germany and other enemies for four years until the end of the war in November 1918.

Great Britain enacted the "Patents, Designs and Trade Marks (Temporary Rules) Act" in August 1914, immediately after the outbreak of war with Germany, and took measures to restrict industrial property rights of enemy nationals. That example sparked a debate on the question of whether Japan should restrict intellectual property rights of enemy nationals. Legal scholars were largely divided between two arguments. The first group argued that the Paris and Berne Conventions had naturally ceased to be effective with the outbreak of the war and therefore there was no need to protect the intellectual property rights of enemy nationals (Germans, Austrians, etc.). The second group argued that the validity of these treaties was unaffected by the war.[18] Then, on April

18 Those who took the former view included Genroku Endō and Tōru Shimizu, while those who took the latter included Saburō Yamada, Rentarō Mizuno, Eiji Shukuri. For example, Saburō Yamada, then a professor of private international law at the Imperial University of Tokyo, argued that what happens to the validity of treaties between belligerents during war depends on the content of the treaty, but treaties like the Paris Convention and the Berne Convention on the protection of private rights do not naturally cease to be valid

15, 1915, the Grand Court (former Supreme Court of Japan) issued a decision in a case concerning trademark rights, interpreting that the Paris Convention had naturally ceased to be in force between Japan and Germany from the beginning of the war until the time of overcoming peace. Furthermore, in 1917, the "Industrial Property Wartime Law" was enacted, which provided for the suspension of applications for industrial property rights by enemy nationals, a system of cancellation of patents and trademark registrations by enemy nationals (a system allowing cancellation when there was a military or public necessity), and a system granting exclusive rights to licensed persons with respect to patents of enemy nationals.[19] The wartime measures ended in 1920. On the other hand, no special measures were taken for copyright of enemy nationals during the war.[20]

3 International Circumstances of Japan during the Interwar Period

3.1 *Political and Diplomatic Environment*

After World War I, international organizations such as the League of Nations (established in 1920), the International Labour Union (1919), and the Permanent Court of International Justice (1922) were established to strengthen international cooperation in various fields.

Japan fought against Germany in World War I and became a permanent member of the League of Nations after the war. Japan also participated in the Versailles Treaty (the Treaty of Peace between the Allied and Associated Powers and Germany). From Japan's political viewpoint, however, the Washington system, established in 1922 after the Washington Conference starting in 1921, was more important than the Versailles system. The Washington system was

---

due to war, and even if they were to cease to be valid, they would not affect vested intellectual property rights. See Itō, Takao, 'Dai Ichiji Sekai Taisen To Kōgyōshoyūken' (World War I and Industrial Property Rights). *Hōgaku Ronsō* 138 (1–3) (1995) 299–327, 301–08.

19 During World War I, 19 trademark registrations for enemy nationals were cancelled, including Bayer's 'Aspirin.' On the other hand, not a single patent was revoked while there were more than 900 patents held by enemy nationals. However, exclusive rights for more than 200 patents were granted to Japanese firms without cancellation of the patents. See Japan Patent Office, Kōgyōshoyūken-seido Hyakunen Shi (*Centennial History of Industrial Property System*) (Tokyo: Hatsumei Kyōkai, 1984) Vol. 1, 410–12.

20 Since the judgment of the Grand Court mentioned above said that the effect of the Paris Convention had been suspended with respect to enemy countries, it is possible that the Berne Convention was also interpreted in the same way. However, there are no known cases in which the protection of the copyrights of enemy nationals actually became a problem.

established at the initiative of the United States, and arrangements were made for naval disarmament, policy toward China, and so on.[21]

Around that time, Japan was trying to strengthen its influence on the Chinese mainland at the time, and Manchuria and inner Mongolia, in particular, were becoming de facto spheres of influence for Japan.

The United States was very critical of Japan's foreign policy, and the negotiations at the Washington Conference turned out to be tough for Japan. However, it was practically impossible for Japan to stand up to the United States, and the Washington regime was realized because a certain amount of compromise was reached between Japan and the United States.[22] The fact that a relatively pacifist political party (Seiyū-kai) was in power at the time may also have contributed to Japan's acceptance of the Washington system.[23]

The Washington system, however, headed toward collapse in the late 1920s. According to Professor Kitaoka, the reasons for the collapse were, first, the growth of Chinese nationalism; second, the recovery of the Soviet Union began as a military power in the late 1920s; third, the London Naval Conference (opened in 1930) which resulted in restrictions on auxiliary ships and left significant acrimony among the Japanese naval forces; and fourth, the Great Depression which occurred in October 1929 and gave significant impact on the Japanese economy.[24]

On the domestic side, party politics lost power and was replaced by the political rise of the military (especially the army). In 1931, Prime Minister Inukai, who represented the political party "Seiyū-kai," was assassinated, and a man from the military was appointed as the next Prime Minister. From then until the defeat of Japan in World War II in 1945, no cabinet was formed by a political party. In 1933, Japan withdrew from the League of Nations, and in 1934, it notified the United States of its abrogation of the Washington Treaty. Japan abandoned the principle of international cooperation and advocated Asiatic Monroeism (a concept that advocated a self-sufficient international order in

21 Kitaoka, *The Political History of Modern Japan* (n 10) 109 (stating '[t]he Versailles Peace Treaty of June 1919 gave shape to this new world order but that was very much primarily concerned with Europe. It was the Washington Conference (November 1921-February 1922) that established the postwar world order for East Asia and the Pacific').

22 Ibid., 110–13 (raising the reasons for the successful conclusion of the Washington system such as the absence of a convincing alternative for Japan, compromises reached over a number of important points of contention, the U.S.-Japan economic relationship, and the weakening of China and the Soviet Union).

23 Banno, Junji. *Nihon Kindai Shi* (*History of Modern Japan*) (Tokyo: Chikuma Shobō, 2012) 336–39.

24 Kitaoka, *The Political History of Modern Japan*, (10) 113–14.

Asia with Japan as the leading power) and accelerated military actions for territorial expansion, starting the Sino-Japanese War in 1937, signing the Tripartite Pact with Germany and Italy in 1940, and then, in December 1941, plunging into war against the United States.

As described above, the international situation during the interwar period, at least from Japan's perspective, needs to be divided into two major periods: the early period when efforts toward international cooperation were made under the Washington system, and the latter period after the mid-1920s, when that regime began to collapse.

3.2 *The Berne Convention during the Interwar Period*

As noted above, after World War I, mechanisms for international cooperation were strengthened. In the field of copyright, the system based on the Berne Convention had already been established, and the war did not affect the continuation of the Berne Union. However, the Versailles Treaty assumed that there had been a break in treaty relations between belligerent Union members and that these were now to be restored.[25] Specifically, Article 286 of the Versailles Treaty provided as follows:

> The International Convention of Paris of March 20, 1883, for the protection of industrial property, revised at Washington on June 2, 1911; and the International Convention of Berne of September 9, 1886, for the protection of literary and artistic works, revised at Berlin on November 13, 1908, and completed by the additional Protocol signed at Berne on March 20, 1914, will again come into effect as from the coming into force of the present Treaty, in so far as they are not affected or modified by the exceptions and restrictions resulting therefrom. (footnotes omitted)

The number of Berne Union member countries expanded during the interwar period, especially in the first half. As for about twenty countries, including Poland (accession in 1920), Austria (1920), Greece (1920), Czechoslovakia (1921), Bulgaria (1921), Brazil (1922), Hungary (1922), Danzig (1922), Romania (1926), Estonia (1927), Ireland (1927), Finland (1928), Canada (1928), Australia (1928), India (1928), New Zealand (1928), South Africa (1928), Thailand (1931), and Liechtenstein (1931) newly concluded the Berne Convention of 1886 during the interwar period. Professors Ricketson and Ginsburg describe the situation as follows:

---

25 Ricketson and Ginsburg, *International Copyright* (n 3)1164.

> Another consequence of the War was the major reordering of a number of new states following the disintegration of the Hapsburg Hohenzollern and Romanov empires. Most of these states moved rapidly to engage themselves within the international order, and for the majority of them this included adherence to the Berne Union. They were joined by those European states which had remained outside the Union prior to the World War I, so that by 1928 almost the entire European continent, except for the newly constituted Soviet Union, was within the Union.[26]

At the 1908 Berlin Conference, it was agreed to hold the next conference within six to ten years in Rome. It was in 1928 that the Rome Conference was actually realized. The revisions achieved at the 1928 Rome Conference were very relevant to Japan.

First, the problem of many reservations that states had made at the ratification of the Berlin Revision was pointed out and discussed. To avoid the total abolition of the reservation system, some states declared abandoning reservations they had previously made.[27] In this context, Japan abandoned its reservation concerning public performance rights and terminated the requirement of indicating the prohibition of public performance in advance of the performance for the protection of public performance rights. This requirement was considered to apply to works of foreign authors.[28] Now foreign authors of musical works were able to enforce their public performance rights in Japan.

Second, the exclusive right of authors to authorize communication to the public by means of radiodiffusion was introduced in a new Article 11*bis*. While it was left to each Union member to determine the conditions under which the right might be exercised, it was also provided that the conditions should not in any circumstances prejudice the moral rights and the rights to equitable remuneration of the author.

Besides the two items explained above, the Rome Conference achieved other revisions, including the recognition of moral rights (Article 6*bis*), inclusion of oral works in the list of works protected (Articles 2 and 2*bis*), and clarification of the term of protection for works of joint authorship (Article 7*bis*).

At the 1928 Rome Conference, delegates agreed to hold the next conference in Brussels in 1935. However, it was delayed partly due to the slow ratification of

26 Ibid., 94.

27 Ibid., 97.

28 This interpretation, however, was problematic from the viewpoint of the consistency with the Berne Convention. See the discussion relating to the 1931 Revision of the Japanese Copyright Act below.

the Rome Revision by Union members (by August 1, 1931, the time of entry into force of the Rome Revision, only thirteen member countries, including Japan, had ratified it.). Eventually, World War II started, precluding international meetings during the war. It was only in 1948 that the next Brussels Revision Conference actually convened. Japan could not participate in this Conference as it was under occupation by the Allied Powers at that time.

4 Situation Related to Copyright in Japan during the Interwar Period

4.1 *The Period to 1931*

4.1.1 Diffusion of Gramophones and the 1920 Revision of the Copyright Act

As mentioned above, in 1899, Japan acceded to the Berne Convention and enacted the Copyright Act to implement the Convention. The primary motivation was not copyright protection per se, but rather to revise unequal treaties and to have Japan recognized by the West as a member of the international community.

However, publishing, theatrical performances, and musical concerts were actively conducted in Japan, and lawsuits over copyright infringement started to be filed sporadically. Furthermore, from the 1890s, phonograph records began to spread, and cases related to copyright infringement by reproducing records also began to arise. The *Tōchūken Kumaemon* Case, decided by the Supreme Court in 1914, is particularly well known. In this case, a German national who got copyright over a recording of a Japanese performer's performance of rōkyoku, a traditional Japanese form of recitation, claimed copyright infringement because the recording had been reproduced without his permission. The Supreme Court denied infringement on the grounds that performances of rōkyoku are not subject to copyright protection (the rōkyoku itself was held to be neither a work of music nor a literally work.).

In 1920, the Copyright Act was revised in response to the opinions that were raised after the ruling in the above case, which called for the protection of phonograms. The first amendment was to include performance and singing as examples of works (this was maintained until the new Copyright Act of 1970, which established neighboring rights). Second, the act of reproducing another person's work on equipment used for the mechanical reproduction of sound was clearly stated to be an infringement of copyright.

4.1.2 The Rome Conference and the 1931 Revision of the Copyright Act

Around 1920, radio broadcasting to the public began in the United States and major European countries. In Japan, radio broadcasting also began in 1925 by an organization that later became the Nihon Hōsō Kyōkai (hereinafter "NHK").

In 1926, an amendment to the Copyright Act was proposed to the Japanese Diet to create exclusive rights for broadcasting, but this proposal was defeated. On the other hand, the 1928 Rome Conference on the Berne Convention recognized exclusive rights for radio broadcasting (Article 11*bis*(1)). The Rome Conference also introduced the system of compulsory licensing (Article 11*bis* (2)) concerning these rights.

Based on the results of the Rome Conference, Japan revised its Copyright Act again in 1931. In the 1931 revision, broadcasting rights were clearly stipulated (although it was considered possible to read broadcasting rights as part of "reproduction" rights even under the previous law). The system of compulsory licensing for broadcasting rights was also introduced. Detailed provisions concerning cinematographic works were also added to the Act.

Of the decisions made at the Rome Conference, the most significant for Japan was the withdrawal of Japan's reservation on performance rights. The reason for the withdrawal is not fully clear, but it seems that while Italy, the host country of the conference, strongly urged other countries to withdraw their reservations, Japan withdrew its reservation on performance rights in order to maintain its reservation on translation rights.

The reservation on performance rights meant to maintain the restriction on the rights that the rights could not be exercised unless the unauthorized performance was prohibited prior to the performance. Such a restriction was provided in the Paris Revision of the Berne Convention but abolished under the Rome Revision. Actually, there was an unclear aspect about the restriction under the Japanese Copyright Act as the Act did not explicitly provide this restriction. Therefore, one interpretation could be that the Paris Revision directly applied to performance rights in Japan, since Article 28 of the Japanese Copyright Act at that time stipulated that the provisions of relevant treaties would apply to the copyright of foreign nationals if the treaty provisions differed from Japanese law. However, it would have been necessary to impose similar restrictions on the copyright of Japanese nationals as well, since treating only the copyright of foreigners unfavorably would be contrary to the principle of national treatment under the Berne Convention. This point seems not to have been clarified at the time of the 1931 revision of the Copyright

Act.[29] In any event, Japan clarified the elimination of reservations on performance rights by a notice of the Ministry of Foreign Affairs when it revised the Copyright Act in 1931.[30]

4.2 *From 1931 to 1939 and Beyond*

4.2.1 The 1931 Copyright Act and Radio Broadcasting

The revised Copyright Act of 1931 came into effect on August 1 of the same year. Radio broadcasting by NHK began in 1925 and had been rapidly spreading, with the number of subscribers (at that time, radio broadcasting required a paid subscription) exceeding one million by the spring of 1932.[31] With the implementation of the revised Copyright Act, NHK had to deal with the broadcasting rights of copyright holders. In March 1932, it concluded comprehensive licensing agreements with domestic organizations of composers and lyricists.[32] These organizations and individual composers and lyricists were eager to charge royalties for reproductions on phonograph records, but not for performances in concerts or for broadcasts. However, when broadcasting rights were enshrined in the law, neither the rights holders nor the users could avoid dealing with the rights to use music in broadcasting.

Negotiations for contracts related to radio broadcasting led to an awareness of the rights of Japanese copyright holders with regard to music copyrights. The right holders demanded an increase in royalty fees in the contract negotiations the following year, but NHK rejected the demand, leading to a situation in June 1932 in which songs by members of the organization of composers (the Association of Composers of Japan) were not broadcast on the radio. However, the composers recognized the disadvantage of not having their works broadcast, and in July 1932, negotiations were concluded with considerable concessions on the part of the composers.

As described above, Japanese copyright holders began to assert their rights to some extent, but a situation arose in which foreign copyright holders asserted their rights in a much more aggressive manner. This phenomenon is known as the Plage Whirlwind.

---

29 JASRAC, *History of Japanese Musical Copyright* (n 5) 351–52.

30 *Centennial History of Copyright Law of Japan* (n 17) 219.

31 Ibid., 220.

32 These organizations appear to have been established as voluntary associations between 1925 and 1926. As of 1932, Japan did not have a system of collecting societies, but it is assumed that these organizations collectively negotiated and concluded contracts with NHK for their member copyright holders.

4.2.2 Plage Whirlwind

4.2.2.1 *Who Was Dr. Plage?*

In 1931, the year when the Copyright Act was amended to specify the broadcasting rights, a German man opened an office in downtown Tokyo. Who was this man, Dr. Wilhelm Plage?[33]

Dr. Plage, a German born in 1888, studied law, economics, and the Japanese language at the University of Berlin, and from 1912 to 1914, worked as a diplomat at the German Embassy in Tokyo and the Consulate in Nagasaki. He then served at the German Embassy in the United States before going into the army and fighting as a field artilleryman on the Western Front in Europe. After the war, he resumed working at the German Embassy in Japan, but resigned from the embassy in 1921. He started working as a German language teacher at high schools (equivalent to colleges in the contemporary education system) in Matsue and Tokyo. From 1930 to December 1933, he was a German teacher at the Metropolitan High School (now Tokyo Metropolitan University). After that, he gave up teaching and devoted himself to copyright-related work.

It is not known how Dr. Plage became involved with copyright, but in 1931 he signed contracts with the Bureau International des Sociétés Gérant les Droits d'Enregistrement et de Reproduction Mécanique (BIEM) in 1931, and with Cartel des Sociétés D'Auteurs de Perceptions non Théatrales[34] and was entrusted with handling the rights managed by these organizations in Japan.

4.2.2.2 *Intensifying Whirlwind*

In July 1932, Dr. Plage appeared at the office of NHK. He claimed that he was an agent handling music copyright in five European countries (Britain, France, Germany, Austria, and Italy) and demanded royalties for the use of music from those countries. As noted above, NHK had concluded royalty agreements with the Japanese rights holders in March 1932, but had continued to make

33 The facts described in 4.2.2 are generally based on Ōie, Shigeo. *Nippon Chosakuken Monogatari: Plage Hakushi Tekihatsu-roku* (*Tales of Japanese Copyright: Dr. Plage's Detection Reports*). *Revised ed* (Sagamihara: Seizan-sha, 1999) 228–47; JASRAC, *History of Japanese Musical Copyright* (n 5) 281–351; and Yoshimura, Tamotsu. *Hakkustu Nihon Chosakuken Shi* (*Excavation of History of Copyright in Japan*) (Tokyo: Daiichi Shobō, 1993) 130–39, 246–55. On the other hand, Tetsuji Mori, *Wilhelm Plage* is not used as a source because its author calls the book a novel.

34 An organization consisting of European collective societies: Société des Auteurs, Compositeurs et Éditeurs de Musique (SACEM) in France; Società Italiana degli Autori ed Editori (SIAE) in Italy; Gesellschaft für musikalische Aufführungs- und mechanische Vervielfältigungsrechte (GEMA) in Germany; Gesellschaft der Autoren, Komponisten und Musikverleger in Austria; and the Performing Rights Society in Britain.

unlicensed use of foreign music without seeking to negotiate on its own. This led to a sudden visit by Dr. Plage and the start of negotiations. In the end, an agreement was reached between the two parties in December 1932, under which NHK would pay 600 yen (about 1.7 million yen in today's currency value) per month for one year from August of the same year for all the music works which Dr. Plage was in charge of.[35] This was the beginning of the Plage Whirlwind.

After this, Dr. Plage enforced copyright on foreign music one after another. He demanded that those who did not pay the required royalties stop using the music, and if they did not comply, he would file a lawsuit against them. According to a survey by the Ministry of Home Affairs at the time, between 1934 and 1938, Dr. Plage was involved in 5 civil and 49 criminal copyright cases. Most of them were resolved before reaching judgment or prosecution.[36] In Japan, copyright awareness had not been well established, and there was a strong tendency to dislike being sued. Therefore, Dr. Plage's attitude toward negotiation was feared by the parties concerned as unreasonably intransigent, lacking consideration and flexibility toward the other party. In addition, his activities were widely reported in newspapers and other media, and became widely known throughout society. His series of actions came to be known as the Plage Whirlwind.

Some of the most prominent examples of the Plage Whirlwind are as follows.

- Cancellation of the broadcast of foreign music due to breakdown of negotiations with NHK

As described above, a contract was concluded between Dr. Plage and NHK until the end of July 1933, but Dr. Plage requested a substantial increase in the royalty fee (from 600 yen to 1,500 yen per month) for the renewal of the contract, and NHK rejected this proposal. The license agreement expired, and from August 1933 to July 1934, no foreign music for which Plage had agency rights was broadcast on the radio. This incident triggered a revision of the Copyright Act to introduce a provision that the

35 While the fee paid collectively to the composers' organization for Japanese compositions for the year beginning in April 1932 was about 1,500 yen, the fee paid for foreign compositions under the agreement with Dr. Plage was much higher (7,200 yen per year). This price difference was a factor in the fierce dispute between the Japanese rights holders' organizations and NHK over the fee increase in 1933.

36 Itō, Nobuo. *Chosakuken Jiken Hyaku-wa* (*One Hundred Stories on Copyright*) (Tokyo: Copyright Research & Information Center, 1976) 136.

authorization by the copyright holder is not required for broadcasting by reproducing phonograph records (see 4.2.2.3 below).

– Lawsuit filed against unauthorized performances of "Madama Butterfly" and "Alt Heidelberg"

In May 1934, Shōchiku Girls Opera Company played adaptations of Puccini's "Madama Butterfly" and Wilhelm Meyer-Forster's "Alt Heidelberg." The copyright holders of the original works (opera and play) asked Dr. Plage's office to enforce their rights, and Plage filed criminal charges against the opera company's directors. However, the criminal case was dismissed by the Tokyo Ward Court in 1936. Japanese newspapers published favorable articles on this ruling. Some Japanese jurists, however, criticized the court's reasoning for its decision -- that Plage had no right to file a criminal complaint, which was necessary for the indictment of crimes of copyright infringement, because he was not registered as a copyright assignee -- as legally unreasonable. However, the prosecutors did not file an appeal.

Dr. Plage then filed a civil suit, for which the Tokyo District Court issued a judgment in 1940 ordering the defendant to pay damages.[37]

– Lawsuit filed against Tokyo Music School concerts

In February and October 1934, the Tokyo Music School (now Tokyo University of the Arts), one of the leading music conservatories in Japan, held concerts to which the Imperial Family and the Minister of Education were invited. The conservatory orchestra performed works by Gustav Mahler and Richard Strauss, but no royalties were paid in response to Dr. Plage's request. Plage, therefore, filed a civil lawsuit against the school and also filed criminal charges. The school immediately settled the case.

– Enforcement of Translation Rights

As mentioned above, Japan reserved the implementation of translation rights at the Paris Conference and maintained a system in which translation of works after ten years of publication was free. In reality, however, many translations of foreign works were published less than ten years after publication without authorization.

Dr. Plage enforced translation rights against such unauthorized translations at the request of copyright holders. Notable examples include cases concerning the publication of unauthorized translations of Benjamin

37 Ibid. 123–26.

Crémieux's "Inquiétude et Reconstruction" and Emil Ludwig's "Juli 14." Both cases were settled out of court.[38]

4.2.2.3 *National Resistance and the End of the Whirlwind*

Dr. Plage's copyright enforcement activities also had the effect of encouraging Japanese copyright holders to assert their rights. For example, as mentioned above, Japanese music copyright holders, realizing that the royalties they were receiving were much lower than those demanded by Dr. Plage for foreign works, asked NHK to raise the royalty rates (although that attempt was virtually unsuccessful). Such a move, however, seems to have strengthened the opposition to Plage in Japanese society as a whole, where awareness of copyright was still low and Plage's activities were seen as giving unnecessary, extra stimulus to Japanese copyright holders. In any case, not only those involved in the business of using copyrighted works, but also newspapers, magazines, and other media condemned Dr. Plage, and even some literary figures published hostile claims against him.

Under such circumstances, national responses were taken to restrict Dr. Plage's activities. First, the Copyright Act was revised in 1934 (effective in 1935). Second, the Intermediary Services Act was enacted in 1939.

The 1934 amendment to the Copyright Act introduced a provision restricting the right to broadcast musical works using a phonographic record on which the work had been legally reproduced, to the effect that the performance right would not extend to the act of broadcasting. After this revision, radio broadcasters were required to obtain authorization for the use of musical works only when broadcasting live performances, and were free to broadcast recordings as long as the source was clearly indicated. In addition, a compulsory licensing system was established for cases where the copyright holder's whereabouts were unknown, and the licensing could not be negotiated.[39] One of the cases in which this system could be used was when the copyright holder had no domicile in Japan, and her agent in Japan was unknown.

38 The case of 'Inquiétude et Reconstruction' was particularly reported by the media in a sensational way partly because the translator died after the publication and that fact attracted sympathy from the public toward the accused rather than Dr. Plage. It appears that the cause of the translator's death was not related to the copyright dispute. Ibid., 130–31; Ōie, *Tales of Japanese Copyright* (n 33) 84.

39 Other amendments included clarification of the rights of producers of phonograms and the creation of a publication right.

Thus, the enforcement of music copyright with respect to broadcasting was greatly restricted.[40] However, Dr. Plage continued to enforce copyright to the use of live performances of music (broadcasts, concert performances, etc.). In 1937, he filed for a preliminary injunction from the court to stop the performance of "Madama Butterfly," in which a world-renowned soprano Tamaki Miura was going to sing. The opera company had no choice but to stop the performance.

In December 1937, Dr. Plage established an organization to manage the copyright of Japanese composers and called on Japanese composers to participate in the organization. Kōsaku Yamada, a famous composer, joined the organization. It signed a contract with European copyright management organizations, and as a result, Yamada received royalties from a German copyright management organization for the use of Yamada's works in Germany. It was reported that the royalties were two or three times higher than the royalties Yamada usually received in Japan. Still, no other prominent Japanese composers participated in Dr. Plage's organization. In contrast, Japanese composers and performers voiced the opinion that a similar organization should be created by themselves. The Ministry of Home Affairs, which was in charge of the copyright system at the time, began considering the creation of a system to regulate copyright management organizations.

Thus, in 1939, Japan's first law regulating copyright management organizations, the Act on Intermediary Business Concerning Copyright (hereinafter the "Intermediary Business Act"), was enacted. The Act placed copyright management business under the government's licensing system, and royalties were subject to approval by the government. In parallel with the enactment of the law, composers and lyricists moved to establish new organizations, and in November 1939, the Japanese Society for Rights of Authors, Composers and Publishers (JASRAC) was established as an incorporated association. On December 28 of the same year, immediately after the Intermediary Business Act came into effect, JASRAC was granted a license to engage in intermediary business under the Act.[41]

Dr. Plage also applied for a license under the Intermediary Business Act in December 1939. However, the government indicated that it would only grant

40 This restriction applied not only to foreign works but also to Japanese works. It lacked a provision for equitable remuneration for copyright holders and might have violated Article 11*bis*(2) of the Berne Convention (Rome Act). See Ōie, *Tales of Japanese Copyright* (n 33) 112.

41 For copyright of literary works, the Japanese Alliance for the Protection of Copyright of Literary Works was established and given a license for intermediary services.

a license to one organization for music copyright, and did not grant it to him. Under the Intermediary Business Act, Dr. Plage could not engage in copyright intermediary services after March 15, 1940. The Ministry of Home Affairs solicited Dr. Plage to work for JASRAC, but this idea did not materialize because Plage and JASRAC could not agree on salary and other matters.

On March 14, 1940, Dr. Plage opened an office in Mukden, Manchuria, and informed relevant parties in Japan that the office would handle copyright related to foreign music. On the other hand, there were growing voices in Japan that Plage's actions violated the Intermediary Business Act, and the National Police Agency conducted voluntary investigations into Plage several times. Dr. Plage did not flinch, and in May of the same year, he again obtained a preliminary injunction on behalf of Puccini's heirs to stop the performance of "Madama Butterfly" starring Tamaki Miura, claiming that it constituted an infringement of their moral rights (more precisely, legal interests based on Puccini's moral rights).[42] In the end, however, Dr. Plage was criminally prosecuted and sentenced to a fine on July 15, 1941. He left Japan on December 12, 1941, on a cargo ship from Yokohama to return to Germany.[43]

5 Analysis

So far, we have observed Japan's copyright-related experiences during the interwar period. Finally, we will summarize the results of our observations again with some additional considerations.

First, during at least the first half of the interwar period, the copyright system became an important instrument for Japan's internationalization, i.e., the formation of a legal system and society consistent with the international order. This point is made even more striking by both the unique characteristics of the copyright system and the situation in Japan at the time.

By the end of the 19th century, the Berne Convention had established the basis of an international scheme for the copyright system. Under the Berne

42 Moral rights were not covered by the Intermediary Business Act.

43 It appears that Plage was not able to return directly to Germany; the cargo ship on which he boarded was caught by a U.S. vessel, and he was forced to cross over to the United States. After working in the United States in the copyright field, he returned to Germany in 1946. In Germany, he worked for GEMA and was its representative to the United States from 1953 to 1964. In 1962, when the president of GEMA visited Japan, Dr. Plage also came to Japan from the United States and met with officials from the Ministry of Education and JASRAC. He died in Germany in 1969.

Convention, the creation and operation of an internationally coordinated system were strongly demanded. In that sense, the copyright system had already been established as a typical example of the international order before the interwar period.

In addition, Japan won the revision of unequal treaties at the end of the 19th century, and the early 20th century and the interwar period was a time when Japan was making efforts to be recognized as a member of the international community in a substantial sense. One of the important pillars of these efforts was the development of the copyright system. In addition, importing scientific, technological, and social scientific knowledge through translation was extremely important for Japan from the late 19th century to the interwar period, and the copyright system was also an important concern for the Japanese government in this regard.

Furthermore, during the interwar period, Japan, for its part, succeeded in forming civil society.[44] As it became common for citizens to enjoy theater, music, opera, literature, radio broadcasts, and other forms of entertainment, the copyright system had a broad impact on society and became a matter of concern for the general public. For the general public, the copyright system may have been a way to learn the fact that the international order also affected civil society.

During World War I, while special wartime measures were taken for industrial property rights, no special measures were taken for copyright. As a matter of fact, it does not seem that copyrights of foreigners were adequately protected in Japan at that time in the first place. Nevertheless, the fact that influential jurists were of the opinion that the protection of private rights must be guaranteed under international law even with an enemy nation at war can be said to represent the peaceful nature of international law pertaining to intellectual property rights.

Second, it is difficult to assess how the copyright system affected Japan's foreign policy and society's perception of international order in the late interwar period. In that period, the military's influence in Japanese politics increased, and society as a whole became more nationalistic. In this context, the Plage Whirlwind, which this chapter has described in detail, was a further example

44 For example, a universal suffrage system was established in 1925, giving all men over the age of 25 the right to vote, regardless of the amount of taxes they paid. It should be pointed out, however, that restrictions on freedom of thought and expression became increasingly severe during the interwar period.

of the opposition to the pressure from foreigners because Dr. Plage, as a foreigner, was a claimant of those rights.[45]

Did the opposition to Dr. Plage's activities lead to criticism and opposition to the copyright system and the Berne Convention? From the published data, it does not appear that Plage's activities led to fundamental criticism of the copyright system. On the other hand, some of the newspaper articles criticizing Plage were against the Berne Convention and, by extension, argued that Japan should withdraw from the Berne Convention. In fact, the argument for withdrawing from the Berne Convention was quite public in Japan from 1930 onward. However, it seems that the argument was much more based on a concern about allowing foreigners to exercise translation rights, rather than on criticism of Dr. Plage's activities. In the background of the argument for withdrawal from the Berne Convention was the fact that the next conference after the 1928 Rome Conference was scheduled to be held in Brussels in 1935, and Japan feared that it would be forced to drop its reservation on translation rights at that conference. However, the Brussels Conference was postponed and did not take place until 1948 due to the outbreak of World War II. In the meantime, the argument for withdrawal from the Berne Convention disappeared spontaneously.

It is important to note that the Japanese government took a firm stance to maintain its participation in the Berne Convention in response to the domestic argument for withdrawing from the Convention. In other words, as the argument for withdrawing from the Berne Convention grew, there were times when Diet members made such an argument, but the government made clear its policy of maintaining its membership in the Berne Convention.[46] Japan's firm stance to maintain its accession to the Berne Convention despite its move to secede from the international order, symbolized by its withdrawal from the League of Nations in 1933, may have been due to the non-political nature of the Berne Convention. In addition, it can be seen that Japan was aware that there were aspects of the international order that it should maintain, and that the copyright system was one of them

45 It would be worth exploring how the nationality of Dr. Plage's (his being a German) affected the reactions of the Japanese government and the Japanese public. At present, this author does not have sufficient sources to give any clear statement of this question. At least, there seems to be no evidence that the German government or German Embassy in Japan exerted pressure on the Japanese government for the sake of Dr. Plage.

46 For example, in 1934, Minister of Foreign Affairs stated at Diet that it would not be appropriate for Japan to withdraw from the Berne Convention from an international perspective.

6 Postscript

Before concluding this chapter, the author would like to comment on the contribution of Dr. Plage to the establishment of the copyright system in Japan. It is undeniable that the Plage Whirlwind had a positive significance. In the first place, there was no question that Dr. Plage's activities were legal until the Intermediary Business Act was enacted. For example, Kōichirō Kunishio, who was a central figure in the drafting of the Intermediary Business Act, wrote as follows:

> Mr. Prage's actions were not illegal by nature in terms of the Berne Convention or Japanese copyright law, but why did the public make an issue of them, and why did the newspapers write about them? I think there were two reasons.
>
> One is that, although the general public was aware of the copyright at the time, it was mostly based on the understanding of copyright as a right to publish, and there was very little knowledge of performance and public performance rights. ....
>
> Another reason was that the royalties he charged for the use of musical works looked very expensive, far removed from the economic reality of the music business at that time. Although the fees may have been low by Western standards, they still seemed unreasonably high by Japanese standards and sentiments.[47]

Dr. Plage's activities dramatically increased Japanese copyright holders' awareness of their rights, especially composers and lyricists. It should also be noted that there were Japanese lawyers who cooperated with Dr. Plage. They made significant contributions to the development and dissemination of Japanese copyright practice.[48] In short, Dr. Plage

47 Kunishio Kōichirō. *Chosakuken Ronbun-shū* (*Papers on Copyright*) (Tokyo: JASRAC, 1987) 137–38. Kunishio was a government official in charge of the copyright system at the Ministry of Home Affairs in the 1930s. After World War II, he served as the chairman of JASRAC.

48 The most prominent lawyer who worked with Dr. Plage was Yoshihiko Kido. Mr. Kido published academic books on copyright law, and served as a Supreme Court Justice from 1963 to 1970. Another lawyer who worked for Dr. Plage was Hiroaki Yamashita. Mr. Yamashita was a university professor of civil law before becoming an attorney. Unfortunately, he died young, in his forties.

should be counted as one of the "people who established copyright" in Japan.[49]

Bibliography

Banno, Junji. *Nihon Kindai Shi* (*History of Modern Japan*) (Tokyo: Chikuma Shobō, 2012).

Editing Committee on Centennial History of Copyright Law of Japan. *Chosakuken-hō Hyakunen Shi* (*Centennial History of Copyright Law of Japan*) (Tokyo: Chosakuken Joho Center (Copyright Research and Information Center), 2000).

Fuess, Harald, 'Unequal Treaties, Consular Jurisdiction, and Treaty Port Society.' In *Routledge Handbook of Modern Japanese History*, Saaler, Sven and Szpilman, Christopher, eds, (Abingdon, Oxon: Routledge, 2020).

Ganea, Peter, 'Copyright History.' In *Japanese Copyright Law: Writings in Honour of Gerhard Schricker*, Peter Ganea, Christopher Heath, and Hiroshi Saitō, eds (The Hague: Kluwer Law International, 2005).

Gordon, Andrew. *A Modern History of Japan: From Tokugawa Times to the Present. 4th ed* (New York: Oxford University Press, 2020).

Itō, Nobuo. *Chosakuken Jiken Hyaku-wa* (*One Hundred Stories on Copyright*) (Tokyo: Copyright Research & Information Center, 1976).

Itō, Takao, 'Dai Ichiji Sekai Taisen To Kōgyōshoyūken' (World War I and Industrial Property Rights). *Hōgaku Ronsō* 138 (1–3) (1995) 299–327, 301–08.

Japan Patent Office. Kōgyōshoyūken-seido Hyakunen Shi (*Centennial History of Industrial Property System*) (Tokyo: Hatsumei Kyōkai, 1984).

Japanese Society for Rights of Authors, Composers and Publishers (JASRAC), ed. *Nihon Ongaku Chosakuken shi* (*History of Japanese Music Copyright*) Vol. 1 (Tokyo: JASRAC, 1990).

Kitaoka, Shinichi. *The Political History of Modern Japan: Foreign Relations and Domestic Politics*. Translated by Robert D. Eldridge and Graham Leonard (Abingdon, Oxon: Routledge, 2018).

Kōichirō, Kunishio. *Chosakuken Ronbun-shū* (*Papers on Copyright*) (Tokyo: JASRAC, 1987).

Mori, Tetsuji. *Wilhelm Plage: Nihon No Chosakuken No Umi No Oya* (*Wilhelm Plage: the Father of the Copyright in Japan*) (Tokyo: Kawade Shobō, 1996).

49 Professor Ōie, who had worked on copyright policy as an official at the Agency of Cultural Affairs before entering the academic, published a book titled: *Chosakuken Wo Kakuritsushita Hitobito* (*People Who Established Copyright*) *2nd ed.* (Tokyo: Seibundō, 2004) and dedicated one chapter to Dr. Plage. Professor Ōie also wrote another book on Dr. Plage's activities in Japan (see Ōie, *Tales of Japanese Copyright*).

Ōie, Shigeo. *Nippon Chosakuken Monogatari: Plage Hakushi Tekihatsu-roku* (*Tales of Japanese Copyright: Dr. Plage's Detection Reports*). *Revised ed* (Sagamihara: Seizan-sha, 1999).

Ōie, Shigeo. *Chosakuken Wo Kakuritsushita Hitobito* (*People Who Established Copyright*) 2nd ed (Tokyo: Seibundō, 2004).

Ricketson, Sam, and Ginsburg, Jane. *International Copyright and Neighbouring Rights: The Berne Convention and Beyond. 3rd ed.* (Oxford: Oxford University Press, 2022).

Seville, Catherine. *The Internationalisation of Copyright Law* (Cambridge: Cambridge University Press, 2006).

Von Lewinski, Silke. *International Copyright Law and Policy* (Oxford: Oxford University Press, 2008).

Yoshimura, Tamotsu. *Hakkustu Nihon Chosakuken Shi* (*Excavation of History of Copyright in Japan*) (Tokyo: Daiichi Shobō, 1993).

CHAPTER 13

IP as Public Property: Early Formation of IP Laws in the Soviet Union

Ekaterina Kirsanova

> The work of a scientist is the property of all mankind, and science is the area of greatest disinterestedness.
>
> M. GORKY

1 Introduction

The beginning of the 20th century seems to be a difficult period in the history of Russia for many reasons: the growing social discontent that led to the revolutionary unrest of 1905, 1914 and 1917, the depletion of the economy, mass strikes, and the withdrawal from participation in the First World War showed the need to reform the political and legal system of the country. Since the main function of law is to streamline the existing economic (or social) relations, the actual reshaping of the state could not lead to the development of legislation in an evolutionary way, respectively, in many respects the legal framework was created anew: in particular, the issue of redistributing property and highlighting its new categories became one of the key aspects of the new legislative developments.

A feature of working with intellectual property legislation at the stage of formation of Soviet statehood was largely the lack of an adequate amount of judicial practice, due to the fact that the issues of protecting exclusive and personal non-property rights were not a priority during that period of historical development. At the same time, it is not worth talking about a complete lack of regulation and interest of the legislator in this area, since one of the priority areas was the aspect of building economic relations with foreign countries, which would be impossible in a situation where the turnover of the results of intellectual activity was excluded. It is not without reason that researchers

 | DOI:10.1163/9789004714663_015

note the difficulty of describing this historical period, the early stage of Soviet legislative developments.[1]

From the point of view of law, there was a radical breakdown of the existing system: in traditional economics, it was designated as a transition between formations. In the language of Marxism, the transition from the capitalist to the socialist formation began as the first stage of communism, which in turn abolished the fundamental category of private property. In addition, the legal system also required not just adjustments, but a complete overhaul. As Ioffe[2] noted, one of the main problems of the initial period was the essence of Soviet civil law, since immediately after the victory of the October Revolution, not only the necessity, but even the possibility of the whole idea of trade relations as a part of capitalist formation was denied. Of course, views changed in the future, however, the subsequent development of the science of law moved considering the socialist nature of state policy.

It is worth noting that the first acts of the Soviet government were of a similar nature to decrees, but at the same time, sometimes their legal significance unjustifiably raises questions.

> modern historians and especially legal scholars do not treat Lenin's writings on international law seriously. However, in the context of a Soviet conception of international law and property, Lenin's writings are key to understanding the overarching spirit of pragmatism/realism, while staying true to core Marxist tenets.[3]

It is also worth noting that, Russian scholars supported by official historical documentation and correspondence, or using expert testimony, have said that the ideological gap between the Russian Empire and the formation of the Soviet Union should not be the sole reason to condemn the state of legal affairs. Rather, the denunciation of treaties concluded by foreign states occurred exclusively in the part that did not correspond to the interests of the new state. A striking example and confirmation of this thesis is the agreement

1 Mamlyuk, Boris, 'Russia & Legal Harmonization: An Historical Inquiry Into IP Reform as Global Convergence and Resistance'. *Washington University Global Studies Law Review* 10(3/4) (2011) 535–592.

2 Olympiad, Ioffe. *Izbrannye trudy po grazhdanskomu pravu: Iz istorii civilisticheskoj mysli. Grazhdanskoe pravootnoshenie. Kritika teorii "hozyajstvennogo prava"* (Selected Works on Civil Law: From the History of Civil Thought. Civil Law. Criticism of the Theory of "Economic Law") (Moscow: Statute Publishers, 2000) 180–182.

3 Mamlyuk, *Russia & Legal harmonization,* (n 1).

with Great Britain dated August 18, 1924, which distinguishes between valid and invalid agreements.[4]

2 Public Property and Soviet Ideology

Contrary to popular belief about the abolition of private property from the very first days of the coup that took place in 1917, this is not entirely true. The institution of private property was contrary to the principles of communism, on which the construction of the Soviet state was planned. However, the simultaneous abolition of private ownership of any kind of objects did not happen: restrictions were introduced on certain types of objects of private property, as well as transactions with them. For instance, this view was often reinforced in Soviet doctrine.[5]

Attitudes towards law, civil relations, the institution of property in general, and intellectual property changed quite significantly after the revolution, and also continued to evolve throughout the entire period of the existence of the Soviet state. A striking stage in the development of the Soviet perception of these concepts, which changed significantly in the 1920s, was the adoption by the Bolshevik Party of the New Economic Policy (NEP), which changed the attitude, legal framework, and the ratio of state and private property.

In essence, the new policy was the proletarian nationalization of land: 'The abolition of private ownership of land, the exclusion of land from private circulation, the prohibition of private transactions with land: sales, leases, gifts, inheritance, etc., the provision of land for use only by state bodies were the main elements of state ownership of land, and therefore it can be argued that already the first decrees on land established the nationalization of land'.[6] In fact, this was the first step towards establishing new rules – community for

4 Expert Opinion of the Head of the Department of History of State and Law of the Law Faculty of Moscow State University. M.V. Lomonosov by Professor V. A. Tomsinov. URL: http://tomsinov.com/Delo/expert_14_02_2011.pdf; La décision de la cour de cassation Pourvoi no G 11-21.947 Arrêt no 406 FS-P+B, 10 avril 2013. URL: http://tomsinov.com/Delo/court.pdf.

5 'Personal property in the USSR is the individual property of Soviet citizens, based on personal labor. It is fundamentally different from private property in capitalist countries and, due to the dominance of public ownership of the means of production, cannot be used for the exploitation of man by man. Bourgeois legislation does not recognize the category of personal property, in contrast to private property'. See *Great Soviet Encyclopedia. 2nd ed.* edn. Vol 25. Vvedensky, BA, ed. (Moscow: State Scientific Publishing House, 1954) 303.

6 Genkin, Dmitry, et al. *Istoriya sovetskogo prava in 1917–1947* (History of Soviet Law 1917–1947) (Moscow: Gosjurizdat, 1949) 73.

the means of production. Furthermore, it would be more correct to speak not about the abolition of private property, but about recognizing the owner of a single subject – the state, which follows from the provisions and acts adopted in the future. 'Land – to the peasants, factories – to the workers' was more of a propaganda slogan, behind which the main principles of the planned economy were hidden: the centralized distribution of resources and the setting of tasks for the implementation of production.

A similar position is held by specialists in related industries: for example, public property was determined as a 'classical form of bureaucratic property', which is characterized by the following features: state monopoly on the means of production and natural resources; concentration of power in the hands of the nomenklatura;[7] dependence relations between the subjects among which the powers of ownership are distributed; bottom-up responsibility; legislative possibility of redistribution of objects of property between business entities.[8]

The first soviet acts establishing public (or so-called public) property also established collective property – that is, collective farm, artel,[9] etc. In practice, there was no significant difference here, except for delegating decision-making on pressing issues of production functioning. At the same time, the question arises – did the institution of private ownership of objects of intellectual rights remain? To decide, it is necessary to start with an understanding of the logic of the division of all objects of civil legal relations in the Soviet state. It was supposed to introduce regulation on a public basis of rights to objects and means of production and the preservation of private ownership of personal items (household).

What we need to pay attention to is that the Soviet legacy, except for the NEP period, which will be discussed later, was based on a policy of abandoning private property in favor of public property. Nevertheless, it is a mistake to believe that private property in the USSR did not exist in principle. Of course, this sounds like an attempt to negotiate with conscience, but the Soviet ideology still recognized personal property: 'The distinguishing feature of communism

7 The term nomenklatura is used to define high-level officials, party leaders who held key administrative posts. In various historical periods, it had an emotional connotation, including a negative one, describing the attitude of the population towards the ruling elites.

8 Leontiev, Gleb, Leonteva, Lyudmila, 'Dialektika svobody i sobstvennosti v obshchestve realnogo utopizma' (Dialectics of Freedom and Property in the Society of Real Utopianism). *Sociodynamics* 4 (2018) 58.

9 Form of association of workers to perform certain economic tasks on the basis of common property (similar in essence to a partnership).

is not the abolition of property in general, but the abolition of bourgeois property'.[10]

Formally, personal property differed from private property according to the following criteria: (a) restriction on objects. For personal property, a restriction was introduced as only consumer goods could be considered. While the means of production cannot be privately owned. The other criteria were (b) the source of personal property of citizens under socialism is labor in social production, while private property allows the existence of unearned income.[11]

Thus, the ideology of the Soviet state in the initial period denied the applicability of private property in relation to the means of production, established state and collective ownership of various kinds of objects, and carried out the nationalization of enterprises. Accordingly, to ensure such a transition, a significant change in the current legislation was required, which led to the abolition of most of the acts of imperial Russia with some exclusions.[12]

3 Status of IP Rights after 1917

Coming closer to the intellectual property and measures of protection one can note that the first legal act to offer a consensus on the legality of the term 'intellectual property' appeared just before the demise of the USSR in 1990-s with the Law of the USSR 'O sobstvennosti v SSSR' (On Property in the USSR).[13]

---

10 Marx, Karl and Engels, Friedrich. *Sochineniya* (Works), 2nd edn. Volume 4 (Moscow: Politizdat, 1955) 438.

11 Hiroshi, Kimura, *Lichnaya sobstvennost v SSSR, ee svyaz s obshchestvennymi fondami potrebleniya i perspektivy ih razvitiya* (Personal Property in the USSR, its Connection with Public Consumption Funds and Prospects for Their Development) (Hokkaido: Hokkaido University Collection of Scholarly and Academic Papers, 1975) 119.

12 These are further discussed in Tomsinov, 'Expert Opinion' (n 4). 'While assuming the property rights of the Russian Empire, the USSR did not renounce its obligations, but only tried to bring them to a reasonable volume, corresponding to the capabilities of the young state, devastated by the world and civil wars, the military intervention of foreign powers in Russian affairs. This is evidenced, for example, by a letter from G. V. Chicherin to the head of the British delegation at the Genoa Conference, dated April 20, 1922. "The Russian Government would be ready to return to the former owners the use of nationalized or confiscated property, or, where this would not be possible, to satisfy the just demands of the former owners, either by direct agreement with them, or in accordance with an agreement, the details of which will be discussed and adopted at this conferences"'.

13 Law of the USSR No 1305-I 'O sobstvennosti v SSSR' (On Property in the USSR). Vedomosti of the Supreme Soviet of the USSR. No 11 (1990).

Since the tsarist era there has been a need to protect the property interests of publishers: the uncontrolled creation and distribution of printed materials reduced the cost of books, in addition, there was a need to control the quality of distributed literary works, which led to the formation of a system of privileges for book printing, the formation of legislation on censorship and the emergence of the first provisions for the protection of exclusive rights.

Starting from 1877, the Code of Laws of the Russian Empire contained provisions on the recognition of typical and new objects (for example, public speeches and private diaries) of the status of objects of copyright, the idea of authorship and the system of collective management of the rights of authors were formed, in particular the emergence of societies for the protection of relevant rights.[14]

Before the revolution of 1917 in Russia there was legal regulation of intellectual property, which, along with legislation in other areas, will later be ideologically recognized as a weapon of oppression (although it is obvious that objectively the functions of intellectual property rights can hardly be described as a means of oppressing the working class). The main intellectual property legislation of the Russian Empire was the Copyright Act of March 20th (April 2nd),[15] 1911, that included 75 articles and fixed the system of rights and obligations of authors and editors, restrictions on public performance, terms of the protection, etc.[16] The law reflected the advanced ideas of the German laws of 1901 and 1907, as well as the Berne Convention in its Berlin version of 1908 the importance of copyright restrictions for socially significant purposes.

All the political and economic changes mentioned above had largely determined the basic concept of intellectual property different to pre-existed traditional rules, which stated intellectual property as one of the types of assets belonging to the subjects of law on an equal basis with other more familiar objects and existing by analogy.[17] The initial period of Soviet statehood (1917–1919) is generally regarded by researchers as controversial years, which

14 Kirsanova, Ekaterina, "Istoriya stanovleniya zakonodatelstva ob intellektualnoj sobstvennosti v otechestvennoj pravovoj sisteme" (The History of the Formation of Intellectual Property Legislation in the Domestic Legal System). *Legal Science* 5 (2020) 38–41.

15 It should be noted that some acts will be dated twice because at the beginning of the 20th century, the Julian calendar was used until On January 24 (February 6), 1918, when the Council of People's Commissars adopted a decree 'On the Introduction of the Western European calendar in the Russian Republic'.

16 Collection of legalizations and orders of the Government. Section I. No. 61 (March 30, 1911). Art. 560.

17 Agarkov, Michail. *Obyazatelstvo po Sovetskomy grazhdanskomy pravu* (Obligation Under Soviet Civil Law) (Moscow: Judicial Publishing House NKJU USSR, 1940) 32–39.

canceled many bourgeois norms, turned the idea of the economic essence of property and the mechanisms for building social relations. The pre-existing criminal and civil legislation in the field of intellectual property was abolished. The Soviet government began to develop and adopt its own regulations governing the creation and use of works of science, literature and art, inventions, and other objects of intellectual property.[18]

After the Revolution in 1917 the previous regulation and protective measures could not exist in the form they used to be before: the established institution of intellectual property seemed logical to be destroyed along with legal system and imperialist ideology in general. Intellectual property objects were the same economic asset, a means of production as land, factories, or any industrial facilities.[19]

The concentration of rights to such objects established a virtual monopoly on its use, made it possible to restrict access or use of the object as a means of generating income. In addition, the rejection of private ownership of objects of intellectual rights would allow their wider use in the creation of developments based on the original object without any restrictions or payments, which could be one of the reasons for the active growth and development of production. Though, the reality was controversial. The Act of 1911 continued to be in force with some changes and in 1918 some objects of copyright (literary, scientific, and other works) were nationalized. This was followed by objects of industrial property, including inventions in the middle of 1919. The results of intellectual activity were declared public property and made available to the state,[20] with the only exception of rights of heirs.[21]

Further development on the legal history of IP in Russia is clearly traced to the example of adopted acts and laws. One of the acts not directly related but affecting the rights of authors and publishers was mostly connected with

18 Aliyev, Samir 'Evolyuciya rossijskogo zakonodatelstva reglamentiruyushchego otnosheniya v sfere intellektualnoj sobstvennosti' (Evolution of the Russian Legislation Regulating Relations in the Sphere of Intellectual Property). *Gaps in the Russian Legislation* 3 (2013) 91–93.

19 See Eugster, Esprit, 'Evolution and Enforcement of Intellectual Property Law in Russia'. *Washington University Global Studies Law Review* 9(1) (2010) 131–151 (noting especially intellectual property rights underwent 'drastic changes in protection' as other rules in the young state).

20 Gavryushkin, Sergey, 'Intellektualnaya sobstvennost: lichnoe pravo i publichnyj interes' (Intellectual property: Personal Law and Public Interest). *IP. Industrial Property* 10 (2019) 45–52.

21 Mamlyuk, *Russia & Legal Harmonization* (n 1).

general rules of censorship: Decree 'O pechati' (On the press)[22] of October 27 (November 9), 1917 restricted the rights and possibilities of publishing houses that were unverified by the authorities. The reason, though, was far from ideological. For instance, publications of criminal nature, distorting facts, and objectively calling for the violation of the established order were considered illegal, and the publisher was limited in the right to conduct business, while press was supposed to be a weapon 'no less dangerous than bombs and machine-guns'.[23] At the same time, it is worth noting that the above restriction, although it can be interpreted as a mechanism for restricting freedom of speech, was more intended to preserve the new legal order that was emerging in a young state, including protecting citizens from falsification and dissemination of data that does not correspond to reality.

In February 1918, the decision of the People's Commissariat of Education 'On the publication of works by Russian writers' announced the nationalization of the right to publish literary works and the procedure for publishing scientific works. Previously used existing publishing contracts (pre-revolutionary treaties) with publishers were declared invalid,[24] and by the Decree of the People's Commissariat for Education of February 14, 1918, several works were nationalized.[25] A list of 58 Russian writers, poets and critics was published, whose works were decided to publish, monopolizing them for 5 years (later the monopoly was extended for another 5 years). The monopoly extended to well-known works of classics, the copyright term for which had expired: the most famous classical works of literature (works of writers, including L.N. Tolstoy, A.P. Chekhov, F.M. Dostoevsky, etc.) and music (works of composers: P.I. Tchaikovsky, M.I. Glinka and others).[26]

At the same time, the authors of works that were not declared subject to nationalization retained the rights by order, except for the possibility of

22 Decree 'O pechati' (On the Press). *Decrees of the Soviet Government* Vol. 1 (Moscow: Institute of Marxism-Leninism, 1957) 24–25.

23 Decree "O pechati" (On the press). *Decrees of the Soviet Government*. (Moscow: Institute of Marxism-Leninism, 1957), Vol. 1. 24–25.

24 Decree of the Council of People's Commissars of October 10, 1919. 'O prekrashchenii sily dogovorov na priobretenie v polnuyu sobstvennost' proizvedenij literatury i iskusstva' (On the termination of contracts for the acquisition of full ownership of works of literature and art). *SU RSFSR* 51 (1919).

25 Kubyshko, Michail, 'Razvitie zakonodatel'stva ob avtorskom prave sovetskogo perioda' (Development of Copyright Legislation in the Soviet Period). *Bulletin of the Moscow University of the Ministry of Internal Affairs of Russia* 10 (2011) 171–174.

26 Aliyev, 'Evolyuciya rossijskogo' (n 18) 92.

inheritance.[27] The limitation of the authors' rights, however, was not carried out on a gratuitous basis: they retained the right to receive royalties, and their heirs had the right to receive maintenance from the state.[28]

Based on the general political course, such a measure was supposed to serve the purpose of increasing the accessibility of literature and other works to the citizens of the young state, that is, copyright in Russia again served the purpose of protecting the consumer rather than the author.

The next act to settle the new system of IP rights in Soviet state was the Decree of the Council of People's Commissars of November 26, 1918 'On the Recognition of Scientific, Literary, Musical and Artistic Works as State Property' established for works the status of 'public property'.[29] Furthermore, the Decree noted that governmental institutions had exclusivity to reproduce and distribute public property. A work declared public property may be reproduced and distributed only by the People's Commissariat of Education or other Soviet institution, by agreement with the People's Commissariat of Education. At the same time, the protection of the rights of authors and their right to determine the future fate and rules of usage of their own work during their lifetime was presumed, and a ban was established on the publication of a work within a 6-month period after the death of the author.[30]

Restrictions were also set for the publication of diaries, personal correspondence and other objects that were not intended to be public. It should be noted that despite the general course of nationalization and the strengthening of the role of the public over the private, the Soviet legal order did not assume the alienation of works free of charge. Rather, the author (or publisher) received monetary compensation for expenses and royalties, which, despite the general rules on the abolition of inheritance, could also claim the needy relatives of

---

27 Decree of the Council of People's Commissars of the RSFSR of November 26, 1918, 'O priznanii nauchnyh, literaturnyh, muzykal'nyh i hudozhestvennyh proizvedenij gosudarstvennym dostoyaniem' (On the Recognition of Scientific, Literary, Musical, and Artistic State Property). *SU RSFSR*, 1918, N 86, art. 900.

28 Decree of the Council of People's Commissars of the RSFSR of November 26, 1918, ibid.

29 Decree of the Council of People's Commissars of November 26, 1918, ibid., with the relevant provision being: 'Any published or unpublished scientific, literary, musical or artistic work, which was not recognized in the hands, can be recognized, according to the establishment of the Commissariat of Education, as the property of the Russian People's Socialist Federative Soviet Republic'.

30 Ibid: 'Works that were not declared public property cannot be reproduced and distributed during the life of the author otherwise than by agreement with the author. Until the expiration of 6 months from the date of the death of the author, no one has the right to publish or republish his works'.

the deceased copyright holder, and it was not even a one-time payment, but a dependency.[31]

Any unauthorized publication, reproduction, distribution, and public performance of works was recognized as a violation of the state monopoly. Similar rules were in force within the framework of the Criminal Code of the Russian Socialist Federative Soviet Republic (RFSRF)[32] adopted in 1922 where article 101 established liability in the form of forced labor for up to one year with or without confiscation of property.

The initiation of mass invention among industrialists and agricultural workers had become an urgent need which was caused by the need to overcome the socio-economic crisis. Some of the causes were, the consequences of the revolution and the civil war (of 1917–1922), a radical economic breakdown, as well as the lack of proper economic management skills at the initial stage of the formation of Soviet statehood. Thus, the role of legislation was to solve the problems, and organize, encourage, and protect invention.[33]

The main rules were adopted in relation to patents by the Decree of the Council of People's Commissars of the RSFSR dated 30th of June 1919 'On Inventions' with additional restrictions on foreign patenting and exemption of the inventor from taxation. Despite the rejection of bourgeois ideology, in the period from October 1917 to June 1919, the Regulation on privileges for inventions and improvements of May 20, 1896, which was a classic 'bourgeois'[34] patent law, the norms of which could not meet the interests of the new government. In short, the provisions of the decree pertained to new principles of the state's attitude to inventions and inventors, a new form of protection of an invention was formed as an object withdrawn from circulation and available to all citizens and organizations, consistent with the Marxist idea of common (collective) ownership of property.[35]

31 Decree of the Council of People's Commissars of the RSFSR of November 26, 1918 (n 27).

32 One of the Union Republics that formed the Soviet State.

33 Talman, Ekaterina, 'Racionalizatory i izobretateli: ot carskoj Rossii do nashih dnej. Istoriya poyavleniya sovremennyh Levshej i Kulibinyh' (Rationalizers and Inventors: From Tsarist Russia to the Present Day – The History of the Emergence of Modern Lefties and Kulibins). https://kachestvo.pro/kachestvo-upravleniya/berezhlivoe-proizvodstvo/ratsionalizatory-i-izobretateli-ot-tsarskoy-rossii-do-nashikh-dney/.

34 The term was used for ideological differentiation with capitalist and other political and legal systems, in fact, pointing to significant differences laid down by the main aspect – the attitude to the basic issues of the economy.

35 Eremenko, Vladimir, 'Retrospektivnyj analiz rossijskogo zakonodatelstva ob izobreteniyah' (Retrospective Analysis of Russian Legislation on Inventions). *IP. Industrial Property* 4 (2019) 43–54.

Hence the point of a new act was that the previously existed rules were to be repealed.[36]

In continuation of the ideas of the Decree, several acts were developed to ensure that the invention is brought to industrial implementation. So, for example, the Regulations on the Committee for Inventions under the Scientific and Technical Department of the Supreme Economic Council of the RSFSR of December 9, 1920, expanded the range of objects of inventive law, which began to act, along with inventions, improvements and models that meet the requirement of utility. In addition, the Regulations on the Committee introduced the institutions of application certificates, where priority was fixed, and copyright certificates, with the help of which the very right of the inventor was established.[37]

It is worth noting that the Soviet ideology itself was largely at odds with generally accepted western patenting rules: Western patent systems were criticized as a formation of a system that prioritized the interests of companies over employees.[38]

Lenin defined the Western patent system as oppressive accusing them of helping capitalists exploit the working class, hindering technological progress using 'preventive' patents[39] (patents that are not obtained to protect a new product, but to protect an existing one by blocking the production of a competitor product). This line of reasoning was also perfect for the time, and the general apathy towards capitalism and property.

Considering that the intellectual property system was formed in the Soviet state in the first years of its existence, the rejection of established rules can be explained from the standpoint of historical logic. The new government could not base its decisions on the 'bourgeois' legislation left over from the imperial period. Accordingly, the law had to change. However, in fairness, it should be

36 Ibid: 'Inventions declared to be the property of the state, related to national defense or especially important for Russia and therefore recognized as especially secret by the relevant People's Commissariat, are not subject to patenting abroad, transfer to third parties or general disclosure'.

'Any invention made on the territory of the Russian Republic must be declared in Russia before it is declared in other countries'.

37 Molchanov A. A., Zaytseva E. V., 'K voprosu o sluzhebhykh obektakhpatentnogo prava' (On Work-Related Objects of Patent Law). *Vestnik Permskogo universiteta. Juridicheskie nauki – Perm University Herald. Juridical Sciences* 44(2) (2019) 314–315.

38 Graham, Loren, 'The Legal System'. In *Lonely Ideas: Can Russia Compete?* (Cambridge: The MIT Press, 2013) 119–126.

39 Vladimir, Lenin. *Sochineniya* (Works), Vol. 22. (Moscow: State Publishing House of Political Literature, 1941) 263.

noted that the formal repeal of the law of 1911 was not even intended to be repealed, in the legal sense it continued to operate in one way or another, in part not contradicting the new legislation.

In general, the initial period of the formation of intellectual rights in the Soviet state was characterized by a tendency for the predominance of public interest, which was also reflected in the Decree of the Council of People's Commissars of the RSFSR of July 29, 1919 'On the abolition of private property in the archives of deceased Russian writers, composers, artists and scientists stored in libraries and museums',[40] as well as in the Decree of the Council of People's Commissars of the RSFSR of October 10, 1919 'On the termination of contracts for the acquisition of full ownership of works of literature and art'.[41]

The change in the approach to intellectual property in the next years taken as a period under review is associated with a revision of the methods of doing business in general. The general course towards nationalization and the transition to a planned economy,[42] the increasing importance of the state as one of the central subjects of economic activity[43] was reflected in the acts regulating the legal regime of intellectual property objects.

4 Locating Public Property: Changes in Economic Policy in 1921–1928

On March 14, 1921, at the tenth Congress of the Russian Communist Party (Bolsheviks) (RCP(b)), a significant event occurred to change the economic

40 Decree of the Council of People's Commissars of the RSFSR of July 29, 1919. 'Ob otmene prava chastnoj sobstvennosti na arhivy umershih russkih pisatelej, kompozitorov, hudozhnikov i uchenyh, hranyashchiesya v bibliotekah i muzeyah' (On the abolition of the right of private ownership of the archives of deceased Russian writers, composers, artists and scientists stored in libraries and museums). SU RSFSR. No 38 (1919).

41 Decree of the Council of People's Commissars of the RSFSR of October 10,1919. 'O prekrashchenii sily dogovorov na priobretenie v polnuyu sobstvennost' proizvedenij literatury i iskusstva' (On the termination of the force of contracts for the acquisition of full ownership of works of literature and art). *Izvestia of the All-Russian Central Executive Committee.* No 229 (1919).

42 Gavryushkin, Sergey, 'Intellektualnaya sobstvennost: lichnoe pravo i publichnyj interes' (Intellectual Property: Personal Law and Public Interest). *IP. Industrial Property* 10 (2019) 45–52.

43 Ragulina, Anastasia, Nikitova, Anna, 'Intellektualnaya sobstvennost: ponyatie, soderzhanie i zashchita' (Intellectual Property: Concept, Content, and Protection). (Moscow: Editorial office of Rossiyskaya Gazeta, 2017) 6–18.

course of the Soviet state.[44] It was a date that marked a new era in Soviet economic experiments with the introduction of the New Economic Policy (NEP) replacing the policy of 'war communism'. Legally, the NEP lasted until October 11, 1931, when a resolution was adopted to completely ban private trade in the USSR. The New Economic Policy was aimed at introducing private enterprise and reviving market relations, with the restoration of the national economy.

The situation in the country, which changed in connection with the adoption of the New Economic Policy (NEP), led to the fact that the regulation of (including intellectual property) by the rules adopted in the first post-revolutionary years could no longer satisfy the demands of the new political and economic course. With the introduction of the NEP, individual property relations were restored, civil circulation was allowed in the form of commodity-money relations. It is worth noting, however, that after the period of war communism, private law enforcement in Russia was technically still in operation, or at least in a limited form. For example, some property rights were settled, such as the right of operational management or the right of economic management.

The position of researchers (of law, economics, and history) is that private property, free trade, and several other elements characteristic of a market economy were revived during the NEP period. In the twentieth century, the institution of private property, as well a market economy, existed in three separate historical periods: before the October Revolution of 1917, during the NEP period (1921–1931), and perestroika in the USSR (since 1985).[45] The main postulates of the new economic policy were as follows: firstly, the recognition of the law of value and commodity-money relations, subject to the plan (change in taxation mechanisms, trade permit, restoration of the principle of payment according to work, cost accounting in enterprises, etc.). Secondly, to a certain extent recognition of the pluralism of property (delivery of concessions under the contract, state capitalism, leasing of land, private property). Thirdly, the admission of the use of hired force under the control of the state; and, fourthly, assigning entrepreneurial and commercial functions to the state.[46]

44 Chesnokov A., Merenkov D., Ershov B., 'Prichiny vvedeniya novoj ekonomicheskoj politiki (NEPa) v SSSR' (Reasons for the Introduction of the New Economic Policy (NEP) in the USSR). *Actual Problems of the Humanities and Natural Sciences* 1–3 (2017) 76–77.

45 Demichev, Alexey, 'Period nepa v rossijskoj istorii cherez prizmu hronodiskretnogo vladeniya' (The NEP Period in Russian History through the Prism of Chrono-Discrete Ownership). *Legal Science and Practice: Bulletin of the Nizhny Novgorod Academy of the Ministry of Internal Affairs of Russia* 3 (4/3) (2018) 63.

46 Rasskazov, Oleg, 'Razvitie grazhdanskogo zakonodatel'stva v period nepa' (Development of Civil Legislation During the NEP Period). *Philosophy of Law* 6 (2008) 74.

As a result, relative freedom of economic activity in comparison with the previous period of war communism (albeit still being controlled by the state) became one of the reasons that stimulated the development of inventions. This was also facilitated by other factors, such as the availability of education, the organization of access to information (for example, against the background of the creation of an open system of libraries), and active educational work. In addition, it should be noted that the transition from the capitalist to the socialist form of ownership with the diversification of objects and the accessibility of the means of production to a wider range of people also led to the expansion of creative opportunities.

Serious attention was paid to the development and registration of inventions. One of the characteristics of the inventive process was assumed to be its mass character, which was determined by its high value in accelerating scientific and technological progress. In 1924 some 1818 inventions were entered into the State Register, and during 1929–32 there were almost 19 393 inventions.[47]

Thus, the period of the NEP is characterized by the rejection of the use of the tools of the planned economy as the only true ones, there was freedom of economic activity, as well as a certain freedom of creativity, which in turn affect the publication activity and the formation of new rules for the functioning of small and medium-sized businesses.

5 Modernization and NEP: The Revival of Private Ownership of Intellectual Property

The foundations of legal principles laid down in the Decree of 1919, such as the criterion for the usefulness of an invention, as well as copyright helped set the stage for a revival of private ownership under the NEP – at least to a degree. The increased role of the state, which is largely considered[48] as the main characteristic of Soviet law, is especially clearly reflected in the formation of national priority and the protection of secret inventions. Article 2 of the Decree for instance noted that secret inventions, in addition to the implementation of the confidentiality regime, were limited in patenting abroad.[49]

---

47 Prokhorov, A.M., ed. *Great Soviet Encyclopedia, 1969–1986*, 3rd ed. (Moscow: State Scientific Publishing House, 1986).

48 Novoselova, Ludmila, *Intellectualnaya Sobstvennost. Patentnoye Pravo* (Intellectual Property Law. Patent Law Textbook, Volume 4). (Moscow: Statute Publishers, 2019) 25–50.

49 Decree of the Council of People's Commissars of the RSFSR of June 30, 1919 'Ob izobreteniyah (Polozhenie)' (On inventions (Regulations)). *SU RSFSR*. No. 34, (1919).

Article 5 noted that the rule of national priority established that inventions eligible for international interaction must be declared without fail on the territory of the Russian Republic, before in other countries (art.5).[50]

The resolutions of the Central Executive Committee of the USSR, the Council of People's Commissars of the USSR 'On patents for inventions'[51] and 'On industrial designs (drawings and models)'[52] of 1924 secured exclusive rights, including orders, as well as the right to transfer a patent by inheritance, however, these resolutions were canceled in 1932[53] and 1936[54] respectively with the adoption and entry into force of new provisions of the legislation.

The main regulatory act in the field of patent law during the development of the new economic policy was the Decree on patents for inventions,[55] put into effect by the Decree of the Central Executive Committee and the Council of People's Commissars of the USSR of September 12, 1924. The Decree on the Enactment of the Decree on Patents for Inventions fixed 'patents for inventions issued by non-Soviet bodies have no validity' but offered a simplified

50 Ibid. According to O.S.Joffe P.I. Stuchka, 'based on the class essence of any law, demanded a class assessment of the nature and purpose of Soviet civil law', as cited in Olympiad, Ioffe. *Razvitie civilisticheskoj mysli v SSSR* (The Development of Civil Thought in the USSR) (Part 1. Selected Works on Civil Law) (Moscow: Statute Publishers, 2000) 199; see also, Stuchka, Petr, *Kurs sovetskogo grazhdanskogo prava: Ucheb. posobie dlya vuzov i komvuzov* (The Course of Soviet Civil Law: Textbook for Universities and Colleges) (Moscow. Publishing House of the Communist Academy, 1927–1931). The Special Part of Civil Law (1931) 62 states: 'For a long time we resisted the introduction of these privileges, which are not characteristic of socialism. – But the privilege won. They didn't get into the Civil Code, but we have special laws, and as long as these rights are expanding, not narrowing'.

51 Decree of the Central Executive Committee of the USSR, SNK of the USSR of September 12, 1924. 'O vvedenii v dejstvie postanovleniya o patentah na izobretenie' (On the Enactment of the Decree on Patents for Inventions). *SZ of the USSR*. No 9 (1924).

52 Decree of the Central Executive Committee of the USSR, Council of People's Commissars of the USSR of September 12, 1924. 'O promyshlennyh obrazcah (risunkah i modelyah)' (On Industrial Designs (Drawings and Models)). *SZ USSR*. No 9 (1924).

53 Decree of the Council of People's Commissars of the USSR of March 28, 1932. 'Ob izmeneniyah v zakonodatel'stve Soyuza SSR v svyazi s izdaniem Polozheniya ot 9 aprelya 1931 g. ob izobreteniyah i tekhnicheskih usovershenstvovaniyah' (On Changes in the Legislation of the USSR in Connection with the Publication of the Regulation of April 9, 1931, on Inventions and Technical Improvements). *SZ of the USSR*. No 24 (1932).

54 Decree of the Central Executive Committee of the USSR, Council of People's Commissars of the USSR of May 27, 1936. 'Ob otmene Postanovleniya CIK i SNK Soyuza SSR ot 12 sentyabrya 1924 goda "O promyshlennyh obrazcah (risunkah i modelyah)"' (On the Abolition of the Decision of the Central Executive Committee and the Council of People's Commissars of the USSR of September 12, 1924 "On Industrial Designs (Drawings and Models)"). *SZ USSR*. No 29 (1936).

55 Novoselova, *Intellectualnaya Sobstvennost* (n 48).

procedure for obtaining a patent in such situations.[56] A provision of the Patent Decree reads:

> Persons who have lost the right to a patent issued by the pre-Soviet government, as well as persons who have made applications to the relevant institutions before the establishment of Soviet power in the given territory, are granted the right to apply for a patent in accordance with the Decree of the Central Executive Committee and the Council of People's Commissars of the SSR on patents for inventions.[57]

The situation in copyright reflected some traits of international protection. The Decree of the Central Executive Committee of the USSR, Council of People's Commissars of the USSR of January 30, 1925 'On the Fundamentals of Copyright',[58] Decree of the All-Russian Central Executive Committee, Council of People's Commissars of the RSFSR of October 11, 1926 'On Copyright',[59] as well as the Resolution of the Central Executive Committee and Council of People's Commissars of the USSR of May 16, 1928,[60] changed the previously established foundations of copyright, and the Decree of the All-Russian Central Executive Committee and the Council of People's Commissars of the RSFSR of October 8, 1928 'On Copyright'[61] began the process of restoring and further forming in the domestic legislation the system of copyright in particular and intellectual

56 Maksarev, Yuri, 'Izobretatel'stvo i racionalizaciya v narodnom hozyajstve SSSR' (Invention and Rationalization in the National Economy of the USSR). In *Great Soviet Encyclopedia* (Moscow: Soviet Encyclopedia Publishing House, 1972) 87–88, noting: 'the novelty of the relevant inventions is discussed in relation to the time of the initial application, provided if the latter was made after January 1, 1910'.

57 Decree of the Central Executive Committee of the USSR, SNK of the USSR of September 12, 1924. 'O vvedenii v dejstvie postanovleniya o patentah na izobretenie' (On the Enactment of the Decree on Patents for Inventions). *SZ of the USSR*. No 9 (1924).

58 Decree of the Central Executive Committee of the USSR, Council of People's Commissars of the USSR of January 30, 1925. 'Ob osnovah avtorskogo prava' (On the Fundamentals of Copyright). *SZ USSR*. No 7 (1925).

59 Decree of the All-Russian Central Executive Committee, Council of People's Commissars of the RSFSR of October 11, 1926. 'Ob avtorskom prave' (On Copyright). *SU RSFSR*. No 72 (1926).

60 Decree of the Central Executive Committee of the USSR, Council of People's Commissars of the USSR of May 16, 1928. 'O vvedenii v dejstvie osnov avtorskogo prava v novoj redakcii' (On the Enactment of the Fundamentals of Copyright in a New Edition). *SZ USSR*. No 27 (1928).

61 Decree of the All-Russian Central Executive Committee, Council of People's Commissars of the RSFSR of October 08, 1928. 'Ob avtorskom prave' (On Copyright). *SU RSFSR*. No 132 (1928).

property rights in general, actually establishing a basic regulation similar to the modern one (both in Russia and in Western legal orders).

Thus, the territorial principle of copyright was established, the author's right to a name, exclusive rights to publish a work or to its public performance, as well as the author's rights to receive remuneration (fee), reflected issues of co-authorship, the rights of editors of ancient works, etc.[62] being fixed in specialized acts such as: the Decree of the Central Executive Committee and the Council of People's Commissars of the USSR 'On the right to transmit by radio and wires the public performance of musical, dramatic and other works, as well as lectures and reports'[63] dated April 10, 1929; the Decree of the Central Executive Committee and the Council of People's Commissars of the USSR 'On the rights customers on architectural, engineering and other technical plans, drawings and drawings made to their orders'[64] dated November 23, 1930.

The legal essence of the listed acts reflected a return to the origins of intellectual property regulation. The rejection of its private law nature and the possibility of being an object of personal property, the violation of the observance of the rights of authors and other nihilistic postulates of the first stage of Soviet reformism showed their ineffectiveness. As a result, there was a need to form clear criteria for the existence of such objects.

In Soviet legislation, the rules for conducting a formal examination and examination on the merits of patents began to take shape. It is assumed that industrial applicability was assessed as a substantive examination. However, industrial applicability was considered already at the stage of formal examination.

Furthermore, the main condition for the patentability of an invention was its novelty.[65] It is worth paying attention to the fact that this criterion is of the most vivid significance for understanding the relationship of Soviet regulation

62 Kubyshko, 'Razvitie zakonodatel'stva' (n 25).

63 Decree of the Central Executive Committee and Council of People's Commissars of the USSR of April 10, 1929. 'O prave peredachi po radio i provodam publichnogo ispolneniya muzykal'nyh, dramaticheskih i drugih proizvedenij, a ravno lekcij i dokladov' (On the Right to Transmit Public Performances of Musical, Dramatic and Other Works, as well as Lectures and Reports by Radio and Wires). *SZ USSR*. No 26 (1929).

64 Decree of the Central Executive Committee and Council of People's Commissars of the USSR of November 23, 1930. 'O pravah zakazchikov na izgotovlennye po ih zakazam arhitekturnye, inzhenernye i inye tekhnicheskie plany, chertezhi i risunki' (On the rights of Customers to Architectural, Engineering, and other Technical Plans, Drawings and Drawings Made to their Orders). *SZ USSR*. No 58 (1930).

65 Kantorovich, Jacov, *Osnovnye idei grazhdanskogo prava* (Basic Ideas of Civil Law) (Kharkov: Juridical Publishing House of the NKJU of the Ukrainian SSR, 1928) 224–225.

to foreign law: 'An invention is not recognized as new if at the time of the application it was within the USSR or abroad, completely or in significant parts described in a printed work or applied so openly that it could be reproduced by a knowledgeable person'.

Foreign registration was not an unconditional preclusive criterion for determining novelty (and, consequently, the patentability of an invention), but was considered when determining registration:

> When examining the novelty of an invention, the examination is based mainly on general technical literature and previous privileges and patent applications. Foreign patent literature is accepted only to the extent possible. <…> Third parties may object to the grant of a patent or challenge the validity of a granted patent, based also on the fact that the invention is known in whole or in part from published foreign patents.[66]

Thus, it is worth noting that the examination was supposed to be carried out not on a formal basis, but rather on the fact of the use of similar objects, that is, it was presumed that in order to be protected as a patent by the Soviet law, an object must be absolutely unique, have no analogues. Which, however, is rather difficult to track since patent protection is usually based on the observance of a formal registration criterion. Accordingly, it can be assumed that the norm was largely declarative in nature.

In addition, many researchers, in particular Graham,[67] spoke about the special mindset of Soviet (and Russian) inventors who were not interested in commercializing the results of their own work, as a result of which some of the objects remained unpatented.

Since during the time of the NEP, the legislator drew attention to the economic component of relations in the field of intellectual property, the reflection of the relevant provisions in the Fundamentals of Copyright of the USSR in 1925, 1928, and the normative legal acts of the RSFSR developed on their basis, made it possible to restore some copyright protection in comparison with the period of war communism. This trend was also reflected in the criminal legislation of the RSFSR. The Criminal Code of the RSFSR of 1926 contained provisions providing for criminal liability for copyright infringement. Interestingly, in contrast to Art. 101 of the Criminal Code of the RSFSR of 1922, located in the chapter 'State crimes', art. 177 of the Criminal Code of the RSFSR

66 Pilenko, Alexandr. *Pravo Izobretatelya* (Inventor's Right) (Moscow: Statute Publishing, 2001) 230.

67 Graham, 'The Legal System' (n 38).

of 1926 was also in the chapter 'Property Crimes'. Such a change in the generic object of copyright crimes indicated a change in the position of the state regarding crimes of this category.[68] Thus, we see a change in the category of protection from crimes that undermine the state system, from crimes against private property of such subjects as citizens and organizations (a partial return to which the implementation of the NEP policy indicates). Furthermore, quite close attention was paid to the protection of the authors' rights: the criminalization of the act as such showed its significance for the country's economy and the state's focus on protecting relations in this area of the economy.

There is an opinion that the 'unusual provisions' of the Soviet legislation, in particular on inventions, gave rise to the idea among Western observers that, at some points, such a system was 'fairer' than Western patenting, which often was on the side of companies, not their employees.[69]

Also, one of the important aspects of the development of intellectual property legislation during this period was the inclusion of the institution of a compulsory license. In the case of a planned economy and public property, such an element could not appear since the right of individuals to the means of production was limited. Nevertheless, a compulsory license as a tool that appeared during the NEP period showed its effectiveness at such a level that it migrated to the modern Russian legislation.

Initially, the logic was to form the obligation of the copyright holder to start using the object on their own or to issue a license for such use. Moreover, short periods were set during which the patent owner must start using the object, or he was deprived of legal protection. Based on the corresponding idea, regulation arose when, under the same circumstances, but already subject to the presence of public interest, a requirement arose to issue 'permission to exploit the invention against the will of the inventor and determine the reward at one's own discretion'.[70]

Some researchers[71] notice differentiated approach of the Decree on Patents of 1924 to solving this problem. For instance, it has been noted that, firstly, the patent holder was deprived of a patent, but only by a court order, and only if it was proved that the failure to implement the invention was intentional.[72] Secondly, if there was no intent, then any interested institution or person has the right to file a petition for the issuance of a compulsory license.[73] Thus,

68 Aliyev, 'Evolyuciya' (n 18).

69 Graham, 'The Legal System' (n 38).

70 Kantorovich, *Osnovnye idei* (n 65) 236.

71 Novoselova, *Intellectualnaya Sobstvennost* (n 48) 25–35.

72 Ibid.

73 Ibid.

it was established in law that compulsory licensing was possible in areas of national defense or of particular importance to the country.[74]

Thus, the tool of compulsory patent, which was very far from the planned economy, has become one of the elements of market regulation, perceived in the framework of the NEP.

Thus, unlike the policy of war communism, which characterized the first period of the formation of Soviet intellectual property legislation, the NEP period significantly changed the approach to the results of intellectual activity, bringing it closer to private law methods. The NEP policy was largely characterized by the weakening of the influence of the state and the planned economy, which led to the need to change the legal methods of interaction. At the same time, the principle of paternalism and the protection of the national system continued to be the main direction of state policy. The intellectual property legislation of the early 20th century is characterized by the introduction of a royalty rate, copyright limits when creating service works.[75]

6 Balancing Public Property and International IP Norms

Turning to international regulation applicable in the young Soviet state, it is worth noting that Russia was not a party to international conventions concerning Intellectual Property until 1952 when the USSR became a member of the Universal Copyright Convention. Also, in 1965 when USSR joined the Paris Convention for the Protection of Industrial Property, and in 1968 it ratified the Stockholm revision of the Paris Convention and announced its participation in the creation of the World Intellectual Property Organization (WIPO). Only in the post-Soviet era did Russia joined to the Berne Convention in 1994. But this does not mean that there was no legal protection on national and international levels during the interwar period.

The regime corresponding to the rules of the Berne Treaty was confirmed in bilateral international treaties, in particular, the Soviet-German Treaty "On the Protection of Industrial Property" of October 12, 1925 which established

74 Resolution of the Central Executive Committee and Council of People's Commissars of the USSR of September 12, 1924 'O vvedenii v dejstvie Postanovleniya o patentah na izobretenie' (On the Enactment of the Decree on Patents for Invention). *Collected Legislation of the USSR* 9 (1924) Art. 97.

75 Salitskaya, Elena, 'Razvitie otechestvennogo zakonodatelstva v oblasti avtorskogo prava: istoricheskij aspect' (Development of Domestic Legislation in the Field of Copyright: a Historical Aspect). *Nauka. Innovation. Education* no 16 (2014) 265–274.

an appropriate regime with respect to the implementation of German IP legislation.[76]

Within the context of the broader international developments of the era, then the legal regulation of intellectual property protection in the Soviet state in the first years should be seen in that context. Being an active participant in political life in the early 20th century, the Soviet State, as the legal successor of the Russian Empire, largely retained external obligations that existed in the sphere of economic relations. Formally, the legislation of the Russian Empire, including intellectual property law, was not repealed where it did not contradict revolutionary ideals. The early Soviet period in general can be regarded largely as a social experiment based on idealistic ideas about the future and allowing for the possibility of using various methods to achieve the set goal. One of these methods was the promotion of active scientific development and industrialization.

Despite the presence of interstate armed conflicts, the academic community continued to develop far beyond the military-industrial complex, which required the enforcement of international principles of law, enshrined in relevant regulations. Although the Soviet state was not a party to international conventions and ratified them much later, it was still necessary to comply with the mechanisms for recognizing and protecting the results of intellectual activity to form a unified system of interaction.

In the Russian Empire, trademarks of enterprises located in another country could be registered in Russia only if there was an agreement with that country that included a condition on the mutual protection of trademarks. From the point of view of international legal regulation, the international treaties of the Russian Empire (with Germany, France, Austria-Hungary, etc.) were short-term and expired at the start of the First World War. The Soviet Union, on the other hand, did not initially commit itself to extending the pre-existing agreements and, in fact, had no international legal obligations in the field of copyright right after the October Revolution.[77]

---

76 Mamlyuk, *Russia & Legal Harmonization* (n 1).

77 See Fedin, Alexandr, 'TAMIZDAT. Poblemy interpretacii' (TAMIZDAT. The Problem of Interpretation). *Modern Studies of Social Problems* 3-1 (2018) 42–45: An interesting phenomenon that has arisen in the field of Russian copyright in terms of its international recognition is the so-called 'tamizdat' ('there published'), which means that the lack of authors' rights protection and recognition of IP rights led to attempts to publish the works in countries that were members of IP Conventions. For instance, Boris Pasternak's *novel Doctor Zhivago*; *The Gulag Archipelago* by Alexander Solzhenitsyn, and poems by Joseph Brodsky were published in this way.

Although for the most part the development of the sphere of intellectual property regulation in Soviet Russia belongs to a later period, the issues of mutual recognition of foreign right holders arose already at the very beginning of the formation of the new state. In some cases, Soviet works were protected without international treaties. The most striking example was the case of Shostakovich v. 20th Century Fox,[78] although it took place somewhat later than the period under consideration.[79] The resulting denial of the right to defense in a New York state court, however, was perceived differently by the French court,[80] due to the different perception of the moral rights of the authors[81].

The essence of the case was to protect the moral rights of the author. The works had become public domain at that time; however, they were used without the consent of the author in a film about the activities of Soviet spies, which, according to the author, negatively affected his good name. Despite the absence of signed agreements, the French and American legal system, however, assessed the author's arguments and the actual violation of his rights.

An important role in shaping the participation of the Soviet state in the world economy, including in the field of intellectual property, was played by the recognition of its statehood by foreign countries. The Anglo-Soviet agreement was the first stage in the resumption of relations with USSR. On May 6, 1921, a temporary Soviet-German agreement was concluded, which recognized the representation of the RSFSR as the legal successor of the Russian Empire in Germany and granted it diplomatic rights and privileges. On December 26, the Italian government approved a preliminary agreement; on September 2, a Soviet-Norwegian trade agreement was concluded, resuming relations between the two countries.[82]

At the same time, no international treaties in the field of intellectual property were signed, and as mentioned earlier, Soviet Russia did not become a

78 Corp., 80 N.Y.S.2d 575 (N.Y. Sup. Ct. 1948), aff'd, 87 N.Y.S.2d 430 (N.Y. App. Div. 1949).

79 Standler, Ronald, 'Moral Rights of Authors in the USA'. http://www.rbs2.com/moral.pdf, but see, Roeder, Martin, 'The Doctrine of Moral Right: A Study in the Law of Artists, Authors and Creators'. *Harvard Law Review* 53 (1940) 554.

80 But see, Society Le Chant du Monde v. Society Fox Europe et Society Foc Americaine Twentieth Century, 1 Gazette du Palais 191, Jan. 13, 1953.

81 Gigante, Alexander, 'Ice Patch on the Information Superhighway: Foreign Liability for Domestically Created Content'. *Cardozo Arts and Entertainment Law Journal* 14(3) (1995) 523—562.

82 Grishin, Alexandr, 'Problema zaklyucheniya sovetsko-anglijskogo torgovogo soglasheniya 1921 goda v rabotah anglo-amerikanskih avtorov perioda "Holodnoj vojny"' (The Problem of Concluding the Soviet-English Trade Agreement of 1921 in the Works of Anglo-American Authors of the Cold War period). *Political Linguistics* 3 (2014) 183–184.

party to international agreements and conventions in the early years. However, it should not be said that the absence of signed agreements were necessarily obstacles in the protection of broadly intellectual property rights during the early Soviet state of the 1920s especially in relation to authors' rights.

One of the significant factors in the policy of the Soviet state was the development of the idea of a world proletarian revolution, which involves cooperation, including from a scientific point of view, with the countries of the sociological camp. Such interaction was unthinkable without the exchange of technologies, patents, etc. In addition, educational institutions and joint scientific centers were organized, allowing joint development based on the highest favor. A feature of Soviet development was the close connection between the creation of intellectual property objects, the transfer of technologies to other countries and material production, as well as the conclusion of trade contracts: when determining suppliers, priority was given to countries in whose scientific and industrial complex investments had previously been made.[83]

Nevertheless, Soviet Russia needed to maintain further international contacts, as evidenced by several agreements, including those establishing the most favored nation regimes. One of the most significant agreements was the Treaty of Rapallo with Germany on the restoration of normal trade relations. Mixed Russian-German joint-stock companies for foreign trade and transport were established at the same time. Germany was interested in military-technical and economic cooperation, unlike other European powers, because 'none of the Western European countries had such experience in relation to working with Russia and such a deep and accurate knowledge of all the conditions of our country as Germany'.[84] The interest of the Soviet side was not only in financial mutual assistance, attracting foreign capital, but also in modern technology and qualified specialists; accordingly, a lot of efforts were made to attract Germany cooperation.[85]

Thus, the agreement established that public and private legal relations would be settled based on reciprocity, for the general settlement of mutual trade and economic relations, and the most favored nation principle. The

---

83 Jacobson, Georgiy, 'Hronika vneshneeconomicheskich svyazei SSSR' (Chronicle of Foreign Economic Relations of the USSR)'. Prokhorov, A.M., ed. *Great Soviet Encyclopedia, 1969–1986,* 3rd ed. (Moscow: State Scientific Publishing House, 1986) 259–264.

84 Krasin, Leonid. *Voprosi vneshnei torgovli* (Questions of Foreign Trade). (Moscow: State Scientific Publishing House, 1928) 305.

85 Erokhina, Olga, 'Koncessii kak forma ekonomicheskogo sotrudnichestva SSSR i Germanii v 20-e gody HKH veka' (Concessions as a Form of Economic Cooperation Between the USSR and Germany in the 20s of the XX century). *Bulletin of VolGU. Series 4, History. Regional studies. International Relationships* 2 (2011) 47.

significance of the agreement is quite high since Russia and Germany were in many respects in partnership and the restoration of normal economic relations played a significant role in reducing the general tension in the post-war period. Germany became a significant (economic) ally after the Russian economy shrank during the Civil War, and because of negotiations in 1921–1922 the development of relations between the two states in various fields proceeded very intensively until 1933.[86]

The politics of the Rapallo treaty is considered by researchers to be the first experience of establishing mutually beneficial relations between states with different social systems: socialist and capitalist. For the USSR, Rapallo was a way out of diplomatic isolation, an opportunity to use the economic potential of Weimar Germany for the industrialization of the country. For Germany, it was also a way of gaining economic benefits from economic cooperation with the USSR.

The countries found themselves in a state of certain isolation from the rest of Europe in connection with the revolutionary events that had taken place and the negative attitudes towards the Versailles settlement. The latter influenced the commonality of interests and further affected the building of mutual assistance relations. But Russo-German relations flourished in all aspects of life covering the political, economic, scientific, and technical cooperation of the two countries, without any desire for armed conflict. And despite the absence of agreements directly regulating IP, the regime established based on diplomatic contacts promoted the mutual recognition of patents and industrial property, as well as joint development.

In later years, additional Soviet cooperation treaties with Germany, for example, the German-Soviet trade agreement of 1925, section 7, provided for the introduction of a national principle of protection for citizens and organizations of the contracting states, mutual recognition of trademarks, priority of initial applications (including those filed before 1914) for trademarks and patents, and also established intention to further develop copyright regulation[87].

But Soviet cooperation went beyond Germany and despite being unrecognized by the United States in the early years, the Soviets cooperated with

86 Khavkin, Boris. *Rossia I Germania. 1900–1945. Spletenie istorii* (Russia and Germany. 1900–1945. Weaving History) (Moscow: New Chronograph, 2014) 80–85.

87 Treaty between the Union of Soviet Socialist Republics and Germany of October 12, 1925. *Collection of Laws and Orders of the Workers' and Peasants' Government of the USSR* No. 28 of April 29. (1926) URL: http://docs.historyrussia.org/ru/nodes/138572-dogovor-mezhdu-soyuzom-sovetskih-sotsialisticheskih-respublik-i-germaniey-ot-12-oktyabrya-1925-g#mode/inspect/page/33/zoom/4.

other nations such as the United Kingdom. This even if the ideologies of the young state were at odds with the external capitalist world. The first contacts between scientists from England and Soviet Russia were established in 1920 after G. Wells visited Moscow and began the exchange of scientific papers on the initiative of M. Gorky. In 1922, the Secretary of the Russian Academy of Sciences, S.F. Odelburg reached agreements on the organization of a regular exchange of scientific papers of the Russian Academy of Sciences and scientific institutions in England. Thus, from the point of view of communication, the trip of the Soviet delegation to Cambridge was of great importance, where it was possible to get acquainted with the work of some physical and physiological laboratories, as well as to establish contacts with several prominent British scientists, such as E. Rutherford, J. Thomson, F. Aston, A. Eddington, M. Dobb, P. Blackett, and others.[88]

During the period under review, contacts in the field of agricultural sciences also became regular in the 1920s. The activities of the Soviet scientist N.I. Vavilov, who was in active correspondence with British biologists and representatives of agricultural science helped with the exchange of necessary information. Publications and monographs of Soviet botanists were regularly sent to England in exchange for similar English editions and abstracts of the latest literature published in Great Britain and its dominions.[89]

Soviet scientists paid serious attention to the problems of the uniqueness of texts, as well as respect for the rights of foreign authors. Despite the absence of national regulation, the format of relations within the framework of scientific activity remained unchanged in comparison with the pre-revolutionary period. In the first half of the 1930s, the exchange was most actively carried out in the field of physics and chemistry and in 1933, Anglo-Soviet scientific cooperation culminated in the First All-Union Conference on the Atomic Nucleus at the Leningrad Institute of Physics and Technology.[90]

There was also an intensive exchange in the field of astrophysics. For example, the Pulkovo Observatory sent scientific literature on a reciprocal basis to observatories in Greenwich, Cambridge, Oxford, Edinburgh, Liverpool, Glasgow, the Philosophical Society in Cambridge, the Royal Astronomical Society in London and Edinburgh, the Astronomical Society in London, etc.[91]

---

88 Zhilinskaya, Irina 'Nauchnie svyazi USSR i Velikobritanii v 1931–1939' (Scientific Relations of the USSR and Great Britain in 1931–1939). *Journal of the National Academy of Sciences of Belarus. Humanitarian sciences* 3 (2011) 80–90.

89 Zhilinskaya, 'Nauchnie svyazi USSR' (n 88).

90 Ibid.

91 Ibid.

Thus, albeit in the absence of signed agreements, the tacit recognition by the union of the rights and legitimate interests of copyright holders ensured the possibility of a safe exchange of products of intellectual activity. In addition, it can be assumed that in the scientific community there was a fairly high level of awareness and assessment of reputational risks, which also helps to ensure compliance with the requirements of non-violation of others' rights.

Along with the relations with Germany or Great Britain Soviet Russia made many attempts to integrate into the world system. At the same time, a significant factor was the actual recognition and protection of intellectual property, as well as the conclusion by the Union of contracts and commercial agreements with the countries of the socialist and capitalist camps. The active participation of representatives of the Soviet state reflects not only the interest of the young state to take part in the development of the scientific environment, but also the readiness of the world community to accept Soviet Russia as an active participant in the development of science and technology.

Chronologically, some of the intellectual property norms in the young Soviet state and attempts to integrate in the world economy concerned participation in industrial and science-intensive partnerships.[92]

In 1918 the first barter deal with a Swedish company for the purchase of agricultural machinery happened. An agreement was signed with Denmark for the supply of garden seeds to Russia. A representative office was established in Sweden for the purchase of goods in Scandinavian countries.

In 1919 a society for Technical Aid (Obschestvo technicheskoy pomoschi) to Soviet Russia has been set up in New York. The Society to Soviet Russia included Russian workers and peasants who emigrated before the revolution, as well as left-wing American proletarians. The society sent working groups that provided technical assistance, as well as shared objects of intellectual property, brought equipment and seeds for reproduction on the territory of the new state.

In 1920 the economic blockade of Soviet Russia was over. The Soviet joint-stock company Arcos was created in London to trade with Great Britain. Trade missions of the RSFSR were established in Great Britain, Sweden, Germany, Austria, Turkey, Iran, and other countries. Agreements with an association of Swedish firms were signed (mainly in the metalworking industry) on the purchase of goods worth 100 million crowns.

In 1925 Pekinskaya konvenciya ob osnovnyh principah vzaimootnoshenij s Yaponiej (The Convention embodying basic rules of the relations between the

92 Jacobson, 'Hronika' (n 83) 259–264.

Union of Soviet Socialist Republics and Japan) was signed. Countries established conditions of reciprocity within the framework of the right of private property, freedom to engage in trade, navigation, crafts, and other peaceful pursuits. They also prescribed the legal basis for concluding concession agreements. Also trade agreements were concluded with Germany and Norway and concession agreements for the development of the Chiatura manganese deposits (with the USA) and for the extraction of gold and other minerals (with Great Britain).

In 1928 an intellectual property rights bilateral treaty was signed with Norway (on the mutual protection of industrial property rights).[93] *The Soviet-Russo bilateral intellectual property treaty established the mutual recognition of intellectual property rights, the provision of national treatment, the 6-month priority principle.* Moreover, the USSR participated in international fairs and exhibitions in Cologne, Berlin, Marseille, Paris, and Prague.

In 1929 an agreement with the American firm 'Ford' on technical assistance in the production of automobiles in the USSR was signed. The project provided for the exchange of experience, the sending of specialists from Soviet Russia for training in production in the United States, as well as the exchange of technical and engineering information. The USSR participated in international fairs and exhibitions in Leipzig, Frankfurt am Main, Ankara, Paris, Lyon, and Prague.

In 1930 France introduced a licensing system for the import of Soviet goods (abolished in 1931). The USSR participated in international fairs and exhibitions in Leipzig, Dresden, Bordeaux Thessaloniki, Milan, Tel Aviv, Paris, Lyon, Leipzig, Milan, Paris, Lyon, Stockholm, and Izmir, etc.

These chronological developments paints some of the young state as an active player in the high-tech market and industrial development in this period. In addition, the active cooperation of states (including the capitalist camp) indicates the ability of the Soviet state to ensure the observance of rights and legitimate interests, including in the field of intellectual property, as well as to act as a party to long-term contracts and confirm the possibility of their execution.

Significant is the fact that the conclusion of the first agreements dates to 1918, when in fact there was not even recognition of a sovereign emerging state. Each of the industrial agreements on the list could not exist if the councils

---

93 Konvenciya mezhdu Soyuzom Sovetskih Socialisticheskih Respublik i Norvegiej otnositel'no vzaimnoj ohrany prav na promyshlennuyu sobstvennost (Convention between the Union of Soviet Socialist Republics and Norway Concerning the Mutual Protection of Industrial Property Rights). Moscow, February 24, 1928. Published in S. 3 for 1928. Dep. II No. 62 Art. 252.

violated the requirements for the protection of intellectual property. Moreover, commercial agreements related, in particular, to the transfer of technologies, and since the agreements were concluded on a voluntary basis, the thesis about the lack of legal recognition and protection in the Soviet state seems doubtful. The transfer of methods and methods for manufacturing products or implementing technological processes was transferred not only at the state level (and interstate agreements), but also by private companies, which clearly characterizes the presence of a commercial interest in cooperation with Soviet Russia.

Given the difficult military-political situation, the participation of the Union in industrial exhibitions and representation in joint ventures with Western countries also seems to be a positive factor. The right of intellectual property, although not fixed by the ratification of international agreements, was nevertheless respected and, presumably, was the basis of long-term relationships and cooperation.

Summing up, it is worth noting the following. The absence of a legal basis for the regulation of intellectual property legislation in post-revolutionary Russia is largely exaggerated. There was no formal recognition of previously existing laws as invalid, despite the absence of signed agreements, there was a 'silent' recognition of international principles for the protection of intellectual property rights.

The transition to a new social system, however, could not be carried out on the same principles that existed before, in connection with which a significant revision was made of the rules governing the rights and obligations of various categories of persons related to intellectual property. Proof of the viability of the Soviet system and the absence of its conflict with the rules recognized by the world communities, enshrined in the relevant concepts, may be the fact of active interaction between individual scientists, commercial structures, and states in the format of partnership in conducting research, participating in joint projects, and creating industrial facilities.

The entry of Soviet Russia into international agreements was delayed due to a few factors: recognition of the new state, awareness of its future policy, concern of the allied (and not only) states about its future behavior in the international arena, as well as significant differences in the applicable legal and economic systems. Nevertheless, the parties made significant efforts to ensure the possibility of peaceful development and interaction. The implementation by Soviet Russia of the basic principles of intellectual property rights, respect for scientific activity and ensuring the effective exchange of ideas and developments in various fields of science and industry characterizes the established sustainable direction of state policy in the field of protection of exclusive rights, as well as the personal non-property rights of authors.

Intellectual property right thus represents a peaceful instrument of legal and political interaction: even in a situation of economic blockade and formal non-recognition of a new state formation, intellectual activity and its protection remained one of the effective ways of interstate dialogue and largely prevented the rupture of any type of ties interrupted by hostilities, as well as revolutionary events in Russia at the beginning of the 20th century.

7 Public Property and IP Discontents

Soviet legislation knew periods of private and public ownership of the means of production, including intellectual property. Moreover, even the application of private law regulation required the introduction of controlling and restrictive elements (for example, compulsory licensing). While the correlation of IP with private property raises only few questions, since it is quite easily correlated with the principles of modern legislation, the interaction between public property rules and the rights of authors (in particular, in the context of exclusive rights) is a matter worthy of discussion.

The perception of the concept of intellectual property is usually carried out through the prism of the criterion of creativity, which implies the existence of certain rights and freedoms of the creator. It must be said that the socialist system was not aimed at the development of individualism. If we talk about the usual balance of private and public interests in intellectual rights, at first glance it seems that the Soviet legislator decided to shift the focus of attention to the public interest.

Such an approach, which essentially establishes the state's monopoly on decision-making regarding intellectual property, cannot but cause discussions on several issues.

In addition to the restrictions related to the financial issue, the previously mentioned Decree 'On the recognition of scientific, literary, musical and artistic works as state property' of November 26, 1918, according to the decision of the People's Commissariat of Education, was recognized as public property. This meant the actual abolition of copyright protection for both published and unpublished works. Also, even if the author did not intend to publish (for example, personal notes, diaries, correspondence, etc.) could now be published not only with the consent of relatives, as it was earlier, but also with the permission of the People's Commissariat of Education without taking into account the desire of the heirs[94] The fact of a monopoly is evidenced by the very text of the document, the final article of which states that for the unauthorized publication, distribution and public performance of works, liability is threatened 'as for violation of the state monopoly'. Moreover, the heirs were deprived of the opportunity to influence the process of the publication.

Formally, it cannot be said that ownership of intellectual property objects was abolished – it was emphasized that, like other means of production, the circulation of information fell into the zone of state control and management. The purpose of the state monopoly, based on the analysis of sources, was to carry out the policy of communism (that is, the ideological struggle against the residual institutions of the bourgeois economic system, in particular with private property), the formation of a different system of perceiving goods as an asset accessible to the people (the general public), which is true not only for tangible objects, but also for intangible assets. Intellectual property objects were thus supposed to be used in two directions: the general cultural development of society, as well as movement towards scientific progress.

The institution of private property could not be used to achieve these goals for different reasons. For instance, because of the ideological rejection of the mechanisms of a market economy, and due to the need to organize a counter economic system, streamline commercial interaction, etc., which largely limited the state's capabilities in operational regulation.

The state, in fact, carried out a nationalization procedure (somewhere with compensation, somewhere without it), the result of which was the declaration of public ownership of IP objects in the initial period. The centralized management of intangible assets made it possible to widely use developments to increase the volume of industry, transfer objects for development in parallel to several research institutes, production organizations, etc. At the same time, such an approach could affect the decrease in the motivation of inventors, which was compensated by other methods of indirect influence: from educational and ideological work to the provision of material benefits for conscientious work.

The public ownership of intellectual property objects in the Soviet interpretation, in fact, did not represent a complete rejection of remuneration for authored work, but revised the rules for its payment, in fact equating the creative component with other professional activities. In addition, since the idea

---

94 Pankeev, Ivan, 'Rossijskoe avtorskoe pravo HKH veka v normativnyh aktah' (Russian Copyright of the XX Century in Regulatory Acts) *Bulletin of Moscow University. Journalism* 3 (2011) 30–33.

of 'unearned' income was unthinkable in a socialist state, inheritance rights were limited.

Drawing analogies with the legislation of a later period, the most obvious example is compulsory licensing, which has survived to meet the needs of public safety, state protection, etc. That is, in fact, the attitude to intellectual property as to public property pursues, circa four goals. The first being, a reduction of the term for the transition of a work into the public domain. Secondly, the acceleration of terms of its practical implementation, thirdly, a different procedure for compensating the work of authors; and fourthly, the abolition of private ownership of the means of production.

The situation changed with the adoption of the new economic policy, which returned the tools of private law regulation, more familiar to the institution of intellectual property. At the same time, the NEP period, although associated with significant relaxations, still established state control over copyright objects, both in terms of censorship and the right of the state to remain the monopoly owner of translations, as well as to carry out the forced purchase of copyright.

8 Conclusion

The initial period of the existence of the Soviet state can be generally characterized as experimental. The young state, being an ideological opponent of the old foundations, selected an adequate format of functioning for itself and the corresponding legal and economic regimes.

The first stage is total nihilism and the rejection of established rules as remnants of the past world order that do not correspond to the values of the new society.

The main principle of the renewed economy was the rejection of private ownership of the means of production in favor of public ownership, that was state controlled. The ideas sent by the Soviet authorities were the ideology of maximum accessibility of benefits for the population, including those benefits (economic and spiritual) that were provided through access to intellectual property.

On the one hand, such a refusal made it possible to make a more active leap in terms of industrial development, since there was no concentration of means of production (as well as patents, copyrights for other objects, etc.). The planned economy, which was formed in a later period, relied on similar principles, softening them, and adapting to civilian life comparing to the first period of the breakdown of the existing system was called war communism.

On the other hand, the sharp restriction of rights turned out to be too aggressive, which led to the need to introduce indulgences for a certain period (NEP), and in the future to consider the mistakes of the first experience.

In terms of the development of intellectual property legislation, the Soviet state followed the general economic policy: the rights were also perceived as subject to transfer to a wider range of persons, the rejection of unearned income was declared, and the procedures for using objects that were previously subject to protection were simplified by canceling the rights to them or reducing the terms exclusive use.

The change in economic policy during the NEP period gave impetus to the formation of a new tool – compulsory licensing, which is still used in Russian legislation and allows balancing private and public interests, as well as meeting the needs of the state.

The problem of removing the pre-existing normative regulation was largely that the adoption of a new legislative framework was postponed, thereby creating a legal vacuum both at the national and supranational levels.

In terms of international politics and the participation of the Soviet state in international conventions and treaties, the young state did not ratify, although it adhered to the fundamental principles of protecting and respecting the interests of other states. Despite the lack of participation in international organizations, a sharp change in political course and the abolition of the previously existing national regulation of the rules of circulation and protection of exclusive rights, the Soviet state actively participated in international scientific and technical activities, educational and research activities, which was associated, among other things, with high assessment of the work of Russian and Soviet specialists in the international market, as well as respect for the boundaries of international law and national foreign regulation.

Bibliography

Agarkov, Michail. *Obyazatelstvo po Sovetskomy grazhdanskomy pravu* (Obligation Under Soviet Civil Law) (Moscow: Judicial Publishing House NKJU USSR, 1940).

Aliyev, Samir 'Evolyuciya rossijskogo zakonodatelstva reglamentiruyushchego otnosheniya v sfere intellektualnoj sobstvennosti' (Evolution of the Russian Legislation Regulating Relations in the Sphere of Intellectual Property). *Gaps in the Russian Legislation* 3 (2013) 91.

Chesnokov A., Merenkov D., Ershov B., 'Prichiny vvedeniya novoj ekonomicheskoj politiki (NEPa) v SSSR' (Reasons for the Introduction of the New Economic Policy (NEP) in the USSR). *Actual Problems of the Humanities and Natural Sciences* 1–3 (2017) 76.

Demichev, Alexey, 'Period nepa v rossijskoj istorii cherez prizmu hronodiskretnogo vladeniya' (The NEP Period in Russian History through the Prism of Chrono-Discrete Ownership). *Legal Science and Practice: Bulletin of the Nizhny Novgorod Academy of the Ministry of Internal Affairs of Russia* 3 (4/3) (2018) 63.

Eremenko, Vladimir, 'Retrospektivnyj analiz rossijskogo zakonodatelstva ob izobreteniyah' (Retrospective Analysis of Russian Legislation on Inventions). *IP. Industrial Property* 4 (2019) 43.

Erokhina, Olga, 'Koncessii kak forma ekonomicheskogo sotrudnichestva SSSR i Germanii v 20-e gody HKH veka' (Concessions as a Form of Economic Cooperation Between the USSR and Germany in the 20s of the XX century). *Bulletin of VolGU. Series 4, History. Regional studies. International Relationships* 2 (2011) 47.

Eugster, Esprit, 'Evolution and Enforcement of Intellectual Property Law in Russia'. *Washington University Global Studies Law Review* 9(1) (2010) 131–151.

Fedin, Alexandr, 'TAMIZDAT. Poblemy interpretacii' (TAMIZDAT. The Problem of Interpretation). *Modern Studies of Social Problems* 3-1 (2018) 42.

Gavryushkin, Sergey, 'Intellektualnaya sobstvennost: lichnoe pravo i publichnyj interes' (Intellectual property: Personal Law and Public Interest). *IP. Industrial Property* 10 (2019) 45.

Genkin, Dmitry, et al. *Istoriya sovetskogo prava in 1917–1947* (History of Soviet Law 1917–1947) (Moscow: Gosjurizdat, 1949) 73.

Gigante, Alexander, 'Ice Patch on the Information Superhighway: Foreign Liability for Domestically Created Content'. *Cardozo Arts and Entertainment Law Journal* 14(3) (1995) 523.

Graham, Loren, 'The Legal System'. In *Lonely Ideas: Can Russia Compete?* (Cambridge: The MIT Press, 2013) 119.

Great Soviet Encyclopedia. 2nd ed. edn. Vol 25. Vvedensky, B.A., ed. (Moscow: State Scientific Publishing House, 1954) 303.

Great Soviet Encyclopedia, 1969–1986, 3rd edn. Prokhorov, A.M., ed. (Moscow: State Scientific Publishing House, 1986) 259.

Grishin, Alexandr, 'Problema zaklyucheniya sovetsko-anglijskogo torgovogo soglasheniya 1921 goda v rabotah anglo-amerikanskih avtorov perioda "Holodnoj vojny"' (The Problem of Concluding the Soviet-English Trade Agreement of 1921 in the Works of Anglo-American Authors of the Cold War period). *Political Linguistics* 3 (2014) 183.

Olympiad, Ioffe. *Izbrannye trudy po grazhdanskomu pravu: Iz istorii civilisticheskoj mysli. Grazhdanskoe pravootnoshenie. Kritika teorii "hozyajstvennogo prava"* (Selected Works on Civil Law: From the History of Civil Thought. Civil Law. Criticism of the Theory of "Economic Law") (Moscow: Statute Publishers, 2000) 180.

Olympiad, Ioffe. *Razvitie civilisticheskoj mysli v SSSR* (The Development of Civil Thought in the USSR) (Part 1. Selected Works on Civil Law) (Moscow: Statute Publishers, 2000).

Jacobson, Georgiy, 'Hronika vneshneeconomicheskich svyazei SSSR' (Chronicle of Foreign Economic Relations of the USSR). Prokhorov, A.M., ed. *Great Soviet Encyclopedia, 1969–1986,* 3rd ed. (Moscow: State Scientific Publishing House, 1986) 259.

Kantorovich, Jacov, *Osnovnye idei grazhdanskogo prava* (Basic Ideas of Civil Law) (Kharkov: Juridical Publishing House of the NKJU of the Ukrainian SSR, 1928) 224.

Khavkin, Boris. *Rossia I Germania. 1900–1945. Spletenie istorii* (Russia and Germany. 1900–1945. Weaving History) (Moscow: New Chronograph, 2014) 80.

Hiroshi, Kimura, *Lichnaya sobstvennost v SSSR, ee svyaz s obshchestvennymi fondami potrebleniya i perspektivy ih razvitiya* (Personal Property in the USSR, its Connection with Public Consumption Funds and Prospects for Their Development) (Hokkaido: Hokkaido University Collection of Scholarly and Academic Papers, 1975) 119.

Kirsanova, Ekaterina, "Istoriya stanovleniya zakonodatelstva ob intellektualnoj sobstvennosti v otechestvennoj pravovoj sisteme" (The History of the Formation of Intellectual Property Legislation in the Domestic Legal System). *Legal Science* 5 (2020) 38.

Krasin, Leonid. *Voprosi vneshnei torgovli* (Questions of Foreign Trade). (Moscow: State Scientific Publishing House, 1928) 305.

Kubyshko, Michail, 'Razvitie zakonodatel'stva ob avtorskom prave sovetskogo perioda' (Development of Copyright Legislation in the Soviet Period). *Bulletin of the Moscow University of the Ministry of Internal Affairs of Russia* 10 (2011) 171.

Leontiev, Gleb, Leonteva, Lyudmila, 'Dialektika svobody i sobstvennosti v obshchestve realnogo utopizma' (Dialectics of Freedom and Property in the Society of Real Utopianism). *Sociodynamics* 4 (2018) 58.

Maksarev, Yuri, 'Izobretatel'stvo i racionalizaciya v narodnom hozyajstve SSSR' (Invention and Rationalization in the National Economy of the USSR). In *Great Soviet Encyclopedia* (Moscow: Soviet Encyclopedia Publishing House, 1972) 87.

Mamlyuk, Boris, 'Russia & Legal Harmonization: An Historical Inquiry Into IP Reform as Global Convergence and Resistance'. *Washington University Global Studies Law Review* 10(3/4) (2011) 535.

Marx, Karl and Engels, Friedrich. *Sochineniya* (Works), 2nd edn. Volume 4 (Moscow: Politizdat, 1955) 438.

Molchanov A. A., Zaytseva E. V., 'K voprosu o sluzhebhykh obektakhpatentnogo prava' (On Work-Related Objects of Patent Law). *Vestnik Permskogo universiteta. Juridicheskie nauki – Perm University Herald. Juridical Sciences* 44(2) (2019) 314.

Novoselova, Ludmila, *Intellectualnaya Sobstvennost. Patentnoye Pravo* (Intellectual Property Law. Patent Law Textbook, Volume 4). (Moscow: Statute Publishers, 2019) 25.

Pankeev, Ivan, 'Rossijskoe avtorskoe pravo HKH veka v normativnyh aktah' (Russian Copyright of the XX Century in Regulatory Acts) *Bulletin of Moscow University. Journalism* 3 (2011) 30.

Pilenko, Alexandr. *Pravo Izobretatelya* (Inventor's Right) (Moscow: Statute Publishing, 2001) 230.

Ragulina, Anastasia, Nikitova, Anna, 'Intellektualnaya sobstvennost: ponyatie, soderzhanie i zashchita' (Intellectual Property: Concept, Content, and Protection). (Moscow: Editorial office of Rossiyskaya Gazeta, 2017) 6.

Rasskazov, Oleg, 'Razvitie grazhdanskogo zakonodatel'stva v period nepa' (Development of Civil Legislation During the NEP Period). *Philosophy of Law* 6 (2008) 74.

Salitskaya, Elena, 'Razvitie otechestvennogo zakonodatelstva v oblasti avtorskogo prava: istoricheskij aspect' (Development of Domestic Legislation in the Field of Copyright: a Historical Aspect). *Nauka. Innovation. Education* no 16 (2014) 265.

Standler, Ronald. *Moral Rights of Authors in the USA*, 2012.

Stuchka, Petr, *Kurs sovetskogo grazhdanskogo prava: Ucheb. posobie dlya vuzov i komvuzov* (The Course of Soviet Civil Law: Textbook for Universities and Colleges) (Moscow. Publishing House of the Communist Academy, 1927–1931).

Talman, Ekaterina. *Racionalizatory i izobretateli: ot carskoj Rossii do nashih dnej. Istoriya poyavleniya sovremennyh Levshej i Kulibinyh* (*Rationalizers and inventors: from Tsarist Russia to the present day. The history of the emergence of modern Lefties and Kulibins*), 2020.

Tomsinov, Vladimir. *Expert opinion of the head of the Department of History of State and Law of the Law Faculty of Moscow State University. M.V. Lomonosov*, 2011.

Vladimir, Lenin. *Sochineniya* (Works), Vol. 22. (Moscow: State Publishing House of Political Literature, 1941) 263.

Zhilinskaya, Irina 'Nauchnie svyazi USSR i Velikobritanii v 1931–1939' (Scientific Relations of the USSR and Great Britain in 1931–1939). *Journal of the National Academy of Sciences of Belarus. Humanitarian sciences* 3 (2011) 80.

Legislations and Decrees

Collection of legalizations and orders of the Government. Section I. No. 61 (March 30, 1911). Art. 560.

Decree "O pechati" (On the press). *Decrees of the Soviet Government*. Moscow: Institute of Marxism-Leninism (1957).

Decree of the All-Russian Central Executive Committee, Council of People's Commissars of the RSFSR of October 11, 1926. "Ob avtorskom prave" (On Copyright). SU RSFSR. No 72 (1926).

Decree of the All-Russian Central Executive Committee, Council of People's Commissars of the RSFSR of October 08, 1928. "Ob avtorskom prave" (On Copyright). SU RSFSR. No 132 (1928).

Decree of the Central Executive Committee and Council of People's Commissars of the USSR of April 10, 1929. "O prave peredachi po radio i provodam publichnogo ispolneniya muzykal'nyh, dramaticheskih i drugih proizvedenij, a ravno lekcij i dokladov" (On the right to transmit public performances of musical, dramatic and other works, as well as lectures and reports by radio and wires). SZ USSR. No 26 (1929).

Decree of the Central Executive Committee and Council of People's Commissars of the USSR of November 23, 1930. "O pravah zakazchikov na izgotovlennye po ih zakazam arhitekturnye, inzhenernye i inye tekhnicheskie plany, chertezhi i risunki" (On the rights of customers to architectural, engineering, and other technical plans, drawings and drawings made to their orders). SZ USSR. No 58 (1930).

Decree of the Central Executive Committee of the USSR, Council of People's Commissars of the USSR of September 12, 1924. "O promyshlennyh obrazcah (risunkah i modelyah)" (On industrial designs (drawings and models)). SZ USSR. No 9 (1924).

Decree of the Central Executive Committee of the USSR, Council of People's Commissars of the USSR of May 27, 1936. "Ob otmene Postanovleniya CIK i SNK Soyuza SSR ot 12 sentyabrya 1924 goda "O promyshlennyh obrazcah (risunkah i modelyah)" "(On the abolition of the decision of the Central Executive Committee and the Council of People's Commissars of the USSR of September 12, 1924 "On Industrial Designs (Drawings and Models)"). CZ USSR. No 29 (1936).

Decree of the Central Executive Committee of the USSR, Council of People's Commissars of the USSR of January 30, 1925. "Ob osnovah avtorskogo prava" (On the fundamentals of copyright). SZ USSR. No 7 (1925).

Decree of the Central Executive Committee of the USSR, Council of People's Commissars of the USSR of May 16, 1928. "O vvedenii v dejstvie osnov avtorskogo prava v novoj redakcii" (On the Enactment of the Fundamentals of Copyright in a New Edition). SZ USSR. No 27 (1928).

Decree of the Central Executive Committee of the USSR, SNK of the USSR of September 12, 1924. "O vvedenii v dejstvie postanovleniya o patentah na izobretenie" (On the Enactment of the Decree on Patents for Inventions). SZ of the USSR. No 9 (1924).

Decree of the Council of People's Commissars of October 10, 1919. "O prekrashchenii sily dogovorov na priobretenie v polnuyu sobstvennost' proizvedenij literatury i iskusstva" (On the termination of contracts for the acquisition of full ownership of works of literature and art). *SU RSFSR*. No 51 (1919).

Decree of the Council of People's Commissars of the RSFSR of July 29, 1919. "ob otmene prava chastnoj sobstvennosti na arhivy umershih russkih pisatelej, kompozitorov, hudozhnikov i uchenyh, hranyashchiesya v bibliotekah i muzeyah" (*On the abolition of the right of private ownership of the archives of deceased Russian writers, composers, artists and scientists stored in libraries and museums*). SU RSFSR. No 38 (1919).

Decree of the Council of People's Commissars of the RSFSR of June 30, 1919 "ob izobreteniyah (Polozhenie)" (On inventions (Regulations)). SU RSFSR. No. 34, (1919).

Decree of the Council of People's Commissars of the RSFSR of November 26, 1918 "O priznanii nauchnyh, literaturnyh, muzykal'nyh i hudozhestvennyh proizvedenij gosudarstvennym dostoyaniem" (On the recognition of scientific, literary, musical, and artistic state property). *SU RSFSR*, 1918, N 86, art. 900.

Decree of the Council of People's Commissars of the RSFSR of October 10,1919. "O prekrashchenii sily dogovorov na priobretenie v polnuyu sobstvennost' proizvedenij literatury i iskusstva" (*On the termination of the force of contracts for the acquisition of full ownership of works of literature and art*). Izvestia of the All-Russian Central Executive Committee. No 229 (1919).

Decree of the Council of People's Commissars of the USSR of March 28, 1932. "Ob izmeneniyah v zakonodatel'stve Soyuza SSR v svyazi s izdaniem Polozheniya ot 9 aprelya 1931 g. ob izobreteniyah i tekhnicheskih usovershenstvovaniyah" (On changes in the legislation of the USSR in connection with the publication of the regulation of April 9, 1931, on inventions and technical improvements). SZ of the USSR. No 24 (1932).

Konvenciya mezhdu Soyuzom Sovetskih Socialisticheskih Respublik i Norvegiej otnositel'no vzaimnoj ohrany prav na promyshlennuyu sobstvennost (Convention between the Union of Soviet Socialist Republics and Norway concerning the mutual protection of industrial property rights). Moscow, February 24, 1928. Published in S. 3 for 1928. Dep. II No. 62 Art. 252.

La décision de la cour de cassation Pourvoi no G 11-21.947 Arrêt no 406 FS-P+B, 10 avril 2013.

Law of the USSR No 1305-I "O sobstvennosti v SSSR" (On property in the USSR). Vedomosti of the Supreme Soviet of the USSR. No 11 (1990).

Resolution of the Central Executive Committee and Council of People's Commissars of the USSR of September 12, 1924 "O vvedenii v dejstvie Postanovleniya o patentah na izobretenie" (On the Enactment of the Decree on Patents for Invention). Collected Legislation of the USSR. 1924. No. 9. Art. 97.

Shostakovich vs Twentieth Century-Fox Film Corp. Corp., 80 N.Y.S.2d 575 (N.Y. Sup. Ct. 1948), aff'd, 87 N.Y.S.2d 430 (N.Y. App. Div. 1949).

Treaty between the Union of Soviet Socialist Republics and Germany of October 12, 1925. *Collection of Laws and Orders of the Workers' and Peasants' Government of the USSR* No. 28 of April 29. (1926).

PART 4

The Emergence of Performers' Rights

CHAPTER 14

'The Pretension Is Nothing; the Performance Everything': The Origin of Performers' Rights and the Creation of the Performer as Artist

Johanna Gibson

> The pretension is nothing; the performance every thing. A good apple is better than an insipid peach.[1]

∵

1 Introduction

In both copyright and in film, the status of and perspective upon performers and auteurs constitute a carefully managed and somewhat hierarchical relationship. Attention to the rights of performers did not start to emerge until the advent of film technology enabled the fixation and reproduction of performances in the late nineteenth century. At the same time, the artistic recognition of film and the nature of its authorship remained in question. During the interwar years, a number of particular developments were instrumental in crafting ultimately the conceptualisation of the film auteur and the film itself as art and indeed a copyright work, including: the influence of film criticism and theory in clarifying the authorship and artistry of film; the advent of sound technologies; and the emerging studio system and management of stardom. This period was a critical time for relevant legal and policy developments. The United Kingdom began to address the protection of performers with a specific legislative response in the form of the Dramatic and Musical Performers Protection Act 1925. Similarly, in the United States, performers had uncertain, if any, protection, but with the advent of sound technology their interests raised real ethical, cultural and commercial questions leading to industry responses

1 Hunt, Leigh. 'Preface' to *The Poetical Works of Leigh Hunt* (London: Edward Moxon, 1832) v–lviii, xi.

 | DOI:10.1163/9789004714663_016

rather than legal rules. Internationally, the Rome Conference of the Berne Convention in 1928 recognised for the first time authors' rights in a performance, but resisted calls for the rights of the performing artists themselves. In the absence of international consensus on the question of performers' rights, which would not be achieved until the Rome Convention in 1961, the structure, culture, and legal context of national industries were critical at this time, and performers' rights thus remained a local issue in a rapidly developing and internationalising industry. In brief, the advent of sound created the performer in copyright law. But there was nothing inevitable about the auteur.

This chapter addresses the developments in the film industry in the interwar period and the role of the motion picture industry in the reform of the wider legal landscape for copyright and performers' rights both then and today. In examining the socio-cultural and legal developments for the industry during this period, it is important to address not only the law but also the surrounding discourse, including the films themselves,[2] as a source of law. The interwar period was also a crucial time for film criticism and scholarship. During this time the industry and art began more explicitly to position directors as authors and performers as directed, giving rise to a compelling authorship narrative, the legacy of which persists today in the law's conceptualisation of the film work and the film author: 'The critics' first objective was to get the film-maker recognized as a creative artist.'[3] Film publications of this period (criticism and theory in particular, but fan magazines as well) are thus very relevant to this discussion as these communications had a particular role in shaping the industry of film, including determining the scope of the film work through a rigorous and sustained examination of authorship. This interdisciplinary context is essential to understand in order to appreciate the instrumentality of the film form and of sound as expressed through the product as well as through commercial and policy developments, concepts which ultimately have been

2 Michèle Lagny argues that, 'Film history … is therefore part of a large ensemble, the socio-cultural history': Lagny, Michèle, 'Film History: Or History Expropriated', *Film History* 6(1) (1994) 26–44, 27. Lagny argues, 'film history should be able to adopt film analysis as a standard practice, so that films can be understood not just within their own existence, but also in relation to other films, in a relatively autonomous complex of moving images. The people who made these images, even those who had seen them (because they work in the film industry or simply because they are used to going to the movies) have their own representation of what a film might have looked like, how motion pictures are made and put together, of what may be shown and what may not (for political, ethical or aesthetic reasons), of what may be done and what may not, for technical and economic reasons' (29).

3 Ferro, Marc, 'Film as an Agent, Product and Source of History'. *Journal of Contemporary History* 18(3) (1983) 357–64, 357.

translated into the conceptualisation of film within the copyright system. Critically, however, all of these influences and stressors converge in the cultural and technological flashpoint of sound films.

The first part of the chapter considers the rapid development of the industry in this period. During these years the industry and the surrounding complex of film criticism and theory engaged in conscientious promotion of film as a distinct art. The legitimation of film as art had significant implications for industry and legal developments alike. This period also saw the rise of the industrial complex of stardom, which contributed to sustaining the separation between filmmaker as artist, and performer as labour and asset. One of the most significant developments at this time, however, was the wider adoption of sound technology and the production of the first talkies, all of which had a particular impact on actors, leading to industry and legal attempts at managing the performance and the performers themselves. Sound in this period operated as both tool and symbol of industrial modernity.[4] The industry's encounters with sound technology are particularly important as these have had a critical role in the origins of performers' rights and beyond.

The second part examines a chronology of key events in relation to the development of performers' rights in this socio-cultural and commercial context: the Royal Assent of the Dramatic and Musical Performers Protection Act 1925 in the United Kingdom; the release in the US of the first talkie, *The Jazz Singer* (1927); the 1928 Rome Conference of the Berne Convention; the release of the first British sound film, *Blackmail* (1928); and the 1930 *Blackmail* litigation on the 1925 Act. This cultural and aesthetic context for the film industry was crucial when going into the international legal environment for the first performers' rights in the 1928 Rome Conference, as well as looking at local industry responses. The final part of the chapter widens this discussion to consider the thorny issue of authorship with respect to an expanding field of the copyright work today and in view of a new frontier of technological challenges with the use of computer-generated imagery, artificial intelligence and deepfakes, and the role of these technologies in the commodification of the contemporary performer and its parts, voice or otherwise.

The final part revisits the significance of the events of the interwar period, their legacy for film and the persistent tropes that render performers, particularly voice performers, at once vulnerable legally and commercially and yet readily appreciated as the first film artists by early audiences and critics alike.

4 Boon, Tim, 'The Cinematic Sound of Industrial Modernity: First Notes'. In *Being Modern: The Cultural Impact of Science in the Early Twentieth Century* Bud, *et al*, eds. (UCL Press, 2018) 40–57.

The history that follows picks up the threads between the visual imagery of the author and master of the work of art, the distortions of the new technologies and productions of sound, alongside the emerging industrial complex of stardom and the development of performers' rights. In doing so the discussion recognises important parallels with contemporary concerns around film sound, including the use of artificial intelligence in filmmaking, and deepfake dubbing and machine translation in particular. The history of film is instructive in understanding the way in which the legal discourse rationalises new technologies in the context of an appeal to author, whether this is understood as the artistry and artist in industrialised consumer cultures of fashion and film, or the "human factor" in contemporary discussions around artificial intelligence as an otherwise mere recording, as it were. Indeed, these contemporary preoccupations are not unlike the criticism of the first film productions. Through encounters with history, the chapter considers whether ultimately, and almost symmetrically, these new commercial, socio-cultural, and inevitably legal challenges will motivate further reforms in performers' protection, almost a hundred years after the first performers' rights legislation.[5]

2 Why Performers' Rights Are (Film) History

A critical reappraisal of film history – not only the production industry but also the film criticism as well as the films themselves – is central to this discussion. Indeed, cinema and cinematographic works are not only socio-cultural and political texts of the period, but also sources of the law itself. The present discussion seeks to chart the various cultural, social, commercial and legal stimuli that positioned and organised the way in which film continues to be viewed and understood today – namely, the concept of authorship (and the particular role of film criticism and theory), the influence of technology (and film sound in particular), and the politics of film labour.

Since the first productions, cinematographic works have struggled with the question of representation and legitimation – from the antagonism towards its status as a technology of reproduction, on the one hand, to the industry's conscientious efforts at distinguishing the film work as a visual art of imagination

5 For a more detailed consideration of the relationship between sound and contemporary challenges and limitations for performers' rights, see Gibson, Johanna, 'All Words and No Performance: A Revolution in Copyright Through Performance in Sound'. In *Reforming Intellectual Property* Ghidini, Gustavo, and Falce, Valeria, eds. (Cheltenham: Edward Elgar, 2022) 95–124.

and performance, on the other.[6] This language and mythology of authorship was critical in early film criticism[7] and even more so with the introduction of sound, and it has proven to be resilient in contemporary scholarship and law, securing a hierarchy of creativity within the law itself. What these apparent poles of creativity share, however, is a relationship to pretence; that is, to deception and artifice. The emphasis on the production of creative work belies a deference to the auteur's creative (deceptive) imagination while at the same time maintaining a preoccupation with the performer's authenticity (the "everyman" of the real world). In other words, the auteur is an artist, the performer a worker; the auteur creates anew, the performer interprets and executes.[8] This distinction at the same time maintains a distance between the authority of the auteur and the labour, as it were, of the performer. Indeed, this stratification of the industry maps clearly onto the stratification of creativity within copyright, with performance commanded, so to speak, by the authority of the author.

The interwar period is an especially important time in the history of cinema, and in the development of performers' rights – two historical phenomena that are closely interrelated for obvious as well as not-so-obvious reasons. As cinema began to dominate the entertainment industry, the labour environment and work opportunities for performers changed dramatically. The interwar years were a period of considerable growth in the cinema industry, during which time it quickly pushed live entertainment to the margins. For example, at the beginning of the twentieth century, just as film was starting to enter the entertainment market, the US entertainment industry was dominated by live performance. In 1900 live performers were responsible for

6 Ferro, 'Film as an Agent' (n 3) 357 explains: 'At the beginning, cinema was something for "helots", it was "mechanical"; in addition, the places where the film-shows were held – fairs, *café-théatres* and the like – were, in Victorian and bourgeois eyes, disreputable, immoral. For a film-maker to try to rank himself with writers and artists was incongruous and obscene'.

7 According to Ferro the mythology of the filmmaker as 'a *type of discourse*, like the writer, the politician or the scientist', ibid, 358. This can be contrasted with the "real-world" identity affixed to the performer as worker. This status of the performer is something which is consolidated within the star system and star as brand (particularly in relation to the studio management and policing of behaviour off-screen). This manifests in the usual approach to protection of voice through image rights where available, passing off and similar, as distinct from anything inherently creative in voice. See Gibson, 'All Words and No Performance' (n 5) 95–124.

8 The relationship between interpretation and execution raises interesting issues with respect to the nature of the director/performer relationship, as discussed later in this chapter. See further Arnold, Richard, 'Do Directors Have Performers' Rights? *Intellectual Property Quarterly* 3 (2022) 134–140.

almost all audience-based entertainment; however, by 1938, live entertainment accounted for less than 3% of all performances,[9] indicating the impact of film on the performing professions.[10] Importantly, the impact upon the performing professions put focus upon the deficient or completely wanting protection for performers as their creativity was revolutionised by new technologies of audience reach and consumer product.

This rapid development of the economic value of the film industry was in part facilitated by the ability to expand dramatically the audiences for performances, not only in terms of class but also in terms of time and location: 'By 1938 motion pictures provided entertainment even at marginal hours and in marginal places ... They gave every consumer the chance to see a superstar such as Chaplin instantly in their own town.'[11] Indeed, the advent of cinema, in conjunction with other technologies of mechanical reproduction (including sound recordings) can be understood as the "industrialisation" of live entertainment into a form of mass communication. At the same time, this period marked the introduction and expansion of sound in film, creating specific issues for performers as well as directing new attention to their contributions. These various factors together brought about a specific set of circumstances that led to the development of the first forms of performers' rights protection in intellectual property systems around the world. In particular, sound was instrumental, so to speak, in achieving the first performers' rights.

9 Bakker, Gerben, 'How Motion Pictures Industrialized Entertainment'. *The Journal of Economic History*, 72(4) (2012) 1036–1063, 1037.

10 Gomery describes the way the powerful producers (Lowe's, Famous Players-Lasky, Universal, First National, PDC, United Artists) pursued a strategy of agreeing a standardised sound system, ultimately consolidating their position with inevitable consequences for performers: 'The reaction was predictable. Realizing their immense economic power, the majors began to cut expenses wherever possible. The most important component of variable costs, the most easily adjusted in the short run was the wage bill for production, an area where most employees were not unionized. Moreover, alternative employment, especially at high wages, existed only in declining industries – vaudeville and the legitimate theatre. Thus, Zukor and his cohorts concluded that they could lower wages for these employees and face little effective opposition. All other producers would follow to save money': Gomery, Douglas, 'The "Warner-Vitaphone Peril": The American Film Industry Reacts to the Innovation of Sound'. *Journal of the University Film Association* 28(1) (1976) 11–19, 14–15.

11 Bakker, 'How Motion Pictures' (n 9) 1037.

3 A Brief History of (Film) Sound

Before the advent of sound, the perspective on the film work within critical circles was as performance and the specific (usually visual) contributions from which might be deciphered a new art. In that the early film industry relied considerably on cinematic productions of the dramatic and literary canon,[12] this "new art" was largely understood as a process of refinement; more specifically, as refinement of performance. From the outset, performance is thus integral to the concept of the film work and not only constituted by authorship but also, in this way, constitutive and legitimating of the author concept. In 1908, in a review of the Film d'art production, *L'Assassinat du Duc de Guise*,[13] Adolphe Brisson explains: 'First, whatever speech alone is able to express – thought, abstract ideas, intense passion – is excluded. We are in a world of the concrete. The actors must perform,' and 'In some way, their movements must be refined, freed of all superfluity, and reduced to the essential.'[14] According to Brisson, 'this work of refinement is a work of art.'[15] This refinement thus produces a kind of artefactual difference: the work. Thus, the author is made by the work – a legal fiction borne of narrative necessity in the writing of the story of film. On the other hand, the movement and performance of the actors is presented as a kind of reproduction or recording of the underlying dramatic work, a performance to be refined by the author, rendering the performance merely adjectival with respect to the dramatic work. In other words, the performance is merely a resource to be refined in service of the film work.

But the introduction of sound complicated this pretence of the authorial film work. As the period in which sound became standard, the interwar years saw growing dissonance among performers and mounting intrusion of the studio-endorsed *auteurial* narrative. Although technologies for film sound, including synchronised sound, had preoccupied inventors since the emergence of film itself, it was not until the interwar period that technological developments attracted more consistent commercial interest from the studios. During this

12 For a fuller discussion of the relationship between the early cinema and theatre, and the theatrical legacy for film art and law, see Gibson, Johanna, 'The Man Behind the Curtain: Developing Film's Double Exposure of Intellectual Property'. In *Intellectual Property and the Law of Nations, 1860–1920* Morris, P. Sean, ed. (Brill, 2022) 207–41.

13 *L'Assassinat du duc de Guise* (1908), André Calmettes and Charles Le Bargy (dirs.), Henri Lavedan (writer). See further Gibson, 'The Man Behind the Curtain' (n 12) 207–41.

14 Brisson, Adolphe, Chronique théâtral: *L'Assassinat du Duc de Guise*, *Le Temps*, 22 November 1908, 3–4. Reproduced in *French Film Theory and Criticism, Volume I: A History/Anthology, 1907–1929* Abel, Richard, ed. (Princeton University Press, 1988) 50–53, 51.

15 Brisson, 'Chronique théâtral' ibid.

period, innovations led to technological advancements that were both interesting and relevant to studio productions, resulting in the production of the first commercial sound films in the late 1920s.[16] At the same time, Hollywood was establishing the star system and the attending facility and structural control over artistic labour for the studio system.[17]

The wider adoption of sound technologies in the late 1920s was thus the first time the film audience heard from the performers themselves, indeed literally.[18] This new voice of cinema complicated the early artistic hierarchy conferred upon film production, in which the industry invested much effort. In particular, hearing from the actors interrupted the simple constructions of the romantic narrative underpinning the film product as it matured to distinguish itself as a purely visual creative form (and art) in and of itself.[19] Further, with the recording of sound broadcasts, new issues began to arise concerning the expropriation of economic value in performance, prompting novel legal developments concerned with the interests of not only authors, but also performers, in relation to their creative work (whether considered property or not).[20] The

16 In the United States, the Warner Bros production, *The Jazz Singer* (1927), Alan Crosland (dir); in the United Kingdom, the British International Pictures Production, *Blackmail* (1929), Alfred Hitchcock (dir). Both films are discussed in more detail later in this chapter.

17 The use of stardom as labour management measure is discussed later in this chapter. See also the discussion in Gibson, 'All Words and No Performance' (n 5) 95–124.

18 Sound effects had been "practised" widely since the first days of cinema, resulting in widely varying audience reactions, but '[w]hen commercial sync sound arrived in the late twenties there was already a tradition of both theory and practice to build on in working out how to make sound, and sound effects, mesh with the pictures. Perhaps this is one reason why the practice of incorporating effects along with other sound elements was so swiftly mastered in the 1930s': Bottomore, Stephen, 'The Story of Percy Peashaker: Debates about Sound Effects in the Early Cinema'. In *The Sounds of Early Cinema* Abel, Richard, and Altman, Charles, eds. (Indiana University Press, 2001) 129–142, 140. See further Bottomore, Stephen, 'An International Survey of Sound Effects in Early Cinema'. *Film History* 11(4) (1999) 485–498. With the advent of sound, sound-era shorts were produced quickly and in considerable quantity. See further the special issue of *Film History* devoted to the early sound short, particularly King, Rob, 'Introduction: Beyond Vitaphone: The Early Sound Short'. *Film History* 23(3) (2011) 247–50; and King, Rob, "The Spice of the Program": Educational Pictures, Early Sound Slapstick, and the Small-Town Audience'. *Film History* 23(3) (2011) 313–39.

19 The emphasis of the visual in film and law is explored in more detail later in this chapter, but this visual hegemony is the critical context in which the early aesthetic of film was established and with which the law conceptualises the work in contemporary copyright, notwithstanding the apparent expanding field of the work in recent copyright jurisprudence: *Levola Hengelo v Smilde Foods* (C-310/17), EU:C:2018:899.

20 This was the subject matter of the first performers protection in the United Kingdom, in the form of the Dramatic and Musical Performers' Protection Act 1925, and the first litigation under the Act in *Musical Performers' Protection Association Ltd v British International*

inter-war period was thus a crucial time socially, culturally, and legally for the development of film and cinema, and sound was indeed at centre stage. These various factors not only coincide historically but also arguably converge in the technology of sound. There is a striking coincidence between the development of film sound, the emergence of the star system, and the sudden noise of film labour and performers' rights in this period. And in the emphasis on achieving economic ends through the protection of the performance, the concept of the performer was deposed as a kind of technology of recording, always in the service of the author and in deference to the underlying copyright work in a kind of feudalism of the surrounding industrial complex of stardom and the studio system.

Prior to the means to record and reproduce the performance, musical performances were otherwise immune to expropriation through copying, and thus effectively invisible as a commercial object, separately from the event of the performance and audience admission prices. As Richard Arnold notes, before such reproduction technologies 'performers did not need protection, for the only way in which their performance could be exploited was by the public paying for admission to a concert or play.'[21] However, there was no such anxiety with regard to the reproduction of actors' performances, which of course had been recorded for at least two decades by this point by the very nature of the cinematographic work, its exhibition and dissemination. Sound, however, altered this landscape considerably. The emergence of film technology, and sound in particular, was thus instrumental in the ultimate creation of the "performer" within the law, in that the ability to record a performance created a kind of artefactual and economic property. In the ability to record (and thus repeat) sound performances, a new economics of performance was put into play. It was thus not until the wider availability of sound recording technology, and the advent of sound in film, that the precarity of the dramatic performer was first recognised in the context of the commercial risks posed by copying. These first forms of performers' rights are considered in more detail later in this chapter, but it is important to note at this stage that recording, indeed "copying", is thus an impetus not merely for the management of rights in the original work; it is the economic and cultural rationale for the recognition of new works in the creative "refinement" that arises through a kind of inventive imitation in new technologies of reproduction. The recognition of

---

Pictures Ltd (1930) 46 TLR 485 (discussed later in this chapter). Similarly, in the Records of the 1928 Rome Conference of the Berne Convention the impact of sound recording is considered at length, as discussed in detail later in this chapter.

21 Arnold, Richard. *Performers' Rights*, 6th edn (London: Sweet & Maxwell, 2021) para 1.41.

rights in film as a copyright work, and ultimately of rights for performers in performing that work, were thus borne out of the possibility of reproduction and the subsequent manifestation of copyright value as an artefact of that risk, by virtue of a new vulnerability to infringement. The risk of copying in and of itself creates the potential for value. In other words, the potential economic expropriation of performance that was made possible through recording created the 'object' of protection for the attention of legal measures, as distinct from the well-being or other concerns of the performers themselves

Thus, in the United Kingdom, the development of technologies of recording (both sound recordings and film) introduced a political and economic interest in protecting first the recordings in 1911,[22] and eventually the performers in 1925.[23] However, it would take several more decades before performers would be recognised at the multilateral level. The nature of performance within international law was largely conceptualised through the author's right to performance, consistent with film criticism's view of the refinement in performance that characterised the film work. There was no international approach to performers' rights until the adoption of the Rome Convention in 1961. And today, with the priority of the copyright work, the non-property rights of the performer are evidence that the distinction between the auteur and the performer continues to manifest through property lines, as it were.[24]

At both the national and international levels, protection for performers remained limited during this period, and set the conceptual groundwork for the framing of modern performers' rights. The dominant approach continues to be that of conceiving any interest in performance as a right attached to the work, rather than the performance in and of itself as a new product, as such. To consider the nature of the film work, the narrative of authorship preoccupied the criticism of the day. What is the art of film in an age of mass communication? Whose art is that?

4 The Art of Film in an Age of Mass Communication

The language of authorship is something of a functional imperative of copyright's architecture, but it was also a favoured and even crucial discourse in

22 Copyright Act 1911.

23 The Dramatic and Musical Performers' Protection Act 1925.

24 *Musical Performers' Protection Association Ltd v British International Pictures Ltd* (1930) 46 TLR 485; Arnold, *Performers' Rights*, (n 21) paras 1–49 to-1–50.

establishing film as "art" in its socially and culturally awkward beginnings.[25] The author is a crucial protagonist in the drama of copyright, and deciphering and delivering a coherent narrative of authorship was part of the fundamental process of cultural and aesthetic legitimation for the nascent film industry. Further, this was consistent ultimately with the "literary" and "textual" character of copyright. The industry's attempt to validate its output (by attaching to theatre and the authority and reputation of established dramatists) as well as the inclusion of cinematographic works within copyright protection, consolidated the importance of writing the story of film as a production of singular authorship and imagination – a work of art, if you will. Ultimately, in the inter-war period, this matured in the figure of the *cinéaste*[26] and ultimately the preferred *auteur*. And while auteur theory in film criticism is largely traced to the criticism of the 1950s, attributed to the French New Wave and *Cahiers du cinéma*,[27] and to Alexandre Astruc[28] and François Truffaut[29] in particular, arguably it was really during the interwar period, when film criticism was maturing and film productions were seeking to distinguish the particularities of their art, that critics began to outline the singularity of the film author, ultimately in the service of the law.

As noted earlier, the film form struggled with perceptions, and was somewhat dismissed as a mere technology of reproduction, not an art form in itself. This was largely in response to film as a form of mass communication and industrialised entertainment, and to its subject matter as a mere recording of life (such as street scenes and stage productions). At the same time, this distinction between film and other arts was in part facilitated by an underlying class narrative that positioned film as a "lower" form of cultural production, while theatre was considered a higher and culturally valuable art. Indeed, in the first decade of cinema it was largely understood as 'a new form

---

25 For more detailed discussion on the cinematic production of dramatic performances, and the work and promotion of Le Film d'Art, see Gibson, 'The Man Behind the Curtain' (n 12) 207–41.

26 For example, *cinéaste* was the preferred term of Louis Delluc and others.

27 Auteurism is largely understood through the movement that became known as *les politiques des auteurs*, for which François Truffaut's essay, published in *Cahiers du cinéma* in 1954, became most commonly associated: Truffaut, François, 'Une certaine tendance du cinéma français'. *Cahiers du Cinema* (1954) 31 January (in English, A certain tendency of French cinema).

28 A Astruc, Du Stylo à la camera et de la camera au stylo, *L'Écran française*, 30 March 1948 (in English, The Birth of a New Avant-Garde: La caméra-stylo).

29 F Truffaut, Une certaine tendance du cinéma français, *Cahiers du Cinema* (1954) 31 January.

of theatre – especially the melodrama whose highly formalized, emotional mode of representation insisted on expressing what language left unsaid.'[30] The influence (which ultimately has become its persistent legacy[31]) of theatre upon the burgeoning film industry led to self-conscious attempts within the emerging industry at establishing and validating the cultural contribution of film through the adaptation (and to a great extent, the mechanical reproduction) of canonical, dramatic works.[32] Consequently, dramatists began to raise concerns that film, as a technology of copying, was threatening their art. It was this conflict between theatre and film that ultimately resulted in the inclusion of film within international copyright protection, at the 1908 Berlin Conference of the Berne Convention.[33] As such, somewhat paradoxically and yet inevitably, it was the perception of film as "copying" that led to its capacity for protection (indeed, as potentially "copied"), anticipating the same paradox when

30 Abel, Richard, 'Before the Canon'. In Abel, *French Film Theory and Criticism* (n 14) 5–35, 19. See further Adolphe Brisson's review of *L'Assassinat du Duc de Guide*, 22 November, 1908, in which he explicitly identifies cinema as both 'a new form of theatre' and as a work of dramatic authorship: see A Brisson, Theater Column: *L'Assassinat du Duc de Guise*, *Le Temps*, 22 November 1908, 3–4. A Brisson, Chronique théâtral: *L'Assassinat du Duc de Guise*, *Le Temps*, 22 November 1908, 3–4. Reproduced in Abel, *French Film Theory and Criticism* (n 14) 50–53.

31 For film and its relationship to theatre, 1908 was a critical year, in which several key developments played out as a drama between classical cultural forms and the mass-reproduction anticipated in film. Crucial events of 1908 included the establishment of the production company, le Film d'art (which emphasised the adaptation of canonical literature and theatre), the inclusion of cinematographic works at the Berlin Conference of the Berne Convention, and the commencement of the *Ben Hur* litigation (*Harper & Bros v Kalem Co.,* No. 2-160 (SDNY Nov 2 1908), reprinted in Transcript of Record, *Kalem v Harper Brothers*, 222 US 55 (1911)), which led to the specific inclusion of film for the first time in the Townsend Amendment to copyright law in 1912 (37 Stat. 488). As will be seen later in this chapter, film criticism was very important in configuring film within the cultural landscape and ultimately within the copyright landscape. Notably, 1908 was also the year the first film columns started to be published: Frey, Mattias. *The Permanent Crisis of Film Criticism: The Anxiety of Authority* (Amsterdam University Press, 2015) 28. See also the Berne Convention for the Protection of Literary and Artistic Works: Berlin Act, 1908: Revised Berne Convention for the Protection of Literary and Artistic Works; Records of the Diplomatic Conference: Convened in Berlin, 14 October to 14 November 1908. See further the discussion in Gibson, 'The Man Behind the Curtain' (n 12) 207–41.

32 Gibson, 'The Man Behind the Curtain' (n 12) 207–41.

33 The Berne Convention for the Protection of Literary and Artistic Works: Berlin Act, 1908: Revised Berne Convention for the Protection of Literary and Artistic Works; Records of the Diplomatic Conference: Convened in Berlin, 14 October to 14 November 1908. See further the extended examination of this relationship between art and law, industry and copyright, in Gibson, 'The Man Behind the Curtain' (n 12) 207–41.

the 1928 Rome Conference considered performers' rights.[34] It would seem that which is capable of copying is, for that same reason, capable of being copied, with interesting implications and wisdoms for many technological flashpoints throughout copyright's history, including those in play today.

Despite the emphasis on the politiques des auteurs in the writings of *Cahiers du cinema*, the preoccupation with film authorship, and arguably the director as auteur, long pre-dates this period and even the pre-war period. Publishing in the early twentieth century under a pseudonym, the film critic known as Yhcam explained the role (and art) of the director in the context of the scenario and its interpretation. As distinct from the later pejorative sense attached to the scenarist as lacking creativity,[35] Yhcam's understanding of the scenarist is in the creative work of interpretation; that is, the director interprets the idea selected for cinematic adaptation (selected from the author of that idea for which that author is paid). Yhcam declared that there is only one author and that one author is the director.[36] In making this assertion, Yhcam is responding to the specific tension between the production model of early cinema and the challenges presented by authors' rights. Yhcam explained this authorship in the context of the dominant production models of the day:

> The Production Company receives ideas for scenarios from any number of people.
>
> A reading committee examines these ideas and selects a certain number of them; the selected ideas are turned over to the directors.
>
> The director constructs a scenario from the selected idea, and he has full discretion to modify the selected idea to his liking, even changing it completely.
>
> The director then explains the scenario to his actors and proceeds immediately to the shooting.
>
> The author of the selected idea receives several francs in payment for it.
>
> In short, there is only one author, properly speaking, and that author is none other than the director.[37]

---

34 The Berne Convention for the Protection of Literary and Artistic Works: Rome Act, 1928: Revised International Convention for the Protection of Literary and Artistic Works; Records of the Diplomatic Conference: Convened in Rome, May 8 to June 2, 1928 ("Rome Act, 1928").

35 Truffaut, 'Une certaine tendance du cinéma français' (n 27).

36 Yhcam, Cinematography, *Ciné-Journal*, 20 April-11 May 1912, reproduced in *Framework: The Journal of Cinema and Media* (1986) (32/33), 160–170, 163.

37 Ibid., 163.

According to Yhcam, 'From the beginning, the film production companies have been terrified of authors or, more precisely, of authors' rights,'[38] a fear attributed to the loss of control over the mise-en-scène, 'something the companies have found comfortable and advantageous.'[39] What is especially striking about Yhcam's account of authorship is the emphasis on interpretation and execution, the language of performers, which resonates with Richard Arnold's work on the film director as performer,[40] to which I will return later in this chapter. For the moment, the emphasis on authorship, and emphatically singular authorship, was becoming instrumental to establishing the emerging art of film as original and creative, and authorship as unitary and whole. As Yhcam proclaimed, 'The cinema-theater has to assert itself as a new ART, with its own original methods, and it should be furious at being considered as a simple reproducer of what is properly called the theater.'[41]

5 But Is It Art?

The quest for film's distinctiveness as a new form of art is throughout the critical work of the interwar period and is entirely implicated in the recognition of film within the copyright system. Indeed, it was the validation of film as art, and in particular as a new and distinct art, that preoccupied the work in the developing professionalisation of film criticism that took hold during the interwar period.[42] Published just before Hitler came to power, Rudolf Arnheim's

---

38 Ibid. Yhcam's insight forecast the might of the studio system. As Aljean Harmetz observed in relation to the studio control in the production of *Casablanca*: 'It was Warner's studio, and he never let his underlings forget it, but Hal Wallis [producer] was the creative force behind *Casablanca*. The French *auteur* theory, the idea that the director is the author of his film, collapses against the reality of the studio system. It is impossible to read through the hundreds of memos Wallis sent and received without understanding how thoroughly he shaped the movie': Harmetz, Aljean. *The Making of Casablanca: Bogart, Bergman, and World War II* (Hyperion, 2002/[1992]) 29. Harmetz goes on to detail examples of memos where the producer "directed" much of the decisions, from costumes to actors' performances: 29–30. Such was Wallis's input that a type of authorial, unitary character is said to be recognisable in his films: 'There was a consistency in the product Warners was turning out during the thirties when Wallis was running the show' (statement of Tom Pryor, quoted in Harmetz, 31).

39 Yhcam, Cinematography, (n 36) 163.

40 Arnold, 'Do Directors Have Performers' Rights? (n 8) 134–140.

41 Yhcam, Cinematography, (n 36) 164.

42 On the professionalising of film criticism and its role in establishing artistic recognition for film, see the extended discussion in Frey, *The Permanent Crisis of Film Criticism* (n 31). Frey notes, 'even in the 1920s the first professional critics continually acted to reassert

Film als Kunst (1932), later published in English as *Film as Art*, advocates for the recognition of film as 'a basically new type of art.'[43] Particularising the art of film, Arnheim explicitly distinguishes the literary and visual, and at the same time recognises unique perspectives and contributions:

> If, then, there is a genuine difference between the literary description of visual matter and the recording in words of things belonging in a non-literary, visual medium, is it not possible that a writer may find it necessary to have his dramatic dialogue completed by – not just accompanied with – a specific kind of visual staging? This indeed would be a basically new type of art, as shown also by the fact that the author himself would have to take care in detail of the visual production since it would represent "the other half" of his work itself rather than simply a subsequent "performance" of it.[44]

The perspective is striking in that it explicitly distinguishes between the (mere) interpretation or performance of an existing literary work, and the creative production of something new. This resonates with the hierarchy of creativity that harries the director-performer relationship today. This distinction is also suggestive of the cultural, social, and legal perspectives upon adaptation in film and the nature of (original) art, as well as the anxieties over adaptation in film and the nature of art: *I preferred the book*. Indeed, this uncertain and at times turbulent relationship between authorship and performance is something that vexes film throughout its history; but at the same time, there is tremendous insight for the nature of creativity and authorship today to be found in an examination of the history and mechanics of this relationship. In this context, Arnheim embraces the aesthetic narrative that compels the unitary author, while at the same time defies that view of the finished and whole work: '*So far, artists have preferred the singular medium*. – The great artists, whose activity represents, as it were, the practical manifestation of the aesthetic laws, have shown little inclination thus far to make use of such a possibility.'[45] This is a point to which I will return, but arguably the anxiety (both

film's rank, calling for more refined productions and cinematic techniques and pointing out the need for individual creativity to enable the cinema to achieve the established arts' level of sophistication' (31).

43 Arnheim, Rudolf. *Film as Art* /[*Film als Kunst*] (University of California Press, 1957/[1932]) 220.

44 Ibid.

45 Ibid., 221.

for the industry and for law) around collaboration is key to understanding the paradoxical interplay between the discourse of art and the creative ordering within the law.

It is in this context that early moves to include cinematographic works within copyright protection,[46] while motivated by film's perceived risk as a technology of reproduction, consolidated its story as a work of singular authorship and imagination – a work of art, if you will. Copyright protection may have acknowledged the role of cinematographic works in dramatic adaptation and the perceived risk of expropriating live performance through recording, but more particularly, it endorsed the emerging cultural value of film as a traditional work of authorship, almost in defiance of its industrial mass-production and collaborative creativity, and certainly in deference to the auteur. A fundamental requirement of this value (and its protection) is the specific contribution of film which is related to but not exactly represented by originality. For copyright to subsist in the work of film itself, it must be more than a simple recording of events or performances (the early business model of recording what was otherwise a stage production).[47] Thus, the "cinematic" becomes relevant not only theoretically but also legally when it comes to understanding the copyright in the film work. What is a film author?

6 What Is a (Film) Author?

The nature of art is thus also the question of authorship. Arguably, the interwar film scholarship was influential in the installation of the director within the auteurism of copyright's architecture. In seeking to achieve artistic recognition for film, early film criticism was instrumental at the same time in constructing the judicial order of film's authorship, as it were. This early film criticism thus also addresses the conceptual challenge of the way in which film is a work in its own right, other than a recording or representation of another authorial work. In the earliest days of film, questions of authorship were largely preoccupied with the scenario (and indeed the story), rather than the film in and of itself, which at the same time facilitated the challenges from dramatists to

46 The Berne Convention for the Protection of Literary and Artistic Works: Berlin Act, 1908: Revised Berne Convention for the Protection of Literary and Artistic Works; Records of the Diplomatic Conference: Convened in Berlin, 14 October to 14 November 1908. See further the extended examination of this relationship between art and law, industry and copyright, in Gibson, 'The Man Behind the Curtain' (n 12) 207–41.

47 Gibson, 'The Man Behind the Curtain' (n 12) 207–41, esp. 16–17.

authorship and originality in film.[48] The growing assertions of auteurial singularity on behalf of both the director and the work were thus critical to establishing not only the art of film but also the protection of film.

In the film criticism of the interwar period, a genuinely conscientious and insightful investigation into the nature of the film work, film authorship, and performance can be found. As part of the developing mythology around the film work, there was a subtle move away from the collaborative perspective towards an emphasis on the singularity of the author (or artist) and the "work of art" of film. Léon Moussinac and Louis Delluc have been credited with introducing the concept of the auteur several decades before André Bazin and others,[49] as the creator and personal responsibility for the film (as art).[50] Aside from using the term *cinéaste* rather than *auteur*, Louis Delluc maintained that the film was a work of singular authorship and sought to remedy this in an important piece of film criticism history, a list of notable *cinéastes* published in his *Paris-midi* column, 10 August 1918, under the title, *D'ou viennent et ou vont nos metteurs en* scène. In this column, Delluc set about rectifying the neglect of the director by developing narratives of inspiration (and thus art) for a list of directors and their craft – André Antoine, Jacques de Baroncelli, Dominique Bernard-Deschamps, Louis Feuillade, Abel Gance, Henri Krauss, Georges Lacroix, and the partnership of Louis Mercanton and René Hervil.[51]

A few years later, in 1921, Léon Moussinac characterised a very similar tension between technicians and scenarists, a bifurcation pronounced forty years later in the politique des auteurs of *Cahiers du cinéma* and the French New Wave. Moussinac identifies two different values or products to be recognised in a film production: 'the argument is the exposition of the generative visual idea of the film; the scenario or script is the practically realized development

48 Gibson, 'The Man Behind the Curtain' (n 12) 207–41.

49 Richard Abel notes, 'Contrary to what was typical in the French film industry, Delluc and Moussinac also argued that the conception of the original scenario and its realization ought to be the work of a single individual. In order to be a film artist rather than a simple *metteur-en-scène* of adaptations, one had to become an *auteur* or *cinéaste*, to use Delluc's favorite term. The two critics were just as insistent that the filmmaker must become an artisan or craftsman as well.' Abel, Richard, '*Cinégraphie* and the Search for Specificity'. In, *French Film Theory and Criticism* (n 14) 203.

50 Richard Abel notes that Delluc, 'came close to enunciating the *auteur* theory (some forty years before its promulgation by *Cahiers du cinema*) in his August 10 column,' and 'in an enthusiastic June 1 review of Douglas Fairbanks' *L'Aventure à New York* (*The Mysteries of New York*, 1915), Delluc linked the cinema to the literary avant-garde': Abel, Richard, 'The Contribution of the French Literary Avant-Garde to Film Theory and Criticism (1907–1924)'. *Cinema Journal* 14(3) (1975) 18–40, 27.

51 Delluc, Louis, 'D'ou viennent et ou vont nos metteurs en scène'. *Paris-midi*, 10 August 1918.

of this idea, and as such it is virtually the realized film.'[52] Prefiguring the much later movement of the French New Wave, Moussinac distinguishes between a more technical type of directing as distinct from the film as a work of art. In the former, 'The task of the *metteur-en-scène* then is roughly parallel to that of the scenario writer ... an excellent technician and no more ... In no case is it his task to dominate the film.'[53] This resembles the way in which auteurism speaks of the scenarist. In the latter, Moussinac characterises quite clearly the director as auteur and outlines the critical authorship of film for both criticism and ultimately for the law itself:

> For films which more precisely claim the title of works of art, on the other hand, there is no question of separating the realization from the conception – here the exceptional case, possible in any creative domain, cannot but confirm the rule. The *metteur-en-scène* becomes his own scenarist. He is truly the original creator, for out of his imagination and his practical skills there arises an absolute insight. And it is in the necessary unity of the work of art that his originality, his creativity individuality, emerges.[54]

Moussinac reconciles this singularity with the collaborative nature of film by noting that while the director may nevertheless 'borrow the *argument* of his film from another's work or for a collaborator to provide him with an argument,'[55] this does not negate the oneness of authorship and authorial perspective that Moussinac sees as necessary for the artistry of film. This 'creative individuality'[56] resonates loudly with the auteurism of copyright's conceptualisation of the work and 'the author's own intellectual creation,'[57] and articulates the concept of a kind of creativity in use, prefiguring copyright's perspective on fair use and fair dealing, transformation and adaptation. As such, borrowing does not divert the perceived wholeness of the film as authorial work, nor the unitary integrity of the original work. When a director borrows, whether from other authors (such as novelists, dramatists, or other directors) or indeed the performers themselves, Moussinac explains this relationship not as one of collaboration but one of singular authorship: 'it is only a pretext for which he *alone* will discover the multiple forms of cinegraphic

52 Moussinac, Leon, 'Cinématographie'. *Mercure de France*, 1 November 1921, 784–91.
53 Ibid.
54 Ibid.
55 Ibid.
56 Ibid.
57 *Infopaq International A/S v Danske Dagblades Forening* (C-5/08) EU:C:2009:465.

development, a general or particular image that he can recreate completely and from which he will make a purely personal work, the same way a painter or sculptor finds in a poem the pretext for a painting or sculpture.'[58] There is a conscious and inventive mastery in this use. And, of course, authorship is for the masters. But who are the masters of the film work?

7 Labour in Vain

The uncertainty around the ownership of film was indeed the background to the anxiety around authors' rights – not only the rights of the scenario authors, but also the increasing emphasis on film authorship for establishing this new art (and new artists). In this context, the "authorship" of performers did not go without consideration. And it is here that critics and theorists during this period offer insightful and compelling critique of the authorial narrative as contrived for film. Béla Balázs, in *Visible Man* (originally published in 1924), notes that the film must stand alone, and that the underlying works, if any, are not for the audience to ascertain: 'In a film the audience has no opportunity of judging whether the director or actors have faithfully reproduced the work of a writer or have distorted his meaning, for it is *their* work alone that the audience perceives.'[59] Notably, whatever the unity of the work, the authorship is a participatory affair: 'The fact is that the director and the actors are the true authors of the film.'[60] Film becomes thus a kind of performance, an interpretation of the underlying work, if any, that stands alone.

However, this is not to abandon any 'original character' created by the director; rather, it is to complicate the contrived chronology of work and performance, with the director thus also a kind of performer. Around a hundred

58 Moussinac, 'Cinématographie' (n 52) 784–91.

59 Balázs, Bela. *Visible Man/[Der sichtbare Mensch]*, R Livingstone (trans), in *Béla Balázs: Early Film Theory* (Berghahn, 2010/[1924]) 18.

60 Balázs, *Visible Man,* ibid. 18. Although writing some decades later, Georges Sadoul explained, somewhat remarkably in defiance of the auteurism that dominated critical discussions at the time, 'In certain cases, the principal "author" might be less the credited director than a star (such as Douglas Fairbanks), a producer (such as Zanuck), a scriptwriter (such as Zavattini), or even a writer whose literary work has been adapted (such as Victor Hugo). A film is almost always a collective creation and each collaborator, from the least technician to the most famous star, in small part or large, is one of the authors.' See Sadoul, Georges, 'Preface', in Sadoul, Georges, *Dictionary of Film Makers* (University of California Press, 1972/[1965]) VI. Sadoul cites Delluc's work as a source of his definition of filmmakers as 'Organizers, directors, artists, industrialists who have contributed something to the artistic industry of the cinema'.

years later, Richard Arnold has argued that the director, through their work of interpretation, is at the same time potentially a performer in the same way that a conductor is a performer in a musical performance.[61] Arnold notes that claiming performers' rights may not matter as much to film directors as it might for other cultural industries (such as theatre).[62] But what is more striking about this potential is what is says about performers as authors, recalling the participatory authorship encountered in early film theory. Indeed, I wish to revive the groundwork for Arnold's compelling argument as found in the critical film theory of the 1920s, particularly given the emergence of those theoretical traditions in the context of a burgeoning industry, an uncertain art, and the somewhat recalcitrant film author. The authorship of film today is still a matter left for domestic legislation, remaining outside the purview of the Berne Convention.[63] Film authorship thus becomes even more emphatically a matter of art. What then is the truth in film?

8 The Truth in Painting, the Deception in Sound

The art of film was thus from the beginning distinguished purely visually, in part of course because this was the silent period of cinema. This painterly aesthetic of cinema is in evidence in the writings of the silent period as well. Raymond Bellour observes in the criticism of the silent period, 'how little they rely on the notion of the *shot*, preferring instead, most often, to speak of images, scraps, fragments, framings.'[64] However, it was not merely a practical constraint that motivated this visual hegemony in film, and this certainly would not explain the lingering emphasis on the visual. In the essay, 'The Two Avant-Gardes,' first published in 1975, Peter Wollen observes that '[d]uring the silent period, the absence of language was not foregrounded; it seemed a natural quality of film, but in retrospect its significance can be seen. Language is still excluded from an enormous number of avant-garde films.'[65] Wollen explains this as the persistently visual aesthetic that attaches to the accepted art of film: 'Again, there are real technical and financial reasons for this, but these practical disincentives coincide with an aesthetic which was itself founded on concepts

61 Arnold, 'Do Directors Have Performers' Rights? (n 8) 134–140.

62 Ibid.,140.

63 Article 14*bis*(2)(a).

64 Bellour, Raymond. *The Cinema Spectator: A Special Memory*, A Martin (trans), in I Christie. Ed. *Audiences* (Amsterdam University Press, 2012) 206–17, 207.

65 Wollen, Peter. *Readings and Writings: Semiotic Counter-Strategies* (Verso, 1982) 96.

of visual form and visual problems which exclude verbal language from their field, and may be actively hostile to it.'[66] Almost fifty years later, arguably this emphasis on the visual continues as an unshakeable aesthetic and a source of legitimation and discernment for the industry and the law alike. And fifty years later again, the visual hegemony of copyright persists in the nature of how an expression of the author's own intellectual creation may be particularised, despite the expanding field of works.[67]

One of the earliest film theorists and critics (as well as a filmmaker himself), Jean Epstein, presents an aesthetic of film authorship in the context of both structural and artistic constraints to be observed in film. As such, Epstein approaches film as a work of interpretation in terms of visual art rather than narrative form, recalling the earlier criticism of Brisson and others. In *The Senses* (1921), Epstein explains: 'Generally speaking, the cinema does not render stories well. And "dramatic action" is a mistake here. Drama that acts is already half resolved and on the healing slope to crisis.'[68] The film is an art of direction, rather than a story of representation. It is a presentation of filmic space and time: 'The cinema is true; a story is false ... So why tell stories, narratives which always assume a chronology, sequential events, a gradation in facts and feelings? Perspectives are merely optical illusions.'[69] For Epstein, this renders cinema (and arguably other visual art) 'ill-suited to the rational framework of the novelette and indifferent to it,'[70] and as such the copyright auteurial narrative itself. Epstein thus presents film as a kind of visual or painterly "use" of the literary authorship of the dramatic work.

This emphasis on the objectivity, or "truth", of the visual reverberates with the visual hegemony of early film criticism and theory, and the emerging (and resilient) concept of the auteur that has been under discussion. Curiously, the introduction of sound was popularly conceived as enhancing the authenticity of the performer, in the context of the star system, with the press equating the introduction of sound 'with realism and truth and the consequent notion that sound technology could reveal more of – and even embarrass – the star.'[71] In

66 Ibid.

67 *Levola Hengelo v Smilde Foods* (C-310/17), EU:C:2018:899.

68 Epstein, Jean, 'Le Sens I bis'. *Bonjour* Cinema (Editions de la sirène, 1921), 27–44. Published in English as *The Senses 1 (b)*, T Milne (trans), *Afterimage* (1981) 10, 9–16. Reproduced in *French Film Theory and Criticism* (n 14) 242.

69 Ibid.

70 Ibid.

71 Slowik, Michael, 'Revealing Reality: Fan Magazine Rhetoric, Sound Technology, and Stardom in the Early Sound Era'. *Journal of Film and Video* 70(2) (2018) 30–45, 30. See further the discussion of sound and stardom later in this chapter.

other words, voice was somewhat outside the management of the frame and the omnipotence of the auteur, being something which is personal to the performer. As such, it has been suggested that 'sound technology required audiences to recalibrate the reality of the silent-era stars they now saw onscreen – that is, to use talking pictures as a means for reflecting upon and reassessing the "true" personalities and talents of the star.'[72] Paradoxically, if sound technology 'peeled back illusion and revealed a greater amount of reality,'[73] arguably this reaffirmed the contribution of the performer as creator, as distinct from tool. With sound, the pretence is nothing, the performance everything.

This emphasis on truth is a trope that is also inflected and deployed throughout the purported objectivity of the intellectual property system. Indeed, it is integral to the question of the work itself and the resolution of audience perception (and the diversity of that perception) in a contrived objectivity and particularising of expression in copyright.[74] Recalling earlier film criticism, this relationship between sound and authenticity is interesting when viewed through those writings and the emphasis on the veracity of the visual in the silent period. The law of film also coincides with this legacy, or indeed copyright itself subscribes to this aesthetic in its operation. The protection of film was and continues to be similarly preoccupied almost entirely and explicitly with the visual artefact within the frame. The earliest protection for cinematographic works was through the protection of individual photographic cells or frames;[75] that is, as "painterly" within the visuality of the law. Narrative is a separable concern (and a separable copyright); therefore, sound is a curious disruption to the painterly aesthetic adopted by the industry. Indeed, when sound began to dominate the landscape, there was a particular resistance to the technology in the European industry due to an overwhelming concern, 'that sound would threaten the progressive development of an essentially *visual* medium.'[76] To recall the language of Jean Epstein, 'The cinema is true; a story is false ... So why tell stories?' In other words, the truth (that is, the art) of film is in painting, the visual. The story is someone else's concern.

72 Ibid.

73 Ibid., 31.

74 *Levola Hengelo v Smilde Foods* (C-310/17), EU:C:2018:899.

75 In the United Kingdom, this was through the Copyright Act 1911 as clarified through *Pathé Pictures Ltd v Bancroft* [1928–35] Macg.Cop.Cas. 403; *Barker, etc., Ltd. V Hulton (£.) & Co. Ltd.* (1912) 28 T.L.R. 496; *Nordisk Films Co Ltd v Onda* [1917–23] Macg.Cop.Cas. 337.

76 Richards, Rashna, 'Unsynched: The Contrapuntal Sounds of Luis Buñuel's "L'Age d'Or"', *Film Criticism* 33(2) (2008/9) 23–43, 25.

This emphasis on the visual as the distinctive art or contribution of film (both culturally and legally) is also the context for the trepidation around sound expressed in the work of Béla Balázs. As well as confounding the visual hegemony of the law, sound threatened the unitary wholeness of the filmmaker's control and thus the singularity of the auteur. At the same time, sound threatened the art of film by returning film, practically speaking, to a technology of recording and the contrivance of narrative. Balázs declares: 'This as-yet undeveloped new technology has attached itself to a highly developed cinematic art, and has thrown it back to the most primitive stage. And it is inevitable that the standard of the content of film will decline in equal measure with the degeneration of its standards of expression.'[77] Sound technology thus introduced an unwelcome uncertainty for the protection of the film work, compromising the author's own intellectual creation, as it were, because its authority was from the performers themselves. Paradoxically, the maturation of the film industry with the production of sound films and talkies in particular, inadvertently accorded with the legacy of a perceptible distinction between the film as recording and the film as work.

Nevertheless, despite these complications for film's aesthetic, the advent of film sound, so to speak, is especially important to the art of film in its explicit resistance to the received conventions of framing; both the law's frame and the industry's frame. At last, the voices of actors could be heard, and the frame of the studio could be breached.

9 Written in the Stars, the Industry of Stardom

The studio management of stars within the industrial complex of stardom is curiously complicit with making film more "literary" and with reconciling film within the dominant "literary copyright" view of copyright more generally. There is also a notable historical coincidence between the introduction of sound to films and the establishing star system. Stars were commodified not in terms of their performance and creativity, but rather, in terms of their celebrity and authenticity (including voice) within the structure and ideology of Hollywood. In this way the star is the asset, and the work and instrumentality of the performer and any skill in performance may be obscured by the vanity of stardom. As such, the performer is merely an instrument of the

77 Balázs, Bela. *The Spirit of Film/[Der Geist des Films]*, R Livingstone (trans), in *Béla Balázs: Early Film Theory* (Berghahn, 2010/[1930]) 183.

auteur, and the auteurism of the industry continues to frame the performer as such. In this way, auteurism is not merely part of the compelling aesthetic narrative, but also part of the industry management of performers: 'The auteur *system* ... allowed studio heads to differentiate their product while maintaining greater control over labor-management relations ... Encouraged to identify themselves as "artists" instead of "workers," auteurs secured their positions by aligning themselves with the interests of management rather than by offering their assistance to those of lower rank.'[78]

This auteurial-powered stratification of the industry was, and arguably continues to be, supported by the awards system and the Academy of Motion Picture Arts and Sciences in particular. The Academy was established at a time of considerable unrest in the industry. Emanuel Levy explains, 'A prime motive for the Academy's foundation was the unionization of the industry in November 1926, when nine major studios and five unions signed the Studio Basic Agreement.'[79] However, a limitation of this Agreement was that it did not apply to actors, writers, or directors, only to technical workers.[80]

> Before the talent groups established their guilds, Mayer decided to take action, and, in December 1926, met with three industry leaders: Actor Conrad Nagel, director Fred Niblo (*Ben-Hur*), and Fred Beetson, head of the Association of Motion Picture Producers. The quartet conceived of an organization that would mediate labor disputes and also improve the public image of Hollywood by helping the Hays office to control controversial screen content.

Thus, the Academy's purpose was overwhelmingly that of protecting the industry from the unionisation of creative workers: 'It's interesting to note that in 1927 the bestowal of merit awards was only of, and not the most, important goal of the Academy.'[81] As Sean Holmes observes, 'the Academy as it operated in the late 1920s and early 1930s was not so much a mechanism for protecting the rights of workers as a means of keeping Hollywood's labour troubles out

78 Clark, Danae. *Negotiating Hollywood: The Cultural Politics of Actors' Labor* (Minneapolis: University of Minnesota Press, 1995) 6–7. See Levy, Emanuel, *All About Oscar: The History and Politics of the Academy Awards* (Continuum, New York, 2003) 40–41. See further the discussion in Gibson, 'All Words and No Performance' (n 5) 125–140.

79 Levy, ibid., 40–41.

80 Ibid., 41.

81 Ibid.

of the public gaze.'[82] Before the unionisation of actors through the establishment of the Screen Actors' Guild in 1933 (and of Equity in Britain before that, in 1930), the Academy and the surrounding system of awards and promotion, was the sole mechanism for arbitrating labour disputes in Hollywood studios:

> The Academy functioned to reinforce the division of labor among actors and to prevent their collective bargaining power against producers. This was achieved by maintaining a hierarchical system of control whereby a small, elite group of actors became the voice for the entire profession … Only the support of their prestigious colleagues would give lower ranked actors the bargaining edge that they needed.[83]

Contemporaneously, the law's purpose, at least in the example of the United Kingdom, was overwhelmingly that of protecting the broadcasting industry, at risk of losing quality product if artists were unwilling to risk the expropriation of their performance. Recording created objects of economic value, by the sounds of things.

10 By the Sounds of Things: *The Dramatic and Musical Performers' Protection Act* 1925

> I say that the man who takes the voice of a performer, and uses it for his own profit without paying for it, ought to stand in the dock.
>
> HANSARD, 27 June 1925[84]

The development of technologies of recording (both sound recordings and film) thus introduced a political and economic interest in a new form of creative work. As already discussed, just as the perceived threat from film as technology of reproduction was addressed through its inclusion in copyright,[85]

82 Holmes, Sean, 'The Hollywood Star System and the Regulation of Actors' Labour, 1916–1934'. *Film History*, 12(1) (2000) 97–114, 111.

83 Clark, Danae, 'Acting in Hollywood's Best Interest: Representations of Actors' Labor During the National Recovery Administration'. *Journal of Film and Video* 42(4) (1990) 3–19, 4.

84 Mr Shaw. HC Deb 27 June 1925 vol 185 cc 1970–9.

85 Cinematographic works were first included at the multilateral level at the 1908 Berlin Conference of the Berne Convention – The Berne Convention for the Protection of Literary and Artistic Works: Berlin Act, 1908: Revised Berne Convention for the Protection

the advent of sound propelled the protection of performers out of concern for the performance.[86] Just a couple of years before the first talkie, the first form of protection of performers in the United Kingdom came into force in 1925,[87] coinciding with the increasing dominance of sound in film production, and the vulnerability to the reproduction, and thus commodification, of sound in illicit recordings as economic things. Performers' rights thus emerged quite explicitly by the sounds of things, as it were.

While it is true that sound was the reason behind this first form of protection in the United Kingdom, the main impetus was largely the vulnerability of voice performances and illicit recording of broadcasts. Thus, although not concerned with sound films as such, the significance of this legislative development was that sound was the critical impetus of the matter and it was through sound that the world turned for performers. Although the rationale was expressed wholly through the expropriation of musical performances in broadcasts, the Act itself was extended to the protection of dramatic performers. Therefore, while it would appear that the recording of the dramatic work in film was itself not sufficient incentive to motivate attention to the potential rights of performers in film, the dominance of sound in film put a spotlight on dramatic performers. Protection of performers became more critical with the increasing dominance of sound film for a number of reasons, both positive and negative; that is, when film started to make them heard. Again, however, it was of questionable efficacy for protection of performers, when the objective was the protection of performance. Whether the protection of broadcasts through the recognition of musical performers, or the protection of theatres (and studios) through the protection of dramatic performers, the protection of performers remained, albeit it indirectly, a dilemma for the author.

The Dramatic and Musical Performers' Protection Act 1925 nevertheless represented a somewhat historic shift in perspective upon the nature of the performer's work, but this protection of performers was implemented explicitly without a right of property in the performance of works.[88] It is notable that the primary sponsor of the Dramatic and Musical Performers' Protection Bill was

of Literary and Artistic Works; Records of the Diplomatic Conference: Convened in Berlin, 14 October to 14 November 1908. See further the discussion in Gibson, 'The Man Behind the Curtain' (n 12) 207–41. In the United Kingdom, this led first to the protection of the cinematographic work (the recording) in the Copyright Act 1911.

86 Copyright Act 1911.

87 The Dramatic and Musical Performers' Protection Act 1925.

88 *Musical Performers' Protection Association Ltd v British International Pictures Ltd* (1930) 46 TLR 485; Arnold, *Performers' Rights* (n 21) paras 1–49 to-1–50.

in fact The Gramophone Company Ltd.[89] While this reflects an overwhelming concern in the recording industry regarding the production of records from broadcasts, rather than the interests of film performers, nevertheless it is evidence of the priority of sound in establishing the performer as creator, resonating with the emergence of sound in film both historically and philosophically. And although, as noted above, the subject of interest was the broadcast of voice performers, notably the first decision under the Act was concerned with film and film music,[90] a decision to which I will return in a moment.

Sir Martin Conway[91] introduced the Bill to the House of Commons, 13 February 1925, as a private member's bill.[92] Sir Martin explained that the purpose of the Bill was the improvement of the quality of the programmes produced by the broadcasting companies.[93] However, this was to be achieved through the mechanism of the protection of artists; in other words, the Bill was ultimately concerned with incentives for performance. Recalling the introduction of protection for cinematographic works in the Berne Convention, the motivation was at first the potential for infringement (as a technology of reproduction) that materialised film's potential as a work for the purposes of copyright.[94] Similarly, when it came to performers' rights, it was in the capacity for infringement of the performance as a separate economic value, and thus the risk to the commercial interests of broadcasting companies, that the potential of the performer as a "creator" was materialised. At the Bill's Third Reading, Sir Martin outlined the risk to performers, and thus the loss of content for broadcasts, presenting the case for a kind of performers' rights as critical to the quality of programming for commercial broadcasts:

> At the present moment it is inadvisable for any first-rate artist to perform for the broadcast, for this reason, that the performance as broadcast can be taken down by a gramophone receiver and a gramophone negative can

---

89 Arnold, *Performers' Rights*, para 1.43.

90 *Musical Performers' Protection Association Ltd v British International Pictures Ltd* (1930) 46 TLR 485.

91 William Martin Conway, 1st Baron Conway of Allington (1856–1937), Member of Parliament for Combined English Universities (1918–1931), Professor of Art, Liverpool (1884–1887) and Slade Professor of Fine Art, Cambridge (1901–1904).

92 By its Second Reading in the House of Lords, the Bill had the support of the nascent Broadcasting Company (established in 1922 and later becoming the public service corporation, the British Broadcasting Corporation (BBC), in 1927), the gramophone companies, and artists themselves. The Bill ultimately received Royal Assent, 31 July 1925.

93 HC Deb 27 June 1925 vol 185 cc 1970–9.

94 Gibson, 'The Man Behind the Curtain' (n 12) 207–41.

> be made. The performer has no protection against this being done, and that illicit gramophone negative can be used to produce records which can be sold. That sale has the effect of breaking contracts between artists and the various gramophone companies, and in order to save their contracts it is impossible for most of them to have their performances broadcast. I have introduced this Bill in order to make it possible to improve broadcast programmes.[95]

The first litigation under the Act[96] described the legislation as addressing, in part, the assertion in the sixth edition of Copinger that, while the owner of copyright has to right to prevent a recording of a performance of their copyright work, 'the actual performer, who may have a valuable interest in his performance, has no such right, since he has no copyright in his skill.'[97] This is a striking metaphor but arguably distracts from what is actually at stake. Copyright does not, as such, protect other skills (for example, literary authorship) deployed in the production of the work. Similarly, the skills in performance would never be the subject directly of intellectual property protection, in and of themselves. Rather, it would be the original creative product arising from those skills. It is in this context that the interpretive work of the performer is relevant to understanding the generation of value, the recognition of original character, and the potential expansion of the work, as discussed later in this chapter. And somewhat paradoxically, beyond the movement and physical expression of the performer, this expansion is vociferously presented in the advent of sound.

11 'You Ain't Heard Nothing Yet': *The Jazz Singer* (1927)

> Wait a minute, wait a minute, you ain't heard nothing yet.[98]

The value of stardom is instrumental in the first talkie, *The Jazz Singer* (1927).[99] The film capitalised not only on Al Jolson's star appeal, but also and more

95 HC Deb 27 June 1925 vol 185 cc 1970–9.

96 *Musical Performers' Protection Association Ltd v British International Pictures Ltd* (1930) 46 TLR 485, 486.

97 James, Francis. *Copinger on the Law of Copyright*, 6th edn. (London: Sweet & Maxwell, 1927) 190. Cited in *Musical Performers' Protection Association Ltd v British International Pictures Ltd* (1930) 46 TLR 485, 486.

98 *The Jazz Singer* (1927), Alan Crosland (dir). First synchronised speech in cinema, uttered by Jack Robin.

99 *The Jazz Singer* (1927), Alan Crosland (dir).

particularly on his voice: '*The Jazz Singer* capitalized on the charisma of Al Jolson ... it was a film which capitalized on the singular appeal of an entertainer whose voice had not been given feature presentation on a motion picture screen until this time.'[100] Earlier audiences had already been treated to Vitaphone promotional screenings of sound shorts, but the sound of these productions was limited to the music (including the replacement of the traditional live orchestra with Vitaphone-recorded music, which often faced considerable criticism).[101] However, the sonic revolution in *The Jazz Singer* was that, for the first time, audiences heard not only the songs but also the dialogue (albeit limited to around just two minutes[102]). Further, the dialogue was largely improvised by the performers, including the very first ever spoken dialogue, Jolson's now legendary, 'Wait a minute, wait a minute, you ain't heard nothin' yet.'[103] This collaborative contribution of performers in this momentous piece of film history recalls Balázs's assertion: 'The fact is that the director and the actors are the true authors of the film.'[104]

However, sound perhaps did more to challenge the auteurism of film than it did to boost the authorship of performers. Indeed, returning to the preoccupation with authenticity and the truth of representation, it is seemingly a further contempt that *The Jazz Singer* deployed voice doubling for Warner Oland.[105] Voice doubling is where an off-screen voice artist performs the audio (usually a musical composition) and the on-screen performer mimes in synchrony, producing the illusions of 'embodiment, the illusion that the body

---

100 Tankel, Jonathan, 'The Impact of the Jazz Singer on the Conversion to Sound'. *Journal of the University Film Association* 30(1) (1978) 21–25, 23.

101 Block, Alex, and Wilson, Lucy, eds. *George Lucas's Blockbusting: A Decade-by-Decade Survey of Timeless Movies Including Untold Secrets of Their Financial and Cultural Success* (HarperCollins, 2010) 59.

102 Tankel, 'The Impact of *The Jazz Singer*' (n 100) 23. Scott Eyman declares, '*The Jazz Singer* offers not just music but an effervescent personality projecting itself in words, bursting through the screen to wrap the audience in an exuberant embrace': Eyman, Scott. *The Speed of Sound: Hollywood and the Talkie Revolution, 1926–1930* (Simon & Schuster, 1997) 15.

103 Goldmark, Daniel, 'Adapting *The Jazz Singer* from Short Story to Screen: A Musical Profile'. *Journal of the American Musicological Society* 70(3) (2017) 767–817, 792. See further 804 (n 19). See also the entry in IMDB, *The Jazz Singer* (1927) https://www.imdb.com/title/tt0018037/?ref_=tttr_tr_tt.

104 Balázs, *Visible Man* (59) 18.

105 Voice doubling is where an off-screen voice artist performs the audio (usually a musical composition) and the on-screen performer mimes in synchrony. See Crafton, Donald. *The Talkies: American cinema's transition to sound, 1926–1931* (University of California Press, 1999) 509–515. See further Spring, Katherine, 'To Sustain Illusion is all that is Necessary': The Authenticity of Song Performance in Early American Sound Cinema'. *Film History* 23(3) (2011) 285–99.

seen onscreen is the source of the voice emanating from the soundtrack, and simultaneity, the illusion that the filming of the image and the recording of the voice occurred concomitantly and in the same space.'[106] Further, from the very first talkie, it would seem that the actor's voice was vulnerable to 'Hollywood's trickery'[107] and that 'Voice-doubling was analogous to the practice of special effects or makeup.'[108] Around a hundred years later, performers' voices are similarly vulnerable to expropriation and commodification, irrespective of the performer.[109] Audiences were willing to accept this separation a hundred years ago: 'Because Hollywood could use technology to craft illusion, there was nothing wrong with exploiting that capability to its fullest.'[110] Recalling the value of the performer's authenticity, the acceptance of technological interventions in performance were and continue to be accepted by audiences, including the use of artificial intelligence to alter performances;[111] but such interventions in the development of screenplays or direction seem less acceptable.[112] With the potential for the commodification of the voice, came the prospect of rights for performers. Once again, this was not in view of the creativity of performer, but rather was in service of the product for the owners, as would be seen at the 1928 Rome Conference of the Berne Convention.

12 The Rome Conference, 1928

The 1928 Rome Conference of the Berne Convention was dominated by concerns arising through new technologies of mechanical reproduction.[113] Notably,

106 Spring, 'To sustain Illusion is all that is Necessary', ibid., 285–86.

107 Crafton, *The Talkies* (n 105) 510.

108 Ibid., 511.

109 Gibson, 'All Words and No Performance' (n 5) 95–124.

110 Crafton, *The Talkies* (n 105) 511.

111 For example, see the discussion in Schofield, Damian, 'Digital Emotion: How Audiences React to Robots on Screen'. *Computer Applications: An International Journal*, 5(1) (2008) 1–20.

112 Explicit distancing from representing AI as autonomous authors is in evidence in existing services in this area. For example, services like ScriptBook describe the technology as "A tale of co-creation between man and machine" and emphasise that their product, DeepStory, a generative AI, is "a worthy artificial co-creator for generating stories" with the human author. See https://www.scriptbook.io/#!/ See further R Haridy (2016) Can AI write a Hollywood film? *New Atlas*, 4 August https://newatlas.com/can-ai-write-film/44610/ See further the discussion in K Farish (2020) AI and the Auteur: Implications of Using Artificial Intelligence in Film Studio Decision-Making, *Jurist*, 27 January https://www.jurist.org/commentary/2020/01/kelsey-farish-ai-and-the-auteur/.

113 Rome Act, 1928 (n 34).

advances in technologies of reproduction have prompted copyright reform at several key stages throughout its history, but not merely because of the risk of copying. Rather, the facility of copying is also a circumstance of new forms of creative work – the process of dealing with the advent of cinematographic works is itself illustrative of this. The inclusion of cinematographic works as protectable works at the 1908 Berlin Conference was prompted by the concerns over the reproduction of theatre through the early business models of the film industry.[114] Although the Rome Conference is frequently lamented as achieving very little, there are nevertheless several key amendments that ushered in a new era for performers in copyright protection, all of which being motivated by sound.

12.1 *The Sounds of Authorship – Article* 2bis

Once again, just as for the introduction of cinematographic works themselves in 1908, technologies of reproduction had revealed a new form of creative work in the mechanical reproduction of live performances and broadcasts. This mechanical reproduction thus uncovered the potential economic value of oral performances and the uncertainty around their management. This prompted the Italian Delegation to the Rome Conference to seek the inclusion of oral works in the list of works in amendments to Article 2 and an accompanying new Article 2*bis*.[115]

The addition of the term "oral works" was met with some opposition from several members, including the British, who called for further detail and more capacity at the national level to vary the conditions and limitations to apply to such protection. This resulted in the change of 'any production' to '*every production* in the literary, scientific and artistic domain' and the expansion of literary and artistic works in Article 2, paragraph 1, with the specific inclusion of '*lectures, addresses, sermons, and other works of the same nature*'.[116] The new Article 2*bis* then left it to Union countries to determine whether to exclude political speeches and legal proceedings,[117] as well as to determine the conditions for the protection and reproduction of such oral works.[118]

---

114 For more detail on these key developments, see Gibson, 'The Man Behind the Curtain' (n 12) 207–41.

115 Records of the Diplomatic Conference: Convened in Rome, May 8 to June 2, 1928.

116 Records of the Diplomatic Conference: Convened in Rome, May 8 to June 2, 1928.

117 Rome Act, 1928: Article 6*bis*, paragraph 1.

118 Rome Act, 1928: Article 6*bis*, paragraph 2.

12.2 *The (Moral) Rights of the Author – Article 6*bis

At the Rome Conference, the Italian Delegation introduced a proposal to recognise, for the first time, the moral rights of the author. This was met with objections from the United Kingdom and other common law countries. The new compromise provision, Article 6*bis*, introduced an immutable relationship between authorship and the work that could not be altered by assignment of the economic rights. This introduced a new relationship to the subject matter beyond a focus on the proliferation of units and towards a clearer emphasis on the author and creative labour. As noted by E Piola Caselli, Vice-Chairman and Rapporteur General of the Rome Conference, the term "moral rights" is 'literally speaking incorrect, as an elliptical expression of the idea that the rights in question are intended to protect certain interests that have a moral content, albeit transformed by this into legal interests.'[119] The introduction and retention of the term "moral rights" in copyright thus introduced moral reasoning for this area of copyright law, and the language of natural rights into the understanding of authorship.

Thus, and perhaps somewhat paradoxically, for cinematographic works in particular, this moral reasoning for protection introduces a compelling incentive to recognise the creative labour of performers and a dilemma for the rationalisation of that work within the legal fiction of the law's auteurism. In other words, that there is a "moral content" to the rights, as explained by the Rapporteur-General, mobilises the potential for recognition of the creative work of the performer as authorship, a discussion motivating contemporary calls for reform.[120] These discussions are assisted by an understanding of the film product, and historically by the advent of film sound, in particular. The singular auteur in relation to the cinematographic work is sustained by the visual hegemony of both law and film. But as will be seen later in this chapter, the history of sound puts the performer at the centre of the innovation and art of cinema, and the amendments in Rome, some hundred years later, ushered in a protracted legal and industry fiction in relation to the cinematographic work.

12.3 *Broadcasting – The Work of Performance in an Age of Mechanical Reproduction – Article 11*bis

The advances in mechanical reproduction prompted not only calls for protection of oral works, but also prompted the Italian Delegation to the Rome

119 Records of the Diplomatic Conference: Convened in Rome, May 8 to June 2, 1928.

120 For example, see Pavis, Mathilde, 'Rebalancing our Regulatory Response to Deepfakes with Performers' Rights'. *Convergence: The International Journal of Research into New Media Technologies* 27(4) (2021) 974–998.

Conference to call for recognition of specific rights in performances, including rights for the performing artists themselves.[121] This was the first attempt to introduce protection for performers in an international forum, once again prompted not by an immutable value in performance as such, but by its manifestation through copying. The perceived risks of copying, as for those perceived in film in 1908, again were addressed through the recognition of creative work, motivated particularly by the risk to phonographic artists through the recording of radio broadcasts.

The view of the Committee, however, was that, despite the ongoing uncertainty in national legislation, 'this new problem … had not yet matured sufficiently for the purposes of an international convention' and the proposal was addressed by 'expressing a formal wish that the countries of the Union consider this interesting question.'[122] This is found in the Voeux or Motions of the Rome Act in which the Conference thus stated 'the wish that the governments which have taken part in the work of the conference will consider the possibility of measures intended to safeguard the rights of performing artists.'[123] While this may have deferred the issue, as discussed below, the revisions to Article 14 arguably reinscribed the industry status quo. Nevertheless, Austria was one member of the Union which was early in recognising wider rights of performers in 1936,[124] including granting moral rights in live performances,[125] in conjunction with rights of fixation, reproduction, and communication to the public.[126] And Italy, the original advocate for protection at the Rome Conference, provided for protection that appeared to acknowledge the "authorship" of performance,[127] and as such the personal and moral dimension of such creative work, in the Law of 22 April 1941.[128]

121 Records of the Diplomatic Conference: Convened in Rome, May 8 to June 2, 1928.

122 Records of the Conference, Rome May 7 to June 2, 1928, 249.

123 *Actes* (1928), Voeu V, relative à la protection des droits des artistes exécutants (Proposition de la Délégation italienne), 350. See further the earlier discussions in the Records of the Berlin Conference 1908 on Mechanical Musical Instruments and Article 13, 206–211. The Berne Convention for the Protection of Literary and Artistic Works: Berlin Act, 1908: Revised Berne Convention for the Protection of Literary and Artistic Works; Records of the Diplomatic Conference: Convened in Berlin, 14 October to 14 November 1908.

124 Law of 9 April 1936.

125 Article 68.

126 Articles 55, 56, 57.

127 Pascal Kamina describes the Italian law as providing for a protection 'akin to author's right': Kamina, Pascal. *Film Copyright in the European Union*, 2nd edn. (Cambridge University Press, 2016) 388.

128 See further the discussion in Kamina, ibid., Chapter 9.

12.4 *The Visual Hegemony of Copyright – Article 14*

As introduced in earlier discussion, reproduction is paradoxically at the heart of originality. This both complicated and facilitated the legitimacy of film as art (in response to film as a technology and medium of mass communication), through the use of classical works to present the "art" of cinema. This visual hegemony is sustained in the records of discussion of Article 14. The French Delegation proposed the inclusion of cinematographic works in Article 2, which was agreed. France also proposed new drafting of Article 14(2) to include the following text: 'cinematographic works shall be protected in the same way as literary, artistic or scientific works,' and to replace the reference to 'performance' with 'adaptation and presentation.'[129] This led to objections from various Union members, including the United Kingdom. Ultimately the Italian proposal for Article 14(2) was accepted; that is, that cinematographic productions will be protected as literary or artistic works, only if the author has given the work an original character. This emphasis on original character, while reasonable within the context of the understanding of the work, nevertheless reinscribed the notion of a singular film "author" and obscured the collaborative contributions to film, including those of the performers with the emerging legal fiction of the "auteur". Notably, there remained no explicit acknowledgement of the director as author of the cinematographic work, and this position continues today, with Article 14*bis*(2)(a) leaving to national legislation the question of the director as author.

13 'Yes, I Heard': *Blackmail* (1929)

Gossiping neighbour:	Morning, Alice. 'eard about the murder?
ALICE WHITE:	Yes, I heard.

Although performers' rights somewhat stalled in Rome, this was followed in the United Kingdom by a key decision under the 1925 Act on what is widely considered to be the first British sound feature, *Blackmail*,[130] thus positioning the film industry and, more particularly, film sound, as central protagonists in the development of performers' rights in the United Kingdom. This was the decision in 1930 in *Musical Performers' Protection Association v British*

129 Records of the Diplomatic Conference: Convened in Rome, May 8 to June 2, 1928.

130 St Pierre, Paul. *Music Hall Mimesis in British Film, 1895–1960: On the Halls on the Screen* (Farleigh Dickinson University Press, 2009) 79.

International Pictures.[131] Before discussing the decision itself, the details of the production must be considered.

The British thriller, *Blackmail*, was produced by British International Pictures (BIP), directed by Alfred Hitchcock, and released 28 July 1929. Filming began originally as a silent production, but reportedly the success of the first US sound film, *The Jazz Singer* (1927), prompted BIP co-owner and producer, John Maxwell, to ask Hitchcock to shoot part of the film as a sound film.[132] Hitchcock, however, complied by effectively reshooting almost the entire film with synchronised sound, achieved through the RCA Photophone sound-on-film process, and both versions were ultimately released. *Blackmail* is particularly significant for the way in which Hitchcock interrogates the relationship between sound and image (and ultimately the tension between listening and looking that persists in film and the way in which the law deals with film),[133] to which I will return in a moment.

Somewhat inevitably, the silent version made more money, since the early success of the sound version was limited by the availability of the necessary technology in cinemas;[134] however, the claims to the importance of the sound version have secured its resilient place in film history. Thus, while sound began to emancipate the creativity of the performer, access to the technology of sound contributed to a persistent studio control of not only the product but also ultimately the distribution. John Belton notes that, 'Film producers were reluctant to convert their total movie output to sound because of the cost of converting all theaters at once,' but for US productions this was less of an issue as 'most big movie houses were owned by studios, and thus first-run conversions took place at a rapid rate.'[135]

---

131 *Musical Performers' Protection Association Ltd v British International Pictures Ltd* (1930) 46 TLR 485.

132 See the summary by the Film Foundation, Out of the Vaults: *Blackmail*, 1929 available at https://www.film-foundation.org/hfpa-blackmail See further the discussion in Belton, John, 'Awkward Transitions: Hitchcock's *Blackmail* and the Dynamics of Early Film Sound'. *The Musical Quarterly* 83(3) (1999) 227–246, 235–236.

133 Elisabeth Weis notes that in *Blackmail*, as well as in the other early Hitchcock film, *Murder!* (1930), 'Hitchcock can be observed trying both to overcome the technical obstacles of early sound shooting and to establish his personal attitudes toward the relationship between sound and picture,' and cites as one of the most famous examples, 'the subjective distortion of the word "knife" in *Blackmail*.' See Weis, Elisabeth, 'The M McDonald, Hitchcock's *Blackmail* and the Threat of Recorded Sound'. *Music and the Moving Image*, 8(3) (2015) 40–51 where McDonald notes the 'daring' use of sound and inaudible dialogue throughout the film, including whispering, mumbling, one-sided telephone calls, and so on.

134 Belton, 'Awkward Transitions' (n 132) 235.

135 Ibid., 228.

13.1 *A Bundle-of-Laughs Theory of Authorship*

Hitchcock played in his own way with the subjugation of sound to image, echoing intellectual property law's own preoccupation with the visual as both objective and particular.[136] This fascination with sound's challenge to the image is found throughout Hitchcock's films in the form of laughter.[137] It is striking that this play is found in this very first sound film, where a clown, and the (silent) laughter painted onto their face, materialises the asynchrony between sound and image. James Naremore discusses Hitchcock's use of laughter in terms of its relationship to genre and argues that the seemingly inappropriate laughter is used to produce comic satire in an otherwise melodramatic moment: 'in each case the audience's laughter derives in part from the feeling that melodramatic convention is being reversed, mocked, or amusingly exaggerated. One might say that the audience takes pleasure in a deliberately "inappropriate" laughter that exposes the solemnity and sentiment of the ordinary murder story.'[138]

This challenge to expectations resonates with the challenge to the "genre" of intellectual property creativity and the emphasis on the visual. In other words, the dominant discourse, be it the rules of the melodrama or the principles of authorship, is challenged by the disruption of the sudden break through laughter. In the film, there is a curious moment where a guard whispers something inaudible to Alice White, to which she responds with a laugh. Alice is the central protagonist who murders Crewe, an artist, when he attempts to attack her. Laughter both opens the reading and at the same time shifts the focus of "objective" scrutiny. This is interesting when compared to John Dewey's historic and influential analysis of laughter, where he maintains it is merely secondary to humour, and concerned more directly with the release following 'a period of suspense, or expectation'.[139] Dewey observes that laughter in a small child is in fact a language of assent: 'it is his emphatic "I do" or "yes" to any suggested idea to which he agrees or which suddenly meets his expectations.'[140] The laughter in *Blackmail* (and elsewhere in Hitchcock's films) both breaks expectations and writes new ones as to the object of attention. This

---

136 *Levola Hengelo v Smilde Foods* (C-310/17), EU:C:2018:899.

137 On the use of humour in Hitchcock's films, as well as specific encounters with laughter, see the more extensive discussion in Naremore, James, 'Hitchcock and Humor'. In *Hitchcock: Past and Future*, Allen, Richard, and Ishii-Gonzáles, Sam, eds. (Abingdon: Routledge, 2004) 22–36.

138 Ibid., 26.

139 Dewey, John, 'The Theory of Emotion: (1) Emotional Attitudes'. *Psychological Review 1* (1894) 553–569, 558.

140 Ibid.

attention becomes enticingly speculative (and productive) yet at the same time seductively compelling when rethinking the attention on the performer, both cultural and legal. In the same way that Hitchcock plays with laughter in *Blackmail*, an ironic silence and historic dialogue with film's progress to sound, Dewey similarly describes laughter as for the most part 'wholly irrelevant to any joke or witticism whatever. It is a constant and repeated "sign" of attaining suddenly to a point … It is a divided activity, part of the kinaesthetic images being fixed upon the immediately present conditions, part upon the expected end.'[141]

13.2 *'Quiet, Alice!'*

Despite this being a sound film (and the first for the British film industry), it is striking that Hitchcock withholds the information of this anticipated exchange. Matthew McDonald describes this in terms that might be understood as a power of Hitchcock's auteurism: 'His message is clear enough: yes, my characters will now speak, but I am in charge of what you will hear.'[142] But in fact it is the characters who whisper, or mumble; it is the characters who control what you hear, as co-conspirators with the director. The "authenticity" of performer and the performer's sound is further complicated by the use of voice doubling for the lead actor, Anny Ondra, whose Czech accent was considered unsuitable for the English character of Alice Crewe.[143] This raises the continuing issue of the relationship between sound and film's neo-colonialism, an issue for contemporary technologies of translation and deepfake dubs.[144] However, it also shows the way in which the advent of sound decolonised film and the idea of a universal cinema language or dominant voice. The authenticity of performers' voices thus unfolded the potential for a participatory and global industry. While the manipulation and voice doubling in *Blackmail* has been considered a directorial control of the performer, at the same time it inserts the creativity and deception of the performer (and the offscreen performer) into the authorship narrative. The performers thus are collaborators and co-conspirators in that authorial deception, if you will.

Paradoxically, this silence (and even the silencing) further reinscribes the contribution of the performer. And with the neighbourhood gossip's

141 Ibid., 559.

142 McDonald, Matthew, 'Hitchcock's *Blackmail* and the Threat of Recorded Sound'. *Music and the Moving Image* 8(3) (2015) 40–51, 42.

143 Ibid., 46–47. See further the negative critical response in the contemporary industry press, e.g., *Variety*, ghosting and Doubling in Talker Publicity, 17 July 1929.

144 Gibson, 'All Words and No Performance' (n 5) 95–124.

compulsive repetition of the word, "knife," which is invariably interpreted as representing Alice's fixation upon the murder, the sound of the word becomes a kind of artefact, with a physicality that overwhelms the primacy of the visual. Sound, as distinct from dialogue, is part of the plot, with part of the detective work including listening in to radio signals. But a particular distinction of the sound version, however, is the inclusion of a song, "Miss Up-to-Date." This song is performed by Crewe, first whistling off-screen, then whistling at the piano, then singing at the piano. It was indeed the music of *Blackmail* that led to the first litigation under the Dramatic and Musical Performers' Protection Act 1925, in 1930 in *Musical Performers' Protection Association v British International Pictures*.[145]

13.3 *'Why This Alarm, for There's Really No Harm'*

Five musicians, all of whom were members of the Musical Performers' Protection Association (MPPA), had performed the music on various dates from May to July 1929 for British International Pictures (BIP). The performers were paid for their performances and had assigned to the MPPA their rights to consent to the production of any records of those performances.[146] BIP had subsequently produced, sold and let for hire the records without having obtained written consent for their production, contrary to the Act. The MPPA brought an action in the High Court seeking: a declaration that the defendants were not entitled knowingly to produce any records from the performances; an injunction to be applied to further production, sales, letting and distribution; and damages, which they claimed arose in relation to the lost benefits from the production.

In making a determination against providing injunctive relief, Mr Justice McCardie concluded, 'Nowhere in the Act is there any indication of an intention to give the performers any "right of property" in the performance of works.'[147] With no right of property or civil liability, only criminal sanctions

145 *Musical Performers' Protection Association Ltd v British International Pictures Ltd* (1930) 46 TLR 485.

146 The terms of that assignment are provided in the decision: 'The assignor doth hereby assign "all that the right of consent to the making of records directly or indirectly from or by means of the assignor's performance of a musical work in conjunction with the film production known as *Blackmail*, and all that the right of consent to the sale, hire, or distribution of such records." Thereupon, written notices of the five assignments were given to the defendants': *Musical Performers' Protection Association Ltd v British International Pictures Ltd* (1930) 46 TLR 485, 487.

147 *Musical Performers' Protection Association Ltd v British International Pictures Ltd* (1930) 46 TLR 485, 488.

(fines) are permitted,[148] an action in the High Court for civil damages is not allowed, and consequently MPPA's claim failed: '[T]his action will not lie unless it can be shown that the Act of 1925 conferred a right of property on the five performers ... A consideration of the Act shows that there are no words providing that it is to be read as one with the Copyright Act'.[149] And as a criminal offence, the judicial intervention is really about industry behaviour and not about the individual performer and their creative labour in the performance, demonstrating a completely different perspective upon the work and one that was wholly consistent with the resistance to unionisation at the time and the continued separation of performers from other kinds of creators. As such, the performers' skills are tools of the industry, and the owners are the producers and studios, as *de facto* authors of the film. The regulatory impact of the legislation appears to be more to do with the labour (and potential labour disputes) than in recognising creative production in the performance itself.

However, the decision introduces some critical issues around the nature of copyright and the distinction from performance. Importantly, Mr Justice McCardie notes that 'The prohibitions of the Act apply as much to non-copyright works as to copyright works,'[150] acknowledging that the "value" at stake in this transaction is generated wholly separately from copyright, in a kind of creative act that is unrelated to the exploitation or production of copyright. This distinction between copyright and the creative labour of performance was explained as central to the rationale of the Act: 'An artist might give, e.g., a brilliant rendering of a non-copyright song or piece of music. The Act of 1911 did not protect his performance from being put upon a master-record and made the subject of large sales by the maker of the record.'[151] This distinction goes to the objective of the Act 'to secure to such a performer some form of protection.'[152] Nevertheless, the objection to property was not made on a critical distinction between the different types of creative labour, but rather on the nature of the industry itself, and the potential burden on the courts if each performer were to be so protected:

---

148 *Musical Performers' Protection Association Ltd v British International Pictures Ltd* (1930) 46 TLR 485, 488.

149 *Musical Performers' Protection Association Ltd v British International Pictures Ltd* (1930) 46 TLR 485, 487–488.

150 *Musical Performers' Protection Association Ltd v British International Pictures Ltd* (1930) 46 TLR 485, 488.

151 *Musical Performers' Protection Association Ltd v British International Pictures Ltd* (1930) 46 TLR 485, 486.

152 *Musical Performers' Protection Association Ltd v British International Pictures Ltd* (1930) 46 TLR 485, 486.

> [O]ften an orchestra (e.g., at the Albert Hall or Queen's Hall) consists of over 100 performers. If the plaintiffs here are correct in saying that each of the five performers had a right of property in his performance, it would follow that the same right would exist if the orchestra was over 100. I am satisfied that parliament foresaw what I have just stated, and intended that it should not be permitted that 100 performers or more should be in a position to bring 100 High Court actions. Moreover, if rights of property had been given by the Act of 1925 it might be difficult to reconcile such rights with those of the owners of the copyright of a piece performed.[153]

Laughter is thus creative and productive, producing something anew. Laughter may also be transgressive and subversive. Women's laughter has been identified as a source of productive and transgressive potential in feminist theory, and indeed Alice's laughter in *Blackmail* is presented as a challenge to the legitimacy of the law. Tania Modleski argues that it accompanies the moment where Alice 'unreasonably demands that the law conform to her, instead of accepting the reverse.'[154] From the play in improvisation to the laughter concealing dialogue, in order to achieve expressiveness through sound, the creativity of the performer was crucial. Humour, laughter, play is at the heart of authorship. And in film, all the authors are merely players.

14 The Second Acoustical Revolution

The interwar period was clearly a crucial period in film development, not least because this was the crossroads at which the path to sound changed not only the art but also the product, and with it the protection of work and author(s) alike. There was nothing inevitable about the singular film author and through a critical reappraisal of film history the rationale for the careful framing of the performer within the industry and by the law is in stark relief. At the same time, however, the very facts of those whys and wherefores outline the contrived abrogation of performers' creativity, and thus the tools for potential reform. The performer is every thing in film. Every thing.

---

153 *Musical Performers' Protection Association Ltd v British International Pictures Ltd* (1930) 46 TLR 485, 488. The Queen's Hall was a concert hall in Langham Place, London, which opened in 1893 and remained in operation until its destruction during the London Blitz of the Second World War, in 1941.

154 Modleski, Tania, 'Rape versus Mans/Laughter: Hitchcock's *Blackmail* and Feminist Interpretation'. *PMLA* (1987) 102(3) 304–15, 305.

Around a century later, film performers are once again facing new technological challenges. With the advent of artificial intelligence in sound and fresh forms of commodification of their creative contributions, performers' rights become a welfare issue.[155] The use of artificial intelligence in relation to performance and sound (including deepfake dubs, translation technology, and replacement of voice actors with artificial intelligence) introduces a new level of instrumentalisation of the performer. Once again sound is at the centre of potential revolution in performance. In the expropriation of voice, the deficiency in copyright's conception of the performer is particularly clear. The wholeness and unity of authorship and the auteur is in stark contrast to the tooling of performers and the elements of performance. Indeed, with the manipulation of voice, the "trust" and "authenticity" that is the currency of performance and the value of the star is put into question. At the same time, the "authorship" of that performance is interrupted and the link between performer and voice is potentially severed, raising the question, 'who – the sound technicians or the actor – actually creates the performance'?[156]

The advent of new sound technologies in this "second acoustical revolution" thus introduces new concerns for the welfare of performers and their connection to their work. Once again the contribution of the performer is being manipulated or even erased in the service of auteurism. While it is beyond the scope of this chapter to consider these technologies in detail, the common issues arising include, in particular, the modifications of performance after the fact (and the patchwork of protection for performers in relation to moral rights, if any, qualified and weakened further by contractual requirements). A further concern is the work of performance and the limitations of protecting performance through approximations of branding and goodwill, as in passing off and defamation, none of which recognises the creativity as such. While the contrived exclusion of the creative and authorial work of performance remains, performers will continue to be vulnerable to the legal fictions that facilitate the expropriation of their contributions. If we can take anything from the advent of the talkies, it is that, performers create a lot more than obligations, to which the attention of legal reform should be paid.

By the sounds of things, the performance is every thing. Every thing.

---

155 Gibson, 'All Words and No Performance' (n 5) 95–124.

156 Marcello, Starr, 'Performance Design: An Analysis of Film Acting and Sound Design'. *Journal of Film and Video* 58(1–2) (2006) 59–70, 59.

Bibliography

Abel, Richard, 'The Contribution of the French Literary Avant-Garde to Film Theory and Criticism (1907–1924)'. *Cinema Journal* 14(3) (1975) 18–40.

Abel, Richard. *French Film Theory and Criticism, Volume 1: A History/Anthology, 1907–1929* (Princeton University Press, 1988).

Arnheim, Rudolf. *Film as Art* /[*Film als Kunst*] (University of California Press, 1957/[1932]).

Arnold, Richard. *Performers' Rights*, 6th edn (Sweet & Maxwell, 2021).

Arnold, Richard, 'Do Directors Have Performers' Rights? *Intellectual Property Quarterly* 3 (2022) 134–140.

Bakker, Gerben, 'How Motion Pictures Industrialized Entertainment'. *The Journal of Economic History*, 72(4) (2012) 1036–1063.

Balázs, Bela, *Visible Man*/[*Der sichtbare Mensch*], R Livingstone (trans), in *Béla Balázs: Early Film Theory* (Bergahn, 2010/[1924]).

Balázs, Bela, *The Spirit of Film*/[*Der Geist des Films*], R Livingstone (trans), in *Béla Balázs: Early Film Theory* (Berghahn, 2010/[1930]).

Bellour, Raymond, *The Cinema Spectator: A Special Memory*, A Martin (trans), in I Christie. Ed. *Audiences* (Amsterdam University Press, 2012).

Belton, John, 'Awkward Transitions: Hitchcock's *Blackmail* and the Dynamics of Early Film Sound'. *The Musical Quarterly* 83(3) (1999) 227–246.

Block, Alex, and Wilson, Lucy, eds. *George Lucas's Blockbusting: A Decade-by-Decade Survey of Timeless Movies Including Untold Secrets of Their Financial and Cultural Success* (HarperCollins, 2010).

Boon, Tim, 'The Cinematic Sound of Industrial Modernity: First Notes'. In *Being Modern: The Cultural Impact of Science in the Early Twentieth Century* Bud, *et al*, eds. (UCL Press, 2018).

Bottomore, Stephen, 'An International Survey of Sound Effects in Early Cinema'. *Film History* 11(4) (1999) 485–498.

Bottomore, Stephen, 'The Story of Percy Peashaker: Debates about Sound Effects in the Early Cinema'. In *The Sounds of Early Cinema* Abel, Richard, and Altman, Charles, eds. (Indiana University Press, 2001).

Brisson, Adolphe, Chronique théâtral: *L'Assassinat du Duc de Guise, Le Temps*, 22 November 1908, 3–4. Reproduced in *French Film Theory and Criticism, Volume 1: A History/Anthology, 1907–1929* Abel, Richard, ed. (Princeton University Press, 1988).

Clark, Danae, 'Acting in Hollywood's Best Interest: Representations of Actors' Labor During the National Recovery Administration'. *Journal of Film and Video* 42(4) (1990) 3–19.

Clark, Danae. *Negotiating Hollywood: The Cultural Politics of Actors' Labor* (University of Minnesota Press, 1995).

Delluc, Louis, 'D'ou viennent et ou vont nos metteurs en scène'. *Paris-midi*, 10 August 1918.

Dewey, John, 'The Theory of Emotion: (1) Emotional Attitudes'. *Psychological Review 1* (1894) 553–569.

Eyman, Scott. *The Speed of Sound: Hollywood and the Talkie Revolution, 1926–1930* (Simon & Schuster, 1997).

Ferro, Marc, 'Film as an Agent, Product and Source of History'. *Journal of Contemporary History* 18(3) (1983) 357–64.

Frey, Mattias. *The Permanent Crisis of Film Criticism: The Anxiety of Authority* (Amsterdam University Press, 2015).

Gibson, Johanna, 'All Words and No Performance: A Revolution in Copyright Through Performance in Sound'. In *Reforming Intellectual Property* Ghidini, Gustavo, and Falce, Valeria, eds. (Edward Elgar, 2022).

Gibson, Johanna, 'The Man Behind the Curtain: Developing Film's Double Exposure of Intellectual Property'. In *Intellectual Property and the Law of Nations, 1860–1920* Morris, P. Sean, ed. (Brill, 2022).

Gomery, Douglas, 'The "Warner-Vitaphone Peril": The American Film Industry Reacts to the Innovation of Sound'. *Journal of the University Film Association* 28(1) (1976) 11–19.

Goldmark, Daniel, 'Adapting *The Jazz Singer* from Short Story to Screen: A Musical Profile'. *Journal of the American Musicological Society* 70(3) (2017) 767–817.

Harmetz, Aljean. *The Making of Casablanca: Bogart, Bergman, and World War II* (Hyperion, 2002/[1992]).

Holmes, Sean, 'The Hollywood Star System and the Regulation of Actors' Labour, 1916–1934'. *Film History*, 12(1) (2000) 97–114.

Hunt, Leigh. *The Poetical Works of Leigh Hunt* (Edward Moxon, 1832).

James, Francis. *Copinger on the Law of Copyright*, 6th edn. (Sweet & Maxwell, 1927).

Kamina, Pascal. *Film Copyright in the European Union*, 2nd edn. (Cambridge University Press, 2016).

King, Rob, 'Introduction: Beyond Vitaphone: The Early Sound Short'. *Film History* 23(3) (2011) 247–50.

King, Rob, '"The Spice of the Program": Educational Pictures, Early Sound Slapstick, and the Small-Town Audience'. *Film History* 23(3) (2011) 313–39.

Lagny, Michèle, 'Film History: Or History Expropriated'. *Film History* 6(1) (1994) 26–44.

Levy, Emanuel. *All About Oscar: The History and Politics of the Academy Awards* (Continuum, 2003).

McDonald, Matthew, 'Hitchcock's *Blackmail* and the Threat of Recorded Sound'. *Music and the Moving Image* 8(3) (2015) 40–51.

Modleski, Tania, 'Rape versus Mans/Laughter: Hitchcock's *Blackmail* and Feminist Interpretation'. *PMLA* (1987) 102(3) 304–15.

Moussinac, Leon, 'Cinématographie'. *Mercure de France*, 1 November 1921, 784–91.

Naremore, James, 'Hitchcock and Humor'. In *Hitchcock: Past and Future*, Allen, Richard, and Ishii-Gonzáles, Sam, eds. (Routledge, 2004).

Pavis, Mathilde, 'Rebalancing our Regulatory Response to Deepfakes with Performers' Rights'. *Convergence: The International Journal of Research into New Media Technologies* 27(4) (2021) 974–998.

Richards, Rashna, 'Unsynched: The Contrapuntal Sounds of Luis Buñuel's "L'Age d'Or"'. *Film Criticism* 33(2) (2008/9) 23–43.

Sadoul, Georges, 'Preface'. In *Dictionary of Film Makers* Sadoul, Georges. (University of California Press, 1972/[1965]).

Schofield, Damian, 'Digital Emotion: How Audiences React to Robots on Screen'. *Computer Applications: An International Journal* 5(1) (2008) 1–20.

Slowik, Michael, 'Revealing Reality: Fan Magazine Rhetoric, Sound Technology, and Stardom in the Early Sound Era'. *Journal of Film and Video* 70(2) (2018) 30–45.

Spring, Katherine, '"To Sustain Illusion is all that is Necessary": The Authenticity of Song Performance in Early American Sound Cinema'. *Film History* 23(3) (2011) 285–99.

St Pierre, Paul. *Music Hall Mimesis in British Film, 1895–1960: On the Halls on the Screen* (Farleigh Dickinson University Press, 2009).

Tankel, Jonathan, 'The Impact of the Jazz Singer on the Conversion to Sound'. *Journal of the University Film Association* 30(1) (1978) 21–25.

Weis, Elisabeth, 'The M McDonald, Hitchcock's *Blackmail* and the Threat of Recorded Sound'. *Music and the Moving Image*, 8(3) (2015) 40–51.

Wollen, Peter. *Readings and Writings: Semiotic Counter-Strategies* (Verso, 1982).

Yhcam, Cinematography, *Ciné-Journal*, 20 April-11 May 1912, reproduced in *Framework: The Journal of Cinema and Media* (32/33) (1986) 160–170.

Cases Treaties and Diplomatic Records

Levola Hengelo v Smilde Foods (C-310/17), EU:C:2018:899.

Musical Performers' Protection Association Ltd v British International Pictures Ltd (1930) 46 TLR 485.

Kalem v Harper Brothers, 222 US 55 (1911).

Infopaq International A/S v Danske Dagblades Forening (C-5/08) EU:C:2009:465.

Pathé Pictures Ltd v Bancroft [1928–35] Macg.Cop.Cas. 403.

Barker, etc., Ltd. V Hulton (£.) & Co. Ltd. (1912) 28 T.L.R. 496.

Nordisk Films Co Ltd v Onda [1917–23] Macg.Cop.Cas. 337.

The Dramatic and Musical Performers' Protection Act 1925.

Berne Convention for the Protection of Literary and Artistic Works: Berlin Act, 1908: Revised Berne Convention for the Protection of Literary and Artistic Works.

Records of the Diplomatic Conference: Convened in Berlin, 14 October to 14 November 1908.

Records of the Diplomatic Conference: Convened in Rome, May 8 to June 2, 1928.
The Berne Convention for the Protection of Literary and Artistic Works: Rome Act, 1928: Revised International Convention for the Protection of Literary and Artistic Works; Records of the Diplomatic Conference: Convened in Rome, May 8 to June 2, 1928.

Index

Printed in the United States
by Baker & Taylor Publisher Services